SUMMARY

OF THE LAW OF

BILLS OF EXCHANGE,

CASH BILLS,

AND

PROMISSORY NOTES.

BY SIR JOHN BAYLEY, KNT.

ONE OF THE JUSTICES OF HIS MAJESTY'S COURT OF KING'S BENC

FROM THE FOURTH LONDON EDITION,

REVISED BY THE AUTHOR.

WITH NOTES AND REFERENCES

TO

AMERICAN DECISIONS,

BY WILLARD PHILLIPS AND SAMUEL E. SEWALL.

Fred B. Rothman & Co.

Littleton, Colorado

1994

Library of Congress Cataloging-in-Publication Data

Bayley, John, Sir, 1763-1841.
Summary of the law of bills of exchange, cash bills, and promissory notes / by Sir John Bayley. -- From the 4th London ed. revised by the author ; with notes and references to American decisions by Willard Phillips and Samuel E. Sewall.
p. cm.
Originally published: Boston : H. Gray, 1826.
Includes index.
ISBN 0-8377-1976-3
1. Negotiable instruments--Great Britain. 2. Negotiable instruments--United States. I. Phillips, Willard, 1784-1873. II. Sewall, Samuel E. (Samuel Edmund), 1799-1888. III. Title.
KD1695.B39 1994
346.41'096--dc20
[344.10696] 94-19793
CIP

Printed in United States of America

The paper used in this publication meets the minimum requirements of American National Standard for Information Sciences—Permanence of Paper for Printed Library Materials, ANSI Z39.48-1984.

SUMMARY

OF THE LAW OF

BILLS OF EXCHANGE,

CASH BILLS,

AND

PROMISSORY NOTES.

BY SIR JOHN BAYLEY, KNT.

ONE OF THE JUSTICES OF HIS MAJESTY'S COURT OF KING'S BENCH.

FROM THE FOURTH LONDON EDITION,

REVISED BY THE AUTHOR.

WITH NOTES AND REFERENCES

TO

AMERICAN DECISIONS,

BY WILLARD PHILLIPS AND SAMUEL E. SEWALL.

BOSTON.

PUBLISHED BY HARRISON GRAY.

1826.

CAMBRIDGE:
University Press—Hilliard & Metcalf.

ADVERTISEMENT

TO

THIS EDITION.

THE present edition of this treatise is taken from the late London edition, prepared by the author himself, whose well known talents and learning, and reputation as a lawyer and a judge of the Court of King's Bench, are a sufficient recommendation of the work, which, as it recently came from his hands, is the fruit of his long experience, accumulated knowledge, and matured judgment. His statements of cases are remarkably concise and complete; he distinguishes the decided points with great accuracy, and lays down general doctrines comprehensively, and at the same time with clearness and precision, so that his work, while it is acceptable and useful to lawyers, may be easily understood and safely followed by others.

A part of the chapter on stamps is omitted, as are also two or three of the British statutes which were inserted at large in the London edition.

A few recent English decisions, and all the American cases within the knowledge of the editors, of which reports could be obtained, have been referred to, or inserted in this edition. As some of these cases embrace new points, the insertion of them rendered it necessary to make corresponding additions to the text, where they could be made without interrupting the connexion. The additions are included in brackets.

BOSTON, April 29th, 1826.

PREFACE

TO

THE FOURTH LONDON EDITION.

THIS edition contains the cases since the last, and a new chapter upon the Forgery of Bills and Notes.

THE profession has sustained a great loss in Mr. Barnes. He was a man of great promise, and most respected where best known: had he been living, this edition would have come from him; but his death, and other circumstances, have induced the original author to prepare and superintend this edition.

BEDFORD-SQUARE, 1822.

TABLE OF CONTENTS.

CHAP. I.

What is a Bill or Note, Form and Obligation.

CHAP. A.

CHAP. II.

Parties to a Bill or Note.

CHAP. III.

Stamps.

CHAP. IV.

Alteration of Bills or Notes.

CHAP. V.

Transfer of Bills or Notes.

CHAP. VI.

Acceptance of Bills or Notes.

CHAP. VII.

Presentment and Notice.

CHAP. VIII.

Payment of Bills and Notes.

CHAP. IX.

Remedy on Bills or Notes, by Action.

CHAP. X.

Remedy upon a Bill or Note by proving it under a Commission of Bankruptcy, or suing out a Commission thereon.

CHAP. XI.

Of the Evidence necessary to entitle the plaintiff to recover upon a Bill or Note.

CHAP. XII.

Defence to an action on a Bill or Note.

CHAP. XIII.

Competence of Witnesses.

CHAP. XIV.

Forgery of Bills or Notes.

A SUMMARY

OF THE

LAW OF BILLS OF EXCHANGE

AND

PROMISSORY NOTES.

CHAP. I.

What is a Bill or Note, Form and Obligation.

A Bill of Exchange is a written order or request, and a Promissory Note a written promise, for the payment of money absolutely and at all events, the one owing its existence and privileges to the law and custom of merchants, the other to the 3d and 4th Anne, c. 9. (1)

---

(1) Before the statute of Queen Anne many attempts were made to put promissory notes on the footing of bills of exchange, but without success, vide Pearson v. Garrett, 4 Mod. 242. Clerke v. Martin, Lord Raym. 757. Salk. 129. Burton v Souter, Lord Raym 774. and Williams v. Cutting, Lord Raym. 825. Salk. 24. 7 Mod. 154. 11 Mod. 24. and see 4 Term. Rep. 151, 152.

'By the 3d and 4th Anne, c. 9, § 1. Whereas it hath been held, that 'notes in writing, signed by the party who makes the same, whereby such 'party promises to pay unto any other person, or his order, any sum of 'money therein mentioned, are not assignable or indorsable over, within 'the custom of merchants, to any other person; and that such person 'to whom the sum of money mentioned in such note is payable, cannot 'maintain an action by the custom of merchants against the person who 'first made and signed the same; and that any person to whom such 'note should be assigned, indorsed, or made payable, could not within 'the said custom of merchants, maintain any action upon such note 'against the person who first drew and signed the same:' Therefore, to the intent to encourage trade and commerce, which will be much advanced, if such notes shall have the same effect as inland bills of exchange, and shall be negotiated in like manner: Be it enacted, that all notes in writing, that after the 1st day of May, in the year of our

The person who makes a bill is called the Drawer, the person to whom it is addressed the Drawee, and the person in whose favour it is made the Payee.

Lord 1705, shall be made and signed by any person or persons, body politic or corporate, or by the servant or agent of any corporation, banker, goldsmith, merchant or trader, who is usually, intrusted by him, her or them, to sign such promissory notes for him, her or them, whereby such person or persons, body politic and corporate, his, her or their servant or agent as aforesaid, doth or shall promise to pay to any other person or persons, body politic and corporate, his, her or their order, or unto bearer, any sum of money mentioned in such note, shall be taken and construed to be, by virtue thereof, due and payable to any such person or persons, body politic and corporate, to whom the same is made payable, and also every such note payable to any person or persons, body politic and corporate, his, her or their order, shall be assignable or indorsable over, in the same manner as inland bills of exchange are or may be, according to the custom of merchants; and that the person and persons, body politic and corporate, to whom such sum of money is or shall be by such note made payable, shall and may maintain an action for the same, in such manner as he, she or they might do, upon any inland bill of exchange, made or drawn according to the custom of merchants, against the person or persons, body politic and corporate, who or whose servant or agent as aforesaid, signed the same; and that any person or persons, body politic and corporate, to whom such note, that is payable to any person or persons, body politic and corporate, his, her or their order, is indorsed or assigned, or the money therein mentioned ordered to be paid by indorsement thereon, shall and may maintain his, her or their action for such sum of money, either against the person or persons, body politic and corporate, who, or whose servant or agent as aforsaid, signed such note, or against any of the persons who endorsed the same, in like manner as in cases of inland bills of exchange.

[Promissory Notes are negotiable in all the States. In some they have been made so by statutes similar to that of Anne, while in others the provisions of that act appear to have been received as law without any express statute upon the subject. But although notes are negotiable in all parts of the Union, so far as to enable an endorsee or assignee to maintain an action in his own name against the maker, yet in the states of Vermont, New Jersey, Pennsylvania, Kentucky and Missouri, endorsees have not in general the privileges of endorsees by the law merchant. In all those states in an action against the maker of a note by the endorsee or assignee, the defendant is allowed to offset all demands which he had against the original payee of the note before notice of the endorsement. In some of the above enumerated states an endorsee cannot sue a remote endorser, and in some he must sue the maker of the note, unless insolvent, before he can bring an action against the endorser, and in all of them he is under some disadvantages. However in most of these States the acts incorporating banks exempt the notes discounted at such banks, and in some cases those lodged in them for collection, from these inconveniences, and place such notes on the footing of bills of exchange. And in New Jersey when a note is expressed to be payable "without dafalcation or discount," in an action upon it by the assignee, the defendant is not allowed to set off his de-

If the Drawee accepts the bill, he is called the Acceptor.

The person who makes a note is called the Maker, and the person to whom it is payable the Payee.

When a bill or note is indorsed, the person indorsing it, is called the Indorser, and the person to whom it is indorsed the Indorsee.

A note while in the hands of the payee, has this resemblance to a bill, that it is for the payment of money absolutely and at all events, and when transferred it is exactly similar to a bill of exchange (2).

Sect. 2.—No particular (3) words are necessary to make a bill or note; any order or promise which from the time of

---

mands against the assignor. A statute of Pennsylvania gives similar privileges to notes dated at Philadelphia, and expressed to be payable "without defalcation," or without set-off. See M'Cullough v. Houston, 1 Dall. 441. as to the law in Pennsylvania; and see Yeaton v. The Bank of Alexandria, 5 Cranch 49, and other cases cited in a note to Ch. ix. post, as to the law in Virginia. See also Griffith's Annual Law Reg. Vols. 3 and 4. pp. 22, 48, 78, 116, 142, 224, 264, 362, 365, 403, 423, 467, 518, 585, 627, 670, 696, 796. 864, 943, 1006, 1068, 1139, 1300.]

(2) In Heylin v. Adamson, Burr. 669. The question was, whether the indorsee of a bill was bound to make a demand upon the drawer as the indorsee of a note must upon the maker, and per Lord Mansfield, "while a note continues in its original shape of a promise from one man "to another, it bears no similitude to a bill; but when it is indorsed, the "resemblance begins; for then it is an order by the indorser upon the "maker to pay the indorsee, which is the very definition of a bill; the "indorser is the drawer, the maker of the note the acceptor; and the "indorsee, the person to whom it is made payable; and all the authori- "ties, and particularly Lord Hardwicke, in a case of Hamerton v. "Mackarell, M. 10 Geo. II. put promissory notes on the same footing "with bills of exchange." And in Brown v. Harraden, 4 Term Rep. 148. where the court decided that three days grace should be allowed on promissory notes, Lord Kenyon observed, that the effect of the statute was, that notes were wholly to assume the shape of bills; and Buller J. added, that the cases cited in the argument showed clearly, that the Courts of Westminster had thought the analogy between bills and notes so strong, that the rules established with respect to the one, ought also to prevail as to the other; that the language of the preamble of the Act was express, that it was the object of the legislature to put notes exactly on the same footing with bills, and that the enacting part pursued that intention. The same doctrine is to be found in Carlos v. Fancourt, 5 Term Rep. 482. Edie v. East India Company, Burr. 1224.

(3) D. Lord Raym. 1397. Str. 629. 8 Mod. 364.

Chadwick v. Allen, Str. 706. A note was in these words: "I do "acknowledge that Sir Andrew Chadwick has delivered me all the

making it cannot be complied with or performed without the payment of money, is a bill or note.

Thus an order or promise to (4) deliver, or that I. S. (5) shall receive money, or to be (6) accountable or (7) responsible for it to him or order, is a good bill or note.

But a mere (8) acknowledgment of a debt without any promise to pay, is not a bill or note.

A note was (9) in these words, "borrowed of I. S. £50, which I promise *not* to pay:" and per Lord Macclesfield, the word *not* shall be rejected, for a man shall never say, I am a cheat and have defrauded.

An order to pay money will be a bill, though instead of the ordinary direction to the drawers, the word *at* is prefixed to their names. (10)

"bonds and notes, for which £400 were paid him on account of Col. "Synge, and that Sir Andrew delivered me Major Graham's receipt "and bill on me for £10, which £10 and £15 5*s.* balance due to Sir "Andrew I am still indebted, and do promise to pay," and upon demurrer to the declaration, the court held it a note within the statute.

(4) D. acc. Lord Raym. 1397.

(5) D. 8 Mod. 364.

(6) Morris v. Lea, Lord Raym, 1396. Str. 629. 8 Mod. 326. Plaintiff sued as indorsee upon a note by which the defendant promised to be accountable to A or order for £100, value received; and after verdict for the plaintiff it was insisted in arrest of judgment, that this was not a negotiable note; sed per cur., no precise words are necessary to be used in a bill or note: Deliver such a sum makes a good bill; by receiving the value the defendant becomes a debtor, and when he promises to be accountable for it to A, it is the same as a promise to pay to A, and it is the stronger, because it is to be accountable to A or order, and it would be an odd construction to expound the word accountable, to give an account, when there may be several indorsees. Judgment for plaintiff.

(7) D. 8 Mod. 364.

(8) Fisher v. Leslie, 1 Esp. N. P. C. 426. An unstamped slip of paper with "I. O. U. eight guineas," written upon it, and signed by the defendant, was offered in evidence under the money counts, and objected to as being either a promissory note, or a receipt, and therefore requiring a stamp; but Lord Kenyon held that it was neither a promissory note nor a receipt, and received it in evidence. But see Guy v. Harris, sittings after Easter Term, 1800, cor. Lord Eldon, C. J. contra, Chitty 243. n.

(9) Cited per Lord Mansfield in Russell v. Langstaffe. B. R. M. 21 Geo III. and in Peach v. Kay, sittings after Tr. 1781, and per Lord Hardwicke, 2 Atk. 32.

(10) Shuttleworth v. Stephens, 1 Campb. 407. In an action against defendant as drawer of a bill, the instrument was in this form: "Two

Especially if from fraud it is written in such a manner as to be intended to escape observation, and to make the instrument pass as a bill. (11)

The order may be addressed to the person making it, in other words, a man may draw upon himself; but in legal operation it is rather a note than a bill. (12)

[The order in a bill of exchange to the drawee, is not revoked by the death of the drawer. (*a*)]

---

months after date pay to the order of J. J. £78 11*s.* value received, T. S.—at Messrs. John Morson and Co." Lord Ellenborough held this was properly declared on as a bill of exchange, and the plaintiff had a verdict.

(11) Allan v. Mawson, 4 Campb. 115. In an action against defendant as drawer of a bill, the insrument was as follows. "Two months after date pay L. H. or order £40, value received, G. M. (at)Srr Jno. Perring and Co's." The *at* was in very small letters in the hook of the S. Plaintiff presented it for acceptance, and on refusal brought this action within the two months: the question was, whether plaintiff was intitled to treat this as a bill of exchange, and Gibbs, C. J. thought he would have been on the authority of Shuttleworth v. Stephens, 1 Campb. 407. had the word *at* been distinctly written; but he left it to the jury whether it was not fraudulently written to escape detection, and to induce a belief that the instrument was a bill, the jury thought it was, and found for plaintiff.

(12) Starke v. Cheeseman, Tr. 11 W. III. Carth. 509. Christopher Cheeseman being in Virginia, drew upon Christopher Cheeseman in Ratcliffe, which in truth was himself; and an action being brought against him upon the bill, he suffered judgment by default, without taking any objection on this ground, though he did upon others, and the plaintiff had judgment.

Dehers v. Harriot, Tr. 2 W. and M. 1 Show. 163. A drew a bill payable by himself in Dublin; an action was afterwards brought thereon, and the plaintiff recovered.

Robinson v. Bland, Burr. 1077. The defendant being at Paris drew a bill for £672 on himself in London; the consideration was partly money lost at play in Paris, and partly money lent at the time and place of play, and upon that ground a case was reserved for the opinion of the court; but no objection was made that the defendant drew the bill upon himself.

Joselyn v. Laserre, Fort. 282. A man may draw a bill upon himself. See also Mar. 3.

[(*a*) Abbot, the master of a vessel at London bound for Boston, and having on board goods consigned to Perkins, drew a bill in favour of one of his (Abbot's) creditors upon Perkins, for the amount of freight to be paid by him. Abbot died, and his estate was insolvent, and after his death, which was known to Perkins, he accepted and paid the bill. Abbot's administrator then sued Perkins for the amount of freight; but the court held that "the draft was an assignment of the money that "might become due for the freight," and that "Abbot's death was not "a revocation of the request on the drawee to accept." Cutts v. Perkins, 12 Mass. R. 206.]

Sect. 3.—Bills and notes must be for the payment of money only; an order or promise to pay money *and do some other act* is not a bill or (13) note.

And they must be for the payment of money in specie: (*a*) an order or (14) promise to pay money *in good East India Bonds,* or in cash, or Bank of England Notes, (15) is not a bill or note.

---

(13) Martin v. Chauntry, Str. 1271, on error from the court of Common Pleas, the court of King's Bench held that a note to deliver up horses and a wharf, and pay money at a particular day, was not a note within the statute, and reversed the judgment which had considered it as such.

[(*a*) A note payable in chattels is not a promissory note under the statute. Jerome v. Whitney, 7 Johns. R. 321; Thomas v. Roosa, 7 Johns. R. 461.

Booth drew an order on Manks in favour of Atkinson for £1642 sterling, payable in the goods of Booth or the proceeds thereof, the Court held that this was not a bill of exchange, because it was not payable in money, and said, "besides it was in the alternative, and payable "on a contingency, and out of a particular fund." Atkinson v. Manks, 1 Cowen, 691.]

(14) Anon. Buller's Ni. Pr. 272. a written promise to pay £300 to B or order, in three good East India Bonds, was held not to be a note within the statute.

(15) Ex parte Imeson, Hil. 1815. Case from Chancery, on the question, whether a country bank was debtor to the holder of certain of their notes, which he had taken from third persons, not from the bank; the notes were for payment some of five guineas, some of one guinea "in cash "or Bank of England notes;" and after argument the court held the bank not debtor to this holder, for these notes were not within the statute, because a delivery of bank notes, which might be of less value than cash, would satisfy them, and they were not absolutely and at all events for payment of money in specie.

Rex v. Wilcox, Easter, 1808. Indictment for forging and uttering a promissory note; the note was to "pay the bearer on demand one guinea "in cash or Bank of England notes;" it was issued by the Pontefract bank. A case was reserved for the consideration of the twelve judges, on the question, whether this was a note within the statute; and a majority of them held it was not; and upon a representation to the crown, the prisoner was pardoned.

[Fales was sued as indorser of a note. The declaration was on a cash note. The note produced in evidence contained the words [Foreign Bills] in brackets at the foot of it. A majority of the Court held that the evidence did not support the declaration, and that such a note was not negotiable, "because the import of the words, *foreign bills*, is not cash, "but something different from cash." Parker J. thought that these words did not destroy the negotiable quality of the paper, because it was not the intention of the parties to affect its transferable quality by them. Jones v. Fales 4 Mass R. 245.

In a subsequent case in an action against the endorser of a promisssory note payable in *foreign money*, the defendant's counsel objected that the

And they must be for a specific amount. A bill or note for a given sum, and for whatever else may be due to the payee, is not, even between the original parties, a bill or note. (16)

Nor is it good for the sum it specifies. (16)

But an order of promise to pay so many "pound" instead of "pounds" is a bill or note. (17)

Negotiable bills or notes made in England for less than (18)

---

note was not negotiable and so that an action could not be maintained by an endorsee in this form. "But the court held the declaration good." Sanger v. Stimpson, 8 Mass. Rep. 260. The grounds of this decision do not appear in the report. Perhaps the court did not consider the note as negotiable, but merely that this was the proper form of declaring by an endorsee against the endorser of a note not negotiable. Parsons C. J. in an earlier case said, that by the common law of the commonwealth "all notes for merchandize may be sued by the promisee against the promiser, and when endorsed by the endorsee against the endorser, who may declare in the same manner, as he might if the notes were negotiable." Jones v. Fales, 4 Mass. R. 245.

The Supreme Court of New York have taken a different view of this subject.—Count on a promissory note "payable in York State bills or "specie." Demurrer. Per Curiam. "The count is good. The note "therein stated is a negotiable note under the statute; and being de-"clared to be payable in *York State bills or specie*, is the same thing as "being made payable in lawful current money of the state; for the "bills mentioned mean bank paper, which is here, in conformity with "common usage and common understanding regarded as cash." Keith v. Jones, 9 Johns. R. 120.

So in a subsequent case, in an action against the endorser of a note payable "in bank notes current in the city of New York." Woodworth. J. delivered the opinion of the Court. "The court will take notice that notes current in the city of New York are of cash value throughout the State; and are distinguished by these words from other bank notes which are received at a discount. From authority I cannot perceive any objection to the note in question. It would have been a note under the statute if payable in bank notes generally; consequently it is valid, as such, when confined to a species of bank paper of known cash value." Judah v. Harris, 19 Johns. R. 144.]

(16) Smith v. Nightingale, 2 Stark. 375. Defendant gave Eastling this note, "I promise to pay James Eastling, my head carter, £65, with "lawful interest for the same, three months after date, *with all other* "*sums that may be due to him.*" Eastling's administratrix sued thereon; Lord Ellenborough thought it no note, even for the £65, but an agreement, and it not having an agreement stamp, he nonsuited the plaintiff.

(17) Rex v. Post, Pasch. 1806. Prisoner altered a note for one pound into a note for ten, by substituting ten for one before the word "Pound" in the body of the note, and also in the corner. It was urged that a note for payment of ten *pound* was not a money note. On a case reserved, the judges were clear that it was, and that a capital conviction of the prisoner for forgery was right.

(18) By 48 Geo. III. c. 88. § 2.

twenty shillings are void; and all negotiable bills or notes made in England (except Bank of England notes, and notes payable to the bearer on demand), for twenty shillings and less than (19) five pounds, unless made conformably with certain regulations, are also void; and the person issuing or negotiating them (20) liable to a penalty not exceeding twenty pounds, nor less than five.

These regulations are, that they specify the name and place of abode of the person to whom or to whose order they are made payable; that they be attested by one subscribing witness; that they bear date at or before the time when they are issued; and be made payable within twenty-one days after the date.

But all notes payable to bearer, issued by the Governor and Company of the Bank of England, are (21) good and valid in law, notwithstanding their being for the payment of less than £5. And the act of the 17th Geo. III., so far as it relates either to the making void of promissory notes, or draughts, or undertakings in writing *payable on demand to the bearer thereof*, for any sum of money less than £5 in the whole, or to the restraining the publishing or uttering and negotiating of any such notes, draughts, or undertakings, was, during the late war, (22) suspended until six months after the ratification of a definitive treaty of peace; and the stamp-act now in force, 55 G. III. c. 184., which imposes stamps on such notes, implies that they are to be considered as valid.

Sect. 4.—A bill or note must purport that the money mentioned in it shall be payable absolutely and at all events; if it purports to make the payment depend on any uncertainty

(19) By 17 Geo. III. c. 30. § 1. made perpetual by 27 Geo. III. c. 16.

(20) By 48 Geo. III. c. 88. § 3. where the bill or note is for less than twenty shillings; and by 17 Geo. III. c. 30. § 2. where such bills or notes as fall within that Act, are not made conformably with the regulations there prescribed.

(21) By 37 Geo. III. c. 28.

(22) By 37 Geo. III. c. 32. and 45 Geo. III. c. 25.

or contingency, the instrument is not, except in certain cases as to the stamp duties, a bill or note; and if it is not a bill or note ab initio, no subsequent (23) event can make it so.

Thus an order or promise to pay money provided (24) the terms mentioned in certain letters shall be complied with, provided (25) I. S. shall not be surrendered to prison within a limited time, provided (26) I. S. shall not pay the money

---

(23) See Colehan v. Cooke, Willes 393. and Hill v. Halford, post 11. and Blankenhagen v. Blundell, post.

[Coolidge sued Ruggles on a note originally given to Skinner, expressed to be payable to bearer, "provided the ship Mary arrived at an European port of discharge free from capture and condemnation by the British." Parker C. J. delivered the opinion of the Court. "We are all of opinion that the written promise declared on is not negotiable in its nature, so that an action may be maintained on it by the name of the assignee, on account of the contingency, on which the payment is made to depend." Coolidge v. Ruggles 15 Mass. R. 387.

A promise to pay a corporation a certain sum upon every share of stock subscribed for by the promiser, "in such manner and proportion, and at such time and place, as shall be determined by the President, Directors, and Co." is not a promissory note within the statute, on account of the contingency. Union Turnp. Co. v. Jenkins, 1 Cain. R. 381.

See Atkinson v. Manks, ante, 6.]

(24) Kingston v. Long, B. R. M. 25 Geo. III. The Plaintiff brought an action as Endorsee against the Defendant, as acceptor, upon an order importing to be payable, *provided the terms mentioned in certain letters written by the drawer were complied with*, and the court held clearly that the plaintiff could not recover, though the acceptance admitted a compliance with the terms, for the order was no bill, until after such compliance, and if it were not a bill when drawn, it could not afterwards become one.

(25) Smith v. Boheme, 3 Lord Raym. 67. cit. Lord Raym. 1362, 1396. Action by payee against the makers upon a note promising to pay plaintiff or order on demand 71*l.* 12*s.* 10*d.* or to surrender the body of Samuel Boheme in an action brought against him by plaintiff. Verdict for the plaintiff and judgment; and on error brought in the King's Bench, the court held that this was not a note within the statute, because the money was not absolutely payable, but depended upon the contingency whether the defendants should surrender Samuel Boheme to prison; and the judgment was reversed 9th of June, 1724.

(26) Appleby v. Biddulph, cit. 8 Mod. 363. 4 Vin. 240—pl. 16. An action was brought on this note, "I promise to pay to T. M. 50*l.* if my brother doth not pay it within six weeks;" and after verdict for the plaintiff, the court arrested the judgment, because the maker was only to pay it on a contingency.

Ferris v. Bond. B. R. Trin. 2 Geo. 4. A note was in these words, "I, John Connor, promise to pay John Ferris or his order 50*l.* with interest, at six months' notice, dated 24th of June, 1803. (Signed,) "I. Connor.—Or else Henry Bond." In an action upon this against Bond, the question was reserved whether this was as to Bond, a note within

by a particular day, provided (27) I. S. shall leave me sufficient, or I shall otherwise be able to pay it, or when I. S. (28) shall marry, is no bill or note on account of the contingency to which the payment is subjected. An order or promise to pay out of my (29) growing subsistence, or (30) fifth payment when due, or out of (31) money when receiv-

---

the statute; and the court after argument held it was not, because Bond's engagement only was to pay if Connor did not; and a rule for a nonsuit was made absolute.

(27) Roberts v. Peake, Burr. 323. The plaintiff as endorsee of a note sued one of the makers; the instrument was in these words: "We promise to pay A. B. 116*l.* 11*s.* value received, on the death of "George Henshaw, provided he leaves either of us sufficient to pay the "said sum, or if we shall be otherwise able to pay it;" and upon a case reserved, the court held it was not a negotiable note, because it was payable eventually aud conditionally only, and not absolutely and at all events, and a nonsuit was entered. See Williamson v. Bennett, post.

(28) Beardsley v. Baldwin, Str. 1151. A note to pay money within so many days after the defendant should marry, was (on consideration) held not to be a negotiable note; and in Pearson v. Garrett, Comb. 227. and 4 Mod. 242. (which was before the statute,) an action having been brought upon a note by which the defendant promised to pay the plaintiff sixty guineas if he (the plaintiff) should be married within two months, the court inclined against the note, because it was to pay money on a mere contingency, and judgment was given on demurrer for the defendant.

(29) Jocelin v. Laserre, Fort. 281. 10 Mod. 294, 316. Evans drew upon Jocelin, and required him to pay Laserre 7*l.* a month out of Evans's growing subsistence. Laserre sued Jocelin, and had judgment, but upon a writ of error that judgment was reversed, because this draught was not a good bill of exchange, inasmuch as it would not have been payable, had Evans died, or had his subsistence been taken away.

(30) Haydock v. Linch, Lord Raym. 1563. Rogers drew upon Linch and requested him to pay Haydock 14*l.* 3*s.* out of the fifth payment when it should become due, and it should be allowed by Rogers. Linch accepted the draught, and Haydock sued him, but the court on demurrer to the declaration held this was no bill of exchange, and gave judgment for the defendant.

(31) Dawkes v. Lord Deloraine, Blackst. 782. 3 Wils. 207. A draught was in these words: "8th of January, 1768, Seven weeks after date, pay Mrs. Dawkes 32*l.* 17*s.* out of W. Steward's money as soon as you shall receive it, for your humble servant, Deloraine. To Timothy Brecknock, Esq." Brecknock accepted the bill, but it not being paid, Mrs. Dawkes brought an action upon it, against Lord Deloraine, who pleaded that Brecknock had not received W. Steward's money, and upon demurrer to this plea, insisted that this was not a bill of exchange. The court after argument, held the objection good; because it was payable out of a particular fund, and on an event which was future and contingent, viz. the receipt of W. Steward's money, whereas a bill ought to be subject to no event or contingency, except the failure of the general

ed, is no bill or note on account of the uncertainty whether the subsistence or payment will become due, or the money be received.

So an order to pay a sum out of (32) rents or (33) other money in the hands of the person to whom it is addressed is no bill, because he may not have rent or other money in his hands sufficient to discharge it.

So a promise to pay (34) *on the sale or produce immediately when sold, of the White Hart inn, St. Albans, and the goods, &c.* is no note : although it be averred in the declaration upon such promise that the White Hart and goods were sold before the action was commenced.

So an instrument in the form of a note, but with a memo-

---

personal credit of the persons drawing or negotiating it. In Wilson 262. is a report from hearsay of a determination that a promise to pay a sum of money, on the receipt of the Payee's wages due from a ship in government service, was a good note: but that may perhaps be questioned, because the maker might never receive the wages.

(32) Lord Raym. 1362. Str. 592. Fort. 282.

(33) Jenny v. Herle, Lord Raym. 1361. 8 Mod. 265. Str. 591. Herle sued Jenny upon a bill drawn by him upon Pratt, and payable to Herle to this effect : " Sir, you are to pay Mr. Herle 1945*l.* out of the money " in your hands belonging to the proprietors of the Devonshire mines, " being part of the consideration money for the purchase of the manor " of West Buckland." Herle had judgment in the Common Pleas, but upon a writ of error, the court of King's Bench held this was no bill of exchange, because it was only payable out of a particular fund supposed to be in Pratt's hands, and the judgment was accordingly reversed.

[See Atkinson v. Manks, ante, 6.]

(34) Hill v. Halford and another in Error, 2 B. and P. 413. The defendants in Error sued Hill as maker of a note, thereby promising to pay them 190*l.* " on the sale or produce, immediately when sold, of the White Hart, St. Albans, Herts, and the goods, &c. value received." The declaration averred a sale of the inn and goods before the commencement of the action. After judgment in K. B. by default, writ of inquiry executed, and general damages recovered, Hill brought a writ of error in the Exchequer Chamber, and the court held that this promise could not be declared on as a note, and therefore reversed the judgment.

[The endorsee sued the maker of the following note. " Trenton, Oct. 29, 1806. This may certify that I do agree to pay unto Solomon Stevens or order forty dollars by the 20th of May, or when he completes the building according to contract." In the Common Pleas the court thought the note payable on a contingency, and so not negotiable, and directed a verdict for the defendant. On Error the Supreme Court " held the note payable absolutely at a day certain," and ordered a new trial. Stevens v. Blunt, 7 Mass. R. 240. The reasons of this decision are not stated by the Reporter.]

randum written upon it, stating that it is taken for (35) securing the payment of all such balances as shall be due from one of the makers to the payee, to the extent of the sum mentioned therein, or that if any dispute shall arise respecting the subject which is the consideration for it, it shall be void, is no note. (36.)

So an instrument acknowledging the receipt of draughts for the payment of money, and promising to pay the money specified in the draughts, is (37) not a promissory note.

---

(35) Leeds & al. v. Lancashire, 2. Camp. N. P. C. 205. The defendant, Marriott, and Ball gave a joint and several promisory note to the plaintiffs for 200*l*. No time for payment was mentioned in the note. On the back was written, "The within note is taken for security of all "such balances as Jas. Marriott may happen to owe to Thos. Leeds and "Co. not extending farther than the within named sum of 200*l*. but this "note to be in force for six months, and no money liable to be called "for sooner in any case." This memorandum was written before the note was signed by the defendant or Ball. It appeared in an action upon this note, that in the course of mercantile dealings, Marriott had become indebted to the plaintiffs, and that on their refusing to deal with him any longer without some guarantee, the above instrument, which the makers represented to be a note, was given. It had a note stamp.—Lord Ellenborough held that as between the original parties it was an agreement, and not a note, and therefore nonsuited the plaintiffs.

(36) Hartley v. Wilkinson, 4 Camp. 127. 4 Maule 25. A note was made payable to Foster or order, for 25*l*. "being the amount of the pur- "chase-money for a quantity of fir belonging to Mr. Hartley." Before the note was signed, this memorandum was endorsed upon it: "This "note is given on condition that if any dispute shall arise between Mr. "Hartley and Lady Wray respecting the fir, this note to be void." In an action upon this note by endorsee against the maker, Lord Ellenborough thought it not a note within the statute, because its payment depended upon there being no dispute between Mr. Hartley and Lady Wray, and he nonsuited the plaintiff. On a motion for a new trial, the court agreed with him, aud refused a rule.

(37) Williamson & al. v. Bennett & al., 2 Campb. N. P. C. 417. The defendants were sued upon the following instrument, which was stamped and declared upon as a promissory note, "Borrowed and received of J. "and J. Williamson (the plaintiffs) the sum of £200 in three draughts, "by W. and B. Williamson, dated as under, payable to us W. Bennett "and S. M. (the defendants) on J. and J Williamson, which we promise "to pay unto the said J. and J. Williamson, with interest. As witness "our hands this 26th day of August, 1802.

"August 26, 1 draught at 2 months £120
" ——— 1 do. ——— 30
" ——— 1 do. ——— 50

£200

(Signed by the defendants.)

For the payment of the money depends upon the draughts being honoured.

So an order from the (38) owner of a ship to the freighter to pay money *on account of freight* is no bill, because the quantum due for freight may be open to litigation, but such an order from the freighter (39) is, because it is an admission that so much at least is due.

And an order to pay money as (40) *the drawer's quarter's half-pay by advance* before the pay will be due, is a good bill, because it will be payable though the half-pay shall never become due.

So a note to pay a sum of money, (41) *being a portion of a value as under deposited in security for the payment hereof ac-*

Lord Ellenborough held that this was not a promissory note. And said there can be no doubt that the money was not payable immediately, and that it was not to be paid at all, unless the draughts were honoured. The plaintiffs were nonsuited.

(38) Banbury v. Lisset, Str. 1211. Gibson drew on the defendants in favour of the plaintiff "on account of freight of the galley Veale, Ed- "ward Champion, and this order shall be your sufficient discharge for "the same." The action was brought against the defendants as acceptors, and they contended it was not a bill of exchange, because it was only payable out of a particular fund; and Lee C. J. was of that opinion, but he left the point to the jury, who found for the defendants on another ground.

(39) Pierson v. Dunlop, Cowp. 571. M'Lintot freighted a ship of which Nichol was captain, and Pierson owner, and being unable to pay the freight, drew upon Dunlop and Co. in favour of Nichol *on account of freight:* Pierson afterwards sued Dunlop and Co. as acceptors, and though other objections were taken, it was never insisted that this was payable out of a particular fund.

(40) Macleod v. Snee, Lord Raym. 1481. Str. 762. 1 Barnard. 12. Macleod was sued in the Common Pleas as acceptor of a bill of exchange drawn by Dundas and endorsed to the plaintiff, dated 25th of May, 1724, by which Dundas required him one month after date "to "pay £9 10*s.* as his (Dundas's) quarter's half-pay from the 24th June, "1724, to 25th September following, by advance," and obtained judgment. Macleod brought a writ of error, and insisted that this was similar to the cases of Jocelin v. Laserre, and Jenney v. Herle, but the whole court was of a contrary opinion; for per cur. this bill was not payable upon a contingency, nor out of a particular fund, but is made payable at all events, and drawn upon the general credit of the drawer, and not out of the half-pay, for it is payable as soon as the quarter begins, and the half-pay was not to be due till three months afterwards.

(41) Haussoullier v. Hartsink, 7 Term. Rep. 733. The defendant issued two notes upon a deposit by one Richardson: one payable to J. S. or bearer, for £25, "being a portion of a value as under deposited in "security for payment hereof according to the receipt in our hands," and specifying the particulars of the deposit: the other, payable to J. S.

cording to the receipt in my hands, or *for value deposited and registered* is a good note, because it is payable at all events.

So an order or promise to pay money when (42) J. S. shall come of age, specifying the day when that event is to happen, is a good bill or note, because it is payable though J. S. die in the interim.

And an order or promise (43) to pay within a limited time after a man's death is a good bill or note, because it must become payable at some time or other, though the exact period is uncertain: and if a bill or note be made payable at ever so distant a day, if it be a day that must come, it is no objection to the bill or note (44).

So an order or (45) promise to pay within a limited time after the payment of money due from government is a good bill or note, because it is morally certain that such payment will be made.

---

or order "for value deposited and registered $\frac{A}{V}$." The plaintiff discounted both notes, bona fide, and for a valuable consideration: and on a case reserved the court said they were clearly of opinion, that though as between the original parties to the transaction, the payment of the notes was to be carried to a particular account, yet the notes were payable at all events, and therefore the plaintiff was entitled to recover.

(42) Goss v. Nelson, Burr. 226. Action on a note payable to an infant "when he (the infant) shall come of age, to wit, 12th June, 1750:" and it was objected in arrest of judgment, that it was uncertain whether the money would ever have been payable, because the infant might have died under 21, but the court held it a good note, because it was payable at all events on the 12th June, 1750, though the infant should have died before that time.

(43) Cooke v. Colehan, Str. 1217. Willes, 393. On error from the Common Pleas, the court held a note payable six weeks after the death of the defendant's father, a good negotiable note, because there was no contingency, whereby it might never become payable, but it was only uncertain as to the time, which is the case with all bills payable so many days after sight.

(44) Per Willes C. J. in delivering judgment in Colehan v. Cooke, Willes's Rep. 394.

(45) Andrews v. Franklin, Str. 24. A note payable two months after a certain ship (in his majesty's service) should be paid off, was objected to, as depending upon a contingency which might never happen: but per cur. the paying off the ship is a thing of a public nature; judgment for the plaintiff. And in Evans v. Underwood, 1 Wils. 262. where an action was brought by an endorsee against the maker upon a note payable on the receipt of the payee's wages from his majesty's ship the Suffolk, the court thought the case like that of Andrews v. Franklin, and after looking into that case *are said* to have given judgment for the plaintiff. Quære tamen, because it was uncertain, though the wages might be paid, whether the maker would receive them.

Sect. 5.—It is not in general essential that a bill or note should be dated.

But negotiable bills or notes, except bank-notes, for between 20*s.* and £5, if made in England, must. (46)

And notes payable to the bearer on demand must not have the dates printed. (47)

And giving false dates to evade the stamp duties upon draughts on bankers, or upon bills or notes not payable within two months after date, or sixty days after sight, will subject the party to a penalty of £100. (48)

If a bill or note is dated forward, of a day not arrived, and any of the parties die before that day, such deaths will be no bar to the remedy of a bonâ fide holder. (49)

So if a blank be left for the date, and that date is afterwards filled up, the manner of filling it up will furnish no ground of objection either to the original parties;

Or to the person who filled it up. (50)

Sect. 6.—Bills and notes are either inland or foreign; inland when made and payable within this kingdom; and foreign, when made or payable abroad. (*a*)

---

(46) See ante, p. 8.
(47) 55 G. 3. c. 184. s. 18.
(48) 55 G. 3. c. 184. s. 12, 13.
(49) See Pasmore v. North, post.
(50) See Usher v. Dauncey, post.

[(*a*) A bill was drawn at Manchester (England) payable in London on a house in Boston (Mass.) and was accepted in the name of the Boston house by a member of the firm, who was then at Manchester, though his domicil was in Boston. In an action upon this bill in Massachusetts against the acceptors, the court held that "it must be considered as a foreign bill, having the same effect as if the payee had sent it to Boston, and it had been accepted here, payable in London." Grimshaw v. Bender, 6 Mass. R. 157.

In New York a bill drawn in one of the United States upon a person within the United States, though not in the same state with the drawer, has been considered as an inland bill; and therefore requiring no protest, since the statute of 9 and 10 W. III. requiring a protest on such bills is not adopted in that State. The case however turned upon another point. Miller v. Hackley, 5 Johns. R. 375.

In South Carolina it was held that a bill drawn in New York upon

It was once doubted whether notes would be intitled to the aid of 3 and 4 Ann. c. 9. unless they were made within this kingdom, (51) but there have been instances (52) (53) since in which actions have been brought upon such notes without exception, (*a*) and 48 G. 3. c. 149. s. 21. prohibited the negotiation or payment of such notes unless they were stamped, and this prohibition is still continued by 55 G. 3. c. 184. s. 29. as to notes payable to the bearer on demand.

And it is no objection to a bill or note that it was made by a British subject in an enemy's country in time of war, if

---

Charleston (S. C.) was a foreign bill, and therefore that a protest for non-acceptance was necessary in order to charge an endorser. *Nott* J. delivered the opinion of the Court. "Sovereignty or jurisdiction over the "subject appears to be the criterion by which to determine the charac-"ter of the instrument. It would seem correct, therefore, to consider "bills between the several States as foreign. They are usually sent "in sets. Exchange is allowed on them; and unless a protest is to be "received as evidence of non-acceptance, the difficulty of proving the "fact would very much obstruct that kind of intercourse between the "States. However they may have been considered in other States, "there has never been but one opinion on the subject in this State." Duncan v. Course, 1 S. Car. R. 100.

In Pennsylvania a bill drawn in one State upon a person residing in another, seems to have been considered a foreign bill. Lonsdale v. Brown, Whart. Dig. 85.]

(51) Carr v. Shaw, B. R. H. 39 Geo. 3. In an action on a promissory note made at Philadelphia, the first count of the declaration stated that the defendant, at Philadelphia, in parts beyond the seas, to wit, at London, &c. according to the form of the statute, &c. made his note in writing, &c. There were also the common money counts. The defendant demurred specially to the first count, and pleaded the general issue to the others. On the demurrer the court intimated a strong opinion that the statute did not apply to foreign notes, and advised the plaintiff to amend: but on the general issue Lord Kenyon said, the note, though not within the statute, is evidence to support any of the money counts, and the plaintiff had a verdict at Guildhall, 1st May, 1799.

N. The pleadings are entered as of Michaelmas Term, 39 G. 3. Roll. 1238.

(52) See Pollard v. Herries, 3 Bos. & Pull. 335, where the plaintiffs recovered upon notes made at Paris. See also Splitgerber v. Kohn, post.

[(*a*) Action by the endorsee against the maker of a promissory note made at Dundee in Scotland. It was contended that the endorsee could sue the maker, only when the note was made in England. Per Curiam. "This is within both the words and the spirit of the act. The words are 'all notes.' It is for the advancement of commerce that foreign as well as inland notes should be negotiable." Milne v. Graham, 1 Barn. & Cres. 192. S. C. 2 Dow. & Ryl. 293.]

it do not appear to have been made for any illegal purpose, and was made payable to a neutral. (53)

Or, if made by a British prisoner of war, if made payable or endorsed to an alien enemy. (54)

Inland bills and notes seldom consist of more than one part: foreign bills in general consist of several.

The several parts of a bill are called a set.

Each part contains a condition that it shall be payable only so long as all the others remain unpaid: in other respects all are of the same tenor.

This condition should be inserted in each part, and should in each mention every other part of the set, for if a man with an intention to make a set of three parts should omit the condition in the first, and make the second with a condition mentioning the first only, and in the third alone take notice of the other two (which, by the way, is the mode pointed out by (55) Molloy, (56) Malynes, and (57) Marius) he might perhaps in some cases be obliged to pay each; for it might be questionable if it would be any defence to an action on the second that he had paid the third, or to an action on the first that he had paid either of the others.

But an omission is not, perhaps, material, which upon the face of the condition must necessarily have arisen from a mistake, as if in the enumeration of the several parts one of the intermediate ones were to be omitted, for instance, "Pay this my first of exchange, second and *fourth* not paid."

Where a bill consists of several parts, each ought to be delivered to the person in whose favor it is made, (unless one

---

(53) Houriet v. Morris, 3 Campb. 303. Payees against maker on note made at Paris in time of war: defendant was a British subject, plaintiffs neutral merchants in Switzerland: the note was given by defendant for watches bought by him in Paris of plaintiffs: it was objected that this was a trading in an enemy's country in time of war, and that a note founded on such trading was not valid: but Lord Ellenborough said, plaintiffs were not enemies, and might legally sell their goods in an enemy's country, and defendant did not appear to have bought them for any illegal purpose. Plaintiffs had a verdict.

(54) See Antoine v. Morshead, and Daubuz v. Morshead, post.

(55) Book 2. c. 10. s. 14.

(56) Book 3. c. 5. p. 261, 262.

(57) P. 7.

is forwarded to the drawee for acceptance,) otherwise there may be difficulties in negotiating the bill, or obtaining payment.

Sect. 7.—A bill or note may fix a particular place for payment.

And where this is what is to be considered as part of a bill or note, it is a variance to omit stating it; (58)

And in an action against the maker of the note, or acceptor of the bill, may make it necessary to allege and prove presentment at that place. (59)

The place is considered part of the instrument where it is incorporated in the body of the bill or note; where it is detached from the body as a memorandum only, not.

Sect. 8.—Bills and notes are made payable to order, or to bearer, or to specified individuals.

A bill or note payable to J. S. or order, is payable to the order of J. S. and negotiable by endorsement. A bill or note payable to J. S. or bearer, is (60) payable to the bearer and negotiable by delivery; and in the latter case J. S. is a mere cypher.

[But a note saying "Due the bearer hereof" a certain

---

(58) Hodge v. Fillis. See post.

(59) Roche v. Campbell. See post.

[But the Supreme Court of Massachusetts, in an action by the endorsee against the maker of a note payable at the Penobscot Bank, held that a plea that the holder of the note was not present at the time and place appointed for payment was bad; and said, "This is no bar to an action on a promise to pay money: and the issue tendered was therefore an immaterial one." Ruggles v. Patten, 8 Mass. R. 480.]

(60) Grant v. Vaughan, Burr. 1516. Vaughan gave Bicknell a draught upon his banker payable "to ship Fortune or bearer." The draught came to the hands of Grant, who sued Vaughan upon it. The defendant contended that this draught was a mere authority to receive the money, and not negotiable, and that point and another being left to the jury, they found for the defendant; but upon an application for a new trial, and cause shewn, the court held clearly that it was negotiable, and a new trial was granted, in which the plaintiff recovered.

sum, "which I promise to pay to A. B. or order," is not a note payable to bearer, but to A. B. or order. (*a*)]

If a bill or note import to be payable to a person not in esse, or his order, and is issued with an endorsement in blank, purporting to be made by him thereon, it is as against the drawer or maker to be considered as a bill or note (61)

[(*a*) The bearer sued the maker of the following note, "Due the bearer hereof, £3 18*s.* 10*d.* which I promise to pay to Abraham Thompson or order." Thompson had not endorsed the note. Per Curiam. "The word, *bearer*, has reference to Thompson, and as the promise is expressly to pay to him or order, another person could not maintain an action on the note without his endorsement." Cook v. Fellows, 1 Johns. R. 143.]

(61) This point has been repeatedly discussed within a few years upon several bills drawn in 1788. A case of the kind had occurred at the London Sittings after Easter Term 1769; Stone v. Freeland, cited 1 H. Bl. 316. in the notes: a bill drawn by Cox on the defendant was made payable to Butler and Co. or their order, and endorsed in their name, and instead of proving that this endorsement was made by Butler and Co., the Plaintiff's own witnesses said, they believed it was made by Cox, and though there was a house under the firm of Butler and Co. with which Cox had dealings, it was proved that the bill had never been in their hands, upon which it was contended that the endorsement being fictitious, the plaintiff could not recover; but by Lord Mansfield, "the intent of the bill was only to enable Cox to raise money, and the reason why it was not made payable to his order was, that there would then have been too many payable to his order in circulation at the same time, which would have had the appearance of fictitious credit; names are often used of persons who never existed;" and it appearing that the defendant promised to pay the bill at the time the plaintiff discounted it, the jury upon the footing of that undertaking found a verdict for the plaintiff. As this case however was distinguishable from those on the bills drawn in 1788, on account of the express undertaking to pay the plaintiff, which (as was admitted by Mr. J. Ashhurst, who held a brief in the cause, in 3 Term Rep. 176.) was the ground of the determination, as this was a nisi prius decision only, and as the amount of the bills in 1788 was very considerable, the point was very strongly contested in the actions on those bills. The first case that came before the court was Tatlock v. Harris, 3 Term Rep. 174. It was an action brought upon a bill drawn by the defendant, as one of several partners in a house at Nottingham upon himself in London, payable to Grigson and Co. or order, and purporting to be endorsed by Grigson and Co. and Lewis and Potter; the defendant was sued upon the bill, and the declaration contained counts upon the bill, and counts for money paid and money had and received. It appeared in evidince that there was no such house as that of Grigson and Co.; that the defendant paid the bill to Lewis and Potter, to whom he was indebted, and they gave him credit in account; and that the plaintiffs discounted it for Lewis and Potter: to this evidence the defendant demurred; and after argument and time taken to consider, the court intimated a strong opinion that the plaintiffs might recover on the counts upon the bill; but the ground of their

payable to bearer; and so is a bill as against the acceptor, if he knew at the time of his acceptance, that the payee was a fictitious person.

---

decision was, that he was entitled to recover on the counts for money paid, and money had and received, because the giving the bill was an appropriation of so much money to be paid to the person who should become holder of the bill, and therefore when the plaintiffs discounted it, they paid the money to the use of the defendant, and when Lewis and Potter gave the defendant credit for the value of the bill, that was money had and received to the use of such persons as should afterwards be the holders of the bill.

The next case was that of Vere v. Lewis, 3 Term Rep. 182. which was brought against the defendant as acceptor, and the only difference between that and Tatlock v. Harris was, that there was no evidence to shew that the defendant had received any value for the bill, and that there was strong evidence to show that the endorsement, in the name of the payee, was made by the defendant; but the court held that the latter circumstance did not vary the question, and that the acceptance was evidence that the defendant had received value from the drawers, and therefore they gave judgment for the plaintiff without argument. Lord Kenyon, Mr. J. Ashhurst, and Mr. J. Buller, thought also that he was entitled to recover on one of the counts of the declaration, which stated the bill to be payable to bearer.

This case was followed by that of Minet v. Gibson, 3 Term Rep. 481. 1 H. Bl. 569. where a bill drawn by Livesay and Co. on the defendants was made payable to John White, or order, and it was found upon a special verdict, that White was a fictitious person, that his name was endorsed upon the bill by Livesay and Co.; that the defendants knew, when they accepted the *bill*, that no such person as John White, whose endorsement was then upon the bill, existed, and that the endorsement was not made by any person of that name, the court of King's Bench thought this case decided by Vere and Lewis, and gave judgment for the plaintiffs; and on a question from the House of Lords, whether the bill might not be deemed in law to be payable to the bearer, Hotham, Perryn, and Thompson, Barons, and Gould J. gave it as their opinions that it might; but Eyre C. B. and Heath J. differed; after which Lord Kenyon, Lord Loughborough, and Lord Bathurst spoke in favour of the judgment, and Lord Thurlow against it, and the judgment was affirmed without a division.

After the judgment in Minet v. Gibson, in the King's Bench, and before its determination in the House of Lords, came on the case of Collis v. Emett, 1 H. Bl. 313. where Livesay and Co. (who were authorized by the defendant to draw for him by his writing his name on a piece of blank paper with a shilling bill stamp thereon,) made a bill payable to George Chapman, or order, and endorsed it with George Chapman's name; and it appearing that there was no such person as George Chapman, the Court of Common Pleas, after two arguments, and time taken to consider, held that the action might fairly be supported on a count that stated the bill to be payable to bearer, and there being such a count in the declaration, they gave the plaintiffs judgment upon it. Vide Bennet v. Farnell, 1 Camp. 180.

[The principles stated in the text with regard to fictitious payees have been fully recognised in various courts in the United States. See

It was for some time unsettled whether it was not essential that a bill or note should be payable either to order, or to (62) bearer, but it is now decided that it is not.

Hunter v. Blodgett, 2 Yeates, 480, which was an action brought against the acceptor of a bill drawn by the same firm of Livesay and Co., mentioned above, and payable to a fictitious payee: and Mussi v. Lorain, 2 Browne, 56.

In an action by the endorsee against the makers of a note, it was declared on as payable to Moses Foster, or order, and by him endorsed. The endorsement was made by Moses Foster of Milford; the defendants contended that Moses Foster of Andover was the person intended. The jury found that the plaintiff had always possessed the note, which was given for money loaned by him to one of the defendants, and "that "no person of the name of Moses Foster had ever possessed any interest "in the note, or been particularly intended as payee." Woodbury J. said, "When a note is made payable to the name of some person, not "having any interest, and not intended to become a party in the trans-"action, whether a person of such a name is or is not known to exist, "the payee may be deemed fictitious." He said that where money passed between the parties, a recovery might in such case be had on the money counts; and that in the present case where only one of the makers of the note received the money, a recovery might be had on the note on a count alleging it to be payable to bearer, "after alleging that "the nominal payee is fictitious." Foster v. Shattuck, 2 N. Hamp. Rep. 446.]

(62) Smith v. Kendall, 6 Term Rep. 123. In an action for money paid and lent, the defendant pleaded the statute of limitations, and the plaintiff replied a latitat sued out 26th Sept. 1793. A note was given in evidence dated 25th June, 1787, and payable to the plaintiff three months after date, but it was not payable either to order or to bearer, and the court on consideration held that it was a good note within the statute, that it was entitled to three days' grace, and consequently that the statute of limitations did not begin to run until those three days had expired, which was on 28th Sept. 1787, and therefore within six years of 26th September, 1793. See also Chadwick v. Allen, ante, p. 3. The old entries also describe the custom upon bills to be to pay the payee without adding any words to make them payable to order or to bearer. Lutw. 231, 277, 891. Vid. 1 Brownl. Rep. 77. Clift. 916.; and see Lord Raym. 1545.

Rex v. Box, 6 Taunt. 325. Indictment for forging a promissory note. The note was as follows: "On demand we promise to pay Mesdames "S. W. and S. D., stewardesses for the time being of the Provident "Daughters Society, held at the Hope, Smithfield, or their successors "in office, £64, with £5, *per cent.* interest, value received this 7th "February, 1815, for F. C. and Co. J. Forster." This society was not enrolled according to 33 G. 3. c. 34., so that these payees were not strictly stewardesses, nor could they legally have successors in office, and it was insisted that this was not in law a promissory note; but on a case for the opinion of the twelve judges, they were unanimously of opinion that it was: that it was not essential a note should be negotiable, that the description of stewardesses was one which went to designate the payees, and the note, if genuine, would have enured to them, and the survivor of them, and the executors and administrators of such survivor, and the conviction of the prisoner was held right.

But where the bill or note is payable otherwise than to the bearer, it must contain the name of the payee.

Uncertainty as to the person to whom the payment shall be made will prevent an instrument from being a bill or note, as making it payable to *A.* or *B.* (63)

[So if no person be named as payee, the instrument is not a bill or note. (*a*)]

If a bill or note is issued with a blank for the payee's name, any *bonâ fide* holder may insert his own name as payee. (64)

[It has been held in New York, in conformity with the English decisions, that a note is within the statute though not payable to bearer or order. Downing v. Backenstoes, 3 Cain. R. 137. Dutchess Cotton Manufactory v. Davis, 14 Johns. R. 238]

(63) Blankenhagen v. Blundell, 2 Barn. and Ald. 417. Declaration on a note by which it was stated that defendant promised to pay J. P. Dahmer or plaintiffs, or his or their order; another count stated Dahmer to be since dead: each count averred that the note was delivered to plaintiffs, and negatived payment to Dahmer: defendant demurred, and on argument the court were clear this was not a note within the statute, because it was not payable in certain either to Dahmer or the plaintiffs, but the claim of either or of the endorsee of either, might be defeated by payment to the other; and if it were not within the statute, when issued, subsequent events could not make it so. It was urged, that in legal operation it was payable to Dahmer and plaintiffs, but the court said they could not take that to be its operation as the declaration was framed, and judgment was given for the defendant.

[(*a*) In an action on the following memorandum—"Boston, 15th May, 1810. Good for one hundred and twenty-six dollars on demand. Gilman & Hoyt"—Mr. Chief Justice Parker, giving the opinion of the court, said, "It is not a negotiable promissory note. It is not payable to bearer. It is not a contract which, *ex proprio vigore*, constitutes a promise to whomsoever shall produce it. Its effect is nothing more than that of a memorandum to the parties to it, to operate as a promise to pay money; or a receipt for money; or proof of a sum of money to be accounted for, according to evidence to show the intention of the parties. It imports no promise to the holder without evidence that it was actually given to him." Brown v. Gilman, 13 Mass. R. 158.]

(64) Cruchley v. Clarance, 2 Maule, 90. In an action by the payee of a bill against the drawer, it appeared that defendant drew the bill in Jamaica, and sent it to England with a blank for the payee's name, that it was put into negotiation here, and afterwards paid to the plaintiff for an old debt, without the blank's being filled up; and that he inserted his own name as payee: plaintiff had a verdict; and on motion for nonsuit or new trial, the court held plaintiff warranted in inserting his own name, for by leaving the blank the defendant authorized any *bonâ fide* holder to fill it up. and the rule was refused.

Cruchley v. Mann, 5 Taunt. 529. Plaintiff brought another action on the same bill against the acceptor: one objection was that the blank was filled up without Clarance's authority, and Clarance gave in evi-

But until the blank is filled up it is not a bill or note. (65)

Unless perhaps where it may be considered in legal operation as payable to the order of the drawer.

Giving a payee a wrong description, if there is no doubt as to the person, is of no (66) consequence.

Sect. 9.—The (67) name of the person making it must be inserted in the body, or subscribed at the bottom of every

---

dence that he did not authorize the insertion; but it appears that Clarance had passed the bill to Vashon, that Vashon had passed it to plaintiff, and that defendant accepted it under Clarance's eye and at Clarance's instance, after plaintiff's name was inserted; the court was clear Clarance's consent must be implied, and a rule for a new trial was refused.

(65) Rex v. Randall. Trin. 1811. The prisoner was indicted for forging a bill of exchange, the bill was payable to   or order (leaving a space for the payee's name), and was in appearance a navy-bill for an officer's wages; the point was saved for the consideration of the judges, whether this could be deemed a bill, there being no payee: it was urged that such a bill authorized any proper holder to fill up the blank as he might choose: but the judges held it was no bill till the blank was filled up, and recommended it to the judge who tried the prisoner to apply to the Crown for his pardon.

(66) See Rex v. Box, ante, p. 21.

(67) Taylor v. Dobbins, Str. 399. The declaration upon a note stated that the defendant wrote it with his own hand, but did not allege that he signed it, and an exception was taken on that ground. Sed per cur. If the defendant wrote it, his subscription to it was unnecessary; it is sufficient if his name appeared in any part. "I, J. S. promise to pay" is as good as "I promise to pay," subscribed J. S.

Elliot v. Cowper, Str. 609. Lord Raym. 1376. 8 Mod. 307. It was objected on demurrer to a declaration on a note, that it alleged only that the defendant made it, but did not state that he signed it; but by the court, if he did not either write or sign it, he did not *make* it, for making implies signing, and making is alleged. Judgment for plaintiff.

Smith v. Jarves, Lord Raym. 1484. The declaration upon a note drawn by Jarves and Baily, stated that Jarves for himself and partner made his note in writing with his own hand subscribed, whereby he promised for himself and partner to pay. It was objected on demurrer, that it was not charged, that Jarves had signed the note for himself and Baily; but the court held the statement showed that Jarvis did sign for himself and Baily, and gave the plaintiff judgment.

Ereskin v. Murray, Lord Raym. 1542. In an action on a bill it was alleged that the plaintiff made his bill in writing, and thereby requested the defendant to pay. It was objected on error, that it did not appear that the plaintiff signed the bill; but it was answered, that the allegation that he made it, and required the defendant to pay, implied that his name was in it, (otherwise he could not request,) and that he or somebody for him wrote it. Judgment for the plaintiff was affirmed.

bill or note, and every bill or note must be written or signed by the person making it, or some one authorized by him for that purpose.

The clerk, who signs bank notes, need not have authority for that purpose under the common seal. (68)

And now by 1 Geo. 4. c. 92. s. 3. his signature may be impressed by machinery.

The signature to a bill or note must import to bind at all events each person who signs it. A note signed A. B. or else C. D. is not as against C. D. binding as a note. (69)

If a person signs his name upon a blank paper, stamped with a bill-stamp, and delivers it to another person to draw such bill as he may choose thereon, he (70) is the drawer of any bill such person shall draw thereon, to which the stamp is applicable.

Sect. 10.—If there be a subscribing witness to a bill or note, the bill or note cannot be read in evidence unless such witness is produced, or his absence properly accounted for.

Sect. 11.—It was for some time matter of controversy whether it was not necessary that a bill or note should im-

(68) Rex v. Bigg, 3 P. Will. 419. On an indictment under 8 & 9 W. III. c. 20. s. 36. for altering and erasing a genuine bank note, it was found upon a special verdict that the person who signed the note was employed by the company to sign notes, but that he had no authority under their common seal: and objection was taken that an authority under their common seal was necessary; many other objections were taken, and what was the opinion of the judges upon each is not stated; but Mr. P. Williams, who argued for the prisoner, says the judges were divided, but the majority of the judges held it to be felony, and the prisoner was transported, not executed.

(69) Ferris v. Bond, ante, p. 9.

(70) Collis v. Emett, 1 H. Bl. 313. Emett signed his name upon a blank paper stamped with a shilling bill-stamp, (the highest stamp then in force for bills,) and delivered it to Livesay and Co. that they might draw thereon such bill as they should please. They drew one for £1551 at three month's date, which was duly transferred to Collis and Co., and Collis and Co. sued Emett thereon. A special verdict was found, principally with a view to another point; the court held Emett answerable, and the plaintiffs had judgment. See Russell v. Langstaffe, post. Pasmore v. North, post. Usher v. Dauncey, post.

port to be for value received, but it is now settled (71) that it need not.

But notes for coals in ships in the port of London must by 3 G. 2. c. 26. s. 7, 8. import to be for value received in coals, and a refusal to insert words to that effect, or taking a note without such words, subjects the buyer and master of the ship to a penalty of £100. (72)

The note however is not, for want of those words, void. (73)

Sect. 12.—A memorandum on a bill or note before it is issued, may, in some instances, be considered as part of the bill or note, and control its operation. (*a*)

As a memorandum, that if any dispute shall arise respecting the consideration, the bill or note shall be void. (74)

But a memorandum upon a note to state where it shall be payable, is not. (75)

Nor a memorandum of acceptance on a note payable after sight. (76)

---

(71) White v. Ledwich, B. R. H. 25 G. III. A declaration upon a bill of exchange was demurred to, because it was not stated to have been given for value received, but the court said, it was a settled point, that it was not necessary, and gave judgment for the plaintiff. The same point is ruled in Macleod v. Snee, Lord Raym. 1481. See also Fort. 282. 8 Mod. 267. 1 Barnard. 88. Lutw. 889. 1 Mod. Ent. 310. 1 Show. 497.

[See also Goshen Turnpike Co. v. Hurtin, 9 Johns. R. 217; Dutchess Cotton Manufactory v. Davis, 14 Johns. R. 238.]

(72) 3 G. 2. c. 26. s. 7. s. 8.

(73) Per Holroyd J. 1. Stark. 463.

[(*a*) As to the effect of a memorandum, see Sanders v. Bacon, post, p. 26.]

(74) See Hartley v. Wilkinson, ante, p. 12.

(75) Exon v. Russell, 4 Maule, 505. At the bottom of a promissory note was written "At Messrs. Brown and Co.'s, bankers, London." In an action against the maker the declaration alleged that defendant made the note, and thereby promised to pay, &c. and made the same payable and to be paid at the house of certain persons described, as Messrs. Brown and Co.'s: there was no averment or proof of presentation at Brown and Co.'s; and on a rule nisi for a nonsuit for want of such proof, and cause shown, the court held that as the "At Messsrs. Brown and Co.'s" was a memorandum only and no part of the note, it was a misdescription to state it as part of the legal effect of the note itself to make it payable there, and on that account the rule was made absolute.

(76) Splitgerber v. Kohn, 1 Stark. 125. Endorsee against maker on

Nor is a memorandum by way of direction to the payee's executors, in case of his death. (77)

Nor a memorandum which cannot be read for want of an agreement stamp. (77)

Nor one which has an attesting witness, and cannot be read on account of his absence. (77)

[The words, "for renewal," written at the foot of a note, do not affect its negotiable quality. (*a*)]

[And a note, with an endorsement upon it, stating the consideration for which it is given, is still a promissory note within the statute. (*b*)]

---

a note made in Prussia, and payable seven days after sight: in the margin were these words, "Accepted on myself, payable every where" [and these words were on the note when it issued]; it was urged that they altered the nature of the note, and should have been noticed in the declaration; but Lord Ellenborough said they constituted no part of the original instrument; they were merely an acknowledgment of a sight of the note; and though they were contemporaneous with the note, their effect was in point of law subsequent.

(77) Stone v. Metcalfe, 1 Stark. 53. 4 Campb. 217. In an action by payee against maker on a note for £1000 and interest, payable months after date, there appeared to be a memorandum endorsed upon the note, but that memorandum was attested by J. S.: it was urged for defendant that he had a right to have the memorandum read as well as the note: but per Lord Ellenborough, "Plaintiff is entitled to have the "note read, having proved defendant's hand-writing; but the endorse- "ment may be an unconnected instrument." J. S. was then called, and proved the endorsement, which was as follows: "Although the within note is payable in months, my will and desire is that it shall not then be called in, and if defendant shall wish for further time, he shall have it without suit at law until three years after my decease:" it was urged that this endorsement made part of the note, and that neither of them could be read, because, taken together, they required an agreement-stamp. Sed per Lord Ellenborough: "I have on one side a perfect "note, and on the other that which, if stamped, might have operated as "a defeasance, but at which, for want of a stamp, I cannot look: but if "the words were incorporated, they are words of mere indulgence and "favour. As to the executors, the case might be different." The plaintiff had a verdict.

[(*a*) In an action by the endorsee against the endorser of a note the words, "for renewal," appeared written near the bottom of the note. These words were proved to be generally understood to mean that the note was intended to meet, or be substituted for, some preceding note; and it was contended that the plaintiff ought therefore to prove himself a *bona fide* holder. But the Court said, "we are of opinion that the words, *for renewal*, did not destroy the negotiable quality of the note." Peirce v. Butler, 14 Mass. R. 303.]

[(*b*) On a note made by the defendants in the common form, payable to Sanders and Ogden, the plaintiffs, was an endorsement signed by the

[The words "*ne varietur*" written upon a note by a notary at the time it is made, as appears to be customary in countries where the civil law is adopted, does not restrain the negotiability of the instrument. (*a*)]

Sect. 13.—The act of drawing a bill implies an undertaking from the drawer to the payee, and every other person to whom the bill may afterwards be transferred, that the drawee is a person capable of making himself responsible for its payment, that he shall, if applied to for the purpose express in writing upon the bill an undertaking to pay it when it shall become payable, and that he shall then pay it: and subjects the drawer on a failure in any of these particulars to an action at the suit of the payee or holder. (*b*)

The making of a note is an express engagement to the payee, or person to whom it shall be transferred, to pay the money mentioned therein, according to its tenor.

---

defendants, saying that the note "is to be delivered" to Sanders and Ogden in consideration of a judgment and execution in favor of S. & O. against S. Tryon "to be assigned to the subscribers." A question was made whether this note could be declared on as a note within the statute. Per Curiam. "The note was well declared upon, as a promissory note within the statute. The endorsement was no part of the note, the effect of it was only to show the consideration, and to operate as a notice to any person who might purchase the note. The delivery of the note was presumptive evidence of an assignment of the judgment, and it stood good, until overthrown by proof on the part of the defendants to the contrary." Sanders v. Bacon, 8 Johns. R. 379.]

[(*a*) Fleckner in Louisiana gave notes for the purchase money of an estate, payable to the vender or order. The notary before whom the contract of sale was executed wrote on each of the notes the words, "*ne varietur.*" In an action by an endorsee of one of the notes, Story J. delivered the opinion of the Court. "There is not the slightest evidence, that by the law or custom of Louisiana the introduction of these words affects the negotiability of these notes: without proof of such law or usage this court certainly cannot infer the existence of such an extraordinary and inconvenient doctrine." Fleckner v. U. S. Bank, 8 Wheat. R. 338.]

[(*b*) A bill of exchange after acceptance may be considered as an assignment of the drawer's funds in the hands of the drawee. "In cases also where an order is drawn for the whole of a particular fund, it amounts to an equitable assignment of that fund; and after notice to the drawee it binds the fund in his hands." "But where the order is drawn either on a general or a particular fund, for a part only, it does not amount to an assignment of that part, or give a lien as against the drawee, unless he consents to the appropriation by an acceptance of the draft." Mandeville v. Welch, 5 Wheaton, 277.]

CHAP. A.

Doctrine of the Lex Loci, *or by the Laws of what place the Liability of the Parties to a Bill or Note is regulated.*

It is a general rule that "the law of the place where a contract is made, is to govern, as to the nature, validity, and construction of such contract. This doctrine has become incorporated into the code of national law in all civilized countries." (*a*) But this rule supposes that the contract is to be executed where it is made; "*the law of the place*," says Lord Mansfield, "can never be the rule where the transaction is entered into with an express view to the law of another country as the rule by which it is to be governed." (*b*) A bill of exchange is made in one place, payable in another, and often endorsed at divers others; and the question arises how far the rights, obligations, and liabilities of the several parties to the bill, are determined by the distinct laws of these places. According to the expression of Lord Mansfield, the rights and obligations of the parties will be governed by the laws of the place to which they had reference in their contract. The validity, and to some purposes the construction, of the contract of the maker, and of each endorser, will be governed by the laws of the place of making or endorsing the bill; but as each of these in effect undertakes that another person, namely the drawee, shall accept and pay the bill on its being duly presented for these purposes; reference is necessarily had to the laws of the place on which the bill is drawn, to determine what must be done by the holder of the bill, and what will be a fulfilment, on the part of the drawee, of the undertaking of the drawer and endors-

---

(*a*) Per Story J. Van Reimsdyk v. Kane & al. 1 Gallis. 375, who cites Hub. de Conflictu Legum, tom. 2. l. 1. t. 3. Emerigon des Assur. tom. 1. c. 4. s. 8. Dig. L. 6 de evictionibus; Casar. Disc. 179, s. 57, Disc. 43. s 19; Disc. 130. s. 28, 33. 34; Decis Rot. Genuæ 38; Straccha, 147. See also Robinson v. Bland. Burr. 1077. Wm. Bl. 256; Smith v. Smith, 2 Johns. 282, and 8 Johns. 146.

(*b*) Robinson v. Bland, Burr. 1077.

ers in respect to the acts to be done by him. If the drawee fail to do what the drawer and endorsers have undertaken he shall do, then reference will again be had to the laws of the places of making and endorsing the bill, to determine what notice the holder must give of its dishonor, and what damage the maker or endorsers must pay. Where the contract appears upon the face of it to be made in reference to the laws of divers places, it will be affected accordingly by those laws respectively; but where a contract has reference to no other place, it will be governed by the laws of the place where it is made. (*a*)

(*a*) The maker and payee of a note were both citizens and inhabitants of Rhode Island, and the maker obtained a discharge under the insolvent laws of that State; it was held that this discharge was a bar to an action by a citizen of Massachusetts, to whom the note was subsequently endorsed. Baker v. Wheaton, 5 Mass. R. 509.

A bill was drawn in France by Bland on himself in England, in favor of Robinson, partly for money lent, and partly for money won at play Lord Mansfield said, "the parties had a view to the English law;" and the court held the bill to be void under the English statute against gambling. It was said however that the debt for which the bill was given could not have been legally enforced in France, though it was valid in the court of honor there. Robinson v. Bland. Burr. 1077. Wm. Bl. 256. And this seems to be a material circumstance, for the legality of the consideration is more properly determined by the laws of the place where the consideration passed, and the contract was made, than by those of the place where it is to be executed.

It was held in New York, in a case on a promissory note made in Canada, payable in England, that English interest only could be recovered on the note, not the New York rate of interest. Scofield v. Day. 20 Johns. R. 102.

The same court held that the ability of the drawer to bind himself is to be determined by the law of the place where the bill is drawn. The drawer of a promissory note made in Jamaica and payable in New York, was under twenty-one years old. It was taken for granted by the court that the note would have been void if made in New York, but as it was not proved that the age of infancy or minority was the same in Jamaica as in New York, the maker was held to be liable; for the court said it did not appear that the maker was not of age to bind himself by his contracts, according to the laws of Jamaica, at the time of making the note. Thompson v. Ketcham, 8 Johns. R. 146.

So a note made in Virginia and payable in New York, was held to be governed by the laws of New York. The note was in the usual form, except that it said, "Witness my hand and seal," and the maker's name had after it the letters L. S. with a flourish. The endorsee brought *assumpsit* upon the note against the maker in New York. Kent C. J. delivered the opinion of the Court. "The note was given in Virginia, and by the laws "of that State it was a sealed instrument or deed. But it was made paya- "ble in New York, and according to a well settled rule, it is to be tested

The endorsement being equivalent to the making of a bill or note, the question occurs whether the liability thus incurred shall be regulated by the laws of the place

---

"and governed by the law of this State. We have never adopted the "usage prevailing in Virginia and some other States, of substituting a "scrawl for a seal. A scrawl with a pen is not a seal and deserves no "notice." Warren v. Lynch, 5 Johns. R. 538.

The liability of the drawer in consequence of notice of the dishonor of a bill was held in New York, to depend on the laws of the place where the bill was drawn; and not on those of the place on which the bill was drawn. A bill was drawn at New Orleans on a house in Philadelphia of which the drawer was a partner; and was protested at Philadelphia for non-acceptance and non-payment, of which due notice was given to the drawer in New Orleans; who was subsequently discharged under the insolvent laws of Louisiana. The Court said "the drawer became conditionally liable for the payment, and the condition was the receiving due notice of the dishonor of the bill, and this notice was given in New Orleans. The circumstance of the bill's being drawn upon a person in another state can make no difference. The whole contract and responsibility of the drawer was entered into and incurred in New Orleans." And it was accordingly held that his discharge in New Orleans exonerated him. Hicks v. Brown, 12 Johns. 142.

It was held in Pennsylvania that the damages for which the drawer is liable on a returned bill, are to be determined by the laws of the place where it is drawn, though the suit is commenced against him on the bill in another place. By the statute of South Carolina, March 22, 1786, on "all bills drawn upon persons resident within the United States, and out of that State, and which shall be *returned* protested, the damages shall be 10 per cent." A bill being so drawn and returned, and a suit afterwards commenced upon it against the drawer, in Pennsylvania, the court adopted the rule of the South Carolina statute in fixing the rate of damages. Hazlehurst v. Kean, 4 Yeates, 19.

A different decision was given upon a very similar case in South Carolina; upon a bill drawn upon Charleston, at Nassau, where the damages upon bills returned protested are 12 1-2 per cent. The bill was accepted at Charleston, but not paid. As the drawer was in Charleston at the time of the dishonor of the bill there was no occasion to return it to Nassau to give notice of the non-payment. In suits in S. Carolina against the drawer and acceptor, the court was of opinion that the holder was not entitled to the damages of 12 1-2 per cent, according to the Nassau rule. Bain v. Ackworth, 1 S. Car. R. 107.

But in a previous case in South Carolina, a different rule seems to have been acted upon. In an action on a bill of exchange drawn in Boston (Mass.) upon persons in S. Carolina, it was left by the court to a special jury of merchants to decide what damages the defendants (probably endorsers—the case does not say) were liable to pay; and whether the damages were to be regulated by the laws and customs of Massachusetts or of South Carolina with regard to bills returned protested. The jury gave interest and 3 per cent. damages, agreeably to the custom of merchants in Boston on inland bills protested. Winthrop v. Pepoon, 1 Bay, 468.

The court of South Carolina however in another case acted upon the rule laid down in Bain v. Ackworth. Cruger in St. Croix drew a bill on himself payable in Charleston, and accepted it himself. After his return

where the bill or note is made, or where it is endorsed, and the courts seem to lean in favor of adopting the laws of the place where the endorsement is made. (*a*)

---

to Charleston the bill was presented to him for payment, and protested for non-payment. A question was made as to interest and damages. The jury who tried the case allowed 12 per cent. interest, the legal interest of St. Croix; and 10 per cent. the South Carolina damages on inland bills. The judges were of opinion that as the contract was to be performed in South Carolina, the damages must be governed by the laws of that State; and that as no law in South Carolina regulated the damages where a man draws upon himself, no damages could be recovered; and with regard to interest, only 7 per cent. interest, the legal rate of South Carolina, from the time of the demand. New trial. M'Candlish v. Cruger, 2 Bay, 377.

A member of a New York house accepted a bill in the partnership name at Manchester, in England, payable in London. The bill being dishonored a suit was commenced upon it in New York against the acceptors, and the question arose whether the plaintiffs were entitled to recover interest at the New York rate of 7 per cent. or the English rate of 5 per cent. By the court, "The bill having been drawn in England, and made payable there, the plaintiffs were entitled to 5 per cent. interest only." Foden v. Sharp, 4 Johns. R. 183.

But in a very similar case in Massachusetts a different decision was given. A bill payable in London was accepted at Manchester, England, by a partner of a house established at Boston, Massachusetts, in the partnership name. The partner who thus accepted for the firm, was domiciled in Boston. The bill being dishonored a suit was commenced in Massachusetts against the acceptors. On a question respecting the rate of damages to be recovered, Parsons C. J., giving the opinion of the court, said, "It is manifest that the remedy contemplated by the parties, in the event of the bill being dishonored, must be sought in this State, where the acceptors lived. The instrument must be considered as a foreign bill, having the same effect as if the payee had sent it to Boston, and it had been accepted here payable in London." And 10 per cent. was recovered for re-exchange, according to the Boston rule, in case of a bill drawn here on a foreign country and returned. Grimshaw v. Bender, 6 Mass. R. 157.

"Where a general order is given to draw bills from a certain place, on account of advances there made, the undertaking is to replace the money at that place." Therefore where Barker of New York had authorized Lanusse to draw bills upon him from New Orleans, which he refused to accept after they were drawn, the Court held that Lanusse might recover from Barker, the legal interest at New Orleans, 10 per cent. from the time the bills were protested. Lanusse v. Barker, 3 Wheat. R. 146.

(*a*) It has been held in New York that a discharge under the insolvent laws of Pennsylvania did not exonerate an endorser from his liability on a note endorsed by him in New York. A promissory note made in Rhode-Island was endorsed in New York by Van Arsdaln, a resident in Pennsylvania, to Van Raugh. Van Arsdaln was discharged of his debts under the insolvent laws of Pennslyvania after a suit had been commenced against him in New York, Van Raugh, the holder of the note,

In one respect a contract may be affected by the laws of a place other than that where it is made, or those to which it has reference, namely, in respect to the remedy, or the means and manner of enforcing it against the contractors. (*a*)

---

not being included in the list of creditors, nor the note mentioned among Van Arsdaln's debts in the proceedings under the insolvent laws of Pennsylvania. Mr. Chief Justice Kent said, "We are of opinion that the discharge is no bar. A discharge under the insolvent laws of another State, will not take away the right of a citizen of this State to sue here upon a contract made here." Van Raugh v. Van Arsdaln, 3 Cain. R. 154.

A case came before the Supreme Court of the United States upon a bill drawn in Barbadoes upon England, and endorsed by Slacum at Alexandria, in the District of Columbia; and the question was whether the 15 per cent. damages on dishonored bills allowed by the laws at Alexandria should be allowed in this case. Mr. Chief Justice Marshall, giving the opinion of the court, said, "Although the drawer of the bill was not liable to the damages of Virginia, the endorser is subject to them, he having endorsed the bill in Alexandria. The endorsement is not simply the transfer of the paper, but a new and substantive contract." Slacum v. Pomery, 6 Cranch, 221.

But in an action in N. Carolina upon a bill drawn in the West Indies, and endorsed in New York, the court said, "The question is whether the damages on a protested bill shall be regulated by the laws of the country where it is endorsed, in an action against the endorser. When a bill is endorsed, the endorser places himself in the situation of the original drawer, and subjects himself to the same duties which he was bound to perform. All that can be understood by an endorsement being in the nature of a new bill, is, that the endorser places himself in the situation of the drawer, and must be answerable to the endorsee in the same manner as the drawer must ultimately be answerable to him. Schermerhorn v. Pelham, Cam. & Nor. 452.

A bill was drawn at Demerara on Clapham of Boston (Mass.) payable to Powers. Lynch, a native citizen of the United States resident at Demerara, by his endorsement guarantied its payment. The bill was returned to Demerara protested for non-payment, and payment was demanded of the drawer in that place. By the law of Demerara any person holding a bill protested for non-payment, and demanding payment thereof from the drawer, thereby loses all remedy against an endorser. Lynch coming to Boston, was sued by Powers upon his endorsement. The Court held that the defendant, being discharged by the law of the place where the contract was made, was not liable to an action in the United States. Powers v. Lynch, 3 Mass. R. 77.

(*a*) An action was brought in New York by an endorsee against the maker of a promissory note dated at Suffield, in Connecticut. By the laws of that State notes were not then negotiable, so as to enable an assignee to sue in his own name, but remained on the footing of choses in action at common law. It was held that the suit was maintainable, whether the contract was to be governed by the law of Connecticut or not. "The admission of the *lex loci* can have reference only to the nature and construction of the contract and its legal effect, and not to the mode of enforcing it." Lodge v. Phelps, 1 Johns. Cas. 139; 2 Cain. Er. 321.

CHAP. II.

Parties to a Bill or Note.

A BILL or note cannot properly be made or endorsed by, nor can a bill be properly addressed to, any person incapable of making himself responsible for the payment, nor can they be properly made payable or endorsed to any person incapable of suing. (*a*)

Sect. 2.—Therefore a bill or note cannot properly be made or endorsed by, nor can a bill be properly addressed to an infant (1), except perhaps where it is drawn, endorsed, or accepted for necessaries. (2)

[(*a*) A note made payable to "the heirs" of a person still living, is good; as the persons intended are sufficiently described. 1 Root, 181]

(1) Williams v. Harrison, Carth. 160. 3 Salk. 197. In an action against the drawer of a bill, the defendant pleaded infancy, and the plaintiff demurred, and the court held clearly without argument, that infancy was a good bar, for the bill was drawn by the defendant as a trader in course of trade, and not for necessaries.

[The promissory note of an infant carrying on trade as adult, cannot be enforced against him by the payee who received it in the course of business, without knowing the defendant's nonage. Van Winkle v. Ketcham, 3 Cain. R. 323.]

(2) Williamson v. Watts, 1 Campb. N. P. C. 552. In an action against the acceptor of a bill, the defendant pleaded infancy, and the plaintiff replied that the bill was accepted for necessaries, on which issue was joined: on opening the case Sir J. Mansfield C. J. said, "This action certainly cannot be maintained. The defendant is allowed to be an infant, and did any one ever hear of an infant being liable as an acceptor of a bill of exchange? The replication is nonsense, and ought to have been demurred to." He said as the point of law was so clear, he felt strongly inclined to nonsuit the plaintiff; but he heard the evidence, and the plaintiff was nonsuited, on proof that the goods, for which the bill had been given, were not necessaries.

[Trueman v. Hurst, 1 Term Rep. 40. An action was brought on a note given for board and lodging, and for teaching the defendant hair-dressing. and upon an account stated; the defendant pleaded infancy, and the plaintiff replied for necessaries. Defendant demurred, and insisted that an infant could not bind himself by a note even for necessaries, and that no action would lie against him on an account stated. The court desired the plaintiff's counsel to confine himself to the last point, from

But if an infant draw a bill to his own order, and endorse it, and the drawee accept it, the acceptance will bind the drawee, and he will be compellable to pay the endorsee, because, by accepting, he precludes himself from disputing the competence of the drawer. (3)

[So it has been held in Massachusetts, that if an infant endorse a note, an action may be maintained upon it by his endorsee against any of the prior parties. (*a*)]

And the drawing, endorsing, or accepting by an infant, is voidable only, not void (4), and if he ratify the act after he comes of age, it will bind him. (*b*)

---

whence it may be inferred that they thought the first was with him, but they decided against him on the last.

It has been held in New York that a negotiable note given by an infant for necessaries is void. Swasey v. Vanderheyden, 10 Johns. R. 33.]

(3) Taylor v. Croker, 4 Esp. N. P. C. 187. In an action against the acceptor of a bill, drawn by Eversfield and Jones on the defendant, in their own favor, and endorsed by them to one S. and by him to the plaintiff; it appeared that both the drawers were infants at the time of drawing the bill. But Lord Ellenborough held that though that might have been a good defence had the action been brought against the drawers themselves, it was no defence in the present action. Verdict for the plaintiff.

[(*a*) Withington made a note to Vose a minor, in payment for his services; Vose for a valuable consideration endorsed it to Bacon, who passed it to Nightingale, all the parties knowing Vose to be a minor. Withington, after having notice of the endorsement, paid the amount of the note to Vose's father. The court held that this payment was no defence to an action upon the note by Nightingale against Withington. Parker C. J. "That an infant may endorse a negotiable promissory note, or a bill of exchange, made payable to him, seems to be well settled in the law merchant; and is no ways repugnant to the common law." "Whether an infant may avoid an endorsement so made, and oblige the promiser to pay him, is a question not arising in this case; for there has been no countermand or revocation of the order to pay, which is implied in his endorsement. If an action should be brought against the infant as endorser, without doubt he may avoid such action by a plea of infancy. But that is a personal privilege which none but himself can set up, in avoidance of any contract in his favor." Nightingale v. Withington, 15 Mass. R. 272.]

(4) Gibbs v. Merrill, 3 Taunt. 307. A bill was accepted by Merrill and Le Blond; Le Blond was an infant. An action being brought against Merrill only, he pleaded that he did not undertake unless jointly with Le Blond. Replication that he did; plaintiff proved Le Blond's infancy, and defendant proved by Le Blond, that he had never disaffirmed the acceptance. The jury found for the plaintiff; but on a rule nisi for a new trial, and time to consider, the court held Le Blond's acceptance voidable only, not void; and that the issue should have been found

As an infant is capable of suing (5) he may be a payee or endorsee.

But it may be questionable in some cases, whether payment should not be made to his guardian. (6)

Sect. 3.—Bills or notes cannot properly be made, endorsed, or accepted by a feme covert, unless where she acts by authority from her husband (7), or where she resides here,

---

for the defendant; they therefore set aside the verdict, but gave the plaintiff leave to amend his replication by stating Le Blond's infancy, and so raising the question whether he was compellable to join him.

[Dutch, whose partner, Green, was a minor, made a note in the partnership name. Green, after coming of age being applied to for payment, said that he would endeavor to procure the money and send it to the plaintiffs, the payees. Parker C. J. who delivered the opinion of the court, said, that this evidence was sufficient to satisfy the jury that Green had ratified the original promise: that no letter of attorney was necessary to authorize Dutch to make this note; and that the note at its inception was only voidable as to Green, not void; and therefore that he might ratify it after he came of age. Whitney v. Dutch, 14 Mass. R. 457.]

(*b*) See 1 Root, 477. Wright v. Steele, 2 N. Hamp. R. 51.

(5) See Teed v. Elworthy, 14 East, 210. Warwick v. Bruce, 2 Maule & S. 205. 6 Taunt. 118.

(6) See Pothier pl. 166. who observes that payment to an infant will be no discharge of the debtor, unless it appear that the payment were beneficial to the infant; if the money were applied to his advantage, the payment will be good; if not, as where the infant squanders it, the party paying will not be discharged. So money *lent* to an infant for necessaries, if duly applied, may in equity be recovered from him. Marlow v. Pitfield, 1 P. Williams, 558. Though it is otherwise at law, 1 Salk. 279. 386. But if an executor pay a legacy to an infant, which the infant's father obtains and dissipates, the executor will be answerable to the infant. Philips v. Paget, 2 Atk. 80. See also Pothier on Obligations, part iii. ch. 1. art. 2, s. 1. pl. 504. and s. 2.

(7) Barlow v. Bishop, 1 East's Rep. 432. Ann Parry was married, but traded in her own name, with her husband's consent. She became indebted to the plaintiff, and to enable her to pay him. the defendant who knew that she was married, gave her a note payable to her or order. She endorsed it in her own name to the plaintiff, and he brought this action. Lord Kenyon thought it not maintainable, but saved the point; and after a rule nisi for a nonsuit, and cause shewn, he said it was clear that the delivery of the note to the wife vested the interest in the husband; that as he permitted her to trade on her own account, and this was a transaction in the course of that trade, he was not prepared to say that had she endorsed the note in his name, it would not have availed; the jury might have presumed that she was authorized by her husband; but the endorsement being in her own name, it was impossible to say it could pass the husband's interest. Rule absolute.

Cotes v. Davis. 1 Campb. N. P. C. 485. In an action by an endorsee

and he is under a civil incapacity of being in this kingdom. (8)

Her living apart from her husband, and having a separate maintenance secured by deed (9), or her trading, by particular custom, on her own account (10), gives her no capacity to draw, endorse, or accept.

If a bill or note be made payable, or endorsed to a feme covert, whose husband is under no civil incapacity, the wife alone cannot, except as agent to her husband, make it available, or sue upon it; (11)

The husband may.

And he may either negotiate it;

Or sue upon it.

And he may either sue upon it in his own name, and treat it as if it were made payable to himself; (12)

Or sue upon it in the joint names of himself and his wife. (13)

[And a note payable to husband and wife, goes to the wife, if she survives him. (*a*)]

---

against the maker of a note made payable to "Mrs. Carter, or order," and endorsed by her in her own name, the defendant offered to show that Mrs. Carter was wife to one Cole; but it being proved that subsequently to the endorsement, and when the note was presented for payment, the defendant had promised to pay it. Lord Ellenborough said the jury might presume that she had authority from her husband to endorse the note, and *that* in the name by which she passed in the world. Verdict for the plaintiff.

(8) Vide Derry v. Duchess of Mazarine, Lord Raym. 147. Salk. 116. Sparrow v. Carruthers cited Blackst. 1197. 1 Term Rep. 6. See also Blackst. 1081, 1082. 1 Term Rep. 9.

(9) Vide Marshall v. Rutton, 8 Term Rep. 545.

(10) Vide Blackst. 1081. Caudell v. Shaw, 4 Term Rep. 361. but see also Lacie v. Phillips. Burr. 1776.

(11) See Barlow v Bishop, ante. p. 35.

(12) Arnold v. Revoult, 1 Brod. & Bingh. 443.

(13) Philliskirk v. Pluckwell, 2 Maule, 393. A note to a feme covert; action thereon by her and her husband. Rule nisi for a nonsuit, but on cause shown, the court held that as a note primâ facie imported a consideration according to its tenor, and the wife might have been the meritorious cause of it, or it might have been given for a debt due to her before marriage, the husband might suffer her to join in suing upon it, and the rule was discharged.

[(*a*) A note and mortgage were made to husband and wife, to secure the purchase money of land which had belonged to the wife. It was

Sect. 4.—If several, who are not partners, join in a note, and it begins with, "I promise," &c. it is several as well as joint, and it will bind each individual separately; (14)

And all jointly. (15)

And it only requires one stamp, if it were the bargain before it was issued that all should join. (15)

But if there were no such bargain, the addition of a fresh signature, after it was once issued, would make a new stamp necessary. (15)

[If a person, not the payee of a note, signs upon the note at the time it is made, an acknowledgment that he is holden as surety for the payment of the note, or endorses an undertaking to pay the note, he is liable as a joint and several promiser. (*a*)]

---

held that the note and mortgage survived to the wife, and did not go to the husband's administrator. Draper v. Jackson, 16 Mass. R. 480.

(14) Lord Galway v. Matthew, post.

[March v. Ward, Peake, 130. A note signed by Bowling and Ward, began "I promise to pay," and in an action against Ward alone, it was objected that the note was *joint only*, and not several; but Lord Kenyon held it was several as well as joint, and said it had been so decided on a case from Chester. "*I* applies to each severally." Verdict for the plaintiff.] [See also Hemmenway v. Stone, 7 Mass. R. 58. Hunt v. Adams, post.]

(15) Clark v. Blackstock, Holt, 474. A note was in this form; "I promise to pay plaintiff or order, £30 with interest, value received; Thos. Jackson, Jno. Blackstock." In an action against Blackstock alone, two objections were made, one that this was the joint note of Jackson and Blackstock: and, secondly, that there should have been an additional stamp for Blackstock's signature; it was ruled that the word "I" made the note several as well as joint; and, secondly, that the necessity of an additional stamp would depend upon this, viz. whether Blackstock's signature was part of the original bargain before plaintiff took the note, or an afterthought, and it appearing to have been part of the original bargain, verdict for plaintiff.

[(*a*) Chaplin made a note for $1500 payable to Bennet. Before the note was delivered to Bennet, Adams signed the following agreement written upon the note. "I acknowledge myself holden as surety for the payment of the demand of the above note." Bennet's administrator brought an action against Adams declaring, 1. Upon a note signed by the defendant solely; 2. On a note made by him jointly and severally with Chaplin Parsons C. J. delivered the opinion of the Court. "The defendant is an original party to the contract. This mode of signing entitles the defendant, if he pays the note, to an indemnity from Chaplin. But, as to the intestate, they must be considered as joint and several promisers. The legal effect of this note does not differ from one written 'For value received *I* promise to pay,' &c., and signed by one with

[So if a person, not the payee of a note, endorses his name upon it at the time it is made, intending to make himself responsible to the payee, he is liable as an original promiser. (*a*)]

---

principal annexed to his name, and by another with surety thus annexed." Hunt v. Adams, 5 Mass. R. 358. In another action between the same parties on another contract not materially varying from the above, the court continued of the same opinion. Hunt v. Adams, 6 Mass. R. 519.

Taber, April 19th, 1806, made a note payable to White on demand. The note was endorsed, "Ap. 19th, 1806. For value received we jointly and severally undertake to pay the money within mentioned to the said Wm. White. John Coggeshall Jr. John H. Howland." White sued Howland on the note, and in one count as a several original promiser. No demand or notice was proved; and Taber became insolvent in 1810. Curia. "We are all satisfied that this case is within the reason of Hunt v. Adams (supra) and that the effect of the defendant's signature is the same as if he had subscribed the note on the face of it as a surety. He is then answerable as an original promiser, equally with Taber, and the count which charges him as a several original promiser is supported by the note in its actual form." White v. Howland, 9 Mass. R. 314. See also Carver v. Warren, 5. Mass. R. 545.]

[(*a*) Moies sold an estate to B. Bird, who agreed to pay for it in part by a note with a sufficient endorser, and proposed to give one of his brothers, Abraham or William, as an endorser or security on the notes. The deed was given, and B. Bird gave his notes payable to Moies. A day or two afterwards one of the notes was brought to Abraham Bird to procure his endorsement. He at first refused to endorse it, saying that it was not negotiable; but finally said he would write his name, to make Moies easy, but would not be accountable for a farthing. Moies sued A. Bird, declaring on a promissory note made by him. Sewall C. J. directed the jury that if Moies conveyed the land to B. Bird upon the expectation of security by the endorsement of Abraham or William Bird as guarantor, and had obtained the defendant's endorsement in consequence of that understanding, they might find for the plaintiff, unless the endorsement had been in fact made with some different intent; and that the endorsement in blank by the defendant was of the same effect as a signature upon the face of the note under the name of B. Bird, in which case the defendant would be considered as surety for B. Bird. On motion for a new trial, Parker C. J. who delivered the opinion of the Court, said, that the effect of the defendant's signature "was to make him absolutely liable to pay the note. He leaves it to the holder to write any thing over his name, not inconsistent with the nature of the transaction. The holder chooses to consider him as a surety binding himself originally with the principal: and we think he has a right so to do." Moies v. Bird, 11 Mass. R. 436.

The plaintiff in one count declared that in consideration of plaintiff's selling Brundige a horse, the defendant guarantied the payment of Brundige's note, given in payment. The evidence was a note made by Brundige payable to the plaintiff or bearer, and endorsed in blank by the defendant. The plaintiff offered to prove the sale of the horse, upon the defendant's agreeing to become surety for the payment, and the making of the note in pursuance of that agreement. Spencer C. J. delivered the

[But if such endorsement be made after the note is passed to the payee, or if there be no evidence to show that the person so endorsing intended to make himself responsible to the payee, no action can be maintained by the payee against such endorser. (*a*)]

---

opinion of the Court. "Under the count on the guaranty the evidence offered was admissible, unless indeed, the promise is within the statute of frauds. I confess, I do not perceive that this case is at all within the statute; the defendant's promise is not to pay on the default of Brundige, but is an original undertaking; and the defendant is as much holden as if he had signed the body of the note." Nelson v. Dubois, 13 Johns. R. 175.]

[(*a*) See Herrick v. Carman, post.

R. and J. Houghton the makers of a note, being applied to by Corbin, the agent of Hodgkins, the payee, for payment, offered security, if farther time should be given. They then procured Bond to endorse his name on the note; and Bond said that he was holden. Corbin some time after wrote a guaranty over Bond's name; and Hodgkins sued Bond as guarantor. Bell J. said, "This is not an action against the party to the original contract. The undertaking of the defendant must be considered as collateral to the original undertaking. It was strictly a promise to pay an existing debt of another." The court held that the action was not maintainable, because there was no memorandum in writing signed by the party, within the meaning of the statute of frauds. Hodgkins v. Bond, 1 N. Hamp. 284.

But in a similar case in Massachusetts, the promise of the guarantor was held not to be within the statute of frauds. Ulen held notes of Butman payable to himself. Kittredge, in consideration of farther time being given, agreed to become security, and endorsed the notes in blank; and being requested by Ulen's agent, to write something over his name, he answered that his name was enough, and that if he wrote it in full, it would not make it stronger. Ulen sued Kittredge as guarantor. By the Court. "We are of opinion that the defendant's name endorsed, with the authority given by him to the plaintiff's agent, to write over it a sufficient guaranty, such guaranty being accordingly written by him, may be considered as a memorandum signed by the party, within the intent of the statute, as fully as if it had been written in the defendant's presence immediately after the signature. And parol evidence was as well admissible to prove this authority, as it is in any case upon a promise in writing, to prove the hand-writing." Ulen v. Kittredge, 7 Mass. R. 233.

Wheeler agreed to sell goods to Moore and Abdy on their giving a note with a good endorser. They afterwards brought him a note signed by them payable to Wheeler, and endorsed in blank by Tillman, and Wheeler then sold them the goods entirely on the credit of Tillman. Wheeler sued Tillman as guarantor; and obtained a verdict in the C. Pleas. Yates J. delivered the opinion of the Court. "For aught that appears Tillman may have put his name on the note as second endorser, on the responsibility of the payee; this is the legal presumption from the appearance of the paper, without any explanatory proof, or a special undertaking on the part of Tillman, who does not appear to have known anything of the original contract between the drawers and payee; nor

If a bill or note is payable to several persons, not in partnership, the right to transfer is in all collectively, not (16) in any individually.

And an endorsement by and in the name of one only, will not give the endorsee a right to sue. (16)

So if a bill is drawn on several persons not connected in partnership, an acceptance by one will bind him, but him (17) only.

[If one of several persons, jointly liable on a bill or note, whether partners or not, dies solvent, and the survivors become insolvent, the assets of the deceased are liable in equity to the payment of the bill or note. (*a*)]

Sect. 5.—Each partner has in general a power to bind the partnership, and therefore a bill or note by one, or an endorsement or acceptance by one, will in general bind all. (18)

---

can the court infer from anything in the case, that he was privy thereto." Judgment reversed. Tillman v. Wheeler, 17 John. R. 326.]

(16) Carvick v. Vickery, Dougl. 2d edit. p. 653. n. 134. A bill was drawn by father and son, who were not partners, payable *to their own order*. The son alone endorsed it, and upon an action by his endorsee against the acceptor, Lord Mansfield thought an endorsement by both parties essential, and nonsuited the plaintiff. A new trial however was afterwards granted. the court, after time taken to consider, being of opinion that by making the bill payable to their own order, the father and son had made themselves partners as to this transaction; but upon the second trial Lord Mansfield said he did not think the question so decided as to preclude evidence which was offered, that by the universal usage and understanding of all the bankers and merchants in London the endorsement was bad, as not being signed by both the payees, and the jury, unâ voce, declared that that was the usage and understanding, and without hearing any evidence upon the point they found a verdict for the defendant.

[Where a note is payable to two joint executors, one of them cannot transfer the note by his separate endorsement. Smith v. Whiting, 9 Mass. R. 334.]

(17) Bull. Nisi Prius, 279. In the case of two joint traders, an acceptance by one will bind both; but if ten merchants employ one factor, and he draw a bill upon them all, and one accept it, this shall only bind him, and not the rest. Mar. 2d ed. 16. Beawes, § 228. 1st. ed. p. 444. Molloy, b. 2. c. 10. § 18.

[(*a*) Jenkins v. De Groot, 1 Cain. Er. 122; Van Reimsdyk v. Kane, 1 Gallis. 630.]

(18) Mason v. Rumsey and another, 1 Campb. N. P. C. 384. A bill

And a note by one, importing to be for all, may bind the partnership, though it begin, "I promise." (19)

[But the partner signing is also liable as a several promiser. (*a*)]

And a bill or note by one in the partnership name will, as between them and an innocent holder, bind the partnership, though the partner making it was prohibited from drawing bills or notes. (20)

---

was drawn on "Messrs. Rumsey and Co."; and T. Rumsey, jun. wrote upon it "Accepted, T. Rumsey, sen." The present action was defended by T. Rumsey, jun. who contended that even if he were a partner, (which he denied,) this acceptance would not bind him. Lord Ellenborough told the jury, that if the defendants were partners, they were both bound by this acceptance. He said the word 'accepted" alone would have been sufficient, and that the effect could not be altered by the addition of "T. Rumsey, sen." The jury found for the plaintiff; and on motion afterwards for a new trial, on the ground of the evidence of partnership not having been sufficient, the court held the Chief Justice's direction right, and refused a rule.

(19) Lord Galway v. Matthew and another, 1 Campb. N. P. C. 403. This was an action against the defendants as surviving partners of T. Whitsmith, on a note drawn thus: "Sixty days after date, I pay Ld. Viscount Galway, or order, £200, value received. For J. Matthew, T. Whitsmith, and T. Smithson (Signed) "J. Matthew." Lord Ellenborough held that it bound the whole firm. S. C. 10 East's Rep. 264.

This signature by the one (presuming his authority) is a good signature by all. See Wilks v. Back, 2 East Rep. 142.

[(*a*) W. Smith, a partner in a country bank, signed notes for himself and partners, beginning, "I promise to pay," and signed "For W. Smith, W. P. Smith, and W. R. Taylor, W. Smith." W. Smith was sued alone upon these notes. He pleaded in abatement that he promised jointly with W. P. Smith and W. R. Taylor. But the court held that he was liable as a several promiser. Hall v. Smith, 2 Dow. & Ryl. 584. 1 Barn. & Cres. 407.]

(20) Swan and others v. Steele and Wood, 7 East Rep. 210. The house of Wood and Payne carried on under the same firm and at the same counting house, two trades, those of wholesale grocers and cotton dealers. The defendant, Steele, was a secret partner in the latter trade, but not in the former. The house was indebted to the plaintiffs, as grocers, and to pay this debt Wood and Payne, without the knowledge of Steele, endorsed to the plaintiffs a bill which they had received on account of the cotton concern. The bill was endorsed in the usual firm of W. and P., and Steele's being a partner was unknown to the plaintiffs. Wood and Payne afterwards became bankrupts, and Payne being dead, this action, by the plaintiffs as endorsees of the bill, was brought against Steele and Wood; and on a case reserved, the only question was, whether the endorsement were good: and the court held the case too clear for argument; and Lord Ellenborough said, that in the absence of all fraud on the part of the endorsee there was no doubt that such endorsement would bind all the partners. Postea to the plaintiffs.

Or though the particular bill or note were a fraud upon the partnership. (21)

But such bills or notes will not bind the partnership as to persons who when they took them knew of the want of authority; (22)

Or of the fraud. (23)

If one partner give a partnership-bill or note for his own private debt without the knowledge of the partnership, it is a fraud upon the partnership. (23)

---

(21) Ridley and another v. Taylor, 13 East's Rep. 175. Ord and Ewbank were linen drapers and partners. The plaintiffs, in Nov. 1806, sold a cargo of coals to Ewbank for £34. 11*s*., and Ewbank in May following gave them £5 in part payment, and a promissory note for the balance. This note was dishonored; and in payment of this balance, Ewbank, on the 7th of Nov. 1807, gave the plaintiffs a bill for £40, dated 20th of October, 1807, drawn and endorsed by him in the partnership name, and accepted by the defendant. The bill was drawn, endorsed, and accepted, before it was produced to the plaintiffs, and it did not appear that they knew that it had been drawn and endorsed by Ewbank. Ewbank afterwards applied to the plaintiffs for the difference between the balance due, and the £40, but they refused to pay it until payment of the note. This bill was dishonored; and the plaintiffs in their account debited Ewbank for the amount. Ord and Ewbank afterwards became bankrupt, and the plaintiffs now sued the defendant as acceptor. A verdict was found for the plaintiffs, subject to the opinion of the court of King's Bench on a case, stating these facts. The court held, that in this case, there being no evidence of covin between the plaintiffs and Ewbank to defraud Ord, and no such gross negligence on the part of the plaintiffs in not inquiring whether Ewbank had authority to transfer the bill, as to render the transaction fraudulent, the plaintiffs were entitled to recover, and they held, that Ord or Ewbank might have been called to disprove Ewbank's authority. The plaintiffs had judgment for the amount of Ewbank's debt.

(22) Lord Galway v. Matthew and Smithson, 10 East's Rep. 264. The defendants and Whitehouse (since deceased) were in partnership as brewers. Matthew applied to the plaintiff to lend his acceptance for £200, to enable him to pay excise duties due from the house, and promised in return to give the note of the firm payable four days before the acceptance. The plaintiff gave his acceptance, and Matthew drew the note and signed it for himself and partners. He then got the acceptance discounted, and applied £180 in payment of partnership debts, reserving the rest to himself. The plaintiff (after Whitehouse's death) was obliged to take up his acceptance, and now sued the defendants on the note. Matthew suffered judgment by default. But Smithson proved that the plaintiff before he took the note had received notice of an advertisement by him warning persons not to trust Matthew on his account, and that he would no longer be liable for drafts drawn by the other partners on the partnership account. And Lord Ellenborough held that the plaintiff having taken the note after such warning could not recover, and therefore nonsuited him; and on motion to set aside the nonsuit the court held it right, and refused a rule.

And though an innocent endorsee may be able to inforce payment the creditor cannot. (23)

And in such case, if an action be brought by such creditor, notice need not be given him that the consideration will be disputed; the nature of the transaction is sufficient notice to him. (23)

[And a person endorsing such a note as surety believing

---

(23) Shirreff v. Wilks and others, 1 East's Rep. 48. In October, 1795, Bishop and Wilks, who were then partners, became indebted to the plaintiffs for goods sold and delivered. Robson became a partner with Bishop and Wilks, in April, 1796, and continued so until the 8th November following, when the partnership was dissolved. On 5th November, 1796, the plaintiffs drew on the partnership for the amount of their demand against Bishop and Wilks, and Bishop accepted the bill in the partnership-firm. The plaintiffs now sued the three partners upon this acceptance. Bishop and Robson were outlawed; and Wilks pleaded the general issue. A verdict was found for the plaintiff, subject to the opinion of the court. Lord Kenyon said he did not know how the case came to be reserved, as he had repeatedly decided the same question at the sittings; the propriety of which decisions had not been canvassed. He said, the consideration of the bill was goods sold to Bishop and Wilks only, when Robson was not a partner. "Then the plaintiffs, knowing this, draw the bill on the three partners, and knowingly take an acceptance from one of them, to bind the other two, one of whom, Robson, had no concern with the matter, and was no debtor of theirs; no assent or knowledge on his part being found. The transaction is fraudulent on the face of it." The other judges concurred. Postea to the defendant.

Hope v. Cust, B. R. M. 1774, cit. per Lawrence J. in Shirreff v. Wilks, 1 East's Rep. 53. Fordyce traded on his separate account, as well as in partnership with others, and being indebted to Hope on his separate account, gave him a general guaranty in the partnership name for his own debt. Lord Mansfield left it to the jury, whether the taking of the guaranty were, in respect of the partners, a fair transaction; or covinous, with sufficient notice to the plaintiff of the injustice and breach of trust Fordyce was guilty of in giving it. The jury found for the defendant.

See also Pinkney v. Hall, 1 Salk. 126. S. C. Lord Raym. 175., and Wells v. Masterman and another, 2 Esp. N. P. C. 731; [and Baird v. Cochran, 4 Serg. & Raw. 397; Livingston v. Hastie, 2 Cain. R. 246; Lansing v. Gaine, 2 Johns. R. 300.]

Green v. Deakin, 2 Stark. 348. Hickman owed Green money, and gave him a draft for the amount in the name of himself and his two partners, Deakin and Bickley: neither Deakin or Bickley knew of the giving of this draft, nor had this been done with their concurrence; Green was not apprized that the other partners were ignorant of the transaction, and it was urged that Deakin should have given notice of his intention to dispute the consideration; sed per Lord Ellenborough, the transaction is intrinsically notice: one partner has no right to bind another without his knowledge by drawing in the partnership name for his private debt. Nonsuit.

it to be good against the partnership, will not be liable upon it to the creditor to whom it is given, who knew it was for a demand against one partner. (*a*)]

If one of several persons who have been in partnership accept a bill in the partnership-name after a dissolution of the partnership, the partnership will not be liable even to a bonâ fide holder for valuable consideration, if the dissolution took place after the date of the bill and before it became due, and proper means were taken to make the dissolution notorious. (24)

[So a note issued by one partner in the partnership name, after the dissolution of the partnership, is not binding upon the partnership, even though it was given for a demand against the partnership; and antedated so as to appear of a date previous to the dissolution. (*b*)]

And if a dissolution is agreed upon, a person who knows of it cannot charge the partnership with a subsequent acceptance by one of the partners in the partnership name, unless he can prove that the intention to dissolve was abandoned, or that the acceptance was for a partnership transaction, and free from fraud. (25)

[(*a*) Livingston v. Hastie, 2 Cain. R. 246.]

(24) Wrightson v. Pullan, 1 Stark, 375. Defendants, Pullan and Hopcroft, had been partners; but on 13th February, 1815, their partnership was dissolved, and on 14th February notice thereof was published in the Gazette. After this date Taylor and Son drew upon Pullan and Hopcroft, and antedated the bill to 1st February, 1815. Hopcroft accepted this bill in the partnership name; after which Taylor and Son paid it to plaintiffs for value. It was urged for plaintiffs, that as the bill was dated before the dissolution, and plaintiffs had taken it bonâ fide and for a valuable consideration, plaintiffs were entitled to recover upon it; but Lord Ellenborough held, that as the partnership had been dissolved before the bill was drawn, Pullan could not be charged by the subsequent act of Hopcroft: and the court afterwards agreed with him, and refused a motion for a new trial.

[(*b*) See Lansing v. Gaine, 2 Johns. R. 300.]

(25) Paterson v. Zachariah, 1 Stark. 71. In an action against A. & B. upon an acceptance by A. in the joint names, they having been in partnership, the defence was, that the acceptance was in fraud of B. after a dissolution to which plaintiff was privy; and it was proved, that before the date of the bill plaintiff had, as attorney, prepared a deed of dissolution, and had sent it for approbation to B.'s attorney; but it did not appear the deed had been executed. Sed, per Lord Ellenborough:— You need not labor this; where an intention to dissolve is made known,

But a dissolution will not protect the retiring partners, if they suffer their names to continue on the partnership premises, and the holder of the bill or note took it bonâ fide, and for value, and without knowledge of the dissolution. (26)

[And if one partner, after committing a secret act of bankruptcy accepts a bill in the partnership name for his own private debt, the partnership is liable on the acceptance to a *bonâ fide* holder, although the partnership was perhaps dissolved in law by the act of bankruptcy. (*a*)

So if one of two partners, after the dissolution of the partnership, give a note in the partnership name on account of a partnership debt, and the other partner afterwards adopt and sanction the act, both partners are liable upon the note. (*b*)

---

and the dissolution is in the course of execution, the burthen is on the other side to shew that the intention has been abandoned. Nonsuit.

(26) Williams v. Keats and Archer, 2 Stark, 290. In an action against defendants as acceptors of a bill, it appeared that they dissolved partnership 18th January, 1817, and that notice thereof was in the preceding night's Gazette; but that the business, (a hatter's,) was carried on as usual by Keats, and that the name, "Keats, Archer, and Co." continued over the door till April; that the bill in question, though dated in December, was not drawn till February; that it was then accepted, in the old partnership name, by Keats; and that plaintiffs took it bonâ fide and for full value in March. Lord Ellenborough thought Archer's permitting his name to remain over the door was notice of a continuance of the partnership; and as there was no proof the plaintiffs knew of its dissolution when they took the bill, they had a right to recover: and they had a verdict accordingly.

[(*a*) Woolcott and Tucker, who had been partners, were sued as acceptors of two bills. The bills were accepted by Woolcott in the partnership name. The acceptance and consideration were private transactions of Woolcott, unknown to Tucker, and not connected with the partnership business. Previously to these acceptances Woolcott had committed an act of bankruptcy, on which a commission subsequently issued. It was contended for the defendant, Tucker, that Woolcott having committed an act of bankruptcy previously to his accepting the bills, the partnership was thereby dissolved and he had no power to bind the firm by an acceptance in their name. But the Court said, "The "case presents no difficulty. The plaintiffs are innocent endorsees, "having taken the bills bonâ fide and for a valuable consideration. "They see the acceptance of Woolcott and Tucker upon the bills; those "persons were then in fact partners, so far as their joint transactions "with the world could make them such; one of them indeed had pre-"viously committed an act of bankruptcy, and in law perhaps the part-"nership was dissolved. But they continued to hold themselves out to "the world ostensibly as partners, and therefore each was bound by the "acts of the other." Judgment for the plaintiffs. Lucy v. Woolcott, 2 Dow. & Ryl. 453.

(*b*) Taylor and Hall had been partners under the firm of John Taylor

If several persons are partners, and one of them signs a note with a name of partnership, all the partners will be bound, unless they can prove that that was not their partnership style. (*a*)]

No *banking* partnership in England, if there be more than six partners, can properly draw, accept, or endorse, any bill or note payable at less than six months after the date; for, by the acts for protecting the Bank of England, such partnerships are not at liberty to borrow, owe, or take up any money on their bills or notes payable at demand, or at less than six months from the borrowing thereof. (27)

But it has been held that this prohibition does not extend to any but banking partnerships. (28)

At least a common partnership cannot make this a defence against an innocent holder, who was ignorant of what number the firm consisted. (29)

& Co. A year after the dissolution of the partnership, Taylor made a note to Eaton on account of a partnership debt. It was proved at the trial before Parker J. that Hall had paid $100 on this note, which was endorsed on it with his knowledge. The judge instructed the jury, that if Hall had adopted and sanctioned the act of Taylor in signing the note for himself and Hall, they ought to find for the plaintiff, although no authority was given at the time of signing. Verdict for plaintiff. And on motion for a new trial the court held that the direction to the jury was correct; but said that upon the whole case they should have been as well satisfied with a verdict for the defendant. Eaton v. Taylor, 10 Mass. R. 54.

(*a*) Elwyn and P. and S. Wittaker were sued as partners, makers of a note. Elwyn signed the note Elwyn & Co. A partnership was proved, but not that the defendants traded under the name of Elwyn & Co. Kent J. delivered the opinion of the Court. "As such a signature imported a copartnership, and a copartnership did exist at the time between Elwyn and the other defendants, I think it is to be *presumed* that such was the name of the firm, and that it was sufficient to cast upon the defendants the burden of proving what was the name of the house or firm, if a different name existed." Drake v. Elwyn, 1 Cain. R. 184.]

(27) 6 Ann. c. 22. § 9. 15 Geo. 2. c. 13. § 5.

(28) Wigan v. Fowler, 1 Stark. 459. In an action against seven partners, as makers of a promissory note for £1000 payable three months after date, the defence was, that the bank acts made this note void: the number of partners did not appear upon the face of the note, nor was there any evidence that plaintiff knew it. Lord Ellenborough thought at the trial, that the bank acts applied to banking partnerships only, and it was with reluctance he saved the point. On motion to enter a nonsuit, he adhered to his original opinion; and it was noticed that plaintiff did not appear to have known how many partners there were when he took the bill, and the rule was refused.

(29) In Broughton v. Manchester Water Works Company, post, 47,

Sect. 6.—Corporations are mentioned in the statute of Anne, as persons who may make or endorse notes, and to whom notes may be payable; and as it gives the like remedy to and for corporations and others as upon inland bills of exchange, it implies, that by the custom of merchants they might, in some cases at least, draw, endorse, accept, or sue upon bills of exchange.

But if the being parties to bills or notes were inconsistent with the purpose for which they were incorporated, that inconsistency might be a bar to any remedy by, or through, or against them, on a bill or note. (*a*)

And English corporations, unless authorized by statute, cannot be parties to bills or notes of less than six months after date. (30)

And this applies to all English corporations; it is not confined to banking corporations. (30) (*a*)

And where an English corporation is empowered by statute to raise money by notes for a special purpose, if it issue notes at less than six months' date, without stating therein

---

this point was relied upon as forming a distinction between the two cases.

[(*a*) A corporation authorized by the act of incorporation to employ their stock solely in advancing money on goods, and the sale of such goods on commission, may lawfully accept bills of exchange, on an agreement of the drawer to deposit goods; the legislature not having required that the goods should be delivered to the company prior to their advancing money on them. Munn v. Commission Co. 15 Johns. R. 44.

So a corporation is bound by a note given by its authorized agent on account of a demand against the corporation, although there is no special clause in its act of incorporation authorizing it to issue notes. Mott v. Hicks, 1 Cowen, 513.]

(30) Broughton v. the Manchester Water Works Company, 3 Barnw. and Alderson, 1. Action against defendants, as acceptors of two bills of exchange payable at three months after date. Demurrer: and the objection was, that they were not liable; they were incorporated for water-work purposes only. One of their acts authorized them to borrow to a limited extent upon bonds under their common seal; but no other power was expressly given, nor was such power necessary for the purposes for which they were established: and the court thought the bank acts (ante, p. 46) an answer to the action, because the acceptance made them debtors and owe money upon the bills.

[(*a*) In most of the States of the United States the privilege of issuing bank paper, *i. e.* notes payable to bearer on demand, intended to circulate as money, is confined to certain incorporated banks; and all other individuals or corporations are prohibited from issuing such notes.]

that they were given for that purpose, the corporation may resist payment, on the ground that they were given for another purpose. (31)

And this will be a defence even against an innocent endorsee. (31)

Sect. 7.—Where a bill or note is drawn by an agent, executor or trustee, he should take care, if he means to exempt himself from personal responsibility, to use clear and explicit words to show that intention.

Thus, if a broker sell goods, and draw upon the buyer in favor of his principal, he will be liable upon the bill, if it be dishonored, unless he use special words to prevent it; (32)

And may be sued thereon by his principal. (32)

So if an agent for A. draw upon B. in favor of C., though he direct B. to place the amount to A.'s debit, he will be personally liable to C. if the bill is not paid, though C. knew he was only agent for A., unless he uses proper words to prevent such liability. (33)

---

(31) Slark v. Highgate Archway Company, 5 Taunt. 792. Defendants were incorporated by 52 Geo. 3. c. 146. (local and personal) and authorized to borrow money to complete their works; they gave a note under their common seal at two months after date for £1000, payable to Nash or order: it did not import to be for money borrowed to complete their works. Plaintiff sued thereon as endorsee. Defence, that it was given for Nash's accommodation, not to complete their works. Gibbs C. J. thought this no defence against an innocent endorsee who had paid the value, and the plaintiff had a verdict; but on a rule nisi for a new trial, the Court of Common Pleas, without assinging their reasons, granted a new trial.

(32) Lefevre v. Lloyd, 5 Taunt. 749. Defendant, as broker, sold cotton for plaintiff at two months' credit, and drew on the buyer for the amount in favor of plaintiff: the bill being dishonored, plaintiff sued defendant on the bill; and Gibbs C. J. at the trial, held, that as defendant had put his name upon the bill, however imprudent that was, all the legal consequences of that act attached upon him, and verdict for plaintiff: and on motion for a new trial, the court agreed with him; for by drawing the bill, defendant removed from plaintiff all consideration of the buyer's responsibility. Rule refused.

(33) Leadbitter v. Farrow, Michaelmas, 1816, in B. R. Plaintiff wanted a bill upon London for £50, and sent to defendant, whom he knew to be agent to the Durham Bank at Hexham: defendant drew a bill accordingly, "Pay to the order of Mr. Leadbitter, £50, value received, which place to the account of the Durham Bank, as advised,

So if an agent employed to buy bills get them payable to himself and endorse them generally, he will be liable upon that endorsement even to his own employer (34); to have

---

C. Farrow. To Messrs. A. and B. London." In an action thereon, the defendant urged that he was not personally liable, or at least that the plaintiff, who knew him to be only agent, could not sue him; but on a case reserved, the court held his signature pledged his own credit, and *that* only, and that he was therefore liable.

[Prince was agent of Higginson, and drew eight bills payable to Mayhew on Higginson, Dodge, and Co. of which house Higginson was the principal, directing them in the bills to place the amount to the debit of Higginson. Mayhew sued Prince as drawer, and the defence set up was, that the defendant was a mere agent of Higginson, for whose use and on whose account the bills were drawn, and that the plaintiff knew that the defendant acted as agent in drawing the bills. Parker J. delivered the opinion of the Court. "The defendant drew the bills putting his own name to them without qualification. He must therefore be considered the responsible drawer. The signer of any contract, if he intends to prevent a resort to himself personally, should express on the contract the quality in which he acts; otherwise he does not bind the party who employs him, and necessarily binds himself." Mayhew v. Prince, 11 Mass. R. 54. But see Van Reimsdyk v. Kane, post, p. 53.

In an action against the drawers of a bill drawn in Philadelphia upon Rotterdam, it appeared that the letters *q. q.* were added after the signatures of the defendants, which the counsel contended meant *qualitate qua*, i. e. in the capacity of agent of the drawers. The defendants offered to prove a custom of the Dutch merchants in Holland and the West Indies, that it was the general understanding of the parties to such bills, that no recourse could be had against the drawers, but that credit was given to the fund or estate on account of which they drew. But the court refused to admit the evidence, not only because the bill was drawn in Philadelphia, but also because the general law of Europe with regard to bills could not be affected by the practice of the Dutch agents of sugar plantations. Verdict for plaintiff. Rheinhold v. Dertzell, 1 Yeates, 39.

But in a case in Pennsylvania, in an action by the payee against the drawer of a bill, the court held that the defendant would be exonerated, from his liability, by proving that between the payee and himself there was no consideration, and that the general understanding was that the drawer was merely an agent of the drawee, and not to be held responsible; and that it was not necessary to show a special agreement to exonerate him. Miles v. O'Hara, 1 Serg. & Raw. 32.

And where a note was made by a corporation payable to a person who was their agent, though the agency did not appear on the face of the note, and the note was endorsed by him with the word "agent" after his name, the Supreme Court of New York held that the endorser was not personally liable to a second endorser who had taken up the note, and who knew at the time the note was made that the first endorser was agent of the corporation. Savage C. J. dissented, considering the agent as personally responsible on his endorsement. Mott v. Hicks, 1 Cowen, 513.]

(34) Goupy v. Harden, Holt. 342. 2 Marsh. 404. 7 Taunt. 159. Plaintiff employed defendant at a commission of 10*s.* per cent. to pro-

exempted himself he should have got the bills made payable to his employer, or should have introduced into his endorsement words to exclude his personal responsibility.

So if a man draw a bill or note as executor of J. S., and sign it in terms as such, yet if it is in a form which implies assets, or will procure forbearance, it will bind him personally. (35)

[So if a person signs a note "as guardian," he is personally liable on the note. (*a*)]

If an executor means to limit his responsibility, he should confine his stipulation, viz. to pay out of the estate; and if an executor endorse, it binds him personally. (36)

So if drainage or inclosure commissioners draw upon the banker appointed by the act, they may be personally liable, unless they use proper words to prevent it, though the bill

---

cure him bills on Portugal, and to transmit them to him in Paris: defendant got bills payable to his own order and endorsed them generally, without restriction: plaintiff afterwards sued him on this endorsement, and defendant insisted that under the circumstances this endorsment did not make him liable to plaintiff; but on rule nisi, to set aside verdict for plaintiff, the court thought it did; for had defendant meant to exclude his liability, he should have given a qualified endorsement; and rule refused.

(35) Childs v. Monins and Bowles, 2 Brod. and Bing. 460. Defendants signed this note, "As executors to J. S. we severally and jointly promise to pay plaintiff £200 on demand, together with interest:" they were sued thereon, and then contended that it only bound them as executors; but on demurrer the court were clear it bound them personally. It admitted assets, and tended to procure forbearance, and as a several note from each would bind the executor of whoever died first, and ultimately the executors of both; an effect it would not have, if it bound them as executors only.

[(*a*) The defendant made two notes, promising "as guardian to A. L. an insane person." The court held that he was personally liable on the notes, after he had ceased to be guardian; and said that he could not make his ward liable on the contract, nor his ward's assets, and that his description of himself, in the notes, could not vary the form of action. Thacher v. Dinsmore, 5 Mass. R. 299.

Fuller, who was guardian of Scott, made a note promising, as guardian of Scott, and signed "Timothy Fuller, guardian." It was held that Fuller was personally liable on the note. Forster v. Fuller, 6 Mass. R. 58.]

(36) King v. Thom, 1 Term Rep. 487. The court held, that upon a bill payable to several as executors, they might sue as executors: and, per Buller J., no inconvenience can arise from their endorsing the bill; for if they endorse, they are liable personally, and not as executors, for their endorsement would not give an action against the effects of the testator.

imports to be drawn on the drainage or inclosure account, and directs the money to be placed to their account as commissioners. (37)

So if a bill is addressed to a man as cashier of a particular company, though it direct him to place it to the company's account, an acceptance upon it by him will bind him personally, unless he uses special words to prevent it. (38)

[If a person become party to a bill or note as the agent of another, and the agency appears on the instrument itself, the principal is bound if the agent had authority; but if the agent had no authority he is liable himself, either as a party to the instrument, or in a special action on the case. (*a*)

---

(37) Eaton v. Bell, Michaelmas, 1821. 5 Barnw. and Ald. 34. Defendants were inclosure commissioners, and plaintiff the banker under the act; the act authorized the commissioners to raise money by rate, and directed that persons advancing money for the purposes of the act should be repaid with interest out of the monies the commissioners should raise: defendants drew on plaintiff in this form: "Messrs. E.—Pay A. or bearer, £40 on account of the public draining, and place the same to our account as commissioners of the Frodsham inclosure:" Plaintiff sued defendants personally; and Dallas C. J. left it to the jury whether credit was given by plaintiff to defendants personally, or to the fund they had to raise: the jury thought it given to defendants personally; and, on case, the court thought them right, and plaintiff had judgment.

(38) Thomas v. Bishop, Ann. 1 Str. 955. A bill for £200 was drawn upon the defendant by the description of *Mr. H. Bishop, cashier of the York Buildings Company, at their house in Winchester-street, London;* and the bill directed him to place the £200 to the account of the company. The defendant accepted the bill; but on being sued insisted that the acceptance did not bind him personally, and gave in evidence that the letter of advice from the drawer of the bill was sent to the company. But Page J. directed the jury to find for the plaintiff, which they did; and upon a rule to show cause why there should not be a new trial, the whole court held the direction right: that the addition to the defendant's name was only to describe him with more certainty, and to point out where he was to be found: that the direction to place the money to the account of the company was for the use of the drawee only: and that the letter of advice could not vary the case against an endorsee, (which the plaintiff was,) because an endorsee could only look to the bill itself.

[(*a*) Colburn was sued as maker of a note signed by him "pro Wm. Gill, J. S. Colburn." The court held that the action would not lie; but that Gill was liable as maker of the note if Colburn had authority to sign it in his name; and that if Colburn had no authority, he was liable to a special action on the case. Long v. Colburn, 11 Mass. R. 97.

In an action against Talbot as maker of a note which he had signed, writing after his name "agent for David Perry," where it was proved that he had no authority to act as Perry's agent, it was held that the

And the agent cannot be bound as a party to the instrument, if the principal is bound by it (*a*), although the agent should misapply the money raised upon it to his own private use. (*b*)

Where the principal authorizes his agent to draw bills for him, and the agent draws a bill signed with his own name, but on the face of the bill directing the drawee to charge it

---

action in this form was not maintainable; but that a special action on the case would be the proper remedy. Ballou v. Talbot, 16 Mass. R. 461.

But in a similar case in New York, the court held that the person falsely representing himself as agent, was liable to an action as maker of the note. The court said, "If a person under pretence of authority from another executes a note in his name, he is bound, and the name of the person for whom he assumed to act will be rejected as surplusage. The party who accepts such a note under such mistake or imposition, ought to have the same remedy against the attorney who imposes on him, as he would have had against the pretended principal, if he had been really bound." Dusenbury v. Ellis, 3 Johns. Cas. 70.]

[(*a*) Chandler was sued as maker of several notes, in the following form: "I, the subscriber, treasurer of the Dorchester Turnpike Corporation, promise" &c. and signed "Gardner L. Chandler, Treasurer of the Dorchester Turnpike Corporation." These notes were given for a debt of the Corporation, and Chandler was duly authorized to make them. By the Court. "The Corporation is itself liable. The consideration moved wholly from them. It is very apparent that the plaintiff did not at the time of receiving the notes look to the defendant's personal security. The whole transaction was on behalf of the Corporation. Their property is liable; the defendant is not." Mann v. Chandler, 9 Mass. R. 335.

See also Mott. v. Hicks, 1 Cowen, 513.]

[(*b*) Darling was sued as acceptor of a bill and on the money counts. The bill was drawn on Darling, "agent of the Commission Company," and accepted thus, "Accepted, Noyes Darling, Agent C. C." Darling had authority to accept bills as agent of the Commission Company. The plaintiffs advanced money to Darling upon this bill; but the bill was drawn and accepted for, and the money appropriated to, Darling's private use, without the knowledge or consent of the company. The Court of Errors of Connecticut held that Darling was not liable to the action. Swift C. J. "Whether a party to an instrument made by an agent in the name of his principal, so as to bind him, but actually made for the benefit of the agent, may, in certain cases, waive his claim on the principal, and bring his action against the agent, as upon his personal contract, is a question not now necessary to decide. The plaintiffs now hold a bill of exchange uncancelled, against the Commission Company of sufficient ability to pay it, accepted by the defendant as their agent so as to be obligatory upon them, and to whom he is accountable for the money received. The express written contract extinguishes the implied one. The plaintiffs then cannot recover on either of the in debitatus counts; nor on the count for the bill of exchange, for that was never accepted by the defendant in his private capacity, but as agent for the Commission Company, so as to be binding on them." Gould J. dissented. Shelton v. Darling, 2 Conn. R. 435.]

to account of his principal, the principal is liable to the holder of the bill, in equity, if not at law. (*a*)

If in such case the agent has no original authority to draw, but the transaction be subsequently ratified by the principal, the latter will be liable as drawer. (*a*)]

Sect. 8.—It is no objection to a bill or note, that it is payable or endorsed to a person who at the time it was given

---

[(*a*) Clark and the firm of Monroe, Snow, & Monroe, were joint owners of the ship Patterson. The ship was sent by the owners on a voyage to Batavia, and B. Monroe, of the house of Monroe, Snow, & Monroe, sailed in her as supercargo. He had authority from the owners, if he thought it best or necessary to complete the lading of the ship at Batavia, to draw bills on their joint account upon Crommelin & Sons, at Amsterdam. B. Monroe at Batavia took up money in joint account of the owners and invested it in a return cargo, and for the amount drew a bill on Crommelin & Sons in favor of Van Reimsdyk, concluding, "charge the same with or without further advice to account of John Innes Clarke, Esq. and Messrs. Monroe, Snow, & Monroe, merchants, Providence, Rhode Island, North America. Your ob't. serv't. Benjamin Monroe." The bill was dishonored, of which the ship owners had due notice, and Monroe, Snow, & Monroe became insolvent and were discharged under the insolvent laws of Rhode Island; and Van Reimsdyk brought a bill in equity in the Circuit Court against Clarke's executors. Story J. said that it was objected that the bill being drawn in the separate name of B. Monroe, no remedy lay against the ship owners. "In equity I find no difficulty in reaching all the parties who were beneficially interested. I do not mean to decide that even at law this bill would be deemed the separate draft of B. Monroe. Perhaps under all the circumstances, it might be questionable, if on the face of the instrument, it might not be susceptible of being construed a partnership draft. But even admitting it to be the separate draft of B. Monroe, the authority confided to him must be deemed to have entitled him to draw in his own name on the joint funds, and to have guarantied to the holder an acceptance and payment by the drawee." He said that it was objected, supposing the bill to be the separate bill of B. Monroe, that the agreement to pay by the joint owners being a parole agreement was within the statute of frauds. But he said there was no foundation for the suggestion, even if the statute could apply to a contract made in a foreign country, because it was a promise to pay their own debt, not that of a third person. Judgment was given for the plaintiff for the full amount of the bill, damages and interest. Van Reimsdyk v. Kane, 1 Gallis. 630. As to what is a sufficient authority to an agent to authorize him to sign a note, or draw or accept a bill, in the name of the principal, see Chomqua v. Mason, 1 Gallis. 342. Emerson v. Prov. Hat. Man. Co. 12 Mass. R. 237; and Munn v. Commission Company, 15 Johns. R. 44. It seems that a general agent has such authority; but not a subagent appointed by the general agent. Emerson v. Prov. Hat. Man. Co. 12 Mass. R. 237. Munn v. Commission Company, 15 Johns. R. 44.]

was an alien enemy, if it were given to him in his own country by a British subject who was then a prisoner there. (39)

And it is no objection to an action on such a bill, that it is brought as to part in trust for an alien enemy. (40)

So it is no objection to an action on such a bill that it was given whilst an act of parliament was in force which made it penal to pay such bills, if after the act expired there was a promise to pay it. (41)

---

(39) Antoine v. Morshead, 6 Taunt. 237. Sir John Morshead, Tyndall, and Estwick, were prisoners of war at Verdun in France. Sir John Morshead drew bills on defendant, some payable to Tyndall, and some to Estwick; they endorsed them to plaintiff, a banker at Verdun. Defendants accepted them; but on being sued thereon at the return of peace, he insisted that the endorsement, as being during war, was void: Gibbs C. J. thought otherwise; and on motion for a new trial, the whole court agreed with him, and the plaintiff recovered.

(40) Daubuz v. Morshead, bart. 6 Taunt. 332. Endorsee against acceptor, on bills drawn by an English prisoner in France in favor of Borau Basti, and endorsed to plaintiff; defence, that plaintiff was only a trustee, except as to a small part, for an alien enemy: but Gibbs C. J. thought plaintiff entitled to a verdict for the whole; and verdict accordingly.

(41) Duhammel v. Pickering, 2 Stark. 90. Defendant was a prisoner of war in France in 1795, and drew four bills on Wishaw in England, payable to La Tailleur, an alien enemy residing in France: by 34 G. 3. c. 9. § 4, if any person paid any bill drawn in France during the war, he was liable to forfeit double value, and the payment was annulled. On the peace in 1802, defendant wrote to La Tailleur's agent, promising payment; this action was brought by La Tailleur's administrator. It was insisted that the statute was a bar to plaintiff's claim; and Lord Ellenborough said, no doubt the bills were void in their creation as bills to be enforced in this country, but they might constitute the basis of a promise on the return of peace; and he thought the promise in defendant's letter removed all doubt on the subject; and plaintiff had a verdict for principal and interest.

CHAP. III.

Stamps.

The paper, parchment, vellum, or other matter, whereon a bill or note made in Great Britain is written, must, except in a few instances, be stamped (1) before the bill or note is written; otherwise the (2) party making, signing, or issuing it, or causing it to be made, signed, or issued, or accepting or paying it, or causing or permitting it to be accepted or paid, will be liable to a penalty of £50, and the bill or note will (3) not be available in law or equity.

And no laches by the holder will make such unstamped bill or note amount to payment of a prior debt (4), even though the bill but for such laches would have been paid. (4)

But an unstamped bill or note may be looked at for a collateral purpose, as to judge whether the party signing it was drunk or sober at the time. (5)

And the forging a bill or note on unstamped paper, or uttering such bill or note with knowledge of its being forged, and with an intent to defraud, is as much an offence as if the bill or note were on paper duly stamped. (6)

Sect. 2.—A note payable to the bearer on demand, made, or purporting to be made, out of Great Britain, or purporting to be made by or on the behalf of any person resident out of Great Britain, (excepting where made and payable in Ireland only,) (7) cannot be negotiated, circulated, or offered or taken in payment, or offered for payment or paid here,

(1) 55 Geo. 3. c. 184. 31 Geo. 3. c. 25. § 19.
(2) By 55 Geo. 3 c. 184. § 11.
(3) 31 Geo. 3. c. 25. § 19. 55 Geo. 3. c. 184. § 8.
(4) Wilson v. Vysar, 4 Taunt. 228.
(5) Gregory v. Frazer, 3 Campb. 454.
(6) Rex. v. Hawkeswood, Pasch. 1783.
(7) By 55 G. 3. c. 184. § 29.

unless it be stamped in like manner as a note of the same tenor and value made in Great Britain, under a penalty upon the party offending therein of £20.

Before this provision, a note made in (8) any part of the King's foreign dominions, (as Jamaica) where by law a stamp was necessary, could not have been received in evidence here, unless it had such stamp as the law of that country was proved to require.

Sect. 3.—A bill drawn in Ireland with blanks for sum, date, and drawee's name, and transmitted to England to have the blanks filled up, though it may require an Irish stamp, will not require an English one. (9)

Sect. 4.—If a bill upon which a person residing abroad is intended to be drawer, is sketched out and accepted here, and then transmitted to such person abroad that he may

(8) Alves v Hodgson, 7 Term Rep. 241. A note was produced in evidence, which had been made in Jamaica; the defendant objected that it ought to have been stamped, and proved the law of Jamaica requiring a stamp. Lord Kenyon thought the objection good, but suffered the plaintiff to take a verdict, with liberty to the defendant to move to enter a nonsuit. In shewing cause against a rule nisi obtained for such purpose, it was urged that the defendant could not avail himself of an objection founded on a revenue law of a foreign country; but Lord Kenyon said, I think we must resort to the laws of the country in which the note was made, and unless it be good there, it is not obligatory in a court of law here. But as the plaintiff might have recovered, without this note, on the quantum meruit, let there be a new trial.

(9) Snaith v. Mingay, 1 Maule and Sel. 87. Bayley and Co. of Waterford, in Ireland, had one partner, Wallace, resident in England, where he carried on a separate trade, and he was restrained by the articles of partnership from drawing bills in the partnership name; they sent him over four signatures made by them as drawers and endorsers on copper-plate impressions, with blanks for dates, sums, and drawees' names; they were to be used by him in his separate trade, and he filled them up and used them accordingly. They were on Irish stamps only; and in an action upon them against the second endorser, it was objected that they ought to have had English stamps; but on a case reserved, the court thought otherwise; because they were bonâ fide *signed* in Ireland, and therefore were to be considered as *made* there.

sign his name as drawer, this is to be considered a foreign bill, and does not require an English stamp. (10)

And the acceptor is liable upon it though it is unstamped. (10)

Sect. 5.—If upon a bill dated abroad the defence is that it was made in England, and has not an English stamp, that defence ought to be made out by distinct evidence, because such conduct to evade the stamp duties would be a very serious offence. (11)

Proof that the drawer was in London so near the date of the bill, that it could not have been drawn on the date at the place from which it is dated, is not sufficient. (11)

---

(10) Boehm v. Campbell, Gow. 56. In an action by drawer against the guarantee of an acceptor, it appeared that the plaintiff lived at Antwerp; that the whole of the bill, except plaintiff's signature, was written here; that the bill was accepted before plaintiff signed it; that it was then transmitted to plaintiff for his signature, and that he signed it at Antwerp. It had no stamp, and it was urged that it was to be considered as made here, and should have had a British stamp; but Dallas C. J. thought it was to be considered as made where it was drawn, and that it was not to be considered as drawn till the plaintiff signed it; and plaintiff had a verdict.

(11) Abraham v. Dubois, 4 Campb. 269. Action on bill dated Paris, 1st March; defence, that it was drawn in London, and proof that the drawer was in London 3d March, at 11 in the forenoon. Per Lord Ellenborough: It is not very probable this bill was drawn in Paris 1st March; but if it were proved ever so distinctly, that it was not drawn in Paris 1st March, it would not follow that it was not drawn there at some other time, or that it was drawn in England Drawing here with a foreign date, to evade the stamp duties, is a very serious offence, and the fact must be made out by distinct evidence. Verdict for plaintiff.

CHAP. IV.

Alteration of Bills or Notes.

If a bill or note is altered in a material part (though by consent of all parties) after it has once issed, it requires (1) a new stamp;

Unless such alteration is to correct a mistake, and merely to make the bill what it was originally intended to have been, for in such a case a new stamp is not necessary. (2)

Where an alteration will vacate a bill or note, it will have that effect, though it is made by a mere stranger. (3)

---

(1) Wilson v. Justice, 1796. A bill of nine months after date was, by consent of all parties, a fortnight after it had been delivered to the payee, altered to ten months after date. Lord Kenyon held a new stamp necessary, and nonsuited the plaintiff.

Bowman v. Nicoll, 5 Term Rep. 537. A bill dated 2d September, and payable twenty one days after date, was, by consent of the acceptor, altered to fifty-one days after date: on 30th September it was with the like consent, and whilst it remained in the drawer's hands, restored to twenty-one days, but the date was altered to September 14th. Lord Kenyon nonsuited, and the court held the nonsuit right.

(2) Kershaw v. Cox, 3 Esp. N. P. C. 246. In an action on a bill, it appeared that the defendant, who was the payee, had *endorsed* the bill to one K., by whom it was passed to the plaintiffs; that they, on discovering that the words, "or order," had been omitted, returned it the day after it was drawn, and the drawer, with the consent of the defendant, then inserted those words. Le Blanc, J. held that no new stamp was necessary; that this was not a new instrument, as in Bowman v. Nicholl, but merely a correction of a mistake, and in furtherance of the original intention of the parties; and the plaintiffs had a verdict. A new trial was afterwards moved for, but the court refused a rule. See 10 East. Rep. 437.

Jacob v. Hart, 2 Stark. 45. In an action on a bill drawn by A. on B., payable to C. or order, B. discovered, when it was in C.'s hands, that by mistake the date was March instead of April, and C. altered it. Some time after B. had accepted it, C. added on the bill, payable at Mr. J.'s, St. Mary Axe; that was the proper place. Lord Ellenborough held both alterations immaterial, and the plaintiff had a verdict.

(3) Master v. Miller, 4 Term Rep. 320. 2 H. Bl. 141. In an action by endorsees against the acceptor of a bill, payable three months after date, to Wilkinson and Cooke, the declaration had one count upon the bill as dated the 20th March, and another as dated the 26th March. The jury found a special verdict, stating that the bill was drawn and dated the 26th March; that it was accepted; and that afterwards, and whilst it remained in the hands of Wilkinson and Cooke, the date was altered from the 26th to the 20th March, without the defendant's know-

And such alteration not only makes a new stamp necessary, but vacates the bill or note, (independently of the stamp laws) except as between the parties consenting to such alteration.

Altering the (4) date, or sum, or (4) time for payment; or inserting words, rendering a bill or note (5) negotiable,

---

ledge, and by some person unknown to the jury. That after such alteration it was endorsed for a valuable consideration by Wilkinson and Cooke to the plaintiffs. After two arguments, Lord Kenyon, Ashhurst, and Grose, Js. held, that the alteration, though by a stranger, vacated the bill; Buller J. differed; but on error, the whole court was so clear that it was vacated, that they would not hear a second argument, and judgment for the defendant was affirmed. See Henfree v. Bromley, 6 East. Rep. 309.

(4) Walton v. Hastings, 4 Campb. 223. 1 Stark. 215. A bill drawn by Brooks in favor of plaintiff was dated 5th July. An agent of plaintiffs presented it for acceptance, and defendant, the drawee, desired to have the date altered to the 10th, which was done accordingly, and then defendant accepted it. Lord Ellenborough held that as the bill was issued before this alteration was made, and was a perfect available instrument, the alteration made a new stamp necessary, and nonsuit.

Outhwaite v. Luntley, 4 Campb. 179. A bill drawn 5th March was endorsed to J. S., who left it for acceptance. The drawees altered the date to 15th March, and then accepted it. In an action on the bill by endorsee against endorser, it was argued that this alteration vacated the bill. Lord Ellenborough was of that opinion, because the bill was a perfect instrument when issued to the endorsee, the alteration might embarrass parties who would expect notice or payment according to the original date, and the alteration made it a new bill, and made a new stamp necessary.

See Wilson v. Justice, and Bowman v. Nicholl, ante, p. 58, and Cardwell v. Martin, infra, p. 62. As to acceptances varying from the tenor of the bill, see Chapter VI.

[See also Stephens v. Graham, 7. Serg. and Raw. 505. Bank of U. S. v. Russell, 3 Yeates, 391.]

Action on a note dated Sept. 10th 1819. The note was in fact made on that day; but was originally written 1809, and had since been altered to 1819. There was no evidence that the maker of the note knew of the alteration. The court held that the alteration in this case was material, and would render the instrument void, unless made by consent of the maker either express or implied, or under circumstances which would rebut the presumption of improper motives in making the alteration. Woodbury J. said, "And whether under all the testimony consent can here be implied, or the presumption be deemed rebutted, that the alteration was fraudulent, should be submitted to a jury." Bowers v. Jewell, 2 N. Hamp. R. 543.

But in Tennessee it has been held that the alteration of the date of the assignment of a note, did not avoid the right of action by the assignee against the maker of the note. Griffith v. Cox, Overton, 210.]

(5) See Kershaw v. Cox, ante, p. 58. n. (2) In Knill v. Williams, 10 East's Rep. 437, Le Blanc, J. said, that Kershaw and Cox could only be supported on the ground that the alteration was merely the correction of a mistake, for the alteration was a very material one.

which was not so originally; or inserting words in a bill or note originally expressed to be for value received generally, stating such value to have been received on a (6) particular account, is a material alteration, and makes a new stamp necessary.

[So procuring a person to sign his name as a witness to a note who did not see the maker sign, is a material alteration. (*a*)

So striking out a special endorsement over the name of an endorser, is a material alteration; but if the alteration be made without any fraudulent intention, the court will permit the special endorsement to be restored. (*b*)]

---

(6) Knill v. Williams, 10 East. Rep. 431. This was an action on a note, by which, nine months after date, the defendant promised to pay to the plaintiff, or order, £100 for value received, *for the good-will of the lease and trade of Mr. F. Knill, deceased.* It appeared at the trial before Le Blanc J., at Hereford, that the words in Italics were added, by consent of both parties, on the day after the note had been signed and delivered to the plaintiff, without any new stamp being impressed upon it; upon this the plaintiff was nonsuited, and a rule nisi to set aside the nonsuit, the whole court held that the alteration was material, and therefore discharged the rule.

[(*a*) Hall whose name was written as the subscribing witness on a note, did not see the defendant sign the note; but the plaintiff long after the date of the note, brought it to Hall, and asked him to sign his name as a subscribing witness, which he did. The court held that this was a material alteration of the note. Homer v. Wallis, 11 Mass. R. 309. In Massachusetts a note executed in presence of a subscribing witness is excepted from the operation of the statute of limitations.]

[(*b*) J. and T. G. Prentiss drew a bill on De Grand payable to the order of T. G. Prentiss. The bill was endorsed, "Pay to the order of J. T. Mason Jr. Tho. G. Prentiss," and afterwards an endorsement by Mason to pay to the order of Nevins and Co. or to Nevins and Co. or order. The bill thus endorsed was accepted by De Grand. Nevins and Co. in order to avoid responsibility as endorsers, erased the endorsement over Mason's name, leaving Mason's endorsement in blank, and sold the bill, which was afterwards passed to Cabot. De Grand refused payment when the bill was presented by Cabot, on account of the erasure. Cabot then brought an action on the bill, and had the endorsement filled up so as to be payable to himself, but the court held that he could not maintain the action. Nevins and Co. repaid Cabot the amount of the bill, and then brought their action against De Grand upon the bill. The plaintiffs asked leave of the court to strike out the words endorsed in Cabot's action, and to restore the original words which made the bill payable to their order. Parker C. J. delivered the opinion of the court. "It being clear that the words now moved to be restored, were stricken out with honest intentions; and that the acceptor has in no way been prejudiced thereby, or can be in any way injured by the restoration; justice requires, and the law allows it to be done. The bill never hav-

But inserting a mere memorandum to say where the bill or note is to be payable, if it give a right direction in that respect, is not. (7)

But altering an acceptance, so as to give an unwarranted place for payment, vacates the acceptance. (8)

And altering the place where a bill or note is payable, if for purpose of fraud, may be a capital forgery. (9)

---

ing been assigned by the plaintiffs, to take effect as was intended, the property remains in them, and they have a right to maintain the action." Nevins v. De Grand, 15 Mass. R. 436.]

(7) Trapp v. Spearman, 3 Esp. N. P. C. 57. In an action on a bill by an endorsee against the acceptor, the defence was, that the bill had been altered, by the insertion of the words, "When due, at the Cross Keys, Black Friars Road." But Lord Kenyon held that the alteration was immaterial, and the plaintiff had a verdict.

Marson v. Petit, 1 Campb. N. P. C. 82 n. Endorsee against acceptor of a bill; after acceptance, the drawer, without the consent or knowledge of the defendant, wrote under his name, Prescott and Co. Lord Ellenborough held it immaterial.

[Woodworth was sued as endorser of a note. After the note was made and endorsed, Kane, the maker, without the knowledge of Woodworth, wrote in the margin of the note, "Payable at the Bank of America, James Kane." The court held that this was not a material alteration, and did not invalidate the note. Bank of America v. Woodworth, 18 Johns. R. 315.

This decision was afterwards reversed in the Court of Errors, who considered the addition of the place of payment as a material alteration. Eighteen votes for reversing, ten, including the Chancellor, for affirming. S. C. 19 Johns. R. 391.]

(8) Tidmarsh v. Grover, 1 Maul. and Sel. 735. Defendant accepted a bill so as to make it payable at Bloxam and Co.'s: Bloxam and Co. failed, and the holder, without defendant's knowledge or consent, struck out their names, and substituted Esdaile and Co.'s. On point reserved whether this alteration vacated the acceptance, the whole court held it did, and plaintiff was nonsuited.

Cowie v. Halsall, 4 Barnew. and Ald. 197. In an action by endorsee of a bill against the acceptor, it appeared that the acceptance was general, and that the drawer, without the defendant's knowledge, added to it "Payable at Mr. B.'s, Chiswell Street;" and on the ground that this was a material alteration and vacated the acceptance, verdict for defendant: A motion was made for a new trial, but the court thought the verdict right, for this alteration would lead to a presentment at B.'s, not at defendant's and the bill might be treated as dishonored, and defendant be arrested thereon, without any presentment where he would expect it, and a rule was refused.

(9) Rex v. Treble, 2 Taunt. 328. Kellaway issued ten pound notes payable at Fordingbridge, or at Wilkinson and Co.'s London: these notes were re-issuable, several of them were paid in town, and stolen on their way back to Fordingbridge. Wilkinson and Co. failed, and the prisoner, who had got one of these notes, covered the names of Wilkinson and Co. with a small piece of paper containing the names of Rams-

[The interlining of a word which the law would have supplied, does not vitiate a bill or note. (*a*)]

Sect. 2.—A bill or note is, primâ facie, to be considered as issued as soon as it is passed away by the drawer or maker, (10) or accepted by the drawee; (11)

Not before. (12)

If two perosns exchange acceptances, each bill is to be considered as issued, and any alteration afterwards will make new stamps necessary. (13)

---

bottom and Co. and re-issued the note: he was indicted for forgery and convicted, and on argument before the twelve judges this was held a forgery, for substituting a solvent house as one of the places of payment instead of an insolvent one varied the credit of the note, and though Kellaway by the real note answered for no payment in London, but at Wilkinson and Co.'s, this alteration made him answerable for it at Ramsbottom's.

[(*a*) A note was written payable on the "the 25th of Dec. in the of our Lord," omitting the word *year*, which word was interlined before the trial. Parsons C. J. delivered the opinion of the court. "The law would have supplied this word, and without the insertion of it the note would have supported a count on a promise to pay on the 25th of Dec. in the year of our Lord 1805. We are therefore of opinion that the actual insertion of the word *year*, which the law would clearly have supplied, is no such alteration as will annul the contract, if it was interlined by the promisee without consent; and if it were an immaterial alteration, the law will reasonably presume an assent of the promisers to the making of it." Hunt v. Adams, 6 Mass. R. 519. See also Bowers v. Jewell, ante, p. 59.

(10) See Walton v. Hastings, ante, p. 59. Outhwaite v. Luntly, ante, p. 59. Knill v. Williams, ante p. 60.

(11) See Tidmarsh v. Grover, and Cowie v. Halsall, ante, p. 61.

(12) Kennerly v. Nash, 1 Stark. 452. Maules drew a bill upon Nash at three months, payable to his (Maule's) order, and sent it to Nash for acceptance: Nash sent it back to Maule, and desired him to let the bill be at four months instead of three: Maule assented, and the bill was altered accordingly. On question whether this made a new stamp necessary, Lord Ellenborough held it did not, and the plaintiff had a verdict.

(13) Cardwell v. Martin, 9. East. Rep. 190. On the 3d of June, 1807, the defendant and Giles and Co. exchanged acceptances; on the 23d, before either of the bills had been passed away, they altered the dates to the 23d; the bills were payable at a certain period after date. Lord Ellenborough thought a new stamp necessary, and nonsuited the plaintiff, with liberty to move to set aside the nonsuit: on motion accordingly, the whole court thought that the exchange of acceptances was a negotiation of each bill, and that the subsequent alteration rendered a new stamp necessary. Rule refused.

N. Each bill was payable to the drawer's order, and plaintiff was a bonâ fide endorsee.

But a bill is not to be considered as issued, so as to make a new stamp necessary, until it is in the hands of some one who is entitled to make a claim thereon; (14)

Though it is accepted and endorsed; (14)

And an alteration thereon without the knowledge of acceptor or endorser, though it will entitle them to consider their acceptance or endorsement vacated if they do not assent thereto, will be binding upon them if they assent. (14)

Sect. 3.—If the date of a bill appear upon production to have been altered, and such alteration is in the hand-writing of the acceptor, the holder must prove that such alteration was made before the bill was parted with by the drawer. (15)

But proof that it was in the drawer's hands after it was accepted, will be primâ facie evidence for that purpose. (15)

---

(14) Downes v. Richardson, B. R. Easter Term, 1822. Upon an issue from chancery, on the question whether Thompson, as acceptor of a bill of exchange, was indebted thereon to Downes, an endorsee; it appeared in evidence that the bill was drawn by Raines to his own order upon Thompson, accepted by Thompson and endorsed by Raines and Lachlan; that its date was the 6th March; that Raines, Thompson and Lachlan were in the habit of putting their names for each other upon bills, and that Thompson and Lachlan put their names upon this bill to enable Raines to pass it: Raines put it into the hands of an agent, and he could not pass it till 10th April, when he paid it for value to Howell, who passed it for value to plaintiff. Before it was paid to Howell, the date was altered to the 16th of March: Thompson did not know of this alteration till after the bill was paid to Howell, but as soon as he knew of it he assented to it. It was urged for defendant, that this alteration made a new stamp necessary; but upon a case reserved, the court thought otherwise; for though the bill had names upon it, so as to give it the semblance of an available bill before it was paid to Howell, it was not in fact an available bill till that payment; no person could have made a claim upon it, and if not, it was not to be considered as issued till that period, and then the alteration was in time; and though Thompson would not have been bound by the bill in its altered state had he not assented to the alteration but might have insisted that the alteration cancelled his acceptance, his subsequent assent bound him, and revived and continued his acceptance.

(15) Johnson v. Duke of Marlborough, 2 Stark. 313. In action by endorsee against acceptor on bill payable to the drawer's order, the bill on production appeared to have been dated originally 29th Decem-

If the bill is put into an agent's hands to pay away, and it is left in doubt whether the date was altered before he paid it away or afterwards, it will not be sufficient. (16)

---

ber, 1816, but the date was altered to 29th January, 1817, and the alteration, which was immediately above the acceptance, was proved to be in defendant's handwriting. Abbot J. intimated, that he must have proof that the alteration was made before the drawer endorsed away the bill, for otherwise a new stamp would have been necessary. Proof was then given that the bill was in the drawer's hands after defendant had accepted it, and that was considered primâ facie proof that it had not been previously negotiated.

(16) In Downes v. Richardson, ante p. 63. it was at first left in doubt when the date was altered, whether before or after the payment to Howell, and then the court inclined against the plaintiff; it was afterwards ascertained that the alteration was before that payment.

CHAP. V.

Transfer of Bills or Notes.

Bills or notes payable to order, or to bearer, or containing any words to make them assignable, may be assigned so as to give the assignee a right upon the bill or note against all the antecedent parties; and bills or notes containing no words to make them assignable may, where the stamp laws do not prevent it, be assigned so as to give the assignee a right upon them against the assignor, but (1) not so as to give him a right against any of the antecedent parties.

[But a bill or note payable to order, may be transferred by the payee by delivery only, so far as to enable the assignee to maintain an action upon it in the name of the original payee. But the defendant in such case may set off any payment or other demands against the payee, which he had previous to notice of the assignment, but none subsequent. *(a)*]

Bills and notes are assigned either by delivery only, or by

---

(1) Hill v. Lewis, Salk. 132. Moore drew one note payable to the defendant, or his order, and another payable to him generally, without any words to make it assignable; the defendant endorsed them to Zouch, and Zouch to the plaintiff; the first objection was that the plaintiff had been guilty of laches, but the jury thought he had not: and it was then urged that the second note was not assignable; and Holt, C. J. agreed that the endorsement of this note did not make him that drew it chargeable to the endorsee, for the words "*or to his order*" give authority to assign it by endorsement; but the endorsement of a note which has not these words is good so as to make the endorser chargeable to the endorsee.

[Ames endorsed a note payable to himself, but not to his order, to secure a debt due from the maker to Josselyn, to whom it was given. Josselyn wrote a guaranty over Ames' name, and sued him as guarantor. No demand or notice was proved. The court held the action not maintainable, because the payee could not "himself warrant to a third person payment of a note payable to himself." But the court said that the plaintiff might cancel what he had written, and instead thereof write, "For value received I undertake to pay the money mentioned to E. J." and upon this endorsement might maintain an action. Josselyn v. Ames, 3 Mass. R. 274.]

[*(a)* Jones v. Witter, 13 Mass. R. 305. Parker C. J. said "There is no sensible ground upon which a writing shall be held necessary to prove an assignment of a contract, which assignment has been executed by delivery, any more than an assignment of a personal chattel."]

endorsement and delivery. Bills and notes whilst payable to order are assignable by the latter mode only; bills and notes payable to bearer, and bills and notes originally payable to order, and endorsed, as (2) they may be, so as to be payable to the bearer, by either.

On a transfer by delivery only, without endorsement, the person making it ceases to (3) be a party to the bill or note; on a transfer by endorsement, he (4) is, according to the legal operation, a new drawer.

No particular (5) words are essential to an endorsemeut; the mere signature (6) of the endorser is in general sufficient.

A promise to endorse, though on sufficient consideration cannot be treated as an actual endorsement. (7)

Nor will it preclude the party from proving that an endorsement afterwards in his name is a forgery. (7)

But delivery without endorsement, where endorsement is essential, and where it is omitted by mistake, will entitle the party to call for an endorsement afterwards; (8)

---

(2) See post, p. 67. [See also Brush v. Reeves, 3 Johns. R. 435.]

(3) Vide Ld. Raym. 442. 774. 929, 930. 12 Mod. 203. 241. 408. 517. 521. Salk. 124. 128.—3 Salk. 68. Comb. 57.

(4) Smallwood v. Vernon, Str. 478. In an action against the endorser of a note, the declaration stated that he became chargeable according to the tenor of the endorsement: and it was objected that the endorsement might appoint the payment at a time different from that mentioned in the note; sed per cur. if it did, it would charge the endorser, for every endorsement is the same as making a new note. Vide 2 Show. 501. Comb. 32. Skinn. 255, 256. 342. 411. 3 Mod. 87. 12 Mod. 36. Ld. Raym. 181. 444. 744. Salk. 125. 132, 133. 3 Salk. 68. Str. 442. 479. 1 Atk. 282. 2 Atk. 182. Burr. 670. 675. Dougl. 613.

(5) Vide Holt. 117. Ld. Raym. 176. 810.

(6) Vide 12 Mod. 192. 244. Salk. 126. 128. 130. Ld. Raym. 444.

(7) Moxon v. Pulling, 4 Camp. 50. Defendant had accepted a bill, he could not pay, and referred the holder to one May, to whom he said he had lent the acceptance. May proposed that plaintiff should take an acceptance of Hullett and Co., and that defendant should endorse it: defendant agreed, and said he would go and endorse it. Four days afterwards May sent plaintiff Hullett and Co.'s acceptance, with an endorsement in defendant's name; and plaintiff gave up defendant's acceptance: the endorsement in defendant's name was a forgery, and defendant being sued as endorser, Lord Ellenborough said, "You cannot establish any agency to endorse: when the promise was given, the bill does not appear to have existed, and all was *in fieri;* defendant might repent and refuse to endorse; he may be liable for breach of promise, but cannot be sued as endorser. Nonsuit.

And if the party who ought to have made it afterwards become bankrupt, will prevent his assignees from claiming the bill or note. (8)

An endorsement which mentions the name of the person in whose favour it is made, is called a full endorsement; an endorsement which does not, a blank one.

A blank endorsement, so long as it continues blank, makes a bill or note payable to the (9) bearer, but the holder may write over it what he pleases. (*a*)

[So where a bill or note is endorsed in blank, and passed to a partnership, it may be filled out to one partner and he may sue upon it in his own name. (*b*)]

And the holder, by writing a direction over the endorsement, ordering the money to be paid to particular persons without adding his own name, does (10) not become an endorser.

---

(8) See Smith v. Pickering, post.

(9) Peacock v. Rhodes, Dougl. 611—633. A bill was drawn by the defendant, payable to Ingham or order. Ingham endorsed it in blank, after which it was stolen; the plaintiff took it *boná fide*, and paid a valuable consideration for it, and acceptance and payment being refused, gave notice to the defendant, and brought this action. A case was reserved for the opinion of the court, and it was contended that this bill was not to be considered as payable to bearer, and that the plaintiff had no better right upon it than the person of whom he took it; but the court said there was no difference between a note endorsed in blank, and one payable to bearer, and the plaintiff had judgment. Francis v. Mott, N. P. before Lord Mansfield, cited Dougl. 612. was a similar case, and the attorney-general, who was for the defendant, after attempting unsuccessfully to show that the plaintiff *knew* the bill was obtained unfairly, gave up the cause.

[(*a*) Williams v. Matthews, 3 Cowen, 252; and Lovell v. Evertson, infra.]

[(*b*) Lovell sued Evertson as endorser of a note. The endorsement was in blank and filled up at the trial in the C. Pleas, payable to the plaintiff. It was proved at the trial that the note was endorsed and delivered for the benefit of Thomas Lovell and Co. and the plaintiff was nonsuited. On Error, Per Curiam. "The note being endorsed in blank, the owner had a right to fill it up with what name he pleased, and the person whose name is so inserted, will be deemed on record as the legal owner, and if not so in fact, he could sue as trustee for the persons having the real interest. But the defendant could have no concern with that question. He was responsible to the person whose name was so inserted in the blank endorsement." Judgment reversed. Lovell v. Evertson, 11 Johns. R. 52.]

(10) Vincent and another v. Horlock and another, 1 Campb. N. P. C. 442. In an action against the defendants as endorsers of a bill, it ap-

As long however as the first endorsement continues blank, the (11) bill or note as against the payee, the drawer, and acceptor, is assignable by mere delivery, notwithstanding it may have upon it subsequent full endorsements.

[And the holder may strike out the subsequent full endorsements, and make himself the immediate endorsee of the first endorser. (*a*)]

A full endorsement may restrain the negotiability of a bill or note. (*b*)

[The holder of a note endorsed in blank, who has written an endorsement over the name of the endorser, making the note payable to an agent, to whom it is transmitted, to obtain payment; may strike out the endorsement when the note is returned to him. (*c*)]

---

peared that the payee had endorsed it in blank to the defendants, and that they had written over the payee's signature, "Pay the contents to Vincent and Co." Lord Ellenborough was clearly of opinion that this was not an endorsement by the defendants; and the plaintiffs were nonsuited.

(11) Smith v. Clark, Peake, 225. A bill was endorsed in blank by the payee, and after some other endorsements was endorsed to Jackson or order; Jackson sent it to Muir and Atkinson, but did not endorse it, and Muir and Atkinson discounted it with the plaintiffs: the plaintiff struck out all the endorsements except the first, which continued blank. This was an action against the acceptor, and it was objected, that the plaintiffs could not recover without an endorsement by Jackson; but Ld. Kenyon held otherwise, and the plaintiffs recovered. The plaintiffs afterwards proved that Jackson desired Muir and Atkinson to discount this bill, but Ld. Kenyon thought the plaintiff's case made out without this evidence.

[(*a*) See Smith v. Clark supra; Thompson v. Robertson, 4 Johns. R. 27; and Ritchie v. Moore, 5 Munf. 388. Morris v. Foreman, 1 Dall. 103.]

[(*b*) Where a note is endorsed to A or order, the property of the note is passed to A, and nothing but cancelling this endorsement, or A's endorsing the note, would divest him of the legal title; not even an assignment by him under hand and seal. Burdick v. Green, 15 Johns. R. 247.]

[(*c*) Spencer C. J. delivered the opinion of the Court. "The defendant is sued as first endorser of a note. Over the name of Peter Smith (the defendant) there was written when the note was presented for payment, 'pay to the order of W. Fish, Esq. Cashier. &c.' This endorsement was thus filled for the safety of transmission, by the plaintiffs' direction, who were owners of the note. The endorsement was afterwards erased, and the note directed to be paid to the plaintiffs. Fish never had any interest in the note. It was sent to him merely to collect, and not being paid, he sent it back. He was the mere servant or agent of the plaintiffs; and it is, I think, clearly settled, that in such a case the plaintiffs had a right to strike out the transfer and make the note payable to themselves." Bank of Utica v. Smith, 18 Johns. R. 230.]

An endorsement is restrictive, which has express words making it so, or is made in favor of a person who cannot make a transfer.

Thus an endorsement in these words, "Pay the contents to I. S. only," "to I. S. (12) for my use;" or (at least when addressed to the drawee) (13) "the within must be credited to I. S.," is restrictive.

An endorsement, "Pay the contents to A. B. on my being gazetted ensign in a given time" is restrictive, and will give no subsequent endorsee a right, unless he is so gazetted. (14)

An endorsement, "Pay to A. or order, for account of B.,"

---

(12) Per Wilmot J. Burr. 1227. Blackst. 299. The payee may check the currency of a bill or note by giving a bare authority to receive the money; as "Pay to A. for my use;" and per Lord Hardwicke in Snee v. Prescott, 1 Atk. 249. Bills and notes are frequently endorsed in this manner, "Pray pay the money to my use," in order to prevent their being filled up with such an endorsement as passes the interest.

(13) Ancher v. Bank of England, Dougl. 615. 637. A bill was drawn by the plaintiffs upon Claus Heide and Co. payable to Jens Mœstue or order. Mœstue endorsed it to this effect: "The within must be credited to Captain M. L. Dahl, value in account," and sent it to Claus Heide and Co. who credited Dahl for the amount, and gave notice to Dahl and the plaintiffs that they had done so; an endorsement by Dahl was afterwards forged upon the bill, and the bank discounted it. Claus Heide and Co. having become insolvent, Fulgberg paid it for the honor of the plaintiffs, and upon the ground that the endorsement had restrained the negotiability of the bill, they brought an action for money had and received against the bank: Lord Mansfield directed a nonsuit, but upon a rule to shew cause why there should not be a new trial, and cause shewn, Lord Mansfield, Willes, and Ashhurst, Js. thought the endorsement restrictive, and that the plaintiffs were entitled to recover; but Buller J. thought otherwise; upon which Lord Mansfield said, the whole turned on the question, whether the bill continued negotiable? and if they altered their opinion, they would mention the case again; but it never was mentioned afterwards, and upon a new trial Lord Mansfield directed the jury to find for the plaintiffs, which they did.

(14) Robertson v. Kensington, 4 Taunt. 30. Bill payable to plaintiff or order: he endorsed it, "Pay the within to Clerk and Ross, or order, upon my name appearing in the Gazette as ensign in any regiment of the line between the 1st and 64th, if within two months from this date:" the bill was at forty-five days after date: defendants accepted it after it was so endorsed: Clerk and Ross endorsed it over, and after passing through several hands it came to the bank, and them defendants paid: plaintiff's name was never in the Gazette, and he therefore insisted the payment by defendants was wrongful, and that he was entitled to the money. He accordingly brought an action, and on a case reserved the court was of that opinion, and decided for the plaintiff.

will not prevent A. from endorsing for value, if it be under circumstances which may induce a belief that such value is to be applied to B.'s use; (15)

But it will from endorsing by way of pledge for the private debt of A; (15)

Or for advances to A. on his own account.

But an endorsement is not restrictive, merely because it expresses what is the consideration for it.

Therefore this endorsement, "Pay the contents to I. S., being part of the consideration in a certain deed of assignment, executed by the said I. S. to the endorser and others," is (16) not restrictive.

And the (17) mere omission of words to give a power of transfer will not make an endorsement restrictive.

---

(15) Treuttel v. Barandon, 8 Taunt. 100. Two bills were endorsed "Pay to J. P. De Roure, Esq. or order, for account of Messrs. Treuttel and Wurtz:" De Roure endorsed them, and gave them to defendants as a security on his own account: he was indebted to them at the time to more than the value of the bills, and they afterwards advanced him money on these bills: De Roure failed, and Treuttel and Wurtz brought trover for the bills. Gibbs C. J. thought this endorsement sufficiently intimated that the bills were not the property of De Roure, and under his direction, verdict for plaintiffs: and on rule nisi for new trial, the court thought, that though he might not be restricted from discounting, and might pass a good title to a person who might suppose they were passed to the use of plaintiffs, he could not pledge them on his own account, and rule discharged.

(16) R. Potts v. Reed, 6 Esp. N. P. C. 57.

(17) Moore v. Manning, Com. 311. A note was drawn by the defendant payable to Statham or order; Statham endorsed it to Witherhead, but did not add "or to his order," and Witherhead endorsed it to the plaintiff. The defendant contended, that as there were no express words to authorize Witherhead to assign it, he had no such power, but the whole court resolved, that as the bill was at first assignable by Statham as being payable to him or order, and as all Statham's interest was transferred to Witherhead, the right of assigning it was transferred also, and the plaintiff had judgment.

Acheson v. Fountain, Str. 557. Bull. N. P. 275. A bill was payable to Abercrombie or order, and he endorsed it thus, "Pray pay the contents to Louisa Acheson." This being stated in the declaration as an endorsement to Acheson or order, it was objected that it was a fatal variance; but upon consideration the whole court was of opinion against the objection, because this was the legal import of the endorsement, and Louisa Acheson was authorized by it to make an endorsement over.

Edie v. East India Company, Blackst. 295. Burr. 1216. A foreign bill drawn upon the East India Company was payable to Campbell or order; Campbell endorsed it to Ogilby, but did not insert the words "or order," or any similar words in the endorsement; Ogilby endorsed it to

A restrictive endorsement precludes the person in whose favor it is made from making a transfer so as to give a right of action against either the person making it, or any of the antecedent parties, and if payment is made to the person to whom such transfer is made, the party paying may, under circumstances, be liable to pay the money a second time (18), or the person receiving it may be liable to refund. (19) (*a*)

---

the plaintiffs. It was insisted that under the endorsement to Ogilby he had no authority to endorse it over, and upon that ground the jury found for the defendants; but upon a rule to shew cause why there should not be a new trial, and cause shewn, the court was clear, that as the bill was originally in its nature negotiable, it continued so in the hands of Ogilby, and that his endorsement was good; and a new trial was granted.

(18) Vide Robertson v. Kensington, ante p. 69. note.

(19) Vide Ancher v. Bank of England, ante p. 69. note.

[(*a*) The Supreme Court of Massachusetts, in one case, seem to be of opinion that a guaranty endorsed on a note, by the promisee, destroys the negotiable quality of the instrument; and that no action can be maintained against him as endorser; or as guarantor, except by the original party to the guaranty. Binney holding a note of Fales, payable to Binney or order, some time after the note became payable, made and signed the following endorsement. "Dec. 13th, 1805. I guaranty the payment of the within note in 18 months, provided it cannot be collected of the promisor before that time." Tyler sued Binney upon this guaranty; but it appeared that Tyler was not the party to whom the guaranty was originally made. Sewall J. delivered the opinion of the Court. "The present plaintiff was not the party to the guaranty or assignment, when it was made: and no evidence has been offered of any subsequent privity or assent between him and the defendant. The guaranty, taken independently of the note, is a promise not negotiable, being conditional and not absolute; and connected with it, the supposition is altogether unreasonable and improbable, of an unlimited currency being intended for the note itself at the risk of the endorser." Nonsuit. Tyler v. Binney, 7 Mass. R. 479.

But in a subsequent case the same court held that such an endorsement did not destroy the negotiable quality of the instrument.

Prince holding a note of Turner payable to himself, endorsed two days after the making of the note, "I guaranty the payment of this note within six months, Andrew H. Prince," and passed it to Faulkner, who passed it Upham. Upham sued Prince as endorser. "Per Curiam. We are all of opinion that the note did not lose its negotiability by this special endorsement, any more than it would, if it had been endorsed with the words, 'without recurrence to the endorser.' The defendant's engagement amounts to a promise that the note should at all events be paid in six months. Now this promise may not be assignable in law; and yet the note itself may be assignable by the party to whom it was so transferred, so that upon non-payment of it by the promiser, the holder would have a right of action against Prince." Defendant defaulted. Upham v. Prince, 12 Mass. R. 14.]

[An endorsement to pay to A at his own risk does not restrain the negotiability of a bill or note (*a*); nor an agreement written on a bill over the name of the endorser to pay damages in case the bill is protested. (*b*)]

An (20) endorsement cannot be made for the transfer of less than the full sum appearing to be due upon the bill or note.

Sect. 2.—A transfer by endorsement will convey no title, except against the person making it, unless it is made by him who has a right to make the transfer: a transfer by delivery may.

Therefore in case of a loss by theft or accident, if the bill or note be assignable by mere delivery, the thief or finder may (21) confer a title by transferring it; if it be assignable by endorsement only, he (22) cannot.

[(*a*) Rice v. Stearns, 3 Mass. R. 225.]

[(*b*) Lajus, payee of a bill of exchange, endorsed it "should the within exchange not be accepted and paid agreeably to its contents, I hereby engage to pay the holder in addition to the principal 20 p. c. damages. Dominique Lajus." In an action against the drawee, Parsons C. J. delivered the opinion of the Court. "The endorsement is evidence of a transfer of the bill, without naming the endorsee; and in this respect the endorsement may be considered as general, and a *bonâ fide* holder may fill it up, by inserting above the express stipulation a direction to pay the contents to his order for value received." The case turned on another point. Blakely v. Grant, 6 Mass. R. 386.]

(20) Hawkins v. Cardy, Ld. Raym. 360. Carth. 466. 12 Mod. 213. Salk. 65. In an action upon a bill drawn by the defendant for £46 19*s*. payable to Blackman or order, the declaration stated that Blackman endorsed £43 4*s*. of it to the plaintiff; the defendant pleaded an insufficient plea, upon which the plaintiff demurred; but the whole court held the declaration bad, because the bill could not be endorsed for less than all the money due thereon, and the plaintiff discontinued his action. And per Gould, J. in Johnson v. Kennion, 2 Wils. 262. where the drawer of a bill has paid part, you may endorse it over for the residue; otherwise not, because it would subject him to a variety of actions.

[Action against the endorser of a note. By one endorsement he had assigned part of the sum mentioned in the note, and the residue by another endorsement. The court held that the action could not be supported, on the ground that an endorsement for part of a note or bill is bad; and if so, these two vitious endorsements could never constitute a good one. Hughes v. Kiddell, 2 Bay, 324.]

(21) Anon. Ld. Raym. 738. Salk. 126. 3 Salk. 71. B. lost a bank bill payable to A. or bearer; C. found it, and assigned it for a valuable

If a bill or note transferable by delivery be lost, the loser should give immediate notice thereof to the drawee, or persons who are to pay it. (23)

And if such persons afterwards pay it to a person who has

---

consideration to D. who got a new bill for it from the bank. Trover was then brought against D. for the first bill, but by Holt C. J. "the action will not lie against *him*, because he took it for a valuable consideration, though it would against C., as he had no title; but payment to C. would have indemnified the bank."

Miller v. Race, Burr. 452. A bank note payable to William Fenney, or bearer, was stolen out of the mail in the night of the 11th of December, 1756, and on the 12th came to the hands of the plaintiff for a full and valuable consideration, in the usual course of his business, and without any knowledge that it had been taken out of the mail; he afterwards presented it at the bank for payment. and the defendant, being one of the clerks, stopped it, upon which an action of trover was brought; and upon a case reserved upon the point, whether the plaintiff had a sufficient property in the note to entitle him to recover, the court was clear in opinion that he had, and that the action was well brought. Vide Lawson and others v. Weston and others, 4 Esp. N. P. C. 56.

Grant v. Vaughan, Burr. 1516. Vaughan gave Bicknell a draught upon his banker payable to "Ship Fortune, or bearer." Bicknell lost it, and the plaintiff afterwards took it, bonâ fide, in the course of trade, and paid a valuable consideration for it: the banker refused to pay it, upon which the plaintiff brought this action against Vaughan. Lord Mansfield left it to the jury to consider, 1st, whether the plaintiff came to the possession of the bill fairly and bonâ fide; and 2dly, whether such draught was in fact and practice negotiable; and the jury found for the defendant: but upon an application for a new trial, and cause shewn against it, the Court was clear that the second point ought not to have been left to the jury, because it was clear that such draughts were negotiable, and if the jury thought the plaintiff took the note fairly and bonâ fide, of which there appeared to be no doubt, he was entitled to recover. A new trial was accordingly granted, in which the plaintiff recovered the money. Peacock v. Rhodes, Dougl. 611. 633. ante, p. 67. note (9.)

By 9 & 10 W. 3. c. 17. § 3. "If any inland bill be lost, or miscarry within the time limited for its payment, the drawer shall, on security given upon request to indemnify him if such bill shall be found again, give another bill of the same tenor with the first." And it should seem that the equity of this statute would comprehend endorsements also, and that the 3 & 4 Anne, c. 9. (which gives the like remedies upon notes as were then in use on inland bills) would extend it to notes. See Walmsley v. Child, 1 Ves. Sen. 341. and see post, Chap. IX., in what cases an action may be maintained, where a bill or note has been lost.

(22) In this case, however, it is advisable for the loser, in order to guard against the forgery of his endorsement, to give immediate notice of the loss to all the antecedent parties, and if payment has been made before such notice could be given, to apprise the payee thereof without delay.

See the case of Smith and another v. Shepherd, in Chitty on Bills.

not taken it *bonâ fide* or paid value for it, they will be responsible to the loser. (23)

The right to transfer a bill or note is in the payee, or in the person to whom it has been transferred from him.

And if a bill or note be deposited with a banker for a particular purpose, and is endorsed so as to give him the right to transfer it, and he (24) 25) negotiate, or (25) pledge it;

---

(23) Lovell v. Martin, 4 Taunt. 799. Plaintiff lost a bill accepted payable at defendant's, and immediately gave notice thereof to the acceptor, and the acceptor communicated the notice to defendants with a request that they would not pay or discount the bill: they afterwards (probably from inadvertence) discounted it for one Powell, who had it from a child who picked it up; when due they wrote a receipt upon it, and debited the acceptor with the amount. Plaintiff brought trover, and there being no proof that Powell took it bonâ fide or paid value, verdict for plaintiff. Rule nisi for nonsuit, on the ground that plaintiff had not demanded the bill of defendants, and without such demand trover would not lie: but the court held the writing a receipt upon it, and debiting the acceptor with the amount, was a conversion; and rule discharged.

(24) Bolton v. Puller, 1 Bos. and Pull. 539. Forbes and Gregory, traders in London, were also partners in the house of Caldwell and Co. in Liverpool. Bolton dealt with Caldwell and Co. and they prevailed with the house in London to let him make his bills payable there; Bolton kept no account but with the house at Liverpool; and they kept the account with the house in London; and the payments on Bolton's bills, when made, were carried by the house in London to *their* account with the house in Liverpool; and by the house at Liverpool to their account with Bolton. In Feb. 1793, he accepted bills payable at the house in London, to the value of £19,702; and to enable the Liverpool house to provide for their payment, he endorsed to them (among other bills) a bill for £4000, and another for £398. These two bills they remitted generally, with many others, to Forbes and Gregory, to whom they were considerably indebted; but before the latter bill arrived, both houses became bankrupt. The acceptances were payable before the endorsed bills. Bolton was obliged to pay all his own acceptances; and the assignees of Forbes and Gregory having refused to deliver up these bills, he brought trover for them. A special verdict was found: and after two arguments, the court were unanimously of opinion, that the assignees were entitled to keep the bills. They admitted, that as Forbes and Gregory were partners in the Liverpool house, they were to be considered as privy to the fact that the bills had been endorsed to that house to enable it to provide for Bolton's acceptances; but they held that the application which had been made of these bills, was the very thing which Bolton intended; and that therefore the privity of the London house in the agreement made between him and the house at Liverpool, could have no effect on the transaction, which, *as between the two houses, had undoubtedly changed the property in the bills:* that for the purpose of providing for Bolton's acceptances, the house at Liverpool was intitled to deal with the bills as it thought fit; that they had therefore a right to remit them to Forbes and Gregory; and as they were indebted

such negotiation or pledging, although it may amount to a gross breach of trust, and defeat the purpose for which the deposit was made, will, as between the person who made the deposit and an innocent holder of the bill or note, be binding upon the former.

[But it has been held that if an agent pass notes belonging to his principal to a third person, as security for collateral liabilities for the agent previously entered into by the person to whom the notes are assigned, the latter cannot retain the notes or their proceeds against the principal. (*a*)]

---

to Forbes and Gregory in more than the amount, the assignees of Forbes and Gregory were intitled to keep them. Judgment for the defendants.

(25) Collins v. Martin, 1 Bos. and Pull. 648. The plaintiff sent bills endorsed in blank to Messrs. Nightingales, to receive the money upon them: they borrowed money of the defendants, and pledged these bills as a security. They afterwards became bankrupt, and the plaintiff brought trover for the bills. There being no evidence that the defendants knew under what circumstances the bills had been left with Messrs. N., or how the plaintiff's account (he being in cash) stood with them, Eyre C. J. thought the action would not lie, and nonsuited the plaintiff. On a rule nisi to set aside the nonsuit, it was urged that though the Messrs. N. might have negotiated the bills, they could not pledge them; but after consideration, the court was unanimous, that they had the power of binding the plaintiff as well by pledging as negotiating the bills, of which they were enabled to hold themselves out to the world as the absolute owners. Rule discharged.

[(*a*) Bay employed Randolph and Savage to sell a schooner for him, with orders to take good notes in payment, and transmit them to him. They sold the vessel and took endorsed negotiable notes from the purchasers. Before Bay could get possession of the notes R. and S. became insolvent, and delivered these notes with others to J. J. and J. C. Coddington, without any request from them, to secure them for certain endorsements and responsibilities which they were then under for R. and S. No new credit was given to R. and S. in consequence of the delivery of the notes. Bay brought a bill in chancery against R. and S. and the Coddingtons, praying that they might be decreed to deliver up, and account to him for, the notes. The Coddingtons did not know that the notes were the property of Bay when they received them; and had disposed of them for cash before being informed of it. The Chancellor, Kent, decreed that the Coddingtons were not entitled to the notes or their proceeds as against Bay, who was the lawful owner of them when they were transferred to the Coddingtons; "inasmuch as they did not receive the notes in the course of business, nor in payment in whole or in part of any then existing debt, nor for cash or property advanced, or debt created, or responsibility incurred on the credit of the notes;" and decreed that they should pay the amount of the notes and interest to Bay. This decree was afterwards affirmed in the Court of Errors. Bay v. Coddington, 5 Johns. Ch. R. 54; Coddington v. Bay, 20 Johns. R. 637.]

An endorsement by a person of the same name with the person entitled to transfer it is (26) void (except against the person endorsing it, and the subsequent endorsers) though the person entitled to transfer it was not particularly described upon the bill or note.

On a bill or note payable to A. for the use of B., the (27) right to transfer is in A.

On a bill or note payable to *several persons*, not in partnership, the right to transfer it is in all collectively, not (28) in any individually.

[After the dissolution of a copartnership, one partner cannot by his endorsement in the partnership name vest in the endorsee the title to a bill or note payable to the partnership. (*a*)]

---

(26) Mead v. Young, 4 Term Rep. 28. A bill payable to Henry Davis or order, was sent by the post, and got into the hands of a wrong Henry Davis, who endorsed it to the plaintiff: there was no description of Henry Davis in the bill, or addition to his name, nor was any fraud imputable to the plaintiff. This was an action against the acceptor, and on his offering evidence to shew that the Henry Davis who endorsed the bill was not the person in whose favor it was drawn, Lord Kenyon was of opinion that the evidence was inadmissible, and he retained that opinion after cause shewn against an application for a new trial; but Ashhurst, Buller, and Gross, Js. held, that unless the endorsement was made by the person to whom the bill was really payable, it was a forgery, and could confer no title, and that therefore it was competent for the defendant to shew that the person who endorsed the bill was not the person in whose favor it was made, and a new trial was accordingly granted.

(27) Evans v. Cramlington, Carth. 5. 2 Vent. 307. Skinn. 264. A bill was payable "to Price or order, for the use of Calvert." Price endorsed it to Evans, after which an extent issued against Calvert, and the money due upon it was seized to the use of the King. These facts appearing upon the pleadings, two points were made upon demurrer; the one, whether Calvert had such an interest in the money as might be extended; and the other, whether Price had power to endorse the bill, or whether he had only a bare authority to receive the money for the use of Calvert; and the Court of King's Bench, and afterwards the Exchequer Chamber, held that Calvert had not such an interest as could be extended, and that Price had power to endorse the bill, and judgment was given for the plaintiff.

(28) See Carvick v. Vickery, ante, p. 40; [and Smith v. Whiting, ante, p. 40.]

[(*a*) Sanford brought an action against Mickles and Foreman, as makers of a note payable to Brown and Olmstead. When the partnership of Brown and Olmstead was dissolved, Olmstead was authorized to take the stock, and collect debts and pay debts due from the company, but no authority was given him to endorse notes. He afterwards endorsed the note to Sanford, "Wm. Olmstead for the late firm of Brown

[A partnership may by endorsement transfer the title to a bill or note to one partner; even where the partner claiming as endorsee of the partnership was the person who made the endorsement. (*a*)

The directors of an incorporated bank, as usually constituted in the United States, may by their vote, without the corporate seal, or by their power of attorney, authorize their president or any other person to endorse a bill or note payable to the bank, and the endorsement by the person thus authorized will pass the property, in the bill or note. (*b*)]

If the right to transfer a bill or note be in a feme sole, and she marry, it (29) devolves upon her husband.

---

and Olmstead." Yates J. delivered the opinion of the Court. "It would be a peculiar hardship to put a partner retired from the whole concern, so completely in the power of the other, as to charge him by negotiating bills given during the partnership. This power being denied, it follows that they must all join in the transfer of a bill negotiable after the dissolution, for the purpose of vesting the title in the endorsee." Sanford v. Mickles, 4 Johns. R. 224.]

[(*a*) Russell v. Swan, 16 Mass. R. 314; Kirby v. Cogswell, 1 Cain. R. 505.]

[(*b*) See Spear v. Ladd, 11 Mass. R. 94; Fleckner v. U. S. Bank, 8 Wheat. 339.

The directors of the Berkshire Bank authorized Larned, one of the directors, by a power of attorney signed by the president and three other directors, to assign any negotiable promissory notes belonging to the bank, to the attorney of the Northampton Bank. Larned endorsed his name as attorney upon a note made by Pepoon, payable to the Berkshire Bank, and the Northampton Bank sued Pepoon as maker of the note. Parker C. J. delivered the opinion of the Court. "We are satisfied that the directors might by their vote or power of attorney authorize the president or any other officer of the bank, to assign over the promissory notes payable to the company." And the court decided that the plaintiffs might fill up the endorsement so as to give effect to it. Northampton Bank v. Pepoon, 11 Mass. R. 288.]

(29) Connor v. Martin, Str. 516. cited 3 Wils. 5. A bill was made payable to Susan Connor, or order, while she was sole: she married, and during her coverture endorsed it to the plaintiff, and upon demurrer and argument the Court of Common Pleas held, that the feme covert could not assign the note, because by the marriage it became the sole right and property of the husband; and by Parker C. J. in Miles v. Williams, 10 Mod. 246, if a note be payable to a feme sole or order, and she marries, her husband is the proper person to endorse it.

M'Neilage v. Holloway, 1 Barnw. and Ald. 218. A bill was payable to a feme sole or order; she married before it became due; her husband brought an action upon it in his own name; and on a rule to shew cause why the judgment should not be arrested on the ground that the wife should have joined in the action, the court held that as this was

If a bill or note be made payable to a feme covert, the right to transfer it is in the husband; the wife cannot transfer unless as agent to him.

But if she do, and the husband promise to pay, it will be evidence (30) that she had authority from her husband to transfer.

If a bill be payable to an infant, an endorsement by him will convey (31) no interest, as against himself; but if he draw the bill, it may against the acceptor. (31)

If the person who has the right to transfer a bill or note die, it (32) devolves upon his personal representative; if he becomes bankrupt, and he holds the bill or note in his own right, on his assignees.

And if the right to a bill or note be in several partners, and some of them become bankrupt, and afterwards endorse it, such endorsement, though made to a creditor of the partnership, will confer (33) no title on the indorsee.

And if the creditor receive the money due upon the bill or note, the solvent partners, together with the assignees of the bankrupts, (33) may recover back the money so received.

---

a negotiable security, the marriage transferred the property to the husband, and entitled him, if he thought fit, to sue alone.

(30) See Cotes v. Davis, ante, p. 35.

(31) See Taylor v. Croker, 4 Esp. N. P. C. 187. ante, p. 33.

(32) Rawlinson v. Stone, 3 Wils. 1. Str. 1260. 2 Barnes, 137. A note was payable to A. B. or order: A. B. died intestate, and his administrator endorsed it to the plaintiff. These facts appearing upon the declaration, the defendant demurred, and contended that the personal representative of the payee had no power to endorse a note; but the Court of Common Pleas, after three arguments; and the Court of King's Bench, upon error brought, were unanimously of opinion that he had; and each court said, it was every day's practice, and the constant usage for executors and administrators to endorse bills and notes payable to the order of their testators or intestates.

(33) Thomason and others v. Frere and others, 10 East's Rep. 418. Thomason, Underhill, and Guest, were partners in trade at Birmingham; and being debtors to the defendants to the amount of £1800, and creditors upon Gamble and Co. for £1450, Underhill and Guest, on the 11th October, 1807, without the consent or knowledge of Thomason, (who was abroad,) endorsed to the defendants a bill drawn by the firm of Thomason, Underhill, and Guest, upon, and accepted by, the agents of Gamble and Co. for this £1450. Underhill and Guest had, on the 7th October, 1807, committed acts of bankruptcy; upon which separate commissions issued on the 19th. The bill for £1450 became due on the 6th December, and was then paid. And to recover this money the

But if a man holds a bill or note, not in his own right, but as a trustee, his bankruptcy will not pass the right to transfer to his assignees. (34)

And if partners hold a bill or note, as trustees, the bankruptcy of one of them will not preclude him and the others from transferring it. (34)

[If after a commission has issued against a bankrupt and before he obtains his certificate, a note be given to him payable to his order, in payment of a debt contracted previously to the bankruptcy, his endorsement will pass a good title to the endorsee, except perhaps against the assignees. (*a*)]

---

present action was brought by Thomason, and the assignees of Underhill and Guest. The house of Thomason, Underhill, and Guest was still indebted to the defendants beyond the amount of the sum now sought to be recovered.—The plaintiffs were nonsuited. But on a rule nisi for a new trial, the court (Lord Ellenborough C. J. absente) held that the endorsement, having been made after an act of bankruptcy, though before the issuing of the commission and for the purpose of paying a partnership debt, was invalid; and they inclined to think that, this action being brought to recover the money received on the bill, which had been thus wrongfully endorsed, the defendants had no right to set off their demand upon the firm, against this claim by Thomason and the assignees. Rule absolute.

(34) Ramsbottom and others v. Cator, 1 Stark. 228. J. and M. Hervey were partners as bankers; defendant delivered them a bill that they might get it discounted; they passed it to plaintiffs, their bankers; but before they did so, J. H. committed an act of bankruptcy, upon which a commission afterwards issued: it was urged for defendant that the bankruptcy of J. H. destroyed his and his partner's right to pass away the bill; but Lord Ellenborough held, that as the Herveys held it upon a special trust, to get it discounted, and not in their own right, no interest in it passed to the assignees of J. H., and though he doubted whether plaintiffs had an interest beyond what the Herveys had, he allowed them to take a verdict, and gave the defendant leave to take the opinion of the court upon the point.—But the defendant did not move it.

[See also Thompson v. Giles, 3 Dow. & Ryl. 733: S. C. 2 Barn. & Cres. 422. A customer was in the habit of endorsing and paying to his bankers bills of exchange not due, which if approved were immediately entered to his credit as "bills" (not as "cash") to their full amount, and he was then at liberty to draw for that amount by checks on the bank. The bankers paid away such bills to their customers, as they thought fit. But there was no evidence of an agreement by the customer, that when the bills were paid in they should become the bankers' property. The bankers becoming bankrupt, it was held that the customer might maintain trover against their assignees for bills paid in by him, and remaining in specie in the hands of the bankers at the time of their bankruptcy, the cash balance, independently of the bills being in the customer's favor at the time of the bankruptcy.]

[(*a*) Bayley J. said, "As against this defendant (the maker of the

If the person who has a right to endorse a bill or note, deliver it over to another for a valuable consideration, and forget to endorse it, he (35) may endorse it after he has become a bankrupt, and the right in it will pass to the person to whom he so delivered it.

So the right to endorse will not devolve upon a bankrupt's assignees, if (36) neither he nor they would have any right to demand payment.

Therefore if a bankrupt draw a bill payable to his own order, having at the time (36) no effects in the hands of the drawee; or if, having effects, he draw it for a sum (37)

---

note) and as against all the world except the assignees, the bankrupt was a person competent to make the endorsement." Drayton v. Dale, 3 Dow. & Ryl. 534. 2 Barn. & Cres. 293.]

(35) Smith and another v. Pickering, Peake, N. P. C. 50. Richardson and Hill drew a bill on the defendant, payable to their own order, which the defendant accepted. The drawers delivered this bill to the plaintiffs for a valuable consideration, but forgot to endorse it. They afterwards became bankrupts, and then endorsed it. The plaintiffs, as endorsees, now sued the defendant as acceptor. Lord Kenyon was clearly of opinion that the endorsement was good, and the plaintiffs had a verdict.

[See also Baker v. Arnold, 3 Cain. R. 279, an action by an endorsee, in which Livingston J. expressed his opinion that where a note had been delivered before it became due, the endorsement, even if made after it became due, should be regarded as relating back to the time of its actual delivery to the endorsee. See also White v. Kibling, 11 Johns. R. 128, in which the same question is raised by the counsel, though the court expresses no opinion upon it.]

(36) Arden v. Watkins, 3 East's Rep. 317. On the 5th of October, 1801, Lewis Jones committed an act of bankruptcy, on which a commission issued on the 31st December, 1801. On the 4th of December, 1801, he drew a bill on Watkins for £100, payable to his own order, and endorsed it to the plaintiff, who paid him the full value. Watkins owed Jones nothing, but accepted the bill to enable him to raise money upon it, and Jones deposited a lease with him as an indemnity: the assignees insisted upon a restoration of the lease, and Watkins refused to pay the bill.—Action on the bill and reference. The arbitrator awarded against Watkins, but stated the facts specially, to enable him to take the opinion of the court. After a rule nisi to set aside the award, cause shewn, and time taken to consider, the court was clear that the defendant was liable: that as Jones had no effects in Watkins's hand, no right to endorse devolved on his assignees, and that therefore his endorsement was effectual, and transferred the property to the plaintiff. Rule discharged.

(37) Willis v. Freeman and another, 12 East's Rep. 656. In an action by the endorsee of a bill against the acceptors, a verdict was found for the plaintiff subject to the opinion of the court upon a case. The case stated, that Anderson, the drawer, being indebted to the plaintiff

exceeding their amount, and the bill be accepted for his accommodation; his endorsement will, in the former case, confer a good title as to the whole sum mentioned in the bill; and in the latter, as to such sum as is not covered by the effects.

So if a trader get a bill by fraud, and become bankrupt, the bill will belong, not to his assignees, (38) but to the person from whom he obtained it; at least, if he promised, before he became bankrupt, to return it.

So if a banker who has a lien on a bill or note for his general balance, delivers it to his customer when it is due, that he may obtain payment, and the customer become bankrupt, the bill or note will nevertheless belong not to the assignees but to the banker. (39)

---

in more than £2000 and being insolvent, proposed to pay the plaintiff a composition of 13*s.* 6*d.* in the pound, together with the costs of an action which had been brought by the plaintiff against him, by a bill upon the defendants. This proposal being acceeded to, Anderson applied to the defendants to accept a bill for £1400, *for his accommodatian.* The defendants accepted the bill, drawn on the 5th of July, and payable on the 10th of November, 1809, having in their hands effects of Anderson's to the amount of £888 16*s.* 8*d.* Anderson had committed a secret act of bankruptcy on the 7th of March, 1809, upon which a commission issued on the 25th of July. The Court of King's Bench held, that to the extent of £888 16*s.* 8*d.* the defendants had a right to resist payment on the ground of their being answerable for that amount to the assignees, to whom these funds devolved upon the act of bankruptcy; and that therefore the endorsement by Anderson to that extent was inoperative: but as to the surplus (£511 3*s.* 4*d.*) for which the acceptance was accommodation, the case of Arden v. Watkins was in point to shew that the endorsement was valid. And they held that the law in this respect had not been altered by the 49th Geo. 3. c. 121. § 8. They therefore ordered the verdict to be entered for this reduced sum of £511 3*s.* 4*d.*

(38) Gladstone v. Hadwen, 1 Maule, 517. Sill and Co. got bills from Hadwen, under color of giving him a security upon some coffee to which however they had no title: on being pressed by Hadwen, they promised to return him the bills, which were on their way from London to Liverpool; but before they arrived, Sill and Co. committed acts of bankruptcy upon which a commission afterwards issued: when the bills arrived, they were delivered to Hadwen, upon which Sill and Co.'s assignees brought trover; but on case and time to consider, the court held that they could not sue for what a court of equity would not have allowed them to keep; and that as Hadwen would never have parted with the bills but for a false pretence and fraud, a court of equity would have compelled the assignees, who claimed under Sill and Co., had they got the bills, to have delivered them up to Hadwen.

(39) Bruce v. Hurley, 1 Stark. 23. Young and Co. bankers at Taunton, sent to plaintiffs, their town bankers, a note of defendant's at two

If a bill or note is made payable to a person who is merely an agent in the transaction, if he endorse generally, without using words to prevent his liability, he will be bound personally. (40)

If an executor or administrator endorse, he binds himself personally, not the assets in his hands. (41)

Sect. 3.—The transfer of a bill or note may be made either before the expiration of the time limited for its payment, or, unless (42) the sum payable thereby be under five pounds, (43) afterwards.

But a man who takes a bill after it is due, takes it subject to all the objections and equities to which it was liable in the hands of the person from whom he takes it. (44)

---

months after date. The day before it became due, plaintiffs sent it to Young and Co. at Taunton, that they might obtain payment from defendant; defendant did not pay it, and whilst the bill was in their hands, Young and Co. became bankrupts. Young and Co. had overdrawn plaintiffs, and plaintiffs sued defendant on this note; and as plaintiffs only sent the note to Young and Co. that they might obtain payment for plaintiffs and act as their agents in that respect, Lord Ellenborough held plaintiffs entitled to recover, and they had a verdict accordingly.

(40) See Goupy v. Harden, ante, p. 49.

(41) See King v. Thom., ante, p. 50.

(42) 17 Geo. 3. c. 30. § 1.

(43) Debers v. Harriott, 1 Show. 163. A bill was endorsed to the plaintiff after it was due, and he had judgment without any objection on this ground.

Mutford v. Walcott, Lord Raym. 575. Holt C. J. said, he remembered a case where a bill was negotiated after the day of payment, and he had all the eminent merchants in London with him at his chambers, and they all held it to be very common and usual, and a very good practice.

(44) Taylor v. Mather, B. R. E. 27 Geo. 3. 3 Term Rep. 83, n. Endorsee of a note against the maker. It appeared to have been endorsed after it was due, and there were many circumstances which led the court and jury to conclude it had been unfairly obtained, upon which the jury found for the defendant. A new trial was refused upon the merits, and per Buller J., "It has never been determined that a bill or note is not negotiable after it is due, but if there are any circumstances of fraud in the transaction, and it is endorsed to the plaintiff after it is due, I have always left it to the jury upon the slightest circumstance to presume that the endorsee was acquainted with the fraud." The rest of the court concurred in this opinion.

Brown v. Davies, 3 Term Rep. 80. Davies drew a note payable to Sandall or order; Sandall endorsed it to Taddy, and he had it presented and noted for non-payment. Davies then paid the money to Sandall

And if such person were agent only, to receive the money for his principal, the person to whom he passes it will be accountable to the principal for whatever he receives thereon, whether it be money,

Or a new bill. (45)

---

and he took up the note from Taddy, but instead of returning the note to Davies, endorsed it to Brown. Brown thereupon sued Davies, and on Davies's offering to prove these facts, Lord Kenyon thought they would not amount to a defence, unless it could be proved that Brown knew them when he took the note, and he rejected the evidence; but upon a rule nisi for a new trial, and cause shewn, Lord Kenyon said, he thought there ought to be further inquiry; it did not strike him at the trial that the note had been noted before Brown took it, and that that circumstance ought to have awakened Brown's suspicion. Ashhurst and Buller Js. thought that the party taking a note after it was due, was to be considered as taking it on the credit of the person from whom he received it, and that whatever would be a defence against the giver would be a defence against the receiver; upon which Lord Kenyon said, he agreed with that, if the note appeared on the face of it to have been dishonored, or if knowledge could be brought home to the endorsee that it had been so; but otherwise he was not prepared to go that length. Grose J. said, if collusion could be proved between the defendant and Sandall, the defendant would not be entitled to insist on the objection; but as the case then stood he thought there ought to be a new trial. Rule absolute.

[Banks v. Colwell, Launceston Spring Assizes, 1788, before Buller J. cited 3 Term Rep. 81. Endorsee of a note payable on demand, against the maker. The note was given for smuggled goods; part of it was paid; and it was not endorsed to the plaintiff till a year and a half after it was given; no privity was brought home to the plaintiff, but Buller J. was clearly of opinion he ought to be nonsuited; and he said it had been repeatedly ruled at Guildhall, that if a bill or note was endorsed over after it was due, the endorsee took it on the credit of the endorser, and stood in his situation.

Brown v. Turner, 7 Term Rep. 630. Pritchard paid some stock-jobbing differences for Turner, and drew on him for the amount; Turner accepted the bill, and after it became due Pritchard endorsed it to the plaintiff for a prior debt. Lord Kenyon however thought that as Pritchard could not have recovered on the bill, the plaintiff could not, and directed a verdict for the defendant; and the court was clearly of opinion that the direction was right, and refused a rule nisi for a new trial. See also Good v. Coe, cit. 7 Term Rep. 427. 429.

The principle stated in the text is fully recognized in many American cases. Gold v. Eddy, 1 Mass. R. 1; Blake v. Sewell, 3 Mass. R. 556; Hemmenway v. Stone, 7 Mass. R. 58; Williams v. Matthew, 3 Cowen, 252; O'Callaghan v. Sawyer, 5 Johns. R. 118.]

(45) Lee v. Zagury, 8 Taunt. 114. Sebag had a bill accepted by defendant, overdue; he sent it to White, that White's correspondent might get the amount for Sebag: White's correspondent endorsed it to Vidal for a debt he owed Vidal, and Vidal not being able to obtain the money, got a new bill from defendant for the amount, and endorsed it

And an order from the principal to prohibit payment of such new bill, will be a bar to any action at the suit of the person to whom the first bill was passed. (46)

[Where a promissory note payable on demand, is endorsed within a reasonable time after the date, it has been held in the United States, that the endorsee has all the rights of an endorsee receiving a negotiable instrument before it becomes due. (*a*) But if it be not endorsed within a reasonable time, it will be considered as overdue and dishonored; and the endorsee will be subject to any defence which would have been available against his endorsers. (*a*)

What is such a reasonable time, is not precisely settled; though it is clear that a note is to be considered as overdue and dishonored a year or even eight or nine months from the date; but not overdue a few days after the date. (*a*)

---

to plaintiffs as his agents. Sebag gave defendant notice not to pay this bill, and an action being brought thereon, the defence was, that plaintiffs were mere agents for Vidal, and that as Vidal took the first bill after it was due, he stood in the place of White; and as White would have been accountable to Sebag for whatever he received in respect of the first bill, Vidal was equally so accountable; and then the second bill was, as against Vidal, the property of Sebag, and Sebag's prohibition to defendant not to pay the second bill, was an answer to the action upon it. Gibbs C. J. was of this opinion, and left it to the jury whether plaintiffs were not mere agents to Vidal, and whether the second bill was not the property of Sebag. The jury found for defendants; and on rule nisi to enter verdict for plaintiffs, the other judges agreed with Gibbs C. J. and rule discharged.

[(*a*) Ayer brought an action against the defendants as makers of a note payable on demand to Page or order, and by him endorsed, without recourse to himself, to Ayer the plaintiff. The defendants at the trial offered to prove that the note was endorsed eight months after it was given, and without the knowledge of Ayer, and for the benefit of Page himself, and that the note was fraudulently obtained by Page. But the evidence was rejected; and verdict for plaintiff. On motion for a new trial,—Parsons C. J. delivered the opinion of the Court. "A note payable on demand is due presently." He considered the length of time of itself sufficient "to let the defendants into any defence which could be made by them if Page were plaintiff. The restricted endorsement also made eight months after the note is due is enough to charge the endorsee with such negligence in making further inquiries, as will subject him to the same defence, that might be made against the endorser." He considered besides, that if Ayer was only trustee of Page, the same defence was admissible, as if Page were the plaintiff of record, whether the note was endorsed before or after becoming due. New trial. Ayer v. Hutchins, 4 Mass. R. 370.

So where a note payable on demand was endorsed eighteen months

So a person receiving a note under circumstances which ought to excite suspicion, or if he be the mere agent or

---

after the date, it was held that the maker might make the same defence against the endorsee, which he could have done against his endorser, the payee. Kent C. J. delivered the opinion of the Court. "This lapse of time must clearly be considered as placing the note in the situation of one due and dishonored, and as imposing on the endorsee the same risk. He takes it on the credit of the person from whom he receives it." Freeman v. Haskins, 2 Cain. R. 368.

See also Loomis v. Pulver, 9 Johns. R. 244.

Dunkin made a note payable on demand to Newton or bearer, dated Jan. 16th, 1805. Newton endorsed it to Losee April 3d, 1805. In a suit on this note by Losee against Dunkin, the Common Pleas allowed the defendant to prove a payment upon it to Newton shortly after the date of the note. On Error—Per Curiam. "There is no precise time at which such a note is to be deemed dishonored. The demand must be made in a reasonable time, and that will depend upon the circumstances of the case, and the situation of the parties. There are no particulars peculiar to this case disclosed; and the court cannot say that it was *erroneous* to let in the defence; for the circumstances of this case might have been such as to justify the conclusion, that the note was dishonored when it was assigned." Losee v. Dunkin, 7 Johns. R. 70.

In a subsequent case, in an action by the endorsee against the makers of a note payable on demand, which had been endorsed to him five months after the date,—Yates J., who delivered the opinion of the Court, said, "Each case ought, perhaps, to be governed by its own circumstances. In the one before us, a number of payments have been endorsed, and the last but a few days prior to the assignment, and about five months after its date. From the last endorsement it may be presumed, that all antecedent payments had been noticed and entered in the same manner; the plaintiff had a right to consider the amount due at the time of the transfer after deducting the payments, to be the true balance; the defendant was, therefore, properly prevented from impeaching the note as given for too large a sum." Sanford v. Mickles, 4 Johns. R. 224.

A note made at Portland, Maine, was, seven days after the date, endorsed by the payee to Thurston in Boston. Thurston sued the maker of the note, and the question was, whether the latter might be permitted to prove in defence, a want of consideration between him and the payee. Parsons C. J delivered the opinion of the Court. "It is certainly a correct principle of law that if the endorsee purchase a note, when from the length of time in which it has been payable, there is reasonable cause to suspect that it has been dishonored, he shall not deprive the maker of any defence, which would avail him against the promisee. But this note cannot be considered as overdue, within the true intent of this principle; as there were no circumstances existing, which ought to have induced in the mind of the purchaser, a suspicion that the note had been dishonored." Thurston v. M'Kown, 6 Mass. R. 76.

See also Hendricks v. Judah, 1 Johns. R 319.

If the maker of a note who has paid it to the payee, neglect to make the defence to an action by an endorsee to whom it was endorsed after the day of payment, he cannot recover the money back in an action

trustee of his endorser, is subject to any defence which his endorser would have been liable to. (*a*)

But the presumption is that the note was transferred within a reasonable time, unless the contrary is proved. (*b*)

What is a reasonable time is a question of law when the facts are settled. (*c*)]

It has been held, that a man who takes a bill after it is due, will stand in the same situation as if he had taken it before, if he held it for value before it was due, and it is re-delivered to him for the same value afterwards; (46)

As if a banker's customer deposits a bill with him for value before it is due, gets it from him again before it is due, and again deposits it with him for value after it is dishonored. (46)

So if a bill or note is returned to an endorser after it becomes due, and he pays the amount, he will be entitled to recover the full amount from the antecedent parties, though some of these parties had lodged securities with the person who held the bill when it became due, and part of the amount had been paid on the securities; (47)

---

againt the promissee. Loomis v. Pulver, 9 Johns. R. 244. Battey v. Button, 13 Johns. R. 187. But the maker may recover the money back, where the note was endorsed before becoming due, so that the payment was no defence to the action by the endorsee; and the declaration in such a case is bad if it do not state the endorsement to have been made before the note became due. Battey v. Button. 13 Johns. R. 187.]

[(*a*) See Ayer v. Hutchins, supra; and Towne v. Hutchins, 6 Mass. R. 46.]

[(*b*) Hendricks v. Judah, 1 Johns. R. 319. And see Webster v. Lee, 5 Mass. R. 334.]

[(*c*) Furman v. Haskin, 2 Cain. R. 368.]

(46) Bosanquet v. Dudman, 1 Stark. 1. Clarkson and Co. banked with plaintiffs, and deposited a bill with them as a security for their engagements on behalf of Clarkson and Co., but before it became due Clarkson and Co. got it back from plaintiffs. After it was dishonored Clarkson and Co. re-delivered it to plaintiffs, but in the interim Clarkson and Co. bought a ship from the drawer, for whose accommodation defendants had accepted, and agreed to give up this bill in part payment, so that Clarkson and Co. could not have sued upon the bill; but Lord Ellenborough held, that when the bill was returned to plaintiffs they returned to their former right, and were not affected by what Clarkson and Co. had done; and verdict for plaintiffs.

At least if such endorser did not know when he took up the bill, that such securities had been so lodged. (47)

And though a man who takes a bill after it is due, takes it subject to the objections to which it was liable in the hands of the person from whom he took it, he is not subjected to every description of evidence to which that person would be liable; (48) therefore, though the entries in that person's books, if made at the time of passing the bill and accompanying that act, might be evidence against him, yet entries which cannot be proved to have been so made, and might have been made afterwards, are not. (48)

And though a bill be endorsed over *before* the time appointed for its payment, yet if acceptance has been previously refused, the endorsee (49) will be liable to the same

---

(47) Buzzard v. Flecknoe, 1 Stark. 333. Plaintiffs endorsed two bills to Lord; Lord held them three months after they fell due, and then called on plaintiffs, who took them up. In the interim Lord had received another bill from the drawer as a collateral security, but plaintiffs did not appear to have known that fact; that bill was afterwards satisfied, and plaintiffs having brought this action against the acceptor, he insisted that the amount of that bill ought to be deducted, on the ground that plaintiffs stood in the situation of Lord; but Lord Ellenborough thought otherwise, because plaintiffs' title did not first commence after the bill became due, but was referable to their prior holding; had they been discharged from the bills, they might have stood in the situation of new holders. Verdict for the whole amount.

(48) Collenridge v. Farquharson, 1 Stark. 259. In an action by endorsee against endorser, it appeared that one Powell was holder when the bill became due, and that he had afterwards endorsed the bill to plaintiff there being accounts between defendant and Powell, which would have regulated the extent to which Powell could have recovered. Defendant offered in evidence Powell's books, to shew how those accounts stood, and insisted that whatever would have been evidence against Powell would be evidence against plaintiff; but Lord Ellenborough held, that though an entry by Powell at the time and accompanying the act would have been evidence, an entry not accompanying the act and which might have been made afterwards for the very purpose of being used in evidence was not, and the plaintiff had a verdict.

(49) Crossley v. Ham. 13 East. Rep. 498. The defendant for the accommodation of Clark, endorsed two bills drawn by Clark in America, upon Dickinson and Co. in London, for £450 each, in favor of the defendant, dated 10th of February, 1804, and payable 60 days after sight. These bills were paid over by Clark to Parry, in February, 1804. The defendant, Parry and Clark, then, and until after the 14th of April, 1808, resided in America. On the 1st of March, Parry endorsed and remitted the bills to his agents in London, with directions to make a payment to the plaintiff, to whom he then, and still, was indebted. On

objections as might have been taken against his endorser, if he take the bill with a knowledge of its having been dishonored;

And if the bill be noted for non-acceptance, he must be taken to have this knowledge.

But if he take the bill without this knowledge, and be a bonâ fide holder for a valuable consideration, he will not be liable to the objection. (50)

And if the holder's immediate endorser might have recovered upon a bill or note, it is no defence to an action by the holder that an (51) antecedent party would have been precluded from recovering upon it.

---

the 26th of April, the bills were presented for acceptance, dishonored, and protested for non-acceptance; and notice thereof was given to the defendant. The plaintiff having been advised of the remittance by a letter from Parry, dated on the 12th of April, applied to Parry's agents for £450; and on the 6th of June they delivered one of the bills to the plaintiff, apprising him of its dishonor, and that therefore he took the bill, subject to all its infirmities. The bill became due on the 29th of June, and payment being refused, this action was brought. The defendant, however, produced at the trial an instrument signed by Parry, dated 14th of April, 1804, by which he agreed that the defendant, on paying one of the bills in London, should be exonerated from paying the other; and the defendant proved his having, on the 2d of July, paid one of the bills, which then remained in the hands of Parry's agents, who delivered it upon payment. This agreement was, until the 2nd of July, unknown to the plaintiff and Parry's agents. A verdict was found for the plaintiff, and a case reserved for the opinion of the court. The court (Le Blanc J. absente) held that the plaintiff, having taken this bill after its dishonor, had taken it with all its infirmities, and subject therefore to the agreement between Parry and the defendant. Postea to the defendant.

(50) Dunn v. O'Keefe, 6 Taunt. 305. 5 Maule. 282. Action on bill drawn by defendants on Ricketts and Co. payable to Sinclair or order, and by him endorsed to plaintiff; breach for non-acceptance; plea, that before endorsement to plaintiff, Sinclair presented it for acceptance, that acceptance was refused, and notice thereof not given to defendants; replication, that it was not so presented, and verdict inde that it was, but non obstante veredicto, judgment for plaintiff. On error it was urged that the presentment by Sinclair, and want of notice inde, discharged defendants entirely from the bill; but the court held, it did not discharge him against an innocent endorsee, who took the bill for a valuable consideration before the time appointed for its payment; and as it was not alleged in the plea that plaintiff knew of the prior dishonor, or that it was endorsed to him after it was due, or that he did not give value for it, judgment affirmed.

(51) Chalmers v. Lanion, 1 Campb. N. P. C. 383. To an action by the endorsees against the acceptor of a bill, one ground of defence was,

The rule as to bills and notes when taken after they are due, is in general applicable also to (52) checks upon bankers.

But it will not apply to such checks where they appear to have been issued long after their date. (52)

A bill or note cannot be (53) endorsed or negotiated af-

---

that the bill had been accepted for a debt contracted in a smuggling transaction, and that though it had been endorsed for value before it became due to a bonâ fide holder, yet that it had been endorsed by him to the plaintiffs after it was due; and it was contended that having been so endorsed to the plaintiffs, it was competent to the defendant to set up the illegality of the consideration as a defence, in like manner as if the action had been brought by the payee. But Lord Ellenborough held, that if the plaintiffs' endorser might have maintained an action upon the bill, the circumstance of the endorsement to them having been made after the bill had become due, was insufficient to let in the proposed defence. And the court of King's Bench concurred in opinion with his lordship.

(52) Boehm v. Sterling, 7 Term Rep. 423. Muilman lent the defendant his acceptance for £2444 14*s*. at three months, and the defendant gave Muilman a check upon his banker for the amount, dated 17th of Feb. 1796. The year was perhaps intended for 1797. On the 20th of January Muilman gave this check to the plaintiff in payment of an old debt. Muilman died before his acceptance became due, and the defendant was obliged to take it up. In an action upon the check, the defendant urged that Muilman could not have sued him upon this check, and that therefore the plaintiff could not, because he took it so many months after it was dated. Lord Kenyon left it to the jury whether the plaintiff took it bonâ fide, and without knowing the circumstances under which Muilman held it. They found for the plaintiff. And on a rule nisi for a new trial, and cause shewn, Lord Kenyon admitted that it was to be considered as a rule that the person who takes a bill after it is due, is subject to the same equity as the party from whom he took it, though the bill did not appear upon the face of it to have been dishonored; and he thought there was no distinction in this respect between checks upon bankers and bills of exchange: but as the defendant had not issued this check until nine months after it was dated, he thought it was not competent to him to object to the time when the Plaintiff took it; the other judges agreed that the rule mentioned by Lord Kenyon was to be considered as settled, but for the reasons given by Lord Kenyon that it did not bear upon this case. Rule discharged.

R. acc. Tinson v. Francis, 1 Campb. N. P. C. 19.

(53) Beck v. Robley, B. R. Tr. 14 Geo. 3. cited 1 H. Blackst. 89 n. Brown drew a bill upon Robley, which Robley accepted, payable to Hodgson or order; Robley did not pay it when it was presented, upon which Brown took it up; Brown afterwards endorsed it to Beck, and Beck brought an action upon it against Robley; but the jury thought that when Brown took up the bill, its negotiability ceased, and found for the defendant; and on a rule nisi for a new trial, the court thought the jury right, and Lord Mansfield said, "When a draught is given payable to A. or order, the purpose is, that it shall be paid to A. or or-

ter it has been once paid, if such endorsement or negotiation would make any of the parties liable who would otherwise be discharged.

But an endorser who pays a bill, may endorse or negotiate it, because his endorsement or negotiation will make no person liable but himself, and those whom he might sue. (54)

---

der; and when it comes back unpaid, and is taken up by the drawer, it ceases to be a bill. If it were negotiable here, Hodgson would be liable, for which there is no color."

(54) Callow v. Lawrence, 3 Maule. 95. Pywell drew on defendant, payable to his own order, and endorsed to Taylor; defendant accepted the bill, but did not pay it; Pywell took it up, and endorsed it to plaintiff. It was urged, that after Pywell had once paid it he could not endorse it, its negotiability was at an end; but on cause shewn the court were clear that Pywell's payment did not terminate its negotiability, because his endorsement would make no person liable but himself and defendant, and defendant had never been discharged. Rule discharged.

[It was formerly held in Massachusetts that a note or bill once paid ceased to be negotiable. See Blake v. Sewell, 3 Mass. R. 556; Boylston v. Greene, 8 Mass. R. 465; and Emerson v. Cutts, 12 Mass. R. 78. But the doctrine stated in the text is now fully established.

The defendants were sued as makers of a note payable to Littlefield, and endorsed by him. Littlefield paid the note at maturity, and afterwards passed it to the plaintiff Guild. The plaintiff was nonsuited at the trial subject to the opinion of the court. Parker, C. J. delivered the opinion of the Court. "In England at this day, the proposition which has been received here without qualification, that a negotiable note once paid, cannot be transferred, is restrained to cases, where by such transfer some party to the bill or note might be prejudiced, or troubled with a suit, who ought to be discharged. As if there be several endorsers, none shall be allowed to transfer it but the last: because if the note is taken up by any prior endorser, and again put in circulation by him, the subsequent endorsers may be exposed to a suit by the new assignee. But where no such consequence will follow, an assignment by the party taking up the bill is lawful, and an assignee may maintain an action upon it in his own name." The court considered the distinction a correct one, and granted a new trial, overruling the cases of Blake v. Sewall, and Boylston v. Greene, supra. Guild v. Eager, 17 Mass R. 615.

So in New York it has been held that the negotiability of a note is not impaired by its being paid and taken up by an endorser, where no party who was not at all events bound to pay it, could be sued in consequence of its being again put in circulation. Havens v. Huntington, 1 Cowen, 387. See also Williams v. Matthews, 3 Cowen, 252. The same doctrine is recognised in Maine. Mead v. Small, 2 Greenleaf, 207.

In a case in N. Hampshire, the court take the position generally, that "it is very clear that where a note has once been paid it ceases to be negotiable." But there were other sufficient grounds for judgment in favor of the defendant. Bryant v. Ritterbush, 2 N. Hamp. R. 212.]

And if a bill or note is paid before it is due, and nothing done upon it to mark such payment, an endorsement afterwards before the time it would have become due, will give the endorsee, if he take it bonâ fide and for a valuable consideration, the same right as if there had been no such payment. (55)

[But if the endorsee, at the time he receives the note, knows that it has been paid by the maker, the endorsee cannot maintain any action upon it against the maker. (*a*)]

If a (56) man endorse a bill or note before the sum or

---

(55) Burridge v. Manners, 3 Campb. 194. Four days before a note became due, some person went to the banker's where it lay, and paid it, and carried it away; it was not cancelled, nor any minute made upon it to denote such payment; within the four days it was endorsed bonâ fide, and for valuable consideration, to plaintiff, and in an action by him against the payee this payment was relied on, and it was urged that after payment it could not be negotiated; sed per Lord Ellenborough, that means payment in due course, not payment by anticipation; had the note been due before plaintiff took it, he would have taken it with all its infirmities, but here was nothing to awaken his suspicion; this payment does not extinguish it more than discounting would; whilst its time is running, it remains negotiable. Verdict for plaintiff.

[In Webster v. Lee, 5 Mass. R. 334, C. J. Parsons says, that "in an action by an endorsee of a note against the maker, the law admits the defendant to prove payment before the endorsement." See also Baker v. Wheaton, 5 Mass. R. 509. But this expression must be restricted to the case of an endorsement after the note becomes due.]

[(*a*) White v Kibling, 11 Johns. R. 128.]

(56) Russell v. Langstaff, Dougl. 496. 514. The defendant, to accommodate Galley, endorsed his name on five copper-plate checks, made in the form of promissory notes, but in blank, without any sums, dates, or times of payment being mentioned therein, and delivered them to Galley; Galley filled them up as he thought fit, and the plaintiff discounted them; the plaintiff knew the notes were blank at the time of the endorsement; Galley not paying them when they became due, the plaintiff brought this action. Hotham, B. before whom the cause was tried, was of opinion, that as the notes were incomplete when the defendant endorsed them, no subsequent act of Galley could make them otherwise, because that would alter the effect of the defendant's endorsement, and he accordingly directed a verdict for the defendant; but upon an application for a new trial, and cause shewn, Mr. Wallace, the attorney-general, gave up the point, though Mr. Lee afterwards argued it, and Lord Mansfield said, "Nothing is so clear as the point; the endorsement on a blank note is a letter of credit for an indefinite sum; the defendant said, trust Galley to any amount, and I will be his security; it does not lie in his mouth to say, the endorsements were not regular." A new trial was accordingly granted, and a verdict having been found for the plaintiff in a similar action before Lord Mansfield, the defendant submitted in this, without going to a second trial.

time of payment be mentioned therein, he will be precluded from saying that his endorsement was prior to the completion or issuing of the bill or note, and this though the holder knew when he took it in what state the bill was at the time of the endorsement.

[So if a person write his name on a blank paper to be used as an endorsement of a note to be written on the other side, and the paper thus endorsed be obtained from him by fraud, and a different note from the one intended to be written on the other side, he will be liable as endorser to a *bonâ fide* holder for a valuable consideration. (*a*)]

[Violett endorsed a blank paper with intent to have a promissory note written on the other side, it was afterwards filled up as intended. The court held that Violett was liable as endorser of the note, and "that he was concluded from saying or proving that it was not filled up when he endorsed it." Violett v. Patton, 5 Cranch, 142.]

[(*a*) Sullivan and Co. being about to be absent from Boston, left with a clerk a number of papers on which the name of the firm was written in blank, some to be used as notes endorsed by the house, and others as notes signed by the house. These papers were to be filled up when money was to be advanced on goods, or to renew the notes of the house at the banks. The clerk was directed to deliver one of the blanks to the promiser of a certain note on which Sullivan and Co. were endorsers, in order to enable him to renew it. The clerk accordingly delivered the promiser one of the endorsed papers. He, afterwards pretending that by some mistake it had become useless to him, and feigning to burn it in the clerk's presence, procured another blank of the clerk, and by a similar contrivance a third and fourth blank, the last of which was used for the purpose intended by Sullivan and Co. Sullivan and Co. were sued by bonâ fide holders as endorsers of one of the first blanks, which had been filled up as a note by the promiser. Verdict for the plaintiffs, subject to the opinion of the court. Parsons C. J. delivering the opinion of the Court said, that this note could not be considered as a forgery of the names of the defendants, although it was a gross fraud, since when the defendants' name was endorsed, it was intended that something should be afterwards written to which their name should apply as an endorsement. He said also that writing the note was not such a fraud as would discharge the endorsers against an innocent endorsee; that since one of two innocent parties must suffer, the loss ought to fall on the endorsers, on account of their laches and misplaced confidence in their clerk which had given the promiser the opportunity to commit the fraud, and not on the endorsees who were not chargeable with any neglect. The court also thought that a different opinion would operate injuriously upon the commercial community. Judgment on the verdict. Putnam v. Sullivan, 4 Mass. R. 45.

"Perhaps if a blind man had a note falsely and fraudulently read to him, and he endorsed it supposing it to be the note read to him," he would not be liable as endorser, because he is not guilty of any laches. By Parsons C. J. in Putnam v. Sullivan, 4 Mass. R. 45.]

And if a man endorse a bill or note with blanks for sum and date, and die before they are filled up, the person filling them up can make no objection on account of his previous death. (57)

And if a bill or note be post-dated (as in most cases it (58) may be) an endorsement before the date (59) will entitle the endorsee to sue the drawer or maker, although the endorser die defore the date of the bill or note.

Upon the transfer of a bill drawn in sets, each part must be delivered to the person in whose favor the transfer is made; otherwise the same inconveniences may follow, which would ensue upon a neglect to deliver each of them to the payee.

The endorsement of a bill or note, implies an undertaking from the endorser to the person in whose favor it is made, and to every other person to whom the bill or note may af-

---

(57) Usher v. Dauncey, 4 Camp. 97. F. D. and three others were partners, and used to draw bills, with blanks for sums and date, to raise money: F. D. drew one 28th February to his own order, and endorsed it in blank, and died 15th March: 22d April the clerk to the surviving partners inserted as the date 27th Feb., and as the sum £1574 and an agent of theirs got it discounted: in an action thereon against the surviving partners, it was urged, that F. D.'s death countermanded all authority in the clerk to fill up a bill with his name to it, and that the bill was therefore void: but Lord Ellenborough thought the clerk's authority emanated from all the partners, and that when he filled up the bill on account of their survivors and for their use, he acted as their agent and bound them, and that the case was within the principles of Russell v. Langstaff. The plaintiff had a verdict, and the court of king's bench refused to set it aside.

(58) See ante, p. 15.

(59) Pasmore v. North, 13 East. Rep. 517. The defendant, on the 4th of May, 1810, drew a bill for £200 on Brook and Co., dated the 11th of May, 1810, payable to Totty or order, sixty five days after date. On the 5th of May, Totty endorsed this bill to the plaintiff for a valuable consideration; and on the same day died. After the 4th, and before the 11th of May, the defendant received effects of Totty's to the amount of about £130 to answer this bill. On the 12th of May, the defendant advised the drawees of the bill having been drawn, and of Totty's death, and desired them not to accept or pay the bill. Acceptance and payment were accordingly refused: and this action was brought against the drawer. A verdict was found for the plaintiff, subject to the opinion of the court of king's bench, on a case reserved. The court, after adverting to the 17 G. 3. c. 30. as to bills for less than £5, and to the 48 G. 3. c. 149. as to post-dating draughts upon bankers, held clearly, that the plaintiff was entitled to recover for the whole amount of the bill; and he had judgment accordingly.

terwards be transferred, exactly similar to that which is implied by drawing a bill, except that in the case of a note, the stipulations with respect to the drawer's responsibility and undertaking do not apply; and a transfer by delivery only, if made on account of an antecedent debt, implies a similar undertaking from the person making it, to the person in whose favor it was made.

And a transfer by delivery, where the bill or note is sold, may imply that it is a genuine bill. (60)

[The endorsement is a new contract by the endorser with the endorsee. (*a*)

And therefore in an action by an endorsee against an endorser, it is no defence that the note as between the maker and payee, is void, or that the name of the maker is forged. (*b*)

Where A. being in possession of a note to which he was not a party, and which had not been endorsed by the payee, endorsed it to B. for a valuable consideration, it was held

---

(60) Jones v. Ryde, 5 Taunt. 488. 1 Marshall, 157. Defendant sold plaintiff a navy bill as and for a bill of £1800, which it imported to be: it turned out that the bill was issued for £800 only, and had afterwards been altered. Government paid the £800 only, and plaintiff who had parted with the bill, paid his vendee the £1000 and called upon defendant to reimburse him; defendant refused, and plaintiff sued him: it was urged for defendant, that both parties were equally innocent; but the court held, that as defendant took upon himself to sell as a bill for £1800 what in fact was a bill for £800, the consideration pro tanto had failed, and plaintiff was entitled to recover it back. In Bruce v. Bruce, 1 Marshall, 165. the same point was decided upon a victualling bill.

[In a case in Massachusetts, it was held, that if a note was sold, the buyer could maintain no action against the seller, though an endorsement upon it proved to be forged, both parties being ignorant of the forgery at the time of the sale. But it was held in the same case, that if the holder of the note intended to purchase merchandize, and the payment by the note was not a part of the original stipulation, but merely an accommodation to him, then the forged note was not a payment, and its amount might be recovered back from him on the original contract for goods sold. Ellis v. Wild, 6 Mass. R. 321.

Payment of a debt by a counterfeit bank note, is no payment, and the amount of the note may be recovered back, from the person paying it. Young v. Adams, 6 Mass. R. 182. See also Markle v. Hatfield, post.]

[(*a*) See Young v. Bryan, 6 Wheat. R. 146.]

[(*b*) Codwise v. Gleason, 3 Day, 12.]

that B. could maintain no action against A. without proof of some special contract between A. and B. (*a*)

A person endorsing a bill or note for the accommodation of the drawer or maker, is liable to the holder in the same manner as any other endorser, although the holder when he received the bill or note knew him to be merely an accommodation endorser. (*b*)

But if an endorsement specifies that there is to be no recourse to the endorser, or that it is at the risk of the endorsee, the endorser is not liable to any action by the endorsee. (*c*)

So the liability of the endorser may be varied by a written agreement of the endorsee. (*d*)

Where the endorsee of a bill resides in the country where the bill is drawn, and endorses it there, he is liable only according to the laws of that country. (*e*)

But where a bill is drawn in one country and endorsed in another, it does not seem fully settled whether the liability of the endorser is to be regulated by the laws of the place of drawing, or of the place of endorsing. (*f*)

If the payee of a note and another person endorse it, they are not joint sureties to the holder, but the payee is liable as first endorser, and the other person as second endorser, and the latter may recover of the former any sum paid by him to the holder of the note. (*g*)]

[(*a*) Birchard v. Bartlett, 14 Mass. R. 279.]

[(*b*) Yeaton v. Bank of Alexandria, 5 Cranch, 49; Violett v. Patton, 5 Cranch, 142; Brown v. Mott, 7 Johns. R. 361.]

[(*c*) Rice v. Stearns, 3 Mass. R. 225; Welch v. Lindo, 7 Cranch, 159.]

[(*d*) In an action against the endorser of a note, the defendant offered in evidence a writing signed by the plaintiff acknowledging an agreement between them that the plaintiff should sue a special writ against the maker, and direct the officer to secure the debt if possible; it was held that the evidence was admissible; and that the defendant might prove that the maker of the note had land conveyed to him, while the execution upon the note was in force against him, which land might have been taken upon the execution. Phelps v. Foot, 1 Conn. R. 387.]

[(*e*) See Powers v. Lynch, ante p. 32.]

[(*f*) See Slacum v. Pomery, and Schermerhorn v. Pelham, ante p. 32 and Van Raugh v. Van Arsdaln, ante, p. 31.]

[(*g*) See Talcott v. Cogswell, 3 Day, 512.]

CHAP. VI.

Acceptance of Bills or Notes.

The doctrine of acceptances applies chiefly to bills; for a note may (1) in general be considered, on comparison with a bill, as accepted when it issues.

But on notes payable a limited time after sight, an acceptance is necessary to fix the time of their becoming due.

An acceptance is an engagement to pay a bill according to the tenor of the acceptance, and a general acceptance is an engagement to pay according to the tenor of the bill.

This engagement is made by the drawee of the bill or some (2) other person, to the (3) drawer or some of the

---

(1) D. acc. 2 Bl. Comm. 470.

(2) Mutford v. Walcott, Lord Raym. 575. 12 Mod. 410. Com. 76. per Holt C. J. "If A. draws a bill on B and B. will not accept, and C. offers to accept for the honor of the drawer, the holder need not acquiesce, but if he does, C. is bound." And per Lord Mansfield and Yates J., in Pillans v. Van Mierop, Burr. 1672, 1674, an acceptance for the honor of the drawer will bind the acceptor.

(3) Pillans and another v. Van Mierop, Burr. 1663. White drew on the plaintiffs at Rotterdam for £800, and proposed to give them credit upon the defendants' house in London; the plaintiffs paid White's bill, and wrote to the defendants to know, "Whether they would accept such bills as they, the plaintiffs, should draw in about a month upon them for £800, on White's credit." The defendants answered, that they would, but White having failed before the month elapsed, the defendants wrote to the plaintiffs not to draw. The plaintiffs did however draw, and on the defendants' refusal to pay the bills, brought this action." The jury found a verdict for the defendants, but upon an application for a new trial, as upon a verdict against evidence, and two arguments upon it, the court was unanimous that the defendants' letter was a virtual acceptance of such bills as the plaintiff should draw to the amount of £800, and the rule was made absolute. See Johnson v. Collings, post, p. 104.

Pierson v. Dunlop and others, Cowp. 571. M'Lintot drew upon the defendants in favor of Nicholl, and gave Nicholl a navy bill assigned to the defendants as a security till the bill of exchange should be accepted; both bills were sent by Nicholl to the defendants, who said, the bill of exchange would not be accepted till the navy bill was paid, but they would receive the money on the navy bill; and they wrote to M'Lintot, saying his bill would receive due honor, but it was drawn too short, being payable before the navy bill: they afterwards received the money on the navy bill, but refused to pay the bill of exchange, upon which this action was brought: the plaintiff obtained a verdict, but the defend-

other parties, and might heretofore have been made upon any bill foreign or inland, before the (4) bill was drawn or (5) afterwards, and either verbally (6) or in writing: but

---

ants had a rule to shew cause why there should not be a new trial, and insisted that the letter to M'Lintot, upon which the jury had in some measure relied, was no acceptance; but on cause shown, Lord Mansfield said, "I consider what the defendants did as an acceptance; it has been truly said, as a general rule, that the mere answer of a merchant to the drawer of a bill, saying he will duly honor it, is no acceptance, unless accompanied with circumstances which may induce a third person to take the bill by endorsement, if there are any such circumstances, it may amount to an acceptance, though contained in a letter to the drawer; in this case, there is great reason to say, that what the defendants did was equivalent to an acceptance; there may be a conditional as well as an absolute acceptance, what then is the declaration by the defendants, but an undertaking that the bill should be accepted when the navy bill was paid; afterwards he writes this letter, which is an admission he looked to the navy bill as the fund out of which the bill of exchange was to be paid." A new trial was refused.

Mason v. Hunt, Dougl. 284. 297. Rowland Hunt in Dominica, wrote a letter to his partner Thomas Hunt in London, stating that he had agreed that Thomas should accept bills for £3600, upon certain conditions; it was doubtful whether those conditions had been performed, but at all events it was clear that the obligation created by this letter was waived; an action was however brought against the Hunts, and after a verdict for the defendants, and an application for a new trial, upon which the court took time to consider, Lord Mansfield said, "There is no doubt but an agreement to accept may amount to an acceptance, and it may be couched in such terms as to put a third person in a better situation than the drawer."

Powell v. Monnier, 1 Atk. 611. Newburgh drew upon Monnier for £50, and sent him a letter of advice, and Monnier wrote for answer that the bill should be duly honored and placed to Newburgh's debit. A bill in chancery was afterwards filed against Monnier's executrix, upon the ground that this letter amounted to an acceptance; and Lord Hardwicke thought it clear that it did, and decreed payment. (See Wynne v. Raikes, post, p. 145. n. (34.)

(4) Vide Pillans v. Van Mierop, and Mason v. Hunt, ante, p. 96, 97. But see also Johnson v. Collings, post, p. 104.

[It is well settled in the United States that an acceptance may be made before the bill is drawn. See Wilson v. Clements, Storer v. Logan, M'Evers v. Mason, Goodrich v. Gordon, and Coolidge v. Payson, post.]

(5) Vide Powell v. Monnier, supra.

(6) Cox v. Coleman. M. 6 Geo. 2. cited arguendo Ann. 75. A foreign bill drawn on defendant was protested for non-acceptance and returned, and afterwards defendant told the plaintiff, "If the bill comes back, I will pay it;" and this was held a good acceptance.

Lumley v. Palmer, Str. 1000. Ann. 74. In an action against the defendant as acceptor of a bill, the acceptance appeared to be by parol only, which Lord Hardwicke C. J. ruled to be sufficient; but Eyre, C. J. of Common Pleas, having ruled it otherwise in Rex v. Meggott,

now by 1 & 2 Geo. 4. c. 78. s. 2., which operates from 1st August, 1821, every acceptance of an inland bill must be in writing upon the bill, or if there be several parts of the bill, on one of such parts. (7)

An acceptance is also either absolute or (8) conditional, and either according to, or (9) varying from, the tenor of the bill.

H. 7. Geo. 2. because of the proviso in 3 & 4 Ann. c. 9. s. 5. "that no acceptance of any inland bill shall be sufficient to charge any person whatsoever, unless the same be under-written or endorsed in writing thereupon," an application was made for a new trial, and the court to settle the point, ordered it to be argued; upon the argument the court held Lord Hardwicke's direction right, on the ground that the statute of Anne was intended to give a holder additional remedies, not to deprive him of any he before had; and Eyre C. J. waived his opinion, and agreed with the court of King's Bench; and this determination is referred to and approved of in Julian v. Shobrooke, 2 Wils. 9. Powell v. Monnier, 1 Atk. 612, and in Pillans v. Van Mierop, Burr. 1662, Lord Mansfield says, a verbal acceptance is binding; and in Sproat v. Matthews, 1 Term Rep. 182, it was taken for granted by the court and bar that a parol acceptance was good. See also Str. 817.

[Ridgway and Balch drew on Shaw, he refused to accept; and the bill was protested for non-acceptance, and at maturity for non-payment. Afterwards on receiving bills of lading of a consignment from Ridgway and Balch, he called on Gilbert and Dean, who held the bill and offered to pay it. They said it had been returned to Philadelphia. He then said that if they would send for it, he would pay it. When the bill was again presented to him, he refused to pay it, having been in the mean time summoned as trustee of Ridgway and Balch. Parker C. J. delivered the opinion of the Court. "The defendant promised Gilbert and Dean, if they would get the bill back, he would accept and pay it; and they obtained the bill. This promise was binding on him." And on the ground of Shaw's liability as acceptor, he was discharged as trustee. Grant v. Shaw, 16 Mass. R. 341.]

(7) By 1 & 2 Geo. 4. c. 78. s. 2. After 1st August, 1821, no acceptance of any inland bill of exchange shall be sufficient to charge any person, unless such acceptance be in writing on such bill; or, if there be more than one part of such bill, on one of the said parts.

(8) Smith v. Abbott, Str. 1152. Defendant accepted a bill *to pay when goods consigned to him were sold;* he sold the goods, and on being sued upon his acceptance, insisted in arrest of judgment that it was not binding, because it was conditional; but the court, on consideration, held, that though the plaintiff might have refused to take it, and have protested the bill, yet as he did take it, it was binding on the defendant.

Julian v. Shobrooke, 2 Wils. 9. The defendant accepted a bill to pay, *when in cash for the cargo of the ship Thetis;* and on being sued, moved in arrest of judgment that a conditional acceptance was not good; but the court held otherwise, and overruled the objection.

Pierson v. Dunlop, Cowp. 571. ante, p. 96. An answer that the bill would not be accepted till a navy bill was paid, was held a conditional acceptance, to pay when the navy bill should be discharged.

(9) Wegerstoffe v. Keene, Str. 214. A foreign bill for £127 18*s.* 4*d.*

An acceptance is seldom made before the bill is drawn by any other person than the drawee; afterwards for the purpose either of promoting the negotiation of a bill where the drawee's credit is suspected, or to save the reputation and prevent the suing of some of the parties where the drawee either cannot be found, is not capable of making himself responsible, or refuses acceptance, it is not uncommon; and it is called an acceptance for the honor of the (10) person on whose account it is made, and enures to the benefit of all the parties subsequent to that person.

Such acceptances for honor as are made with the former view, are considered as made on account of the person in possession of the bill at the time they are made, and such as are made with the latter, unless they declare the contrary, on account of the drawer.

Acceptances for honor may be made by the drawee, or any other person. Thus, if a bill be drawn by A. on account of B, and the drawee be unwilling to accept on account of B, he (11) may accept for the honor of A. and on his account.

So the drawee may accept for the honor of an endorser.

---

was drawn on the defendant, and he accepted it to pay £100 part thereof; he was sued upon this acceptance, and on demurrer to the replication, insisted that a partial acceptance was not good within the custom of merchants; but the court held otherwise, and judgment was given for the plaintiff.

Walker v. Atwood, 11 Mod. 190. A bill was drawn on the defendant 8th of April, and no time fixed for its payment; it was presented to defendant 18th of April, and he accepted it to pay 8th of September; this being stated in the declaration, the defendant demurred, and insisted that as no time was prescribed for the payment, the bill was payable at sight, and then a promise to pay two or three months after sight was not an acceptance within the custom of merchants; but the court held, it was an acceptance within the custom, and the demurrer was overruled.

Petit v. Benson, Comb. 452. A bill was accepted to be paid, half in money and half in bills; and the question was, whether there could be a qualification of an acceptance; and it was proved by divers merchants that there might, for he that might refuse the bill totally might accept it in part; but that the holder was not bound to acquiesce in such acceptance.

(10) Vide Lutw. 899. Beawes, s. 34. 1st ed. p. 418. s. 40. 42. 1st. ed. p. 419.

(11) Beawes, § 33. 2d ed. p. 421. Marius, 21.

And if the drawee refuse acceptance, or if he accept and afterwards abscond, or (12) become bankrupt, any other person may accept for the honor of the drawer or of an endorser.

But after a general acceptance by the drawee, another person (13) cannot make a second acceptance in order to guaranty the acceptor's credit.

If however such second acceptance be written on the bill, the party for whose benefit it is made (14) may sue the person who made it, as upon a collateral undertaking to guaranty the payment of the bill, if it has the stamp proper for such an undertaking.

A person who accepts for honor, is only liable if the original drawee does not pay. (14)

And to charge such acceptor, there must be a presentment for payment to such original drawee. (14)

And if the acceptor for honor pay, he is (15) entitled to have recourse for repayment to the person for whose honor he made the acceptance, and to all other parties who are liable to that person.

---

(12) See ex parte Wackerbarth, 5 Ves. 574. and infra, n. (15.)

(13) Jackson v. Hudson, 2 Campb. N. P. C. 447. This was an action on a bill drawn by the plaintiff on I. Irving, and accepted by him; and under his acceptance the defendant wrote "accepted, Jos. Hudson, payable at, &c." The defendant was sued as acceptor. The plaintiff offered to prove that he had had dealings with Irving, and had refused to trust him further, unless the defendant would become his surety; and that the defendant, in order to guaranty Irving's credit, wrote this acceptance on the bill. Lord Ellenborough said, that this was neither an acceptance by the drawee, nor by a person for the honor of the drawer: but that it was a collateral undertaking that the bill should be paid, and ought to have been declared upon as such. Nonsuit.

It seems, however, that after an acceptance supra protest for the honor of one party, there may be a similar acceptance for the honor of another. Beawes, § 72. 2d ed. p. 422.

(14) Hoare v. Cazenove, 16 East. 391. A foreign bill was drawn on Penn & Hanbury; they refused acceptance, and it was protested for non-acceptance. Defendant accepted it for the honor of the first endorsers; but did not pay; action inde, defence, that it had not been presented for payment when due to Penn & Hanbury, nor protested for non-payment by them; and on case and time to consider, the court held such presentment and protest essential, because they considered defendant's acceptance as conditional if Penn & Hanbury did not pay; and Penn & Hanbury might have funds when the bill became due, though they had none before.

(15) Beawes, § 47. 49. 2d ed. p. 422. and see ex parte Wackerbarth,

An acceptance of this description is not made on a foreign bill until after a (16) protest (either for non-acceptance, or (where the acceptor absconds or becomes bankrupt) for want of better security), and from this circumstance it is called an acceptance *supra protest.*

If a bill is drawn on several partners, an acceptance by one, though in his own name only, will bind (17) all; but if drawn on several persons not connected in partnership, an acceptance by one will bind him, but him (17) only.

And if an acceptance by one of several partners be a fraud on the others; or if the one has no authority to bind the others by accepting bills; a person who is (18) privy to such fraud, or who (18) has received notice of such want of authority, cannot, by taking such acceptance, acquire a right to sue the partnership.

On a bill drawn upon a man by the description of servant, a general acceptance will (19) bind him personally.

An acceptance after the bill is drawn may be made even after (20) the time appointed for its payment.

---

5 Ves. 574. The acceptor of a bill having become bankrupt, and the holders having protested it for better security, Christen and Bowen accepted it for the honor of the drawers; and having paid it, now claimed to be entitled to dividends out of the bankrupt's estate. The chancellor said, that he had spoken to persons in trade on the subject, and that the result was, that the person accepting for the honor of the drawer had a right to come upon the acceptor. He said, however, that the justice of the case required that they should go in the first place against the drawer, if the acceptor had no effects, and directed an inquiry to be made whether the original acceptor or Christen and Bowen had effects of the drawers in hand.

(16) Beawes, 2d ed. p. 421. Marius, p. 21. See Evans on Bills of Exchange, p. 35.

(17) See ante, p. 40, note (17)

(18) See ante, c. 2. p. 41 to 46.

(19) See Thomas v. Bishop, ante, p. 57. n. (38.)

(20) Jackson v. Piggot, Lord Raym. 364. Salk. 127. Carth. 450. 12 Mod. 212. In an action against the acceptor of a bill, the declaration stated, that it was dated 25th March, 1696, payable one month after date, and that in April, 1697, it was shewn to the defendant, and he promised to pay it according to its tenor and effect; after verdict for the plaintiff, it was moved in arrest of judgment, that the promise was void, because as the day of payment was past at the time of the acceptance, it was impossible to pay the bill according to its tenor and effect; but it was answered for the plaintiff, that it amounted to a promise to

In such case an acceptance to pay according to the tenor, will (21) be considered as a general acceptance to pay upon demand.

Upon the acceptance of a bill payable at a given time after sight, if the words of acceptance and the date are in one hand-writing, and the drawee's name under it in the drawee's, the presumption is that the words of acceptance and the date were either upon the bill when he signed his name, or put there afterwards with his consent, because that is the usual course. (22)

A written acceptance is either made upon the bill or (23) elsewhere.

On a written acceptance by the drawee, his name need not appear; and any words written by him upon the bill, not putting a direct negative upon its request, as, "accepted," (24) "presented," "seen," (24) the day of the

---

pay generally; and of that opinion was the court, and they accordingly gave judgment for the plaintiff.

Mutford v. Walcot, Lord Raym. 574. Salk. 129. 12 Mod. 410. Com. 75. is precisely to the same effect. [See also Grant v. Shaw, ante, p. 98.]

(21) Vide Jackson v. Piggott, and Mutford v. Walcot, supra.

(22) Glossop v. Jacob, 4 Campb. 227. 1 Stark. 70. Action against acceptor on bill payable sixty days after sight; the acceptance was, "Accepted, 25th October, 1814. B. Jacob." The signature only was Jacob's; whose the other words were did not appear: but it was proved to be usual for a clerk to write "accepted," and the date, and for the drawee then to subscribe his name; and Lord Ellenborough, on objection, said he should leave it to the jury to presume the words were written with defendant's privity when he accepted the bill, unless defendant could give some other date to the transaction. The jury presumed accordingly, and verdict for plaintiff.

(23) Vide Pillans v. Van Mierop. Mason v. Hunt, Powell v. Monnier, and Pierson v. Dunlop, ante, p. 96, 97. [See also Goodrich v. Goodwin, and Coolidge v. Payson, post, p. 106.]

(24) Anon. Comb. 401. per Holt C. J. If the drawee underwrites a bill "presented such a day, or only the day of the month," it is such an acknowledgment of the bill as amounts to an acceptance; and this was declared by the jury to be the common practice.

Powell v. Monnier, 1 Atk. 611. A bill was sent by the post to the drawee for acceptance; he entered it in his bill-book (which was his practice with all bills he received whether he meant to accept them or not), wrote upon it the number of the entry, and kept it ten days; on the tenth he wrote upon it the day of the month, and returned it, saying he could not accept it; and per Lord Hardwicke, "It has been said to be the custom of merchants, that if a man underwrites any thing, be it

month, or a (25) direction to a third person to pay it, is primâ facie a complete acceptance.

It has indeed been said, (26) that an express refusal to accept, written on a bill, is an acceptance; but this is not the case, unless it is accompanied with a conduct which shows an intent to create a belief that it is accepted.

On a written acceptance on the bill by any other person than the drawee, it should seem essential that his name should appear.

A promise to accept an existing bill, if made upon an (27) executed consideration, or if it (28) influence any per-

---

what it may, it amounts to an acceptance; but if there were nothing more than this in the case, I should think it of little avail to charge the defendant;" but he decided that a letter the drawee had written, amounted to an acceptance. Vide ante, p. 97.

(25) Moor v. Whitby, B. R. Tr. 10 Geo. 3. Bull. Ni. Pri. 270. A bill drawn by Newton on Whitby, was presented for acceptance, and Whitby wrote upon it, "Mr. Jackson, please to pay this note, and place it to Mr. Newton's account. R. Whitby." It was insisted that this was no acceptance, but merely a direction to Jackson to pay it out of a particular fund, and if there was no fund there was to be no payment; sed per cur. this is a direction to Jackson to pay the money, and it signifies not to what account it is to be placed; that is between Jackson and Whitby only, this is clearly an acceptance.

(26) In Ann. 75. is this note: "Underwriting or endorsing a bill thus, 'I will not accept this bill,' is held by the custom of merchants a good acceptance;" but by Lord Mansfield in Peach v. Kay, in sittings after Trinity Term, 1781. "It was held by all the judges that an express refusal to accept, written on the bill, where the drawee apprized the party who took it away what he had written, was no acceptance; but if the drawee had intended it as a surprise upon the party, and to make him consider it as an acceptance, they seemed to think it might have been otherwise."

(27) Vide Pillans v. Van Mierop, ante, p. 96.

(28) Vide Pierson v. Dunlop, and Mason v. Hunt, ante, p. 96, 97.

[The doctrine stated in the text is recognized by the court in M'Evers v. Mason, 10 Johns. R. 207.]

Clarke and others v. Cock, 4 East's Rep. 57. Woodward authorized the defendant to receive certain African bills, of which he sent him a list, and apprized him that he had drawn upon him for the amount. The defendant, by letter, acknowledged the receipt of the list, and assured Woodward that the bills he had drawn on him "should meet with due honor." The plaintiffs, who were Woodward's bankers, and greatly in advance to him, having refused to give him further credit, he endorsed to them the bills which he had so drawn upon the defendant, and at the same time either communicated the purport of the defendant's letter, or else represented his having made an absolute promise to accept, but did not show the letter itself: and the plaintiffs, on the faith of defend-

person to take or retain the bill, is, where 1 & 2 Geo. 4. c. 78. s. 2. does not apply, a complete acceptance as to the person to whom the promise is made in the one case, and the person influenced in the other, and as to all the subsequent parties in each.

But a promise to accept a bill to be afterwards drawn, is (29) no acceptance of the bill when drawn, unless some per-

---

ant's promise, advanced to Woodward the full amount of the bills. The defendant afterwards wrote to Woodward, that the African bills had been attached, and Woodward in answer desired them to refuse acceptance of the bills drawn on him. The defendant did in fact receive the amount of the African bills before the bills drawn on him became due; but this amount was afterwards attached in his hands, and upon that attachment he paid over the money so received. This action was brought against the defendant as acceptor of the bills drawn by Woodward; a verdict was found for the plaintiffs, subject to the opinion of the court. The court held that this was a good acceptance, and that the subsequent circumstances had not done it away; and therefore awarded the postea to the plaintiff. Lawrence J. said the defendant might have resisted the attachment on the ground of his acceptances, which would have been a defence to him.

(29) Johnson v. Collings, 1 East's Rep. 98. Collings owed Ruff £23, 10*s.* 6d. Ruff applied for payment, and Collings said that if Ruff would draw for it at two months he would pay it. Ruff drew accordingly, and endorsed the bill to the plaintiff, but did not mention to him Collings's promise. The plaintiff now sued Collings, on the ground, that his promise to Ruff was virtually an acceptance. But Le Blanc J. thought that as it was not made to a third person, nor with circumstances which might induce a third person to take the bill, it was no acceptance, and nonsuited the plaintiff. On a rule nisi for a new trial, and cause shewn, the whole court thought it no acceptance: and Lord Kenyon thought that the admitting a promise to accept, made before the existence of the bill, to operate as an actual acceptance of it afterwards, even though a third person were thereby induced to take the bill, was carrying the doctrine of implied acceptances to the utmost verge of the law, and he doubted whether it did not go beyond the proper boundary. Rule discharged.

[Mason, Hodgson, & Co. were sued as acceptors of a bill. The evidence to support the acceptance consisted of letters written by the defendants to Proctor, their agent, before the bill was drawn, in one of which they agree to allow Proctor a commission upon all consignments of produce to them, and state that they "advance in anticipation of property on the receipt of bills of lading and invoices, with orders to insure, from 2-3 to 3-4 the probable proceeds;" and that he may "confidently assure any shippers that their drafts under the above circumstances will meet honor." The bill was drawn by Jephson on account of a shipment made by him to the defendants on the recommendation of Proctor, and he had forwarded bills of lading and invoices with orders to insure, and the bill drawn was for less than two thirds of the probable proceeds. The bill at the request of the drawer was made

son be thereby (30) induced to take or retain the bill; and indeed it may be doubted, whether in any case, a promise to accept a non-existing bill, would (31) now be considered as an acceptance of the bill when drawn. (*a*)

And a promise to accept, made upon an executory consideration, is in no case (32) binding, so long as such consideration remains executory, unless it influence some person to take or retain the bill.

[The doctrine may be considered as established in the United States, that a written promise to accept a non-existing bill, is binding as an acceptance, if the holder of the bill receives it upon the credit of such promise. (*b*)

Although the holder receives the bill from the drawer in payment of a pre-existing debt. (*b*)

---

payable to Proctor and by him endorsed. But it did not appear that the plaintiff purchased the bill, or that the drawer drew it, on the credit of the letter, or that either of them had any knowledge of it. The court held that even if an endorsee could in any case avail himself of such a promise as amounting to an acceptance, yet he could not in this case, as the bill was not taken upon the credit of the promise contained in the letter. M'Evers v. Mason, 10 Johns. R. 207.]

(30) Vide Pierson v. Dunlop, and Mason v. Hunt, ante, p. 96, 97, and Johnson v. Collings, supra.

(31) Vide Johnson v. Collings, ante, p. 104. n. (29).

[(*a*) But it is clear that the person promising to accept bills to be drawn, if he refuse to accept them when drawn, is liable in damages for a breach of contract to the party to whom the promise is made. Laing v. Barclay, 1 Barn. & Cres. 398; S. C. 2 Dow. & Ryl. 530. See also M'Evers v. Mason, 10 Johns. R. 215.]

(32) In Pillans v. Van Mierop, ante, p. 97. n. (3). Burr. 1666. Lord Mansfield says, "It was argued upon at the trial, that this imported to be a credit given to the plaintiffs in prospect of a *future* credit to be given by them to White, and this credit might well be countermanded before the advancement of any money, AND THIS IS SO."

[(*b*) Goodwin, one of the owners of the sloop Hope, wrote a letter of instructions to Napier the master, previous to a voyage, in which he said, "Should you unfortunately be captured by an English cruiser, you will endeavor to ransom the vessel and cargo, as low as possible, say not to exceed two thousand dollars; your draft on me or my brother will be duly honored." The vessel being captured, the master for her ransom drew a bill on Gordon for $[illegible]000, payable to Stewart or order, and gave Stewart the letter of instructions, and the vessel was released. Goodrich & Deforest, as endorsees of Stewart, brought an action against Gordon as acceptor. They had received the letter of instructions at the same time with the bills. Thompson C. J. delivered the opinion of the Court. "The testimony is very full to show, that the letter of the defendant authorizing the drawing of the bill accompanied it at all

But such promise is not binding as an acceptance, unless the bill is drawn within a reasonable time after the promise is made. (*a*)

And where a bill was drawn two years after the promise was made, in order to procure the drawer's release from arrest, the person making the promise was held not to be bound as acceptor. (*a*)

---

times, and that it was upon the credit of that letter that the bill was taken by the plaintiffs. It was an authority given for the express purpose of enabling the captain to draw the bill, which was an act done for the benefit of the defendant, and according to his instructions; and I think it binding upon him as an acceptance; and this is the opinion of the Court." Goodrich v. Goodwin, 15 Johns. R. 6.

Coolidge & Co. wrote to Cornthwaite & Cary, saying, "If Mr. Williams feels satisfied on this point," (referring to a bond given by Cornthwaite & Cary to Coolidge & Co.) "he will inform you, and in that case your draft for $2000 will be honored." Cornthwaite & Cary gave Payson & Co. a bill for $2000 on Coolidge & Co., and Payson & Co. after ascertaining from Williams that he was satisfied with the bond, received the bill in payment of a pre-existing debt from Cornthwaite & Cary, upon the faith of the above letter. Payson & Co. sued Coolidge & Co. as acceptors of the bill. Marshall C. J. delivered the opinion of the Court. "Upon a review of the cases which are reported, this court is of opinion, that a letter written within a reasonable time before or after the date of a bill of exchange, describing it in terms not to be mistaken, and promising to accept it, is, if shown to the person who afterwards takes the bill on the credit of the letter, a virtual acceptance binding the person who makes the promise. This is such a case." "The mere circumstance that the bill was taken for a pre-existing debt has not been thought sufficient to do away the effect of a promise to accept." Coolidge *v.* Payson, 2 Wheat. 66, affirming the judgment of the Circuit Court, which appears in 2 Gallis. 233, Payson v. Coolidge. See also Storer v. Logan, infra.]

[(*a*) See Coolidge v. Payson, supra.

Hinckley having expressed dissatisfaction with a settlement of accounts between him and Clements, the latter wrote the former a letter containing the following words, "Reperuse the accounts, make out a statement according to your own wishes, and draw upon me here for the balance, which shall be punctually honored." Two years after this letter was written, Hinckley, being arrested by Wilson, a creditor, drew a bill on Clements in favor of Wilson for $2405 80. Acceptance being refused, Wilson brought a suit against Clements, declaring, 1. Upon the bill as accepted. 2. Upon a promise to accept such bills as should be drawn. 3. For money had and received. The court held that the action could not be maintained; and, without deciding that an action would not lie, had the bill been seasonably drawn, yet that "the length of time alone was a sufficient reason why the defendant's promise should not be considered as conclusively binding on him." Sedgwick J. who delivered the opinion of the Court, said, "It would in my opinion be unreasonable to hold the defendant at all responsible for any bill which

A letter agreeing in unqualified terms to accept a non-existing bill, is not binding on the writer as an absolute acceptance, where the holder of the bill is informed at the time of receiving it, that the acceptance depends upon a certain specified contingency. (*a*)]

A promise in a letter that a bill then drawn (33) "shall meet with due honor; or that the writer will (34) "accept or certainly pay" it, is, where 1 & 2 G. 4. c. 78. does not apply, an acceptance.

Hinckley might be induced, within two years to draw upon him, to obtain a release from imprisonment." Wilson v. Clements, 3 Mass. R. 1.]

[(*a*) Storer, as payee, sued Logan, Lenox, & Co. as acceptors of two bills, drawn by Weeks & Son. The evidence to prove the acceptance, was a letter from Lenox addressed to Weeks & Son, in which he engages that his firm shall accept certain bills to be drawn by Weeks & Son; the plaintiff received the bills on the credit of the letter, and it was admitted that they were drawn pursuant to the authority given by the letter. At the trial before Sewall J. the defendant was admitted to prove that at the time the letter was shown to the plaintiff, he was informed, "that the undertaking to accept was to be understood conditionally, and depended altogether upon certain shipments to the defendants which the drawers were then engaged in making; and that if these shipments failed, the bills would not be paid." Verdict for defendants, subject to the opinion of the Court. Sewall J. delivered the opinion of the Court. He said that the letter amounted to an acceptance of any bill drawn "pursuant to the license and credit given, and negotiated upon the faith of that engagement."—"We concur in opinion that the delivery of the letter was subject to an explanation by parol testimony. The holder of the bill possesses with it a letter, which is evidence of an acceptance or a credit to the drawer, until this evidence is controlled by the circumstances communicated to the payee of the bill, the plaintiff in this action, and the manner in which he became possessed of a letter and promise not addressed to him is made to appear. Thus controlled, there is no evidence of an absolute, but only of a conditional and restricted promise to accept: which under the circumstances proved did not amount to an acceptance." Judgment on the verdict. Storer v. Logan, 9 Mass. R. 55.]

(33) See Clarke v. Cock, ante, p. 103. n. (28), and Pierson v. Dunlop, ante, p. 96. n. (3).

(34) Wynne v. Raikes, 5 East's Rep. 514. On 9th Nov. 1801, Brown in America, drew on the defendants in London, a bill for £500 at sixty days after sight; and on the same day wrote to them, that he had valued on them for £5,548 by divers bills, of which he requested their acceptance. The bill for £500 which was one of those bills, was endorsed by the payees to the plaintiffs in London, for a valuable consideration. On 2d Jan. 1802, the plaintiffs, on receiving the bill, presented it for acceptance, which was refused. On 13th January, 1802, the defendants wrote to Brown, stating, that as their prospects of security had improved, they would "accept or certainly pay all the bills which had then ap-

And this, although the letter was not received until (35) after the bill had become due; and although no person had been (35) induced by such promise, to take the bill.

But to make a promise, in a letter to the drawer, where the bill is payable to a third person, amount to an acceptance, it ought to be in terms which do not admit of doubt. (36)

An answer in reply to a letter of advice from the drawer desiring it may be honored, that the bill shall have attention, will not, in general, amount to an acceptance. (36)

And it will make no difference, though this answer is communicated to an endorsee before he takes the bill. (36)

But if, by the course of dealing between the parties, these words are considered as an acceptance, they will have that effect.

So in cases not within 1 & 2 G. 4., a verbal promise to accept, though the party expressly defer a written acceptance, as where he says, "Leave the bill and I will accept it," is a (37) complete acceptance. And a verbal promise

---

peared." The bill for 500*l.* had so appeared. This letter was received by Brown in America on 19th March, 1802. The plaintiffs presented the bill for payment on 6th March, sixty-three days after the presentment for acceptance and on payment being refused, brought this action on the bill. At the time when the bill was drawn, Brown was indebted to the defendants, and still continued to be so, to the amount of 5,000*l.* A verdict was found for the plaintiffs subject to the opinion of the Court of King's Bench. The court held that the case of Powell v. Monnier was in point; that this was a good acceptance. Postea to the plaintiffs.

(35) See Wynne v. Raikes, preceding note.

(36) Rees v. Warwick, 2 Barnew. 113. 2 Stark. 411. Action against defendant as acceptor of a bill drawn by Denison and Co., to the order of Johnson and Co., dated 3d May; 4th May, Denison and Co. wrote to defendant, "We yesterday valued on you, favor Johnson and Co. for 100*l.*, which please to honor:" defendant answered, "Your bill 100*l.* &c. shall have attention." This letter was shewn by Denison and Co. to Johnson and Co., and by them before he took the bill to plaintiff; it was insisted this amounted to an acceptance: Bayley J. thought not; but it being suggested that in the dealings between these parties, these words had that meaning; other letters from defendants were read in evidence, but they did not prove the point: the jury intimated their opinion that these words, per se, did not amount to an acceptance; and nonsuit with liberty to plaintiff to move to enter a verdict; motion accordingly; but the court were also of opinion that these words by no means imported an unequivocal acceptance of the bill, and as the jury were of that opinion in this case, the nonsuit was right.

(37) D. Molloy, B. 2. c. 10. § 20. Mar. 2d ed. 17.

to accept a returned bill when it shall come back, is binding (38) if it do come back.

Saying, " Send the bill to my counting house, and I will give directions for its being accepted," is not of itself an acceptance; the bill must be sent to the counting house. (39)

An answer by the drawee when a bill is called for, " there is your bill, it is all right," is no (40) acceptance.

[And the drawee's saying to a person not a party, nor acting for a party to the bill, that " he must pay it" or " would have to pay it," is not an acceptance. (*a*)]

Saying, when a bill is presented for payment, " that it will be paid," if said with reference to immediate payment, will not amount to an acceptance, if the person who brought the bill declines the immediate payment (41) because he makes an ulterior demand.

Especially if the drawee has before refused to accept. (41)

---

(38) Cox v. Coleman, ante, p. 97. note (6). [And see Grant v. Shaw, ante, p. 98.]

(39) Anderson v. Hick, 3 Campb. 179. Acceptance being refused by the drawees, the holder remonstrated with the managing partner, who said, " If you will send it to the counting-house again, I will give directions for its being accepted." In an action against the drawees as acceptors, it was urged that without proof of the bill's being again sent to the counting-house, this answer was an acceptance. Sed per Lord Ellenborough, it was only a conditional promise to accept, and could not operate as an acceptance till the bill was sent back.

(40) Powell v. Jones, Espinasse, 17. In an action against the defendant as acceptor of a bill, the only evidence to prove the acceptance was, that when the bill was called for, he returned it, and said, " There is your bill, it is all right." Lord Kenyon thought that these words could by no implication amount to an acceptance, and nonsuited the plaintiff. Vide ante, p. 103. note (26).

[(*a*) Martin v. Bacon, 2 S. Car. R. 132.]

(41) Anderson v. Heath, Trin. 1815, 4 Maule, 303. A bill for 2000*l.* at sixty days' sight was presented to defendants, the drawees, 2d August, 1814, for acceptance, which they refused, and it was protested. At the end of the sixty days, 4th October, it was brought for payment, and one of defendants said, "This bill will be paid; but we cannot allow you for a duplicate protest," which was charged, and he was about to pay the bill; but the clerk who brought it said, " he could not receive the payment without all the charges, without further orders;" and he went away for instructions: he returned in half an hour; but in the interim defendants had learned the drawer had failed, and they refused payment. An action was brought on the ground that the saying, " the bill would be paid," was an acceptance; but, on case, the court held it was not; it was said alio intuitu, acceptance did not enter into the

[A supercargo or other agent cannot by drawing a bill on his principal bind the latter as acceptor, unless the agent have special authority for the purpose. (*b*)]

In cases to which 1 & 2 G. 4. does not apply, the drawee's keeping a bill presented for acceptance, (42) may amount to an acceptance;

And so may his destroying it.

But if there is a refusal to accept, and the holder submits

---

contemplation of either party at the time; they thought of immediate, not future payment; defendants did not think of giving a pledge, nor the clerk of receiving one. Nonsuit.

[(*b*) See Scott v. M'Lellan, 2 Greenleaf, 199.]

(42) Harvey v. Martin, King's Bench, sittings after Michaelmas Term, 1806. In an action by the payee and holder of a bill against the defendant as acceptor, it appeared that the bill was drawn in Guernsey, where the drawer and the plaintiff resided, on the defendant, who lived in Cornwall, dated 13th March, 1805, at three months; within a fortnight after it was drawn, the plaintiff sent it to the defendant, desiring him to accept it, and remit it to S. Dobree, the plaintiff's correspondent in London. On 13th April, 1805, the plaintiff, finding that the bill had not been sent to S. Dobree, wrote to the defendant requesting him to accept and send it, stating, that though he considered the keeping the bill as tantamount to an acceptance, yet that it was not the same to him, as S. Dobree would not give him credit for it until he received it accepted. The defendant, however, did not accept the bill, or remit it, or give any notice of his refusal so to do. On the 1st of June the defendant signed a letter, admitting that he had kept the bill, though told by the plaintiff that he considered his doing so as tantamount to an acceptance, "as he intended to have paid it," but having no effects of the drawer's, he refused to pay: and on 4th July, when the bill was protested for nonpayment, he said he had neglected to write an acceptance upon it, thinking it of no consequence, "as he meant to pay it." Lord Ellenborough referred to a MS. case of Trimmer v. Oddie, mentioned post, p. 118., in which Lord Kenyon expressed an opinion, that a mere keeping of a bill was an acceptance; and said he inclined to entertain the same opinion; but should leave that question to the jury on the custom. Gibbs, however, for the defendant, admitting that he could not answer the case, a verdict was found for the plaintiff. And on an application to Lord Ellenborough to certify for a special jury, his lordship refused, saying that this was a clear case; but that if it had not been attended with such strong admissions on the part of the defendant, but had been a mere case of a bill kept by the drawee, he should have thought it a fit case for a special jury to decide, whether such detention of the bill amounted to an acceptance.

See Scaccia de Commerciis et Cambio, fol. 383, num. 335., who, in enumerating the different acceptances, mentions that which is made "tacite per receptionem, et *detentionem* literarum." See also Pothier Contrat de Change, part. I. c. 3. § 3. p. 39, who observes, that the ordonnance having directed that an acceptance should be in writing, had rendered inadmissible the "*acceptation tacite*" resulting from the drawee's having received and retained the bill.

to that refusal, but omits taking the bill away, a subsequent destruction by the drawee is not necessarily an acceptance. (43)

If a bill is sent by the post to the drawee for acceptance, and that has been the course between the holder and drwee, a neglect by the drawee to return it for ten or twelve days whilst he is waiting to see if the drawer sends him funds, is no acceptance. (44)

Though he keeps it at the instance of the drawer on a promise from him of funds. (44)

At least, it is not, if by the course of dealing between the holder and the drawee, the former is apprised that the latter will accept, without delay, when he has funds, and that he will not accept without. (44)

A fortiori the holder cannot insist upon it as an acceptance, if he makes no remonstrance on account of the delay whilst the bill is kept, or when it is returned unaccepted. (44)

And query whether when the holder sends the bill by post to the drawee and thereby makes him his agent, whether any neglect by the drawee will have any other effect than

---

(43) Jeune v. Ward, 1 Barnew. 653. 2 Stark. 326. Godfrey was entitled to a 200*l.* legacy under a will, to which defendant was an executor, and he drew upon defendant for 150*l.* at sight in favor of plaintiff, who was a creditor: the bill was drawn 28th May; on 29th plaintiff went to defendant, who lived in the country, and left the bill for acceptance: in June plaintiff wrote to defendant's solicitor, Egerton, saying defendant had refused to accept the bill, desiring his assistance to get payment from the drawer: Egerton apprised him when the legacy was to be paid, and Godfrey having received it without paying plaintiff, plaintiff applied to defendant to return the bill, to which defendant replied, that having also been applied to by Godfrey's mother to send it her, he had, to avoid trouble, destroyed it. Plaintiff brought an action on the ground that the destruction was tantamount to an acceptance; and of that opinion was Lord Ellenborough, and verdict for plaintiff. On rule nisi for a new trial, and cause shewn, Lord Ellenborough retained his opinion; and Holroyd J. thought, that in general destruction was equivalent to acceptance, but as there was a refusal to accept and plaintiff seemed to consider deft. not liable in June, he thought there ought to be a new trial, to put the facts upon the record: Bayley and Abbot Js. thought, under the circumstances, the destruction was no acceptance; and rule absolute. Bayley J. doubted whether, in any case, destruction would do more than subject to an action of trover.

that of subjecting the drawee to a special action for the negligence. (44)

By the usage of trade, a banker in London will not render himself responsible by retaining a check drawn on him, (45) provided he return it at any time before five o'clock in the evening of the day on which it is drawn.

An acceptance to pay when remitted for, is (46) a conditional acceptance.

So an answer by a drawee who lived in London, that a ship was consigned to him and a person in Bristol, and that

---

(44) Mason and others v. Barff, M. 59 G. 3. 2 Barnew. 26. Brankstone used to draw on defendants for wool he sent them: August 1814, plaintiff, who used to discount the bills, sent one by letter to defendants, and defendants returned it accepted, but said, it would be well for the future if plaintiffs would inquire whether the wools were delivered to the carrier, and the invoices and the carrier's acknowledgement sent, and in such case the bills would be accepted without delay: 25th February, plaintiffs sent another bill for acceptance, which arrived 27th; but defendants not having received remittance of the invoice, &c. omitted returning it till 8th March, and then sent a letter to say they could not accept because they had not received the invoice, &c., and said they had kept it during the interval on a promise from Brankstone that the invoice should be sent: this letter arrived 11th March, on which day, before its arrival, plaintiffs sent another bill for acceptance, making no mention of the other bill: defendants kept both bills till 25th March, and then sent back both unaccepted. Plaintiffs insisted their conduct amounted to an acceptance of both, and they brought an action on the case; but on argument, the court was clear against plaintiffs, for as they knew the bills would be accepted without delay if the invoices, &c. were sent, they must have concluded, from the delay, that defendants were waiting for them: that their making no remonstrance when they wrote on 11th March, implied that they so considered it, and their making no reply to the letter of the 8th of March, shewed that they did not then consider silence as an acceptance, and had they meant so to consider it, they should at once have written to say so to defendants, because that would have prevented his keeping the second bill, and would have put him upon getting funds for the first. Nonsuit.

(45) Fernandez v Glynn, 1 Campb. N. P. C. 426. n. In this case it was decided, that by the custom in London, a banker might return a check at any time before five o'clock of the day on which it was drawn. And although the check had been cancelled by mistake, yet having been returned within the time, the banker was holden to be discharged.

(46) Banbury v. Lissett, Str. 1211. The drawee accepted a bill "*for Lissett and Galley, of Leghorn, to pay as remitted from thence at usance*," and it was objected, in an action against him, that there was no evidence to shew he had a remittance, and that his acceptance was conditional only. Lee C. J. declared he so understood it; but he left it to the jury, and they found for the defendant upon another point, and gave no opinion upon this.

till he should know to which port the ship would come he could not accept, connected with a subsequent answer that the bill was a good one, and would be paid though the ship should be lost, was (47) held a conditional acceptance only; it being clear that the drawee looked for an opportunity of reimbursing himself, and had three events in contemplation,—the ship's arrival at Bristol, her arrival at London, and her loss; in the two latter he should have the opportunity, and therefore accepted; in the former he should not, and did not accept.

But an answer by the drawee, that he would pay if I. S. would not, but that he must first apply to him, not that he thought he would pay, but because he judged it right to put him to the trial, with an assurance to the holder that he might rest satisfied of the payment, was, before 1 and 2 G. 4., held (48) an absolute acceptance.

---

(47) This was the case of Sproat v. Matthews, 1 Term Rep. 182. The ship did arrive at London, and the defendant disposed of the cargo; but it appearing that upon the defendant's answer that the bill would be paid though the ship should be lost, the plaintiff noted the bill for non-acceptance, Buller J. held that the acceptance was conditional only, and that the noting shewed the plaintiff did not choose to take it, and he directed a nonsuit; and upon a rule to shew cause why there should not be a new trial, the court, viz. Willes, Ashhurst, and Buller, Js. concurred that the acceptance was conditional only, but Willes, J. thought if there were a doubt whether it was conditional, or whether the plaintiff had precluded himself from insisting upon it, all the facts should have been left to the jury, and he was therefore of opinion that the nonsuit should be set aside; but the other judges thought differently, and the rule was discharged.

(48) Wilkinson v. Lutwidge, Str. 648. Two bills drawn on the defendant were sent to him by the plaintiff's agent for acceptance, and he wrote for answer, "The two bills which you sent me, I will pay if the owners of the Queen Anne do not: and they living in Dublin must first apply to them: I hope to have their answer in a week or ten days. I do not expect they will pay them, but I judge it proper to take their answer before I do, which I request you will acquaint Mr. Wilkinson with, and that he may rest satisfied of the payment." He afterwards wrote, "I have not had an opportunity of sending the bills to the owners of the Queen Anne, but will take the first opportunity, and shall then remit to the gentlemen concerned, according to my promise." One of the bills he paid, but being sued upon the other, he contended that his acceptance was conditional only, to pay if the owners of the Queen Anne did not; but Raymond C. J. held it an absolute acceptance, and that the attempt to procure payment from the owners of the Queen Anne was to be made by him, and was wholly for his benefit and accommodation, but that the plaintiff was to have his money at all events. The jury found accordingly for the plaintiff.

If a man purposes making a conditional acceptance only, and commits that acceptance to writing, he should be careful to express the conditions therein; for it may at least be doubted whether parol evidence of such conditions would be admissible; if it were, the onus of proving them would be upon the acceptor, and the proof would be of no avail if the holder, or any person under whom he claims, took the bill without notice of such conditions, and gave a valuable consideration for it.

A conditional acceptance becomes absolute, as soon as its conditions are performed.

Thus an answer by the drawee, that he could not accept until a navy bill should be paid, was thought (49) to operate as an actual acceptance upon the payment of the navy bill.

So an answer that the bill would not be accepted till certain goods against which it was drawn arrived, was held virtually an acceptance when they did arrive, and were received. (50)

But if the drawee says he cannot accept without further directions from I. S., and I. S. afterwards desires him to accept, and draw upon A. B. for the amount, the (51) mere drawing upon A. B. will not make this an acceptance, although the actual payment of the bill upon him may.

---

(49) Pierson v. Dunlop, ante, p. 96.

(50) Miln v. Prest, Holt, 181. 4 Camp. 393. Endorsee against defendant as acceptor, and question whether what defendant had written or said amounted to an acceptance. The drawer bought wheat for defendant, and in a letter to him defendant said he would accept bills for it when they received notice that the wheat was shipped; this letter had been shewn to plaintiff, (before he took the bill;) when the bill was presented for acceptance, defendant said he would not accept till the wheat arrived; the wheat afterwards arrived, and defendant accepted it and sold it; Gibbs C. J. was clear that the letter would have been no acceptance, had it not been shewn to plaintiff; but he said a conditional acceptance was valid if the conditions were performed; this wheat arrived, and defendant had it and sold it; and he was clear what defendant had done was equivalent to an acceptance, and verdict for plaintiff.

(51) Smith and another v. Nissen and another, 1 Term Rep. 269. Taubert ordered goods of the defendants, and desired them to draw on the plaintiffs for the amount, which they did; the plaintiffs wrote two letters to the defendants, one saying they could not accept, because the defendants had sent more goods than were ordered, but that they had written to Taubert for further directions; the other saying they had

An acceptance varying from the tenor differs from it either in the (52) sum, the (53) time, the (54) place, or (55) mode of payment.

The effect of accepting a bill in such way as to make it payable at a banker's, or elsewhere than at the drawee's residence or place of business, (56) has of late been matter of great controversy and difference of opinion, but the point is now settled by 1 and 2 G. 4. c. 78. (57)

By that statute, if the acceptance merely makes it payable at a particular house, without any further expression in such acceptance, it is to be deemed a general acceptance. (57)

If it make it payable at that house *only*, a qualified one. (57)

Though any acceptance varying from the tenor bind the person making it, the holder of a bill is entitled from the

---

written to Taubert and were waiting his answer before they could accept, but had desired the holder to keep the bill; in the mean time, Taubert desired the plaintiffs to accept, and draw on Goverts for the amount; they accordingly drew on Goverts, who refused to accept, and upon that they paid the bill for the honor of the defendants, and brought an action against them for money paid; the plaintiffs had a verdict, but the defendants moved for a new trial, on the ground that the drawing on Goverts was an acceptance of the bill drawn by the defendants. Sed per cur. What the plaintiffs did, did not amount to an acceptance, for they never meant to make themselves liable, unless the bill they drew was accepted and paid, and a rule was refused.

(52) Vide Wegerstoffe v. Keene, ante, p. 98. note (9).

(53) Vide Walker v. Atwood, ante, p. 99. note (9).

Paton v. Winter, 1 Taunt. 420. The drawee altered the time of payment of a bill from one month to two, and accepted it; the holder kept it the two months, and then presented it for payment; the court held that this was an acquiesence in the alteration, and the holder having brought an action on the case against the acceptor for having mutilated the bill, they directed a nonsuit.

(54) Bishop v. Chitty, and Smith v. De la Fontane, post.

(55) Vide Petit v. Benson, ante, p. 99. note (9).

(56) See post.

(57) By 1 and 2 G. 4. c. 78. After 1st August, 1821, if any person shall accept a bill of exchange, payable at the house of a banker or other place, without further expression in his acceptance, such acceptance shall be deemed and taken to be, to all intents and purposes, a general acceptance of such bill; but if the acceptor shall in his acceptance express that he accepts the bill payable at a banker's house or other place only, and not otherwise or elsewhere, such acceptance shall be a qualified acceptance of such bill, and the acceptor shall not be liable to pay the said bill, except in default of payment when such payment shall have been first duly demanded at such banker's house or other place.

undertaking of the drawer and endorsers to expect an absolute acceptance by the drawee, (58) (or if there be several not connected in partnership by (59) each,) for the payment of the full (60) sum of money mentioned therein (61) according to its tenor, specifying (62) (if none be mentioned for the purpose) a place for its payment, and (63) expressing, if the bill be payable within a limited time after sight, the time of its presentment for acceptance ; and may reject any other.

If upon the offer of any other acceptance the holder does any act expressing a refusal to take it, as if he gives notice to any of the antecedent parties generally that acceptance is refused, or notes the bill for non-acceptance, the offer (64) is not binding.

There is a case (65) however in which it has been supposed to have been decided, that if the holder strikes out an acceptance which varies from the tenor of the bill, and substitutes an acceptance according to the tenor, he may afterwards restore the acceptance he struck out, and that such acceptance will continue binding, but it has (66) been

---

(58) Mar. 2d ed. 22.

(59) Molloy, B. 2. c. 10. § 18, 19. Mar. 2d ed. 16.

(60) Molloy, B. 2. c. 10. § 20. Mar. 2d ed. 17. Beawes, § 218. p. 443.

(61) Molloy, B. 2. c. 10. § 28. Mar. 2d ed. 21. Beawes, § 221. p. 444. See Boehm v. Garcias, 1 Campb. 425. where Lord Ellenborough held that the holder was not bound to take an acceptance to pay in a different kind of currency from that mentioned in the bill.

(62) Mutford v. Walcot, Lord Raym. 575. per Holt C. J. "If a bill be payable at London, and the person on whom it is drawn accept it, but names no house where he will pay it, the party that has the bill is not bound to be satisfied with this acceptance."

(63) Beawes, p. 452. Where a bill is drawn payable at so many days' sight, the acceptance must express the day it is made.

(64) Sproat v. Matthews, ante, p. 113. note (47), and Bentinck v. Dorrien, post. p. 119. note (71).

(65) Price v. Shute, Beawes, § 222. 1st ed. p. 444. Moll. B. 2. c. 10. § 28. A bill was drawn, payable the 1st of January, and the drawee accepted it to pay the 1st of March: the holder struck out the 1st of March, and substituted the 1st of January, and sent the bill for payment on that day, which the acceptor refused: the holder then struck out the 1st of January and restored the 1st of March, and in an action on this bill, the question was, whether these alterations did not destroy the bill; and Pemberton C. J. ruled that they did not.

(66) In Master v. Miller, 4 Term Rep. 330. Lord Kenyon in commenting on the case of Price v. Shute, observes, that the books do not

doubted whether the determination went farther than to decide that the alteration in the acceptance (though it annulled the acceptance and discharged the acceptor) did not leave the bill in statu quo as to the other parties.

An alteration in a material point certainly vacates an acceptance. (67)

And an alteration by substituting or adding a new place for payment is an alteration in a material point (67)

An acceptance once completed and issued (68) cannot be revoked.

And there are cases (69) in which it was held, that if the drawee wrote an acceptance upon a bill he could not afterwards cancel it, though he cancelled it whilst the bill re-

---

say against whom the action was brought; and it could not have been against the acceptor, because his acceptance was struck out by the party himself who brought the action; and he concludes, "that on the person to whom the bill was directed refusing to accept the bill as it was originally drawn, the holder resorted to the drawer;" however Buller J. 4 Term Rep. 336., says he cannot consider this case in any other light than as an action against the acceptor, because the books only state what passed between the holder and the acceptor.

(67) Tidmarsh v. Grover, 1 Maule 735. Defendant accepted a bill "payable at Bloxham and Co.'s." Bloxham and Co. failed; the holder struck out their names, and without defendant's knowledge or consent inserted "Esdailes."—The point was reserved whether this alteration vacated the acceptance, and the court held it did, and ordered a nonsuit to be entered.

Cowie v. Halsall, 4 Barnew. and Ald. 197. Endorsee against acceptor. It appeared that the acceptance was general, and that the drawer, without the acceptor's knowledge, added to the acceptance "payable at Mr. B.'s, Chiswell-street," and on the ground that this was a material alteration, and vacated the acceptance, verdict for defendant. Motion for a new trial; but the court thought the verdict right, for this alteration would lead to a presentment at B.'s, not at defendant's, and the bill might be treated as dishonored, and defendant be arrested thereon, without any presentment where defendant would expect it; and rule refused.

(68) See Marius, p. 20, and the cases mentioned in the two next notes.

(69) Thornton and another v. Dick and another, 4 Esp. N. P. C. 270. A bill drawn on the defendants, payable three months after sight, was, on the 1st of October, left with them by the plaintiffs for acceptance. It was not called for until the 11th; when it appeared that the words, "Accepted the 1st of Oct. 1799. Q. Dick and Co." had been written upon the bill, and afterwards nearly obliterated by ink. The words however were still legible. At the time of drawing the bill the defendants were in advance to the drawer. The plaintiffs, as endorsees,

mained in his possession, and before it had been called for by the holder. But the contrary has since (70) been decided.

---

sued the defendants as acceptors. The acceptance and subsequent cancellation were admitted: and the only question was, whether the cancellation, having been made before the re-delivery of the bill, had discharged the acceptor. Lord Ellenborough said, that if a party once accepted a bill he had done the act, and could not retract; and that there was no difference in point of legal effect, whether the bill were payable after sight or after date. Verdict for the plaintiffs.—Trimmer v. Oddie was cited; in that case however the declaration contained counts against the drawee for having mutilated the bill.

Trimmer v. Oddie, 1800. A bill was left for acceptance and accepted, but the acceptance was afterwards cut off, and the bill returned in that mutilated state. Lord Kenyon was clearly of opinion, that the acceptance once made could not be revoked, and that the acceptor was still bound. This case was cited in Bentinck v. Dorrien, 6 East. Rep. 200., and the Hamburgh ordinance was referred to as having been recognised by Lord Kenyon to be the law of merchants here: and Lord Ellenborough said, "The rule is certainly laid down in the Hamburgh ordinance as stated, that an acceptance once made cannot be revoked; though, to be sure, that leaves the question open as to what is an acceptance, whether it be perfected before the delivery of the bill." And Lawrence J. in the case last mentioned, 6 East. Rep. 201., said, "When the general question shall arise, it will be worth considering how that which is not communicated to the holder, can be considered as an acceptance while it is yet in the hands of the drawee; and where he obliterates it before any communication made to the holder." From this it would appear, that Mr. J. Lawrence had taken the same view of this question as Pothier, who cites from La Serra, ch. 10. a case where the holder of a bill having left it for acceptance, the drawee, before he returned it, cancelled an acceptance which he had written and signed upon it, and it was adjudged that this acceptance was annulled; and observes, "La raison est, que le concours de volontés qui forme un "contrat, est un concours de volontés que les parties se sont reciproque-"ment déclarées; sans cela, la volonté d'une partie ne peut acquérir, "de droit à l'autre partie, ni par conséquent être irrévocable. Suivant "ces principes, pour que le contrat entre le propriétaire de la lettre "et celui sur qui elle est tirée, soit parfait, il ne suffit pas que celui-ci "ait eu pendant quelque temps la volonté d'accepter la lettre, et qu'il "ait écrit au bas qu'il l'acceptoit; tant qu'il n'a pas déclaré cette "volonté au porteur, le contrat n'est pas parfait; il peut changer de "volonté, et rayer son acceptation."—Traité du Contrat de Change, part. 1. ch. iii. § 3. pl. 44.—See also Emerigon Traité des Assurances, ch. ii. § 4. p. 45., who observes, that La Serra "pose en maxime, que "tant que l'acceptant est maitre de sa signature, c'est-à dire, qu'il n'a "pas délivré la lettre de change, il peut rayer son acceptation."—See also Stevenson on Bills, p. 162—164.

(70) Cox v. Troy, 5 Barnew. and Ald. 474. A bill on defendant and Co. for £938. 16*s.* 10*d.* payable sixty-one days after sight, was put into their bill box for acceptance the 24th of May, 1820; they wrote an acceptance upon it, and dated it 24th May, 1820; the bill was not called for till the 27th of May, and before that time the acceptance was

And before this decision it was adjudged, that if upon such a cancellation, the holder noted the bill for non-acceptance, he (71) precluded himself from insisting that the acceptance was binding.

And if an acceptance is struck out before a bill left for acceptance is called for, the drawee is not compellable to shew in evidence why it was struck out, or when, or by whom. (72)

And it makes no difference though the bill is left beyond the usual time with the drawee, if the delay is imputable not to the drawee but to the holder.

The obligation also of a complete acceptance may be (73) waived.

---

erased by inking it over: when, or by whom that was done, did not appear. Plaintiffs brought an action on the ground that the writing the acceptance bound the drawee, and that he could not afterwards cancel his acceptance: but on case, the court were clear the acceptance might be cancelled at any time before it was delivered out by the drawee, and they ordered the postea to be delivered to the defendant. Plaintiff had leave to turn the case into a special verdict. See also ante, p. 117. note (69).

(71) Bentinck v. Dorrien and another, 6 East. 199. This action which was by an endorsee against the defendants as acceptors of a bill, was referred; and the arbitrator, after reciting in his award that the plaintiff on the 31st of May, left the bill with the defendants for acceptance, that they signed an acceptance thereon, but that, on the 1st of June, and *before the bill was called for*, they cancelled that acceptance, and that the plaintiff thereupon noted the bill for non-acceptance, declared himself to be of opinion, that by such noting the plaintiff had precluded himself from insisting that the defendants had bound themselves to pay the bill, and therefore awarded in favor of the defendants. A rule nisi was obtained for setting aside this award, on the ground that the acceptance was irrevocable. But after cause shewn, the court held that whether such acceptance could or could not be revoked, the plaintiff had, at all events, by noting the bill for non-acceptance, precluded himself from contending that the acceptance was valid. Rule discharged. See Sproat v. Matthews, ante, p. 113. note (47).

(72) See Cox v. Troy, ante, p. 118.

(73) Vide Walpole v. Pulteney, and Black v. Peele, post. p. 120., and Mason v. Hunt, post. p. 120. note (76);—and in Dingwall v. Dunster, post. p. 123. note (84), the whole court held, that though nothing short of an express agreement would discharge the acceptor, an express agreement would.

Whatley v. Tricker, 1 Campb. 35. The endorsees of a bill, knowing that it had been accepted for the accommodation of the drawer, and possessing goods of the drawer's, from the produce of which they expected payment, said, (at a meeting of the acceptors' creditors) that "they looked to the drawer, and should not come upon the acceptors."

This waiver may be either expressed or implied.

An (74) agreement to consider an acceptance as at an end, or a (75) message to the acceptor upon an accommodation bill, that the business was settled with the drawer, and he need give himself no further trouble, is an express waiver; the receipt (76) of the known consideration of the acceptance, an implied one.

In consequence of which the latter assigned their property for the benefit of their creditors, and paid them 15*s.* in the pound. The drawer's goods, however, proved to be of little value, and he became insolvent, upon which the endorsees sued the acceptors. Lord Ellenborough said, that if the plaintiff's language amounted to an unconditional renunciation of all claim upon the acceptors, whereby the latter had entered into the arrangement with their creditors, the acceptors were discharged; if only to a conditional promise, not to resort to the acceptors, if satisfied elsewhere, they were not. The jury found for the plaintiffs.

(74) Walpole v. Pulteney, cited Dougl. 236, 237—248, 249. Walpole held a bill accepted by Pulteney, but agreed to consider his acceptance as at an end, and wrote in his bill-book, opposite the entry of this bill, "Mr. Pulteney's acceptance at an end." Walpole kept the bill from 1772 to 1775, without calling upon Pulteney, and then brought this action. The jury found a verdict for the plaintiff; but the court of exchequer thought the verdict wrong, and granted a new trial, upon which the jury found for the defendant.

(75) Black v. Peele, cit. Dougl. 236, 237—248, 249. Black arrested Peele as acceptor of a bill drawn by Dallas, but on finding that the acceptance was an accommodation one, his attorney took a security from Dallas, and sent word to Peele that he had settled with Dallas, and that Peele need give himself no further trouble; Dallas afterwards became bankrupt, upon which Black again sued Peele; but it was held, that as Black had in express words discharged Peele, the action could not be maintained.

(76) Mason v. Hunt, Dougl. 284. 297. ante p. 97. note (3). Rowland Hunt agreed that his partner, Thomas Hunt, should, on consignment of a cargo, and an order for its insurance, accept bills for £3,600. The cargo was consigned, the order for insurance given, and Thomas Hunt effected the insurance, but he refused to accept the bills; after some negotiation, the plaintiff being the holder, signed a memorandum, by which, after stating that the consignment had been made on account of the bills, and that the Hunts, being apprehensive that the net proceeds might not be sufficient to discharge them, had refused to accept, he accepted the bill of lading and policy, and undertook to apply the net proceeds, when in cash, as far as they would go, to the credit of the payee, in part payment of the bills; the plaintiff afterwards sued the Hunts; and insisted that Rowland Hunt's agreement was an acceptance; but after a verdict for the defendant, and time taken to consider upon a rule to shew cause why there should not be a new trial, the whole court was clear that by the memorandum the plaintiff had waived all right to insist on Rowland Hunt's agreement, for it was obvious that the whole consideration of the acceptance was the consignment, upon which there would be a commission, and the policy, and these the plaintiff had taken to himself.

But a declaration by the holder that he should look to the drawer for payment, and that he wanted no more of the acceptor than another debt, not connected with the bill, will not be sufficient to discharge the acceptor. (77)

Though in consequence of that declaration, the acceptor pays the other debt. (77)

If the holder of a bill receives a part of the money from the drawer, and takes a promise from him upon the back of the bill for the payment of the residue at an enlarged time, it (78) is for a jury to say whether this is not a waiver of the acceptance.

Where a bill has been accepted for the mere accommodation of the drawer, it has been held, that if the holder, knowing that circumstance, give time to the drawer, he (79) will discharge the acceptor.

---

(77) Parker v. Leigh, 2 Stark. 228. In an action against the acceptor on a bill for £300, the defendant proved that he owed plaintiff £700, or warrants of attorney, and that plaintiff had said, that as to the £300 bill, he should look to the drawer for that, and that he wanted no more from defendant that what was included in the warrants of attorney, and that in consequence of this declaration, defendant paid plaintiff what was included in the warrants of attorney; but Lord Ellenborough held, that as plaintiff had not expressly renounced all claim upon this acceptance, it continued binding, and the plaintiff had a verdict.

(78) Ellis v. Galindo, B. R. M. 24 Geo. 3. cited Dougl. 250. note. James Galindo drew upon his brother for £30 in favor of the plaintiff; when the bill became due, James paid the plaintiff £3 15*s.* 4*d.* and endorsed a promise to pay the remainder in three months. Three years elapsed, and then the plaintiff sued the drawee upon his acceptance. Lord Mansfield thought the defendant discharged, and nonsuited the plaintiff. An application was made for a new trial, when Lord Mansfield said, he thought the case did not interfere with that of Dingwall v. Dunster, but a rule to shew cause was granted; after cause was shewn, Lord Mansfield said, "The doubt is, whether the question should not have been left to the jury, it being a question of intention arising out of the circumstances." Willes J. thought it should have been left to the jury; and per Buller J. "I rather think the case should have gone to the jury; but I am not therefore of opinion that there ought to be a new trial; the endorsement could not have been meant as an additional security, for the drawer was equally liable before. I should have left the question to the jury, but with very strong observations; and as the demand is so small, I do not think there ought to be a new trial." Rule discharged.

(79) Laxton v. Peat, 2 Campb. N. P. C. 185. The holder of a bill, knowing that it had been accepted for the accommodation of the drawer, received part payment from the drawer, and gave him time for pay-

But this has been doubted. (80) (81) (82)

Especially if the holder, when he took the bill, did not know it was an accommodation acceptance. (81)

Or if it were duly presented, when due, to the acceptor, and he promised payment. (82)

Telling an accommodation acceptor that he shall not be troubled about the bill, will not discharge him, though the party knew him to be an accommodation acceptor only, if such party held for value. (83)

---

ment of the remainder; he now sued the acceptor; but Lord Ellenborough held, that the acceptor was a mere surety, and by time having been given to the principal, was discharged. Nonsuit.

(80) Raggett v. Axmore, 4 Taunt. 730. In an action against the acceptor of a bill, motion for new trial, on the ground that it was an accommodation acceptance, and that the holder had given time to the drawer. Sed per Mansfield C. J. there was no sufficient evidence that it was an accommodation acceptance; nevertheless, excepting in the case in Campbell, it never was known that any thing passing between other parties could discharge an acceptor; but it is unnecessary to decide that question.

(81) Fentum v. Pocock, 5 Taunt. 192. Endorsee against acceptor, on bill drawn by Beazley. Defence, that plaintiff had taken a cognovit from Beazley, payable at a future day, without defendant's privity or consent; that defendant's was a mere accommodation acceptance, and that plaintiff knew it was so when he took the cognovit from Beazley: Mansfield C. J. thought this no answer to the action; and verdict for plaintiff. On rule nisi for nonsuit, and cause shewn, two cases were cited, in which Lord Ellenborough, under similar circumstances, held the acceptor discharged; but the court thought those cases wrong; and rule discharged. Mansfield, C. J. noticed that plaintiff did not know, when he took the bill, that it was an accommodation acceptance, but he disclaimed proceeding on that ground.

(82) Kerrison v. Cooke, 3 Campb. 362. Endorsee against acceptor. Defence, that it was an accommodation acceptance to accommodate the drawer, that plaintiff knew it, and that on the bill's becoming due, plaintiff gave time to the drawer without the concurrence of defendant; and Laxton v. Peat was cited as in point: when the bill was due it was presented to defendant, and he promised payment; per Gibbs J. "Grave doubts have been entertained of Laxton v. Peat, and this case may be distinguished from it; here payment is demanded of defendant, and he promises payment. I think the giving time under these circumstances to the drawer did not discharge the acceptor." Verdict for plaintiff.

Sed vide Adams v. Gregg—the next case.

(83) Adams v. Gregg, 2 Stark. 531. Defendant accepted a bill to accommodate Holmes, and plaintiff knew it; Holmes paid it to plaintiff for an old debt; when it became due, defendant could not pay it, and one Jones gave plaintiff the amount, on a stipulation that he should, if necessary, stand in plaintiff's situation. Defendant asked Jones to give up the bill, which he refused, but he said defendant should not be troubled about it. Jones afterwards sued defendant in plaintiff's name; defend-

But a neglect to call upon an acceptor, or an indulgence to any of the other parties, though for ever so long a time, shall (84) not be considered as a waiver.

If the holder of a bill agree not to sue the acceptor, upon his making an affidavit that the acceptance is a forgery, he will be (85) precluded from suing him, if such affidavit be made and sworn, though it be false.

---

ant insisted she was discharged. Abbott C. J. seemed to think she would have been, had Jones given time to the drawer, or disabled himself for a moment from suing him; but he thought Jones's declaration that defendant should not be troubled, no discharge, and plaintiff had a verdict.

(84) Dingwall v. Dunster, Dougl. 235. 247. Dunster lent Wheate his acceptance, which became due 13th December, 1774; it was then in the hands of Dingwall, but he, finding that Wheate was the real debtor, wrote to his attorney in February and November, 1775, for payment, received interest upon the bill from Wheate, and suffered several years to elapse without calling on Dunster; on 13th of February, 1775, Dunster wrote to thank Dingwall for not proceeding against him, and said he had been informed by a person Dingwall had sent, that Wheate had taken up the bill; but Dingwall took no notice of this letter: he afterwards sued Dunster, for whom the jury found; but upon a rule to shew cause why there should not be a new trial, the whole court held there was nothing in the plaintiff's conduct to discharge Dunster; that it meant nothing more than an indulgence to him, and that he would try to recover from the drawer if he could; but by Lord Mansfield, no use had been made of the defendant's letter; probably the fact did not warrant him in asserting that a person the plaintiff sent had told him Wheate had taken up the bill; had the plaintiff by any thing in his conduct, confirmed him in such a belief, it might have altered the case.

Anderson v. Cleveland, 13 East's Rep. 430. n. In an action by an endorsee against the acceptor of a bill, no demand was proved till three months after the bill was due, and when the drawer had become insolvent. But by Lord Mansfield, the acceptor of a bill, or maker of a note, always remains liable. The acceptance is proof of having assets in his hands, and he ought never to part with them, unless he be sure that the bill is paid by the drawer.

(85) Stevens v. Thacker, Peake, N. P. C. 187. The plaintiff, who was endorsee of a bill, presented it to the defendant, as acceptor, for payment. The defendant said the acceptance was a forgery, and offered to make an affidavit that he had never accepted the bill. The plaintiff at first agreed not to sue him, if he would make such affidavit; but being afterwards convinced that the defendant had accepted the bill, refused to receive the affidavit, and brought this action. The affidavit had been engrossed, but not sworn. It was urged, that the plaintiff could not recede from his agreement. But Lord Kenyon said, that had the affidavit been sworn, he should have held that the defendant had discharged himself from this action, though such affidavit had been false. But not having been sworn, the defendant was still liable, unless he could prove the acceptance a forgery. Verdict for the plaintiff.

CHAP. V.

Presentment and Notice.

The receipt of a bill or note implies an undertaking from the receiver to (1) every party to the bill or note who would be entitled to bring an action on paying it, to (2) present in proper time the one, where necessary, for acceptance, and each for payment, to (3) allow no extra time for payment, and to give (4) notice without delay to such person of a failure in the attempt to procure a proper acceptance or payment; and a (5) default in any of these respects will discharge such person from all responsibility on account of a non-acceptance or non-payment, and unless (6) the bill or note were on an improper stamp, make it (7) operate as a satisfaction of any debt or demand for which it was given.

[Where a bill or note is endorsed after it is due, though the strict rules as to demand and notice do not apply, yet in order to charge the person then endorsing it, a subsequent

---

(1) Vide post.
(2) Vide post.
(3) Vide Tindal v. Brown, post.
(4) Vide post.
(5) Vide post.
Syderbottom v. Smith, Str. 649. In an action against the endorser of a note, Eyre, C. J. of the Common Pleas, directed the jury to find for the defendant, because the plaintiff had not proved diligence to get the money from the maker; being of *the old* opinion that the endorser only warrants upon default of the maker.

Gee v. Brown, Str. 792. The holder of an inland bill gave the acceptor time, by intervals, from 14th of May, when the bill became due, to 7th of June, and then sued the drawer; but their being no notice to him, Eyre, C. J. held the loss ought to fall on the plaintiff.

(6) See Wilson v. Vysar, ante, p. 55.

(7) By 3 and 4 Anne, c. 9. § 7. It is enacted, that if any person doth accept any such bill of exchange, for and in satisfaction of any former debt, or sum of money formerly due unto him, the same shall be accounted and esteemed a full and complete payment of such debt, if such person accepting of any such bill for his debt, doth not take his due course to obtain payment thereof, by endeavoring to get the same accepted and paid, and make his protest as aforesaid, either for non-acceptance or non-payment thereof.

demand must be made on the drawee or maker, within a reasonable time, and notice given to the endorser. (*a*)

And in such a case the want of a proper presentment and notice, is not excused by the holder of the note's using due diligence to collect it of the maker, even if the endorser knows that the money has not been paid by the maker. (*b*)

A waiver by an endorser of a bill or note of all right to notice, does not excuse the holder from making a presentment on the drawee or maker. (*c*) (*d*)

It has been doubted in New York whether an action could be brought against an incorporated bank on one of its own notes, without making a previous presentment for payment. (*e*)]

The presentment is to be made where the bill or note is payable.

[(*a*) Ecfert v. Des Coudres, 1 S. Car. R. 69; Rugely v. Davidson, 2 S. Car. R. 33; Dwight v. Emerson, 2 N. Hamp. R. 159; M'Kinney v. Crawford, 8 Serg. & Raw. 351. Berry v. Robinson, 9 Johns. R. 121. Swift C. J. said, "The endorsement of a bill or note after due is equivalent to drawing a new bill payable at sight; and demand must be made by the endorsee of the drawee of the bill or maker of the note, and notice given to the endorser, as in cases of bills payable at sight." Bishop v. Dexter, 2 Conn. R. 419.]

[(*b*) M'Kinney v. Crawford, 8 Serg. & Raw. 351.]

[(*c*) Berkshire Bank v. Jones, 6 Mass. R. 524.]

[(*d*) Where the selectmen of a town drew an order upon their town treasurer, it was held that no action could be maintained against the town, without proving a presentment for payment to the treasurer. Mellen C. J. delivered the opinion of the court. "The case may be compared to that of a draft by a man on his banker; or a note payable at his banker's, or by his agent, in which cases it seems settled that the draft or note must be presented at the place appointed." Varner v. Nobleborough, 2 Greenleaf, 121.]

[(*e*) In the case of the Bank of Niagara v. M'Cracken, the defendant, being sued as maker of a note, was allowed to set off notes of the bank which he held, and which he had tendered in payment of his own note, without proving a presentment of them for payment; and Woodworth J., who delivered the opinion of the Court, said, that as the notes were not payable at any particular place, an action might have been sustained on them without a demand at the bank. 18 Johns. R. 493. But in a subsequent case, the court appear to consider the question as to the necessity of a presentment of a bank note, in order to charge the bank, as still open; and they consider that M'Cracken's having tendered the notes of the bank in payment of his own note, was equivalent to a demand of payment. Jefferson County Bank v. Chapman, 19 Johns. R. 322.]

If the drawee or maker cannot be found at the place where the bill or note is payable, and it appears that he never lived there, or has (8) absconded, the blll or note is to be considered as dishonored, especially if he cannot be heard of at any of the banking-houses there ; (9) if he has only removed, the holder (10) must endeavor to find out to what place he has removed, and make the presentment there.

[Where no place of payment is specified, in a bill or note, a presentment at the residence of the drawee or maker, is sufficient, even if he be out of town at the time. (*a*)

---

(8) Anon. Lord Raym. 743. "The custom of merchants is, that if B., upon whom a bill of exchange is drawn, absconds before the day of payment, the man to whom it is payable may protest it, to have better security for the payment, and to give notice to the drawer of the absconding of B." Proved by merchants at Guildhall, Tr. 6 W. and M., before Treby C. J.

[In a case in Massachusetts, the court held that where the maker of a note, having become insolvent, left the country before it became due, the plaintiff was excused from demanding payment of him, in order to charge the endorsers. Widgery v. Munroe, 6 Mass. R. 449.

And in another case, the same court held that where the maker of a note absconded before it became due, the holder was discharged from his obligation to make a presentment, in order to charge the endorser. Putnam v. Sullivan, 4 Mass. R. 46.

Van Ness, J. in a case in New York decided that where the maker of a note was notoriously absent in a foreign country, there was no need of showing diligent inquiry for him, or of making a demand at his last place of residence or business. But in this case it appeared that the maker of the note at the time it fell due was actually resident in a foreign country, having no domicil or place of business in New York. Cummings v. Fisher, Anth. N. P. 1.]

(9) See Hardy v. Woodroffe, post.

(10) Collins v. Butler, Str. 1087. The maker of a note shut up his house before the note became due, and in an action against an endorser, the question was, whether the plaintiff had shewn sufficient in proving that the house was shut up? and Lee C. J. thought not, but that he should have given in evidence that he inquired after the maker, or attempted to find him out. Vide Bateman v. Joseph, p. 228. n. (105).

[Where the residence of the maker of a note is not known to the holder, the presumption is, that he resides at the place where the note is dated, and that is the proper place to make inquiry for him. Duncan v. M'Cullough, 4 Serg. & Raw. 480.

See also Rugely v. Davidson, 2 S. Car. R. 33. as to the diligence to be used to make a demand upon the maker of a note, and to ascertain the place to which he has removed.]

[(*a*) Moodie v. Morrall, 1 S. Car. R. 367.

But a demand of payment at a place where the maker of a note once

So a presentment at his place of business is sufficient, if made in business hours, even if it be shut, and no person left there to answer inquiries. (*a*)

If the maker of a note where no place of payment is specified, remove from his place of residence, after the making of the note, and before it becomes due, to another place within the same State or government, a demand must still be made upon him, in order to charge an endorser, (*b*) but if he removes to a place out of the State or government, no presentment is necessary. (*c*)]

---

boarded, he residing at another place at the time of the demand, is altogether nugatory. Freeman v. Boynton, 7 Mass. R. 483.

So a demand at a store formerly occupied by the maker of a note, but not occupied by him at the time of the demand, is not sufficient to charge an endorser. Bond v. Farnham, 5 Mass. R. 170.]

[(*a*) Shed v. Brett, 1 Pick. 413.]

[(*b*) In an action against the endorser of a note, he pleaded specially, that the maker of the note had, shortly after the making thereof, and before it became payable, removed from the city of New York to Kingston in Ulster county, in the same State, there permanently to reside, which was well known to the plaintiff, and that no demand had been made upon the maker. Demurrer. Thompson C. J. delivered the opinion of the court. "In a case decided in this court, the drawer of the note had removed to Canada; the note was drawn and dated at Albany, though not made payable at any particular place, it was held that a demand at Albany was sufficient to charge the endorser." "I am inclined to think where a note is not made payable at any particular place, and the maker has a known and permanent residence within the State, the holder is bound to make a demand at such residence. As the demurrer, therefore, in this case admits the permanent residence of the maker to have been at Kingston, when the note fell due, and that known to the plaintiff, he was bound to demand payment of the note at that place; and not having done so the endorser is discharged." Judgment for defendant. Anderson v. Drake, 14 Johns. R. 114.]

[(*c*) In an action against the endorser of a note, it appeared, that when the note was made, and until within ten days of its falling due, the maker was a housekeeper in the District of Columbia, but that he then removed into the State of Maryland, to a place about nine miles out of the district. The holder of the note did not know the place to which the maker had removed. A notary called to present the note at the former place of residence of the maker, and protested it for non-payment; but it did not appear that any inquiries were made to ascertain where he then resided. Johnson J. delivered the opinion of the court. "The party must be considered as lying under the same obligations, as if, having made inquiry, he had ascertained that the maker had removed to a distance of nine miles, and into another jurisdiction. We think that reason and convenience are in favor of sustaining the doctrine that such a removal is an excuse from actual demand. No other rule can be laid down

If on a presentment, it appears that the drawee or maker is dead, the holder (11) should inquire after his personal representative, and if he lives within a reasonable distance, present the bill or note to him.

If in the absence of a drawee, a bill has been accepted by his agent, and at the time when the bill becomes due, the drawee be still absent, presentment for payment (12) should be made to such agent.

If a bill or note is made payable at a banker's, it is (13) sufficient to present it for payment at the banker's, and if the banker is himself the holder, it is (13) sufficient for him to see whether he has effects in hand.

[So if a bill or note be payable at a particular place, if the bill or note is at that place on the day of payment, and any person there authorized to receive payment and give up the note, it is sufficient to charge the endorser. (*a*)

---

which will not leave too much latitude as to place and distance." M'Gruder v. Bank of Washington 9 Wheat. R. 598.

See also Anderson v. Drake, supra.]

(11) Molloy, B. 2. c. 10. § 34. "If a bill be accepted, and the party dies, yet there must be a demand made of his executors or administrators: and in default of payment, a protest must be made."

(12) See Philips v. Astling, post.

(13) Saunderson and others v. Judge, 2 H. Bl. 509. A note made payable at the plaintiffs' was endorsed to them; when it became due, the maker having no effects in their hands, they wrote to one of the endorsers to say it was not honored, and afterwards brought an action against him; but it appearing that they had made no demand on the maker, they were nonsuited; on shewing cause, however against a rule for a new trial, the court held, that it was sufficient to present the note where the maker made it payable, and as the persons at whose house it was made payable were themselves the holders, it was sufficient for them to refer to their books, and see whether they had effects in hand; and a new trial was granted.

[(*a*) In a suit by the Berkshire Bank against the endorser of a note payable at the Berkshire Bank, Sedgwick J. at the trial nonsuited the plaintiffs because there was no proof of a demand on the promiser. Parsons C. J. delivered the opinion of the court. "As the plaintiffs held this note, we must presume it was in their bank; and there it was made payable. The nonsuit ought to be set aside; and if on the trial the plaintiffs can show that on the day of payment the note was at the bank, and that the servants or officers of the plaintiffs were there during the usual bank hours, to receive payment and give up the note, they will be entitled to recover, as by the terms of the note, they were not holden to demand

And the endorser is discharged if the note is not at the place on the day of payment, although a personal demand is made on the maker. (*a*)]

If a bill or note is made payable at a particular house, that house is the proper place at which to make the presentment, whether such house be mentioned in the body of the bill or note, or in a marginal note only, or in the acceptance only. (14)

And if such house be mentioned in the body of a note, a presentment there is necessary even to charge the maker. (15) (*b*).

---

payment but at the bank, which was impracticable, through the default of the maker." Berkshire Bank v. Jones, 6 Mass. R. 524.

See also Woodbridge v. Brigham, infra, and Bank of America v. Woodworth, post, p. 134. Lincoln & Kennebec Bank, v. Page, 9 Mass. R. 155, seems contra.

(*a*) In an action against the endorsers of a note payable at the Hartford Bank, it appeared that the note was not at the Hartford Bank, or in the possession of any officers of the Bank, or presented there by any person, on the day it became payable, or payment seasonably demanded of the maker personally. The court held that the action could not be maintained. Parker, C. J. delivered the opinion of the court. "The general rule is, that a demand must be made on the maker of the note, *on the day it falls due.* The exception is, that when the note is payable at a particular place, such demand need not be made, if the holder, or any one for him is *at the place*, with the note, so that he may receive the money and give up the note. This exception is to be strictly complied with, in order to charge the endorser, without a demand upon the maker." Woodbridge v. Brigham, 13 Mass. R. 556. This case was reported erroneously in 12 Mass R. 403.]

(14) Ambrose v. Hopwood, 2 Taunt. 61. In an action against the drawer of a bill, the declaration stated the bill to have been accepted by the drawee, payable at Messrs. Freeman's and Co., No. 6. Church-street, Bermondsey, Southwark, and averred that the bill was in due manner presented to them for payment, not saying in *Church-street*, &c. and dishonored. On special demurrer for other causes (which were abandoned) it was contended that there was no due averment of a presentment for payment, and that this objection, which was *not one of the causes* assigned, went to the substance of the case. The court held the objection fatal, but permitted the plaintiff to amend on payment of costs.

See Garnett v. Woodcock, 1 Stark. 475.

(15) Sanderson v. Bowes and others, B. R. M. 52 Geo. III. In an action on twelve country bank notes, for £1. 1*s.* each, issued by the defendants from their banking house at Workington, the declaration contained a count upon each note, stating that the defendants made a certain promissory note, "and thereby, on demand, promised to pay at the banking house at Workington, to one R. N. or bearer," the sum

And so it is if it be printed on the note, though by way of memorandum only. (16)

---

of £1. 1*s.*; and that thereby the defendants became liable, and promised to pay, according to the tenor and effect of the note. There was, however, no averment of a presentment for, or demand of, payment at the banking house; but only the usual allegation, that the defendants, "although often requested," (without saying where) had refused to pay. To these counts there was a general demurrer and joinder; and after argument, the court held, that there being no privity between these parties but in respect of the note, and that being a contract to pay at a particular place, a demand of payment at that place was in the nature of a condition precedent to the plaintiff's right to recover; and there being no averment of such demand, the defendants were entitled to judgment; and they gave judgment accordingly.

Dickinson v. Bowes, 16 East. 110. Action against the makers on fifty-six guinea notes; they were dated Workington Bank, and ran thus: "On demand I promise to pay at the banking house here to R. W. or bearer, the sum of one guinea, value received." Proof was given that thirty-two were presented for payment at the banking house at Workington, and payment refused; but there was no such proof as to the to the other twenty-four, and on point saved, the court held that the plaintiff could only recover in respect to the thirty-two, and judgment accordingly.

Howe v. Bowes, 16 East. 112. Action on a similar note for five guineas against the makers, instead of averring presentment plaintiff alleged that defendants became insolvent, and ceased and wholly declined and refused to pay at the banking house aforesaid, the sum specified in any note issued by them, and he proved that the shop was shut up and no notes paid there for some time before the action; the jury considered this proof as making out the averment, and verdict for plaintiff: and on rule nisi to set aside the verdict, and cause shewn, the court thought the verdict right; the shutting up the shop was in substance a refusal to make any payments there, and rule discharged. But on error, the Exchequer chamber thought the allegations in the declaration not sufficient to excuse a presentment, and reversed the judgment. 5 Taunt. 30.

[But it has been held in New York that a presentment of a bill of exchange at the place where it is payable is not necessary in order to charge the acceptor. In an action against the acceptor of an inland bill made payable at the Bank of Utica, the declaration did not state any presentment for payment at the bank; and was demurred to on that account. Spencer C. J. delivered the opinion of the Court. "I must think that the time and place of payment are merely modal, forming no essential part of the contract; that it is incumbent on the defendant whether the payee was at the place at the time appointed or not, to show in his defence, that he was there ready and willing to pay, and that the payee did not come, &c.; that the consequences of the absence of the payee under such circumstances, unless he makes a subsequent special demand, and there be then a refusal, are merely that he must be content with receiving the sum originally payable, and if he sue without having made a special demand, he loses all claim to damages and costs, and will himself be subject to them. This I consider not only entirely equitable between the parties, but the old and settled law

And if such house be mentioned in an acceptance, and the acceptance makes the bill payable there *and not otherwise or elsewhere*, a presentment there will be necessary to charge the acceptor. (17)

---

of the land, and such was the opinion of the court in Foden v. Sharp," (4 Johns. R. 183, which see.) Yates and Platt, Js. concurred; Van Ness and Woodworth, Js. dissented. Judgment for plaintiff. Walcott v. Van Santvoord, 17 Johns. R. 248.

And in Massachusetts it appears to have been held that where a note is made payable at a particular place, no presentment at that place is necessary in order to charge the maker. In an action against the maker of a note payable at the Penobscot Bank, the plaintiff alleged in his declaration that the promisee was at the bank on the day the note fell due, and demanded payment; the defendant pleaded that the said promisee was not then ready or present at the bank to receive payment, and did not demand payment of the defendant; and tendered an issue to the country. On demurrer the plea was adjudged insufficient. And the Court says, "The holder of the note's not being present at the time and place appointed for payment, is no bar to an action on a promise to pay money: and the issue tendered was an immaterial one." Ruggles v. Patten, 8 Mass. R. 480.]

[(*b*) In a case in New York, where a note was made payable at a particular bank, and a demand was made on the maker personally and not at the bank, and no objection was made to the demand, it was held that the demand was sufficient. This however was not an action against an endorser, but was a case in which one partner having given his own note for a partnership debt, the question was, the note being unpaid, whether the holder had used such diligence to obtain payment of the note, as would enable him to maintain a suit for the original demand against the partnership. Herring v. Sanger, 3 Johns. Cas. 71.]

(16) Trecothick v. Edwin, 1 Stark. 468. The whole of a note, except the names of the parties, sum, and date, was printed; and at the bottom was printed, "at Barclay, Tritton, and Co.'s." In an action against the maker, a question was made whether it was necessary to prove a presentment at Barclay and Co.'s; and Lord Ellenborough held it was, because the stipulation being printed, must have been on the note at the time the note was made, and was to be considered part of the note. The proof was then given, and the plaintiff had a verdict.

(17) See 1 and 2 Geo. 4. ante, p. 115.

Callaghan v. Aylett, 3 Taunt. 397., 2 Campb. 549. In an action against the acceptor of a bill, it appeared that the bill was accepted, payable at Messrs. Ramsbottoms', bankers, London; and two objections were taken to the plaintiff's right to recover; first, that there was a variance between the acceptance proved, which was a special one, and that averred in the declaration, which was general; and secondly, that there was no proof of a presentment for payment at the place where the bill, by the acceptance, had been made payable. A verdict was found for the plaintiff, subject to the opinion of the court upon these points, which were reserved. A rule nisi to set aside this verdict and enter a nonsuit, was obtained; and after cause shewn, the court (Mansfield C. J. absente) held, that the place where a bill is made payable must be considered as part of the contract between the acceptor and the

But where a particular house is mentioned in a note by way of marginal memorandum only, presentment at that house may not be necessary to charge the maker; (18)

---

holder; that this was a special and qualified acceptance, binding the acceptor to pay at Ramsbottom's, and not universally. They said, it seemed fair that when a party had provided funds at his banker's for the due satisfaction of a bill, he should be allowed to protect himself from the risk of being arrested upon it by a malicious creditor. They referred to Parker v. Gordon, 7 East. 385., and said it could make no difference (for this purpose) whether the action were against the drawer or acceptor. Rule absolute.

Gammon v. Schmoll, 5 Taunt. 344. Bill directed to defendant, Bath: the declaration alleged that he accepted it, "payable at Batson's, London;" there was no averment of a presentment at Batson's. Demurrer on that ground; and after argument, the court held the averment essential, and the declaration, for want of it, bad.

Rowe v. Young, 2 Brod. 165. Bill directed to defendant at Torpoint, Devon: the declaration alleged that he accepted it, payable at Sir John Perring and Co.'s, bankers, London: the action was by an endorsee; and on error, objection that there was no averment of presentment at Sir John Perring's, and the House of Lords held the objection fatal; and judgment for plaintiff below reversed.

[Bishop v. Chitty, Str. 1195. Chitty, the drawee of a bill, wrote upon it, by way of acceptance, "Messrs. Caswell and Mount pay this bill when due for Thomas Chitty:" it became due 2d of January, 1741: Caswell and Mount paid till the 19th, when they stopped; and no notice was given to Chitty of its non-payment till the 21st; and Lee C. J. held that Chitty was discharged, for though the holder might have refused this acceptance, he had agreed to it, and it was in nature of a draught, which is considered as payment when a reasonable time to receive it in has clapsed. However, in Smith v. De la Fontaine, B. R. T. 25 Geo. 3., where an action was brought against the acceptor of a bill upon an acceptance to pay at his banker's, and the plaintiff could not prove a presentment at the banker's, notwithstanding which the jury found for him; the court held the proof unnecessary, and refused to grant a new trial. Bishop v. Chitty, was cited.]

(18) In Wild v. Rennards, 1 Campb. N. P. C. 425. n. Bayley J. held, that if a prommissory note be made payable at a particular place, there is no necessity for proving, in an action against the maker, that it has been presented there for payment. And upon this case being cited in Sanderson v. Bowes, Bayley J. said, that as far as he could recollect, the place was not incorporated with the body of the note; it was only mentioned in a memorandum at the bottom. And in Callaghan v. Aylett, 2 Campb. N. P. C. 551, and Sanderson v. Judge, 2 H. Bl. 509., the same distinction is taken.

Price v. Mitchell, 4 Campb. 200. At the bottom of a note was written, "At Vere and Co's, 77, Lombard-street." In an action against the maker, it was urged that plaintiff ought to prove a presentment at Vere and Co.'s; but as the direction was only at the foot of the note, and not part of the note, Gibbs C. J. thought otherwise, and the plaintiff had a verdict.

Nor is it, (since 1 and 2 Geo. 4. c. 78., on acceptances made after 1st August, 1821,) to charge an acceptor, where the acceptance mentions that house without further expressions to make it the exclusive place of payment. (19)

And where a bill is so accepted as to make it necessary even to charge the acceptor that it should be presented for payment at a particular place, a neglect to present it there the very day it becomes due will not discharge the acceptor, unless the money is lost in consequence of such neglect. (20)

If the money is lost in consequence, it may. (20)

[If the maker of a note appoint a particular place at which it may be presented for payment, a presentment for payment at that place will be sufficient to charge an endorser, (*a*) even if the place of payment is appointed by the

---

(19) See 1 and 2 Geo. 4. ante p. 115.

Fenton v. Goundry, 13 East's Rep. 459. Drawer against acceptor of a bill. The declaration stated, that the defendant accepted the bill, payable at Sykes and Co.'s, and thereby became liable and promised to pay according to the tenor and effect of the bill and of his acceptance. There was no averment of a presentment for payment at Sykes and Co.'s, nor of any demand upon the defendant other than the common allegation that the defendant, "although often requested," had not paid the bill. The defendant demurred specially, and assigned for cause, the want of an averment of a due presentment for payment. And after argument, the court (Le Blanc J. absente) held, that the place mentioned in the acceptance was only an intimation to the holder where the acceptor was to be found; that it formed no part of the contract that the bill should be presented there; and that the acceptance, though stated to be payable at a particular place, bound the party to pay the bill generally and universally. The court, however, being desirous of looking into the case of Callaghan v. Aylett, which was cited, gave judgment nisi for the plaintiff; but they did not mention the case again in the course of the term, and the judgment therefore stood for the plaintiff.

Head v. Sewell, Holt, 363. Action against acceptor on acceptance payable at Messrs. Harrisons', Picket-street. Gibbs C. J. held proof of presentment at that place not necessary.

(20) Rhodes v. Gent, 5 Barnew. 244. In an action on an acceptance, payable, when due, at Messrs. P. and H.'s. bankers, London, it was proved that the bill was presented for payment at Messrs. P and H.'s. but that such presentment was not until several days after the bill became due. Abbott C. J. thought the plaintiff nevertheless entitled to a verdict; and on motion to set aside the verdict, all the judges in court, viz. Abbott C. J., and Holroyd and Best Js., held, that as the bill had been presented at the banker's, and the non-payment arose not because the bankers had failed, but from some other cause, and the acceptor was not prejudiced by the postponement of the presentment, such postponement was no defence to him; and a rule was refused.

[(*a*) In an action against the endorser of a note, it appeared that notices according to the forms of banks in Boston were left for the maker

maker by a memorandum on the note made subsequently to the endorsement, and without the knowledge or consent of the endorser. (*a*)]

If a check upon a banker be lodged with another banker, a presentment by the latter at the clearing house is (21) sufficient.

---

and endorser, at one Metcalf's shop in Cornhill, Boston, by direction of the maker and endorser respectively. The court held the demand and notice sufficient. Curia. "The agreement of the promiser that notice left for him at a certain shop in Boston should be equivalent to a more formal demand upon him, removed the necessity of resorting to his house or place of business, to make such demand; and his failure to pay on such notice rendered the endorser, who had seasonable information, absolutely liable." State Bank v. Hurd, 12 Mass. R. 172. See also Whitwell v. Johnson, post.]

[(*a*) Woodworth endorsed a note made by Kane, payable in sixty days, for Kane's accommodation. After the note was made and endorsed, Kane, without the consent or knowledge of Woodworth, wrote in the margin, "Payable at the Bank of America, James Kane." In a suit against Woodworth as endorser, a presentment at the Bank of America and notice to him were proved; and the Supreme Court of New York held that he was liable. Spencer C. J. delivered the opinion of the Court. "On the ground that the memorandum in the margin of the note in this case, did not alter the contract, as between the immediate parties to the note; as it was an appointment of the place where the maker would pay the note; and as I think, upon authority that has not and cannot be shaken, the maker had a right to make such appointment, a demand of payment at the Bank of America was sufficient." But he questioned whether appointing a very distant place of payment without the knowledge of the endorser, might not be a fraud upon him, so as to discharge him from his liability. Bank of America v. Woodworth, 18 Johns. R. 315.

This case was afterwards reversed by the Court of Errors, on the ground, as it seems, that the memorandum made by Kane was a material alteration of the contract, and so discharged the endorser; or that if the alteration was not material, and the original contract remained untouched, then there was no sufficient demand on the maker. The Chancellor, Kent, was in favor of affirming the opinion of the Supreme Court. His opinion contains a very elaborate examination of the cases. He took the following positions. 1. That the plaintiffs being *bonâ fide* endorsees, who received the note without knowing of any dissent to the memorandum on the part of the endorser, were only required to make a demand at the place named in the memorandum. 2. That the note endorsed was like an inland bill, and therefore that the maker of the note after the bill was returned to him, had a right to appoint a place for payment, as none was mentioned in the note, in the same manner as the acceptor of a bill might designate a place for payment. 3. That the memorandum was no part of the contract, but was sufficient to justify the holder in calling at such a place for payment, and being refused he had a right to look to the endorser. Eighteen senators were for reversing; nine concurred with the chancellor. Woodworth v. Bank of America, 19 Johns. R. 391.]

(21) See Robson v. Bennett, post. p. 195, n. (47)

[Where a bill is drawn upon a person resident in A, but is made payable in B, a large city, without specifying any particular place in B, it is sufficient for the holder in order to charge the prior parties, either to present the bill to the drawee for payment at his place of residence, or to have the bill at the place where it is payable on the day of payment, and there have it protested without making any inquiry for the drawee. (*a*)]

A presentment should be made at a seasonable time.

If by the known custom of any place, bills and notes are only payable within limited hours, a presentment *there* out of those hours is unreasonable.

And so is a presentment out of the hours of business to a

[(*a*) An action was brought against the endorsers of a foreign bill drawn upon Rathbone, Hughes, and Duncan, merchants at Liverpool, payable sixty days after sight in London. Acceptance had been refused, and the declaration averred that when the bill was due, it was presented to the drawees at Liverpool, who refused to pay the same, and that it was then protested at Liverpool for non-payment. Demurrer, because the declaration did not allege a presentment for payment in London, or diligence to find any person to whom to present the bill for payment, or a protest in London. Kent C. J. delivered the opinion of the Court. "A good cause of action arose upon the protest for non-acceptance; and were we to admit that the subsequent demand of payment and protest for non-payment were void acts, by being made at Liverpool, that part of the declaration alleging the subsequent demand and protest might be rejected upon demurrer as surplusage. But we are of opinion that at no place of payment in London was designated, the demand of payment and protest for non-payment, were well made upon the drawees personally, at Liverpool. A general refusal to pay was a refusal to pay according to the face of the bill. It was equivalent to a refusal to pay in London." Mason v. Franklin, 3 Johns. R. 202.

In another action against the drawer of a bill drawn upon Rathbone, Hughes, and Duncan of Liverpool, payable in London, in which case also the bill was not accepted, the declaration did not state a presentment for payment to the drawees in Liverpool, but averred that the bill when payable was protested at London for non-payment, and that the holders did not know where to present the same for payment in London. Demurrer, because the plaintiffs did not allege a presentment of the bill to the drawees for payment, or any endeavors to find the drawees or inquiries made for them. Kent C. J. delivered the opinion of the Court. "It was not incumbent upon the plaintiffs to state that inquiry was made in London for the drawees. *Lex neminem cogit ad vana seu inutilia.* An attempt to search for them in such a city as London would have been without any object or effect. Nor were the holders bound to go elsewhere to seek the drawees, as the bill had directed the payment to be in London. They were in London on the day of payment ready to

person of a particular description, as a (22) banker in a place where, by the known custom of that place, all persons of his description begin and leave off business at stated hours. (*a*)

But to an acceptor not so circumstanced (23), eight

---

receive payment; and they did all that they were enabled to do, they caused the bill to be there protested." Boot v. Franklin, 3 Johns. R. 208.]

(22) Parker v. Gordon, 7 East's Rep. 385. The drawee accepted the bill, payable at Davison and Co.'s, his bankers; at the part of the town where Davison and Co. lived, bankers shut up at six o'clock. The bill was not presented for payment until after six, when the shop was shut up, and the clerks gone. In an action against the drawer, Lord Ellenborough held that this was not a good presentment, and nonsuited the plaintiff: and on motion for a new trial, the court held, that if a party took an acceptance payable at a banker's, he bound himself to present the bill during the banking hours; and therefore rule refused.

N. Lawrence and Le Blanc Js. said, the holder was not bound to take such an acceptance.

Elford v. Tred, 1 Maule and Selw. 28. The drawee accepted a bill, payable at his bankers', Hodsoll and Co.; the only evidence of a presentment was by a notary's clerk, between half after six and seven in the evening: the banking-house was then shut, and the answer at the private door was "no orders." Lord Ellenborough allowed plaintiff to take a verdict, with liberty to defendant to move to enter a nonsuit; rule nisi: and on cause shewn, the court thought this presentment too late; that it furnished no ground for presuming that there had been a prior presentment by the holder within the banking hours; but that plaintiff might have an opportunity of proving such a presentment, they allowed him to have a new trial on his paying the costs.

[(*a*) But where a bill or note is payable at a bank, a presentment for payment at the bank after it is closed as to other business, is sufficient, if it be made within the usual time for making such presentments.

Action against an endorser of a note payable at the Mechanics Bank in the city of New York. The note was presented for payment at the bank on the day it became due at about fifteen minutes after three o'clock P. M. It was proved that this was the usual hour to call for notes, though the bank closes at three o'clock P. M.; that the officers of the bank were all present, and they never deliver notes for protest, until after the banking hours; and that payment will be received even after banking hours, if the officers are present. Spencer C. J. delivered the opinion of the court. "The bill was properly presented at the bank for payment; and although it was a quarter of an hour after the usual time for closing the bank as to other business, it was yet within bank hours; for it appears that these fifteen minutes, according to the general course of doing business at this bank, was the usual and accustomed time for such presentment; and of the course of doing business there the defendant ought to have informed himself." Bank of Utica v. Smith, 18 Johns. R. 230.]

(23) Barclay v. Bailey, 2 Campb. N. P. C. 527. This was an action against the drawer of a bill. At eight o'clock in the evening of the day on which it became due, it was presented at the house of the acceptor in London, for payment; and the answer given was, that the acceptor

o'clock in the evening is not an unseasonable hour for making a presentment. (*a*)

And no objection can be made to a presentment on the ground of its being at an unseasonable hour if a person is stationed there at the time to give an answer. (24)

Therefore a presentment at a banker's out of the usual hours will be unobjectionable, if the banker or any agent on his behalf, is there at the time of such presentment. (24)

A presentment for acceptance is not (25) necessary, except upon bills payable within a limited time after sight.

---

had become bankrupt, and had removed into another quarter of the town. It was, however, proved that a person had been stationed at the house from nine o'clock till four, for the purpose of taking up this bill, but that it was not presented within those hours. Lord Ellenborough held, that the acceptor being a common trader, not a banker, the presentment was good; and said, that eight o'clock in the evening, could not be considered an unseasonable hour for demanding payment at the house of a private merchant who had accepted a bill. Verdict for the plaintiff.

Morgan v. Davison, 1 Stark. 114. A bill made payable at Herring & Co.'s (not bankers), Copthall-court, was presented there between six and seven in the evening of the day it became due; there was only a girl there, who was left to take care of the counting-house. In action by endorsee against drawer, Lord Ellenborough held this a sufficient presentment, the hour being one at which the holder might reasonably expect to find the party in his counting-house.

[(*a*) But carrying a bill or note not payable at any particular place to the place of business of the maker or acceptor, and finding it shut, will not be a sufficient presentment for payment unless it be done in business hours. Shed v. Brett, 1 Pick. 413.]

(24) Garnett v. Woodcock, 1 Stark. 476. In an action against the acceptor, on a bill made payable in London, and accepted payable at Dennison and Co.'s, plaintiff proved a presentment at Dennison and Co.'s between seven and eight o'clock in the evening, and that a boy returned for answer "no orders." It was insisted that this presentment, being at a London banker's, was at an unseasonable hour: but Lord Ellenborough said, if the banker appointed a person to attend to give an answer, a presentment at any time whilst that person was in attendance would be sufficient. Plaintiff had a verdict, and a rule to set it aside was refused.

(25) Molloy, B. 2. c. 10. § 16. "If a bill is drawn upon a merchant in London, payable to I. S. at double usance, I. S. is not bound in strictness of law to procure an acceptance, but only to tender the bill when the money is due."

Beawes, § 266. p. 453. "There is no obligation to procure acceptance to a bill payable at a day certain, as the time goes on, whether accepted or not; but it is otherwise with bills payable at so many days sight." See also Mar. 12, 13, and Blesard v. Hirst, and Goodall v Dolley, post.

No (26) certain time is fixed within which this presentment must be made, but it should (27) be made within a reasonable time.

What shall be deemed a reasonable time must depend upon the particular circumstances of each case.

Keeping it a whole day, exclusive of the day of receiving it, without negotiating it or sending it for acceptance, is not necessarily an unreasonable delay. (28)

No delay warranted by the common course of business is improper, nor is any delay which is occasioned by keeping the bill in (29) circulation at a distance from the place where it is payable; but a delay by locking it up for any length of time (30) is.

If a bill payable abroad at a certain time after sight is taken in a course of negotiation, (31) it is not necessary to send it by the first opportunity to the place where it is payable.

Indeed in all cases where a bill is remitted to a factor or agent, it may be his duty to apply for an acceptance, and he may be answerable for any loss his principal may suffer by a neglect; but this neglect does not affect the bill, if payable otherwise than after sight, nor the principal's right thereon. Vide Beawes, § 49, p. 420, Mar. 12, 13.

(26) Per Eyre C. J. and Heath J. H. Bl. 569. 570.

(27) Per Eyre C. J. 2 H. Bl. 569.

(28) Fry v. Hill, 7 Taunt. 397. Plaintiff took a bill at Windsor on Friday, payable in London a month after sight. What he did with it did not appear, but it was not presented for acceptance till Tuesday: it was left to the jury whether there was a default to present within a reasonable time, and they found for plaintiff; and on motion for a new trial, the court said, it would still be a question for the jury whether there had been a presentment in reasonable time; and as they had passed their judgment on that point, rule refused.

(29) See ante, n. (27).

(30) Per Buller J. 2 H. Bl. 170. See Muilman v. D'Eguino, infra, n. (31).

(31) Muilman v. D'Eguino, 2 H. Bl. 565. In debt on bond conditioned to pay certain bills drawn on India at sixty days after sight, in case they should be returned protested, defendant pleaded that they were not presented for acceptance within a reasonable time after the drawing: it appeared that they were drawn 5th of March, 1793; that they were endorsed on that day by defendant to plaintiffs, who procured them for a house at Paris; that plaintiffs sent immediate advice to the house at Paris, and on receiving their directions on 30th of April, sent them to India, where they arrived the 3d of October; on the 5th of October, the holder wrote to the drawee, who was from home, desiring him to accept the bills, and on the 17th of October, he sent an answer of re-

Upon a presentment for acceptance, the bill should be left with the drawee (32) twenty-four hours, unless in the interim he either accepts or declares a resolution not to accept.

---

fusal; some of the bills were thereupon protested 29th of October, and the rest 1/th of November. Eyre C. J. left the case to the jury, but told them, he thought the bills had been sent to India in time, as they were put up here for negotiation, and were therefore liable to be delayed, and that they were presented in India in time after their arrival. The jury found for the plaintiff; and on a rule to shew cause why there should not be a new trial, and cause shewn, the court was satisfied with the verdict, and plaintiff had judgment. Eyre C. J. said, "It is not necessary to lay down any new rule as to bills of exchange payable at sight, or within a given time afterwards; if it were, I should feel great anxiety not to clog the negotiation of bills circumstanced like these. It would be a very serious and difficult thing to say, that a person buying a foreign bill, in the way these were bought, should be obliged to transmit it by the first opportunity to the place of its destination. There would also be a great difficulty in saying *at what time* such a bill should be presented for acceptance. The courts have been very cautious in fixing any time for presenting for acceptance an inland bill, payable at a certain period after sight, and it seems to me more necessary to be cautious with respect to a foreign bill payable in that manner. I think, indeed, the holder is bound to present the bill in reasonable time, in order that the period may commence from which the payment is to take place; but the question, what is reasonable time, must depend on the particular circumstances of the case; and it must always be for the jury to determine whether any laches are imputable to the plaintiff." Per Buller J. "The only rule I know of, which can be applied to the case of bills of exchange, is, *that due diligence must be used.* Due diligence is the only thing to be looked at, whether the bill be foreign or inland, and whether it be payable at sight, at so many days after, or in any other manner. But I think a rule may thus far be laid down as to laches, with regard to bills payable at sight, or a certain time after sight, namely, that they ought to be put in circulation; and if a bill drawn at three days sight were kept out in that way for a year, I cannot say there would be laches; but if instead of putting it in circulation, the holder were to lock it up for any length of time, I should say that he would be guilty of laches, but farther than this, no rule can be laid down." Per Heath J. "No rule can be laid down as to the time for presenting bills payable at sight, or at a given time afterwards. In the French ordinances of 1673, in Postlethwaite and Marius, it is said, 'That a bill payable at sight *or at will* is the same thing.'"

Goupy v. Harden, Holt, 342. 7 Taunt. 159. 2 Marsh. 454. A bill drawn in London 12th May, 1815, at thirty days after sight, on a house at Lisbon, was remitted by defendant to plaintiff at Paris. Plaintiff endorsed it to a house at Genoa; they negotiated it, and it was not till 22d August that it reached Lisbon, and was presented for acceptance; before that time, viz., on 15th July, the drawer failed, and on that account acceptance was refused. It was urged for defendant, that it was unwarrantable in plaintiff to send the bill to Genoa, instead of transmitting it to Lisbon for acceptance: but Gibbs C. J. thought otherwise;

But a bill or note must not be left (unless it is paid) on a presentment for payment; if it be, the presentment is (33) not considered as made until the money is called for.

[A demand of payment, by a person who has not the bill or note with him at the time, is not a sufficient presentment. (*a*).

---

and the jury said such a bill might be sent round the world before it was presented for acceptance, and found for the plaintiff. On motion for a new trial, Gibbs C. J. relied upon Muilman v. D'Eguino, in which, he said, the point had been deliberately considered, and he was clearly of opinion that the plaintiff had not taken the risk upon himself by sending the bill into circulation; and the jury having been of opinion that the bill had been presented in reasonable time, a rule was refused.

[A bill was drawn in Augusta, Ga. March 6th, 1819, upon persons in New York, payable sixty days after sight to Ross and Starr or order, and was by them endorsed to Robinson. The mail goes from Augusta to New York in ten days, and leaves Augusta three times a week, and the mail of March 10th was lost. The bill was presented for acceptance May 20th, 1819. The court held that this was not such a delay to present the bill as discharged the drawers. Spencer C. J. delivered the opinion of the court. "I do not find that where a bill of exchange has been drawn payable at sight, or any specified number of days after sight, that there is any definite or fixed rule when the bill shall be presented for acceptance, other than this, that due diligence must be used. And it is certain with respect to such bills, and particularly where they are negotiated by the payee, there is much more latitude as to the time of presentment, than where the bill has a fixed period of payment. Now here the bill was put in circulation by Ross and Starr; and although it is probable that the first of exchange was lost, by the loss of the mail, we are not authorized to consider that as a fact in the case; but I cannot say that upon such a bill there has been laches." Robinson v. Ames, 20 Johns. R. 146.

A bill was drawn in Antigua upon London, payable at ninety days after sight, dated July 18th, 1817, it was endorsed by the payee, and by two other parties. Packets go from Antigua to London regularly once in every month or forty days. The bill was presented for acceptance Jan. 16th, 1818. It was held that there was no laches in presenting, and that the drawer was not discharged in consequence of the delay. Gowan v. Jackson, 20 Johns. R. 176.]

(32) Vide Mar. 2d ed. 16. Moll. b. 3. c. 5. § 1. Lord Raym. 281.

(33) Hayward v. Bank of England, Str. 550. Hayward kept cash at the bank, and paid in a banker's note; the runner to the bank left it the next morning, and called for the money in the afternoon, but in the interval the banker had stopped; and though this appeared to be the usual practice at the bank, King C. J said, it was dangerous to suffer persons to deal with notes in that manner, and that the Common Pleas were of that opinion in the like case; and he directed the jury to find for the plaintiff, which they did. Sed vide Turner v. Mead, and Hoar v. Da Costa, post. p. 144 and 145.

[(*a*) Freeman v. Boynton, 7 Mass. R. 483; Haddock v. Murray, 1 N. Hamp. R. 140.

It was held in a case in New Hampshire, where the note was in a bank

A presentment by any person in possession of a bill or note *bonâ fide*, is sufficient to charge the parties to the instrument, and no letter of attorney or other writing from the proprietor of the bill or note, is necessary to give an authority to another person to make a presentment. (*a*)]

The time when a presentment for payment must be made depends upon the time when a bill or note is payable.

A bill or note payable on demand must not be kept locked up; if it be, the loss will fall on the holder. (34)

And it will be no excuse that it would not have been paid had it been presented sooner. (34)

A bill or note payable on demand, is payable immediately upon presentment; and unless put into circulation must be presented within a reasonable time after the receipt. (*b*)

---

a few rods from the house of the maker, that a letter sent to the maker's house informing him of this fact and requesting payment, was a sufficient presentment to charge an endorser. 1 N. Hamp. R. 80.]

[(*a*) Freeman v. Boynton, 7 Mass. R. 483; Bank of Utica v. Smith, 18 Johns. R. 230; Hartford Bank v. Stedman, 2 Conn. R. 489; Morris v. Foreman, 1 Dall. 193.

A presentment of a note for payment was made by a notary public at the request of the endorsee, the court said that there was no room for question that the demand was sufficient. Parker C. J. said, "The demand may as well be made by an agent, as by the principal, and there is no need of a power of attorney or any written instrument to constitute an agent for this purpose." Shed v. Brett, 1 Pick. 401.]

(34) Breching v. ———————— Holt, 315. Plaintiff took of defendant at Tunbridge, on the 5th, before the Maidstone post went out, a £20 Maidstone bank note, payable on demand; he kept it till the morning of the 7th, and then sent it by the carrier who reached Maidstone at nine in the morning of the 7th; the post of the 6th reached Maidstone an hour sooner; the bank did not open that day: Gibbs C. J. held that there were laches in plaintiff, and he directed a nonsuit.

[(*b*) Redfield and Beers made two notes dated Jan. 31st, 1814, payable on demand to Nickerson. Nickerson endorsed the note for the accommodation of R. and B. R. and B. informed Nickerson that the money would not be demanded immediately. A demand was made on R. and B. Sept. 23d, 1814, and immediate notice of non-payment given to Nickerson. The holder and the other parties to the note all resided in Boston. In an action against Nickerson as endorser, Parker C. J. charged the jury, that a demand on this note must be made in a reasonable time; and that what was reasonable time was a question of law arising from the facts which appeared; and that the delay of eight months was unreasonable. Verdict for defendant. Parker C. J. delivered the opinion of the court. "A promissory note payable on demand, is like a bill payable at sight. As in the latter case the holder must present his bill for acceptance within a reasonable time, in order

It has (35) not been expressly decided whether what shall be considered as a reasonable time is to be taken as a question of fact for the determination of the jury, or as a question of law for the determination of the court. In Darbishire v. Parker, (36) Lawrence J. intimated very decidedly that it

---

to charge the drawer, so in the former the endorsee must make demand of payment on the promiser within a reasonable time, in order to charge the endorser. Was the demand in this case made in a reasonable time? The jury have said no, and they were perfectly justified in returning that answer." Field v. Nickerson, 13 Mass. R. 131.

In an action in New York against the endorser of a note payable on demand, where the holder of the note, the maker, and the endorser, all resided in the city of New York, and no demand was made on the maker until more than five months after the date of the note, it was held that this was an unreasonable delay, and that the endorser was discharged. Sice v. Cunningham, 1 Cowen, 397.

In an action against the endorser of a note payable on demand, dated September 4th, 1819, where no demand was made until after May 6th, 1820, Story J. said, "Payment of a note payable on demand, must be demanded within a reasonable time, otherwise the endorser is discharged." "Unless there be circumstances in the case which account for the delay, a neglect to demand payment of such a note for more than seven months is an unreasonable delay, and discharges the endorser." Martin v. Winslow, 2 Mason, 241.]

(35) See ante, Muilman v. D'Eguino, p. 138. note (31). Tindal v. Brown, post, p. 161. note (74). Appleton v. Sweetapple, post, p. 146. note (43). Hankey v. Trotman, post, p. 146. note (45), and Hilton v. Shepherd, Hopes v. Alder, and Darbishire v. Parker, infra, note (36).

(36) Whether it is the province of the judge or of the jury, to decide upon the reasonableness of notice, has never been expressly determined. In Tindal v. Brown, post. p. 161. note (74), Lord Mansfield considered it as a question partly of fact and partly of law: Ashhurst and Buller Js. as a question of law. In the two cases of Hilton v. Shepherd, and Hopes v. Alder, 6 East's Rep. pp. 14. 16. note, Lord Kenyon considered it as a question for the jury, under all the circumstances of accident, necessity, and the like. But the judgment of Lawrence J. in Darbishire v. Parker, shows it was his decided opinion that it was an inference of law, to be drawn by the court from the facts, which (as in all other cases) were to be found by the jury.

Darbishire and another v. Parker, 6 East's Rep. 3. The plaintiffs received at Manchester notice of the dishonor of a bill, between eight and nine o'clock in the morning of the 12th of August. The post from Manchester to Liverpool, where the drawer resided, set off between twelve and one o'clock at noon. They however sent no notice by the post of that, or the next day, but sent it by a private hand on the 13th, by which it was delivered about nine o'clock at night, two hours later than it would have arrived had it been sent by the post. Lord Ellenborough left it to the jury, whether reasonable notice had been given, and they found for the plaintiffs. A new trial was moved for, on the ground of a misdirection, and a rule nisi granted. The court, without entering into the general question, held that the case deserved recon-

was a question of law for the judges, and yet in many instances since it has been treated as a question of fact for the jury. (37)

---

sideration; inasmuch as the plaintiffs appeared, at all events, to have been guilty of laches, whether the notice should have been sent by the post of the 12th or by that of the next day, having failed in doing either. Rule absolute. In this case, Lawrence J. on the general question, whether reasonable notice be a question of law or of fact, said, "It must be recollected, that the facts stated in the report of Tindal v. Brown were afterwards found in a special verdict, in which the jury did not find whether the notice were reasonable or not; on which special verdict this court gave judgment for the plaintiff, and that judgment was unanimously confirmed in the Exchequer Chamber. But if reasonable notice were a question of fact, and not of law, I am at a loss to know how those judgments are to be sustained; for the jury did not find the fact of reasonable notice, but left that as a question of law to be inferred from all the circumstances. But if it were a question of fact, there ought to have been a venire de novo in that case." In Ball v. Wardell, Willes, 204, 6., where a custom was pleaded for the inhabitants of a town to walk and ride over a certain close of the plaintiff's at all *seasonable* times, what was to be deemed a *seasonable* time was considered to be a question of law, arising out of all the circumstances; of which Lord C. J. Willes, says, "the court were the proper judges, as in the case of *reasonable time*, reasonable fines," &c. "For," he adds, "what is contrary to reason cannot be consonant to law, which is founded on reason; and therefore the reasonableness in these and the like cases depends on the law, and is to be decided by the judges." And in the same case he says, "issues may be joined on things which are partly matters of fact, and partly matters of law; and then, when the evidence is given at the trial, the judge must direct the jury how the law is; and if they find contrary to such direction, it is a sufficient reason for a new trial."

See also Anderson v. Royal Exchange Assurance Company, 7 East's Rep. 43., in which Lord Ellenborough, in speaking of the time within which the assured may abandon the property insured, says, "an abandonment must be made within a reasonable time; and I rather conceive that it is the province of the judge to direct the jury as to what is a reasonable time under the circumstances." See also Bateman v. Joseph, post. See also Co. Lit. 56 *b*. "Reasonable time shall be adjudged by the discretion of the justices before whom the cause dependeth: and so it is of reasonable fines, customs, and services, upon the true state of the case depending before them; for reasonableness in these cases belongeth to the knowledge of the law, and therefore to be decided by the justices." "For nothing that is contrary to reason is consonant to law."

[In a case in New York, Kent C. J., in delivering the opinion of the court, says, "The questiou of reasonable notice is a compound of law and fact, to be submitted to a jury." Taylor v. Bryden, 8 Johns. R. 136.

In the case of Hussey v. Freeman, Sewall J. says, "The endorser is entitled to seasonable notice: and what is seasonable notice is a question of law, to be decided by the court, as soon as the facts necessary to the decision are ascertained." 10 Mass. R. 84.

Upon a bill or note payable on demand or at sight, and given for cash by a person who makes the profit by the money on such bills or notes a source of his livelihood, it is difficult to say what length of time such person shall be entitled to consider unreasonable; but upon such bills or notes given by way of payment, or paid into a banker's, any time beyond what the common course of business warrants, (38) is.

Upon a bill or note of this kind given by way of payment, the course of business seemed formerly to allow the party to keep it, if it was payable in the place where it was given, until the (39) morning of the next day of business after its

---

See also Field v. Nickerson, ante, p. 141; and Haddock v. Murray, 1 N. Hamp. R. 140; and Whitwell v. Johnson, 17 Mass. R. 453.

In another case in New York, Spencer J. said, "What is reasonable notice, is a mixed question of law and fact; but when the facts are ascertained it becomes purely a question of law." Bryden v. Bryden, 11 Johns. R. 187.

But in Pennsylvania, what is reasonable notice appears to have been considered a question of fact, on which the jury were to decide. Robertson v. Vogle, 1 Dall. R. 252; Steinmitz v. Currie, 1 Dall. R. 234 and 269; Bank of North America v. Pettit, 4 Dall. R. 127; Bank of North America v. M'Knight, 2 Dall. R. 158; Warder v. Bell, 1 Yeates, 531; Gurly v. Gettysburg Bank, 7 Serg. & Raw. 324.]

(37) See Fry v. Hill, ante, p. 138, note (28). and Goupy v. Harden, ante, p. 139.

(38) See Turner v. Mead, infra, note (39).

(39) Ward v. Evans, Ld. Raym. 928. A banker's note was paid to the plaintiff's servant at noon, and presented for payment the next morning, at which time the banker stopped payment. On a case reserved, the court held it was presented in time; and judgment was given for the plaintiff.

Moor v. Warren, Str. 415. The defendant gave the plaintiff a banker's note at two o'clock in the afternoon, and he tendered it for payment the next morning at nine: the banker stopped a quarter of an hour before; and Pratt C. J. told the jury the loss should fall on the defendant, there being no laches in the plaintiff, who had demanded the money as soon as was usual in the course of dealing, and that keeping the note till next morning, could not be construed giving a new credit to the banker; and the jury found for the plaintiff. In Holmes v. Barry, Str. 415. the circumstances were the same; and King C. J. of the Common Pleas, gave a similar direction, and the jury found accordingly.

Fletcher v. Sandys, Str. 1248. A banker's note was paid to the plaintiff after dinner, and he sent it for payment the next morning, but the banker had stopped payment; and Lee C. J. ruled that there were no laches in the plaintiff, and that in all these cases there must be a reasonable time allowed, consistent with the nature of circulating paper.

Turner and others v. Mead, Str. 416. The defendants paid the Sword Blade Company (the plaintiffs) two banker's notes at three

receipt, and till the next post, if payable elsewhere; but (40) not longer.

Thus where a note of this kind, payable in London, was given there in the morning, a presentment the next morning

---

o'clock in the afternoon; and the next morning their servant left them at the banker's in order to call for the money in the evening, it then being the custom with the plaintiffs and the bank to send out their notes in the morning and to call for the money in the afternoon. The plaintiffs' servant called for the money between four and five in the afternoon, and the banker had just stopped payment; and because the plaintiffs had done nothing more than was usual in leaving the notes in the morning without taking the money, Pratt C. J. directed the jury to find for them, which they did.

Hoar v. Da Costa, Str. 910. The defendant paid the plaintiff a banker's note at twelve: he put it into the bank at one, and at ten the next morning the runner from the bank carried it with other notes, and left them, as was then usual, to call again for the money: he called at eleven, and was told the banker's servant was gone to the bank: he called again at two, when the banker said he was going to stop, and refused payment; but he paid small notes till four o'clock. The defendant gave notice to the plaintiff the next morning: the question was, whether this note was payment to the plaintiff. It was insisted for the defendant, that if the note had been tendered by itself it would have been paid; and for the plaintiff, that if there had been no demand there would have been no laches, being within a day after the receipt. Raymond C. J. said there was no standing rule, and left it to the jury, who found for the plaintiff.

(40) Manwaring v. Harrison, Str. 508. On Saturday the 17th of September, about two o'clock, Harrison gave Manwaring a banker's note, dated the 5th of September, and payable to Harrison or order on demand; Manwaring paid it away the same afternoon to J. S., and he presented it for payment on the Tuesday morning as soon as the shop was open: but the banker stopped payment at that time. Manwaring paid the money to J. S., and brought this action to recover it from Harrison. Pratt C. J. left it to the jury, whether there had been any neglect; and observed, that as Harrison had kept it eleven days, he probably would not have demanded payment sooner than J. S. did. The jury wished to leave it to the court whether there had been a reasonable time: but the Chief Justice told them they were the judges of that; upon which they found for the defendant, and gave it as their opinion, that a person who did not demand a banker's note in two days, took the credit on himself.

East India Company v. Chitty, Str. 1175. At half past eleven in the morning of the 18th of January, the defendant paid the East India Company's cashier a banker's note, and they did not send it for payment till the next day at two, at which time the banker stopped payment. The question was, who should bear the loss? and upon examining the merchants, it was held, that the company had made it their own by not sending it out the afternoon they received it, or at farthest the next morning; and the jury found accordingly for the defendant.

was held (41) sufficiently early; a presentment at two the next afternoon too (42) late.

In (43) a later modern case, where a similar note was given in London at one, and not presented till the next morning, two juries held the delay unreasonable, but it was against the opinion of the court.

But in a very recent case, where such a note payable in London was given in the country, it was held that the person receiving it was not bound to send it to London till the following day. (44)

And that the person receiving it in London was not bound to present it till the next day. (44)

A bill or note of this kind, given by way of payment to a banker, must (45) be presented by him as soon as if it had been paid into his hands by a customer.

---

(41) Ward v. Evans, Moore v. Warren, Holmes v. Barry, Fletcher v. Sandys, ante, p. 144. note (39).

(42) East India Company v. Chitty, supra.

(43) Appleton v. Sweetapple, B. R. M. 23 Geo. 3. A bill payable in London on demand was given to the plaintiff in London at one o'clock in the afternoon, and he did not present it till the next morning; the question was, whether he presented it in time? Lord Mansfield left the point to the jury, who found for the defendant; but the court granted a new trial, because the question was a matter of law upon which the judge should have decided; the jury found again for the defendant, but against the judge's direction; a second new trial was granted, and the jury again found for the defendant; and then the court refused to interfere.

(44) Williams v. Smith, Pasch. 1819, 2 Barnew. and Ald. 496. At ten o'clock on Friday morning, defendant paid plaintiff at Wantage, (eighteen miles from Newbury,) 450*l.* in Newbury bank notes, payable at Newbury or London: plaintiff sent them to the Wantage bank the same day, to remit to London, but they declined on account of the risk, and halves of them were sent to London by Saturday's coach, and the other halves by Sunday's post: they were presented for payment on the Tuesday, but no Newbury notes were paid in London after the Monday, nor at Newbury after the Saturday. Newbury is a two-days' post from Wantage, and the post for London leaves Wantage at half after five in the evening; on case, it was urged for defendant, that plaintiff should have sent the notes to London by the Friday's post, or if not that they should have been presented for payment the day they arrived in London, in either of which cases they would have been paid; but the court held, plaintiff had till the day after they were received, i. e. till Saturday, to send them to London, and the banker there had till the day after he received them, i. e. till Tuesday, to present them, and postea to plaintiff.

(45) Hankey v. Trotman, Blackst. 1. The plaintiff was a banker, and

And it has been held that a bill or note of this kind if payable at the place where the banker lives, must be presented the next time the banker's clerk goes (45) his rounds.

But if a London banker receive a check by the general post, he is not bound to present it for payment (46) until the following day.

And where a person in London received a check upon a London banker between one and two o'clock, and lodged it soon after four with his banker, and the latter presented it between five and six, and got it marked as a good check, and the next day at noon presented it for payment at the clearing house; the court held that there had been no unreason-

---

had a bill on the defendant, for which the defendant paid him a draught upon another banker at twelve at noon, and the plaintiff got it marked for acceptance that night; before the next morning the banker on whom it was drawn stopped. The question was, whether the plaintiff or defendant should bear the loss? The jury found a verdict for the defendant, and upon a rule to shew cause why there should not be a new trial, and cause shewn, the court (Wright J. dubitante) held that it was a question of fact, whether the plaintiff had sufficient time for receiving the money, of which the jury were the proper judges; and the verdict stood.

But see the cases of Rickford v. Ridge, and Robson v. Bennett, in the two following notes. In the last-mentioned case, Mansfield C. J. said, that Hankey v. Trotman had been overruled by Appleton v. Sweetapple. See 2 Taunt. 394.

(46) Rickford and others v. Ridge, 2 Campb. N. P. C. 537. The plaintiffs, bankers at Aylesbury, gave the defendant cash for a check upon Smith and Co., bankers in London; and in an action to recover this money, it appeared that they took the check on the 13th of June, but instead of sending it to London by the post of that day, which they might have done, they sent it by a morning coach on the 14th; and their bankers, to whom it was directed, received it between three and four o'clock on the same day, and presented it at Smith's house at noon on the 15th, when payment was refused. It was proved that bankers to the west of St. Paul's, where the plaintiffs' bankers resided, sent out checks and bills for payment only once in the day, and that generally before the arrival of the post; and therefore such as arrived by the post on one day generally remained with them until the following morning; so that had this check arrived by the post on the 14th, it would not have been presented until the 15th. The question therefore was, whether such practice were reasonable. It was admitted that a different practice prevailed to the east of St. Paul's. Lord Ellenborough said he could not hear of any arbitrary distinction between one part of the city and another. That in towns where posts arrived at different hours, it would be impossible, or at least unreasonable, to require that bankers should present bills and checks on the same day on which they were

able delay, either by the (47) holder in not presenting it for payment on the first day, which he might have done, or by his (47) banker in presenting it at the clearing house only, on the following day at noon: it being proved to be the usage among such bankers, not to pay checks presented by one banker to another after four o'clock, but only to mark them if good, and to pay them the next day at the clearing house. (*a*)

---

received. That the practice here proved, that checks received in the course of one day should be presented on the following day, appeared to him to be subservient to general convenience, and consistent with the law merchant, which merely required checks to be presented with reasonable diligence. Verdict for the plaintiffs.

(47) Robson v. Bennett, 2 Taunt. 388. On the 11th of September, between one and two o'clock, the defendants gave the plaintiffs a check upon Bloxam and Co., their bankers, in payment for goods. The plaintiffs lodged the check with Messrs. Harrisons, their bankers, a few minutes after four; and they presented it between five and six to Bloxam and Co., who marked it as good. It was proved to be the usage among London bankers, not to pay any check presented by or on behalf of another banker after four o'clock, but merely to mark it if good, and pay it the next day at the clearing house. On the 12th at noon, Harrisons' clerk took this check to the clearing house; but no person attended for Bloxam and Co., who stopped payment at nine on that morning, and the check was therefore treated as dishonored. The plaintiffs in going with the check to Harrisons' passed Bloxam's house. On a case stating these facts, the court held, that there had been no laches in the plaintiffs in not presenting the check to Bloxam and Co. on the 11th for payment; or in his bankers in not presenting it at the banking house, but merely at the clearing house; and therefore gave judgment for the plaintiffs.

See also Reynolds v. Chettle, 2 Campb. N. P. C. 596.

[(*a*) A check on a bank is in form and reality a bill of exchange; and a demand of payment at the bank must be made in order to charge the drawer of the bill. Cruger v. Armstrong, 3 Johns. Cas. 5.

But though it is a general rule that a check on a bank must be presented at the bank within a reasonable time; yet where a check is presented at the bank a long time after the date, and payment is refused for want of funds of the drawer, and not on account of the insolvency of the bank, the drawer is still liable to the holder of the check.

A check drawn by Warren on a bank in New York 28th March, 1800, payable to bearer, was presented at the bank 20th October, 1800, for payment, which was refused, for want of sufficient funds of Warren, he having in the meantime drawn large sums from the bank. The court held that he was liable for the amount of the check to the holder. Kent J. "In the case of Cruger v. Armstrong I considered it a settled rule that a check must be presented for payment in a reasonable time, otherwise the holder takes upon himself the risk of the banker's responsibility; and that drawing a check was an appropriation of as much money as it amounted to in the hands of the bank. In the present

[A bill or note must be presented for payment on the very day on which it becomes due. (*a*)]

If a man takes a bill on the eve of its becoming due, and it is payable at a distant place, he must not keep it by him so as to prevent its being presented for payment on the day it becomes due. (48)

---

case the bank did not fail, but it was the act of the defendant himself which defeated the payment of the check, by drawing out the money, which, in good faith, was to be considered as appropriated for the payment of the check. Although checks are now considered substantially the same as inland bills, I know no case which goes the length of exonerating the drawer, where the responsibility of the bank has remained good, and where he was himself the cause of the non-payment by withdrawing the money." Conroy v. Warren, 9 Johns. Cas. 259.

So an order drawn by a debtor in favor of his creditor must be presented to the drawee within a reasonable time, otherwise the drawer is discharged.

Jones gave Brower an order on Smith dated December 9th, 1804; and Smith at the time it was drawn agreed with Brown to pay the money in about ten days; the order was not presented then, and Smith would have paid the money had the order been presented within two or three weeks from the date; the order was afterwards presented to Smith several times during the winter and also in March, 1805, when Smith had become embarrassed and unable to pay his debts. The court held that independently of the neglect to present at the time Smith agreed to pay it, and independently of the neglect to give notice, Jones was discharged by the negligence of Brower, whereby the money was wholly lost. Brower v. Jones, 3 Johns. R. 230.]

[(*a*) Johnson v. Haight, 13 Johns. R. 470.

But the strict rules as to presentment and notice have not been enforced in all our States.

In a case in New Hampshire where the holder and maker resided about fifteen miles apart, and in a thinly settled country, a presentment eight days after the note fell due, was held to be sufficient to charge the endorser. Haddock v. Murray, 1 New Hamp. R. 140.

In a case in Pennsylvania in 1792, where notice of non-payment of a note was not given to an endorser until four or five days after it became due, M'Kean C. J. observed that before the Revolution it was not usual to give notice to an endorser or even to call upon the maker as soon as a note became due; and that to have done so would have been considered harsh and unreasonable. Bank of N. America v. M'Knight, 2 Dall. R. 188. See also 2 Dall. 233, and Gurly v. Gettysburgh Bank, 7 Serg. & Raw. 324.]

(48) Anderton v. Beck, 16 East. 248. 26th December plaintiff received in Yorkshire a bill payable in London, 28th; he kept it till the 29th, and then sent it to the Lincoln bank, who forwarded it to London without delay, and it was received in London and presented for payment 2d January; plaintiff had no correspondent in London; the bill was dishonored, and in an action for goods sold, the question was, whether this bill was payment? Bayley J. thought it was, and verdict for defendant; and on motion to enter verdict for plaintiff, the court held, that as plain-

And if he takes it so near the time of its becoming due, that it will be impossible to present it on the day it becomes due, he must lose no time in forwarding it, or putting it into circulation, so that it may be presented without delay. (48)

If a bill is payable at either of two places, the person taking it has the option at which to present it; and it cannot be imputed as laches in him that he presented it at the most distant, and that if he had presented it at the other it would have been paid. (49)

A (50) bill or (51) note importing to be payable within a

---

tiff submitted to take this bill, he was bound to use due diligence in presenting it, and that he had been guilty of laches in keeping it from the 26th to the 29th; he might have sent it off the 27th or 28th. Rule refused.

[But in a case in Massachusetts where the maker of a note resided at a distance from the endorsee, the court held that a reasonable time should be allowed after the note became due, to transmit it, the endorsee having a right to wait for payment at his own residence, before he was obliged to follow the maker to his house to make the demand. In that case the note fell due on the fourth of June, the holder residing at Boston, and the maker and endorser at Wiscasset, about two hundred miles from Boston, and the court appeared to think that a demand on the ninth or tenth of June at Wiscasset would have been seasonable, but the case turned upon another point. Freeman v. Boynton, 7 Mass. R. 483.]

(49) Beeching v. Gower, Holt. 313. Plaintiff took of defendant at Tunbridge, on 5th March, a 10*l.* Kentish bank note, payable on demand at Maidstone or at Messrs. Ramsbottom's, London. Plaintiff sent the note to London the same day, and it was presented at Ramsbottom's on the 6th, but they ceased paying that day; the Kentish bank paid all the 6th, so that had it been sent to Maidstone it would have been paid; defendant insisted that plaintiff ought to have sent it to Maidstone, which was nearer, and where plaintiff had a clerk; Gibbs C. J. was clear that as the note was payable at either place, plaintiff had his option at which to present it; and verdict for plaintiff.

(50) Colman v. Sayer, 1 Barnard. B. R. 303. In an action upon an inland bill payable six days after sight, one question was, whether three days' grace are allowed where a bill is payable at certain days after sight, as well as where it is payable upon sight? and Raymond C. J. said they were allowable in one case as well as in the other. Another question was, whether they were allowable upon inland as well as upon foreign bills? and the common serjeant and foreman of the jury said it was the constant practice in the city to allow them in both cases; upon which Raymond C. J. said he would not alter it; but the plaintiff was nonsuited on another point.

(51) Brown v. Harraden, 4 Term. Rep. 148. In an action on a note dated the 13th of September 1789, and payable the 2d of November, the declaration stated a presentment and refusal on the 2d of November. The defendant pleaded a tender on the 5th, and the plaintiff replied a bill of Middlesex sued out the 4th: rejoinder, that defendant

limited time after a certain event, or (52) at sight, is not in fact payable until (53) two days afier the expiration of that time, nor unless the third be a day of public rest, until (53) three.

These extra days are called days of grace.

---

was not liable to pay the note at the time the bill of Middlesex was sued out, and surrejoinder that he was. Demurrer and joinder. The question therefore was, whether three days' grace were to be allowed on promissory notes? and after argument the court was unanimous that they were. The same point was taken for granted in Smith v. Kendall, ante, p. 21, note (21). See Dexlaux v. Hood, Bull. Ni. Pr. 274. Ward v. Honeywood, Dougl. 62. May v. Cooper, Fort. 376.

(52) See Coleman v. Sayer, ante, note (50), and in Janson v. Thomas, B. R. T. 24 G. III. Buller J. mentioned a case before Willes C. J. in London, in which a jury of merchants was of opinion that the usual days of grace were to be allowed on bills payable at sight. But see Poth. pl. 12. 172. 198.

(53) Tassell v. Lewis, Lord Raym. 743. "In case of foreign bills of exchange, the custom is, that three days are allowed for the payment of them; but if it happens that the last of the three days is a Sunday, or great holiday, as Christmas day, &c. upon which no money used to be paid, there the party ought to demand the money upon the second day, otherwise it will be at his own peril. Merchants in evidence swore this to be the custom of merchants, and it was approved by Holt C. J. See also 2 Bl. Com. 469. Mar. 2d. ed. 25.

[The rules as to days of grace in the United States are generally the same as those stated in the text. Farnum v. Fowle, 12 Mass. R. 89; Jackson v. Richards, 2 Cain. R. 344; Johnson v. Haight, 13 Johns. R. 470; Bussard v. Levering, 6 Wheat. R. 102; Norton v. Lewis, 2 Conn. R. 198; Widgery v. Munroe, 6 Mass. R. 449; Shepard v. Hall, 1 Conn. R. 329.

In the United States the fourth of July is generally considered a day of public rest, and it has been held in New York that if the third day of grace falls on that day, a demand must be made the preceding day.

In a case in New York where the third day of grace fell on the fourth of July, the jury found by a special verdict that it was the general practice and usage of the city of New York ever since 1784, where the last day of grace fell on the 4th of July to demand payment and give notice on the third. The court held the demand sufficient. Benson J. delivered the opinion of the court. "Whenever a practice, usage, or custom hath obtained for a length of time, so as that it may be presumed to be generally known; then all contracts to which it may be applicable, shall be interpreted and governed by it." Lewis v. Burr, 2 Cain. Er. 195.

The Supreme Court of Massachusetts formerly held that a promissory note was not entitled to grace, unless expressly made payable with grace. Jones v. Fales, 4 Mass. Rep. 251. But merchants were never satisfied with this doctrine. And Mr. Dane says, "when the court gave the opinion in Jones v. Fales, as to grace, it was new. Gentlemen, old in practice, understood that we had adopted the English law as to this, as we had the other parts of that law, in regard to negotiable contracts." 1 Dan. Dig. 413. A statute has recently been passed in Massachusetts giving days of grace to promissory notes. St. 1824, c. 130.]

Different (54) countries vary in the number of days allowed by way of grace; and in two cases some years ago it was proved, (55) that at Hamburgh the holder of a bill is not bound to present it until the eleventh day after the time limited for its payment, where the eleventh is a post day; that if the eleventh be not a post day, he must present it the next preceding post day; but that (56) if the drawee reside not at Hamburgh, but at Lubeck or Bremen, or other places near Hamburgh, and in daily intercourse with it, the holder need not present it until the eleventh day, although the eleventh be not a post day. (*a*)

---

(54) Beawes, § 260. 1st ed. p. 449. The number allowed by the Hamburgh ordinance, art. 16., is twelve.

(55) Goldsmith and another v. Shee, C. P. cor. Lord Eldon, 20th of December, 1799. A bill for £500 drawn on Katter at Hamburgh, at three usances, was dated the 25th of June, 1799; it was presented for payment the 4th of October, which was a post day. In an action by the endorsees against the payee, the defence was, that the presentment was improper: but it was proved in evidence as the settled usage at Hamburgh, that although it is usual to pay bills on the day they become due, the holder may, if he pleases, keep them a certain number of days, called respite days; and that the number of respite days is eleven where the eleventh is a post day; but where the eleventh is not a post day, the respite days extend to the preceding post day only, the holder being obliged at his peril to protest, and send off the protest by the eleventh day. Verdict for the plaintiffs.

But this is not consistent with the Hamburgh ordinance, art. 17; in which it is stated that the holders may postpone the protest until the twelfth day, if it be not a Sunday or holiday.

(56) Goldsmith and another v. Bland and another, C. P. cor. Lord Eldon, 1st of March, 1800. A bill for £998, 9*s*. 9*d*. drawn on Treviramus of Bremen, but payable in Hamburgh at three months, was dated the 15th of June, 1799; it was not presented or protested until the 26th of September, which was not a post day: another bill for £261, 7*s*. 2*d*. addressed to Voeg, in Lubeck, payable in Hamburgh, at three months, was dated the 26th of June, 1799; it was not presented or protested until 7th of October, which was not a post day. In an action on these bills against the defendants as endorsers, it was proved that it was optional in the holder of a bill at Hamburgh, whether he would present and protest it on the post day before the eleventh day after the day limited for its payment, the eleventh not being a post day, or whether he would keep it until the eleventh: and one witness proved, that where the drawee lived at Lubeck or Bremen, it was the constant usage to keep the bill until the eleventh, whether it was a post day or not, there being posts from Lubeck and Bremen to Hamburgh every day. Verdict for the plaintiffs for £1633. See the proceding note.

[(*a*) It is the custom of the banks in the District of Columbia to demand payment of notes on the *fourth* day after the time limited for payment, instead of the third; and it was held, that a demand on the fourth

In this country [England] upon the last day of grace, and within a reasonable time before the expiration of that day, a bill or note must be presented for payment.

But if the holder makes a second presentment on that day, the drawer or maker is (57) entitled to insist on paying it when such presentment is made, without paying the fees of noting or protesting, notwithstanding such presentment is made after the banking hours, and for the purpose of noting and protesting.

A presentment on the second day of grace, where the third is not a day of public rest, is a (58) nullity.

Upon a bill or note payable within a limited time after sight, the time must be computed from its (59) presentment

---

day upon the maker of a note held by one of these banks was sufficient to charge an endorser who was acquainted with the custom. Renner v Bank of Columbia, 9 Wheat. R. 581.]

(57) Leftley v. Mills, post, p. 166. note (83).

(58) Wiffen v. Roberts, Espinasse, 261. A bill was dated 1st November, 1798, and payable three months after date: in an action against the drawer, it appeared that the only presentment for payment was on the 3d of February, which was only the second day of grace, and the day following was not a day of public rest; and Lord Kenyon held, that the non-payment by the acceptor the day before the bill became regularly due, was not such a default in him as could authorize the holder to have recourse to the drawer, and the plaintiff was nonsuited.

[So a bill at five days sight accepted Oct. 1st, is due Oct. 9th, and a presentment for payment Oct. 8th is too early, and will not charge the parties to the bill. Mitchell v. Degrand, 1 Mason, 179.

So a demand on the day of payment expressed in a note without reckoning any days of grace, and notice to the endorser predicated on that demand, are wholly nugatory. Griffin v. Goff, 12 Johns. R. 423; Farnum v. Fowle, 12 Mass. R. 89.

So a demand on the day before a note becomes due, is not sufficient to charge an endorser. Henry v. Jones, 8 Mass. R. 453.]

(59) Beawes, § 252. 1st ed. p. 447.; but Mar. 2d ed. p. 19., says from the day of acceptance, or protest for non-acceptance. By the Hamburg ordinance, art. 26. "If a bill of exchange, at or after sight, should not be accepted immediately on its being presented, but it should be done afterwards, such acceptance is to be considered as made on the first day of *presentment*." Pothier, pl. 13. says, from the day of presentment *and* acceptance. See Campbell v. French, 6 Term Rep. 200.

[Where a bill payable at so many days sight, is presented one day and accepted the next, the number of days must be computed from the day on which it is accepted, not from the day on which it was presented; the acceptance cannot be considered as relating back to the presentment. A bill payable in so many days after sight means so many days after legal sight; and a general acceptance is an agreement to pay in so many after the acceptance, for that is the sight which the drawee admits and refers to. Mitchell v. Degrand, 1 Mason, 176.]

for acceptance; and upon a bill or note payable within a limited time after the date, where it has no date, from (60) the day it issued.

The calculation of the time depends upon the different modes of computing time.

All places with which we are in the habit of negotiating bills compute their time, as we do, (except that Russia adheres to the old style) by years reckoned in a series from the birth of our Saviour, and divided each into twelve months, and 365 (or in every fourth year 366) days.

Upon a bill drawn at a place using one style, and payable at a place using the other, if the time is to be reckoned from the date, it shall be computed according to the style of the place at which it was drawn; otherwise according to (61) the style of the place where it is payable; and in the former case the date (62) must be reduced or carried forward to the style of the place where the bill is payable, and the time reckoned from thence.

Thus on a bill dated the 1st of March, old style, and payable here one month after date, the time must be computed from the corresponding day of February, new style; and on a bill dated the 19th of February new style, and payable at Petersburgh one month after date, from the corresponding day of March, old style.

Where the time after the expiration of which a bill or note imports to be payable is limited by months, it is to be computed by (63) calendar, not lunar months.

Thus on a bill or note payable one month after date, and dated the 1st of January, the (64) month will not expire till the 1st of February.

---

(60) Armitt v. Breame, Lord Raym. 1076. An award which directed the removal of some scaffolds within fifty-eight days from the date of the award, had no date; and an objection being taken upon this ground, the court said that the time was to be computed from the delivery.

(61) Vide Mar. 2d ed. p. 25. Beawes, § 251. 1st ed. p. 447.

(62) Mar. 2d ed. p. 22.

(63) Mar. 2d ed. p. 19.

[Leffingwell v. White, 1 Johns. Cas. 99.]

(64) Vide Mar. 2d ed. p. 24. Beawes, § 253. 1st ed. p. 447.

Where the time is computed by days, the day on which the event happens is to be (65) excluded.

Thus on a bill or note payable ten days after date, dated the 1st of January, the time does not expire until the 11th.

Instead of an express limitation by years, months, or days, we continually find the time on bills drawn or payable at Amsterdam, Rotterdam, Hamburg, Altona, Paris, or any place in France, Cadiz, Madrid, Bilboa, Leghorn, Genoa, or Venice, limited by *the usance*, that is, the usage between those places and this country; because, in the infancy of bills, all bills between this country and any of those places respectively were usually made payable after the same interval.

An usance between this kingdom and Amsterdam, Rotterdam, Hamburg, Altona, Paris, or any place in France, is one calendar month from the date of the bill; an usance between us and Cadiz, Madrid, or Bilboa, two; an usance between us and Leghorn, Genoa, or Venice, three.

A double usance is double the accustomed time; an half usance, half.

Where it is necessary to divide a month upon an half usance, which is the case where the usance is either one month or three, the division, (66) notwithstanding the difference in the length of months, contains fifteen days.

The bankruptcy or known insolvency of the drawee or maker is no (67) excuse for a neglect to make a presentment, or to give notice; (*a*)

---

(65) Bellasis v. Hester, Lord Raym. 280. Lutw. 1591. Upon a bill payable ten days after sight, Treby C. J. was of opinion, that the day on which the bill was seen by the drawee was not to be reckoned one of the ten, because then a bill payable one day after sight would be payable the day it was seen; but Powell and Neville Js. held the contrary, and judgment was given according to their opinion. However, in May v. Cooper, Fort. 376., the court seemed to consider a note payable ten days after date, and dated the 21st July, as payable the 31st (not allowing, however, any days of grace); and in Coleman v. Sayer, 1 Barnard B. R. 303., in an action upon a bill payable six days after sight, one question was, whether the day of sight was to be reckoned one of the six? and Raymond C. J. said it was not; and the modern practice is conformable to his opinion. [See also Avery v. Stewart, 2 Conn. R. 69., and Mitchell v. Degrand, ante, p. 153.]

(66) Mar. 2d ed. p. 23.

(67) In Russell v. Langstaffe, Dougl. 497. 515., Lee said, arguendo, that it had frequently been ruled by Lord Mansfield at Guildhall, that

Nor is a general ceasing to pay. (68)

[But where an endorser of a note receives sufficient security for the purpose of indemnifying himself against his endorsement, he is liable to the holder of the note, though there has been no demand or notice. (*a*)

And it has been held in an action against the endorser of a note who had received a general assignment of all the maker's property, that the endorser was liable without any demand or notice, although the assigned property was not sufficient to secure the endorser against his other responsibilities for the maker, exclusive of the note in suit. (*a*)

---

it is not an excuse for not making a demand on a note or bill, or for not giving notice of non-payment, that the drawer or acceptor has become a bankrupt, as many means may remain of obtaining payment by the assistance of friends or otherwise; and Lord Mansfield, who was in court, did not deny the assertion: this dictum was also referred to, arguendo, in Bickerdike v. Bollman, 1 Term. Rep. 408.

Esdaile & al. v. Sowerby & al. 11 East. Rep. 114. In an action by the endorsees of a bill drawn by Cheetham on Hill in favor of the defendants, and by them endorsed to the plaintiffs, a verdict was found for the plaintiffs, and a case reserved. The bill, which was payable in London, became due on Saturday the 20th of February, when it was presented for payment, and dishonored. By mistake, notice of non-payment was not given to the defendants, who resided at Liverpool, until the 27th of February, whereas it ought to have been given on the 24th, and they refused payment on the ground of this laches. Before the bill became due, the drawer had stopped payment and become bankrupt, and the acceptor was insolvent. The drawer had himself apprized the defendants of his situation at the time of his stopping payment, and that this bill would not be paid; and they knew that the acceptor had no funds but such as the drawer furnished him with: and on the 25th of February they admitted to the plaintiff's agent that they knew of the insolvency of the drawer and acceptor. It was contended that notice of the dishonor was unnecessary; but the court was clear that the insolvency of the drawer and acceptor, and the knowledge of it, did not dispense with the necessity of giving notice of the dishonor of the bill to the defendants. Postea to the defendants. See also Smith v. Beckett, and Brown v. Massey, post.

[(*a*) The doctrine stated in the text is fully recognized in the United States. And it makes no difference whether the drawer or maker was insolvent and known to be so at the time of drawing the bill or note, or became so subsequently. Crossen v. Hutchinson, 9 Mass. R. 205; Garland v. Salem Bank, 9 Mass. R. 408; Jackson v. Richards, 2 Cain. R. 343; Barton v. Baker, 1 Serg. & Raw. 334; Sandford v. Dillaway, 10 Mass. R. 52: Farnum v. Fowle, 12 Mass. R. 89; Buck v. Cotton, 2 Conn. R. 126; Edwards v. Thayer, 2 Bay, 217.

But a contrary doctrine has been held in Tennessee. Overton, 260.]

(68) See Howe v. Bowes, ante, p. 130.

[(*a*) Farnham was sued as endorser of a note made by Barker. Before the note became due Barker became insolvent, and stopped pay-

The right to insist upon a demand and notice may be waived or modified by custom, or the agreement of the parties. (*a*)

Thus where it is the custom of banks to notify the maker of a note without presenting the note itself, or to notify him before the note falls due, if the maker of the note is ac-

---

ment, and assigned all his property to Farnham, to secure him against this and other endorsements. The whole property assigned was not sufficient to secure him against the other notes, exclusive of the one in suit. No sufficient demand was made upon the maker. Farnham after notice to him offered to pay the note in foreign bills, but the plaintiffs refused to receive them. It was held that Farnham was liable as en dorser. Parsons C. J. delivered the opinion of the Court. "The defendant had no right to insist upon a demand upon the maker. He must be considered as having waived the condition of his liability, and as having engaged with the maker, on receiving all his property, to take up his notes. And the nature of this engagement cannot be varied by an eventual deficiency in the property; because he has received all there was. This intent of the parties is further supported by the offer of the defendant to take up this note if the plaintiffs would receive foreign bank notes in payment." Bond v. Farnham, 5 Mass. R. 170.

In an action against Small as endorser of a note made by Allen, no sufficient demand or notice being proved, it appeared that Small held a mortgage of Allen's real estate, as collateral and sufficient security for the amount of the note. Mellen C. J. delivered the opinion of the Court. "These facts present a stronger case in favor of the plaintiff than those in the case of Bond v. Farnham, (supra). There the property pledged was not a *sufficient* indemnity to the endorser, but it was all that the maker had. Here it is proved to be sufficient. If the endorser has protected himself from eventual loss by his own act in taking security from the maker, such conduct must be considered as a waiver of the legal right to require proof of demand and notice. And the facts before us clearly show such a waiver in the present case." Mead v. Small, 2 Greenleaf, 207.

So in a case in Pennsylvania, where the maker of a note had made a general assignment of all his property, to an endorser, to indemnify him for his advances and endorsements, it was held that the holder was excused from proving a regular demand and notice in order to charge the endorser. Barton v. Baker, 1 Serg. and Raw. 334. See also Corney v. Da Costa, post.

A different doctrine seems to have been held in New-York. To excuse a want of regular notice to an endorser, the plaintiff offered to prove, that the maker had failed before the note became due, and that he had conveyed his property in trust to secure and indemnify the defendant against his endorsement, and that the trust fund was sufficient for this purpose. The plaintiff was nonsuited; and the court refused to set aside the nonsuit, without saying anything as to the effect of the evidence above stated. Ireland v. Kip, 11 Johns. R. 231.]

[(*a*) See Renner v. Bank of Columbia, ante, p. 152; and the cases in the next note. See also Hartford Bank v. Stedman, 3 Conn. R. 489.]

quainted with this custom, such a notice will be a sufficient presentment to charge the endorser. (*a*)

[(*a*) It is the usage of the banks in Boston, where a note is payable with grace, to notify the promiser on the first day of grace, that the note will become due on the last day of grace, and request him to make payment, by sending a printed notice to this effect by the messenger, who does not take the note with him; and on the last day of grace to notify the endorser that the note is not then paid. In an action against an endorser, where the maker and endorser had been notified in conformity with this usage, and it was proved that the defendant was cognizant of this usage, and had in other cases conformed to it, the court held that this evidence was proper to go to the jury, to infer from it an agreement of the defendant to waive a legal demand on the maker, and to be bound by the demand and notice in conformity with the usage of the banks. Jones v. Fales, 4 Mass. R. 245.

In Widgery v. Munroe, 6 Mass. R. 449, a similar case to the foregoing, the court held that notice to the maker of a note in conformity with the usage of a bank, of which the endorser was cognizant, was sufficient to bind him.

The Lincoln and Kennebec Bank v. Page is to the same effect. Sewall J., who delivered the opinion of the Court, said, "It is incumbent upon the holder of a note, to prove, in maintaining an action against an endorser, a demand upon the promiser, as soon as the note became due, and notice to the endorser." But, he said, that the endorser might waive or modify his right to require such demand and notice. "When this is done by an express stipulation, there can be no doubt: and where he continues to endorse notes, and to deal with a bank, where by the known usage, or by the by-laws of the bank, these privileges have been taken to be waived or modified; his dealings and contracts are to be understood and enforced with the constructive effect of such usage." Lincoln and Kennebec Bank v Page. 9 Mass. R. 155.

See also Blanchard v. Hilliard, 11 Mass. R. 85; and Weld v. Gorham, 10 Mass. R. 366.

In a subsequent case the same court held that the endorser of a note who was not acquainted with the usage of the bank at which the note was payable, as to demand and notice, was not bound by a demand and notice in conformity to such usage. Peirce v. Butler, 14 Mass. R. 303.

But in a later case the same court held that a demand upon the maker of a note in conformity with the usage of a bank of which he was cognizant, was sufficient to charge an endorser.

Johnson was sued as endorser of a note made by E. and M. Toppan. The note being lodged in one of the Boston banks, the makers were notified according to the custom of the Boston banks, of which the makers were cognizant. But Johnson resided at Newburyport, and there was no evidence that he had any knowledge of the usage of the Boston banks. Verdict for plaintiffs, and motion for new trial. Parker C. J. delivered the opinion of the Court. "If the endorser has seasonable notice of the fact of non-payment, when the note is due, it must be immaterial to him, in what form the demand upon the maker was made. If there has been such a demand as the maker was bound by, so that he had no right to refuse payment; it is not easy to see how it concerns the endorser, whether the legal forms had been complied with, or waived by the promiser." Judgment on the verdict. Whitwell v. Johnson, 17 Mass. R. 449. See also State Bank v. Hurd, ante, p. 133.]

Where one person was a member of two partnerships, one of which signed, and the other of which endorsed a note, it was held that a presentment for payment was still necessary in order to charge the endorsers. (*a*) (*b*)]

Sect. 2.—Notice (69) must be given of a failure in the attempt to procure an acceptance, though the application for such acceptance might have been unnecessary; otherwise the person guilty of the neglect may loose his remedy upon the bill.

But such neglect will be no bar to a subsequent endorsee, if he took the bill before it became due, and gave value for it, and was ignorant that acceptance had been refused. (70)

[(*a*) Swift C. J. said, "It is true one of the defendants must, in legal consideration, have known that the note was not paid; but he equally well knew, that the note, when it became due, had not been presented to the makers, and payment demanded; he knew the fact that exonerated the defendants from all liability on their endorsement; and it would be strange logic to say that this knowledge rendered the defendants liable." Dwight v. Scovil, 2 Conn. R. 654.]

[(*b*) In Massachusetts where the maker of a note died, and an administrator was appointed before the note became payable, the day of payment falling within a year from the time of his appointment, it was held that the holder might maintain an action against an endorser without proving a demand upon the administrator at the maturity of the note. This decision was on the ground that in Massachusetts the administrator is not obliged to pay any debt of the deceased, except such as are particularly privileged, within a year from the time of his appointment. Hale v. Burr, 12 Mass. R. 86.]

(69) Vide Blesard v. Hirst, and Goodall v. Dolley, post.

(70) O'Keefe v. Dunn, 6 Taunt. 305. (1815. Trin.) A bill at one month after date was drawn by defendants, payable to Sinclair or order: Sinclair presented it for acceptance, and acceptance was refused, but no notice was given to defendants: Sinclair endorsed the bill to plaintiff for a valuable consideration, before the month from the date expired, but plaintiff had no notice of the prior refusal to accept: when the bill became due it was duly presented for payment, payment was refused, and notice thereof given to defendants. Action inde: defendants pleaded the presentment for acceptance by Sinclair, the refusal and want of notice thereof; plaintiff traversed the presentment and refusal, and after verdict thereon for defendants, rule nisi to enter judgment for plaintiff non obstante veredicto: after cause shewn, and time to consider, Gibbs C. J., Heath, and Dallas, against Chambre J., were of opinion that plaintiff was entitled to judgment; that the bill did not necessarily require presentment for acceptance; that defendants therefore had not, by the nature of the instrument, stipulated for such presentment; but that, on the contrary, they had, by its form, agreed that it

So if the drawee offer a partial or conditional acceptance, or an acceptance at an extended period, or if any other person offer an absolute one, though the holder may be willing to acquiesce in such acceptance, he must (71) give notice.

In that case, however, if he wishes to have the power of availing himself of it, he should mention in his notice the acceptance offered; for a notice generally of non-acceptance shews (72) he did not acquiesce in such offer.

A neglect to give notice, upon the refusal of any thing more than a conditional acceptance, is done away by the completion of those conditions before the bill becomes payable; and a neglect, upon the refusal of any thing more than a partial acceptance, discharges the persons entitled to it only from their responsibility as to the payment of the residue.

[Where the holder of a bill presented it for acceptance, and the drawee being out, was asked by his clerk to leave it, but the holder of the bill had it protested, but did not give immediate notice to the parties to the bill, it was held that they were discharged, notwithstanding the bill was accepted on the next day by the drawee, and was afterwards protested for non-payment. (*a*)]

---

should be negotiable till the period for payment arrived; that an innocent endorsee therefore might be deluded, and the negotiation of such bills defeated, if his remedy were to be destroyed by a fact of which he had no notice, and as to which there was nothing to raise a suspicion. Rule absolute. And on error, the judgment was affirmed in the king's bench. Ante, Dunn v. O'Keefe, p. 88.

(71) Vide Mar. 4th ed. p. 21. Beawes, § 221. 2d. ed. 445.

[See also Lenox v. Leverett, 10 Mass. R. 1.]

(72) Vide Sproat v. Matthews, ante, p. 113. note (47).

[(*a*) A bill drawn on Stevenson, was presented for acceptance September 30th at his counting room. Stevenson being out, his clerk proposed that the bill should be left, and said that Stevenson would accept it on his return. The bill was left; but Mitchell, the holder, had it immediately protested for non-acceptance. The next day Stevenson told a person sent by Mitchell, that he would accept the bill, and send it to Mitchell in the course of the day. No notice of the protest for non-acceptance was sent to the drawer, until the bill was protested for non-payment. In an action against the drawer, the court held that he was discharged. Story J. said, that the payee was not bound to consider what passed between him and Stevenson's clerk as a non-acceptance; but that he might properly have waited till the next day, a reasonable

The notice must come from the (73) holder, or some party entitled to call for payment or reimbursement; and though there is no prescribed form for it, ought to import that (74)

---

time, to ascertain the intentions of the drawee. "But he elected to consider the bill as dishonored on the 30th of September, and protested it accordingly for non-acceptance. And the question now is, whether as to all the other parties to the bill, he is not bound by that act; I am very clear that he is. When a bill is once dishonored, the holder is bound to give notice by the next practicable mail, to the parties whom he means to charge. No such notice was given in this case. But it is said that on the 1st of October, and before the mail from Boston was closed on that day, the drawee accepted the bill, and thereby notice became unnecessary. Assuming that the evidence clearly shows an acceptance, still where once a bill is dishonored, the right of the other parties to notice immediately and absolutely attaches, and no subsequent acts between the holder and drawee can vary that right." Mitchell v. Degrand, 1 Mason, 176.]

(73) Ex parte Barclay, 7 Ves. 597. Barclay was endorsee and holder of two bills drawn by Kemp upon Dearlow, and endorsed by Clay to Barclay. These bills were dishonored, of which Clay gave notice to Kemp; and on petition by Barclay to be allowed to prove these bills under a commission of bankruptcy issued against Kemp, one question was, whether this notice from Clay, and not from Barclay the holder, were sufficient. And Lord Eldon C. J., after referring to Tindal v. Brown, held that the notice ought to have come from the holder, and dismissed the petition. See Jameson v. Swinton, post.

[See also Williams v. Matthews, 3 Cowen, 252.]

(74) Tindal v. Brown, 1 Term Rep. 167. 186. A note which became due on the 5th of October, was presented at ten in the morning, and the maker not being at home, word was left for him where it lay; the holder sent again on the 6th, when the maker promised to take it up within the banking hours, which were from nine to four; on the 7th, the holder sent again to the maker, and the note not being paid, gave notice to the defendant, who was an endorser, but the defendant said he had made it his own; the maker had told defendant on the 6th, that he could not pay it, and desired the defendant would: all the parties lived at Bristol. The jury found for the plaintiff; but upon a rule to shew cause why there should not be a new trial, and cause shewn, the court granted a new trial. Lord Mansfield said, "What is reasonable notice is a question partly of fact, and partly of law: it may depend in some measure on facts; such as the distance at which the parties live, the course of the post, &c.; but wherever a rule can be laid down with respect to this reasonableness, *that* should be decided by the court, and adhered to for the sake of certainty. Per Willes J. "New credit was given to the maker, and I cannot consider notice from the maker equal to notice from the holder." Ashhurst J. "The reasonableness ought to be settled as a question of law; the next day at the most is as long as is necessary in a case like this; if the parties live at a small distance, this is a sufficient time; if at a greater, they should write by the next post. Notice means something more than knowledge, because it is competent to the holder to give credit to the maker: it is not enough to say that the maker does not intend to pay, but that the holder does not intend to give credit; the party ought to know whether the holder

the person to whom it is given is considered liable, and that payment from him is expected. (*a*)

It has indeed been held, that notice from the acceptor to the drawer that he had not been able to pay it, and that it was then in plaintiff's hands, was sufficient; but that might,

---

intends to give credit to the maker, or to resort to him." Per Buller J. "*When* the post goes out, is a matter of fact; when that is established, it is a matter of law, what notice is reasonable; as to giving time, the holder does it at his peril, and that is enough to decide the case; the purpose of giving notice is to let the party know that he is looked to for payment, that he may have his remedy over by an early application; if it shews that the holder has given time, it discharges the party: it ought to purport that the holder looks to him for payment, and a notice from another person cannot be sufficient; it must come from the holder." Upon the second trial there was contradictory evidence whether the notice from the maker was on the sixth or the seventh, and the jury found again for the plaintiff; but the court said it was a verdict against law, and granted another new trial.

[(*a*) Where the maker of a note was absent from the State at the time the note fell due, and a demand made at his dwelling house; it was held that an endorser was chargeable although the notice to him did not state the absence of the maker. Sanger v. Stimpson, 8 Mass. R. 260.

The notice to an endorser, which was sent on the last day of grace, January *sixth*, called the note "Jotham *Cushing's* note;" the name of the maker being in fact Jotham *Cushman;* and also said that the note became due January *third.* In an action against the endorser the judge (Parker) directed the jury to find for the plaintiff, if they believed that the defendant must from the notice have necessarily known what note was intended; which they accordingly did. And the whole court considered the direction correct, and judgment on the verdict. Smith v. Whiting, 12 Mass. R. 6.

A notice sent to an endorser by a notary public, who had presented the note for payment, did not state who was the holder of the note, nor at whose request the notice was sent. The notice was held sufficient. Parker C. J. giving the opinion of the court, said, "No particular form is necessary; the great object of the notice is to put the party affected by it on his guard; and if he is informed of the two principal facts, that the note is dishonored, and that the holder looks to him for payment, he may easily acquire all other knowledge necessary for his safety." Shed v. Brett, 1 Pick. 401.

The maker of a note paid a part of the amount on the day it became due, a general notice to the endorsers not stating this part payment, was held sufficient to charge them. James v. Badger, 1 Johns. Cas. 131.

A note was made for $1216.50, at the bottom of the note were the figures $1216.52. The notice of non-payment sent to the endorser described the note as given for the latter sum. In an action against the endorser the judge left it to the jury, whether the note produced, and the one described and intended by the notice were the same. Verdict for the plaintiff. A motion for a new trial was refused. The court said, "The law does not prescribe any form of notice to an endorser. It is not perhaps requisite to specify the amount of the note. The notice was sufficient to put the defendant on inquiry." Reedy v. Seixas, 2 Johns. Cas. 337.]

perhaps, have been on the ground that the acceptor wrote for the plaintiff, and as his agent. (75)

[But notice to the drawer, from a drawee who refuses acceptance, is not sufficient. (*a*)]

A notice from the holder or any other party will enure to the benefit of every other party who stands between the person giving the notice and the person to whom it is given. (76)

Therefore a notice from the last endorsee to the drawer, will operate as a notice from each endorser.

It is nevertheless prudent in each party who receives a notice, to give immediate notice to those parties against whom he may have a right to claim; for the holder may have omitted notice to some of them, and that will be no protection (77); or there may be difficulties in proving such notice.

Though a holder, or any other party, gives no notice but to the person of whom he took the bill, yet if notice is communicated without laches to the prior parties, he may avail himself of such communication, and sue any of such prior

---

(75) Rosher v. Kieran, 4 Campb. 87. Endorsees of bill against drawer, and the question was, whether defendant had had due notice of the bill's dishonor? It was proved, that, on the day the bill became due, the acceptor wrote to defendant that he had not been able to pay the bill, and that it was in plaintiff's hands: Lord Ellenborough held this sufficient, and verdict for plaintiff. See Stewart v. Kennet, 2 Campb. 177.

[(*a*) See Stanton v. Blossom, post p. 163.]

(76) Wilson v. Swabey, 1 Stark. 34. In an action by endorsee of a bill against the drawer, it appeared that notice was communicated to Lewis, an endorser, the day after the bill became due, and that Lewis gave defendant notice the next day: it was objected, that plaintiff had not given defendant notice: but Lord Ellenborough said, notice from any person who was party to the bill was sufficient, and plaintiff had a verdict.

[Stafford v. Yates, 18 Johns. R. 327 is to the same effect.]

(77) Edwards v. Dick, 4 Barnew. 212. In an action by endorsee against drawer, it appeared that the acceptor made the bill payable at a particular place, and it did not appear that plaintiff had given the acceptor notice of its dishonor: but on motion for nonsuit on that ground, the court held it sufficient in order to warrant a suit against defendant, that notice was given to him; he could not object that a third person had not had notice: if he was entitled to a remedy over against the acceptor, he should have given him notice. Rule refused.

[See Morgan v. Woodworth, 3 Johns. Cas. 89.]

parties; it is no objection in such case that there was no notice immediately from the plaintiff to the defendant. (78)

[A notice from a notary public to whom a bill or note has been handed for the purpose of having him present it and give notice, is sufficient; so from any person having a parol authority, or the mere possession of the bill or note. (*a*) (*b*)]

To give this notice, in the case of a foreign bill, effect, it is (79) necessary that a minute of the non-acceptance or

---

(78) See note (76).

[Stanton v. Blossom, 14 Mass. R. 116. Putnam J. delivered the opinion of the court. "Lord Ellenborough held that notice from any person who was a *party to the bill* was sufficient. But the drawee who refuses to accept, is not a party: and notice from him is in no degree better than notice from a stranger." "The holder himself, *or some one authorized*, must give the notice. Now the endorser who has been notified by the holder, of the dishonor of the bill, may, by reason of his liability, be considered as authorized to notify the drawer for the benefit of the holder as well as himself; both having an interest in the matter."]

[(*a*) Bank of Utica v. Smith, 18 Johns. R. 230; Hartford Bank v. Stedman, 2 Conn. R. 489; and see other cases cited p. 141 note, (*a*). In Hartford Bank v. Barry, 17 Mass. R. 94, the court held that the cashier of a bank, might by his endorsement on a note belonging to the bank, authorize a third person to make a demand and give notice; it being part of his official duty to see that the proper steps were taken to charge the parties to notes. But the court appeared to entertain no doubt that any person to whom the note was sent for the purpose, would be sufficiently authorized to make a demand and give notice, without any endorsement by the cashier.]

[(*b*) It is the custom of the banks in New York where a note is left with them for collection, to have a demand made on the maker, and notice given to the endorser. If where a note is left for collection, the bank neglects to give the notice, in consequence of which the owner of the note is damnified, he may maintain an assumpsit against the bank for a breach of the implied promise to give notice.

But if the bank employs a competent and faithful agent for the purpose of notifying the parties to the note, the bank is not answerable for his default or neglect. And it seems that a notary being a public officer, and usually employed to protest notes and notify endorsers, is a competent agent. But if the bank gives the note to an agent who is not competent, it will be liable for his default. Smedes v. Utica Bank. 20 Johns. R. 372. Utica Bank v. Smedes, S. C. 3 Cowen, 662.]

(79) Rogers v. Stephens, 2 Term. Rep. 713. In an action against the drawer of a foreign bill, it appeared that the bill had been noted for non-acceptance, but there was no protest, and this was pressed as a ground for a nonsuit. Lord Kenyon admitted the objection, but upon the other circumstances thought this a case in which a protest was not necessary. See post, note (117).

Gale v. Walsh, 5 Term. Rep. 239. In an action against the drawer of a foreign bill, it was reserved as a point whether it was necessary to prove a protest; and the court thought it so clear upon the motion to

non-payment, and a solemn declaration on the part of the holder against any loss to be sustained thereby, (which minute and declaration is called a protest) should be made out by a notary public, or if there be no such notary in or near the place where the bill is payable, by an inhabitant in the presence of two witnesses; and in some cases a copy, or some other memorial of it, should accompany the notice.

Such protest may also be made on the (80) non-acceptance of an inland bill, if such bill is for the payment of 5*l.*, or upwards, within a limited time after date, and the value

---

enter a nonsuit, that they suggested to the plaintiff's counsel the expediency of making the rule absolute in the first instance; and upon their acquiescence it was accordingly done; they afterwards however wished to have it opened, upon an idea that the drawer had no effects in the hands of the drawee, but it appearing upon the report that that idea was not founded, the rule stood. And in Brough v. Parkins, Lord Raym. 993. 6 Mod. 80. Salk. 131. Holt C. J. says, "A protest on a foreign bill is part of the custom." See also Orr. v. Maginnis, post.

[It was formerly held in several cases in the United States, that in an action on the protest for non-payment of a foreign bill, it was not necessary to aver in the declaration, or produce at the trial, a protest for non-acceptance. Morris v. Foreman, 1 Dall. 193. in 1787; Brown v. Barry, 3 Dall 365, in 1797; Clark v. Russell, 3 Dall. 415, in 1799.]

(80) By 3 & 4 Anne, c. 9. § 4. Whereas by an act of parliament in the 9th year of the reign of his late majesty King William the Third, entituled, "An act for the better payment of inland bills of exchange," it is, among other things, enacted, "that from and after presentation and acceptance of the said bill or bills of exchange, (which acceptance shall be by the underwriting the same under the party's hand so accepting,) and after the expiration of three days after the said bill or bills shall become due, the party to whom the said bill or bills are made payable, his servant, agent, or assigns, may, and shall cause the same bill or bills to be protested in manner as in the said act is enacted; and whereas by there being no provision made therein for protesting such bill or bills, in case the party on whom the same are or shall be drawn, refuse to accept the same by underwriting the same under his hand, all merchants and others do refuse to underwrite such bill or bills, or make any other than a promissory acceptance, by which means the effect and good intent of the said act in that behalf is wholly evaded, and no bill or bills can be protested before or for want of such acceptance by underwriting the same as aforesaid;" it is enacted, that from and after the first day of May, 1705, "in case, upon presenting of any such bill or bills of exchange, the party or parties, on whom the same shall be drawn, shall refuse to accept the same, by underwriting the same as aforesaid, the party to whom the said bill or bills are made payable, his servant, agent, or assigns, may and shall cause the said bill or bills to be protested for non-acceptance, as in case of foreign bills of exchange; for which protest there shall be paid two shillings, and no more."

is expressed therein to have been received, or (81) after an acceptance written on such a bill, for its non-payment.

But (82) if a man draw or endorse a bill on this country abroad, and afterwards comes here, a notice to him here need not be accompanied by the protest, or any memorial of it.

At least he cannot object to such notice, unless he applied for the protest on receiving the notice.

---

(81) By 9 & 10 W. 3. c. 17. § 1. "Whereas great damages and other inconveniences do frequently happen in the course of trade and commerce, by reason of delays of payment, and other neglects on inland bills of exchange in this kingdom;" it is enacted, that from and after the 24th day of June, 1698, all and every bill or bills of exchange drawn in, or dated at and from any trading city or town, or any other place in the kingdom of England, dominion of Wales, or town of Berwick upon Tweed, of the sum of 5*l.* sterling or upwards, upon any person or persons of or in London, or any other trading city, town, or any other place (in which said bill or bills of exchange shall be acknowledged and expressed the said value to be received) and is and shall be drawn payable at a certain number of days, weeks, or months after date thereof, that from and after presentation and acceptance of the said bill or bills of exchange, (which acceptance shall be by the underwriting the same under the party's hand so accepting) and after the expiration of three days after the said bill or bills shall become due, the party to whom the said bill or bills are made payable, his servant, agent, or assigns, may and shall cause the said bill or bills to be protested by a notary public, and in default of such notary public, by any other substantial person of the city, town, or place, in the presence of two or more credible witnesses, refusal or neglect being first made of due payment of the same; which protest shall be made and written under a fair written copy of the said bill of exchange, in the words or form following:

Know all men, that I, A. B., on the day of at the usual place of abode of the said have demanded payment of the bill, of the which the above is the copy, which the said did not pay, wherefore I the said do hereby protest the said bill. Dated this day of

(82) Cromwell v. Hynson, 2 Esp. N. P. C. 511. Endorsee against the endorser of a foreign bill. When the endorsement was made, Hynson (a master of a ship) was in Jamaica where the bill was drawn, but his residence was at Stepney. The bill was presented for acceptance, dishonored, and protested; and then sent to Hynson's house for payment, with notice of non-acceptance. Hynson was not then in England, but the bill was shewn to his wife, and the circumstances stated to her. It was urged, 1st, that notice should have been sent to Jamaica. 2dly, that the demand on the wife was not sufficient; and, 3dly, that a copy of the protest should have been sent with the notice; but Lord Kenyon overruled all the objections, and the plaintiff had a verdict.

Robins v. Gibson, 3 Camp. 334. 1 Maule, 288. Endorsee of bill drawn at Buenos Ayres, against drawer; before the bill became due

And a (83) protest cannot properly be made on any other inland bills.

And a protest upon an inland bill is never necessary where (84) the bill is for the payment of less than £20; and on such as are for the payment of more, though the 3d and 4th Ann. c. 9. s. 5. contain words which primâ facie import that a neglect to (85) procure it would preclude the holder from

---

defendant returned to this country: the bill was dishonored, and notice thereof left at his house, but no notice given of its being protested: Lord Ellenborough held the notice sufficient; and on motion for new trial, the court agreed with him: Lord Ellenborough said, it did not appear that defendant requested to have the protest; he had notice of the bill's dishonor, and as circumstances alter, the rule respecting notice changes; if the party is abroad he cannot know of the protest but by having it: being here, he might have inquired to ascertain that fact. Rule refused.

(83) Leftley v. Mills, 4 Term Rep. 170. An inland bill for £20 7s. payable 14 days after sight, became due 24th April, 1790. A banker's clerk called with it for payment in the morning, and the acceptor not being at home, left word where it lay; after six, another of the clerks, who was a notary, noted it, and between seven and eight the first clerk went with it again. The acceptor tendered him the amount of the bill, and sixpence over; but he insisted on 2*s.* 6*d.* for the noting, and *that* sum not being paid, an action was brought against the acceptor, who pleaded the tender. Lord Kenyon thought a tender of the amount of the bill at any time of the day it was payable, was sufficient; upon which the jury found a verdict for the defendant. A rule to show cause why there should not be a new trial, was afterwards granted; and upon cause shewn, Lord Kenyon thought the acceptor had till the last minute of the day of grace to pay the bill, and that it could not be noted or protested till the following day. Buller J. thought they were payable any time of the last day of grace upon demand, so as such demand was made within reasonable hours; and that they might be protested on that day. Grose J. declined giving any opinion on these points; but the whole court concurred, that the bill in question could not be noted, because it was payable within a limited time after sight, and the statute authorizes the noting of such inland bills only as are payable after date. Lord Kenyon also thought that the sixpence tendered was sufficient for the noting, and the rule was discharged.

(84) By 3 & 4 Anne, c. 9. § 6. it is provided, that no such protest shall be necessary, either for non-acceptance or non-payment of any inland bill of exchange, unless the value be acknowledged and expressed in such bill to be received, and unless such bill be drawn for the payment of £20 sterling or upwards; and that the protest hereby required for non-acceptance shall be made by such persons as are appointed by the act of 9 & 10 W. 3. c. 17. to protest inland bills of exchange for non-payment thereof.

(85) Brough v. Parkins, Tr. 2 Anne, Lord Raym. 992. 6 Mod. 80. Salk. 131. In an action against the drawer of an inland bill, it was insisted upon for error, that it did not appear by the declaration, that the bill had been protested; sed per Holt C. J. "on an inland bill no

recovering against the persons entitled to notice any special damages or costs occasioned by the non-acceptance or non-payment and interest, yet it hath not generally that effect. (86).

---

protest was necessary by the common law, and the statute does not destroy or take away the party's action where there is no protest; nor is the want of a protest any bar of the action; but the act seems only to take away from the plaintiff his interest and damages where he has not made a protest, or to give the drawers a remedy against him by way of action for their costs and damages"—and the judgment was affirmed.

Harris v. Benson, Tr. 5 G. 2. Str. 910. In an action against the drawer of an inland bill after an acceptance, Raymond C. J. ruled, that for want of a protest according to 9 & 10 W. 3. c. 17. the drawer could not be charged with interest. In Lumley v. Palmer, Ann. 77. Lord Hardwicke says, "At common law there was no way to charge the drawer of an inland bill with interest and costs after a protest; and therefore the first act was made, that after acceptance by underwriting, these bills might be protested for non-payment, and that thereupon interest and charges should be paid by the drawer from the time of the protest, the statute does not say the original sum, for that is recoverable without protest, but interest and charges."

Windle v. Andrews, B. R. Trin. 59 G. 3. 2 Barnew. 696. In an action against the drawer of an inland bill, in which the requisites specified in 3 & 4 Ann. c. 9. § 6. occurred, rule nisi to strike out the interest from the verdict, on the ground that there had been no protest; but on cause shewn, the court held the want of a protest no ground for disallowing interest where notice of the dishonor of the bill had been duly given; that the object of 9 & 10 W. 3. and 3 & 4 Ann. c. 9. § 4. was to give interest, damages, and costs in cases in which it was supposed they were not recoverable at common law, not to deprive a plaintiff of them in any case in which the common law would give them; that the 5th section, which contained the words of deprivation, was by way of proviso only, to qualify the additional benefit that statute and the statute of William were supposed for the first time to give; that the proviso in the 8th section contained words to secure to a plaintiff all his common law rights, and that the right to damages was a common law right; that it was upon this principle only that the constant allowance of interest where there was no protest could be explained; that the 5th section contained words to annul parol acceptances; and in Rex v. Meggott, Hil. 7 Geo. 2. ante, p. 97. Eyre C. J. of K. B. held that they had that effect; that this notion was corrected in Lumley v. Palmer, ante, p. 97. in Mich. Term, 8 Geo. 2. upon the principle now adopted by the court, that the 5th section of 3 & 4 Ann. c. 9. deprived a party of no remedy he had at common law; that that case must be considered as having virtually overruled Harris v. Benson, which was in Tr. 5 Geo. 2., and that from that time, for any thing which appeared to the contrary, parol acceptances had been held binding, and interest had been allowed against the drawers and endorsers of all inland bills, though no instance could be shewn in which any such bill had been protested.

(86) By 3 & 4 Anne, c. 9. § 5. it is provided, that if such (see § 4. ante, p. 165.) bill be not accepted by such underwriting, or endorsement in writing, no drawer of any such inland bill shall be liable to pay any costs,

A protest may (87) also be made on the non-payment of coal notes, given pursuant to 3 Geo. 2. c. 26. § 7. (*a*)

A foreign bill should be noted for non-acceptance or non-

---

damages, or interest thereupon, unless such protest be made for the non-acceptance thereof, and within 14 days after such protest the same be sent, or otherwise notice thereof be given to the party from whom such bill was received, or left in writing at the place of his or her usual abode: and if such bill be accepted, and not paid before the expiration of three days after the said bill shall become due and payable, then no drawer of such bill shall be compellable to pay any costs, damages, or interest thereupon, unless a protest be made and sent, or notice thereof be given, in manner and form above-mentioned. Nevertheless every drawer of such bill shall be liable to make payment of costs, damages, and interest upon such inland bill, if any one protest be made of non-acceptance or non-payment thereof, and notice thereof be sent, given, or left as aforesaid.

(87) By 3 Geo. 2. c 26. § 7., be it enacted, That from and after the 24th day of June, 1730, all lightermen and other buyers of, or contractors for, coals on board of any ship or vessel in the port of London, shall, at the time of the delivery of such coals, either pay for the same in ready money, or for such part thereof as shall not be so paid, shall give their respective promissory note or notes of their hands for payment thereof, expressing therein the words *value received in coals*, payable at such day or days, time or times, as shall for that purpose be agreed upon between such lighterman or other buyer of or contractor for coals, and the master or owner of such ship or vessel, or his agent or factor on his behalf; and that all such notes, in case of non-payment at the respective days and times therein mentioned, shall and may be protested or noted in such manner as inland bills of exchange may now be; and in default of such protesting or noting by any endorsee, and notice thereof given by such endorsee to the respective endorser or endorsers, within twenty days after such failure of payment, such respective endorser or endorsers, to whom such notice shall not be given, shall not be chargeable with or liable to answer or pay such sum of money, as shall be mentioned to be payable in or by such note or notes, nor any part thereof; any law, usage, or custom to the contrary thereof notwithstanding.

[(*a*) It is usual in the United States to have bills drawn in one State, and payable in another, protested, when dishonored, though such bills are frequently called inland bills. Whether such bills are to be considered as strictly *inland*, in the sense in which that word is used in the English law-books, and whether a protest is necessary to entitle the holder to recover the amount of the bill from the prior parties, seem not to be settled; but in many States a protest is essential in order to entitle the holder to the statute damages. See ante, p. 15, note (*a*). It cannot be safe to neglect to protest such bills.

It is also a common practice in many of the States to protest promissory notes for non-payment; though it is not necessary. Young v. Bryan, 6 Wheat. 146; Union Bank v. Hyde, 6 Wheat. 572; Nicholls v. Webb, 8 Wheat. 326; Bank of North America v. M'Knight, 1 Yeates, 145; Payne v. Winn, 2 Bay, 374.

A protest is said to be necessary in Delaware on the non-payment of promissory notes. 4 Griff. Law. Reg. 1069.]

payment on the (88) day on which acceptance or payment is refused; but it would seem that the protest (89) may be formally drawn up at any future period, provided that, in the event of a suit, it be drawn up before the commencement of such suit. (*a*)

A protest for (90) non-acceptance of an inland bill may be made in like manner as for non-acceptance of a foreign bill; but a protest for (91) non-payment of an inland bill cannot be made until the day after such bill has become due.

---

(88) In Buller's Nisi Prius, 272. it is said, "The use of noting is, that it should be done the very day of refusal, and the protest may be drawn any day after by the notary, and be dated of the day the noting was made." See Chitty on Bills, 163—4.

In Leftley v. Mills, 4 Term Rep. 174., Buller J. says, "With regard to foreign bills of exchange, all the books agree that the protest must be made on the last day of grace." This however is not said with reference to any distinction between the time of noting the bill, and that of formally drawing up the protest; but merely, as furnishing an argument, to shew within what time payment must be made; and the argument is equally conclusive, whether the party have the power of noting or of protesting the bill on the last day of grace. Indeed the noting is in effect an incipient protest.

(89) Chaters v. Bell, 4 Esp. N. P. C. 48. In an action by an endorsee against an endorser of a foreign bill, it appeared that the bill became due on the 24th of April, when payment was demanded and refused, and the bill noted for non-payment. Regular notice of the dishonor was given to the defendant, but he refused payment because there was no protest. On 14th of May, the protest was formally drawn up, and this action was afterwards brought. Lord Kenyon said, "He was of opinion, that if the bill was regularly presented and noted at the time, the protest might be made at any future period." A verdict was found for the plaintiff, but the point was reserved: and on the case coming on to be tried again on a venire facias de novo before Lord Ellenborough, his lordship expressed his concurrence with the opinion of Lord Kenyon. See the preceding note.

Mr. Selwyn, in his abridgment of the Law of Nisi Prius, 379. says, That a case was reserved in Chaters v. Bell, for the opinion of the court, and that the court, after argument, conceiving the question to be of great importance, directed it to be turned into a special verdict; but that the sum in dispute being small, and the parties unwilling to incur the expense of a special verdict, the recommendation of the court was not attended to, and the case was not mentioned again.

[(*a*) Though a protest must be produced at the trial of an action against the endorser of a foreign bill, it is not necessary that the notice to him should be accompanied by the protest. Lenox v. Leverett, 10 Mass. R. 1.

But in a previous case, Parsons C. J. says, "As to notice of the protest of a foreign bill, a copy of the protest should be given or offered to the drawer, or due diligence used to furnish him with this notice before he can be charged." Blakely v. Grant, 6 Mass. R. 386.]

(90) See 3 & 4 Ann. c. 9. § 4. ante, p. 165. n. (80).

(91) See 9 & 10 W. 3. c. 17. § 1. ante, p. 166. n. (81). which enables

A notice the day the bill or note becomes due, is not too soon ; for though payment may still be made within the day, non-payment on presentment is a dishonor. (92)

To such of the parties as reside in the place where the presentment was made, the notice must be given at the farthest, by the expiration of the (93) day following the failure ; to those who reside elsewhere, by (94) the post of that or the next post day.

---

persons to make such protests "after the *expiration* of three days" after the bill has become due.

(92) Burridge v. Manners, 3 Campb. 193. Endorsee of note against payee ; the note was presented the forenoon of the day it became due, when payment was refused, and in the afternoon of that day plaintiff sent notice of its dishonor to defendant ; it was urged that this notice was too soon, because the maker had the whole day to pay the note ; but Lord Ellenborough thought it a sufficient notice, for as soon as the maker refused payment the note was dishonored. The plaintiff had a verdict.

[Many cases in the United States recognise the law as stated in the text. Shed v. Brett, 1 Pick. 401 ; Corp v. M'Comb, 1 Johns. Cas. 328 ; Bussard v. Leyering, 6 Wheat. R. 102 ; and Lindenberger v. Beall, 6 Wheat. R. 104.]

(93) Tindal v. Brown, ante, p. 161, note (74). Muilman v. D'Eguino, ante, p. 138. note (31).

Smith v. Mullet, 2 Campb. N. P. C. 208. In an action against an endorser of a bill, the only question was, whether the plaintiff had given due notice of its dishonor to one Aylett, his immediate endorser. All the parties resided in London: the bill became due and was dishonored on the 19th of May, a Saturday. The holder (who had received it from the plaintiff) gave notice to the plaintiff on the Monday ; and plaintiff sent notice to Aylett on Tuesday, by the twopenny post, but so late that it did not reach Aylett till Wednesday. Lord Ellenborough said, he thought there could be no rule more convenient than that where all the parties resided in London each should have a day to give notice ; here a day had been lost. He therefore nonsuited the plaintiff.

(94) Malynes, B. 3. c. 6. § 1. 1st ed. p. 265. Mar. 2d ed. p. 24.

[In a case where the evidence seemed to leave it doubtful, whether notice to an endorser was put into the post-office, on the day on which the note fell due, or on the next, C. J. Parker, in delivering the opinion of the Court, said, "It cannot be requisite, nor do we find that it has ever been required to give notice to an endorser, living in another town, by the very next mail after the dishonor of the note, or on the same day. The next day is early enough : and if there be two mails aday, whether the notice goes by the first or second of these mails, we think, is immaterial: provided it was put into the post-office early enough to go by a mail of that day." Whitwell v. Johnson, 17 Mass. R. 449.

See also Robinson v. Ames, 20 Johns. R. 146.

Where the evidence proved notice to an endorser given *within three days* after advice received of the dishonor of a bill, where the holder and endorser resided in the same city, it was held that it did not prove a reasonable notice. Bryden v. Bryden, 11 Johns. R. 187.

Each party has a day for giving notice. (95)

And he will be entitled to the whole day, though the post by which he is to send it, goes out within the day. (95)

Therefore, where the notice is to be sent by the post, it will be sufficient if it is sent by the post of the following day. (95)

Where a party receives notice on a Sunday, he is in the same situation as if it did not reach him till the Monday; he is not bound to pay it any attention till the Monday; (95)

And has the whole of Monday for the purpose. (95)

So if the day on which notice ought thus to be given be a (96) day of public rest, as Christmas-day or Good Friday,

---

Notice sent from Portland to an endorser of a note at Cape Elizabeth, a distance of four miles, eight days after the dishonor of the note, there being no mail between the two places, was held to be too late. Hussey v. Freeman, 10 Mass. R. 84.]

(95) Bray v. Hadwen, 5 Maule 68. Plaintiffs paid into their bankers at Launceston a bill on London. On Sunday morning, 17th July, about half after eight, the Launceston bankers received a letter from London announcing its dishonor; Monday evening they put into the post a letter to plaintiffs at Tavistock to give them notice; that post did not leave Launceston till twelve on Tuesday; a post left Launceston for Tavistock at twelve on Monday. Plaintiffs forwarded notice without delay to the person who endorsed the bill to them, and that person immediately forwarded notice to defendant, who was an earlier endorser. Two queries were made; one, whether the Launceston bankers were not bound to have sent notice to plaintiff by Monday's post; and, secondly, whether plaintiff should not have given notice immediately to defendant, and not have left it to the later endorser to give that notice: Graham B. overruled both objections, and verdict for plaintiff: and on motion for new trial, the court held it was now the settled rule that each party was entitled to an entire day for the purpose of giving notice, and that the Launceston bankers therefore were not bound to send their notice by the Monday's post, but had the whole of Monday to put in their letter; and that, as there was no delay in transmitting notice to defendant, he could not protect himself on the ground of want of notice, and rule refused.

Wright v. Shawcross, 2 Barnew. 501. Plaintiff received notice by a letter on a Sunday of the dishonor of a bill: he did not send notice to defendant till Tuesday's post, which set out in the evening; he might have sent it in the evening of Monday by the Monday's post. But on motion for new trial, after verdict for plaintiff, the court held plaintiff was not bound to open the letter till Monday, nor bound to send notice till the Tuesday, and therefore rule refused.

(96) See Smith v. Mullet, ante, p. 171., and Haynes v. Birks, and Scott v. Lifford, post. p. 174. note (98). See also Tassell v. Lewis, ante, p. 151. note (53), and 39 & 40 Geo. 3. c. 42. enacting, that with respect to noting and protesting bills and notes which become due on Good Friday, that day shall be considered like a Sunday or Christmas-day.

[It has been held in several cases in the United States, where a bill

or a day of (97) similar sanctity according to the religion of the party bound to give notice, the notice need not be given until the following day.

If the holder of a bill or note place it in the hands of his banker, the banker is only bound to give notice of its dishonor to his customer, in like manner as if he were himself the holder, and his customer were the party next entitled to notice. (98)

And the customer has the like time to communicate such notice as if he had received it from a holder. (98)

And therefore by thus placing a bill or note in a banker's hands, the number of persons from whom notice must pass, is increased by one. (98)

Thus notice sent by a London banker to a London customer, the day after the dishonor, (98) is in time ; and if the customer communicate that notice the day following, that (98) will be in time also.

---

or note was dishonored on Saturday, that notice on Monday was sufficiently early. Jackson v. Richards, 2 Cain. R. 343 ; James v. Badger, 1 Johns. Cas. 131 ; Williams v. Matthews, 3 Cowen, 252.]

(97) Lindo v. Unsworth, 2 Campb. N. P. C. 602. Notice of the dishonor of a bill was sent to the plaintiff in London, on the 8th of October; but he being a Jew, and the 8th of October being the day of the greatest Jewish festival throughout the year, on which all Jews are prohibited from attending to secular affairs, gave no notice by the post of that day to the defendant, who lived at Lancaster, but sent it to him by the post of the 9th. Lord Ellenborough held, that the plaintiff was excused by his religion from giving notice on the 8th; and that the notice sent by the post on the 9th was sufficient. The plaintiff had a verdict.

(98) Haynes v. Birks, 3 Bos. and Pull. 599. In an action against the endorser of a bill, it appeared that the bill, which had been endorsed in blank and deposited by the plaintiff in the hands of his bankers, became due on Saturday, October 1st. On that day, at two o'clock, it was presented for payment by the bankers, and payment being refused, it was again presented between nine and ten at night by a notary, and again dishonored; the bankers sent the bill, and notice of its dishonor, to the plaintiff on the Monday, and the plaintiff gave notice to the defendant on Tuesday, about noon : the plaintiff lived at Knightsbridge, and the defendant in Tottenham-court-road. The only question was, whether this notice was sufficient. A verdict was found for the plaintiff, with liberty to defendant to move to enter a nonsuit. On motion accordingly, it was urged that the bankers were to be considered as the agents of the plaintiff, and that the defendant was entitled to the same notice as if the bill had remained in the plaintiff's hands: but the court thought that reasonable diligence had been used, and therefore

[And where a bill or note is sent by the holder to his agent for him to obtain payment, and he gives seasonable notice to his principal of its dishonor, he does all that he is required to do; and a notice from the principal will be sufficient to charge the prior parties to the bill or note, though a notice sent directly by the agent would have reached them much sooner. (*a*)]

---

refused a rule. Lord Alvanley, however, said, that if a bill be returned to a banker, he is bound to give notice to his principal that very day, if he can do so by using ordinary diligence.

Scott v. Lifford, 9 East's Rep. 347. A bill due on the 4th of June, was presented on that day, by Down and Co. the plaintiff's bankers, who lived in London; the plaintiff lived in London also, and they gave him notice on the 5th. The defendant (the drawer) lived at Shadwell; and on the 6th the plaintiff sent notice to him by the twopenny post. Lord Ellenborough left it to the jury, whether the plaintiff had communicated the notice in reasonable time; and they thought he had. And on a motion for a new trial, Lord Ellenborough said, he could not say that the plaintiff, omissis omnibus aliis negotiis, was bound to post off immediately with notice; it was sufficient if reasonable diligence had been used. The court thought the verdict right, and refused a rule.

Langdale v. Trimmer, 15 East. 291. Plaintiff paid a note into Drummonds, his bankers; it became due 25th February, was presented and dishonored; they presented it again the 26th, a little before five, and payment being again refused, they gave notice directly to plaintiff, who lived in Holborn; by the next day's post, plaintiff gave notice to defendant, who lived at Farnham. Lord Ellenborough thought both notices in time, and after verdict for plaintiff, and motion for a new trial, the court agreed with him; they thought the banker was to be considered as a distinct holder, not as identified with his customer, and that the banker had till the next day to give notice to his customer, and the customer till the day following; and the rule was refused.

[(*a*) Noble, the defendant, master of an American ship, being at Madras and bound to Portsmouth in New Hampshire, the place of his residence, endorsed to the plaintiffs, residents at Madras, a bill of exchange drawn in New South Wales, and payable in London. They sent it to their agents in London to obtain payment of the drawees. The bill was duly protested for non-acceptance and non-payment, and within a reasonable time returned with the protests to the plaintiffs at Madras. The plaintiffs sent seasonable notice to Noble at Portsmouth. But their agents in London might have sent him notice much earlier. The court held that the notice was sufficient to charge Noble as endorser. Parsons C. J. giving the opinion of the court, said, "a person appointed a factor to cause a bill to be presented, is entrusted with no other powers, and it is his duty to notify his principal. The factor may not know to which of the prior parties to the bill the principal intends to resort, and if he does, he may not know their domicils, as he has no interest in the bill, or privity with the parties." He said that the principal was not bound to give this information to his factor. "There is no difference between the cases of a bill sent to a factor to procure acceptance, and of a bill remitted to a correspondent in payment, if the bill be dishonored." Colt v. Noble, 5 Mass. R. 167.

It is no excuse for not giving notice the next day after a party receives one, that he received his notice earlier than the preceding parties were bound to give it; and that he gave notice within what would have been proper time if each preceding party had taken all the time the law allowed him. The time is to be calculated according to the period when the party in fact received his notice. (99) (*a*)

Nor is it any excuse that there are several intervening parties between him who gives the notice and defendant to whom it is given; and that if the notice had been passed through those intervening parties, and each had taken the time the law allows, the defendant would not have had the notice sooner. (99) (*b*)

So in a case in New York the court held that the duty of an agent who had received a bill to procure payment, "extended no farther than to give notice to his principal, of the non-acceptance and non-payment, and to transmit the reqnisite protests, in order that the holder might give notice" to the prior parties. Tunno v. Lague, 2 Johns. Cas. 1.]

(99) Turner v. Leech, 4 Barnew. 451. Plaintiff was the eleventh endorser to a bill, defendant the eighth; plaintiff endorsed it to Bennett, Bennett to Fletcher, Fletcher to Hordem, and Hordem to Sansom and Co.; it was dishonored Saturday, 30th August, and on Monday, 1st September, Sansom gave notice to Hordem; this reached Hordem the 2d. and the same day he gave notice to Fletcher; Fletcher sent notice to Bennett on the 3d, and this notice reached Bennett on the 4th; he did nothing till the 8th, and then he gave notice to plaintiff, who paid the bill. Plaintiff sued defendant, and on case plaintiff urged that Bennett's laches had not discharged defendant, because defendant had notice as soon as he would, had each party between him and Sansom taken the time the law allowed them; but the court was clear that defendant was discharged, and judgment for defendant.

[It was held in a case in New York, where an agent had received a bill in order to procure payment, that if the agent himself undertook to give notice to the drawer, it would be sufficient, if it was given as soon as it could have been received from the holder; although the notice would not have been sufficiently early, if the agent had been the proprietor of the bill. Tunno v. Lague, 2 Johns. Cas. 1.]

[(*a*) In a case in New York it was held that the prevalence of a malignant fever which put a stop to all business at the place of residence of the drawer of a bill, was a sufficient excuse for not giving notice to him until November of a protest for non-payment made in September. Tunno v. Lague, 2 Johns. Cas. 1. But Van Ness J. in a subsequent nisi prius case, ruled that the prevalence of an epidemic was no excuse for not giving notice during its continuance. Roosevelt v. Woodhull, Anth. N. P. 35.]

[(*b*) In case of a note payable on demand, it seems that although the holder is not required to make an immediate demand on the maker, yet when he has made a demand and payment is refused, immediate notice must be given to an endorser in order to charge him. See Shaw v. Griffith, 7 Mass. R. 494.]

[It is not necessary that notice to an endorser should be given within the hours of business. (*a*)]

Sending a verbal notice to a merchant's counting-house (100) is sufficient; and if no person be there in the ordinary hours of business, it is (100) not necessary to leave or send a written one.

Sending a verbal notice to a man's place of business, at a time when he or some of his people might reasonable be expected there, is sufficient; it is not necessary to leave or send a written notice, or to send to the house where he lives. (101) (*b*)

[(*a*) Jameson v. Swinton, 2 Taunt. 224. In an action on a bill by the plaintiff, who was the endorsee of Elsham, against an endorser, the defence was, that due notice of the dishonor, which took place on the 10th of July, had not been given. Elsham (the last endorser) who lived at Back-hill, Holborn, received notice on the 10th at four o'clock in the afternoon, and he gave notice on the 11th, between eight and nine o'clock at night, to the defendant, who lived at Islington, Lawrence J. held, that this was sufficient to entitle Elsham to recover from the defendant, and therefore sufficient to enable the plaintiff, who received the bill from Elsham, to recover. Verdict for the plaintiff; and on motion to set it aside, it was urged, that the notice should have been given within the hours of business, but the court held the notice sufficient. Rule refused.]

(100) Goldsmith and al. v. Bland and al. at Guildhall, cor. Lord Eldon, 1 March, 1800. The plaintiffs sued the defendants as endorsers of two foreign bills, and to prove notice the plaintiffs shewed that they sent a clerk to the defendants' counting-house, near the exchange, between four and five o'clock in the afternoon; nobody was in the counting-house; the clerk saw a servant girl at the house, who said, that nobody was in the way, and he returned, having left no message with her. Lord Eldon told the jury, that if they thought the defendants ought to have had somebody in the counting-house at the time, he was of opinion, that the plaintiffs had done all that was necessary by sending their clerk; that the notice was in law sufficient, if the time was regular, whether the defendants were solvent at the time or not. The jury thought, that the defendants ought to have had somebody in the counting-house at the time, and that the plaintiffs had done all that was necessary. Verdict for the plaintiffs for 1633*l.*

(101) Cross v. Smith, 1 Maule, 545, Smith and Co. had a bill for 3176*l.* drawn by Fea and Co. accepted by Tuke, payable at Smith, Payne, and Smith's, due 12th of April, 1810; this bill they remitted to Smith, Payne, and Smith, their correspondents. Tuke banked with Smith and Co.; 6th of April Tuke directed Smith and Co. to write to Smith, Payne, and Smith, not to pay this bill; they did so, and when the bill was due it was protested, and sent to Smith and Co. at Hull. Fea and Co. had a counting-house at Hull, where they were merchants, and one lived within a mile, and the other within ten of Hull. The morning after Smith and Co. received the bill, their clerk went to give notice, and called at the counting-house of Fea and Co. about half after

But telling a man's attorney that a bill is dishonored, is no notice, unless the attorney has more than usual powers. (101) (*b*)

Though the endorser of a bill receive directions from the acceptor, to send word to the house at which it is payable to forbid its payment, and he does so, he is not bound to give any notice of those directions to any of the parties to the bill. (101)

And he is entitled to act as though he had received no such directions. (101)

---

ten; he found the outward door open, the inner one locked; he knocked so that he must have been heard had any one been there; waited two or three minutes and went away; on his return he saw Fea and Co.'s attorney, and told him. The next morning he went again at the same hour, but with no better success. No written notice was left, nor was any notice sent to the residence of any of the partners. Fea and Co. became bankrupts, and their assignees insisted that Smith and Co. had made this bill their own, and were not entitled to carry it to the debit of Fea and Co.; first, because they ought to have given notice of the directions they received from Tuke, to prevent payment by Smith, Payne, and Smith; and secondly, because calling at the counting-house without leaving a written notice, and without sending one to the residence of some one of the partners, was not sufficient notice of the bill's dishonor. On case, and time to consider, the court thought the notice to the attorney nothing, because he was not the proper person to receive such a notice; but they held, that Smith and Co. were not bound to give notice of the directions they had received, and that it would have been a breach of confidence in them to have done so; and they held, that going to the counting-house at a time it should have been open, was sufficient; and that it was not necessary to leave a written notice, or to send to the residence of any of the parties; postea to defendants.

Bancroft v. Hall, Holt, 476. Endorsee of bill against drawer. Plaintiff received notice of the bill's dishonor at Manchester, 24th of May; the same day he sent a letter by a private hand to his agent at Liverpool, to give defendant notice; the agent called at defendant's counting-house about six or seven, P. M., but the counting-house was shut up, and defendant did not receive notice till the morning of the 27th, Monday. Two points were ruled,—that sending by a private hand to an agent to give notice was sufficient; secondly, that it was sufficient for the agent to take the ordinary mode to give notice; the ordinary time of shutting was eight or nine.

[(*a*) Where the endorser of a note shut up his house in town soon after the note was made, and before it became due, and retired to his house in the country, intending however only a temporary residence in the country; it was held that a notice left at his house in town, being put into the keyhole, was sufficient to charge him. Stewart v. Eden, 2 Cain. R. 121.]

[(*b*) Where the holder of a note payable on demand, gave it to an endorser for him to collect the money of the maker, this was held not

And it is the same if the holder of the bill receive those directions.

Sending (102) notice by the post is sufficient though it is not received; and where there is no post, it is sufficient to send by the ordinary mode of conveyance. (*a*)

---

to be sufficient notice to charge the endorser. Agan v. M'Manus, 11 Johns. R. 180.]

(102) Saunderson v. Judge, ante, p. 128. note (13). The holder of a note wrote to the defendant, who was one of the endorsers, to say it was dishonored, and put the letter in the post, but there was no evidence that it ever reached the defendant, and the court held, that sending the letter by the post was quite sufficient. S. P. Kufh v. Weston, 3 Esp. N. P. C. 54. See also Scott v. Lifford, 9 East's Rep. 347. and 1 Campb. N. P. C. 246. In this case the parties lived in London and its vicinity, within reach of the twopenny post; and notice of the dishonor of a bill was sent by that conveyance, and the court of king's bench held that it was sufficient. The notice however must appear to have been put in in due time. Hilton v. Fairclough, 2 Campb. 633.

[So it has been held that putting a notice into the postoffice is conclusive evidence of notice; even if the party to whom it is directed can prove that he never received it. Shed v. Brett, 1 Pick. 401. See also Munn v. Baldwin, 6 Mass. R. 316.]

[(*a*) The sufficiency of a notice sent by the mail is well established in the United States, where the person to be charged resides in a different town or place from that in which the presentment is made. Munn v. Baldwin, 6 Mass. R. 316; Lincoln and Kennebec Bank v. Hammatt, 9 Mass. R. 159; Bussard v. Levering, 6 Wheat. R. 102; Linderberger v. Beall, 6 Wheat. R. 104; Shepard v. Hall, 1 Conn. R. 329.

But where he resides in the same place, a notice to him put into the post-office is not sufficient; but the notice to him must be personal, or left at his residence or place of business. Ireland v. Kip, 10 Johns. R. 501, and S. C. 11 Johns. R. 231; Smedes v. Utica Bank, 20 Johns. R. 372; Shepard v. Hall, 1 Conn. R. 329.

In an action against the endorser of a note, who resided within the limits of the city of New York, at Kip's Bay about three and a half miles from the post-office, a place to which the letter carriers do not carry letters, it was held that a notice for him put into the post-office was not sufficient. Ireland v. Kip, 10 Johns. R. 501.

In a new trial of the same case, the plaintiff offered to prove besides the putting the notice in the post-office that the defendant had given directions to the letter carriers of the post-office, to leave all letters that came to the post office for him at a broker's in Frankfort street in the city of New York, that the letter carriers called at the post-office three or four times every day, and took out and delivered all letters left there, and that the defendant usually called or sent every day for his letters to the house in Frankfort street. It was held this evidence was not sufficient to maintain the action, without proof that the notice was actually delivered. Ireland v. Kip, 11 Johns. R. 231.

Where there is no post-office in the town in which the party resides, perhaps a notice sent to the nearest post town would be sufficient. Shed v. Brett, 1 Pick. 401; Ireland v. Kip, 11 Johns. R. 231.

And a notice sent directed to the post-office, to which the person to

Therefore in the case of a foreign bill it (103) is sufficient to send it by the first regular ship bound for the place to which it is to be sent; and (103) it is no objection, that if sent by a ship bound elsewhere, it would by accident have arrived sooner, though the holder wrote other letters by that ship to the place to which the notice was to be sent. (*a*)

---

be notified usually resorts for his letters, is sufficient, although he resides in a different town in which there is also a post-office. Reid v Payne, 16 Johns. R. 218

Where the mail to the place of residence of the party to be notified, is sometimes sent by one route, and sometimes by another, a notice sent by either route is sufficient.

The endorser of a note owned by the Bank of Utica, payable at a bank in the city of New York, resided at Peterborough. Notice of non-payment to Smith was enclosed at New York to the cashier of the Utica Bank, who took it from the post-office in Utica, and put it into the post-office in Utica again the same day directed to the endorser at Peterborough, in season to go by the same mail as if it had been originally directed to Peterborough and not taken out of the office at Utica. There is another mail route to Peterborough, and had the letter gone by that route, it would probably have reached Peterborough a day or two sooner than it did. The court held the notice sufficient. Spencer C. J. delivered the opinion of the court. "I consider the mode adopted in this case, in the same light as if the notary had sent a notice directed to the defendant *via* Utica; in which case I can conceive no possible objection to the notice, for it is expressly in proof, that it was as usual to send letters to the defendant by the way of Utica, as by the other route. The law does not exact of the holder of a note or bill that he shall give the earliest possible notice of its dishonor. It requires of him only reasonable diligence." Woodworth J. dissented. Bank of Utica v. Smith, 18 Johns. R. 230.

The Hartford Bank held a note payable at the Middletown Bank. After a presentment for payment by a notary and refusal, he enclosed a notice directed to the endorser without any place of residence, in a letter to the cashier of the Hartford Bank requesting him to complete the direction. The cashier received the letter from the post-office at Hartford, and the endorser residing at that place returned the notice to the post-office after adding the word "*Hartford*." The notice was held to be sufficient to charge the endorser. Hartford Bank v. Stedman, 3 Conn. R. 89.]

(103) Muilman v. D'Eguino, ante, p. 138, note (31). To debt on bond conditioned to pay certain bills drawn on India at sixty days' sight, in case they should be returned protested; defendant pleaded that he had not notice so soon as he should have had. It appeared that notice was sent by the first English ships, but that by the accidental conveyance of a foreign ship not bound for England, and by which the holder wrote to England upon other matters, notice might have been sent sooner, and would have arrived sooner; but Eyre C. J. told the jury, that notice by the first regular ships bound for England was sufficient, and that it was not necessary to send notice by the chance conveyance of a foreign ship. The jury found for the plaintiff, and the court was satisfied with the verdict, and refused a new trial.

[(*a*) But where a bill drawn in the United States upon London was

And it is not essential the notice should be sent by the post where there is one; sending to an agent by a private conveyance, that he may give the notice, will be sufficient, if the agent give the notice, or take due steps for the purpose, without delay. (104)

And it will be of no consequence though the notice by the agent is not quite so early as notice by the post would have been. (104)

Where it is not known where a party lives, due diligence must in general be used to find out. (105) (106)

And where such diligence is unsuccessful, it will excuse want of notice. (105)

---

protested in London for non-payment June 3d. and a notice with the protest forwarded June 19th, by which delay it appeared that the opportunity of a packet was lost: the court held that this was an inexcusable delay unless satisfactorily accounted for. Lenox v. Leverett, 10 Mass. R. 1.]

(104) See Bancroft v. Hall, ante, p. 177.

(105) Bateman v. Joseph, 12 East's Rep. 433. In an action by an endorsee against the payee and first endorser of a bill, it appeared that the plaintiff received notice of its dishonor on the 30th of September, in time to have given notice to the defendant on that day; he gave no notice however until the 4th of October; to excuse which, his clerk proved that the plaintiff did not know the defendant's residence until that day. Lord Ellenborough left it to the jury, whether the plaintiff had used due diligence to find the defendant's residence. They found for the plaintiff; and on motion for a new trial, the court refused the rule, saying, whether due notice had been given was a question of law, but whether due diligence had been used to discover the place of residence of a person entitled to notice, was a question of fact.

[Action against the drawers of a bill dated at New York, and drawn upon a house in that place. The defendants resided in Petersburg (Va.) The clerk of the notary who protested the bill made diligent inquiry for the drawers' place of residence at the banks and elsewhere, and being informed that they resided in Norfolk, (Va.) he sent a notice by post directed to them at that place, and another addressed to them at New York. It was held, that as it did not appear that the holder knew of their residence, he had used due diligence, and that the drawers were chargeable. Chapman v. Lipscombe, 1 Johns. R. 294.

See also Reid v. Payne, 16 Johns. R. 218.

Where the drawer of a foreign bill had been absent from the State for several years, the Supreme Court of Massachusetts thought that evidence of notice having been left at his former place of residence, would support an averment of due diligence in the declaration. Blakely v. Grant, 6 Mass. R. 386. But it does not appear from the case as reported, why a notice might not have been sent to the drawer, or that he had not some known domicil or place of business in the foreign country where he drew the bill.]

But merely inquiring at the house where a bill is payable, is not due diligence for finding out an endorser. (106)

Inquiry should be made of some of the other parties to the bill or note, and of persons of the same name. (106)

Calling on the last endorser, and last but one, the day after the bill becomes due, to know where the drawer lives, and on his not being in the way calling again the next

---

(106) Beveridge v. Burgis, 3 Campb. 262. In an action by the endorsee of a bill against the endorser, the excuse for not giving notice to defendant was, that plaintiff did not know his residence, but the only inquiry he proved was at the house where the bill was made payable. Sed per Lord Ellenborough, how could he expect information there? he might have inquired of other parties to the bill, or of persons of the same name in the directory: ignorance may excuse notice, but reasonable diligence must be used to obtain knowledge. Nonsuit.

[In a case in which the residence of the drawer of a bill was in a different place from that in which the bill was drawn, and no notice was given to the drawer of the dishonor of the bill, and no inquiry made to ascertain his residence, it was held that he was discharged.

In this case the counsel for the plaintiff contended that the place where the bill is drawn must be taken to be the residence of the drawer, and not being there when the bill was dishonored, notice was dispensed with. But Tilghman C. J. said he could find no such principle. Fisher v. Evans, 5 Binn. 541.

A different opinion seems to be expressed in a case in South Carolina. Action against the endorser of a note dated at Charleston. A notice to the endorser was left at a house where he usually lodged when in town, he then being absent. The case however does not state whether Charleston was his usual residence or not. Bay J. delivered the opinion of the court. "Charleston, being the place where the note was drawn and endorsed, shall be presumed to be the residence of both (maker and endorser) for every mercantile purpose; and the use of due diligence; to find out either of them there will answer the demands of the law upon this subject." Moodie v. Morrall, 1 S. Car. R. 307.

Action against the drawer of a bill drawn at Alexandria, D. C. on New York. The bill being protested for non-payment, two letters containing notice were immediately after put into the post-office at New York, one directed to the drawer at New York, and the other to him at Alexandria; and a third notice for him was left at the counting-house of the acceptors. It did not appear that any inquiries were made as to the drawer's place of residence. He in fact resided at Fairfield in Connecticut, and this was publicly known, and particularly to one of the acceptors of the bill. It was held that the notice given was not sufficient; and that the drawer was discharged, because due diligence had not been used to ascertain his place of residence. Barnwell v. Mitchell, 3 Conn. R. 101.

Action against the endorser of a promissory note payable at the Bank of Utica. When the note fell due, notice of its non-payment was given by a letter put into the post-office, directed to the defendant at Canandaigua. The defendant in fact lived at Ovid, in the county of Seneca, and had resided there for ten years previous. It was proved

day, and then giving the drawer notice, may be sufficient. (107) (*a*)

But if a party when he passes a bill or note declines saying where he lives, and undertakes to call upon the acceptor to see if the bill is paid, he cannot complain of want of notice. (108)

Notice to one of several partners, is notice to all: and when a bill has been drawn by a firm upon one of the partners, and by him accepted and dishonored, it is (109) unnecessary to give notice of such dishonor to the firm; for this must necessarily be known to one of them, and the knowledge of one is the knowledge of all.

---

that the book-keeper who gave the notice was informed by the cashier and some of the directors of the bank, that the defendant resided at Canandaigua. Spencer J. delivered the opinion of the court. "The notice is bad. With ordinary diligence the place of his abode might have been ascertained; and it must be the plaintiff's loss, not the defendant's, that the notice was not given." Judgment for defendant. Bank of Utica v. De Mott, 13 Johns. R. 432.]

(107) Browning v. Kinnier, Gow. 81. Defendant endorsed to Newman, Newman to Maberly, Maberly to Chesterman, and Chesterman to plaintiff; the bill became due 23d November; on the 24th plaintiff applied to Chesterman to know where defendant lived; Chesterman could not tell, and referred him to Maberly; he called on Maberly at 4 P. M., but Maberly not being at home, he did not repeat his call till the next morning, and then Maberly gave him the information, and he gave defendant notice. Dallas C. J. thought reasonable diligence had been used, but he left the question to the jury, who were of the same opinion.

[(*a*) So where the traveller of a house receives a bill or note, he is not bound when he passes it to his principals to inform them of the places of residence of the parties to the instrument; and if the bill is dishonored, it is sufficient for the holders to send and obtain the requisite information as soon as possible from their traveller, and afterwards to notify the parties they intend to charge, even if a delay of several days takes place in obtaining this information. Baldwin v. Richardson, 2 Dow. & Ryl. 285; 1 Barn. & Cres. 245.]

(108) Phipson v. Kneller, 4 Campb. 285. 1 Stark. 116. Plaintiff, the holder of a bill, asked defendant, the drawer, where he lived; he said, he had no regular residence, but lived amongst his friends, and he would call himself upon the acceptor, and see if the bill was paid. Lord Ellenborough held that this dispensed with all notice, and threw it upon defendant to inquire; and plaintiff had a verdict.

(109) See Porthouse v. Parker and another, post, in which Lord Ellenborough held that the plaintiff was not bound to prove that the defendants had received express notice of the dishonor of the bill, assigning the reason mentioned in the text.

[But where a note was made payable to, and endorsed by, two persons not partners, it was held that the written acknowledgement of one of

[So where the drawer of a bill is a partner in the house on which it is drawn, he is chargeable without any notice being given him of the dishonor of the bill. (*a*) (*b*)]

If the holder gives due notice of the bill's dishonor, but intimates that he expects it will be paid in a given time, and that he will keep it that time without putting more expense upon it unless the person written to objects, it will be no answer to an action afterwards against the person written to, that he had no notice upon the expiration of the extended time of non-payment. (110)

The law does not require a second notice when the extended time expires. (110)

But if the party written to, sustain any damage from not having such notice, he may perhaps be entitled to bring an action on that account. (110)

---

them that he had received due notice, was not sufficient to charge them both. Shepard v. Hawley, 1 Conn. R. 368.

See also Dwight v. Scovil, ante, p. 205.

Where the selectmen of a town drew an order upon the treasurer of the town, the court held that a presentment was necessary before an action could be brought against the town, but seemed to think that in case of presentment and non-payment, it would not be necessary to give notice to the selectmen. Varner v. Noble, 2 Greenleaf, 121.]

[(*a*) In an action against J. Jackson, as drawer of a bill, on which due notice of non-acceptance had not been given, it was proved that the drawer was a partner in the firm of Jackson and Brothers, the drawees. It was held that he was chargeable without any notice. Spencer C. J. delivered the opinion of the court. "In the absence of all other proof, the bill must be considered as drawn by one partner of the firm on the firm itself, in relation to the partnership business; and if so, then a knowledge of one of the firm of the dishonor of the bill, is, in point of law, knowledge by the whole firm. D. Jackson, the partner in London, had notice that the bill was refused acceptance, for he was the person who had refused. Although J. Jackson is alone sued on the bill, yet it must be deemed a partnership transaction; and a knowledge by one of the firm of the dishonor of the bill, is all that ought to be required." Gowan v. Jackson, 20 Johns. R. 176.]

[(*b*) Where the second of a set of exchange was accepted and protested for non-payment; and the protest together with the first of the set was sent back and presented to an endorser, and payment requested of him, it was held that the notice was sufficient. Kenworthy v. Hopkins, 1 Johns Cas. 107.]

(110) Foster v. Jurdison, 16 East. 105. Endorsee against drawer. When payment was refused, plaintiffs apprised defendants thereof, but added, they had reason to believe a friend would advance the money for the acceptor in a few days, that they would therefore hold it till the end of the week without putting more expense upon it, unless they heard from defendant to the contrary; the bill was not paid, but no further

The (111) drawer of a bill, and every endorser of a bill or note, is, primâ facie, to be presumed entitled to bring an action on paying it, and therefore entitled to insist on a want of notice, or on a neglect to make a proper presentment, but the (112) contrary may be proved.

[If the endorser of a note be dead at the time it becomes due, and there be executors or administrators, at that time, known to the holder, notice must be given to them; but if there be no personal representatives at the time, a notice sent to the residence of his family is sufficient; and it is not necessary to give notice afterwards to executors or administrators subsequently becoming such. (*a*)]

A surety, though not a party to a bill or note, may be discharged by want of notice and neglect to present, if it is probable he would otherwise have been safe. (113)

---

application was made to defendant for near two months: action, and Wood B. being of opinion that plaintiff should have given a second notice at the end of the week, and the jury thinking that certain circumstances proved, did not amount to a waiver of the want of such notice, verdict for defendant: but on rule nisi for a new trial, and cause shewn, the court thought plaintiffs had done all the law merchant required by giving one notice, that they then, at the highest, made themselves agents for defendants, to endeavor to get payment, and if any damage resulted to defendant for want of notice, it might perhaps entitle him to call on defendant as his agent by action, but that it was no defence to the action. Rule absolute.

(111) Vide Bickerdike v. Bolman, post, p. 192. note (119); and Rogers v. Stephens, post, p. 187. note (117).

(112) Bickerdike v. Bolman, post, p. 192. note (119); Rogers v. Stephens, post, p. 187. note (117); and Goodall v. Dolley, post, p. 189. note 118).

[(*a*) Action against the executors of an endorser. The endorser died at sea before the note fell due; but neither was his death known to the holders of the note, nor his will proved, until some time after. A notice of non-payment directed to the endorser, was left at his last residence, another sent to his family in the country by the post-office, and a third left with his reputed agent. Verdict for plaintiffs; and motion for new trial, on the ground that notice ought to have been given to the executors within a reasonable time after probate of the will. Spencer C. J. delivered the opinion of the Court. "The holders of the note gave all the notice in their power to give, when the note fell due. The rights of the holder of a note or bill, are to be determined by his acts, when the note or bill becomes due; and if he then gives such notice, as under the existing state of facts the law requires of him, his rights are fixed, and he cannot be required to superadd any other notice at a future period." Merchants Bank v. Birch, 17 Johns. R. 25.

In a previous case, where the endorser died before the note became due, and his will was not proved until some time after, it was held that

As if the parties who ought to have paid were solvent when the bill or note became due, and have failed since. (113)

But a person not party to a bill or note, cannot complain of laches or want of notice, unless he can shew it has done him prejudice. (114)

Therefore he cannot complain if the person who ought to have paid the bill or note were insolvent when it should have been paid. (114)

---

a notice left at his former residence, wás sufficient. Stewart v. Eden, 2 Cain. R. 121.]

(113) Philips v. Astling, 2 Taunt. 206. The declaration stated, that in consideration that the plaintiff would sell and deliver to Davenport and Finney certain goods, to be paid for by a bill to be drawn by Davenport and Finney on Houghton at six months, the defendants undertook to guaranty the payment of such bill. It then averred delivery of the goods, acceptance of the bill, its presentment for payment, and dishonor. At the trial, it appeared that Houghton was at sea when the bill became due, which was on the 14th of July, 1808; but that he had an agent residing in London, authorized to accept bills, and who had accepted this. That no presentment for payment was made to this agent when the bill became due. That on the 16th of July, the plaintiff gave Davenport and Finney notice that the bill remained unpaid, but no notice was given to the defendants. In February, 1809, Davenport and Finney became insolvent, and Houghton was declared a bankrupt in July, 1809, after which payment was demanded of the defendants. A verdict was found for the plaintiff, but the court, upon a rule nisi for a nonsuit, after referring to Warrington v. Furbor, (infra,) said, that here the insolvency of the drawers and the bankruptcy of the acceptor, did not happen until long after the bill became due, and that for any thing that appeared, if the money had been demanded either of the drawer or acceptor, the bill might have been paid; but that the necessary steps not having been taken to obtain paymant from the parties who were liable upon the bill, and solvent, the guarantee must be discharged, and therefore they made the rule absolute.

(114) Warrington and another v. Furbor and another, 8 East. Rep. 242. The plaintiffs guarantied the payment of the price, to the extent of £1000, of goods to be sold by one Martin to the defendants, at six months' credit. The goods were furnished, and the defendants accepted a bill at six months, for the value. This bill became due on the 3d of December, 1801; but on the preceding 21st of November the defendants became bankrupts. The plaintiffs were therefore obliged to pay the £1000, and now brought this action to recover the same. It was objected that the plaintiffs had not proved a presentment of the bill to the defendants for payment, without which, it was urged, that Martin could not have recovered against the plaintiffs, and therefore that the latter had paid the money in their own wrong. Lord Ellenborough held the proof unnecessary; this not being an action on the bill, and the defendants having been recently stripped of all their property; and the plaintiffs had a verdict; and on rule nisi to set it aside, and cause shewn, the court held the verdict right: and Lawrence J. said,

And in an action on a bond from the drawer or endorser of a bill, conditioned to pay it in a limited time after it becomes due, if the acceptor does not, it is no defence that the bill was not duly presented for payment. (115)

Or that due notice of its dishonor was not given to the defendant. (115) (*a*)

---

the guarantees were not prevented from showing that they ought not to have been called upon at all, for that the principal debtors could have paid the bill if demanded of them. Rule discharged.

Swinyard v. Bowes, 5 Maule, 62. Action for goods sold. Defence, that plaintiff had drawn on Chesner, a debtor of defendant, for the amount, and had given defendant no notice of the dishonor of that bill; Chesner was bankrupt the week after the bill became due, and was not in a condition in the interim to pay it. Bayley J. thought the defendant not within the custom of merchants, because he was not party to the bill; and as he did not appear to have been prejudiced by the want of notice, the not giving it him furnished no ground of defence; and on motion for new trial, the court thought him right, and rule refused.

[See also Holborow v. Wilkins, 2 Dow. & Ryl. 59, 1 Brod. & Bing. 10.]

(115) Murray v. King, 5 Barnew. 165. In an action against the payee of a bill, on a bond from him and the drawer to pay the bill in a month after it became due, if the acceptor did not, defendant pleaded that the bill was not duly presented for payment, and secondly, that defendant had not due notice of its dishonor. Plaintiff replied, that the acceptance was a forgery; and defendant rejoined, that he did not know it when the bill became due. Plaintiff demurred, and on argument, the court held the pleas bad, for the condition was silent as to the presentment and notice; and had it been intended that a neglect as to presentment or notice should have avoided the bond, the obligors should have taken care to have had words to express that intention.

[(*a*) It has been held in several of the United States that a guarantor of a note is in all cases liable, whether there has been a presentment and notice to him or not.

Rightmere, the payee of a note, endorsed on it "For value received, I sell, assign, and guaranty the payment of the within note to John Allen or bearer." In an action by Allen against Rightmere, it was held that it was not necessary for the plaintiff to prove a demand and notice. Spencer C. J. delivered the opinion of the Court. "The defendant insists that he stands in the situation of an endorser merely; but such is not the fact. The undertaking here is not conditional; it is absolute that the maker shall pay the note when due, or that the defendant will himself pay it." Allen v. Rightmere, 20 Johns. R. 365.

Little, the payee of a note, by a written endorsement guarantied its payment in six months, and passed it to Kinsman & Cobb before it fell due. In an action against the guarantor by them, no demand was proved on the maker, but about eighteen months after the note fell due, Cobb sued the maker in his own name, but had been able to collect nothing. The defendant proved that the maker of the note had sufficient visible property to pay all his debts for a long time after the note fell due. It was held that the defendant was liable on his guaranty. Mellen C. J. delivered the opinion of the Court. "The guaranty in its

Payment of (116) part, or (117) a promise to pay after full notice of the default, sufficiently evinces that the party

---

terms, is *absolute*, that the note should be paid in six months. It was the duty of the defendant upon such an engagement to see that the maker paid the money within the time specified; and if he did not, to take notice of his neglect, and pay the amount himself." Cobb v. Little, 2 Greenleaf, 261.

On a note made by Phelps, payable to Williams, Oct. 1st, 1806, Granger endorsed and signed a guaranty, "for value received," that the maker "was and would continue to be until the day of payment, of sufficient responsibility to pay the note;" and a promise to the payee, if the note was not paid, "by the 5th day of September, 1807, that he [Granger] would on that day pay the same to Williams." To an action on this contract, brought after Sept. 5th, 1807, Granger pleaded that Phelps was always able to pay the note until the date of the writ, that the defendant was a surety without funds, and that no notice was ever given to the defendant, or demand made on him previously to the date of the writ; and that no suit had ever been brought against Phelps. In the Court of Errors of Connecticut this plea was adjudged bad. Trumbull J. said, "This is not the case of a mere endorsement. No act was required on the part of Williams for obtaining the money of Phelps. He was merely bound to receive it, if offered. No special notice was necessary on that day in order to render Granger liable; for his engagement became immediately absolute on the failure of Phelps to pay. No special demand previous to the commencement of a suit was necessary." Williams v. Granger, 4 Day, 444.]

(116) Vaughan v. Fuller, Str. 1246., was an action against the endorser of a note, and it being proved that the defendant had paid part, Lee C. J. held, that *that* made the proof of a demand upon the maker unnecessary. See Lundie v. Robertson, Horford v. Wilson, Gibbon v. Coggon, and Potter v. Rayworth, post.

(117) Rogers v. Stephens, 2 Term Rep. 713. In an action against the drawer of a foreign bill, an objection was taken that there was no protest; but it appearing that the defendant had no effects in the hands of the drawees when the bill was drawn, or afterwards, and that on being pressed for payment by the plaintiff's agent after the bill was dishonored, he had said, it must be paid; Lord Kenyon thought a protest or notice unnecessary, and directed the jury to find for the plaintiff, which they did: a rule was afterwards granted, to show cause why there should not be a new trial, and it was stated *then*, and upon the shewing cause, that the defendant had really been prejudiced by the want of notice to the amount of the bill, that he had advanced money to one Calvert to the amount before the bill was drawn, that Calvert desired him to draw on the drawees as Calvert's agents, that he did so on a supposition that Calvert had effects in their hands; that he afterwards settled with Calvert, and upon a reliance that the bill was paid, delivered him up effects to more than the value of the bill, and that Calvert was since insolvent; that the defendant was prepared with evidence to this effect, but that Lord Kenyon delivered it as his opinion, that it did not make a protest or notice necessary; Lord Kenyon did not recollect that this evidence was offered, but he and all the court thought it answered by the defendant's admission that the bill must be paid, because that was an admission that the plaintiff had a right to resort to him upon the bill, and that he had received no damage by the want of notice, and was a promise to pay. The rule was discharged.

could not have sued on paying the bill or note, and consequently that he cannot insist on want of notice, or of a

---

Anson v. Bailey, Bull. Nisi Prius, 276. Tne endorsee of a note presented it for payment, but the maker pretended that the payee had promised not to endorse it over without acquainting him, and so put off the endorsee from time to time for three weeks; at the end of that period the endorsee wrote twice to the payee, stating what he had done, and the maker's excuse; the payee answered, that when he came to town he would set the matter right; and upon an action by the endorsee against the payee, the jury found for the plaintiff, though the maker became bankrupt before the second letter was written, and though he continued solvent for three weeks after the note was due.

Wilkes v. Jacks, Peake, 202. In an action against Jacks as endorser of a bill drawn by Vaughan on Eustace and Holland, it appeared that notice had not been given to the defendant, upon which the plaintiff offered to shew that Vaughan had no effects in the hands of Eustace and Holland; sed per Lord Kenyon, "That circumstance will not avail plaintiff; the rule extends only to actions brought against the drawer; the endorser is in all cases entitled to notice, for he has no concern with the accounts between the drawer and the drawee." The plaintiff then proved a letter from the defendant acknowledging the debt, and promising to pay, and upon *that* he had a verdict.

[In a suit against the endorser of a note, no demand on the maker was shown, but a promise to pay by the endorser after he was notified and called on for payment, and circumstances which tended to prove his knowledge of the neglect to make a presentment, were proved at the trial. Parker C. J. instructed the jury "that if the defendant when he made the promise to pay knew that no demand had been made on the maker," they should find for the plaintiff; which they did. Motion for a new trial. "Per Curiam. A promise of this sort to be binding must be made with a knowledge of the circumstances which operate to discharge the party; and the jury in this case have decided that there was such knowledge." Judgment on the verdict. Hopkins v. Liswell, 12 Mass. R. 52.

In an action against an endorser of a note who had not been duly notified of non-payment, it was proved that after the note became due, he had admitted his liability upon the note, and offered to pay it. At the trial the defendant's counsel moved that the plaintiff should be nonsuited unless he further proved that "when the defendant made his promise he knew that he was discharged in law by the insufficiency of the notice." The judge overruled the objection, and verdict for the plaintiff subject to the opinion of the Court. Spencer C. J. delivered the opinion of the Court. "It must be shown by the plaintiff affirmatively and clearly, that the defendant knew, when he made the subsequent promise, that he had not received regular notice. An endorser may believe that due notice has been given, inasmuch as notices need not be personally served, and under an ignorance of the facts consider himself liable when he is not." Nonsuit. Trimble v. Thorne, 16 Johns. R. 152.

In a similar case, Story J. said, "A promise to pay with a full knowledge of all the facts, is binding upon the endorser, although he might otherwise be discharged. But if he promise in ignorance of material facts affecting his rights, it is not a waiver of those rights." Martin v. Winslow, 2 Mason, 241.

See also Pierson v. Hooker, 3 Johns. R. 68; Duryee v. Dennison,

neglect to present; a payment or promise without notice of the default does (118) not.

[Where an endorser of a note, who was discharged by the laches of the holder, afterwards paid him the money, under an ignorance of the facts which discharged him, it was held that he might recover the money back. (*a*)

---

5 Johns. R. 248; Donaldson v. Means, 4 Dall. 109; Ladd v. Kenney, 2 N. Hamp. R. 340.]

(118) Blesard v. Hirst and another, Burr. 2670. The defendants endorsed a bill to the plaintiff, and he endorsed it over; his endorsee presented it for acceptance a month before it was due, and acceptance was refused; it was afterwards presented for payment, and payment was refused, of which notice was given to the defendants, but they had no notice of the refusal to accept. The drawer was a bankrupt before the bill was due, but he continued in credit three weeks after the presentment for acceptance. Three days after the notice, one of the defendants called on the plaintiff at Bradford, on his way to Leeds, and said he would take up the bill as he returned; but on his return he said he was advised he was not bound to do it, upon which this action was brought; and on a case reserved the court held, that though the holder might not have been obliged to present the bill for acceptance, yet as he did he ought to have given notice of the refusal, and that by not doing so he had taken the risk upon himself, and notwithstanding the promise of one of them the defendants had judgment.

Goodall v. Dolley, 1 Term. Rep. 712. A bill drawn in favor of the defendant, payable the 11th of January, 1787, was presented for acceptance by the plaintiffs the 8th of November, 1786, when acceptance was refused: they gave no notice to the defendant till the 6th of January, and then did not say when the bill was presented; upon which the defendant proposed paying by instalments, but the plaintiffs rejected that offer, and brought this action. Heath J. thought the defendant discharged for want of notice, and that his offer to pay being made under an ignorance of the circumstances was not binding, and the jury, under his direction, found a verdict for the defendant. Upon cause shewn against a rule for a new trial, the court thought the direction and verdict right, and discharged the rule.

See Lundie v. Robertson, Horford v. Wilson, Gibbon v. Coggon, and Potter v. Rayworth, post.

[See also Crain v. Colwell, 8 Johns. R. 299; Martin v. Winslow, ante; Hussey v. Freeman, 10 Mass. R. 84; Fotheringham v. Price, 1 Bay, 291.

But in Walker v. Laverty, 6 Munf. 487, it appears to be held that the promise of the drawer of a bill not duly notified, to pay it, was binding on him, whether he knew the facts as to the laches of the holder, or not.]

[(*a*) Cross left a note in the Salem Bank for collection, on which Garland was endorser. The note fell due while Garland was absent from Salem, his place of residence; but there was no sufficient demand or notice. On his return to Salem he paid the money, which the bank passed to the credit of Cross. Three days afterwards Garland having ascertained the facts, reclaimed the money of the bank, it still remaining there, not paid over to Cross, forbade their paying it over to any person,

A promise to pay by a party to a bill or note, who is discharged by the laches of the holder, must be explicit and deliberately made in order to be binding. (*a*)

Even a confession of judgment is not conclusive evidence of the waiver of the right to presentment and notice (*b*); nor is taking security (*b*) (*c*); nor using exertions to obtain payment from a prior party. (*d*)

---

gave notice that he had paid it by mistake, and tendered the note to the cashier and officers of the bank. The bank afterwards paid over the money to Cross. And Garland brought a suit against the bank to recover back the money paid. Sewall J. charged the jury "that the defendants were not entitled to retain the money paid, unless the payment had been made by the plaintiff voluntarily, and with a knowledge of all the circumstances, and an intended waiver of his legal advantage and discharge." Verdict for the plaintiff; and on motion for a new trial judgment on the verdict. Garland v. Salem Bank, 7 Mass. R. 408.

In Glen on Bills, 187, is a similar case, where a party to a bill discharged by the laches of the holder, recovered back the amount paid by him.]

[(*a*) Coffin, the endorser of a bill, had not been notified of its non-acceptance. When called on for payment by the agent of the holder, who had the protest for non payment with him, Coffin said that this was the first notice he had of the bill's being protested for non-acceptance; that he was not prepared to meet the payment; but that in a few days he would look round, and make preparations for the settlement of it; and other expressions to the same effect. It was held that Coffin was not liable. Sedgwick J. delivered the opinion of the Court. "What a man says under the surprise of a sudden and unexpected demand for money, ought to be construed with a good deal of strictness. We are all satisfied that what the defendant said of paying money, from the payment of which he was discharged by law, ought not to bind him." May v. Coffin, 4 Mass. R. 341.

An endorser of several bills, on one of which he was chargeable, speaking generally of them, to a person not a party, said, "*that he would take care of the bills, or see them paid.*" It was held, whichever of the expressions he used, that he did not make himself liable on the other bills, of whose dishonor he had not been duly notified. Van Ness J. delivered the opinion of the Court. "A subsequent promise to pay under a knowledged of the fact of want of notice, ought to be made out clearly and unequivocally. It would be dangerous to fix an endorser without notice, and perhaps withont knowledge of the *laches* of the holder, upon such loose conversation with a third person." Miller v. Hackley, 5 Johns. R. 375.

The endorser of a note, on the maker of which there had been no regular demand, being sued, a short time before the trial said that "he knew of no defence." Spencer J. delivered the opinion of the Court. "Here there is no promise. The defendant knew of no defence. This is extremely slight; and by no means waives any objection which the law puts into his hands." Griffin v. Goff, 12 Johns. R. 423.]

[(*b*) The endorser of a note, where there had been no demand on the maker, being sued, at first confessed judgment, the makers of the note

A conditional promise to pay, or an offer to pay in a certain manner, is not binding as a waiver of the rights acquired by the neglect of the holder, if the terms be not accepted. (*a*)

It has been held in some cases that a promise to pay made by a party knowing the facts which discharge his liability, but ignorant of the law, would not render him liable. (*b*)

---

after the action brought having given him security, which however turned out to be worthless; but the judgment was afterwards opened, and he let into a defence. It was held that the confession of judgment, though evidence, was not conclusive evidence, of an acknowledgment of liability; and that if the defendant made it being unacquainted with his rights, or through imposition, it did not render him liable; and "that taking the indemnity, being after action brought, if taken under the impression of a regular demand and notice, and the endorser believing himself to be liable, was no waiver" of his rights. Richter v. Selin, 8 Serg. & Raw. 425.

See also Warder v. Tucker, 7 Mass. R. 449.]

[(*c*) The endorser of a note, after it fell due believing himself liable upon it, took an assignment of a chose in action from the maker, and also received some money, to indemnify him from his endorsement. It was held in an action against the endorser, that the plaintiff was not excused from proving a demand and notice. Tower v. Durell, 9 Mass. R. 332.]

[(*d*) Hussey v. Freeman, 10 Mass. R. 84.]

[(*a*) The endorser of a note who had not been duly notified, offered the holder to take up the note, and give his own note payable in a year; but the holder requiring an endorser on the new note, nothing was done. In a suit by the holder against the endorser, it was held that the endorser was not liable. Thompson C. J., giving the opinion of the Court, said, "The promise or offer of the defendant was qualified or conditional, and having been rejected by the plaintiff, was not binding on the defendant." Agan v. M'Manus, 11 Johns. R. 180.

See also Sice v. Cunningham, 1 Cowen, 397; and Crain v. Colwell, 8 Johns. R. 299.]

[(*b*) In an action against the endorser of a bill, it appeared that the had not been duly notified of its non-acceptance. After receiving notice of the bill's being protested for non-acceptance and non-payment, he wrote a reply to the holders in which he expressed hopes of recovering property of the drawers sufficient to indemnify the holders, acknowledged his accountability to them, and engaged to do all that was in his power to make payment. Curia. "Although the defendant, when he first received notice from the plaintiffs of the protest of the bill, considered himself as liable by law to pay the plaintiffs the amount of it, yet his ignorance of the law shall not bind him to fulfil an engagement made through mistake of the law." Nonsuit. Warder v. Tucker, 7 Mass. R. 449.

See also May v. Coffin, supra.

In a case of the same kind Parker J. in delivering the opinion of the court, said. "The facts reported do not show any direct promise to pay; and even if they did, it is well settled that a promise under such circumstances as show an ignorance that the party was legally dis-

If before a note falls due, the endorser agrees to pay it, in consideration of time to be given him, this promise renders a demand and notice unnecessary. (*a*)]

Proof that the drawer had no effects nor any ground to expect any in the hands of the drawee from the time the bill was drawn until it became payable, and that he had no other valid foundation to expect payment by the drawee is (119)

---

charged, is without consideration and void." Freeman v. Boynton, 7 Mass. R. 483.

In Ladd v. Kenny, 2 N. Hamp. R. 340, the court seem to think that a promise to pay by an endorser, who is discharged by the laches of the holder, made with a knowledge of all the facts, but under a mistake of the law, would render him liable.]

[(*a*) On the day before a note became due, a demand was made on the maker, and notice given to the endorser, and the latter then agreed with the holder to pay the note in considerations of time being given him. It was held that this promise was "a waiver of strict demand and notice." Norton v. Lewis, 2 Conn. R. 478.]

(119) Rogers v. Stephens, ante, p. 187. note (117).

Bickerdike and another, assignees of Reichard, v. Bollman, 1 Term Rep. 405. The only question upon a case reserved was, whether a bill the bankrupt had drawn in favor of the petitioning creditor, upon a man who then, and from that time till the bill became due, was one of the bankrupt's creditors, had discharged so much of the petitioning creditor's debt, no notice having been given of its dishonor to the bankrupt; and the court, after argument, were of opinion it had not, because the reason why notice is in general necessary, is, that the drawer may without delay withdraw his effects from the drawee, and that no injury may happen to him from the want of notice; but where the drawer has no effects in the hands of the drawee, he cannot be injured, and is not entitled to any notice.

Goodall v. Dolley, ante, p. 189. note (118). In this case upon the application for a new trial, the plaintiff's counsel offered an affidavit that the drawer had no effects in the hands of the drawee, but the court thought *that* made no difference, the action being brought against the payee, but by Buller J. "Had the action been against the drawer, I should have been willing to let in the affidavit; that would be like the case of Bickerdike v. Bollman: if the drawer has no effects in the hands of the drawee he cannot be injured by want of notice."

Legge v. Thorpe, 12 East's Rep. 171. This was an action by an endorsee against the drawer of a foreign bill drawn upon C. B. Wyatt, payable one month after sight, of which acceptance had been refused. The declaration negatived effects in the hands of the drawee, or any consideration for the bill. It appeared at the trial that the defendant had no effects in Wyatt's hands, and that the latter had therefore refused acceptance; but that Wyatt was one of the executors of Weeks, and that Weeks's executors had desired the defendant to employ the payee of this bill to do some carpenter's work on Weeks's property, and the defendant therefore drew this bill on Wyatt to settle with the payee. Wyatt denied that he had assets to pay the bill. The only question was, whether a protest for non-acceptance were necessary. Lord Ellenborough thought not, and a verdict was given for the plaintiff, but the

sufficient, at least primâ facie, to shew, that the drawer would be entitled to bring no action on paying the bill and has therefore no right to insist on the want of notice, &c. and it (120) has been doubted whether the drawer would be at liberty to shew the contrary.

It is no excuse for not giving notice to the drawer that he had no effects in the drawee's hands when the bill was drawn or became due, if he had effects on their way to the drawee. (121)

Unless the drawer gets back those effects, and would stand indebted in the amount to the drawee, if the drawee paid the bill. (121)

It is no excuse for not giving notice to the drawer that he had no offects in the drawee's hands, if the drawer would be entitled on taking up the bill to sue either the acceptor; (122)

Or any other party; (122)

As if he and the acceptor lent their names to the payee or a subsequent endorsee. (122)

---

point was reserved; and on a rule nisi for a nonsuit, and cause shewn the whole court held that this case was governed by those of Bickerdike v. Bollman, and Rogers v. Stephens, and discharged the rule.

[Where the drawer had no funds in the hands of the drawee, it was held that notice to the drawer of non-payment was not necessary, in order to charge him, even though the bill had been accepted by the drawee. Hoffman v. Smith, 1 Cain. R. 157.]

(120) In Rogers v. Stephens, ante, p. 187. note (117), Mr. J. Ashhurst said, "Admitting the proof offered had been given, I do not think it clear it would take the case out of the common rule; for the law being now established, that notice to the drawer of a non-acceptance is not necessary where he has no effects in the hands of the drawee; when the plaintiff found the drawees of this bill had none of the defendant's effects in their hands, he knew he was not bound by law to give the defendant notice; he was not bound to take cognizance of any private transaction between the drawer and a third person not appearing on the face of the bill."

(121) Rucker v. Hiller, 3 Campb. 217. 16 East, 43. In an action by the endorsee of a bill against the drawer, it appeared that the drawer had no effects in the drawee's hands, but that he had shipped goods which were on their way to the drawee: the drawee refused to accept, but no notice thereof was given to the drawer; and it was insisted, that as the drawee had not received effects, defendant was not entitled to notice: Lord Ellenborough thought otherwise, as the drawer was in expectation that the goods he had shipped would reach the drawee; and nonsuit: on motion to set aside the nonsuit, it did not appear but that

It is no excuse for not giving notice to the drawer that he had in fact no funds in the hands of the drawee if he had made a provision to have such funds there, and might reasonably expect they were there. (123)

As if he drew upon a cargo he shipped for this kingdom, and such cargo was in the hands of a broker, who was to pay the proceeds to the drawee. (123)

---

the drawer might have been prejudiced by want of notice, and the rule refused.

(122) Corey v. Scott, 3 Barnew. 619. Endorsee against drawer, on bill drawn by defendant on Gordon, and accepted by him, payable to defendant, endorsed by him to Lough, and by Lough to plaintiff; no evidence of notice to defendant; excuse that defendant had no effects in Gordon's hands; answer, that Lough was to provide for the payment, and that Gordon, and defendant Scott both lent their names to accommodate him. Abbott C. J. thought this rebutted the excuse from want of effects; and nonsuit: and on rule nisi to enter verdict for plaintiff, and cause shewn, the court was clear defendant was entitled to notice, for had he taken up the bill he might certainly have sued Lough, if not Gordon: he was, therefore, in a situation in which want of notice might have hurt him, and if so he was entitled to notice; and rule discharged.

(123) Robins v. Gibson, 3 Campb. 334. To excuse want of notice to the drawer of a foreign bill, the drawee proved that he had in fact no funds of the drawer in his hands from the time the bill was given till its becoming due: but he said the bill was drawn on a cargo shipped by the drawer for England, that the cargo was in the hands of a broker for sale, and when it was sold, the proceeds were to be paid to him to answer the bill: and Lord Ellenborough held, that under these circumstances, as the bill was drawn on expected funds, the drawer was entitled to notice: plaintiff then proved notice, and had a verdict.

And see 1 Bos. and Pull. 655; and 12 East, 175.

[In an action against the drawers of a bill protested for non-acceptance, it was proved that the drawees had no funds in their hands when this bill was presented, having accepted bills previously drawn by the defendants to a greater amount than the funds in their hands; and that the want of funds arose from a fall in the price of cotton shipped by the drawers to the drawees. It was held that the action could not be maintained without proving seasonable presentment and sufficient notice of the dishonor to the drawers. Spencer C. J. delivered the opinion of the court. "It has repeatedly been decided, that where there are any funds in the hands of the drawee, so that the drawer has a right to expect the bill will be paid, or where there are not any funds, yet, if the bill was drawn under such circumstances as induced the drawer to entertain a reasonable expectation that the bill would be accepted and paid, the person so drawing it is entitled to notice; and *a fortiori* he is entitled to have the bill duly presented." But judgment was given for the plaintiff in this case, because the court thought that there had been no laches. Robinson v. Ames, 20 Johns. R. 146.

See also French v. Bank of Columbia, 4 Cranch, 141.

Where the drawer had funds in the hands of the drawee at the time of drawing the bill, but those funds were attached in the hands of the

If the drawer had effects in the hands of the drawee at the time when the bill was drawn, it has been held he (124) is entitled to notice of non-acceptance; although at the time when the bill was presented for acceptance, and from thence until presentment for payment, he had not any.

So if he had effects in the hands of the drawee, when the bill was presented for acceptance, it has been held he will be entitled to notice of non-acceptance (125), although he was indebted to the drawee greatly beyond the amount of such effects.

Notice to the drawer is not necessary, though he had supplied the drawee with goods, if those goods were supplied

---

drawee by the trustee process of Massachusetts, before the bill was presented for acceptance, it was held that the drawer could not be charged without due notice of the non-acceptance being proved. Stanton v. Blossom, 14 Mass. R. 116.]

(124) Orr and others v. Maginnis, 7 East. Rep. 359. In an action by the payees against the drawer of a foreign bill, payable at ninety days after sight, the declaration averred presentment for acceptance and refusal, presentment for payment and refusal, and protest for non-payment; it then averred, that at the time of making the bill, and from thence until presentment for payment, the defendant had no effects in the hands of the drawees. At the trial it appeared, that at the time of *drawing* the bill, the defendant had effects in the hands of the drawees, but to what amount did not appear: but that when the bill was presented for acceptance, and thence until presentment for payment, he had not any. The bill was only noted for non-acceptance, but was protested for non-payment: no notice of non-acceptance was given to the defendant. The plaintiffs had paid the amount of the bill to an endorsee. They were nonsuited for want of proving protest for, and notice of, non-acceptance. On motion to set aside the nonsuit, Bickerdike and Bollman, and other cases, were cited to shew that no notice, and therefore no protest, was necessary. But Lord Ellenborough said, that that case went on the ground that there were no effects in the hands of the drawee at the time when the bill was drawn; and the other cases followed on the same ground; but that no case had extended the exemption to cases where the drawee had effects of the drawer's in his hands at the time when the bill was drawn, though the balance might vary afterwards, and be turned into the opposite scale. Rule refused.

(125) Blackhan v. Doren, 2 Campb. N. P. C. 503. This was an action against the drawer of a bill for £250 payable after sight; of which acceptance had been refused; and to excuse the want of notice of non-acceptance, it was proved that when the bill was presented, though the drawer had effects in the hands of the drawees to the amount of £1500, yet that he owed them £10,000 or £11,000. And that they had appropriated the effects to go in satisfaction of this debt. This appropriation, however, was without the defendant's privity. Lord Ellenborough held, that a notice was necessary, and nonsuited the plaintiff.

[See also Robinson v. Ames, ante, p. 194.]

upon a credit which had not expired, and the drawer could entertain no reasonable expectation that the drawee would pay the bill; (126)

And could have no remedy againt him for not doing so. (126)

The drawer is entitled to notice, though he had no effects in the hands of the drawee at the time the bill was drawn, or at the time it was accepted, if he had before it became due. (127) (128)

And it has been held that the drawer is entitled to notice, if he has any effects in the hands of the drawee at the time the bill becomes due. (128)

Though such effects are not equal to the sum in the bill. (128)

And if there are several bills in the hands of the same owner becoming due on different days, the drawer is entitled to notice as to each, though the effects in the drawee's hands are not equal to any of the bills. (128)

And a neglect to give notice will discharge the drawer as to all. (128)

It is no excuse for not giving notice to the drawer that the bill, before it became due, had been accidentally destroyed, and that he had refused to give a new bill according to 9 & 10 W. 3. c. 17. (128)

The drawee's insolvency is no excuse for not giving notice. (128)

---

(126) Claridge v. Dalton, 4 Maule, 226. Defendant drew upon Pickford for £300, at two months after date: defendant had supplied Pickford with goods to the amount of £200, and between June and September he supplied him with £70 worth more; but, according to their course of dealing, the goods were to be paid for by acceptance at the end of the year. Defendant being sued by an endorsee, insisted upon want of notice: but on point saved the court held, that under the circumstances, as he had no ground for expecting that Pickford would pay the bill, and as notice could have done him no service, he had no right to object to the want of it; and rule nisi for nonsuit discharged.

(127) Hammond v. Dufresne, 3 Campb. 145. Action against drawer on bill for £301: proof, that at the time the bill was drawn and accepted, defendant had no effects in the hands of the drawees; but it appearing, that before the bill became due he paid £400 for them, Lord Ellenborough held want of notice not excused; and nonsuit.

(128) Thackray v. Blackett, 3 Campb. 164. Plaintiff had two bills for £1833 each, drawn by defendant on Preston and Co., due the 13th

Though notice to the drawer may be dispensed with, where it is shewn he had no effects in the hands of the drawee, or any right to expect payment by him, yet evidence (129) cannot be received for the purpose of shewing that the drawer has not, from the insolvency of the drawee, or other causes, been prejudiced by the want of such notice.

It is no excuse for not presenting a bill in due time, and giving notice to the drawer, that the acceptor had told the drawer he could not take up the bill and the drawer must, and that the acceptor had given the drawer part of the amount for that purpose. (130)

But the money so given may be recovered by the holder of the bill against the drawer as money had and recéived to the holder's use. (130)

---

and 20th of April, 1810; they were accepted, but before they became due they were, by mistake, destroyed by Preston and Co: plaintiff applied to defendant for new bills in their stead, according to 9 & 10 W. 3. c. 17. but defendant would not give them. Preston and Co. became insolvent before April, 1810, owing defendant £1000: the bills had been drawn for defendant's accommodation, but during their currency defendant came under engagement for Preston and Co., which created the debt from them of £1000. On the 13th and 20th of April, 1810, payment of each sum was demanded of Preston and Co. and refused, but no notice thereof was given to defendant. Lord Ellenborough thought defendant entitled to notice as to each sum, and discharged by want thereof as to each, and nonsuited plaintiff, and B. R. refused to set aside the nonsuit.

(129) Dennis v. Morrice, 3 Esp. N. P. C. 158. In an action on a bill, brought by an endorsee against the drawer, it appeared that no notice had been given to the defendant of non-payment by the acceptor: to excuse which the plaintiff offered to prove, that, in fact, the defendant had not been prejudiced by the want of such notice. But Lord Kenyon said, the only case in which notice is dispensed with, is where the drawer had no effects in the hands of the drawee. This would be extending the rule still further than ever has been done, and opening new sources of litigation, in investigating whether, in fact, the drawer did receive a prejudice from the want of notice or not. He rejected the evidence, and nonsuited the plaintiff.

(130) Baker v. Birch, 3 Campb. 107. In an action against the drawer of a bill for £23, it appeared, that before it became due the acceptor told defendant he could not pay it, but defendant must, and that he gave him five guineas towards it; but the bill was not presented for payment till some days after it became due, nor was proper notice given of its dishonor; and Lord Ellenborough held defendant discharged upon the bill for want of notice, but he thought plaintiff entitled to recover the five guineas as so much money received to his use; and verdict accordingly.

It is (131) no excuse for not giving notice to the drawer, that on an apprehension that the bill would be dishonored, he lodged other money, which he had of the drawee's, in the hands of the endorser, on an undertaking by the endorser, that he would return it whenever it should appear that he was exonerated from the bill; for his having other money of the drawee's does not entitle him to apply it to the dishonored bill, unless he has due notice of the dishonor.

Nor (132) is it any excuse for not giving notice, &c. to the drawer of a bill, if he had effects in the hands of the drawee, that the drawee represented to the drawer when the bill was drawn, that he should not be able to provide for it, and that the drawer thereby understood that he should have to provide for it.

---

(131) Clegg v. Cotton, 3 Bos. and Pull. 239. Endorsees against the drawer of a bill. The bill was drawn in America on Cullen, of Liverpool, in favor of Miller and Robertson, and by them endorsed to Booth and Co., and it afterwards came to the plaintiff's hands. It was dated in 1794, and drawn at ninety days' sight. In 1800, the defendant having other effects of Cullen's in his hands, deposited them with Miller and Robertson and Booth and Co., on an undertaking from them that they would return these effects whenever it should appear that they were exonerated from this bill. Cullen afterwards became bankrupt: the defendant was arrested, and then said that he should apply to Cullen's assignees to bail him, for he had lodged property in America to answer the bill, and if he was discharged by want of notice, he should pay it over to them. Acceptance and payment were both refused, but no notice was ever given of it to the defendant. Chambre J. nonsuited the plaintiff on the ground that the defendant was discharged for want of notice: and on rule nisi to set aside the nonsuit, and cause shewn, the court held, that the special circumstances did not excuse the want of notice; that there was no fraud in the defendant, which was the ground of the rule for dispensing with notice; and that when Miller and Robertson, and Booth and Co. were exonerated, which they also were by want of notice, the money deposited with them belonged to Cullen's assignees. Rule discharged.

N. It did not appear that the defendant had got back the property which he deposited, but that circumstance was not relied on.

(132) Staples v. Okines, Esp. 332. In an action against the drawer of a bill, the defence was want of notice; the plaintiff thereupon called the acceptor, who proved that when the bill was drawn he was indebted to the defendant in more than the amount of the bill, but that he then represented to the defendant that it would not be in his power to provide for the bill when it should become due, and that it was therefore then understood between them, that the defendant should provide for it, and it was contended that this superseded the necessity of giving the defendant notice; but Lord Kenyon held it did not, and nonsuited the plaintiff

It is no excuse for not presenting for payment, that defendant, the drawer, told the holder the day the bill was due that he hoped the bill would be paid, and he would see what he could do, and endeavor to provide effects ; (133)

And though the drawee said the preceding day that he had no effects. (133)

If the drawer had no effects in the hands of the drawee, it does (134) not entitle him to notice that the payee had, except the bill is drawn to accommodate the payee.

But proof that the drawer had no effects in the hands of the drawee, or any ground to expect payment by him, is no evidence that the payee or any of the endorsers could not have brought an action on paying the bill, and therefore does not excuse the want of notice to them. (135)

If the payee of a note lend his name merely to give it credit, and to enable the maker to raise money upon it, and knows at the time that the maker is insolvent, it has been

---

(133) Prideaux v. Collier, 2 Stark. 57. In an action against the drawer on a bill due 23d May, it appeared that plaintiff, the holder, applied to the drawee the 22d, and received for answer that he had no effects, but the drawer would probably provide them: the next day plaintiff saw the drawer, who said he hoped the bill would be paid, he would see what he could do, and endeavour to provide effects: plaintiff did not present the bill that day, and on question whether his neglect was excused, Lord Ellenborough held it was not, and plaintiff was nonsuited.

(134) Walwyn v. St. Quintin, 1 Bos. and Pull. 652. In an action by endorsee against the drawer of a bill, it appeared to have been drawn to accommodate the payee, who had placed securities to raise money in the hands of the drawee. The defendants had no effects in the hands of the drawee; and no notice having been given to him of the dishonor of the bill, the question was, whether that were made necessary by the payee's having effects in the hands of the drawee. Eyre C. J. directed a verdict for the defendant, with liberty to the plaintiff to move to enter a verdict for him. After rule nisi accordingly, cause shewn, and time taken to consider, the court held, that the defendant was not entitled to notice. But postea to the plaintiff on another ground.

(135) Goodall v. Dolley, ante, p. 189. note (118); Wilks v. Jacks, ante 188. note (117).

[See also Warder v. Tucker, 7 Mass. R. 449; Fotheringham v. Price, 1 Bay, 291.

If the endorser at the time of making his endorsement, knows that the drawer has no funds in the hands of the drawee, quære whether the endorser is entitled to notice in order to charge him. See Fenwick v. Sears, 1 Cranch, 259.]

holden that he (136) is not entitled to notice, and that it (136) is no defence for him that the note was not properly presented for payment. (*a*)

But inasmuch as the payee, in that case, would, upon paying the note, have a clear right of action upon the note, against the maker, it would seem that he is entitled to notice of the dishonor, or to make non-presentment in time a

---

(136) De Berdt v. Atkinson, 2 H. Bl. 336. In an action against the payee of a note, it appeared that the note was not presented for payment till the day after it became due, and that no notice was given to the defendant till five days after such presentment; but it also appearing that the defendant gave no value for the note, that he lent his name merely to give it credit, and that he knew at the time that the maker was insolvent, Eyre C. J. directed the jury to find for the plaintiff, which they did. A rule to shew cause why there should not be a new trial was afterwards granted, and upon cause shewn, per Eyre C. J. "If the maker is not known to be insolvent, insolvency will not excuse the want of an early demand; but knowledge excludes all presumption, which would otherwise arise; here the money was to be raised upon the defendant's credit; he meant to guarantee the payment, and no loss could happen to him from the want of notice." And per Buller J. "The general rule is only applicable to fair transactions, where the bill or note has been given for value in the ordinary course of trade, it is said insolvency does not take away the necessity of notice; that is true where value has been given, but no further; here the defendant lent his name merely to give credit to the note, and was not an endorser in the common course of business." Heath and Rooke, Js. concurring, the rule was discharged.

The court appears to have proceeded upon a misapplication of the rule which obtains as to accommodation acceptances; in those cases the drawer, being himself the real debtor, acquires no right of action against the acceptor, by paying the bill, and suffers no injury from want of notice of non-payment by the acceptor. But in this case the maker was the real debtor, and the payee a mere surety, having a clear right of action against the maker, upon paying the note; and therefore entitled to notice to enable him to exert that right.

[(*a*) It has been repeatedly decided in the United States, that the endorser of a note is entitled to notice, even if the maker of the note is notoriously insolvent when it is made, or becomes so previously to its maturity. See the cases cited ante, p. 156. note (*a*).

And a person who endorses a note merely for the accommodation of the maker, cannot be charged as endorser, unless there has been a regular demand of payment, and due notice given him of the non-payment. Marshall C. J. in delivering the opinion of the Court, said, "In point of reason, justice, and the nature of the undertaking, there is no case in which the endorser is better entitled to demand strict notice, than in the case of an endorsement for accommodation, the maker having received the value." French v. Bank of Columbia, 4 Cranch, 141.

So the endorser of a bill is entitled to notice, notwithstanding the drawer of the bill becomes insolvent, and leaves the country, before the holder of the bill receives information of its dishonor. May v. Coffin, 4 Mass. R. 341.]

ground of defence; and it was soon afterwards held, that where the payee of a note lent his name merely to guarantee a debt from the maker, and expected it would not be paid, and had desired the banker at whose house it was payable to send it to him and he would pay it, he was discharged by a neglect to present in proper time (137); and in a later case, where the name was lent to give the maker credit with his bankers, the court thought notice to the payee essential. (138)

And in a (139) subsequent case, where a bill was drawn

---

(137) Nicholson v. Gouthit, 2 H. Bl. 609. Gouthit and Burton undertook to guarantee an instalment on the debts of Greens, and for that purpose Greens drew notes payable to Gouthit at Drury and Co.'s, which Gouthit and Burton endorsed, after which they were delivered to the creditors. Before they became due Gouthit inquired at Drury and Co.'s if they had any effects, and on their saying they had not, he desired them to send the notes to him, and he would pay them; many notes were accordingly presented and paid, but the note in question not being presented till three days after it was due, Gouthit refused to pay it. Burton had supplied him with money to take up all the notes, but as this was not presented when due, he had returned the money destined to pay it. An action was brought against Gouthit, and upon the trial, Eyre C. J. thought, as he knew the note would not be paid at Drury and Co.'s, and had provided money for it, and as his endorsement was by way of guarantee, he was not injured by the delay; and that the request to send the notes to him was either a waiver of notice, or notice by anticipation; but on a rule nisi to enter a nonsuit, and cause shewn, though he thought the justice was clearly with the plaintiff, he thought he could not recover, for though the endorsement was by way of guarantee, it was liable to all the legal consequences of an endorsement, and Gouthit's promise to pay was only to pay such as should be duly presented at Drury's. Heath and Rooke, J. were of the same opinion, and the rule was made absolute.

(138) Smith and others v. Beckett, 13 East. Rep. 187. In an action against the payee and endorser of a note, drawn by Canning, dated the 28th of October, 1809, and payable on demand; it appeared that the defendant had lent his name to this, and other notes, merely to enable Canning to obtain credit with the plaintiffs, his bankers, he having then lately stopped payment, which was well known to all the parties. The plaintiffs made advances for six months upon these notes, which advances they afterwards renewed without any communication with the defendant. On the 28th of May, 1810, Canning became bankrupt, and payment of him was afterwards demanded and refused; but no notice of this dishonor was given to the plaintiffs. Lord Ellenborough thought a notice necessary, and therefore nonsuited the plaintiffs. And on a motion to set aside the nonsuit, De Berdt v. Atkinson was cited; but the court held clearly that a notice was necessary, especially as the advances had been renewed without the defendant's knowledge. Rule refused.

(139) Brown v. Maffey, 15 East. 216. Action on a bill drawn by

for the accommodation of a remote endorsee, and the names of all the prior parties were lent to him, it was holden, in an action against one of those parties, an endorser, that the latter was entitled to notice of the dishonor of the bill, because, upon paying it, he would be entitled to sue such endorsee for repayment.

But if the payee of a note lends his name, and takes effects of the drawer to answer it (140), he is not entitled to notice, because he is the proper person to pay it, and would be entitled to no remedy over on making the payment.

It is no excuse for not giving notice to the payee, that the drawer and drawee are non-existing persons, and that their names were used for the purpose of fraud, unless the payee was privy to the fraud; (141)

So it is no excuse that there was a parol agreement between plaintiff and defendant, that payment should not be demanded till certain estates were sold. (142)

Whitmarsh on J. and H. Neale, payable to Fiander or order, endorsed by Fiander to the defendant, by the defendant to Cosier, by Cosier to Wood, and by Wood to the plaintiff. The bill was drawn for Wood's accommodation, and all the prior names were lent to him. It did not appear that the defendant knew that any name was lent, excepting his own. The bill was dishonored, but notice of the dishonor was not sent to the defendant. Bayley J. thought the notice necessary; because if the defendant had paid the bill, he would have been entitled at least to have sued Wood, and therefore nonsuited the plaintiff. A rule nisi was granted to set aside the nonsuit, and De Berdt v. Atkinson, and Sisson v. Tomlinson, 1 Selwyn's Ni. Pri. 357. n. were cited, but on cause shewn, the court thought it clear that the defendant was entitled to notice. Rule discharged.

(140) Corney v. Da Costa, Espinasse, 302. Da Costa and Co. compounded with their creditors, and to secure the composition drew notes in favor of the defendant, which he endorsed to the creditors. The defendant took effects of Da Costa and Co. at the time to the amount of the composition; and an action being brought against him upon one of these endorsements, he insisted that he had no notice of the non-payment of the note until five weeks after it was due; but Buller J. held he was not entitled to notice, and the plaintiff had a verdict.

[See several similar cases, p. 156. note (*a*).]

(141) Leach v. Hewitt, 4 Taunt. 731. Cattle drew a bill in the name of Rogers, Crooke, and Co. upon Rogers and Co., 83, Lombard Street, payable to defendant or order, and got defendant to endorse it: there were no such houses as Rogers, Crooke and Co., or Rogers and Co., but Cattle used those names for the purpose of fraud. Action against defendant by a bonâ fide holder; defence, want of notice: Mansfield C. J. told the jury, that if defendant was a party to the fraud, he was not entitled to notice, but if he acted innocently, he was: the jury thought

[Where the money raised upon a note is received by an endorser, and he is the person ultimately to pay, notice to him of non-payment by the maker is perhaps not necessary. (*a*)

Where the maker of a note is not in a situation to pay it, and before it falls due the endorser proposes to the holder to pay it in a certain manner, and pending the negotiation for this purpose the note becomes due, the endorser thereby waives his right to insist on demand and notice. (*b*)]

Upon an acceptance payable at a banker's, notice of non-payment need not be given to the acceptor, for he makes the bankers his agents; presentment to them is presentment to him, and refusal by them is refusal by him; (143)

Especially where what he has in their hands when the bill becomes due is so much below the amount of the bill, that he could have no reasonable expectation they would pay it. (143)

And it makes no difference, though he had enough in their hands when the bill was drawn. (143)

---

he acted innocently, and nonsuit: and on motion for new trial, the court held him entitled to notice, and rule discharged.

(142) Tree v. Hawkins, post.

[(*a*) By Thompson C. J. in Agan v. M'Manus, 11 Johns. R. 180.]

[(*b*) In an action against the endorser of a note it appeared, that before the note became due, he informed the plaintiff's attorney who held the note, that one of the makers was out of the State, and that the other had absconded; but he said that he was secured for his responsibility, and requested time to pay the note; and offered to give a new note with an endorser, to which the plaintiff's attorney assented, and pending the negotiation for that purpose the note fell due, and no demand was attempted to be made or notice given. It was held that the endorser was liable on his endorsement. Leffingwell v. White, 1 Johns. Cas. 99.]

(143) Smith v. Thatcher, 4 Barnew, 200. Drawer against acceptor on a bill for 300*l*., accepted, payable at Messrs. Coutts and Co.'s: no proof was given of notice to defendant when the bill was dishonored; but it appeared, that though he had 712*l*. at Coutts's when the bill was drawn, he had only 41*l*. when the bill became due, and on the ground of the inadequacy of that sum to pay the bill, Bayley J. directed a verdict for plaintiff. On motion for a new trial, Abbot C. J. expressed a strong doubt whether notice need, in any case, be given to the acceptor, because the banker was his agent; but he and the other Judges held, that where the effects were insufficient, as here, notice was not necessary. Rule refused.

Treacher v. Hinton, 4 Barnew, 413. Endorsee against acceptor, on

So upon a note payable at a banker's, notice of non-payment need not be givèn to the maker. (144)

A person who has been once discharged by laches from his liability on a bill or note, is always discharged. And therefore where two or more parties to a bill or note have been so discharged, but one of them, not knowing of the laches, pays it, he pays it in his own wrong, and (145) cannot recover the money from another of such parties.

[The commencing of a suit by holder of a note against the maker, does not render notice to the endorser unnecessary. (*a*)

Where a note is void for illegality of consideration between the maker and payee, an innocent endorsee of the payee may recover against him, though there has been no demand or notice. (*b*)]

---

bill addressed to defendant at Plymouth, and accepted by him, payable at Sir John Lubbock and Co.'s, bankers, London. Plaintiff proved the acceptance, and presentment at Sir John Lubbock's, but there being no evidence of notice to defendant of the bill's dishonor, Abbot C. J. nonsuited plaintiff, with leave to move to enter a verdict for plaintiff: rule nisi accordingly; and on cause shewn, the court thought the notice not necessary; that the acceptance was not a cheque upon the banker, but merely made the banker the acceptor's agent, and then it was his duty to see that his agent did his duty.

(144) Pearse v. Pemberthy, 3 Campb. 261. Action against the maker of a note payable at Were, Bruce, and Co.'s: the place of payment being a material part of the instrument, it was urged that defendant should have had notice of the note's dishonor, for the answer being "not sufficient effects," shewed there were some effects there. Lord Ellenborough thought notice unnecessary, and verdict for plaintiff.

(145) Roscow v. Hardy, 12 East. Rep. 434. Acceptance of a bill was refused; of this however the holders gave no notice, but when the bill became due, again presented it for payment, and that being refused, they called upon the plaintiff, an endorser, for payment, and he, being ignorant of their laches, paid it. He now sued the defendant as his endorser, who set up the laches of the holders as a defence; and the plaintiff was nonsuited. On motion to set aside this nonsuit, it was urged, that the plaintiff ought not to be prejudiced by the laches of subsequent holders, of which he was ignorant, without the means of information. But the court held that his ignorance, which had prevented his availing himself of this laches as a defence, could not alter or revive the liability of the defendant, who had been discharged by the same laches.

[(*a*) Harwin v. Lowell, 2 S. Car. R. 193.]

[(*b*) M'Dugall, the payee of a note given to him for an illegal consideration by the maker, endorsed it to Copp. Copp, having failed in an action brought by him against the promiser, sued M'Dugall as endorser;

and the court held, that the consideration between the maker and M'Dugall being illegal, Copp might maintain his action against M'Dugall, without proving a demand, and notice of non-payment. Sewall J. giving the opinion of the court, compared this to the case of a bill, where the drawer has no funds in the hands of the drawee or acceptor, "the endorser standing in the relation of the drawer, and the promisor being acceptor:" and said, "when the promise or acceptance is void, as it is in case of usury between the drawer and acceptor, if he will resort to that defence against his promise, the contract becomes, as it respects the endorser, a draft accepted without funds, that is, in the case of a promissory note." Copp v. M'Dugall, 9 Mass. R. 1.]

CHAP. VIII.

Payment of Bills and Notes—to and by whom, and when.

PAYMENT should be made to the (1) proprietor of the bill or note, or to some person authorized by him to receive payment.

If the proprietor die, payment should be made to his (2) personal representative; if he become bankrupt, to his assignees; if he be an infant, to his guardian; and payment to the (3) infant himself, may be good; at least if it be beneficial to him.

In the case of a married woman, payment should be made to (4) her husband.

Payment *to* a bankrupt will be (5) good, if made bonâ fide, and without notice of the bankruptcy: and accepting a bill drawn by a trader, after a secret act of bankruptcy (6),

---

(1) Pothier, pl. 164.

[The payee of a note left it in the care of his son, with directions not to receive payment from the maker. The maker however, with a knowledge of these directions, paid the money to the son before it became due, and received the note from him. It was held that the payee might maintain trover for the note against the maker, because the son had no authority to receive the money. Kingman v. Pierce, 17 Mass. R. 247. See Cod. de Com. Liv. 1. Tit. 8. sec. 9. no. 2. 3.]

(2) A bonâ fide payment of a debt to a person who has the probate of a will purporting to be the creditor's, will discharge the debtor, if the creditor be dead, though the will afterwards turn out to be a forgery, and the probate be annulled on that ground; because such payment is made on the authority of the probate: but it is otherwise (per Ashhurst and Buller, Js.) if the creditor be living, because in such case the probate is a mere nullity. Allen v. Dundas, 3 Term Rep. 125.

(3) See Pothier, pl. 166., and ante.

(4) See Connor v. Martin, ante, p. 77. n. (29), and Barlow v. Bishop, ante, p. 35. n. (7).

(5) By 1 Jac. 1, c. 15. § 14. it is provided, "That no debtor of the bankrupt be hereby endangered for the payment of his or her debt, truly and bonâ fide, to any such bankrupt, before such time as he shall understand or know that he is become a bankrupt."

(6) Wilkins v. Casey, 7 Term Rep. 707. A factor was indebted to his principal in £222, 18*s.*; the principal committed an act of bankruptcy, and drew on his factor for £222, 18s.; the factor did not know of the act of bankruptcy, and accepted the bills: before they became due, a commission issued, notwithstanding which the factor paid them; the assignees sued the factor for the £222, 18*s.*; and on a case reserved,

will be protected as much as payment, though the bill do not become due until it is notorious that a commission against him has issued. The acceptance, which creates an obligation to pay, is within the protection of 1 Jac. 1. as much as actual payment.

And payment to a bankrupt, or accepting on his account, even after a commission issued, will be as much protected as a payment before, if the party paying or accepting knew nothing, and had not the means of knowing, of such commission. (7)

And payments *to* a bankrupt are entitled to a different consideration from payments *by;* vacating the former makes the party pay twice, vacating the latter only puts one creditor on the same footing with the rest.

Payment *by* a bankrupt to a bonâ fide creditor in respect of a (8) bill really and bonâ fide drawn, negotiated, or accepted by the bankrupt in the (9) usual and ordinary course

---

insisted that though the statute (1 Jac. 1. c. 15.) would protect a *payment* before notice of the bankruptcy, it would not a mere acceptance. Sed per Lord Kenyon, the statute ought to receive a liberal construction; giving goods in exchange would have been a payment, though not in money; and so is giving an acceptance, if the bill be paid when due. The other judges concurred, and the defendant had judgment.

(7) Sowerby v. Brooks, 4 Barnew. and Ald. 523. On 7th October a commission issued against Carbutt, but it was not gazetted till 5th November. 30th October Sowerby accepted a bill drawn on him by Carbutt for £95, 4*s*., a sum he owed Carbutt; he had no reason to suppose at that time that the commission had issued, or that Carbutt was a bankrupt or insolvent. Carbutt's assignees sued Sowerby for the old debt, and he relied on his acceptance, which he paid when due, as a discharge: the court of common pleas thought it no discharge, on the ground that the issuing of the commission was notice to all the world of the bankruptcy; but the facts being stated in a special verdict, the court of king's bench on error thought otherwise, and reversed the judgment.

(8) See 19 Geo. 2. c. 32. § 1. post, p. 208. n. (10). The statute only mentions bills; whether it may be construed to extend to notes, has not been decided. See Harwood v. Lomas, infra.

(9) Harwood and another v. Lomas, 11 East's Rep. 127. Odell being indebted to the defendant in £400, gave him, in August, 1805, his note for that sum, payable at twelve months, with interest half yearly. Part only of the money being paid, the defendant, in 1806, arrested Odell for the residue, and in Hilary Term, 1807, obtained judgment, which was affirmed on error the 5th of February, 1808; and the next day (the 6th of February) Odell paid the amount of the damages, interest, and costs. Odell had committed an act of bankruptcy on the 27th of January, 1808; on which a commission issued dated the 19th of February,

of trade and dealing, will be (10) valid; provided the party paid be ignorant of the bankruptcy or insolvency of the bankrupt.

The statute giving this protection to payments by bankrupts, mentions bills, but is silent as to notes.

Whether it extends to notes has not been decided; and it is in terms confined to bills drawn, &c. in the usual and ordinary course of trade.

But all payments *by* and *to* any bankrupt bonâ fide made more than two calendar months before the date of his commission, will, notwithstanding any prior act of bankruptcy, be (11) good; provided the party so paid or paying, had not any notice of such prior act of bankruptcy, or that the bankrupt was insolvent, or had stopped payment.

[Where a due bill or note is not negotiable, payment to the promisee personally is sufficient to discharge the promiser, although the instrument has been assigned to a third person, unless the promiser has "direct and positive notice of the assignment." (*a*)]

1808. In an action by his assignees to recover this money, the only question was, whether the payments by the bankrupt were protected by the 19 Geo. 2. c. 32. The court inclined to think that it was incumbent on the party receiving the money to shew that the payment was protected by the statute. But it being admitted that the note had been given for the balance of an account stated, consisting (inter alia) of money lent to the bankrupt, the court, without expressing any opinion as to whether the statute could be construed to extend to notes, held that this note could not be said to have been given in the ordinary course of trade and dealing. Postea to the plaintiffs.

(10) By 19 Geo. 2. c. 32. § 1. it is enacted, "That from and after the 29th of October, 1746, no person who is or shall be really and bonâ fide a creditor of any bankrupt, for or in respect of goods really and bonâ fide sold to such bankrupt, or for or in respect of any bill or bills of exchange really and bonâ fide drawn, negotiated, or accepted by such bankrupt, in the usual or ordinary course of trade and dealing, shall be liable to refund or repay to the assignee or assignees of such bankrupt's estate, any money, which before the suing forth of such commission, was really and bonâ fide and in the usual and ordinary course of trade and dealing, received by such person of any such bankrupt, before such time as the person receiving the same shall know, understand, or have notice that he is become a bankrupt, or that he is in insolvent circumstances."

(11) By 46 Geo. 3. c. 135. § 1. it is enacted, "That in all cases of commissions of bankrupt hereafter to be issued, all conveyances by, all payments by and to, and all contracts and other dealings and transactions by and with, any bankrupt, bonâ fide made or entered into more

After a foreign bill has been protested for non-payment, any person may pay it (under protest) for the (12) honor of the drawer or of an endorser (*b*); and he is entitled to demand repayment not only from the person for whose honor he made the payment, but from (13) all other parties who are liable to that person.

[Where one bill of a set having been protested for non-payment, and returned, the drawee afterwards makes payment to the holder on another of the set, such payment is good. And if a party to the bill, ignorant of this payment, subsequently pays the bill, to the person to whom the protested bill of the set has been returned, he may recover back such payment, as money had and received to his use. (*c*)]

---

than two calendar months before the date of such commission, shall, notwithstanding any prior act of bankruptcy committed by such bankrupt, be good and effectual to all intents and purposes whatsoever, in like manner as if no such prior act of bankruptcy had been committed; provided the person or persons so dealing with such bankrupt had not at the time of such conveyance, payment, contract, dealing, or transaction, any notice of any prior act of bankruptcy by such bankrupt committed, or that he was insolvent or had stopped payment."

[(*a*) Meghan v. Mills, 9 Johns. R. 64.]

(12) Beawes, 2d ed. pl. 50. and vide ante, p. 100.

[(*b*) A person who wishes to pay a bill tor the honor of any party to it, must be ready at the time and place of payment.

An action was brought against Henderson and Cairns as endorsers of a bill drawn in the United States upon a house in London. Frears and Cairns, of Birmingham, were the agents of the defendants. After acceptance had been refused by the drawees, Frears informed Wallis, the holder of the bill, that if it was not paid, he and his partner would pay it, and requested Wallis to let them have the bill, if not paid by the drawees, which he promised to do. Payment having been refused by the drawees, Frears called on Wallis, and offered to pay the bill and expenses, if Wallis would let them have the bill. Wallis informed him that he had sent the bill to the post-office to be sent to America. The defendants had funds in the hands of Frears and Cairns, with which they might have taken up the bill. Per Curiam. "The facts stated afford no ground of defence. If the agents meant to carry into effect the agreement with Wallis, they should have stood ready to pay and take up the bill in London where it was payable. Indeed the agreement with Wallis was a *nudum pactum;* the agents were not compellable to pay at any time." Denston v. Henderson, 13 Johns. R. 322.]

(13) Beawes, 2d ed. pl. 57., vide ante, p. 100., and Mertens v. Winnington, post, p. 213. n. (3), Hall v. Pitfield, post, p. 213. n. (4), and ex parte Lambert, post, p. 214. n. (5).

[(*c*) Durkin and Henderson having a bill in London, endorsed and sent it to M'Bride their agent at New York for him to sell it. M'Bride endorsed and sold it to the defendants. They endorsed and sent it to

Payment of a bill or note should not be made (14) *before* it has become due;

If it be, it is at the peril of the person paying.

A check upon a banker was lost, and paid to a stranger the day before it *bore date;* the banker was obliged to repay the money to the loser. (15)

Pigou and Co. of London, in payment of a debt from them to Pigou and Co. for about the amount of the bill. The first of the set having been duly presented was sent back to the defendants at New York, under protest for non-payment. And M'Bride, on notice being given him, paid the defendants the full amount of the bill and 20 per cent. damages. The defendants on the same day made a remittance to Pigou and Co., being partly to pay the balance on account of which the bill was remitted. The drawees of the bill had however, previously to the payment in New York, paid the amount with interest and charges to Pigou and Co. on the second of exchange; but this was not known to M'Bride when he paid the bill. Durkin and Henderson brought an acton for money had and received to recover back the amount paid by M'Bride. Per Curiam. "The payment by the drawees must be considered as valid, although it was after protest for non-payment, because Pigou and Co. were the holders of the bill as general endorsees, and the legal title was in them. The notice to M'Bride, the bill having already been paid by the drawees, and the subsequent payment by him, were consequently founded in mistake. It was upon the assumption of a fact which did not then exist. The plaintiffs are entitled to recover back the whole sum paid, and the 20 per cent. inclusive and interest." Durkin v. Cranston, 7 Johns. R. 442.]

(14) Marius, 4th ed. p. 31., who observes, that if the drawee pay a bill before it has become due, and it appear that the payee was merely the factor or agent of the person who delivered it to him, and that person countermand the payment before the maturity of the bill, but after such payment by the drawee the latter may be obliged to repay the money." [See also Cod. de Com. Liv. 1. art. 144. 145. Tit. 8. § 9.]

(15) See Da Silva v. Fuller, Chitty, 2d ed. 112. n.

CHAP. IX.

Remedy on Bills or Notes, by Action.

Upon a non-acceptance or non-payment, the holder of a bill or note may sue all the persons liable to him on account of such non-acceptance or non-payment, and he may sue them either at the same time or successively.

[The pledgee of a bill or note to whom it has been en dorsed, may maintain an action upon it, against any of the prior parties. (*a*)

So an agent to whom a note has been endorsed for collection, may bring an action upon it in his own name. (*b*)

Where a note is payable to A, "agent of B," A may sue upon it in his own name. (*c*)

So the payee of a note, who is an officer and member of a company consisting of many persons, must sue in his own name, though his official character be stated in the note; and it is no defence that the defendant is a member of the same company. (*d*) (*e*)

[(*a*) Bowman v. Wood, 15 Mass. R. 535.]

[(*b*) Little v. Obrien, 9 Mass. R. 423.]

[(*c*) Buffum brought a suit against the maker of a note, and styled himself in his writ, agent of the Providence Hat Manufacturing Company, and declared that the defendant, "for value received of the said company, promised the said Buffum, as agent thereof to pay him," &c. to his damage in his said capacity, &c. By the court. "The contract was with the agent personally, and his adding his character to his name in the writ and declaration, amounts only to a description of his person. Let the defendant be called." Buffum v. Chadwick, 8 Mass. R. 103.]

[(*d*) Forrest, president of a commercial company consisting of four or five hundred members, sued Crossfield and Van Ness in his own name upon a note payable to Forrest, president of the commercial company, and taken on account of goods of the company sold by them. Van Ness was a partner in the commercial company. Marshall C. J. giving the opinion of the court, said, "The principle that a company cannot sue its members does not apply to this case; nor does the principle, that a partner cannot sue a partner on a partnership transaction, apply to any case where a note in writing is given for money, not to a firm, but to an individual member. The legal title is in Forrest, who recovers in his his own name, as a trustee for the company." Van Ness v. Forrest, 8 Cranch, 30.]

[(*e*) But where a bill was endorsed to the treasurer of the United

When a person endorses a bill or note to another, and it afterwards comes back to the possession of the endorser, he shall be presumed to be the rightful holder, and need not produce any receipt or re-endorsement in order to maintain an action upon it. (*a*)

The endorsee of a negotiable note cannot bring a suit upon it in the name of an endorser without his consent. But the assignee of a note not negotiable may bring an action upon it in the name of the payee. (*b*)]

An endorser, an acceptor for the honor of an endorser or drawer, or the (1) drawer, is, after payment by him, holder;

States, it was held that an action might be brought upon it it in the name of the United States.

A bill purchased by the United States was endorsed to Tucker, "treasurer of the United States," who received it in that capacity, for their account. Tucker endorsed the bill as treasurer to Willinks and Van Staphorst, who presented it for acceptance and the bill being dishonored, returned it to the Secretary of the Treasury. In an action by the United States against an endorser of the bill, Livingston J. delivered the opinion of the court. "If it be generally true, that where a bill is endorsed to the agent of another for the use of his principal, an action, cannot be maintained in the name of such principal, (on which point no opinion is given,) the government should form an exception to such rule, and the United States be permitted to sue in their own name, whenever it appears, that they alone were interested in the subject matter of the controversy."

"It is next said that the title of the United States was divested by Tucker's endorsing the bill to Willinks and Van Staphorst, which endorsemeut appeared upon the bill at the trial, and is still on it. The mere returning of this bill, by Willinks and Van Staphorst to the Secretary of the Treasury, is presumptive evidence of the former having only acted as agents or as bankers of the United States. But if this agency were not established, the opinion of the court would be the same. After an examination of the cases on this subject, (which cannot all of them be reconciled), the court is of opinion, that if any person who endorses a bill to another, whether for value or for the purpose of collection, shall come to the possession therof again, he shall be regarded, unless the contrary appear in evidence, as the *bonâ fide* holder and proprietor of such bill, and shall be entitled to recover, notwithstanding there may be on it one or more endorsements in full subsequent to the one to him, without producing any receipt or endorsement back from either of such endorsees, whose names he may strike from the bill or not, as he thinks proper." Dugan v. The United States, 3 Wheat. R. 172.]

[(*a*) See Dugan v. The United States, supra. Welch v. Lindo, 7 Cranch, 159, is contra.]

[(*b*) Mosher v. Allen, 16 Mass. R. 451.]

(1) Louviere v. Laubray, 10 Mod. 36. The plaintiff drew a bill upon the defendant, which the defendant accepted, but afterwards refused to pay; upon this the bill was endorsed to the plaintiff, and the question was, whether he could maintain an action as endorsee? and, per Parker

but he holds in his original capacity, not (2) as upon a transfer from the person he has paid.

So the bail of any of the parties who are sued, or (3) any persons who pay the bill or note on account of any of the parties, become, on payment, holders; and they hold as upon a transfer from the person for whom they made the payment, not (4) as upon a transfer from the person they have paid. (*a*)

C, J., upon evidence that he had effects in the hands of the defendant enough to answer the bill, and consequently that the acceptancee was not upon the honor of the plaintiff, the action is well brought, but if there were no effects, the action would not lie; and the plaintiff recovered.

Symonds v. Parminter, 1 Wils. 185. 4 Bro. Parl. Cas. 604. The plaintiff drew a bill upon the defendant to the order of Cleer and Co., which the defendant accepted, but did not pay; the plaintiff paid it, and brought this action. The declaration stated that the plaintiff drew the bill; that the defendant accepted it, but did not pay it; that the plaintiff became liable, and paid it; by reason whereof the defendant became liable, and promised. The defendant demurred, and afterwards moved in arrest of judgment, and contended that the action would not lie; but the court, after two arguments upon the demurrer, and one on the motion in arrest of judgment, were of opinion that it would, and judgment was given for the plaintiff. The defendant brought a writ of error in parliament, but did not appear at the bar to support it, and the judgment was affirmed.

(2) Bishop v. Hayward, 4 Term Rep. 470. The plaintiff declared upon a note payable to himself or order, endorsed by him to the defendant, and by the defendant endorsed back again to him, and obtained a verdict; a rule was granted to shew cause why the judgment should not be arrested, on the ground that according to the statement in the declaration the plaintiff would be liable upon his endorsement to pay the defendant the sum for which the verdict was given; and upon cause shewn, the court held the objection good, because as the plaintiff had not stated it to be otherwise, his endorsement was to be considered as a legal existing endorsement: had any circumstances existed which exempted the plaintiff from answering upon his endorsement to the defendant, they should have been disclosed on the record. And see Louviere v. Laubray, ante, p. 212. note (1).

[But see Britten v. Webb, infra.]

(3) Mertens v. Winnington, Espinasse, 112. A bill was drawn by the defendant, and endorsed by Burton, Forbes, and Gregory; the plaintiff paid it for the honor of Burton, Forbes, and Gregory, and brought this action against the defendant as drawer; the defendant contended that a person who paid for the honor of one of the parties could only sue that party; but Lord Kenyon said, "he was to be considered as an endorsee paying full value for the bill," and he directed the jury to find for the plaintiff.

(4) Hall v. Pitfield, B. R. H. 17 Geo. 2. The endorsee of a note sued the maker, and on payment by his bail permitted them to sue the endorser in his (the endorsee's) name, but the court held that the payment

And they stand, with respect to other parties to the bill or note, in the situation of the party for whom they made the payment, and consequently unless he could have sued upon the bill or note, they (5) cannot.

[A first endorser or his agent cannot maintain an action upon a bill or note against the second endorser. (*b*)]

---

by the bail discharged the endorser, and that the action could not be maintained.

[(*a*) The payee of a note who endorses it for the accommodation of the maker, by paying the note to the holder, acquires a right to sue the maker upon it. Havens v. Huntingdon, 1 Cowen, 387.

So an accommodation endorser paying a note may bring an action against the maker upon it; and this notwithstanding a prior endorser at whose request the plaintiff endorsed the note, raised money upon it for his own use in fraud of the maker. Robertson v. Williams, 5 Munf. 381.]

(5) Ex parte Lambert, 13 Ves. 179. Adams and Co. drew two bills on Lane and Co., which the latter accepted. Lambert took up both these bills for the honor of the drawers. A commission of bankruptcy afterwards issued against the acceptors, and the drawers also failed: Lambert received a dividend upon the bills from the estate of the drawers, and claimed the balance from the estate of the acceptors. But it being proved that the drawers had no effects in the hands of the acceptors, and that the acceptances were for the accommodation of the drawers, the claim was rejected; and upon petition, the Lord Chancellor said that Lambert could not make a title stronger than that of the drawers, nor oust the assignees of the defence which they would have had against them. Petition dismissed.

[(*b*) In an action against the second endorser of a bill drawn by the plaintiffs, payable to their own order, and by them endorsed, the count alleged that by an agreement between the plaintiffs and defendants, the latter endorsed the bill as security for its payment by the acceptor, and for that purpose only, and that the endorsement from the plaintiffs to the defendant was without consideration, and for the purpose of procuring the defendant's endorsement, and making the bill negotiable. On demurrer, judgment was given for the defendant. Bayley J. said, "This count is contradictory; it alleges in the first instance that the plaintiffs by their endorsement appointed the money to be paid to the defendant, and then that they did not appoint the money to be paid to the defendant, for that the endorsement was ineffectual. As to the special agreement there was no consideration for it. Besides, the plaintiffs are not at liberty to set up a parol contract inconsistent with a written contract, and that would be the effect of enabling them to recover on this declaration against the defendant." Britten v. Webb, 2 Barn. & Cres. 483; 3 Dow. & Ryl. 650.

In an action against Herrick, the second endorser of a note, it was held that the defendant might prove that the plaintiff was the mere agent of the payees, the first endorsers, and that this was a complete defence to the action. Herrick v. Carman, 10 Johns. R. 224.

On another trial of this case it was proved that the maker of the note had given it to Carman & Co., the payees, with Herrick's name endorsed upon it, in payment for goods sold by them to him, which they

An action (6) may be brought for non-acceptance before the expiration of the time limited by a bill for its payment. (*a*)

---

had refused to let him have without security; and that the plaintiff, knowing these circumstances, bought the note of Carman & Co. But it was held that the action could not be maintained. Spencer J. delivered the opinion of the court. "The plaintiff purchased the note, with a full knowledge of all the facts in the case; his right therefore cannot be superior to that of Carman & Co. It does not appear that Herrick endorsed the note for the purpose of giving the maker credit with Carman & Co., or that he was informed of the use to which the maker meant to apply the note. In the absence of any proof to the contrary we must intend that Herrick meant only to become the second endorser, with all the rights incident to the situation. He must have known that though the first to endorse, his endorsement would be nugatory, unless preceded by that of the payees of the note." Herrick v. Carman, 12 Johns. R. 159.]

(6) Bright v. Purrier, Bull. Ni. Prius, 269. A foreign bill payable one hundred and twenty days after sight was presented for acceptance, but acceptance being refused, the holder brought an action immediately against the drawer; the defendant objected that he was not liable till the expiration of the one hundred and twenty days, and offered to call witnesses to prove that such was the custom of merchants; but Lord Mansfield said the law was clearly otherwise, and refused to hear the evidence; so the plaintiff recovered.

Milford v. Mayor, Dougl. 55. The defendant drew a bill of exchange, which the drawee refused to accept, upon which the plaintiff arrested him before the bill became due; these facts appearing upon the affidavit to hold to bail, a rule was obtained to shew cause why the defendant should not be discharged; but upon shewing cause, Buller J. said, "It is settled that if a bill is not accepted, an action will lie immediately against the drawer, because his undertaking that the drawee should give him credit is not performed; there have been many actions of this sort;" and Willes and Ashhurst, Js. concurring, the rule was discharged.

[(*a*) The law as stated in the text is fully recognised in the United States. The right of action of the holder of a bill is complete upon giving notice of the non-acceptance, he is under no obligation to present for payment; and this right is not lost by a neglect to present for payment, or to give notice of the non-payment. Mason v. Franklin, 3 Johns. R. 202; Robinson v. Ames, 20 Johns. R. 146; Winthrop v. Pepoon, 1 Bay, 468; Watson v. Loring, 3 Mass. R. 557; Weldon v. Buck, 4 Johns. R. 144; Miller v. Hackley, 5 Johns. R. 375; Sterry v. Robinson, 1 Day, 11; Taan v. Le Gaux, 1 Yeates, 204.

In an action against the endorser of a bill protested for non-acceptance, and non-payment, it appeared that he had been notified of the non-acceptance, but not of the non-payment. The defendant's counsel contended that although a right of action accrued on the non-acceptance, yet that it was merged in the new right of action arising on the protest for non-payment, and that this new right was lost by the neglect of notice. By the court. "When acceptance is refused by the drawee, a right of action accrues to the holder after due notice. He is not bound to demand payment at the time the bill falls due, nor to protest for non-payment, nor to retain the bill for that purpose; but he may bring an action against all parties liable, immediately on the refusal of the drawee to accept." Lenox v. Cook, 8 Mass. R. 460.]

And such an action may be brought against an (7) endorser, as well as against the drawer.

[Where a note is payable by instalments at different times, an action may be maintained for each instalment as soon as it falls due. (*a*)

So where interest on a note is payable annually, an action lies for each year's interest immediately upon its falling due, and before the principal becomes due. (*b*)

An action brought against an endorser before notice is sent him, cannot be maintained, although notice is afterwards seasonably given him. (*c*) But an action may be brought against an endorser as soon as notice to him is put

---

(7) Ballingalls v. Gloster, 3 East. Rep. 481. John Gloster drew a bill on Jackson, payable to Anthony Gloster's order, and the latter endorsed it to the plaintiffs. Jackson refused acceptance, on which the plaintiffs immediately sued Anthony Gloster, without waiting until the bill, which was drawn at ninety days' sight, would have been due. The plaintiffs had a verdict, with liberty to the defendant to move for a nonsuit. On rule nisi accordingly, it was urged that an endorser stood in a situation different from that of a drawer; and that although a drawer might be sued immediately on non-acceptance, an endorser could not until the expiration of the time limited for the payment of the bill; but the court was clear that the case of an endorser was not distinguishable from that of a drawer, and that every endorser was a new drawer. Rule discharged.

[(*a*) Tucker v. Randall, 2 Mass. R. 283.]

[(*b*) Greenleaf v. Kellogg, 2 Mass. R. 568; Cooley v. Rose, 3 Mass. R. 221.]

[(*c*) N. Eng. Bank v. Lewis, 2 Pick. 125. In an action against the endorsers of a note, it appeared that a notary made a seasonable demand on the maker, and afterwards on the same day, but after this suit was brought, notified the endorsers. All the parties lived in Boston. After a verdict for the defendants, Parker C. J. in giving the opinion of the court, said, "that the notice was not sufficient for the purposes of this action, because it was not given until after the action was commenced. Where the endorser lives in a different town from the holder, the law considers putting the notice seasonably into the post-office as using due diligence, or as a constructive notice. Here all the parties lived in the same town, and proper notice might have been given by a minute's walk, and to commence the action before giving such notice was not using due diligence." Afterwards the plaintiff's counsel said, "If it will make any difference, we can show that the notice was in the hands of the notary before the writ was in the hands of the officer." C. J. "That question was put in our discussions, and it was thought that it would make no difference."

In a previous case the court seem to have been of opinion, that an action brought before the notice was put into the post-office, might be maintained. Stanton v. Blossom, 14 Mass. R. 116.]

into the post-office, before he can have received it by the regular course of the mail. (*a*)]

All the antecedent parties are liable to the holder on account of a non-acceptance or non-payment; and if the bill or note was transferred to him for a precedent consideration by delivery, the person who delivered it is also liable to be sued for such consideration. (*b*)

[Where the acceptor of a bill resided in a different place from that in which it was payable; it was held that the person for whom it was drawn was not liable to the acceptor, for any loss accruing to him by the bankruptcy of parties to bills remitted by him to meet his acceptance. (*c*)

[(*a*) Parker C. J. delivered the opinion of the Court. "Another objection is that the action was commenced too soon. By course of mail the notice could not have reached the defendant until after the writ was served. The putting the letter into the post-office is notice in itself. The receipt of notice, or time for it to be received is not necessary." Shed v. Brett, 1 Pick. 401.

But in a case in Pennsylvania, it was held that an action brought against an endorser, after notice to him was sent to the post-office, but before it could have reached him by the regular course of the mail, could not be maintained; the Court being of opinion that a letter put into the post-office could be considered notice only from the time at which it ought to be received by the regular course of mail. Smith v. The Bank of Washington, 5 Serg. & Raw. 318.]

[(*b*) In Virginia the holder of a note cannot sue his endorser, unless he has previously brought a suit against the maker if solvent. But if the maker is insolvent, so that a suit against him would be fruitless, an action may be brought against the endorser without first suing the maker. Clark v. Young, 1 Cranch, 181; Yeaton v. The Bank of Alexandria, 5 Cranch, 49; Violett v. Patton, 5 Cranch, 142; Saunders v. Marshall, 4 Hen. & Mun. 455.

If the maker is not insolvent, and no suit has been brought against him, the endorser is not liable, though the maker is out of the reach of the process of the court, and the endorser has been secured by the maker for his endorsement. Dulany v. Hodgkin, 5 Cranch, 333.

In the same State no action at law can be maintained, by an endorsee against a remote endorser. Mandeville v. Riddle, 1 Cranch, 290; Harris v. Johnston, 3 Cranch, 311. The case of Dunlop v. Silver 1, Cranch, 367, Appendix, is contra.

But the holder may recover against a remote endorser, by a suit in equity. Harris v. Johnston, 3 Cranch, 311; Riddle v. Mandeville, 5 Cranch, 322.]

[(*c*) Forbes v. Eldridge, 9 Mass. R. 497. The defendant having consigned a vessel to the plaintiffs in Dublin, his agents by his authority drew a bill on the plaintiffs, payable at sixty days' sight in London; the plaintiffs accepted the bill payable at Johnson and Co.'s, in London, and remitted bills to Johnson and Co. to reimburse them. These bills did not fall due until after the maturity of the first bill; and the parties to

Where A. authorizes B. to draw upon certain persons in partnership to a certain amount, and the partnership being dissolved, B. draws a bill upon one of the partners, which is accepted and paid, B. is liable to the acceptor for the amount of the bill. (*a*)]

If the holder sues all the persons liable at the same time, it was at one time (8) supposed that the court or a judge would not stay proceedings in any one action but upon payment of the money recoverable in that, and the costs in such of the rest in which judgment had not been obtained; but it is now settled that in the (9) case of a regular bill, where the acceptor is the proper person to provide for payment, he is the only person against whom the plaintiff is entitled to

---

them became bankrupt before they became due. The plaintiffs sued the defendant to recover the loss upon these bills. But it was held that the action would not lie. The Court said, "The acceptor does not act as agent of the drawer of a bill. He accepts on his own terms and for his own convenience. Whether funds were placed in London to meet the acceptance at a profit or a loss to the plaintiffs, was no concern of the defendant's, and he cannot be liable for the result."]

[(*a*) Jennings and Roddy gave Watson a letter of credit on Penoyer and Co. saying in it, "Mr. Watson is authorized to value on you on our account, for ten thousand dollars." Penoyer and Co. having dissolved their partnership, Watson drew a bill on Penoyer alone, which Penoyer accepted and paid. It was held that Penoyer might maintain an action against Watson for the amount of the bill; as Jennings and Roddy were not liable, they only being liable on account of bills drawn on the partnership. Penoyer v. Watson, 16 Johns. R. 100.]

(8) Golding v. Grace, Blackst. 749. The endorser of a bill obtained a rule nisi to stay proceedings on payment of the debt and the costs of the writ; the plaintiff insisted that he was entitled to be paid for drawing declarations against the defendant and the drawer; and it was agreed, that if any was to be paid for, the plaintiff was entitled to be paid for both; but the court held that the application to pay debt and costs was made so early, that the plaintiff was only entitled to the costs of the writ.

(9) Smith v. Woodcock, Same v. Dudley, 4 Term Rep. 691. The holder of a bill brought actions against the acceptor, the drawer, and two endorsers; the drawer and one of the endorsers obtained a rule nisi to stay proceedings against them on payment of the bill and costs of the actions against *them:* the plaintiff insisted that the costs of the other actions should be also paid: sed per cur. "that is only necessary where the application comes from the acceptor, who is the original defaulter, and against whom all the costs occasioned by his default may be recovered." Rule absolute.

[It has been held in Connecticut, that the acceptor of a bill was not liable to the costs of a suit against the drawer on account of the non-payment, notwithstanding the acceptor had in his hands funds of the drawer sufficient to pay the bill. Barnwell v. Mitchell, 3 Conn. R. 101.]

the costs of *all* the actions, and that each of the other parties is entitled to a stay of proceedings upon paying the debt and the costs in the action against him. (*a*)

The maker of a note stands in this respect in the condition of the acceptor of a bill.

And where it appears that some of the actions are friendly and collusive, not to obtain payment but to increase costs, it is probable the costs of those actions would not be included.

Though the holder may recover judgments in all the actions, he (10) can only once recover the sum payable by the bill or note, and the costs; and if he rejects a tender of such sum and costs, the (11) court will make an order to restrain him from taking out execution.

If the holder at first sue some only of the persons liable, he may at any time before satisfaction sue all or any of the rest. (*b*)

[(*a*) In a case in Massachusetts, where separate actions had been brought against the maker and endorser of a note; and judgment obtained against the endorser, which was afterwards satisfied, it was held that the action against the maker could not be maintained any longer, and judgment was given for the defendant for costs. Gilmore v. Carr, 2 Mass. R. 171. But see the remarks of Sewall J. upon this case in Porter v. Ingraham, 10 Mass. R. 88; and 1 Dane's Dig. 415.

See also Tarin v. Morris, 2 Dallas, 115.

The holder of a note in New York brought two actions, one against the maker, the other against the endorser, at the same term. It was held that the plaintiff was entitled to the costs of both suits. Per Curiam. "The statute allowing a recovery of costs in one suit only, when several suits are brought upon the same instrument, does not apply to this case; but to cases in which separate suits are brought upon the same note or bond where one suit would have served." Austin v. Bemiss, 8 Johns. R. 275.]

(10) Ex parte Wildman, 2 Vez. 115. Per Lord Hardwicke, "In cases of bills of exchange or promissory notes, where there is a drawer and endorser, perhaps more than one judgment is against all, but there can be but one satisfaction."

(11) Windham v. Withers, Str. 515. The plaintiff having obtained judgments against the drawer and endorser of a note, the principal in one, and the costs in both were offered him, which he refused; and the court granted a rule to restrain him from taking out execution, and intimated that they would have punished him, had he taken out execution upon both judgments.

[In a suit against the bail of an endorser of a note, where a judgment against the maker had been paid, after judgment recovered against the endorser; judgment was given *pro forma* for the penalty of the recognizance, but the plaintiff was only entitled to levy for the costs of the original suit against the principal, and the costs of this suit. Wattles v. Laird, 9 Johns. R. 327.]

And the difference between extinguishment and satisfaction is to be remembered; the holder's claim upon a bill or note may be extinguished as to some parties, and remain entire as to others; if his claim is satisfied as to any, it is satisfied as to all.

Taking security of a higher description, as a bond or judgment, for the money due upon a bill or note, extinguishes the holder's claim upon the bill or note, as against the party giving that security (12): it does not satisfy it. (*c*)

So obtaining judgment on a bill or note is an extinguishment as between the parties, not a satisfaction. (*d*)

[(*b*) Mere delay by the holder to sue the maker of a note, does not affect the liability of an endorser. Powell v. Waters, 17 Johns. R. 176.

In an action against the endorser of a note, it was proved that after the note became due, he requested the holder to sue the maker, which was not done; that the amount might then have been collected of the maker, who afterwards became insolvent. The court appeared to think that the endorser was not discharged by this neglect; and said, "Though in the nature of a surety, he is answerable upon an independent contract, and it is his duty to take up the bill when dishonored." Trimble v. Thorne, 16 Johns. R. 152.

So the mere delay of the second endorser for a length of time to take up a note, does not affect his right of action against the first endorser. Stafford v. Yates, 18 Johns. R. 327.]

(12) Bac. Abr. tit. Extinguishment, D. vol. iii. p. 106.

[(*c*) Taking a mortgage from the maker of a note as collateral security, does not discharge an endorser. Ligget v. The Bank of Pennsylvania, 7 Serg. & Raw. 218.

Where the holder of a dishonored bill received security from the drawer, and afterwards gave it up, it was held that the endorser was not thereby discharged.

The holder of a bill protested for non-acceptance, received security from the drawer; but he afterwards gave up the security on learning that a large part, and probably the whole, of the money would be paid by the drawee. The greater part of the money was paid at maturity. In an action against an endorser for the remainder, the Court said, "That as the holder had not given time to the drawer, but had only taken further security, the endorser was not discharged: that it was no more than if the holder had commenced an action, and attached the goods of a party to a bill or note, in which case another party would not be discharged, even though the creditor should discontinue that suit, or release the attachment." Hurd v. Little, 12 Mass. R. 502.]

[(*d*) If an action against the maker of a note be brought in the name of one only of two persons jointly interested in the note; they are not thereby estopped from maintaining a joint action against a guarantor or endorser. Cobb v. Little, 2 Greenleaf, 261.

A judgment against one of two joint makers of a note, is no bar to a joint action against both.

In a suit against Mandeville and Jamesson upon a note declared on as having been made by them trading under the name of Jamesson,

But taking a warrant of attorney to enter up judgment, is not, unless judgment is actually entered up, even an extinguishment. (13)

Obtaining (14) a judgment is no satisfaction, even as to the parties subsequent to him against whom the judgment is obtained.

And (15) the actual taking of a man in execution, and discharging him upon a letter of licence, is no satisfaction as to any of the antecedent parties. (*a*)

Nor (16) is it a satisfaction, that one of the parties has

Mandeville pleaded in bar a judgment against Jamesson upon this note in favor of the plaintiff. On demurrer the plea was held bad. Sheehy v. Mandeville, 6 Cranch, 253.]

(13) R. Norris v. Aylett, 2 Campb. 329.

(14) Claxton v. Swift, 2 Show. 441. 494. Lutw. 882. To an action against the endorser of a bill, the defendant pleaded that the plaintiff had recoverad a judgment against the drawer, and that the judgment was still in force; and upon demurrer, the court of king's bench held the plea good, but the court of exchequer chamber held otherwise, and the judgment was reversed.

(15) Hayling v. Mulhall, Blackst. 1235. A bill was endorsed by Sheridan to Boon, and by him to the plaintiff: he sued Boon, and took him in execution, but discharged him upon a letter of license; he then sued Sheridan, for whom the defendant became bail; and upon an action against the defendant, *he* contended that the debt was satisfied by the imprisonment of Boon: but the court was clear it was not, and Mulhall was obliged to pay the money. Vide post.

[(*a*) Committing the maker of a note on execution is no satisfaction of the note, and no bar to an action against an endorser. And where the gaoler without authority released from confinement the maker of a note who had been committed, and received the amount of the judgment from a third person, and then tendered it to the assignee of the judgment, who refused to receive it, it was held that an action might still be maintained against an endorser. Porter v. Ingraham, 10 Mass. R. 88.

In an action by the endorsee of a note against an endorser, it appeared that an officer having an execution obtained in a suit against the maker, took personal property of less value than the debt, but did not sell it, and afterwards relinguished the property to the debtor, and took his body; it was held that the endorser was still liable to the full amount of the note, without deducting the value of the property taken on the execution. Sheldon v. Ackley, 4 Day, 458.]

(16) M'Donald v. Bovington, 4 Term Rep. 825. A bill drawn by M'Donald on Bovington, was endorsed to Thompson, who charged Bovington in execution upon it; Bovington was discharged as an insolvent, and then Thompson sued M'Donald and recovered. M'Donald paid the bill, sued Bovington, and charged him in execution; and on a rule nisi to discharge him, and cause shewn, it was urged that Bovington had satisfied the bill by being charged in execution at the suit of Thompson. Sed per Lord Kenyon, nothing can be clearer than that he has not; it was a mere formal satisfaction as to Thompson, not like actual pay-

been charged in execution on the bill or note and discharged as an insolvent, unless as to the party at whose suit he was so charged.

[A discharge of one of two joint makers of a note, under an insolvent law, will not operate as a discharge of the other. (*a*)

Proving a bill or note under a commission of bankruptcy against one of the parties to it, does not discharge any of the other parties. (*b*)]

If a customer deposit with his banker bills or notes of a third person *on account*, and they are suffered to remain with the banker after they are due, it will be no satisfaction of them, that at the time they became due, and at subsequent periods, the balance between the banker and his customer was in favor of the customer. (17)

And if the balance is afterwards against the customer, the banker may sue the third person on such bills or notes. (17)

If a bill or note is mislaid, and an agent for one of the parties tenders payment, on condition that the bill or note is delivered up, such tender is no satisfaction of the demand;

---

ment; and when M'Donald was obliged to pay the bill, a new cause of action arose against the defendant by the payment, without regard to what passed in the former action; and per Buller J. the consequence would be, that because the drawer was obliged to pay the holder, the acceptor would be discharged without paying either. Rule discharged.

[(*a*) Tooker v. Bennet, 3 Cain. R. 3.]

[(*b*) Kenworthy v. Hopkins, 1 Johns. Cas. 107.]

(17) Attwood v. Crowdie, 1 Stark. 483. Defendants lent their acceptances for the accommodation of Mattingley and Co., to two bills at three and four months after date, payable to Mattingley and Co., or order; Mattingley and Co. having been pressed by their bankers for security, sent them these and other bills on account: at the time these bills became due, and at several periods afterwards, the balance between Mattingley and Co. and the bankers was in favor of Mattingley and Co; but Mattingley and Co. failed, and the balance then was the other way: the barkers sued defendants upon these acceptances; defendants insisted that as the balances were against the bankers when these bills became due, and afterwards, these bills must be considered as satisfied, or at least that plaintiffs must stand as if the bills had been endorsed to them after they became due: but Lord Ellenborough held, that as the bills were sent *on account*, which must have meant the floating account, though there were periods at which the plaintiffs had no claim upon them, and they might have been demanded back, yet, as they were suffered to remain, the plaintiffs' claim reverted when by fresh advances the balance turned in their favor, and plaintiffs had a verdict.

and if the agent fail with the money in his hands before the bill or note is found, it will be no answer to an action upon the bill or note against the principal. (18)

But payment of interest shall cease from the time of such tender. (18) (*a*)

(19) Discharging, or (20) giving time to any of the par-

---

(18) Dent v. Dunn, 3 Campb. 296. An executor deposited money with an agent to pay notes of the testator: plaintiff had some of the notes, but could not find them: the agent tendered him the money if he would give up the notes, but they could not be found, and the agent failed with the money in his hands: plaintiff afterwards found the notes, and brought this action. It was urged for defendant, that plaintiff ought to bear the loss, for had he not mislaid the notes, they would have been paid. Sed per Lord Ellenborough, here was only a tender, which could not extinguish the debt; plaintiff did nothing to make the stakeholder his agent; he continued defendant's agent: verdict for plaintiff, but interest to the time of the tender only.

[(*a*) The payee of a dishonored bill, to whom it had been remitted by the drawer in payment of à debt, returned the first of the set to the drawer, requesting credit for the amount and a remittance. It was held that an action could not after this be maintained against the drawer upon the second of the set by an agent of the payee to whom he had endorsed it; and that the redelivering the bill to the drawer and desiring a remittance, must operate as a legal extinguishment of the bill. Ingraham v. Gibbs, 2 Dall. 134.]

(19) Ex parte Smith, 3 Bro. C. C. 1. Lewis and Potter endorsed certain bills and notes to Esdaile, and became bankrupt. Esdaile proved the amount of the bills and notes under their commission, and afterwards received a composition from the acceptors of the bills, and the makers of the notes, and gave them a full discharge, without the knowledge of the assignees of Lewis and Potter. On petition by the assignees to have the debt in respect of the bills and notes expunged, the chancellor held that, by discharging the acceptors and makers, without the consent of the endorser, the latter was discharged also. To the same effect is the case of ex parte Wilson, 11 Ves. 410. See also Smith v. Knox, 3 Esp. N. P. C. 46.

[See also M'Fadden v. Parker, 4 Dallas, 275.]

(20) English v. Darley, 2 Bos. and Pull. 61. The holder of a bill sued the endorser and acceptor, and took out execution against the acceptor, but received 100*l.* from him, and took his bond and warrant of attorney for payment of the remainder by instalments, with interest and costs, excepting only a nominal sum to enable him to support actions against the other parties: he then brought on to trial this action against the endorser. Lord Eldon thought that the bargain to give indulgence to the acceptor was a bar, and nonsuited the plaintiff; and on motion for a new trial, the court was clear that the nonsuit was right; because giving time to the acceptor was a pledge that he should have time from all the other parties. and the holder had no right to give such pledge and yet hold the other parties liable.

Gould v. Robson, 8 East. Rep. 576. The holder of a bill, upon its becoming due, received part payment from the acceptor, and took a bill from him at a future short date for the remainder, and agreed to

ties, is a discharge of every other party, who, upon paying the bill or note, would be entitled to sue the party to whom such discharge or time has been given; (*a*)

Unless the right to sue in such case result from facts out of ordinary course, as from the signatures being accommodation signatures.

And if the party who would be entitled to sue assent (21)

---

keep the original bill in his hands in the interim, as a security. He now sued the defendants as endorsers, and this was relied upon as a defence. Lord Ellenborough thought at the trial, that it did not amount to a giving time to the acceptor, and the plaintiff had a verdict; but upon motion for a new trial, he and the court were satisfied that it did, and a nonsuit was entered.

Laxton v. Peat, 2 Campb. N. P. C. 185. Endorsee of a bill against the acceptor. It appeared that the bill had been accepted for the accommodation of the drawer, which circumstance was known to the plaintiff, who gave value for the bill. When the bill became due, the plaintiff received part payment from the drawer, and gave him time to pay the remainder, without the concurrence of the defendant. Lord Ellenborough held, that this being an accommodation bill, within the knowledge of all the parties, the acceptor could only be considered as a surety for the drawer; and in the case of simple contracts, the surety is discharged by time being given, without his concurrence, to the principal. Nonsuit.

And see Rees v. Berrington, 2 Ves. Jun. 540. Rees became surety in a joint and several bond conditioned for the payment to the obligee, of a certain sum with interest by two instalments; the first on the 31st of December, 1789, and the second on the 31st of December, 1790. In September, 1790, the whole sum being unpaid, the obligee took promissory notes from the principal obligor, for payment of the debt by instalments at extended periods, which notes were afterwards exchanged for others payable at more distant days. This arrangement was without the knowledge of Rees. The principal obligor afterwards became bankrupt; and the executor of the obligee sued Rees, the surety. And on a bill filed for an injunction, the chancellor held, that the surety was discharged by this indulgence having been given without his consent to the principal. See also 2 Bos. and Pull. 62.

[(*a*) The law as stated in the text is recognised in many cases in the United States. Moodie v. Morrall, 1 S. Car. R. 367; Sharpe v. Bingley, 1 S. Car. R. 373; Scarborough v. Harris, 1 Bay, 177.

The holder of a note, after it became due, agreed with the maker for a consideration paid him, to wait ninety days without suing. It was held that the endorsers of the note were discharged by this agreement. Hubbly v. Brown, 16 Johns. R. 70.

But where the drawer of a bill on paying it would have no right to sue the acceptor, it seems that the discharge of the acceptor does not discharge the drawer. See Sargent v. Appleton, p. 225.]

(21) Clarke v. Devlin, 3 Bos. and Pull. 363. Atkinson, the acceptor of a bill, having been arrested by the holder, offered him a warrant of attorney for the amount of the bill, payable by instalments: this offer the holder mentioned to the defendant, the drawer, proposing to accept

to the giving time, or if, knowing of its having been given, he (22) promise to pay the bill or note, his liability will be continued in the former case, and revived in the latter; and it will make no difference in the latter case, though the promise were made under a misconception of the law, the party believing himself to be still liable, unless the holder is instrumental in raising that belief.

[It has been held that the drawer of a bill was not discharged by the holder's releasing the acceptor, where the drawer retained money on purpose to pay the bill. (*a*)

---

of it; who said, "you may do as you like, for I have had notice of the non-payment." In fact he had had notice. The court held that this amounted to an assent on the part of the defendant to the security being taken, and therefore that the defendant was not discharged by this indulgence to the acceptor.

(22) Stevens v. Lynch, 12 East. Rep. 38. The defence in this action, which was by an endorsee against the drawer of a bill, was, that the plaintiff had given time to the acceptor; in answer to which, it was proved that the defendant knew of such time having been given, but that, conceiving himself to be still liable, three months after the bill became due, he said to the plaintiff, "I know I am liable, and if Jones (the acceptor) does not pay it, I will." Upon this, Lord Ellenborough directed a verdict to be found for the plaintiff; and upon a motion for a new trial, the court held the direction right, and refused a rule.

[(*a*) In an action against Appleton, as drawer of a bill, it appeared that he was agent and supercargo of Smith, the drawee, in his brig Levant at Marseilles, and having in his hands a balance due to Sargent, the payee, for goods consigned to Appleton, and by him sold, and the proceeds invested on account of Smith. For this balance the bill was drawn and accepted by Smith, but payment was refused, Smith having become insolvent. Smith soon after, by indenture, to which the plaintiff was a party, assigned the Levant, and her earnings, and other property to his creditors, subject to the payment of any bills which Appleton had drawn or might draw on him, for the purchase of a cargo for the Levant. The creditors, in consideration of this assignment released Smith, the acceptor, from all demands. Appleton, the defendant, had retained sufficient property of Smith's for the purpose of discharging this bill. After this assignment, the defendant in letters to the plaintiff, expressed an intention of paying the bill, and acknowledged his liability; but he was forbidden to pay it by one of Smith's creditors, a party to the indenture. The plaintiff had received nothing under the assignment. Sewall J. directed a verdict for the plaintiff. Sedgwick J. giving the opinion of the court, said, "It is true as a general rule, that where the holder of a bill discharges the acceptor, all other parties are thereby discharged. The rule would apply in this case, if on a recovery against the defendant, he could maintain an action against Smith, the acceptor. But it is impossible this could be the case; for the bill would be paid by the defendant with money which belonged to Smith, and had been retained for the express purpose. It is the opinion of the court, that the direction of the judge was right." Sargent v. Appleton, 6 Mass. R. 85.]

The endorser of a note is not discharged, in consequence of discharging the maker, where it is done with the consent of the endorser, (*a*) or where the holder in making the discharge, expressly reserves all his rights against the endorser, and the endorser's rights against the maker. (*b*)

Where the holder of a note, after a suit brought against the endorser, released the maker by a writing not under seal and without consideration, it was held that the release was void, and was therefore no bar to the suit against the endorser. (*c*)

Where a bill is accepted, but dishonored by non-payment, receiving from the acceptor, as security, a new bill payable

---

[(*a*) Bruen and Sons were holders of a note made by Shelton and Beach, endorsed by Marquand. After the making of the note S. and B. assigned their property by indenture to Marquand and others, in trust for their creditors, and their creditors released all demands. One of the firm of Bruen and Sons became a party to this indenture on behalf of the partnership. Marquand was also a party as a creditor. The creditors in this instrument were divided into three classes, and those of the first class were to be first paid. In the schedule of the first class, was written, "Isaac Marquand endorsed to M. Bruen and Sons, 500 dollars." Bruen and Sons received a dividend under this assignment from Marquand and the other assignees. In an action by Bruen and Sons against Marquand as endorser, Van Ness J. delivered the opinion of the court. "The reason for holding the endorser discharged, by the discharge of the maker, certainly does not apply here, viz. that the remedy by the former against the latter is materially affected or taken away; because the defendant, who is a party to the assignment, not only as a trustee, but as a creditor to a large amount, *as a creditor*, released Shelton and Beach from their liability over to him, on this note. If the intention of the parties was to preserve the liability of the endorser, it was competent for them to do so. The intent of the parties clearly appears to have been that both the holders of the note and the defendant should set the makers free, but the remedy against the endorser should remain. It was, no doubt, for this reason that the debt in question was put in the first class. The makers intended to secure (as far as they could) their endorsers, as honorary creditors. As between the holders of this note and the makers, there was no reason for giving it a preference, but as between the makers and endorser it was otherwise." Bruen v. Marquand, 17 Johns. R. 58.]

[(*b*) R. and H. Stewart, holding a note made by Waring, endorsed by Eden, released Waring from all claims which they had against him on the note, "excepting always that he shall be responsible to the executors of Eden, deceased, and to them only;" and the same instrument declared that it was not to affect the claim of R. and H. Stewart against the said executors. It was held that this instrument was no bar to an action by R. and H. Stewart against the executors of Eden, the endorser. Stewart v. Eden, 2 Cain. R. 121.]

[(*c*) Crawford v. Millspaugh, 13 Johns. R. 87.]

at a future day, does not discharge the drawer of the first bill, unless there is an agreement by the holder not to sue upon the first bill. (*a*)

So where the holder of a bill drawn by A and accepted by B, but protested for non-payment, drew a bill upon A and B jointly for the amount of the first bill and damages, which was accepted by B, but not by A, it was held that A, the drawer of the first bill, was not thereby discharged. (*b*) (*c*)]

Release to payee of note, does not discharge the maker; (23)

Though the note were an accommodation note; (23)

Unless that fact were known to the releaser when he gave the release. (23) (*d*)

[(*a*) Pring v. Clarkson, 2 Dow. and Ryl. 78, 1 Barn. and Cres. 14.]

[(*b*) Furse at New York drew a bill on Angove in England, which came by endorsement to Suckley. The bill was accepted, but was protested for non-payment, and returned to Suckley. He then drew another bill on Furse and Angove jointly, at sixty days' sight, for the amount of the first bill and 20 per cent. damages. Suckley sent this bill to his partner, Holey, in England. This bill was accepted by Angove, but not by Furse, and was returned to Suckley unpaid. Suckley then sued Furse upon the first bill. Yates J. delivered the opinion of the court. "Holey's act in taking the acceptance of Angove alone, did not bind the plaintiff, and consequently could not discharge the liability of Furse as drawer of the original bill, on the ground of an agreement for an extension of the time of payment, or the giving of a new credit. No such agreement had ever existed between the parties. The new bill being for an existing debt, could not affect the original liability of Furse; for it is a settled rule of law, that a bill shall not be a discharge of a precedent debt, unless it be so expressly agreed between the parties." Suckley v. Furse, 15 Johns. R. 338.

[(*c*) Where the holder of a note sued the maker, and after issue joined took a *relicta* and *cognovit*, and gave the defendant a stipulation not to issue execution on the judgment to be entered on the cognovit, until a certain day, before which day, according to the course and practice of the court, he could not have brought the cause to trial, and obtained judgment, the court seemed to be of opinion that this was not such an indulgence or giving time, as would discharge the endorser. Hallett v. Holmes, 18 Johns. R. 28.]

(23) Carstairs v. Rolleston, 5 Taunt. 551. Assignees of first endorsee of note against the maker. Plea, that defendant made the note as surety for the payee, and not on his own account, and that plaintiff had released the payee from the note and from all claims and sums of money due thereon: there was no allegation that plaintiff knew that defendant was only surety, and on demurrer the plea was held bad, and plaintiff had judgment.

[(*d*) If the endorser of a note before it becomes due releases to the maker all actions, causes of action, and demands, which the former has

Agreeing after a bill has become due, and been regularly protested for non-payment, and notice thereof given, not to press the acceptor, will (24) not discharge the drawer. (*a*)

Nor will (24) receiving part of the money on account from an endorser.

[Receiving a partial payment from any party to a bill, or note, will not discharge any other party. (*b*)]

---

or may have against the latter, by reason or means of any act, matter, cause, or thing previously to the date of the release; if the endorser afterwards pays and takes up the note, he cannot maintain an action against the maker for money paid to his use. Coe v. Hutton, 1 Serg. and Raw. 398.]

[(*a*) Where judgment has been obtained against the maker of a note, the holder may issue an execution on the judgment or not, as he pleases; and the endorser is not discharged in consequence of any negligence of the holder in his endeavors to obtain the money of the maker.

In a case where judgment had been obtained against both the maker and endorser of a note, and the judgment creditor had issued a fieri facias against the maker, at the request of the endorser, and on which it appeared probable that a great part of the money might have been raised, but afterwards countermanded it, it was held that the endorser was not entitled in equity to an injunction against proceeding upon the judgment obtained against him. Livingston J. delivering the opinion of the court, said, " If the endorser suffers any injury by the negligence of the judgment creditor, it is clearly his own fault, it being his duty to pay the money, in which case he may take under his own direction the judgment obtained against the maker. By an act of Maryland it seems expressly provided, which is, perhaps, only declaratory of the common law, that an endorser may tender to a plaintiff the amount of a judgment which has been recovered against the maker of a note, and obtain an assignment of it." Lenox v. Prout, 3 Wheat. R. 520.]

(24) Walwyn St. Quintin, 1 Bos. and Pull. 652. In an action by endorsees against the drawer of a bill, it appeared that after the bill had become due and been protested for non-payment, though no notice thereof had been given to the defendant, he having no effects in the hands of the acceptor, the plaintiffs received part of the money *on account*, from the endorser; and that to an application from the acceptor, stating that it was probable he should be able to pay at a future period, they returned for answer that they would not press him. It was urged that either of these facts discharged the drawer: but the court after argument, and time taken to consider, held that they did not, and awarded the postea to the plaintiff. Eyre C. J. said, that, had this forbearance to sue the acceptor taken place before noting and protesting for non-payment, so that the bill had not been demanded when due, it was clear that the drawer would have been discharged: it would have been giving a new credit to the acceptor. But that after protest for non-payment, and notice to the drawer, or an equivalent to notice, a right to sue the drawer had attached, and the holder was not bound to sue the acceptor: he might therefore forbear to sue him.

Giving time to the payee will not discharge the drawer, for indulgence to the payee cannot affect the drawer: he may nevertheless pay and enforce his remedies. (25)

Giving time to the acceptor will not discharge the drawer, if the acceptance was to accommodate the drawer, and the drawer, as between him and the acceptor, is the person to pay the bill. (26)

Discharging any of the endorsers will be a discharge of all (27) subsequent, though not of prior, endorsers.

An agreement between holder, drawer, and acceptor, that the acceptor shall pay, discharges the drawer, if the acceptor is to pay to a limited extent only;

As the bill without expenses. (28)

[(*b*) James v. Badger, 1 Johns. Cas. 131. See also Lynch v. Reynolds, post.

In an action against one of several joint promisers of a note, it was held to be no bar, that one of the others had paid his share or proportion of the money, and that in consideration thereof the payee had acquitted all the promisers. Ruggles v. Patten, 8 Mass. R. 480.]

(25) Claridge v. Dalton, 4 Maule, 226. Endorsee against drawer. Defence, that plaintiff's agent had given time to the payee: it did not appear that plaintiff had authorized him so to do: but on rule nisi for a nonsuit, and cause shewn, the court expressed a clear opinion, that if he had it would not affect the drawer or give him any ground of defence, and rule discharged.

(26) Collott v. Haigh, 3 Campb. 281. In an action against the drawer of a bill, it appeared that plaintiffs had given time for some weeks to the acceptor, but it appearing also that the acceptance was an accommodation acceptance, without value, Lord Ellenborough was clear that the drawer continued liable; for the reason why indulgence to the acceptor without the drawer's consent discharges the drawer is because it may affect his remedy over against the acceptor; and that reason does not apply where he is not entitled to a remedy over. Verdict for plaintiff.

(27) Smith v. Knox, 3 Esp. N. P. C. 46. Per Lord Eldon, "It is said that the holder may discharge any of the endorsers after taking them in execution, and yet have recourse to the others. I doubt of the law as stated so generally; I am disposed to be of opinion, that if the holder discharge a prior endorser, he would find it difficult to recover against a subsequent one."

So also in English v. Darley, 2 Bos. and Pull. 62. Lord Eldon, after adverting to the inaccuracy of the marginal abstract of the case of Hayling v. Mulhall, said, had the plaintiff first sued a prior endorser and discharged him from execution, it would have afforded a sufficient objection to an action against a subsequent endorser. See Hayling v. Mulhall, ante, p. 221, n. (15).

(28) De la Torre v. Barclay, 1 Stark. 7. The drawers of a bill having become bankrupts, an agreement was entered into between their assignees, the holder (plaintiff), and the acceptor, by which the ac-

Taking the separate notes of one of several partners, at distant dates, as a collateral security, will not discharge the others, if the party insists at the time it shall not prejudice his claim upon the partnership, and he does not bind himself to wait till the notes are due; (29)

Though the partnership is dissolved before such notes are given: (29)

Otherwise, if he do bind himself to wait. (29)

Receiving dividends under a commission of bankruptcy is a satisfaction pro tanto only. (*a*)

[But where a person took up a note for the honor of an endorser, and afterwards assented to the discharge of the maker as an insolvent, signed his petition, and made affidavit of his debt as being money paid to the use of the maker; it was held that the endorser was discharged. (*a*)]

---

ceptor agreed to pay the amount of the bill, provided he were not called upon to pay more: the agreement recited the bill, the acceptance, and the probability it would be sent back for non-payment. Plaintiff having afterwards sued the drawers, Lord Ellenborough held this new agreement, which varied the condition of the acceptor, was a waiver of the right of action against defendants, who were represented by their assignees, and nonsuit.

(29) Bedford v. Deakin, Bickley, and Hickman, 2 Stark. 178. Defendants were drawers of a bill, which was dishonored; they dissolved partnership, and Hickman became bankrupt: Bickley afterwards proposed to give his own notes at four, eight, and twelve months as a security, and one Rushbury added his name as surety: plaintiff, who held the bill, agreed to take the notes, reserving to himself the security he held from the three, and he retained the bill. Interest was calculated on the notes till they would become due. In an action afterwards upon the bill against the three, it was urged, that the taking these notes discharged Deakin and Hickman: Lord Ellenborough said, he should have acceded to the objection had plaintiff agreed to postpone his remedy upon the bill, but as he had not, and on the contrary, had retained the bill, and expressly reserved to himself that security, he thought the taking the notes did not alter the original liability of the three defendants; and the plaintiff had a verdict.

[(*a*) D. Lynch, Jr., as agent of J. Lynch, sold goods to Reynolds, for which he took his note, endorsed it, and had it discounted. Reynolds failing, D. Lynch, Sen. took up the note for the honor of the endorser, and afterwards assented to the discharge of the maker, signed his petition, and made affidavit of his debt as being money paid to the use of the maker in taking up the note. After the discharge, J. Lynch paid D. Lynch, Sen. the amount of the note, and then sued Reynolds for money paid to his use. Per Curiam. "If the holder of a bill or note, compounds with the acceptor or maker, without the assent of the other parties to it, he thereby discharges them from their liability. Taking a sum of money in part payment and accepting a dividend, would not

After a partial satisfaction, the holder must (30) not in an action take a verdict for more than the sum remaining due; if he do, the court will (31) either make him correct the verdict, and pay any expense the mistake may have occasioned, or grant a new trial.

Satisfaction of a bill or note, as to one of several partners, is a satisfaction as to all; and if a person is a partner in two

---

produce the same effect; for these acts are advantageous to the other parties. But if the holder does an act which takes away and destroys the remedy of the other parties against the maker, upon the very note, he forfeits his right to call upon the endorsers. Here the holder took upon himself, in effect, to discharge the maker of the note from his liability to pay the debt; and we have a right to intend, that the defendant could not have obtained a discharge under the insolvent act, unless D. Lynch, Sen. had united in his petition. D. Lynch, Sen. must have considered himself as having no further claim upon the other party, for he swears that the money was paid for the use of the defendant. We are of opinion that the payment made by the plaintiff to D. Lynch, Sen. was made in the plaintiff's own wrong, it could not have been enforced at law: and therefore cannot be the basis of a suit against the defendant." Lynch v. Reynolds, 16 Johns. R. 41.]

(30) Bacon v. Searles, 1 H. Bl. 88. Upon a bill for £95, 10*s.* the drawer paid the plaintiff £60, 10*s.* and on an action against the acceptor, *he*, the acceptor, paid the residue with the interest into court; the plaintiff however proceeded, and after a verdict for the defendant, with liberty to the plaintiff to move to enter a verdict for him, he contended that the acceptance having made the defendant liable for the whole, and a personal contract not being divisible, he was entitled to recover, and to stand as a trustee for the drawer, but the court held otherwise, and the verdict stood.

Pierson v. Dunlop, Cowp. 571. In an action against the acceptor upon a bill for £300, the plaintiff took a verdict for the whole sum: the defendant filed a bill against him in the Exchequer, and he admitted in his answer that he had previously received £180 from the drawer; this (among others) was urged as a ground for a new trial, and after cause shewn, Lord Mansfield said, "The verdict is certainly taken for £180 more than was due; there was no admission of this payment at the trial, which was very wrong, and has been the occasion of filing a bill in the Exchequer, therefore there ought to be a deduction of the money received, and a proportionable part of the interest, together with all the costs in the Exchequer;" and though the court discharged the rule for a new trial, they made the plaintiff remit the £180 with interest upon it from the time it was paid, and pay the costs of the bill and answer in the Exchequer.

However, in Johnson v. Kennion, 2 Wils. 262., the defendant drew a bill for £1000 in favor of Benson or order, and Benson endorsed it to the plaintiff; Benson paid the plaintiff £232, notwithstanding which he took a verdict against the defendant for the whole £1000, and upon a rule nisi for a new trial upon this ground, the court are represented to have held that he did right; but in Bacon v. Searles, supra, Wilson J. considered the report inaccurate, and the authority questionable.

(31) See Pierson v. Dunlop, supra.

firms, satisfaction as to one firm is (32) so as to both. What would bar one firm will bar the other, and it will make no difference though one common partner is, in fact, ignorant of the circumstances which constitute the satisfaction.

Thus if one house receive funds from the drawer to take up a bill, and misapply them, no other house to which any member of the first house belongs can sue the drawer;

Or if he stands in the place of the drawer, the acceptor. (32)

In an action upon a bill or note, the plaintiff is in general entitled to recover the money payable thereby, with (33) interest, (*a*) and (34) all incidental expenses occasioned by non-acceptance or non-payment.

The interest is, in general, to be computed from the time the bill or note would regularly have been payable, and it is, in general, to be carried down to the time when final judgment may be signed. (35)

---

(32) Jacaud and Gordon v. French and others, 12 East's Rep. 317. Jacaud was in partnership with Blair in Ireland, and with Gordon here. Jacaud and Gordon had a bill drawn by Farrell and Co. on defendants, and Farrell and Co. had supplied Jacaud and Blair with funds to pay this bill: Blair misapplied those funds, and on an action on the bill by Jacaud and Gordon, the defence was, that the misapplication by Blair was a misapplication by Jacaud also, and that after being guilty in one house of disappointing payment by misapplying the payment-fund, he could not endeavor to enforce payment in another: and on case the court was of that opinion, and the postea was awarded to the defendants.

(33) D. Mar. 2d ed. 13. Blaney v. Bradley, Blackst. 761. By the court. "Interest is due on all bills of exchange and notes of hand payable at a day certain, or after demand, if payable on demand." See also Bunb. 129. 2 Term Rep. 58.

[(*a*) In an action for three years' interest upon a note with interest payable annually, interest was allowed in Massachusetts on each year's interest from the time it became payable to the time of the judgment. Greenleaf v. Kellogg, 2 Mass. R. 568.

So in New Hampshire, in an action on a note with interest payable annually, though the court refused to allow compound interest, yet they allowed simple interest on the annual interest. Pierce v. Rowe, 1 N. Hamp. R. 179.

But in another case, in Massachusetts, in an action on a note with interest payable annually, the court refused to allow interest on the annual interest. Hastings v. Wiswall, 8 Mass. R. 455.]

(34) Vide Mar. 2d ed. 13. In Simmonds v. Parminter, ante p. 213. note (1), the plaintiff recovered interest, exchange, and re-exchange; and in Auriol v. Thomas, (post, p. 238. n. (45.) 10*s.* per pagoda in lieu of interest, exchange, and all other charges.

(35) Robinson v. Bland, Burr. 1077. In an action upon a bill of ex-

Thus, upon a bill or note payable on presentment, interest (36) must be computed from the presentment.

But if a bill or note payable at a given time after date be for a specified sum, "bearing interest," interest shall be computed from the date. (37)

It has, indeed, been held (38), that if a party entitled to notice of the dishonor of a bill or note, offer to pay it within a reasonable time after the notice is given, he is not liable for interest from the time of the dishonor: but perhaps there might be risk in acting upon that decision.

---

change, and for money lent, a case was reserved, and the court was of opinion that the plaintiff could not recover upon the bill, but that he might for the money lent; but they took time to consider, with a view to settle the future practice, to what time the interest upon money lent should be computed, and afterwards determined that it should be computed to the time of giving judgment.

(36) Blaney v. Bradley, ante, p. 232. note (33). Cotton v. Horsemanden, Pract. Reg. 357. The court held, that in actions upon promissory notes, payable on demand, interest should be given from the time of the demand proved; but in this case, where it appeared upon the face of the note to be for money lent, interest should be given from the date of the note. 9 Mod. 138. By the court, interest upon a bill of exchange commences from demand made.

(37) Kennerly v. Nash, 1 Stark. 452. Action on bill at four months after date for £25, 4*s*. bearing interest; and per Lord Ellenborough, these words entitle plaintiff to interest from the date of the bill; without them, he would have been entitled to it from the time it became due.

Hopper v. Richmond, 1 Stark. 507. By the terms of a note defendant undertook to pay legal interest on demand: Lord Ellenborough held, that must mean from the date of the note.

(38) Walker v. Barnes, 5 Taunt. 240. A bill for £10, due 11th June, was presented for payment on that day, and dishonored. On the 12th notice was sent by letter to the drawer, and early on the 13th he tendered the £10; the £10 was not accepted, and on an action against the drawer, it was urged for the plaintiff, that the tender was insufficient, for that defendant ought to have tendered the interest from the 11th to the 13th; but on the point being reserved, the court held it sufficient, if the drawer, within a reasonable time after the notice, tendered the principal without the interest; and judgment was given for the defendant.

Note, the interest would have been under three farthings,—one fifteenth part of ten pence. But quære, whether non-payment by the drawee was not a breach of the drawer's contract, and whether the holder was not entitled to interest for not receiving on the 11th what defendant undertook he should receive on that day. It may be observed, however, in support of this decision, that the constant form in assumpsit against a drawer or endorser, makes him promise only for the amount of the money mentioned in the bill. It is silent as to interest. It is, however, silent also as to expenses.

Where all that is due is tendered, and the holder has mislaid the bill or note, so that he cannot give it up, and payment is, on that account, postponed, the interest shall be computed up to the time of such tender only. (39)

The language of 3 & 4 Anne seems to imply, that a neglect to procure a protest upon any inland bill for the payment of £20, upon which a protest might have been made, (39), would preclude the holder from recovering such interest or expenses from any person entitled to notice of the non-acceptance or non-payment; but the contrary is now settled. (40)

Whether it would preclude the holder of a coal-note given under 3 Geo. 2. c. 26. § 7. is not decided.

A jury is not bound to give interest upon a bill or note, and where the bill or note has lain dormant for many years without any claim being made upon it, they may properly refuse it. (40*)

And for any time that it has been in the hands of an alien enemy, interest ought not to be allowed, because during that time payment of the principal would have been illegal. (40*)

[On a note made in one place, payable in another, interest is recoverable according to the legal rate of the place where it is payable. (*a*)

---

(39) See 3 & 4 Anne, c. 9. § 5. ante, p. 168. note (86).

(40) See Windle v. Andrews, ante, p. 168. n. (85.)

(40*) Du Belloix v. Lord Waterpark, Hilary, 1822. Payee against maker on note for £800 of 27th December, 1787, payable six months after date. The cause was tried in 1821; there was was no evidence of any claim upon the note from the time it was made, and for many years of the intermediate time plaintiff had been an alien enemy: the jury asked if they were bound to give interest, and Abbot C. J. told them *that* was for their consideration; and they gave none. A motion was made to increase the verdict by adding the interest, or for a new trial, but the court was clear that the question of interest was within the province of the jury; that it was in the nature of damages for the non-payment of the debt, that they were to say whether there should be any and what damages on that account, and that in this instance there was no ground for saying they had not exercised their discretion rightly. Abbot C. J. added, that during the time the plaintiff was an alien enemy, it would have been illegal to have paid him the debt, and that for that interval therefore damages could not legally have been given: the rule was refused.

[(*a*) Scofield v. Day, 20 Johns. R. 102.]

So if a bill be drawn in one country, and payable and accepted there, in an action against the acceptor, interest is recoverable only according to the legal rate of that country, although the suit is brought in another country. (*a*) (*b*)]

[(*a*) Foden v. Sharp, ante, p. 31.]

[(*b*) Where a note is discounted at less than the legal rate of interest, interest at the legal rate is recoverable against an endorser in an action on the note by the party that discounted it. Mechanics' Bank v. Minturn, 19 Johns. R. 244.

Where the endorsee of a note purchases it from the endorser, the former can recover of the latter only the consideration actually paid, though less than the amount of the note. But the maker is liable for the full amount. Braman v. Hess, 13 Johns. R. 52; Munn v. Commission Company, 15 Johns. R. 44. See also Brown v. Mott, 7 Johns. R. 361; and Wiffen v. Roberts, 1 Esp. R. 261.

An endorsement is however *primâ facie* evidence of a full consideration. Riddle v. Mandeville, 5 Cranch, 322. It is otherwise if it be made without recourse. Welch v. Lindo, 7 Cranch, 159.

In an action upon three notes payable with 3 per cent. interest per annum if paid at maturity, "if not, 6 per cent. interest to be paid;" and upon a fourth payable without interest "until the note is out, if not paid then, lawful interest until paid;" the notes not having been paid when they fell due, judgment was given for their amount, with 6 per cent., the lawful interest, from the date to the time of the judgment. Dagget v. Pratt, 14 Mass. R. 177.

In an opinion of Chanceller Kent, on a case submitted to him since his retiring from office, as to the necessity of producing the very bill of the set which was protested and the original protest, in giving notice to the drawer or endorser of a bill, he says, "This question about the production of the identical number of the set that was accepted and protested, affects nothing but the point of *interest.* If the holder calls on the drawer or endorser for payment, and shows him a copy of the protest and one of the set of bills, but not the one that was accepted and protested, and the drawer offers to pay the bill and protest and damages, and re-exchange, *provided the bill itself be produced*, and not otherwise, and it is not produced, is he bound to pay *interest* from that time? I am of opinion that he is not bound to pay interest, *until the bill be produced*, or its loss accounted for, for he is not in *default of payment* until then. The drawer is *entitled* to the accepted bill if he is obliged to pay it, and if he offers to pay, but insists on the bill previously, and the other party for his own convenience chooses to retain it, or leaves it abroad, I conclude that interest will not begin to run *until a redemand accompanied by the bill.*" Though the preceding remarks refer only to the case of a bill accepted and protested for non-payment, yet the author inclines to the same opinion with regard to a bill protested for non-acceptance.—He cites Beawes' Lex Merc. 424. § 74. "No drawer or endorser is obliged to make restitution on sight of the protest alone, nor on sight of the protest and the unaccepted bill, when one of them hath been accepted; but he is obliged to give a satisfactory security to the remitter on his producing only the protest, and to make payment when this and the accepted bill are presented together."—He also cites Code de Commerce, Art. 148, 151. See also Dent v. Dunn, ante, p. 223.]

The only incidental expense in the case of the person who made the presentment is the charge of the notice and protest; in the case of any antecedent party, that of the return of the bill or note must be added.

Upon a foreign bill the (41) re-exchange forms a part of the expense of the return, aud let the bill be returned through ever so many hands, the (41) drawer is liable for the re-exchange upon each return.

And the (42) drawer is liable for the re-exchange and every other expense arising from the non-acceptance or non-payment, notwithstanding the dishonor of the bill is expressly ordered by the country on which it is drawn.

But the acceptor is (43) not liable for re-exchange; his contract cannot be carried farther than to pay the sum specified in the bill, together with legal interest, where interest is due.

[It has been held, that the endorser of a note, who has been sued by the endorsee, and obliged to pay the costs of the suit, cannot in an action against the maker, compel him to pay those costs, in addition to the amount of the note. (*a*)

---

(41) Mellish v. Simeon, 2 H. Blackst. 378. A bill was drawn in London upon Paris, and negotiated through Holland; before it became due the French government prohibited the payment of any bill drawn in England, in consequence of which it was dishonored, and sent back through the different hands by which it had before been negotiated, to London; the re-exchange between Paris and Holland, raised the bill from £603, 19*s.* 10*d.* to £905, 13*s.* 9*d.*, and the re-exchange between Holland and London to £913, 4*s.* 3*d.*, which the plaintiff (the payee) paid; and upon an action by him against the drawer, Eyre C. J. left it to the jury, whether the defendant was liable for the re-exchange occasioned by returning the bill through Holland, and they found that he was. An application was made for a new trial upon the ground that the defendant was not liable for the re-exchange, because there was no default in him, the payment being prohibited by the government of France; but the court held it immaterial why the bill was not paid, that as it was not paid, he was liable to all the consequences, of which the re-exchange was one, and the rule was refused.

(42) See the preceding note, (41). Vide Detastet v. Baring, 11 East's Rep. 265.

(43) Thus in Napier v. Schneider, post., the court was clearly of opinion that the defendant, who was acceptor of a bill, was not liable for re-exchange. S. P. R. acc. in Woolsey v. Crawford, 2 Campb. 445.

[(*a*) Simpson v. Griffin, 9 Johns. R. 131. The court says, "If the endorser of a note be duly fixed, he ought to pay it, without waiting to

Where the endorsee of a note sued the maker, and failed to recover on account of the illegality in the consideration between the maker and payee, it was held that in an action by the endorsee against the payee who had endorsed the note to him, he could only recover the principal and interest of the note, and not the costs or expenses of the suit against the maker. (*a*)]

If, by the terms of a note, the holder has the option of being paid either at the place where it was made, or, "according to the course of exchange" between that place and another, he (44) may insist upon being paid according to such course of exchange as exists between them at the time when the note becomes due. (*b*)

And it makes no difference, that at the time when the

---

be sued. It is his own fault or misfortune that subjects him to costs. He can only look to the maker for the amount of the note." Simpson v. Griffin, 9 Johns. R. 131. But see Jones v. Brooke, post, ch. xiii. note (8), and Smith v. Woodcock, ante, p. 218. note (9).]

[(*a*) Copp v. M'Dugall, 9 Mass. R. 1.]

(44) Pollard v. Herries, 3 Bos. and Pull. 335. The defendant gave the plaintiff a note for payment, at seven days' sight, of 1200 livres Tournois, and interest, drawn at Paris, and expressed to be "payable as above in Paris, or, at the choice of the bearer, at the Union bank in Dover, or at my usual residence in London, according to the course of exchange upon Paris." In an action on this note the defendant paid £18, 16*s*. 6*d*. into court. The jury found a verdict for the plaintiff, with £40, 6*s*. 10*d*. damages, subject to the opinion of the court upon a case stating the making of the note, and the due presentment in London, and that, at the time when the note was made, there was a direct course of exchange between London and Paris, that that exchange had fallen, and before the note became due had altogether ceased; that, according to the last direct course, £18, 16*s*. 6*d*. would be sufficient to pay the note: that when the note became due there was no direct course, but that a circuitous course of exchange through Hamburgh existed, and that, according to that circuitous course, the £59, 3*s*. 4*d*. would be due upon the note. The court held, that the plaintiff had a right to insist upon being paid according to such circuitous course, and the verdict therefore was entered for £40, 6*s*. 10*d*.

[(*b*) But in an action brought in New York on a note made in Canada payable to the plaintiffs, residents in England, "with interest until paid in England," it was held, that "the plaintiffs were not entitled to any allowance on account of the difference of exchange with England:" but that they were entitled to English interest up to the time of the judgment, not to the time when the money might in the ordinary course of business be remitted to England. Scofield v. Day, 20 Johns. R. 102.

In South Carolina it is provided by statute that in any action on any bill or for any debt payable in any other country, the jury may give a verdict for such difference of exchange as shall be just. St. S. Car. 1796. 2 Brev. Dig. 48. See also note (*a*), p. 238, post.]

note was made there was a direct course, and at the time when it becomes due, there is no direct, but only a circuitous course of exchange between them.

On the return of a bill drawn here for the payment of pagodas in the East Indies, the (45) practice is to allow for the sum payable by the bill interest and all incidental charges, after the rate of 10*s.* for each pagoda, and five per cent. thereon from the expiration of thirty days after notice of the bill's dishonor; and it has been (45) determined that this practice was lawful, even where the price allowed for each pagoda on the discount of the bill was only six shillings and six-pence. (*a*)

---

(45) Auriol v. Thomas, 2 Term Rep. 52. Upon executing a writ of inquiry on a bill for the payment of 800 star pagodas returned protested from India, it appeared that the usage was to charge 10*s.* per pagoda for bills returned from India protested, and five per cent. after the expiration of thirty days from the notice to the defendant of the bill's dishonor, which included all incidental charges, and that the defendant had agreed to pay accordingly; upon which the jury assessed the damages at 10*s.* per pagoda, with the five per cent., though the plaintiff discounted the bill at the rate of 6*s.* 6*d.* a pagoda; that being then the current price. A rule nisi was obtained to set aside the inquisition, on the ground that this allowance was exorbitant, and the agreement for it usurious; but the court, on cause shewn, thought otherwise, and discharged the rule.

[(*a*) In most of the United States damages, in addition to the principal sum and interest, are recoverable on bills, both foreign and inland, returned dishonored.

The rule as to damages on bills drawn in Massachusetts upon places out of the United States, as it existed till very lately, appears from the opinion of the Court, delivered by Parsons C. J. in Grimshaw v. Bender. "The rule of damages on foreign bills, established by the law merchant, is in our opinion, absolutely controlled by the immemorial usage of this State. Here the usage is to allow the holder of the bill the money for which it was drawn at par, and also the charges of protest, with *American* interest on those sums from the time when the bill should have been paid; and the further sum of one tenth of the money for which the bill was drawn, with interest upon it from the time payment of the dishonored bill was demanded of the drawer. But nothing has been allowed for re-exchange, whether it is below or at par. This usage is so ancient that we cannot trace its origin; and it forms a part of the law merchant of the commonwealth." 6 Mass. R. 187. In Barclay v. Minchin, 6 Mass. R. 162, damages were assessed by the same rule.

In a manuscript opinion of Judge Jackson, given since his retiring from the bench, he says, that "the damages and interest, on a protest for non-acceptance, are computed in like manner as on a protest for non-payment;" and that the holder of a foreign bill drawn in this State, and protested for non-acceptance, is, according to the decision in Grim-

The action usually brought on account of a bill or note, is a special action of assumpsit thereon, but perhaps a spe-

---

shaw v. Bender, (supra,) "entitled to interest on the amount of the bill and charges, from the date of the protest for non-acceptance." He adds, "It is true the Chief Justice speaks of the interest as due, 'from the time when the bill should have been paid;' but I understand that as equivalent to saying 'from the time when the bill was protested for non-payment,' or 'from the time of the breach of the contract of the drawer or endorser.'" But in the same opinion the rule as to interest on dishonored bills, is considered as being incorrectly laid down by C. J. Parsons. And the author expresses his opinion, that in an action against a drawer or endorser interest is recoverable only from the time notice is given of the dishonor of the bill; conformably to what is conceived to be the rule as to interest in such case in England. This opinion is on the ground that the "10 per cent. damages are given instead of the expenses or damages on re-exchange, and are to be considered in all respects the same, excepting that they are fixed at an immutable rate, instead of varying with the actual rate of exchange."

By a statute of Massachusetts lately passed it is enacted, that where any bill is drawn or endorsed in the State after the first of April, payable at any place beyond the Cape of Good Hope, in Africa, Asia, or the islands thereof, shall be refused acceptance or payment, the drawer or endorser shall, on due notice and demand thereof, pay the contents of such bill, at the par value thereof, together with twenty per cent. thereon, in full of all damages, interest, and charges; and where any bill so drawn or endorsed and payable at any other place out of the United States, is dishonored, the drawer or endorser, shall on due notice and demand thereof, pay the contents of such bill at the current rate of exchange at the time of demanding payment, and five per cent. damages on the contents of such bill, together with interest on such contents from the time when such bill shall have been refused acceptance or payment, which shall be in full of all damages, charges, and expenses. Mass. St. March 4th, 1826.

When any bill drawn or endorsed in Massachusetts payable at any place without the State and within the United States, is protested for non-acceptance or non-payment, the drawer or endorser besides the contents of the bill, the costs, and interest, is liable to pay damages to the holder at the following rates, viz. three per cent. if payable in any of the New England States or New York; five per cent. if payable in New Jersey, Pennsylvania, Delaware, Maryland, Virginia, or District of Columbia; six per cent. if payable in North Carolina, South Carolina, or Georgia; and nine per cent. if payable in any other part of the United States. One per cent. damages are also recoverable on bills for $100 or more drawn or endorsed in Massachusetts and payable at any place in the State, if it be seventy five miles or more distant from the place where the bill is drawn or endorsed. Mass. St. 1819, c. 41; St. 1820, c. 2.

In New York the holder of a bill drawn there payable at a place out of the United States, protested for non-acceptance or non-payment, is entitled to recover of the drawer or endorser, the amount of the bill at the rate of exchange on the place on which the bill was drawn, at the time of notice given to the party to be charged, and twenty per cent. damages on the amount of the bill at the rate of exchange, the expenses

cial action (46) of debt, debt on an indebitatus, or an (47) indebitatus assumpsit, might be maintained thereon.

---

of the protest, and interest on the aggregate amount of the bill and damages from the time of notice given to the party to be charged. Hendricks v. Franklin, 4 Johns. R. 119; Weldon v. Buck, 4 Johns. R. 144; Graves v. Dash, 12 Johns. R. 17; Denston v. Henderson, 13 Johns. R. 322.

The rule formerly acted on by the Supreme Court of New York, was the same as that above stated, except that the amount of the bill was calculated at the par of exchange. Spencer J. says, "The twenty per cent. was in lieu of damages, in case of re-exchange, and because there was no course of exchange from London to New York, and to avoid the constant uncertainty and fluctuation of exchange." Hendricks v. Franklin, 4 Johns. R. 119. But this decision has been overruled by the Court of Errors, who have fixed the rule as above stated. Graves v. Dash, 12 Johns. R. 17.

The damages on bills drawn or endorsed in Maine, and payable within or out of the United States, are precisely the same as those above stated with regard to Massachusetts, previously to the statute of Massachusetts of March 6th, 1826. Laws of Maine, 318, statute passed February 28th, 1821.

The damages on bills drawn in Connecticut or Delaware, payable out of the United States, returned protested, are twenty per cent. 3 Griff. Law Reg. 80; 4 Id. 1069.

The holder of a bill drawn or endorsed in Rhode Island payable in any place out of the United States, and returned protested for non-acceptance or non-payment, is entitled to recover of the drawer or endorser ten per cent. damages, charges of protest; and interest from the date of the protest. On bills drawn in the State, and payable in any other part of the United States, five per cent. damages, the charges of protest, and interest from the date of the protest, are recoverable. Laws of R. I. Ed. 1798, p. 444. See also Brown v. Van Braam, 3 Dall. 344.

The damages given on bills drawn or endorsed in Pennsylvania, payable out of the State and within the United States, (except in Louisiana,) are five per cent.; if payable in Louisiana or any other place in North America or its islands, (except the northwest coast of America, Mexico, or any of the West India or Bahama islands,) ten per cent.; if payable in Madeira, the Canaries, Azores, Cape de Verd Islands, Spanish Main, or Mexico, fifteen per cent.; in Europe or its islands twenty per cent.; in any other part of the world, twenty-five per cent. Interest is given in all these cases on the amount of the bill, damages, and charges of protest, from the time of notice; and the amount of the bill and damages is to be determined by the rate of exchange, or value of the money or currency mentioned in such bill, at the time of notice. 7 Laws of Penn. 434.

It was formerly held in this State that the holder of a bill protested for non-acceptance, but not for non-payment, was not entitled to the twenty per cent. damages, but only to such a sum as would purchase a new bill for the same amount, with interest from the time of notice. The court in this case instructed the jury, that if no current rate of exchange was settled, there could be no safer rule than to give damages at the par of exchange. Taan v. Le Gaux, 1 Yeates, 204.

The damages on bills drawn in Ohio on persons living within the

And assumpsit will lie upon a bill or note against a corporation, where such corporation is empowered by statute to issue, indorse, or accept bills or notes. (48)

United States, and out of that State, returned protested for non-acceptance or non-payment, are ten per cent.; if drawn on persons out of the United States, fifteen per cent. 3 Griff. Law Reg. 404.

The damages in Indiana are the same as in Ohio. 3 Griff. Law Reg. 468.

The damages on bills drawn in Illinois payable out of the United States are twenty per cent.; on those payable within the United States ten per cent. 3 Griff. Law Reg. 424.

Upon a bill drawn in Maryland payable in any other State, duly protested, the holder can recover so much current money as will purchase a good bill on the same place at the current rate of exchange, and also eight per cent. damages upon the *value* of the principal sum mentioned in such bill, and costs of protest, and interest upon the value of the principal from the time of protest; and upon a bill payable out of the United States, the *value* of the bill is recoverable at the rate of exchange, fifteen per cent. of that value, damages, costs of protest, and interest on the value of the principal sum in the bill from the time of protest. Stat. of Mar. 1785, c. 38. 1 Laws of Maryland, Maxcy's Ed. 558.

The damages on protested bills, drawn in Virginia upon any place out of the United States, are fifteen per cent., and interest from the date of the protest. 1 Virg. Rev. Code, c. 77, § 1. p. 113; 2 Virg. Rev. Code, c. 72, § 1. p. 100. See Slacum v. Pomery, 6 Cranch, 221. The damages on inland bills returned protested are one per cent. 3 Griff. Law Reg. 363.

Any bill drawn in Kentucky, on a person out of the United States, and protested, draws interest at the rate of ten per cent. from the date until paid; but not more than eighteen months interest from the date until it is presented protested to the drawer or endorser. Toulmin's Kentucky Laws, 267, Statute Feb. 6, 1798. No other damages are recoverable upon any bills drawn in Kentucky. 4 Griff. Law Reg. 1141.

On any bill drawn in Missouri payable out of the United States, returned protested, twenty per cent. damages are recoverable; and on a bill payable out of the State, and in the United States, ten per cent. 4 Griff. Law Reg. 627.

In North Carolina upon the protest of bill drawn in that State, payable out of the United States, ten per cent. interest is chargeable from the date until payment is made, but not more than eighteen months interest is allowed, previously to its being presented protested to the drawer or endorser. The *damages* on such bills are fifteen per cent. with costs and charges of protest; and the damages on the protest of bills drawn in the State and payable in the United States, are ten per cent. with costs, and charges of protest. 3 Griff. Law Reg. 225.

The holder of any bill drawn in Tennesee, and protested, is entitled to recover ten per cent. interest from the date to the time of payment, but not more than eighteen months interest previously to its being presented protested to the drawer or endorser; and also fifteen per cent. damages on the sum expressed in the bill, with the costs and charges of protest. 4 Griff. Law Reg. 799.

The damages on bills drawn in South Carolina, and returned protested, if payable out of that State, and within the United States, are ten per

31

Debt (49) may be maintained by the payee against the maker of a note expressed to be for value received.

---

cent.; if payable in any other part of North America or any of the West India islands, twelve and a half per cent.; if payable in any other part of the world, fifteen per cent. In all these cases all charges, and interest from the time when the bill becomes due, are recoverable; and the damages are to be liquidated by the difference of exchange on the place where the bill is payable. St. S. Car. 1796, 1 Brev. Dig. 487.

The damages in Alabama and Louisiana are the same as in Missouri, stated above. 4 Griff. Law Reg. 586, 697.

In Mississippi ten per cent. damages are recoverable upon foreign bills drawn in that State and returned protested. 4 Griff. Law Reg. 670.

It has been held in New York, that where a bill is remitted to pay an antecedent debt, no damages are recoverable against the remitter.

In an action by the endorsee against the endorser of a foreign bill returned dishonored, it appeared, that the bill had been remitted by the defendant for the payment of goods which he had purchased of the plaintiff. The court said, "The plaintiff ought not to be allowed the twenty per cent. damages: the practice on this point we believe to be settled. The reason for that allowance does not apply where a bill is remitted to pay an antecedent debt." Kenworthy v. Hopkins, 1 Johns. Cas. 107.

The person to whom a bill is remitted in payment of an antecedent debt, or a person to whom he endorses it after it is dishonored, and who is acquainted with the circumstances, cannot recover the twenty per cent. damages against an endorser prior to the remitter. The remitter of the bill is the person entitled to the damages, "he having encountered all the hazard and inconvenience of the remittance." Thompson v. Robertson, 4 Johns. R. 27

And where it appeared from a receipt of the payee of a bill, that when paid it was to be in full for the balance of an account due from the drawer to the payee, the bill being dishonored, it was held in Pennsylvania that the payee was not entitled to recover the twenty per cent. damages. Chapman v. Steinmitz, 1 Dallas, 261.

So where a bill had been remitted by the endorsers in payment of an antecedent debt, and being dishonored, the endorsees to whom it had been remitted, received from the drawer his note for the amount of the bill and twenty per cent. damages, and gave him up the bill, it was held that the endorsers might recover from their endorsees the amount of the twenty per cent. damages included in the drawer's note, notwithstanding his failure before it became due. Keppele v. Carr, 4 Dallas, 155.

Where a bill was drawn, as additional security for a bottomry bond, previously given by the drawer, the captain of a vessel of which the drawee was owner, it was held that the drawer was not liable to damages on the dishonor of the bill. Hazelhurst v. Kean, 4 Yeates, 19.

It is often made a question, by the law of what place the damages on a protested bill are to be regulated. See on this subject, Hazelhurst v. Kean, ante p. 30; Slacum v. Pomery, ante, p. 32; Shermerhorn v. Pelham, ante, p. 32; Bain v. Ackworth, ante, p. 30; Winthrop v. Pepoon, ante, p. 30; M'Candlish v. Cruger, ante, p. 30; Grimshaw v. Bender, ante, p. 31.

The acceptor of a bill is in no case liable to pay damages. Bain v. Ackworth, 1 S. Car. R. 107.

But where principals directed their agent to draw on them for the

[So debt may be maintained by the drawer of a bill payable to himself, against the acceptor, where it is expressed to be for value received. (*a*)]

---

amount of purchases made by him on their account, and the agent in consequence drew upon his principals, who refused to accept the bills, and the drawer was in consequence obliged to pay the amount of the bills and damages to the holders, it was held, that the drawer might recover of the drawees the amount of the bills and damages thus paid, on a count for money paid to their use, and that the bills might be given in evidence on that count. Riggs v. Lindsay, 7 Cranch, 500.]

(46) In Anon. Hardr. 485. It was held that the payee of a bill could not maintain debt agaiest the acceptor, because there was no privity between them, and because the acceptance was a collateral undertaking only. [See also Smith v. Segur, 2 Hen. & Munf. 394; and Wilson v. Crowdhill, 2 Munf. 302.] In Welch v. Craig, Str. 680. 8 Mod. 373. it was held that debt will not lie npon a note; but it does not appear by or against what particular party that action was brought. In 1 Mod. Ent. 812. pl. 13., it is said that debt will lie against the maker of a note, not against the endorser. And in Morgan's Precedents, 458, is an entry of a declaration in debt by the administratrix of the payee of a note against the maker; and in Rumball v. Ball, 10 Mod. 38, an action of debt was brought upon a note.

(47) In Brown v. London, 1 Freeman, 14. 1 Mod. 285. 1 Vent. 152. It was held, that an indebitatus assumpsit would not lie upon the acceptance of a bill, Twisden J. dubitante. And there is a dictum to the like effect in Comb. 204. But in another report of Brown v. London, Lev. 298, the court is stated to have resolved in favor of the defendant, because the custom was not set out in the count. In Skinn. 346, it is said it will only lie against the drawer upon a bill importing to have been given for value received. In Salk. 125. 12 Mod. 37, it is laid down generally, that an indebitatus assumpsit will not lie upon a bill; and in 12 Mod. 345, it is held that the payee of a bill importing to have been given for valne received, may maintain an indebitatus assumpsit against the drawer. And it may be observed, that the demand of an endorsee upon a bill or note against endorser, drawer, maker, or acceptor, is continually allowed as an item of set-off under the statutes of set-off.

(48] Murray v. East India Company, 5 Barnew. and Ald. 204. Assumpsit against the East India Company as acceptors of certain bills of Exchange: it was urged, that assumpsit could not lie against a corporation; but the court, without intimating how that would be in general, held, that as the East India Company was, by 53 G. 3. c. 155. § 57., and other acts, expressly authorized to accept bills, those statutes were to be considered as virtually making them liable to the ordinary remedies upon bills, and consequently to the action of assumpsit.

(49) Bishop v. Young, 2 Bos. and Pull. 78. This was an action of debt by the payee, against the maker of a promissory note, expressed to be for value received. The first count of the declaration was upon the note; and upon general demurrer to this count, the court, after time taken to consider, held, that in this particular case, the action of debt was maintainable. But Lord Eldon, who delivered the opinion of the court, said, "We do not say how the case would stand if the action were brought by any other person than he to whom the note was originally given, or against any other person than him by whom it was signed and made, or if the note itself did not express a consideration upon the face of it." Judgment for the plaintiff.

But instead of suing upon the bill or note, the holder may use it merely as evidence in another action.

A bill is primâ facie evidence of money lent by the payee to the drawer, and a note of money (50) lent by the payee to the maker, and each consequently of money (51) had and received by the drawer or maker to the use of the holder, and of money paid by the holder to the use of the drawer or maker. (*b*)

[The case of Lindo v. Bank of Alexandria, 1 Cranch, 343. is contra. But see a note to this case in 1 Cranch, Appendix, 462.]

[(*a*) The plaintiffs declared in debt as the drawers of a bill payable to themselves or order, *for value received in goods*, against the defendant as acceptor. On demurrer, Bayley J. delivered the judgment of the court. "There is an immediate privity between the plaintiff and defendant independently of the bill. The defendant is immediate debtor to the plaintiff, and he contracts by his acceptance to pay that debt. Under these circumstances we think the action of debt maintainable. Had there been a want of immediate privity between the parties, or had the bill omitted to specify the consideration, the case might have been different." Priddy v. Henbrey, 1 Barn. and Cres. 674. 3 Dow. and Ryl. 165.]

(50) Clarke v. Martin, Lord Raym. 758. Holt C. J. expressed his disapprobation of declaring upon promissory notes (before the statute) as if they were within the custom of merchants; and assigned as a reason, "because there was so easy a method, as to declare upon a general indebitatus assumpsit for money lent." The same was laid down in 12 Mod. 380. and in Burr. 1525, Lord Mansfield says, "I do not find it any where disputed, that an action upon an indebitatus assumpsit generally, for money lent, might be brought on a note payable to one or order." And see Smith v. Kendall, ante p. 21. n. 62.

(51) Grant v. Vaughan, Burr. 1516. The bearer of a note payable to "Ship Fortune, or bearer," brought an action upon it, and inserted a count for money had and received. Lord Mansfield left it to the jury whether such a note was negotiable, and whether the plaintiff took it fairly, and they found for the defendant; but upon a rule nisi for a new trial, the court was clear the first point should not have been left to the jury; and per Lord Mansfield, "Upon the count for money had and received, the case is clear beyond dispute; for undoubtedly an action for money had and received to the plaintiff's use, may be brought by the bonâ fide bearer of a note payable to bearer. It was certainly money received for the use of the original advancer of it, and if so, it is for the use of the person who has the note as bearer;" and Wilmot and Yates, Js. expressed themselves to the same effect. A new trial was granted, and the plaintiff recovered.

[So it was held that the holder of a note payable to Wm. Douglass or bearer might recover against the maker on the money counts. Pierce v. Crafts, 12 Johns. R. 90.

If the second endorser of a note pay part of the sum due upon it, to the holder, who retains possession of it, he may recover the amount so paid, of the first endorser, on a count for money paid to his use; but in such case the second endorser not having possession of the note, cannot maintain an action upon the note itself. Butler v. Wright, 20 Johns. R. 367.]

An acceptance is (52) also primâ facie evidence of money had and received by the acceptor to the use of the holder, and of money paid by the holder to the use of the acceptor,

---

[(*b*) A check upon a bank may be given in evidence on the money counts, in an action by the bearer against the drawer. Cruger v. Armstrong, 3 Johns. Cas. 5.

A check upon a bank drawn by a person borrowing money, in favor of the lender, both parties knowing there were no funds in the bank, and it not being intended to be presented there, is evidence of money borrowed, and the amount of the check is recoverable on the money courts. Cushing v. Gore, 15 Mass. R. 69.

So a note may be given in evidence on the money counts, in an action by the payee against the maker. And the plaintiff is entitled to recover, though the defendant has fraudulently obtained possession of the note. Arnold v. Crane, 8 Johns. R. 62.

So a note for a certain sum payable in certain lands may be given in evidence under the money counts, in action by the payee against the maker, where the latter is unable to convey the lands from defect of title. Smith v. Smith, 2 Johns. R. 235.]

(52) Tatlock v. Harris, 3 Term Rep. 174. In an action at the suit of the indorsee of a bill payable to a fictitious payee against the acceptor, who was also one of the drawers, the delaration contained counts for money paid and for money had and received; it appeared upon the evidence, that the defendant was indebted to one of the endorsers, and sent him this bill, for which he was credited in account, and that the plaintiff paid *that* endorser the value of the bill: and upon a demurrer to the evidence, the court held that the plaintiff was entitled to recover under the counts for money paid and money had and received, and he had judgment accordingly.

Vere v. Lewis, 3 Term Rep. 182. This was a similar action to that of Tatlock v. Harris, except that the defendant was not one of the drawers, and there was no evidence that he received any value for the bill; upon which it was urged the plaintiff could not recover upon the money counts; but the court said the acceptance was evidence that he had received value from the drawers, and the plaintiff had judgment.

Thompson v. Morgan, 3 Campb. 101. Plaintiff drew on defendant, payable to plaintiff or order, defendant accepted it; plaintiff sued on the acceptance, but there being a variance between the bill as stated, and the real bill, plaintiff resorted to the money counts. Lord Ellenborough at first doubted, because indebitatus assumpsit would not lie on the bill against the acceptor; but it being pointed out to him that plaintiff was drawer and payee, so that there was no intermediate party between plaintiff and defendant, he admitted the bill as evidence under the count for money had and received; but he would not allow interest. Verdict for plaintiff.

[S. Penniman drew on J. Penniman in favor of A. Penniman or order, for the net proceeds of certain notes in the hands of its drawee after deducting his own demands. A. Penniman accepted the order. It was held that an endorsee of the payee might maintain an action for money had and received, against the acceptor. Story J. said, " It is true, that the instrument is not negotiable. But by his acceptance the defendant undertook to hold the proceeds, after deducting his own demands, for the account of such person as should by the endorsement of the payee

and (53) an endorsement of money lent by the endorsee to the endorser.

But if it appear that at the time of accepting the drawee says he has nothing in his hands except a bill of the drawer's for a large amount, but that he expects the drawer will remit, and will therefore take all risks upon himself, the acceptance will not be evidence of money had and received by the acceptor to the use of the holder, unless there is proof that the larger bill is paid; (54)

Or other money remitted;

With that proof it will. (54)

Proof that the drawee has received a remittance from the drawer specifically for payment of the bill, will also make

---

on the draft entitle himself to the proceeds. The plaintiff is the regular endorsee or appointee of the payee, and after notice of this fact, the defendant must be considered as holding money for his use; and under such circumstances the law will imply a promise to pay the same over to him." Weston v. Penniman, 1 Mason, 306.]

(53) Kessebower v. Tims, B. R. E. 22 G. 3. Lord Mansfield held, that the endorsee of a note might maintain indebitatus assumpsit for money lent, against the person who endorsed it to him.

[So a negotiable note endorsed by the defendant to the plaintiff, may be given in evidence on a count for money had and received. State Bank v. Hurd, 12 Mass. R. 172.

Although a note be *primâ facie* evidence under a count for money had and received, in an action against an endorser; yet where he is merely an accommodation endorser, and the money for which the note is made, is paid to the maker, and for his sole use, the endorser is not liable on such a count. Page v. The Bank of Alexandria, 7 Wheat. 35.]

(54) Whitwell v. Bennett, 3 Bos. and Pull. 559. This was an action by the endorsee against the acceptor of a bill. The bill was incorrectly stated, and the plaintiff was therefore obliged to resort to the money counts. The evidence was, that when the defendant accepted the bill (which was for £30), he said, that though the drawer had not remitted to him, he expected that he would, and that, as he had a bill of his for £80, which would be paid, he would take all risks upon himself. Lord Alvanley directed a verdict for the plaintiff, with liberty to the defendant to move for a nonsuit. Rule nisi accordingly; and on shewing cause against this rule, it was urged, that if the bill for £80 was paid, the defendant was liable as for money had and received; and that, as the defendant had not at the trial produced that bill, the presumption was, that it was paid. The court said, that if that bill was paid, the action for money had and received would be maintainable, on the ground of the defendant's specific appropriation of that money to the payment of the plaintiff's demand; but that the declaration being upon the bill for £30, it was a surprise upon the defendant to call for proof of the non-payment of the other bill; and that therefore it would be too much to presume payment of that bill. Rule absolute.

the drawee, though he has not accepted the bill, answerable to the holder for money had and received, if he has done any thing which can be deemed a pledge to the holder for so applying it.

And proof that the acceptor's banker has received the money from the acceptor specifically for the bill, will make the banker liable to the holder for money had and received, if he does any thing which can be deemed a pledge to the holder. (55)

Taking the bill as agent to the holder to receive payment thereon, if payment is offered, is such a pledge, and will make him answerable for money had and received, if the money is paid to him whilst the bill is so in his possession;

At least if it be owing to such possession that he receives the payment. (55)

But a specific remittance will not make the drawee, if he do not accept, answerable to the holder as for money had and received, unless there is something which can be deemed a pledge to the holder; without such pledge there is no privity between the holder and the drawee, and the drawer is the only person who can call the drawee to account for the misapplication. (56) (*a*)

---

(55) De Bernales v. Fuller, 2 Campb. 426. 14 East. 590. Plaintiff held a bill accepted by Puller, payable at defendants', Puller's bankers; plaintiff sent the bill to his own bankers, and they, according to the course amongst bankers, sent it to defendants'. Puller found the bill was at defendants', and sent the money there to pay it: defendants' clerk took the money, but refused to give up the bill, and defendants insisted on keeping the money for a debt Puller owed them. Plaintiff thereupon brought an action for money had and received. Lord Ellenborough thought it not maintainable, and the defendants had a verdict; but, on an application for a new trial, and cause shewn, the court held, that as defendants made themselves agents for plaintiff by taking the bill from his bankers, and as they would not have had the money paid them had they not had possession of the bill, they were not at liberty to say they did not receive the money for plaintiff's use: a new trial was accordingly granted, and plaintiff afterwards had a verdict.

(56) Yates v. Bell, 3 Barnew. and Ald. 643. Ingram remitted £800 to defendant to take up, amongst others, a bill for £743, but that bill being returned dishonored, defendant wrote to Ingram that he should carry the money to his credit: the bill coming back, the holder brought an action against the defendant for money had and received, on the ground that defendant was bound to apply the money to his bill. Abbot C. J. thought be was not, and nonsuited; and on a rule to shew cause

An acknowledgement of the debt by the defendant will enable the holder to recover upon a count for the account stated. (57)

Against the very person also from whom he received the bill or note, the holder may sue for the consideration upon which the bill or note is given. (*a*)

For, in general, a bill or note is (58) no satisfaction of

---

why the verdict should not be entered for plaintiff, and cause shewn, the court held the nonsuit right, for there was no privity between plaintiff and defendant, unless defendant assented to apply the money as Ingram directed; if he did not follow Ingram's directions, he might be accountable to Ingram, but not to the plaintiff, and the rule was discharged.

Stewart v. Fry, 7 Taunt. 339. A bill made payable at defendant's was dishonored for want of advice; the same day defendant received the money from Aspinall, the to pay it, and he sent to plaintiff, who had presented it, but the bill was returned to Ireland. Aspinall called back the money, and defendant paid him: the bill came back to plaintiff, and he sued defendant for the money; the jury found for defendant, and on rule nisi for a new trial, the court held the verdict right, and discharged the rule.

S. P. upon a remitttance to pay a common debt, Williams v. Everitt, 14 East. 582.

[(*a*) See Mandeville v. Welch, ante, p. 27.]

(57) Highmore v. Primrose, 5 Maule, 65. In an action against the acceptor of a bill, plaintiff was precluded from recovering on the special count because of a variance, but he proved that defendant had acknowledged the acceptance, and pleaded inability to pay; and upon the point reserved, the court held, this entitled plaintiff to a verdict on the count for the account stated, and he had judgment accordingly.

(58) Puckford v. Maxwell, 6 Term Rep. 52. The defendant having been arrested by the plaintiff for £80, gave a draft for £45, and promised in a few days to settle the remainder, on which the plaintiff consented to his being discharged out of custody. The draft was dishonored, and the defendant was again arrested on the same affidavit. On rule to shew cause why he should not be discharged out of custody, and cause shewn, it was urged, that the draft, having been accepted as part payment, could not be treated as a nullity. But per Lord Kenyon: In cases of this kind, if the bill which is given in payment, do not turn out to be productive, it is not that which it purports to be and which the party receiving it expects it to be, and therefore he may consider it as a nullity and act as if no such bill had been given. These questions have frequently arisen at nisi prius, where they have always been determined the same way. Rule discharged.

Owenson v. Morse, 7 Term Rep. 64. The plaintiff bought some plate of the defendant, and gave him some country bank-notes in payment; the notes were dishonored, on which the defendant refused to deliver the plate. The plaintiff brought trover, and insisted that the notes were payment; but on a case reserved, the court held that they were no payment unless the defendant had agreed to take them as payment, and to run the risk of their being paid. Nonsuit entered. See also Tapley v. Martens, 8 Term. Rep. 451.

[The vendor of flour agreed to take the note of Lyon in payment.

any debt or demand for which it has been given; it is only primâ facie evidence of payment, rendering it necessary that the party receiving it should (59) account for it, before he will be entitled to recover the consideration. (*a*)

The vendee a few days after tendered Lyon's note, and demanded the flour; the vendor refused to deliver it, Lyon having failed in the mean time. It was held that no action lay for not delivering the flour. Spencer J. delivered the opinion of the court. "The offer by the plaintiff to pay in the note of a bankrupt, was not an offer of payment. On an agreement to accept notes in payment, if before the delivery of the articles purchased the notes turn out not to be good, a tender of them is not to be considered payment, unless it was part of the agreement to take them as such, and to run the risk of their being paid. Roget v. Merritt, 2 Cain. R. 117.]

(59) Kearslake v. Morgan, 5 Term R. 513. Assumpsit for goods sold and delivered, and for money lent. The defendant pleaded the general issue; and that as to £4, 14*s*. 6*d*. one W. P. made his note for £10, payable to the defendant or order, at a time which elapsed before the commencement of the suit: and that the defendant, before the note became due, endorsed it to the plaintiff "for and on account of the said sum of £4, 14*s*. 6*d*., and the sum of £5, 5*s*. 6*d*.," paid by the plaintiff to the defendant, and that the plaintiff accepted the note "for and on account" of those sums. To this plea there was a general demurrer, and it was urged, that the plea ought to have alleged that the note was received in *satisfaction* of the debt. But the court, on argument, held the plea good, and advised the plaintiff to withdraw his demurrer, and reply; which he did.

Dangerfield v. Wilby, N. P. C. 159. The declaration contained a count upon a note made by the defendant, payable to the plaintiff and the money counts. At the trial the note was stated to have been lost, but no evidence of that fact was offered. It was proved, however, that on the money being demanded, the defendant had apologized for not having paid the money *on account of the note*. This was the whole of the plaintiff's case; and he contended that the note was only evidence of the consideration (which was stated to have been money lent), and that he might abandon the note, and go for the consideration. But Lord Ellenborough said, that as the note for any thing that appeared in evidence was in existence, it might still be in circulation, so that the defendant might be subjected twice to the payment of the same demand; without therefore proving the note lost, the plaintiff was not entitled to recover. Nonsuit.

[(*a*) The principles stated in the text are recognized in a great number of American cases.

See Pintard v. Tackington, 10 Johns. R. 104; Clark v. Young, 1 Cranch, 181. In the last case it was held that an action might be commenced on the original cause of action, without proving an offer to return the note before the institution of the suit.

Where the attorney of the plaintiff took the note of the sheriff for the amount of an execution, without agreeing that it should be payment, and without giving a discharge of the execution, it was held that the execution was still valid against the judgment debtor, and that the usual

But the holder will be precluded from recovering for the consideration, if it appear that the bill or note has been,

---

remedies on the execution might be pursued for the benefit of the sheriff, by leave of Court. Cheever v. Mirrick, 2 N. Hamp. R. 376.

Barber being indebted to Tobey for rent, procured Coffin to give a note payable to Tobey or order in four months for a part of the amount: Tobey gave a receipt in full for the rent. Coffin failing, the note was not paid. Tobey then sued Barber for the rent. Per Curiam. "The taking of the note was no extinguishment of the debt due for the rent. It is a rule well settled and repeatedly recognized in this court, that taking a note either of the debtor or a third person, for a pre-existent debt, is no payment, unless it be expressly agreed to take the note as payment, or unless the creditor parts with the note, or is guilty of *laches*. There is no evidence in this case, that the plaintiff agreed to run the risk of the solvency of Coffin, and to take the note as absolute payment, except it be the receipt itself, and that is not enough to establish such a positive agreement." Tobey v. Barber, 5 Johns. R. 68.

Murray and Co. being indebted to Governeur and Kemble in the sum of $5000, as the first instalment, on an agreement of the latter to sell a house to the former; Governeur and Kemble purchased of Murray and Co. bills drawn by them on one of their partners in London to the amount of $25,000 and on paying for the same, deducted $5000, and gave a receipt for the same as the first instalment. The question was whether this was a payment of the first instalment, the bills being dishonored, and the evidence not shewing that it was agreed to be considered as payment. Kent J. said, "It is a settled rule that a bill shall not be a discharge of a precedent debt, unless it be so expressly agreed by the parties." Murray v. Gouverneur, 2 Johns. Cas. 438.

A mortgage was given to secure payment of a note, the note was afterwards taken up, and a new note given for the same sum and interest to the date of the new note; it was held that the mortgage was not thereby discharged; as the first note was not *paid*. Elliot v. Sleeper, 2 N. Hamp. R. 525.

See also Suckley v. Furse, ante, p. 227.

Where the defendant had given his note to the plaintiffs on account of a pre-existent debt, in an action for the original debt, Spencer J., who delivered the opinion of the Court, said, "Technically speaking a negotiable note or bill of exchange is not an extinguishment of an antecedent debt: yet it has been held an extinguishment *sub modo*. In the King's Bench, a note or bill has been held to be an extinguishment of a simple contract debt, the defendant being liable to pay the money to a third person." He said he was disposed to adopt this rule with this qualification, "that where a negotiable note has been given for a prior debt, not to suffer the plaintiff to recover on the original consideration, unless he shows the note to have been lost, or produces and cancels it at the trial." The court directed the plaintiffs to cancel the note and file it with the court, which was accordingly done. Holmes v. De Camp, 1 Johns. R. 34.

In another case it was held that giving a note was not payment of a book-debt;—and that it only suspended the right of action during the period allowed for payment of the note: and that the note not having been paid, the plaintiff was entitled to recover the amount of the book-debt, with *interest* from the time the note was payable. Putnam v. Lewis, 8 Johns. R. 304.

To the common counts in assumpsit the defendant pleaded that he

by (60) laches, made to operate as a satisfaction of the debt or demand for which it was given; or if he originally re-

---

had given his prommissory note to the plaintiff for the same promises, which the plaintiff received in full satisfaction, and which the plaintiff had endorsed and delivered to a third person. Spencer J. "The plea is defective, for the mere giving of a negotiable note, or its endorsement to a third person, does not extinguish the original cause of action, provided the payee can show it to be lost, or can produce it to be cancelled; and *non constat* that it cannot be done in this case." Burdick v. Green, 15 Johns. R. 247.

It has been held in various cases that a receipt in full, is open to explanation, and does not preclude the creditor from showing the circumstances under which it was given. Putnam v. Lewis, 8 Johns. R. 304; Tobey v. Barber, supra; Johnson v. Weed, supra; Bartsch v. Atwater, 1 Conn. R. 409.

It has been decided in many cases that taking the note of one partner or joint debtor, does not discharge a prior debt. Herring v. Sanger, 3 Johns. Cas. 71.

Townsend, one of the owners of the ship Eleanor, ordered supplies for her, which were furnished by the plaintiffs, and charged in their books to "Ship Eleanor, Mr. George Townsend and owners," and he some time after gave his note to the plaintiffs for the amount, who gave him a receipt which stated that they had received his note in full for supplies of ship Eleanor. Townsend died, and his estate proved insolvent. The plaintiffs then brought this suit against the other owners of the Eleanor, for the supplies furnished. It did not appear that the plaintiffs knew at the time of the sale that the defendants were part-owners. Per Curiam. "The taking of the note of Townsend, and giving a receipt in full, is no extinguishment of the original debt, unless the note was paid. There is no evidence that the plaintiffs *knew* that the defendants were part-owners. The case of Reed v. White, proceeds on the ground that the plaintiff had taken the ship's husband exclusively for his debtor, knowing there were other owners, and after a settlement of account between them and the ship's husband." Judgment for the plaintiffs. Schemerhorn v. Loines, 7 Johns. R. 310.

Rogers and Bement, being partners, were indebted to Smith and Marshall. April 22d, 1816, Bement wrote to Smith and Marshall, that their firm was dissolved, and that he had assumed the debt due to Smith and Marshall. Smith and Marshall in reply wrote, "We observe your partnership is dissolved, and that you have assumed our debt, which we are satisfied with." Bement afterwards paid part of the money, which he directed to be placed to "the credit of the late firm of Rogers and Bement," and August 15th, 1816, gave his note to Smith and Marshall for the balance, and they gave him a receipt for the note, "when paid to be placed to the credit of Rogers and Bement." Bement became insolvent in Nov. 1817. Smith and Marshall then sued Rogers and Bement on the original contract, having never sued Bement or made any demand on Rogers, until after Bement's insolvency. Bement's note had been assigned, and this action was brought for the benefit of the assignees. The Court were of opinion that nothing had been done by the plaintiffs which discharged the firm of Rogers and Bement; and said there must be judgment for the plaintiffs, on their filing the note given by Bement with the clerk of the court, to be cancelled. Smith v. Rogers, 17 Johns. R. 340.

Muldon and Montgomery furnished stores for the ship Cadmus, owned

ceived the bill or note (61) as cash, and took upon himself the risk of its being paid; or if it was transferred to him by

---

by Jenkins and Son, and Whitlock and Jenkins, and about two months after the sale took the notes of the ship's husbands, Jenkins and Son, at twelve months for the amount, giving a receipt which declared the note to be received "*in full* for stores for ship Cadmus." The note not being paid, and Jenkins and Son becoming insolvent, Muldon and Montgomery brought an action for the stores against all the owners. Muldon and Montgomery knew Whitlock and Jenkins to be part owners when the stores were furnished. Jenkins and Son had charged these stores in their account with Whitlock and Jenkins, but the account was never settled, and Whitlock and Jenkins had never paid Jenkins and Son anything on account of the stores. Sutherland J. "No principle of law is better settled than that taking a note from *one of several joint debtors* or *from a third person,* for a *pre-existing debt,* is no payment, unless it *be expressly agreed to be taken as payment, and at the risk of the creditor.* Nor does the taking a note and giving a receipt for so much cash, in full of the original debt, amount to evidence of such express agreement to take the note in payment. Jenkins and Son gave their note as the agents of the defendants. It was *their* note in judgment of law; and not having been paid, the plaintiffs have a right to resort to the original cause of action." He seemed to think it of no consequence that the plaintiffs knew who were the other owners. "The defendants have not been misled or injured in consequence of the manner in which the plaintiffs dealt with Jenkins and Son. They have not settled with them upon a different principle, or paid them money, which they would not otherwise have done." Judgment for the plaintiffs. Muldon v. Whitlock, 1 Cowen, 290.

Kean and Foster, being partners, owed Dufresne a note. Their partnership being dissolved, Kean gave his own note to Dufresne, and Dufresne got it discounted, and applied the proceeds to the credit of Kean and Foster. Dufresne had to take up this note himself, and then sued Kean and Foster on their note. Per Curiam. "The note set up as an extinguishment of the debt of Kean and Foster, was not parted with by Dufresne, but for the purpose of raising money for Kean and Foster. Therefore it can be no extinguishment." Kean v. Dufresne, 3 Serg. and Raw. 233.

Chapman v. Durant, 10 Mass. R. 47, is contra.

Some of the above cases make a distinction between a note given for a pre-existing debt, and one given at the time of contracting the debt; but it appears from the following cases that a diversity of opinion exists as to the propriety of this distinction.

In an action for goods sold, it appeared that a note of a third person had been taken and a receipt given, and there was evidence on both sides as to the agreement of the vendor in taking the note, and the jury found for the plaintiff, the Supreme Court of New York refused to set aside the verdict; and the Court said, that taking the note of a third person for goods sold is no payment, if it turns out afterwards to be of no value, "unless there be a clear and special agreement that the vendor shall take the paper absolutely as payment." Johnson v. Weed, 9 Johns. R. 310.

Van Ness agreed to give Whitbeck $90 dollars for a horse, if he would take Deane's note in payment payable in six months; Whitbeck took the note of Deane payable to Whitbeck himself, and delivered the

way of (62) sale; unless indeed, in the two latter cases, it be proved that the person transferring the bill or note (63)

---

horse. Deane not paying the note at maturity, Whitbeck sued Van Ness for the price of the horse. The Court held that "the note of a third person, agreed to be taken in payment for goods sold at the same time, was taken at the risk of the vendor of the goods," and consequently that the action was not maintainable. And Spencer J. said, "Though I assented to the decision in Johnson v. Weed, and still believe it to be correct, the reasoning of the judge who gave the opinion went further than I intended, and as I understand those of my brethren who assented to the decision, further than they meant to go." Whitbeck v. Van Ness, 11 Johns. R. 409. But see Bartsch v. Atwater, 1 Conn. R. 409.

It has been held, that the note of an agent given for a debt of his principal, at the time of contracting it, does not discharge the right of action against the principal.

N. Talcott, as agent of Talcott and Bowers, exchanged a ship of theirs for a brig of U. and C. Porter; and gave the notes of N. and D. Talcott, under which name he traded, payable at different times, for the difference in value between the brig and ship. N. Talcott failed before the notes became due, having charged Talcott and Bowers with the difference in value between the vessels, and being largely indebted to them. In an action against Talcott and Bowers after the maturity of the notes, the jury found that there was "no evidence of any agreement or mutual understanding, that the said Talcott and Bowers were or were not bound to the plaintiffs for the amount of the notes of N. and D. Talcott in the event of their insolvency." Woodworth J. "Is N. Talcott to be considered a third person within the meaning of the rule laid down in Whitbeck v. Van Ness? He was an agent merely, and represented the defendants. The note of Talcott is not the note of a third person, nor does it operate as payment unless so agreed. I am on the whole of opinion, as Talcott was merely an agent, and as there does not appear to have been any agreement not to look to the defendants, they are liable." Sutherland J. was of the same opinion as far as regarded the principal case, though he seems to think that the note of a third person is not payment of a debt cotemporary with the giving of the note, any more than of an antecedent debt, unless there is an express agreement to receive it as payment. Porter v. Talcott, 1 Cowen, 359.

But where an agent received property of his principal out of which to pay a debt due from the principal to a third person, and the creditor took the note of the agent payable at a future day, and the agent failed before the note became due, having sold the property, and the creditor joined with other creditors of the agent in discharging him; it was held that the creditor could not maintain an action against the principal on his original demand, because he had trusted the agent beyond what the principal did, and without his consent. Tudor v. Whiting, 12 Mass. R. 212.

In Massachusetts it has been held that a negotiable note given in consideration of a simple contract debt due, is a discharge of the simple contract. Thacher v. Dinsmore, 5 Mass. R. 299; Chapman v. Durant, 10 Mass. R. 47; and Wiseman v. Lyman, 11 Mass. R. 369.

In the case of Maneely v. M'Gee, Parsons C. J. says, "At common law a promissory note given by a debtor to pay his creditor a subsisting

knew at the time that it was of no value; (*a*) [or unless the signature of any party to it be forged. (*a*)]

---

debt, is no discharge of the debt. But in this State it has long been settled, that when a debtor gives to his creditor his negotiable note for a debt due on simple contract, the legal presumption is that the note was received in payment. This presumption arises from the consideration that if the creditor could compel payment of the original debt, the debtor might afterwards be obliged to pay the note to an endorsee, and thus be twice charged." Maneely v. M'Gee, 6 Mass. R. 143. But does the reason given establish the propriety of the peculiar rule adopted in Massachusetts? According to the rule of the common law a debtor is in no danger of being twice charged, since in an action on the original contract, it is held to be necessary for the plaintiff to produce and give up the note, before he can prevail.

It has been held in Massachusetts that where the underwriter in a policy of insurance, acknowledges the premium paid, and the assured has afterwards a right to the return of the premium, he may recover the same in an action for money had and received; although he gave his promissory note therefor, which remains unpaid in the hands of the underwriter. Hemmenway v. Bradford, 14 Mass. R. 121. See also Russell v. Degrand, 15 Mass. R. 35.

In the case of Varner v. Nobleborough, in Maine, Mellen C. J. says, "The legal presumption arising from the fact of drawing a negotiable order, or making a negotiable note, which are received by the creditor, is, that they were intended to be, and in fact are, an extinguishment of the original cause of action. But this presumption may be controlled or explained by the agreement of the parties, or by proof of circumstances or usages inconsistent with such presumption." 2 Greenleaf, 121.

In Connecticut in an action of book debt, the defendant gave in evidence a receipt by the plaintiff acknowledging the recept of a bill of exchange, which when paid was to be in full of the plaintiff's account: and it appearing that this bill had been protested, the defendant produced a receipt by the plaintiff acknowledging the receipt of the amount of the bill by a bill on another person; the court refused to admit evidence on behalf of the plaintiff that the latter bill was not paid. Anderson v. Henshaw, 2 Day, 272.

But even in Massachusetts a promissory note not negotiable, does not operate as payment of a pre-existing demand in consideration of which it is given. Greenwood v. Curtis, 4 Mass. R. 93.

And a negotiable note is no discharge of a debt for which it is given, where it is the agreement or understanding of the parties that it is not to be considered payment. Maneely v. M'Gee, 6 Mass. R. 143.

Maxwell, in payment for boards purchased by him of Tucker, gave an order in favor of the latter on a third person, payable on the return of the brig Cataract owned by Maxwell from a voyage. The order was accepted, and Tucker gave Maxwell a receipt in full. After the usual time for the voyage had long elapsed, the vessel not returning, Tucker sued Maxwell on the original contract; and it was held that the action was maintainable, unless the defendant could prove that the plaintiff was to take the risk of the voyage. Tucker v. Maxwell, 11 Mass. R. 143.]

(60) Vide ante, chap. vii. p. 124.

[Defendant bought goods of the plaintiff, in payment for which he

A bill or note will satisfy a preceding debt, if the holder makes it his own by laches. (64) (*a*)

---

gave a bill of exchange drawn and accepted by two other persons, and endorsed by defendant in blank. The plaintiff having lost the bill brought an action for the goods sold. The Court said, "that the plaintiff having taken a bill, by losing which, he had deprived the defendant of all means of recovering over, he should not turn round and sue the defendant for goods which had already cost him their full value." Champion v. Terry, 3 Brod. & Bing. 295.—7 Moore, 130.

Where a party to whom a bill had been endorsed neglected to have it protested for non-acceptance, it was held that he could maintain no action on the original contract on account of which the bill was endorsed to him. Duncan v. Course, 1 S. Car. R. 100. See also Brower v. Jones, ante, p. 149; and Henry v. Donaghy, Addison, 39.]

(61) In Owenson v. Morse, 7 Term Rep. 66. ante, p. 248. n. (58), Lord Kenyon said, "If the defendant had agreed to take the notes as payment, and to run the risk of their being paid, that would have been considered as payment whether the notes had or had not been afterwards paid." See also Clark v. Mundal, 1 Salk. 124.

(62) Fydell v. Clarke and another, 1 Esp. N. P. C. 447. The plaintiff had been in partnership with his brother R. Fydell; and the latter, on his own account, but in the partnership name, drew certain notes to the amount of £8000, which he discounted with Hurlock and Co., bankers. The plaintiff, after his brother's death, voluntarily paid the £8000 to the bankers, supposing that his brother had received the amount of these notes in *money:* he afterwards discovered that they had only given other bills and notes, which they had not endorsed, in lieu of his brother's notes, some of which bills and notes to the amount of £4300 proved unproductive; and to recover that sum the present action was brought against the defendants, who were trustees of the insolvent estate of the bankers, and who had reserved funds to answer the event of the action. Lord Kenyon said, that the bankers by not endorsing the bills and notes, had refused to pledge their credit to their validity, and that R. Fydell must be taken to have received them on their own credit only; and that therefore the action could not be supported. Nonsuit.

Ex parte Shuttleworth, 3 Ves. 368. Newton gave the bankrupt before his bankruptcy, cash for a bill, but refused to allow the bankrupt to endorse it, thinking the bill better without his name. He now proved the amount under the commission, and on petition to have the debt expunged, the chancellor granted the petition, observing that this was a sale of the bill. [See also Wilkings v. M'Kinzie, Cam. and Nor. 448.]

(63) In Fenn v. Harrison, 3 Term Rep. 759. Lord Kenyon said, "It is extremely clear that if the holder of a bill send it to market without endorsing his name upon it, neither morality or the laws of this country will compel him to refund the money for which he sold it, if he did not know at the time that it was not a good bill. If he knew the bill to be bad, it would be like sending out a counter into circulation to impose upon the world, instead of the current coin. In this case, if the defendants had known the bill to be bad, there is no doubt but that they would have been obliged to refund the money.

[(*a*) The principles stated above are fully recognized in many American cases.

In an action against two partners for goods sold, it is a good plea in bar, that the note of one partner was given and received by the plain-

As by not presenting it for payment when due; (65) (*a*)
Though it were taken from a third person; (65)

---

tiff for and in *discharge* of the account for the goods sold. Marshall C. J., in delivering the opinion of the Court, says, "The note of one of the parties or of a third person may, by agreement, be received in payment." Sheehy v. Mandeville, 6 Cranch, 253. See also Van Ness v. Forrest, 8 Cranch, 30; Willie v. Green, 2 N. Hamp. R. 333; and Campbell v. Mosby, 4 Munf. 287.

In an action against Camp and Downing, as makers of a note, it appeared that the plaintiff had given the note up to Downing and received his separate note for it, but Downing afterwards took back his own note, and returned the partnership note to the plaintiff, on the plaintiff's telling him, that if he did not do so, he should work for him no longer. Thompson C. J. delivered the opinion of the Court. "The facts in the case necessarily lead to the conclusion that when the individual note of Downing was taken, and the partnership note delivered up, it was intended and agreed to be considered as payment of the note in question, and it operates as a satisfaction of the partnership note." Judgment for the defendant. Arnold v. Camp, 2 Johns. R. 409.

Where the selectmen of a town had given a creditor of the town an order on their town treasurer, payable to the creditor or order, for the amount due him, it was held that an action could not be maintained against the town without proving a presentment of the order to the town treasurer. Varner v. Nobleborough, 2 Greenleaf, 121.

But where A. received from B. a check on a bank merely to hold as evidence of the amount due from B. to A. and not to be presented at the bank, and A. passed it to C. in payment of a debt; and C. after ascertaining the purpose for which the check was drawn, and that B. had stopped payment of it, brought an action against A. without having presented the check for payment, Thompson C. J. said that A. had committed a fraud both on B. and C. and directed a verdict for the plaintiff for the amount of the check and interest. Devoe v. Moffatt, Auth. N. P. 161.

In an action by Watts against Willing on a bond in which Willing was surety for Bird, it appeared that Bird had delivered certain bills of exchange to Watts, which it appeared by an endorsement on the bond when paid were to be credited in part payment. The bills were not paid, and Watts had furnished accounts in which he had charged 20 per cent. damages on the bills. He did not offer to return the bills at the trial. The Court said, that the two circumstances of retaining the bills in his own hands, and of charging 20 per cent. damages, showed an election to receive them as payment; and that their amount must be credited in this action. Watts v. Willing, 2 Dall. 100. See also the opinion of Sedgwick J. in Wiseman v. Lyman, 7 Mass. R. 286.

Where a debtor remitted to his creditor a bill of exchange drawn by a third person, which when paid was to discharge the debt, and the bill being dishonored, the creditor, contrary to the request of the debtor, delivered up the bill to the drawer, and took his note for the principal, interest, and damages, payable at a future day; it was held that the original debt on account of which the bill had been remitted was discharged. Keppele v. Carr, 4 Dallas, 155.

Johnson, on account of goods sold by him to Harris, received from him a note of other persons endorsed by Harris, which when paid was to be in full. Johnson endorsed this note to Dunlop, who sued Harris

And in such case plaintiff must prove the bill was duly presented; (65)

---

upon it, but failed to recover, because the law of Virginia gave him recourse only to the maker or his immediate endorser. Johnston sued Harris on the original contract for goods sold, and obtained judgment in the Circuit Court of the District of Columbia. On Error, Marshall C. J. delivered the opinion of the court. "The judgment is to be reversed, for error in directing the jury that the action was maintainable on the original contract, after the note received as conditional payment had been endorsed." The court thought that Harris was entitled to have the note returned that he might have his remedy against the previous parties to it; and also because they thought that Dunlop, the holder, might maintain a suit against him in equity, though not at law. Harris v. Johnston, 3 Cranch, 311.

Where a note was given on account of money paid, which was void on account of its also including a sum in consideration of forbearance, it was held that an action might be maintained on the original contract for the payment of money. Johnson v. Johnson, 11 Mass. R. 359.

Roberts bought goods on account of the Providence Hat Manufacturing Company of the plaintiffs, and gave a note for the amount signed, "for the Provid. Hat Man. Co. Frink Roberts." Roberts had no authority to sign such a note, though he had authority to buy goods. It was held that taking the note did not extinguish the implied promise to pay for the goods; and that the company were liable in an action for goods sold and delivered. Emerson v. Prov. Hat Man. Co. 12 Mass. R. 237.

Willson sold Foree a horse and chaise, and agreed to take in part payment the note of Whaley at Willson's own risk. In an action by Willson on the original contract of sale, it was held, that he might be allowed to prove, that the defendant at the time of the sale, knowing Whaley to be insolvent, represented to the plaintiff that he was a man of property; and that the plaintiff offered to return the note before bringing the action. The court said, "The taking of the note under a fraudulent misrepresentation was no payment, and any term of payment which the note may have implied became void." Willson v. Foree, 6 Johns. R. 110.

Snyder v. Findly, 1 Coxe, 48, is a similar case, and decided on the same ground.

In an action for cattle sold, where the defendant had paid the plaintiff for them in bank notes, one of which turned out to be forged, but it did not appear that either party knew it to be so at the time of the sale, it was held that the plaintiff might recover the amount of the counterfeit note with interest. Kent C. J. delivered the opinion of the court. "The negotiable note of a third person, and a bank note, are equally promissory notes, for the payment of money; and if the receiver may be presumed in the one case, and not in the other, to have taken upon himself the risk of the solvency of the maker, there is no presumption in either case, that he assumes upon himself the risk of forgery." Markle v. Hatfield, 2 Johns. R. 455. See also the cases ante, p. 94. note (60).

Where one of two copartners obtained money on a note payable at a future day, and on which he had forged the name of an endorser, the other partner being ignorant of the forgery, it was held that the lender might bring an action for money had and received before the maturity

But he need not prove notice to such third person of the bill's dishonor. (65)

---

of the note, against both partners, the money having gone to their use. Manufacturers and Mechanics Bank v. Gore, 15 Mass. R. 75.

In another case of the same kind, against partners, as makers of a note, and also on the money counts, where the name of an endorser had been forged on the note by one partner, of which the other was ignorant; it was held that both partners were liable on the money counts, though there was no evidence that the money obtained went to the use of the partnership. It was objected in this case that no civil action could arise out of a felony. Parker C. J. giving the opinion of the court, said, "As far forth as the objection goes against the recovery by the plaintiff as endorsee of the note it is well founded. For to maintain the action in that shape, he must prove the handwriting of the supposed endorser. But we see no objection to his recovering upon the money counts. He does not claim the money through or under a forgery; but merely on the ground that money was advanced by him on the faith of a security, which turns out to be wholly worthless."—"General copartners are bound by the acts of each other, when the name of the firm or house is pledged to any extent; unless the person who takes a security of that sort, has knowledge of some limitation of the authority of the partner who undertakes to bind the firm. The note was still the note of the partnership notwithstanding the forgery of the endorser's name. And the money being obtained upon a note payable by the company, both partners must be considered answerable." Boardman v. Gore. 15 Mass. Rep. 331.

Taking a note from a debtor, and afterwards giving it up to him in consequence of his fraudulent representations, does not extinguish the original debt.

Crane gave Arnold his notes for money lent him by Arnold. Crane afterwards executed a deed of land to Arnold for this debt; and Arnold gave Crane the deed to get it recorded, which Crane offered to have done; and Arnold gave up the notes to Crane. But Crane did not get the deed recorded, and sold the land to another person, who had his deed recorded. Crane refused to pay the money or return the deed or the notes. It was held that Crane having obtained possession of the notes by a fraud, there was no payment or extinguishment of the original debt; and that Arnold might recover against him on the common money counts. Arnold v. Crane, 8 Johns. R. 62.

Hollingworth as agent of Manly sold goods to Lewis, for which he took Lewis's note. Lewis fraudulently representing himself insolvent, Hollingworth returned his note to him, on the delivery of goods charged at exorbitant prices. The court had no doubt that the note was no extinguishment of the original cause of action. Lewis v. Manly, 2 Yeates, 200.]

(64) Bridges v. Berry, 3 Taunt. 130. Defendant accepted a bill for 119*l.* due 20th October, but did not pay it: plaintiff was the holder: defendant afterwards lodged in plaintiff's hands as a security, a bill drawn by defendant upon one Ivory, for 117*l.* 11*s.* 2*d.* and paid plaintiff the difference: this bill was dishonored, but no notice thereof was given to defendant: action by plaintiff on both bills. It was admitted at the trial that defendant was discharged from the second bill, but it was urged that he continued liable on the first: but Mansfield C. J. and the court held he did not, and nonsuit; and rule to set it aside refused.

See Swinyard v. Bowes, p. 186. note (114).

[A forged check on a bank, which is received by the bank from a *bonâ fide* holder, and either paid or passed to his credit, is equivalent to the payment of so much money to the bank, and the bank cannot in the one case recover back the amount of the check, or in the other retain it. (*a*)]

If the holder of a bill or note employ a particular agent to get it discounted, but refuse to endorse it, and the agent guarantee its payment, the principal will (66) not be bound by such guarantee; and not being bound, a subsequent

---

(65) Bishop v. Rowe, 3 Maule, 362. Plaintiff sued the drawer and acceptor of a bill, and proved the necessary facts: defendant gave in evidence that after the bill was due, and part paid, one Tucker, who had been connected with the bill, but had not endorsed it, drew for the balance on Lewis at two months, and gave plaintiff the draught: plaintiff could not prove that the draught was presented for payment, but he nevertheless had a verdict: the court however thought that proof essential, and granted a new trial. On the second trial plaintiff gave this proof, but he could not prove that he had given notice to Tucker of the dishonor: the point was saved, whether he was bound to give this proof? and on rule nisi for nonsuit, and cause shewn, the court held it sufficient for him to prove presentment and non-payment, for that shewed there had been no payment in fact; and if the defendant insisted there had been such neglect as amounted to payment in law, he should have shewn it. The rule was discharged.

[(*a*) Levy sent a check to the U. S. Bank purporting to be drawn by Wharton upon that bank, between eleven and one o'clock. The bank received the check, credited it to Levy as cash, and charged it to Wharton. The check was a forgery, but Levy was a *bonâ fide* holder. Between three and four the same afternoon the bank discovered the forgery, and sent notice to Levy. Levy, on first being informed of the forgery, said, "If the check is a forgery, it is no deposit." The bank refusing to pay Levy the amount of the check, he brought a suit against it to recover that sum. Shippen C. J. charged the jury, "When the check was credited to the plaintiff as cash, it was the same thing as if it had been paid. In the latter case the bank would have appeared as plaintiffs; and every mistake which could have been corrected in an action by them, may be corrected in this action, and none other. Now the law seems to be well settled that where a bill of exchange to which the drawer's name is forged has been paid by the drawee, it is too late for him to question the handwriting. The effect of the *acceptance* of a forged bill is not quite so clear. Some of the authorities decide that the acceptor is bound because his acceptance gives a credit to the bill. But the modern cases notice another reason for this liability which we think has much good sense in it, namely, that the acceptor is presumed to know the drawer's handwriting, and by his acceptance to *take this knowledge upon himself*." As to what Levy said, "it was the expression of an opinion of what he should be obliged to do, rather than what he was willing to allow, and being under a mistake of his right he is not bound by it." Levy v. Bank of the United States, 1 Bin. 27; S. C. 4 Dall. 234.]

promise by him to pay the amount of the bill or note, will be (66) nudum pactum.

But if no restraint be imposed on such agent, the principal (66) may be bound by his guarantee; at least such guarantee will be a (66) sufficient consideration to support a subsequent promise by the principal to pay the bill or note.

[A mere endorser of a note, is not liable as guarantor. (*a*) (*b*)

A promise made to endorse the bill or note of another person, on request, on the payment of a certain per centage by the holder, will not be binding, unless the request to endorse be made within a reasonable time. (*c*)]

---

(66) Fenn v. Harrison, 3 Term Rep. 757. and 4 Term Rep. 177. The defendants employed F. Huet to get a bill discounted, but said that they would not endorse it; F. H. employed his brother James H. and said he would indemnify him if he would endorse it; James endorsed it, and the plaintiffs discounted it; the bill being dishonored the plaintiffs applied to the defendants who promised to take it up, but did not; and this action for money had and received and money paid, was brought against them. Lord Kenyon told the jury, that if they thought that James H. had made himself answerable as agent for the defendants, that was a sufficient consideration for their promise. A verdict was found for the plaintiffs; and on a rule nisi for a new trial, and cause shewn, Lord Kenyon inclined to think the verdict right; because though the agent had exceeded his authority, he thought the principal bound by what he did: the other judges differed, because F. H. was a *particular* agent only: and the rule was made absolute. On the next trial it did not appear that the defendants had told F. H. that they would not endorse the bill. A verdict was found for the plaintiff, and on a rule nisi for a new trial, and cause shewn, the whole court thought the verdict right, because as F. H. was not restrained as to the mode of getting the bill discounted, the defendants were bound by his act. But Buller and Grose, Js. said, that if the facts had been the same, they should have continued of their former opinion. Rule discharged.

[(*a*) A count upon a guaranty that a note endorsed by the defendant to the plaintiff was given for a valid and legal consideration, and a promise to indemnify, is not supported by mere evidence of an endorsement, as "this is not the legal effect of an endorsement." Copp v. M'Dugall, 9 Mass. R. 1. See also Hopkins v. Liswell, 12 Mass. R. 52; and Josselyn v. Ames, ante, p. 65.]

[(*b*) It seems that withdrawing a note from a bank where it has been lodged for collection, is of itself a sufficient consideration for the promise of a third person not a party, to the holder, to pay the note, although a regular demand is afterwards made on the maker, and sufficient notice given to an endorser. Stewart v. Eden, 2 Cain. R. 150.]

[(*c*) Ives and Co. signed an agreement to endorse any bill or bills which Stubbs might give Payne and Co. in part payment of an order

In case of a transfer by delivery, no action can be brought against the deliverer, except on account of the consideration.

[In an action against the maker of a note by an endorser who has taken it up, the plaintiff cannot recover without producing the note at the trial. (*a*)]

If a bill or note be destroyed by fire or other accident, an action may perhaps be brought thereon as if it were in esse. (67)

[And it has been held, where all the bills of a set miscarried, that an action lay for the original consideration given for them. (*b*)]

But if a bill or note be lost, there can be no remedy upon it at law, unless it was in such a state when lost that no person but the plaintiff could have acquired a right to sue thereon. (68)

---

for lace then executing for him, Payne and Co. to allow five per cent. on the amount of the bills for the guaranty. Stubbs shipped the goods to India, and in part payment accepted a bill drawn on him by Payne and Co. at eighteen months, the usual period of credit in the India trade. Payne and Co. kept the bill seventeen months and ten days, and then, finding Stubbs had become insolvent, applied for the first time to Ives and Co. for their endorsement, tendering the commission. Ives and Co. refused to accept the commission, or to endorse the bill. It was held that no action lay for Payne and Co. against Ives and Co. on this agreement, because the request to endorse was not made within a reasonable time. Payne v. Ives, 3 Dow. and Ryl. 664.]

[(*a*) Morgan v. Reintzel, 7 Cranch, 275.]

(67) See Pierson v. Hutchinson, infra. Mayor v. Johnson, post. p. 264. [An action on a lost bill was maintained in South Carolina, the letter bag of the vessel in which it was sent having been thrown overboard. Anderson v. Robson, 2 Bay, 495.]

[(*b*) All the bills of a set miscarried on their passage to Europe, and of course before acceptance. The manner of the loss is not stated in the case. The owners of the bill applied to the drawers for another bill of the same tenor and date, offering to indemnify against the former bills, the drawers refused to give it. It was held that an action for money had and received lay in favor of the purchasers of the bill against the drawers. Murray v. Carrett, 3 Call, 373.]

(68) Pierson v. Hutchinson, 2 Campb. N. P. C. 211. In an action by an endorsee against the acceptor of a bill, it appeared that the bill had been lost after endorsement, and the plaintiff had offered the defendant an indemnity. But Lord Ellenborough nonsuited the plaintiff, saying, that if the bill had been proved to have been destroyed, he should have had no difficulty in receiving evidence of its contents, and in directing the jury to find for the plaintiff; but that having been lost, after endorsement by the payee, it might still be in the hands of a bonâ fide endorsee for value, who might sue the defendant upon it. And as to

As if it were specially endorsed to plaintiff, and had no endorsement from him upon it. (69)

Where it is so specially endorsed, [or is not negotiable,] an action may perhaps be brought thereon. (69)

Where the person paying is entitled to require an indemnity, the only remedy on a lost bill is in equity: a court of equity can inquire into the sufficiency of an indemnity; a court of law cannot. (*a*)

The acceptor is not liable to be sued upon a *lost* bill, if the loss was before the bill was due, though he promises to pay it after knowing of the loss, unless there is some new consideration for such promise. (70)

---

the indemnity, he said a court of law could not inquire into its sufficiency.—S. P. ruled by Lord Eldon. See ex parte Greenway, 6 Ves. 812.

[But in an action at law on a lost bill in Pennsylvania, the court appear to have directed the plaintiffs to indemnify the defendant. Meeker v. Jackson, 3 Yeates, 442.

In an action against the maker of a note, which was lost *after* it became *due*, the plaintiff was nonsuited, on the ground that it was not sufficient to prove its loss without proving its destruction. Curia per Woodworth J. "Although the note was due when it was lost, yet in an action by a *bonâ fide* holder against the maker, he would be exposed to the hazard of showing that fact by evidence. It would therefore be a hard doctrine which should place the maker in this situation, without requiring an indemnity. In such cases, it is better to leave the party to his remedy in equity, where a suitable indemnity will be provided against any subsequent recovery." Judgment affirmed. Rowley v. Ball, 3 Cowen, 303.]

(69) Long and another v. Bailie, 2 Campb. N. P. C. 214. This was an action against the acceptor of a bill of exchange, payable to the order of the drawer, and by him specially endorsed to the plaintiffs. It was proved that a person took the bill to have it compared with the affidavit to hold to bail, that a copy was then taken, and that the bill was afterwards stolen from such person. The correctness of this copy and the special endorsement were proved, and upon this the plaintiffs had a verdict.

[Where an action was brought on a promissory note as a lost note, and it did not appear that the note was negotiable, or if negotiable, that it had ever been endorsed, and the existence and contents of the note were fully proved, and the circumstances showed that it had been lost or destroyed, it was held that the action was maintainable. Pintard v. Tackington, 10 Johns. R. 104.

In an action against the endorser of a note, where the note was lost, but had been produced a few days before in the trial of an action against the maker, it was held that secondary evidence of the contents of the note might be admitted. The case does not state whether the endorsement was full or in blank. Renner v. Bank of Columbia, 9 Wheat. 581.]

[(*a*) See Rowley v. Ball, supra.]

The holder's only remedy is to enforce the giving a new bill under the statute. (70)

If a bill is lost after action brought thereon, and defendant suffer judgment by default, the court will, on a copy verified by affidavit, refer it to the master to see what is due thereon; (71)

Especially if the bill has been shewn to defendant, and he has admitted his signature, and promised payment. (71)

But if the bill is lost after action brought, and defendant resists the action, and puts the plaintiff to prove the bill, the loss will be no excuse for the non-production of the bill, and plaintiff will not be able to recover. (72)

And it will make no difference though the bill is of so old a date that the statute of limitations has attached upon it. (72) (*a*)

---

(70) Davis v. Dodd, 4 Taunt. 602. Action on bill payable to Allen or order, accepted by defendant, and endorsed generally to plaintiff: plaintiff lost it before it was due, but defendant after knowing of the loss, promised repeatedly to pay it. Lord Ellenborough however held the action not maintainable, and nonsuit; and on motion for a new trial, the court agreed with him: they thought defendant under no moral obligation to pay plaintiff, who by his negligence had exposed defendant to the danger of being compelled to pay another holder, and that his subsequent promise, their being no new consideration, was nudum pactum: they said, enforcing the giving a new bill under the statute, seemed to be plaintiff's only course.

(71) Brown v. Messiter, 3 Maule. 281. The acceptor of a bill desired to see the bill, and then he admitted the acceptance, and promised payment; he suffered judgment by default; and the bill having been stolen from plaintiff's attorney's pocket, rule nisi to refer on production of copy verified by plaintiff's attorney, and on cause being shewn, rule absolute.

(72) Poole v. Smith, Holt. 144. In action by endorsee against acceptor, it appeared that a few days before the trial the bill was picked out of the pocket of the plaintiff's attorney's clerk; and that defendant had admitted the acceptance, but said it had been satisfied between him and the drawer: the bill had been due above six years. Gibbs C. J. thought the non-production of the bill called upon him to nonsuit plaintiff, and that the statute of limitations made no difference: he said the rule was salutary, and ought not to be relaxed.

[(*a*) In an action brought in 1815 upon a note, which had been lost in 1797, it was objected that the note might still be in existence, and be again demanded of the defendants by a *bonâ fide* holder. But the court thought that after so great a lapse of time, it was incumbent on the defendants to show either that the note existed, or that it had been demanded of them; and that it must be presumed that no demand would now be made. Peabody v. Denton, 2 Gallis. 351.]

If a bill or note transferable by delivery is cut in halves, and half lost, the holder cannot sue at law upon the other half. Payment at law cannot be enforced unless the entire instrument is produced, or unless there is proof that the entire instrument, or whatever part of it is wanting, has been destroyed. (73)

[In an action on a bill, where the first of the set had been protested for non-payment, the plaintiff after proving the loss of the protested bill, was allowed to give in evidence the third of the set, and a duplicate protest of the first of the set. (*a*)

It has been held by the Supreme Court of the United States, that secondary evidence of the contents of a lost note was admissible, without a special count upon a lost note. (*b*)]

A special count upon a bill or note states in their order all the facts necessary to maintain the action.

To give a full idea of this count, and open the way to the observations necessary to be made upon it, I shall insert a comprehensive one in assumpsit upon a foreign bill, which will sufficiently elucidate those on inland bills or notes, and those in debt.

Count in assumpsit upon a Foreign Bill.

London } John Mills v. Thomas Roper and Stephen Howe.
to wit. } For that whereas on (1) the 1st day of January, 1789, at (2) London aforesaid, in the parish of St. Mary le Bow, in the ward of Cheap, certain persons (2[a]) using the

---

(73) Mayor v. Johnson, 3 Campb. 324. Plaintiff's traveller took a 5*l.* country bank-note, payable at Stamford or London, and cut it in halves, and sent the two halves to plaintiff; one half only arrived, the mail containing the other was stolen: plaintiff sued on the half which arrived; but as plaintiff could not shew that the other half was destroyed, Lord Ellenborough held the action could not be supported, and nonsuit.

N. He assigned as a reason, that the stolen half might immediately have got into the hands of a bonâ fide holder for value, and that such holder would have had as good a right as plaintiff: but, quære—If a man who takes half a note does not take it at his peril.

[(*a*) Usher v. Gaither, 2 Har. & M'H. 457.]

[(*b*) Renner v. Bank of Columbia, 9 Wheat. R. 581.]

style and firm of Gaunt and Co. according (3) to the usage and custom of merchants, from time immemorial used and approved of, made (4) their certain bill of exchange in writing, their (5) copartnership, style, and firm aforesaid, being thereunto subscribed, bearing (6) date the day and year aforesaid, and (7) directed to one Henry Hunt, at Venice, in Italy, in parts beyond the seas, and (8) thereby requested the said Henry, at double usance (*a*), to pay in Venice (8[2]) that their first of exchange (second (9) and third of the same tenor not paid) to the said (9[2]) Thomas and Stephen, or (10) their order, a certain sum of foreign money, (10[2]) called in the said bill seven hundred ducats, value (10[3]) received, and then and there (10[4]) delivered the said bill to the said Thomas and Stephen, which (11) said bill the said Henry Hunt, afterwards, to wit, on (12) the day and year aforesaid, at Venice, to wit, at London aforesaid, in the parish and ward aforesaid, on sight thereof, duly according to the usage and custom of merchants accepted, payable at A. B. and Co.'s, Venice (12[2]); and the said Thomas and Stephen (12[3]) afterwards and before the payment of the said sum of money in the said bill mentioned, or of any part thereof, to wit, on the day and year aforesaid, at London aforesaid, in the parish and ward aforesaid, by their certain endorsement (*b*) in writing then and there made upon the said bill, (12[4]) their proper hands being thereunto subscribed, according to the usage and custom of merchants, appointed the (13) contents of the said bill to be paid to one Peter White, or (14) his order, and then and there delivered the said bill so endorsed to the said Peter; and (15) the said Peter afterwards and before the payment of the said sum of money in the said bill mentioned, or of any part thereof, to wit, on the day and year aforesaid, at London aforesaid, in the parish and ward aforesaid, by his certain endorsement in writing then and there made upon the said bill, his proper hand being thereunto subscribed, appointed the contents of the said bill to be paid to the said John, and then and there delivered the said bill so endorsed to the said John, of (16) which said endorsements the said Henry afterwards, to wit, on the day and year aforesaid, at London aforesaid, in the parish and ward aforesaid, had notice; and the said John in fact says, that (17) an usance mentioned in any bill of exchange drawn in London and payable in Venice, is, and at the several times aforesaid was three calendar months from the date of the said bill, and no other time whatever; and (18) that afterwards, and when the said bill had according to the tenor and effect thereof become payable, to wit, on (19) the 4th day of July, in the year aforesaid, at Venice aforesaid, to wit, at London aforesaid, in the parish and ward aforesaid, the said bill was duly, according to the usage and custom of merchants, and according to the tenor of the said acceptance thereof, shown and presented to the said Henry at A. B. & Co.'s aforesaid, at Venice aforesaid, for payment; and the said Henry was then and there requested to pay the said sum of money in the said bill mentioned, but the said Henry did not then (19^2) or there pay the said sum of money in the said bill mentioned, or any part thereof, but wholly neglected and refused so to do; neither (20) did he pay the said second or third of exchange in the said bill mentioned, or either of them; nor (21) did the said persons so using the style and firm of Gaunt and Co. pay the said sum of money in the said bill mentioned, or any part thereof, or the said second or third of exchange; and thereupon the said John, afterwards, to wit, on the day and year last aforesaid, at Venice aforesaid, to wit, at London aforesaid, in the parish and ward aforesaid, according to the usage and custom of merchants, caused the said bill to be protested (22) for non-payment, of all which premises the said Thomas and Stephen afterwards, to wit, on the day and year last aforesaid, at London aforesaid, in the parish and ward aforesaid, had (23) notice; and by reason thereof, and by force of the usage and custom of merchants, became liable to pay to (24) the said John the said sum of money in the said bill mentioned, or the value thereof, when (25) they the said Thomas and Stephen should be thereunto afterwards requested: and (26) being so liable, they the said Thomas and Stephen, in consideration thereof, afterwards, to wit, on the day and year last aforesaid, at London aforesaid, in the parish and ward aforesaid, undertook, and to the said John then and there faithfully promised, to pay to him the said sum of money in the said bill mentioned, or the value thereof, when they the said Thomas and Stephen should be thereunto afterwards requested: and (27) the said John avers, that the said 700 ducats in the said bill mentioned, on the day and year last aforesaid were, and from thenceforth hitherto have been, and still are of great value, to wit, of the value of *l.* of lawful money of Great Britain, that is to say, at London aforesaid, in the parish and ward aforesaid; yet the said Thomas and Stephen (although often requested) have not nor hath either of them paid to the said John the said sum of money in the said bill mentioned, or any part thereof, or the value thereof, or of any part thereof, but hath wholly neglected and refused, and still neglects and refuses so to do; wherefore the said John says he is injured, and hath sustained damage to the value of *l.* and therefore he brings suit, &c.

1. "On, &c." Upon a bill or note importing to be payable within a limited time after the date, and dated on a particular day, this (74) must be that day: on a bill or note importing to be payable within a limited time after the date, and not dated, the day (75) it issued, if it can be ascertained, otherwise (76) the first day the plaintiff knew and can prove that it existed.

2. "At, &c." On a foreign bill this must be the place at which it bears date; but where the drawing of the bill must be proved upon a trial, some place in England or Wales should be subjoined under a videlicet, thus, "at Venice in Italy, to wit, at London," &c.

---

(74) Stafford v. Forcer, 10 Mod. 511. cited Str. 22. In an action on a note dated in 1704, defendant pleaded that the cause of action did not accrue within six years; the plaintiff replied a bill filed in 1714, and that the cause of action accrued within six years of that time; and after verdict for the plaintiff the court arrested the judgment, because it was stated that the note was made and dated in 1704, and then the cause of action must have accrued above six years before 1714.

(75) Vide ante, p. 154. n. (60).

(76) Vide Beawes, § 190. p. 439.

In an action against the drawer, the want of subjoining such place may be taken advantage of by special demurrer to the count, but by special demurrer (77) only.

In an action on a foreign note, it may be stated to have been made at any place in England, without naming the foreign place. (78)

Inland bills and notes, though they may bear date at a particular place, may be alleged to have been made any where in England or Wales.

2ª. "Certain persons." A bill or note may be stated according to its legal operation.

Thus a joint or several note, or a note importing in the body of it to be made by several persons, but signed by one only (79), may be stated as a several note.

Nay, where the plaintiff in an action against one of two makers of a joint or several note, stated that the defendant and another made their certain note, &c. and thereby jointly or severally promised to pay, the court held it (80) well

---

(77) Vide 16 and 17 Car. 2. c. 8. § 1., 4 Ann. c. 16. § 1.

(78) Houriet v. Morris, 3 Campb. 303. In an action on a note dated at Paris, the statement was, that defendant at London &c. made his note, &c.; it was urged that it should have been stated to have been made at Paris, to wit, at London, &c. but Lord Ellenborough said the contract was transitory, and the statement sufficient.

(79) Roberts v. Peake, Burr. 322. A note signed by the defendant alone, but importing in the body of it to have been made by the defendant and another person, was declared upon as the several note of the defendant, and it was agreed that it might be declared upon according to its legal operation; but judgment was given for the defendant upon another ground. See Siffkin v. Walker, 2 Campb. N. P. C. 308.

(80) Butler v. Malissy, Str. 76. In an action on a note, the declaration stated that the defendant and another did jointly or severally promise to pay; and upon demurrer, the court held it bad, and the plaintiff obtained leave to discontinue. And in Ovington v. Neale, Str. 819., Lord Raym. 1544., the plaintiff declared upon a note by which the defendant and another jointly or severally promised to pay; and upon error, the court of king's bench held it bad, because the plaintiff had not shewn a title to bring a separate action against the defendant, for he only says he has this or some other cause of action; and judgment for the plaintiff was reversed. However, in Rees v. Abbott, Cowp. 832., the declaration upon a note stated that the defendant and another made their note, by which they jointly or severally promised to pay; and upon error after judgment by default, Butler v. Malissy, and Ovington v. Neale, were cited as in point. Sed per Lord Mansfield, "If *or* is to be considered in this case a disjunctive, the plaintiff is to elect, and by the action he has made his election to consider the note as several; but in this case it is synonymous to *and*, and both and each promise to pay." Judgment affirmed.

after judgment by default; notwithstanding, as the truth of either member verifies a disjunctive proposition, the note might have been joint.

And in an (81) action against one of the several makers of a joint note, or one (82) of several drawers of a joint bill, if it be stated as a several one made by one alone, the objection can only be taken by plea in abatement.

A bill or note made by a servant for his master may be stated to have been made by the master, because that (83) is its legal operation.

3. "According, &c." It is (84) not requisite to set out any part of the custom, and even a reference to it is (85) unnecessary.

In actions upon notes, instead of referring to the custom of merchants, the count refers to the statute, but this reference is unnecessary.

4. "Made." Where a man signs his name upon a blank paper, stamped with a bill stamp, and delivers it to another to draw above the signature what bill he pleases thereon, and he draws one accordingly, the (86) bill may be stated to have been made by the person whose signature it bears.

[It is not necessary to set forth in a declaration that one

---

(81) Per Buller J., Rees v. Abbot, supra; and see Rice v. Shute, Burr. 2611., and Abbot v. Smith, Blackst. 947.

(82) Evans v. Lewis, E. 1794. cit. 1 Barnew. and Ald. 226. In an action against defendant as drawer of a bill, the declaration stated that he made his certain bill of exchange &c.; it appeared in evidence that the bill was drawn by defendant and another person jointly: the point was saved whether this was a variance, and the court on motion were of opinion it was not, and that the only mode by which the defendant could have made the objection was by plea in abatement.

(83) See ante, p. 268.

(84) Soper v. Dible, Lord Raym. 175. In an action upon a bill the defendant demurred, because the declaration did not set out the custom, the court held it unnecessary, and said the better way was to omit it.

(85) This was determined in Ereskine v. Murray, Lord Raym. 1542., on error after judgment by default; and see Lord Raym. 88., Carth. 83. 269, 270; Lutw. 279.

(86) Collis v. Emett, 1 H. Blackst. 313. Emett signed a piece of blank paper stamped with a bill stamp, and delivered to Livesay and Co. that they might write above his signature such bill as they should please: they wrote one accordingly; and an action being brought thereon against Emett, in which it was stated that he drew the bill, the court thought the statement proper; and upon a special verdict stating these facts, the court gave judgment for the plaintiff upon a count which alleged that the bill was drawn by the defendant.

of the partners of a firm made or endorsed a note in the name or style of the partnership: it is sufficient to declare upon it according to its legal effect, as made or endorsed by the partners. (*a*)]

5. "Their, &c." A signature, when essential, is (87) implied by the preceding word "made;" this allegation, therefore, is not strictly necessary, and had better be omitted, lest there should be a (88) variance between the signature stated and that proved.

6. "Bearing, &c." This allegation (89) also may be dispensed with; for it shall be intended, when the date is material, that a bill or note was dated when drawn.

Where the date is immaterial, and this allegation is omitted in the declaration, this intendment shall (90) not operate

---

[(*a*) Manhattan Company v. Ledyard, 1 Cain. R. 192.]

(87) This was ruled upon demurrer in Elliot v. Cooper, Lord Raym. 1376., Str. 609., and Smith v. Jarvis, Lord Raym. 1484.; and on error after judgment by default, in Ereskine v. Murray, Lord Raym. 1542. Vide ante, p. 23. n. (67).

(88) Jones and another v. Mars and another, 2 Camp. N. P. C. 305. The declaration in an action against the drawers of a bill stated it to have been made by the defendants, "their own proper *hands* being thereunto subscribed." The bill was in fact signed by only one of them "Mars and Co." Lord Ellenborough doubted whether the variance was material; but refused to nonsuit the plaintiffs. He said had it been "their own proper *hand*," he should have held it clearly sufficient.

[In an action against John and George Pease, as makers of a note, the declaration did not aver that they were partners, but said that the defendants made the note, "their own proper hands and names being thereunto subscribed." It was held that a note signed by the defendant, George, with the name of the firm, John and George Pease, did not support the declaration. Pease v. Morgan, 7 Johns. R. 468.]

See also Levy v. Wilson, 5 Esp. N. P. C. 180., post, 278. and Helmsley v. Loader, 2 Campb. N. P. C. 450., and Heys v. Heseltine, 2 Campb. 604.

[A declaration upon a note stating it as made "under the hands" of the defendants, was held to be supported by a note produced in evidence signed with the defendants' names by an agent. Phelps v. Riley, 3 Conn. R. 266.]

(89) De la Courtier v. Bellamy, 2 Show. 422. In an action upon a foreign bill payable at double usance from the date thereof, the declaration stated that the drawer on such a day drew the bill, but the date was not set forth. An exception was taken on this ground; but, by the whole court, "It is well enough; we will intend it was dated when it was drawn:" judgment for the plaintiff. S. P. R. acc. Hague v. French, 3 Bos. and Pull. 173.

(90) Coxon v. Lyon, 2 Campb. N. P. C. 307. n. The declaration stated that the defendant, on the 3d of Feb. 1810, made his bill, requesting the drawee to pay on a particular day. The bill was in fact

so as to render a variance between the date of the bill and the day on which it is stated to have been drawn fatal.

7. "Directed, &c." In an action against the acceptor upon a bill directed to him, or, in his absence, to I. S., the (91) conditional direction to I. S. need not be stated.

So in an action against the acceptor of a bill, though the bill were directed to him and another person, it may be described as directed to him, without naming the other person. (92)

In an action against an acceptor, if the bill were not directed to him, it has been held to be a fatal variance to state that it was. (93)

If a bill is directed to Messrs. A., B., and Co., it is no variance in setting out the bill according to its tenor to put *Mess^s.* A., B., and Co., without putting the *r*, instead of Messrs. with it. (94)

[A declaration on a bill stating it as directed to A. C., meaning B. C., and presented to A. C. *alias* B. C., has been held sufficient on demurrer. (*a*)

---

dated the 6th of Feb. 1810, but no date was stated in the declaration. Thompson B. held that the variance was immaterial.

(91) Anon. 12 Mod. 447. A bill directed "to A., or, in his absence, to B," began thus: "Gentlemen, pray pay, &c." A. accepted it; and in an action against him on his acceptance, the declaration described the bill as directed to A., without any notice of B.; and Holt C. J. held it well.

(92) Mountstephen v. Brooks, 1 Barnew. and Ald. 224. In an action against three as acceptors of a bill, the declaration stated that J. S. made his bill directed to defendants, and thereby requested them to pay, &c.; it appeared in evidence, that it was in fact directed to them and one Richard Smith, with whom they were in partnership, and that it was accepted by him and them. Lord Ellenborough thought this a variance, and nonsuited the plaintiff; but on an application for a new trial, he changed his opinion; and the rest of the court concurring with him, a new trial was granted.

(93) Gray v. Milner, 2 Stark. 336. In an action against the acceptor of a bill, the declaration stated that the bill was directed to the defendant; it appeared to have no direction: Lord Ellenborough held this a fatal misdescription, and nonsuited the plaintiff.

(94) Rex v. Oldfield, Mich. 1815. An indictment for forging an endorsement upon a bill imported to set out the bill according to its tenor; the bill was directed to "Messrs. Masterman and Co.;" but upon the indictment the *r* in Messrs. was omitted, and it stood Mess^s. ; the point was saved for the consideration of the twelve judges, and they were unanimous that as it appeared by the context that Mess^s. must mean Messrs., the variance was immaterial, and the conviction unobjectionable.

[(*a*) Sterry v. Robinson, 1 Day, 11.]

A declaration on a promise to A. B. by the name of C. D. is sufficient. (*a*)]

8. "In Venice." If a bill or note in what is strictly part of it, fixes a specific place for payment, it is a fatal variance to omit stating it in setting out the bill or note. (95)

On the other hand, if it be stated as the import of the bill or note that the money should be paid at a specific place, when the provision for that purpose is not strictly part of the bill or note, it is a fatal variance. (96)

In such case, however, stating that the party made the bill or note, and that he *then and there* made it payable at a specified place, without stating that he *thereby* made it so payable, is not fatal. (97)

[(*a*) A declaration on a note, averring that the defendants "promised the Medway Cotton Manufactory, (the plaintiffs,) by the name of Richardson, Metcalf, and Co." was on demurrer held sufficient. Medway Cotton Manufactory v. Adams, 10 Mass. R. 360.]

(95) Roche v. Campbell, 3 Campb. 247. A note was in this form, "31 days after date I promise to pay J. S. or order, at the house of N., No. 6. Grafton-street, Dublin, £40, &c." In an action by endorsee against endorser, the bill was described generally to pay J. S. or order, without naming the place; and it was urged that this was a misdescription, for it implied that the note was payable generally, while it was only payable at one given house. Lord Ellenborough thought it a fatal misdescription, and nonsuited plaintiff.

Hodge v. Fillis, 3 Campb. 463. A bill was addressed to Messrs. Fillis and Co. Plymouth, "payable in London;" they accepted it, payable at Sir John Perring and Co.'s, London. In an action against them the first count, in stating the bill, omitted to allege that the address made it payable in London. Lord Ellenborough thought the omission fatal on that count; but on proof of a promise by defendants to pay after the bill was due, he thought the plaintiff entitled to recover on other counts; and verdict accordingly.

[The declaration on a note stated no place of payment; the note offered in evidence was "negotiable and payable at the Office of Discount and Deposit of the Bank of the United States at Lexington." It was held that the variance was fatal. Sebree v. Dorr, 9 Wheat. R. 558.]

(96) Exon v. Russell, 4 Maule and Selw. 505. At the bottom of a note was written, "at Messrs. Brown and Co.'s, bankers, London:" in stating the note, the declaration alleged that defendant made the note, and thereby promised to pay, &c. and made the same payable, and to be paid according to the tenor and effect, at the house of persons described as Messrs. Brown and Co., bankers, London. On rule nisi for a nonsuit upon another ground, the court thought it a misdescription of the note to state as its import that it was made payable at a particular place; for as the place was mentioned by way of memorandum only, and not as part of the contract, that was not its import; and on that ground the rule for a nonsuit was made absolute.

(97) Hardy v. Woodroffe, 2 Stark. 319. In an action against the

[*a* "At double usance." If a note is payable at a certain time after date, and the count upon it either states no time of payment, or states it to be payable on demand, the variance is fatal; (*a*) even upon executing a writ of inquiry. (*b*)

But it is sufficient to declare on a note according to the terms of it. And therefore a declaration which stated no time of payment, was on demurrer held to be good. (*c*)]

9. "Second, &c." In an action upon a bill consisting of several parts, if the plaintiff has each part, it may be doubted whether he need take notice of this condition, because all the parts collectively make an unconditional bill; and where he has not each part, it should seem more correct to state that the drawer made his certain bill of exchange in writing in three parts, his proper hand being subscribed to each of the said parts, bearing date, &c. and directed, &c. and by each of the said parts requested, &c; but the form I have adopted is the usual one.

9[2]. "To the said Thomas and Stephen." A bill or note importing to be payable to a fictitious person, and to be endorsed by him, may be stated to be payable to the person in

---

maker of a note, it was alleged in the declaration that defendant made the note, &c. and that he then and there made it payable at No. 32, Castle-street, Holborn; the defendant had written upon the note "payable at No. 32, Castle-street, Holborn," and Abbott J. held that memorandum supported the statement in the declaration; and the plaintiff had a verdict.

[(*a*) Sebree v. Dorr, 9 Wheat. R. 558; Page v. Bank of Alexandria, 7 Wheat. R. 35.]

[(*b*) Sheehy v. Mandeville, 7 Cranch, 208.]

[(*c*) The declaration on a note mentioned no time of payment. Demurrer. Per Curiam. "It is to be presumed that the declaration states the note according to the terms of it, and that is sufficient. The conclusion of law is, that where no time of payment is specified in the note, it is payable immediately. The declaration then shows a cause of action, and the plaintiff is entitled to judgment." Herrick v. Bennett, 8 Johns. R. 291.

But such a declaration has been held in Connecticut, on error, not to be sufficient, on the ground that the declaration should state the contract to be to pay on demand, according to the *legal effect* of the note, no time of payment being specified, and that it was not sufficient to declare according to the terms of the note, which was merely the evidence of the contract. Bacon v. Page, 1 Conn. R. 404.]

whose favor the endorsement is made, or if it import to be endorsed in blank, it may be stated to be payable to (98) bearer.

A bill or note intended to have been made payable to A. that he might guarantee the payment to B., but through ignorance or mistake made payable to B. and by him endorsed to A., and then endorsed back by A. to B., may perhaps (99) be stated to have been made payable to A.

The payee of a bill or note payable "to his order," may (100) state it to have been made payable to himself.

If the intended payee's name is miswritten, so as to give it a different sound and make it a different name, it may be stated to have been made payable to the person intended, and evidence may be given to shew who was intended. (101)

10. "Or order, &c." In an action by the assignee of a bill or note, it is necessary to shew that the bill or note authorizes a transfer; in an action by the payee (102), not.

[(98) Vide ante, p. 19. n. (61). In Vere v. Lewis, ante, p. 20. note (61)., Lord Kenyon, Ashhurst, and Buller, Js. thought that the plaintiff might recover on the count which stated that the bill was drawn payable to bearer; and in Collis v. Emett, ante, p. 20. n. (61). it was so decided.

(99) Bishop v. Hayward, 4 Term Rep. 470. A note payable to the plaintiff or order was endorsed by him to the defendant, and endorsed back again by the defendant to him; these facts being stated on the declaration, the court arrested the judgment. It was suggested in the argument that the plaintiff had refused to take the note, unless the defendant put his name upon it, and that as he was made payee, his endorsement was mere form; and per Lord Kenyon, "Had it been understood by all parties that the note, though nominally payable to the plaintiff, was substantially to be paid to the defendant, it should have been declared on according to its legal import, as was held in Minet v. Gibson; a name may be omitted in the declaration, if the legal operation of the instrument requires it." [But see Britten v. Webb, ante, p. 214.]

(100) Frederick v. Cotton, 2 Show. 8. In an action against the acceptor of a bill, it was objected, in arrest of judgment, that the bill was stated to be payable to the order of the plaintiff, and no order was alleged; but the court resolved without any difficulty, that money to be paid to a man's order was due to himself; and judgment was given for the plaintiff.

(101) Willis v. Barrett, 2 Stark. 29. E. Willis sued as payee of a note: the note, when produced, imported to be payable to E. Willison, but Lord Ellenborough allowed evidence to prove that plaintiff was the person meant; and he had a verdict. [See also Medway Cotton Manufactory v. Adams, ante, p. 272.]

(102) See ante, p. 21. note (62). Moore v. Paine, Ann. 283. In

10². "Money." If a bill or note is for money of the same appellation as ours, but of different value, it must not be stated as if it were for our money; (103)

As if it be for so many pounds, and is drawn and payable in Ireland, it must not be stated to be for so many pounds generally, without something to shew that pounds Irish were meant. (103)

10³. "Value received." It is not necessary to state that a bill or not was for value received.

And if it be so stated, and the statement give a wrong meaning to those words, it will be a fatal misdescription. (104)

Upon a bill payable to the drawer's order, if the bill is for value received generally, without saying by whom, it is giving them a wrong meaning to state it as for value received by the drawer. (104)

---

error upon a judgment by default in an action upon a note, it was objected that it was only stated to be payable to the plaintiff, and not *to his order;* but by Lord Hardwicke, that has been overruled often: the judgment was affirmed.

[In an action by the endorsee of a note against the maker, the declaration did not state the note to be payable to order. After judgment for want of a plea, and a writ of inquiry executed and returned, judgment was arrested for this defect in the declaration. Barriere v. Nairac, 2 Dall. 249.

The declaration in an action by the assignees of a note against the assignors, did not state the note to be payable to order, the note offered in evidence was payable to the defendants "or their order." The variance was held to be fatal. Sebree v. Dorr, 9 Wheat. R. 558.]

(103) Kearney v. King, 2 Barnew. and Ald. 301. In an action against the acceptor the declaration stated that A. B. at Dublin, to wit, at London, drew a bill on defendant requiring him to pay the sum of £542, 1*s.* 8*d.* The bill, when produced, appeared to be drawn in Ireland, and to be payable in Ireland, and though it was for £542, 1*s.* 8*d.* sterling, that sum Irish was only equal to £500, 7*s.* 9*d.* English; and on rule nisi for a nonsuit, and cause shewn, the court were clear that the bill, as stated, must be taken to have been for English money; and the bill produced being for Irish, there was a clear variance; and the rule was made absolute. [S. P. Sprowle v. Legge, 1 Barn. & Cres. 16; 2 Dow. & Ryl. 15.]

(104) Highmore v. Primrose, 5 Maule and Selw. 65. A bill payable to the drawer's order was for value received generally; the declaration stated that it was for value received by the drawer. The court thought that value received by the drawer could be no foundation for his drawing to his own order, and considered this a variance; but there being an acknowledgement of the debt by the defendant, the plaintiff recovered on the account stated.

If the bill is payable to a third person, it is not. (105)

10[4]. "Delivered, &c." It is (106) not necessary to state that the drawer of a bill "delivered" it to the payee; it is implied in the allegation that he "made" the bill.

If it be stated that the bill was delivered to the drawee, and that he accepted it, it is (107) not necessary to allege that he delivered it back.

11. "Which, &c." Except in actions against acceptors, or on bills payable a limited time after sight, the acceptance need not be stated. If stated, though unnecessarily, it has been held at nisi prius that it (108) must be proved.

12. "On, &c." Where the time of payment depends on the presentment, and the action is against the drawer of a bill, or the endorser of a bill or note, this should be the

---

(105) Grant v. Da Costa, 3 Maule and Selw. 351. In an action against the acceptor on a bill payable to J. S. or order, it was stated to be for value received by the drawer; on production, it appeared to be for value received generally: and on a rule nisi for a nonsuit, the court held that the meaning of value received on such a bill, payable to a third person, was, that the value had been received by the drawer of the payee; that it was natural the drawer should give the drawee that information; but why should he tell him that he, the drawee, had had value from the drawer? and yet that could be the only other object of the words. Rule discharged.

(106) Churchill v. Gardner, 7 Term Rep. 596. In an action by the payee of a bill against the acceptor, the declaration stated that the drawer made his certain bill of exchange, but there was no allegation that he delivered it to the plaintiff, and the defendant demurred specially for that cause. But the court was clearly of opinion that there was no foundation for the objection, the delivery of the bill to the plaintiff being sufficiently implied in the allegation that the drawer "made" the bill.

(107) Smith v. M'Clure, 5 East. Rep. 376. The plaintiff declared on a bill payable to his own order, and averred that he delivered it to the defendant, to whom it was addressed, and that he accepted it according to the custom of merchants, by reason of which premises, &c. the defendant became liable to pay. The defendant demurred specially, because it was not alleged that the defendant delivered back the bill: sed per Lord Ellenborough, the acceptance must be considered as perfect; and if so, it gave the plaintiff a right to sue upon it: if, after the acceptance, the defendant improperly detained the bill, the plaintiff might nevertheless sue him upon it. Judgment for the plaintiff.

(108) Jones v. Morgan and another, 2 Campb. 474. In an action on a bill, drawn on Burt by the defendants, payable to their own order, and endorsed by them to the plaintiff, the declaration unnecessarily stated an acceptance by Burt. And Lord Ellenborough was of opinion, that the plaintiff having stated an acceptance, was bound to prove it.

very day of the presentment; in other cases, exactness as to the day is not requisite.

If, however, the plaintiff allege in terms that the acceptance was made before the time limited by a bill for its payment, it has been laid down that he will (109) be precluded from giving in evidence an acceptance afterwards; but this may perhaps be doubted. (110)

Though the time of payment depend upon the presentment, as in bills payable a given time after sight; yet, if the action is against the acceptor, exactness as to stating the day of presentment is not essential. (111)

12². "At A. B. and Co's." If an acceptance import to make the bill payable at a banker's, or any other particular place, this need not be stated in an action against the acceptor, nor, perhaps, in an action against the drawer or an endorser, unless the acceptance is prior to the 1st of August, 1821, or unless it expresses that the party accepts the bill payable there, and not otherwise or elsewhere. (112)

If this be expressed in the acceptance (112), or if the acceptance be prior to 31st August, 1821, the acceptance must be stated as a special acceptance, to pay at such place. (113)

12³. "Afterwards, &c." It is (114) not a material va-

---

(109) Jackson v. Pigott, Lord Raym. 364., 12 Mod. 212. In an action against the acceptor of a bill, per Holt C. J. "If the plaintiff declares that the acceptance was before the day appointed for the payment, and that the defendant accepted to pay according to the tenor and effect of the bill, and it appears upon the evidence that the acceptance in fact was after the day of payment, this would be against the plaintiff."

(110) See Young v. Wright, infra note (114).

(111) Forman v. Jacob, 1 Stark. 46. Endorsee against acceptor on bill dated Constantinople, and payable fifty days after sight. The declaration averred an acceptance on the day the bill bore date, whereas the acceptance was not till five weeks afterwards: it was objected that this was a fatal variance; but Lord Ellenborough held otherwise, and plaintiff had a verdict.

N. The date was 11th August, the acceptance 19th September.

(112) See 1 & 2 G. 4. c. 78. § 1. ante, p. 115.

(113) See Rowe v. Young, ante, p. 132.

(114) Young and another v. Wright, 1 Campb. N. P. C. 139. This was an action by endorsees against the drawer of a bill. The declaration stated all the endorsements to have been made before the bill became due; but it appeared that the immediate endorsement to the

riance, that an endorsement is stated to have been made before, and is proved to have been made after, the bill became due.

[*b* "Their certain endorsement," &c. Where the declaration on a note stated it to be endorsed by A. B, and the note produced had the word *agent*, endorsed after A. B's name, the variance was held to be immaterial. (*a*)]

12[4]. "Their proper hands." This is an unnecessary allegation, being implied in the preceding words ; it is better to omit it, because there are cases in which it may occasion risk. For instance, if a bill be endorsed by procuration, and it be thus stated to have been made by the hand of the party himself, the variance (115) will be fatal.

[In an action by an endorsee against the acceptor of a bill, an averment that a bill had been endorsed to certain persons trading under the firm of H. and F. and that they endorsed the bill by procuration of one J. D. is supported by evidence that J. D. one of the firm of H. and Co. endorsed this bill, and was in the habit of endorsing bills by procuration in the name of H. and F., an old firm which had ceased to exist, though all other business of H. and Co. was carried on in the name of H. and Co. only. (*b*)]

---

plaintiffs had been made after the bill had become due. Lord Ellenborough, on the authority of Russell v. Langstaffe, Dougl. 514. (ante), held that the variance was immaterial; he said that this was the converse of that case, but was to be governed by the same principle.

[(*a*) A declaration on a promise to indemnify the second endorser of a note if he had to pay it, stated the note to be made by a company payable to A. B. or order, and by him endorsed; the note produced had the word *agent*, endorsed upon it, after A. B's name, and he was proved to be agent of the company. The variance was held immaterial, although a majority of the court thought that A. B. by endorsing the word *agent* after his name, avoided all personal liability as endorser. Mott v. Hicks, 1 Cowen, 513.]

(115) Levy v. Wilson, 5 Esp. N. P. C. 180. In an action by an endorsee of a bill, the declaration stated the endorsement to have been made by the payee "his own handwriting being thereunto subscribed." The bill appeared to have been endorsed by procuration. Lord Ellenborough held this variance fatal, and nonsuited the plaintiff. See also Jones v. Mars, ante, p. 270.—[Phelps v. Riley, ante, p. 270. is contra.]

[(*b*) In an action by an endorsee against the acceptor of a bill, the declaration averred that the bill had been endorsed to certain persons trading under the firm of Habgood and Fowler; and that Habgood and Fowler endorsed the bill by procuration of one John Dickson.

13. "The contents." On an endorsement for less than the full sum mentioned in the bill or note, the plaintiff must (116) shew that the residue was paid.

14. "Or his order." These (117) words are unnecessary.

A full and blank endorsement are stated in the same manner.

15. "And the said Peter, &c." Every endorsement essential to a transfer must be stated; unnecessary ones may (118) be omitted.

Where the plaintiff would omit an endorsement, he should represent that which precedes the endorsement to be omitted to have been made in favor of the person who is endorsee upon that which follows.

The evidence proved that the firm of Habgood and Fowler ceased ten years before the endorsement; but that a new firm of Habgood and Co. had been established, and that Dickson, one of the firm, was in the habit of endorsing bills by procuration in the name of Habgood and Fowler. Habgood and Co. did not do any other business under the name of Habgood and Co. nor did it appear that the other partners knew that Dickson endorsed this bill. Abbott C. J. said, "As between an innocent holder and the acceptor, there was proof to satisfy the allegation, that there were persons trading under the firm of Habgood and Fowler, though the business was carried on by the new partnership under the name of Habgood and Co." Bayley J. was of the same opinion, and said, "If the other members of the new firm knew that Dickson used the name of Habgood and Fowler from time to time, they are to be bound by what he does." Holroyd J. thought, that it would be enough in this action by the endorsee against the acceptor to prove the handwriting of Dickson, without showing the actual existence of such a house as Habgood and Fowler. Williamson v. Johnson, 2 Dow. and Ryl. 281. S. C. 1 Barn. and Cres. 146.]

(116) Hawkins v. Gardner, 12 Mod. 213. The declaration stated that the defendant drew a bill for 46*l.* 19*s.* payable to Blackman or order, and that Blackman endorsed 43*l.* 4*s.* thereof to the plaintiff; the court held, that an endorsement for part only of what was due upon the bill was bad, and said, if Blackman had brought an action for part, he must have acknowledged satisfaction for the residue.

(117) Vide ante. p. 70.

(118) In Peacock v. Rhodes, ante, p. 67. note (9.) the bill was payable to Ingham, and endorsed by him and by John Daltry; the plaintiff declared as endorsee of Ingham, and recovered.

Chaters v. Bell and others, 4 Esp. N. P. C. 120. The declaration stated, that a bill was drawn payable to Curry, by him endorsed to the defendant, and by the defendant to the plaintiff. There were in fact several intermediate endorsements between Curry and the defendant, which were omitted in the declaration; and it was contended that the plaintiff should have either declared, as the immediate endorsee of the payee, or have stated all the endorsements. But Lord Ellenborough overruled the objection. Vide Waynam v. Bend, and Critchlow v. Parry, post.

Thus if a bill payable to A.'s order be endorsed by him in blank, and delivered to B. and endorsed by B. to C., if C. would omit stating B.'s endorsement, he should state that A. endorsed it immediately to him, C.

16. "Of which, &c." This (119) allegation is unnecessary.

17. "That an usance, &c." A neglect to shew the duration of an usance is (120) fatal upon demurrer, (unless perhaps where it is alleged that the bill was presented on the day it was payable) but upon demurrer only. (121)

18. "And that, &c." In an action against the maker of a note or the acceptor of a bill, the presentment is never stated, unless the bill or note is made payable either by the original frame of it, or by the form of the acceptance at a particular place only. (122)

---

(119) Anon. Pract. Reg. 358. In an action by an endorsee of a note against the maker, the defendant demurred, and showed for cause, that it was not alleged that he had notice of the endorsement; but by the court, there is no need of notice. Judgment for the plaintiff.

Reynolds v. Davies, in error, 1 Bos. and Pull. 625. In an action by an endorsee against the maker of a note, the declaration stated the endorsement and delivery by the payee, and then averred (in the usual form) the defendant's liability and promise to pay to the plaintiff. There was no averment of notice of such endorsement. The defendant demurred specially, but did not assign such want of notice as a cause of demurrer. After judgment in the king's bench for the plaintiff Davies, a writ of error was brought in the exchequer chamber, and such want of notice assigned as error. But Eyre C. J. said the promise to pay contained in this note is to the payee or his order; immediately then on the order being made to the endorsee, the promise attaches: nor can we add the qualification of notice to a promise which was not orignally qualified with that circumstance. Judgment affirmed.

(120) Buckley v. Campbell, Salk. 131. The plaintiff declared upon a bill drawn at Amsterdam and payable in London, at two usances, and did not shew what the two usances were: and the court gave judgment for the defendant, because they could not take notice of foreign usances, which are longer in one place than another.

(121) Smart v. Dean, 3 Keb. 645. In an action on a bill from Paris, payable here at double usance, the defendant pleaded payment; and on issue taken thereon, demurred, and objected that it was not alleged that double usance was two months: sed non allocatur, "It being a known term among merchants, that usance is a month, double two months; and being averred he had not paid in two months, it is well enough, the defendant having waived advantage hereof by pleading payment;" but by Twysden J., had it been on demurrer to the declaration, the plaintiff should have averred a particular custom that usance signifieth a month. Judgment for the plaintiff.

(122) Vide Fenton v. Goundry and Callaghan v. Aylett, ante, p. 133.

In an action against the drawer of a bill, or the endorser of a bill or note, it is essential to state either that (123) the bill or note was presented, that the drawee or maker could not be found, or that the defendant, had he paid the bill, would have no remedy against them.

If a bill be stated to have been accepted payable by certain persons at a particular place, so as to make presentment at that place essential, an averment in an action against the drawer of a presentment to those persons generally, without saying at that place, is insufficient.

---

note (19). See also Sanderson v. Bowes, ante, p. 129. note (15), with which it is difficult to reconcile, in principle, the case of Fenton v. Goundry. The acceptance seems to be as much the original contract of the acceptor of a bill, as a note is the original contract of the maker.

(123) Mercer v. Southwell, 2 Show. 180. The declaration against the drawer of a bill stated that the drawee did not accept, but did not allege that the bill had been shewn or tendered to him; and upon demurrer on this account, the omission was held fatal, for otherwise it would be in the plaintiff's power to charge the drawer, when perhaps the drawee was ready to pay the money according to the tenor of the bill, if it had been tendered to him.

Rushton v. Aspinall, Dougl. 654.—680. In an action by endorsee against endorser upon a bill payable three months after date, the declaration stated that the bill, after the making thereof, to wit, on the same day and year aforesaid (referring to the day the bill bore date), was presented for acceptance, and accepted; yet the drawer, although afterwards, to wit, on the same day and year aforesaid requested, did not pay, of which the drawer, the payee, and first endorser, and the acceptor had notice: by reason whereof defendant became liable to pay; and being so liable, on the same day and year promised to pay. After verdict and judgment for plaintiff, the court of king's bench, upon a writ of error brought, held the declaration bad; because it did not shew that payment was demanded of the acceptor when the bill became due, or that notice was given to the defendant of his refusal to pay; and that though it was stated that he had promised to pay, that promise was stated as an inference of law, and the declaration did not contain premises from which that inference could be drawn; and the judgment was reversed. See also Parker v. Gordon, ante, p. 136. note (22), and Ambrose v. Hopwood, infra.

[But in an action against the endorser of a note in New York, the declaration which merely alleged a demand of payment of the maker in general terms, viz. "although often requested," &c. and did not state any demand on him on the last day of grace, was held good after verdict, on motion in arrest of judgment. Per curiam. "Even if the objection were good on demurrer, it is now too late. The fault is no more than the defectively setting out of a title, which is always cured by a verdict." Leffingwell v. White, 1 Johns. Cas. 99.

In Wilson v. Lenox, 1 Cranch, 194, the question whether an averment or presentment to the drawee for payment is essential, was argued, but no opinion was given by the court.]

But an allegation that it was presented to them "according to the tenor and effect of the bill, and the acceptance thereof," will (124) be sufficient.

If the drawee or maker cannot be found, it is (125) sufficient to aver generally that he was not found, without stating that any inquiry was made after him.

On an allegation that the bill or note was presented, and acceptance or payment refused, the plaintiff cannot (126) give in evidence that the drawee or maker could not be found. (*a*)

---

(124) Huffam v. Ellis, M. 51 G. 3. In an action against the drawers of a bill, the bill was stated in the declaration to have been accepted by Robertson, payable at the house of Kensington, Styan, and Adams, and a presentment to them was averred to have been made "according to the tenor and effect of the said bill, and the said acceptance thereof," without saying *at the house:* to this the defendant pleaded a judgment recovered, and judgment was given by the court of King's Bench for the plaintiff, the defendants having failed to produce the record of the judgment pleaded. On error to the House of Lords, the want of an averment of a presentment at the *place* where it was made payable, was assigned for error: and Ambrose v. Hopwood was cited. But the House of Lords affirmed the judgment of the Court of King's Bench. 10th of April, 1811.

(125) Starke v. Cheeseman, Carth. 509. In an action upon a bill drawn by the defendant on C. C. of Radcliffe, London, the declaration merely stated that the said C. C. at Radcliffe aforesaid, or elsewhere within the kingdom of England, was not found; and, after judgment by default, it was objected in arrest of final judgment, that it was not shewn that any inquiry had been made after him; but it was answered, that it was according to the custom among merchants, and the common form in the like cases, and judgment was given for the plaintiff.

(126) R. Leeson v. Pigott, sittings after Trinity, 1788; and see Smith v. Bellamy, 2 Stark. 223.

[It has been held in several American cases that the averments of demand and notice in the declaration on a bill or note, were sufficiently supported by evidence of any thing which rendered a demand or notice unnecessary. See Stewart v. Eden, and Norton v. Lewis, infra.

In an action against the endorser of a note, one count alleged a demand on the makers on the day on which it became due. The court seemed to be of opinion that evidence of due diligence to obtain payment without an actual demand, would support the averment. But it was not necessary to decide the question, as the second count stated that one of the makers had absconded, and alleged a regular demand on the other, according to the facts. Williams v. Matthews, 3 Cowen, 252.

So where no demand had been made of the maker on account of his absence in a foreign country, it was held by Van Ness J. at nisi prius, that an averment of presentment in the common form was sufficient. Cummings v. Fisher, Anth. N. P. 5.]

[(*a*) It has been held that the usual averments of demand and notice

But if a note be made payable at a particular town, and the maker has no residence there, a presentment at the banking-houses there will justify and support an allegation that it was presented there to the maker. (127)

[It seems that the averment of a demand upon the maker of a note, and his refusal to pay, is sufficiently supported by evidence of a presentment at the store of the maker in his absence. (*a*)]

If the allegation be that the bill was presented by one J. S., that part of the allegation which states that the presentment was by J. S. is immaterial. (128)

In an action against the acceptor of a bill or maker of a note payable on demand, a (129) presentment need not be stated.

19. "On, &c." Unless there is an express averment that the presentment was made on the day when the bill or note

---

in a declaration on a note, are satisfied by proof of a promise to pay the note in consideration of time given, although there has been no sufficient demand or notice. Hosmer J. said, that this mode of declaring, "relying on proof of an excuse for the omission to make demand, or give notice, had too frequently been sanctioned to remain questionable." Norton v. Lewis, 2 Conn. R. 478.]

(127) Hardy v. Woodroffe, 2 Stark. 319. Action against the maker of a note made payable at Guilford, and allegation that plaintiff shewed and presented the note to defendant at Guilford for payment thereof: plaintiff proved that he presented the note at two banks at Guilford, and that defendant lived in London: it was objected that this proof did not support the allegation; but Abbott J. thought otherwise, and that a presentment at Guildford, defendant not being there, was a presentment to defendant; and verdict for plaintiff.

[(*a*) Stewart v. Eden, 2 Cain. R. 121. Livingston J. who delivered the opinion of the court, said, that "the present averment was sufficiently supported by testimony, that the makers, on inquiry at their store, could not be found; and that payment was therefore demanded of a clerk, who said they were out of town, and had left no instructions to pay the note."

(128) Boehm v. Campbell, Gow. 55. In an action by drawer against guarantee of acceptor, averment that the bill was presented for payment by one J. S. at the place where the acceptance made it payable: plaintiff proved a presentment there, but not by J. S.; and Dallas, C. J. held the substantive part of the allegation proved, and plaintiff had a verdict.

(129) Rumball v. Ball, 10 Mod. 38. Debt upon a note, by which the defendant acknowledged himself indebted, and promised to pay on demand: it was urged in arrest of judgment, that it was not alleged that there had been a demand; but the court held the allegation unnecessary.

became payable, this (130) must be that very day; where there is such averment, exactness as to the day is, probably, immaterial.

In an action against the acceptor of a bill payable a limited time after sight, if the declaration allege a presentment for payment, mistaking the day on which such presentment was made is immaterial. (131)

Especially if it is alleged that it was presented when it became due and payable, and it was in fact presented on the day it became due, (131)

19². "Did not, &c." In an action against the maker upon a note payable at the house of a third person, if a presentment there is stated, it is not necessary to state a special refusal there: the general allegation at the end of the declaration, that defendant did not pay, will be sufficient; for payment at that house would have been payment by him, and it would not be true that he had not paid, had there been a payment there. (132)

---

(130) See Rushton v. Aspinall, ante, p. 281. note (123).

(131) Forman v. Jacob, 1 Stark. 46. In an action by endorsee against acceptor on a bill payable fifty days after sight, the declaration alleged an acceptance 11th August, and that when the bill became due and payable, viz. on 3d of October, it was presented for payment. It appeared in evidence that the acceptance was not till the 19th of September, nor the presentment for payment till the 11th of November; and it was urged that these mistakes were fatal: Lord Ellenborough thought not, and the plaintiff had a verdict.

[A declaration against the drawer of a bill averred, that when it "became due and payable according to the tenor and effect thereof, to wit, on the 31st of March, 1822," it was duly presented for payment. On special demurrer stating for cause, that the 31st of March was Sunday, the declaration was held sufficient. The court said, "The presentment is stated to have been made when the bill became due and payable, according to the tenor and effect thereof. That is quite sufficient, as the tenor and effect of the bill will appear upon the face of it. Besides, as it is laid under a *scilicet*, the precise day is not material, and need not be proved." Bymer v. Russell, 7 Moore, 266. S. P. Norton v. Lewis, 2 Conn. R. 478.]

(132) Butterworth v. Lord Le Despencer, 3 Maule and Sel. 150. Payee against maker on note payable at the house of Wright and Co. A presentment at Wright and Co.'s was stated, and it was alleged at the end of the declaration that the defendant, although often requested, had not paid, &c.; but there was no special allegation of non-payment upon the presentment at Wright and Co.'s. Defendant demurred on this ground; but on argument, the court was clear that the general allegation of non-payment sufficiently negatived any payment at Wright and Co.'s, and judgment was given for the plaintiff.

20. "Neither, &c." Where the plaintiff states that the sum of money mentioned in the bill was not paid, this allegation is not (133) necessary.

21. "Nor, &c." This (134) allegation is unnecessary.

22. "Protested, &c." The protest (135) need not be stated in an action on an in inland bill; in an action on a foreign one the plaintiff (136) must either state it, or (137) shew that it was not necessary; but the omission can (138) only be taken advantage of by a special demurrer.

---

(133) Starke v. Cheeseman, Carth. 509. The declaration stated that the defendant made three bills of exchange, all of the same date and contents, and by the second required the drawee (the first and third of the said bills not being paid) to pay, &c.; that the drawee was not to be found, and the said sum of money in the said bill mentioned was not paid: after judgment by default, it was objected in arrest of judgment, that there was no averment, that the first and third bills were not paid; but it was answered, that the allegation *that the money in the said bill mentioned* was not paid supplied the want of the averment, because the sum was the same in all the bills; and the plaintiff had judgment.

East v. Essington, Lord Raym. 810. Salk. 130. Assumpsit against the acceptor of the following bill, "Pray, pay this my first bill of exchange, the second and third not being paid." After verdict for the plaintiff, it was moved in arrest of judgment, because there was no averment, that the second and third were not paid: sed non allocatur; for per curiam, though it had been ill upon demurrer, yet it is aided by the verdict; for if the second or third had been paid, the jury would have found non-assumpsit.

Wegersloffe v. Keene, Str. 214. In assumpsit against the acceptor upon a bill by which the drawer requested him to pay "that his first bill (his second not being paid)" the declaration stated that the defendant promised to pay the money, but had not; the defendant pleaded an insufficient plea, and upon demurrer to the replication, objected that there was no averment that the second bill was not paid; but the objection was overruled, and judgment given for the plaintiff.

(134) Vide post, c. 11.

(135) See Brough v. Parkins, ante. p. 167. note (85).

(136) Salomons v. Stavely, cited Dougl. 2d ed. 684. n. 144. The court held, on the authority of the precedent in Dunstar v. Pierce, Lill. Ent. 55. that the neglect to allege a protest in an action on a foreign bill, was matter of form only, and could not be taken advantage of on a general demurrer.

[See Patterson v. Becher, 6 Moore, 319.]

(137) In Rogers v. Stephens, supra, p. 187. note (117). Lord Kenyon, and afterwards the court, held a protest for non-acceptance not necessary to support an action against the drawer, because it appeared he had no effects in the hands of the drawee. See Legge v. Thorpe, ante, p. 192. note (119). And see the form of averring that the drawer had no effects in the hands of the drawee, in Legge v. Thorpe, 12 East. Rep. 171.

(138) Vide supra, note (136).

In stating the protest, if the plaintiff allege, "*that* (139) *he protested the bill or caused it to be proteseed,*" it will be unobjectionable, if the defendant pleads over.

23. "Notice." If the defendant is primâ facie entitled to notice, it is essentially necessary to state that he had (140) notice, or to shew that he was not entitled thereto.

Under an allegation of notice, it may be questionable whether evidence can be given of what would excuse notice (141), or whether to let in such evidence, the facts to excuse notice should not be pleaded specially. (141)

---

(139) Witherby v. Sarsfield, 1 Show. 125. The declaration upon a foreign bill stated that the plaintiff "protested it, or caused it to be protested;" the defendant pleaded that he was not a merchant, and upon demurrer had judgment. A writ of error was brought; and it was then, for the first time, urged that the allegation that the plaintiff protested the bill or caused it to be protested, was uncertain; but the court thought it well enough, reversed the judgment below, and then judgment was given for the plaintiff.

(140) See Rushton v. Aspinall, ante, p. 281. n. (123). And see the form of averring that the drawer of a bill had no effects in the hands of the drawee, in Legge v. Thorpe, 12 East. Rep. 171.

[A statute of Virginia gives an action of *debt* against the endorser of a bill, but says nothing of the notice to be given him. It was held that it was still necessary in an action against him to aver and prove a notice of protest, and that the omission to aver it in the declaration was fatal. Slacum v. Pomery, 6 Cranch, 221.]

(141) Corey v. Scott, B. R. Tr. 1 Geo. 4. 3 Barnew. 619. In an action by endorsee against drawer, the declaration stated presentment for payment and dishonor, whereof drawer afterwards, &c. had notice: at the trial there was no evidence of notice, but plaintiff proved that defendant had no effects in the drawer's hands: defendant rebutted this proof by shewing that he and the acceptor only lent their names to a subsequent endorser, and therefore that defendant on paying the bill would have been entitled to sue the acceptor and that subsequent endorser. Under these circumstances Abbott C. J. held notice necessary, and nonsuited, giving plaintiff leave to move to enter a verdict: rule nisi accordingly. On cause shewn, it was urged that under the allegation of notice plaintiff had no right to give evidence of what went only to excuse want of notice, and of that opinion were Bayley and Holroyd, Js.; but on the merits, they agreed with Abbott C. J., that defendant was entitled to notice; and the rule was discharged. See 12 East, 171.

[In a case where notice to the defendant was averred in the declaration, Parsons C. J., delivering the opinion of the court, said, that the facts proved were "not evidence of the notice stated in the declaration. But had the use of due diligence been averred, instead of notice being in fact given, the case would have shown sufficient evidence of such diligence." Blakely v. Grant, 6 Mass. R. 386. The case however turned on another point. But see Norton v. Lewis, ante, p. 283, and Williams v. Matthews, ante, p. 282. It is held that a subsequent promise to pay is evidence to support the averment of due notice. See the cases in Ch. xi. note (22).]

[A general averment of notice is sufficient. (*a*)

If the endorser of a note dies before it becomes due, notice should be alleged to his executors, not to him. (*b*)]

24. "To the said John." In an action upon a bill or note stated upon the count to be payable to the order of the plaintiff, it is sometimes (142) usual, though (143) unnecessary, to insert here an allegation that the plaintiff made no order; but the better way upon a bill or note made so payable, is to state according to the legal operation, that it was made payable to the plaintiff, and then this allegation would be impertinent.

25. "When, &c." In an action against the acceptor of a bill or maker of a note not payable immediately upon presentment, instead of alleging that the defendant became liable, and promised to pay *when he should be thereunto afterwards requested*, he is stated to have become liable, and promised to pay *according to the tenor and effect of the bill and acceptance* in the one case, and *of the note* in the other.

26. "And, &c." This clause is unnecessary in an action against either the (144) acceptor of a bill or the maker of

---

[(*a*) The declaration against the drawer of a bill, after the usual averments of non-acceptance, and protest, &c. proceeded, "of all which said premises, the said defendant afterwards, to wit, on —— at —— had notice." On demurrer, it was objected that the notice to the defendant of the protest for non-acceptance and non-payment was not sufficiently averred. Kent C. J. delivered the opinion of the court. "The general averment of notice of all the antecedent promises was sufficient, and is conformable to approved precedents." Boot v. Franklin, 3 Johns. R. 208.]

[(*b*) See Stewart v. Eden, post.]

(142) It was done in Fisher v. Pomfret, Cart. 403.

(143) Vide Frederick v. Cotton, ante, p. 274. note (100).

See Lill. Ent. 90. 29, 41. 44, 55. 73. Lutw. 1589.

Sheldon v. Occarsen, Tr. T. 41 Geo. 3. 12 June, 1801. C. B. Roll. 715. Special demurrer to a declaration on a bill stated to be payable to the *order* of the plaintiff; and the cause assigned was, that it was not stated that the plaintiff had made no order: the court said, that it was too clear for argument, and gave judgment for the plaintiff. Best Serj. was to have argued for the defendant. S. P. Smith v. M'Clure, 5 East. Rep. 476.

(144) Wegersloffe v. Keene, Str. 214. In assumpsit against the acceptor, an objection was taken to the promise as stated; sed per Fortescue J., "The plaintiff need not set out any promise. In Lowther v. Conyers, which was upon a promissory note, they left out super se assumpsit, and yet it was held well enough, for the law raises a promise."

a note; and it may be doubted whether (145) it is essential in any other.

[But in an action against the executors of the endorser of a note, who died before it became due, it was held that an averment in the declaration of notice to the endorser, and a promise by him, could not be supported. (*a*)]

27. "And the said, &c." This averment is not, it is apprehended, ever necessary; the want (146) of it is certainly cured by verdict.

In an action by a person who has paid a bill under protest, for the honor of drawer or an endorser, it is sufficient for him to allege that he, according to the usage and custom of merchants, paid the bill: he need not specify to whom he paid it. (147) (*a*)

---

(145) Starke v. Cheeseman, Carth. 509. Salk. 128. After judgment by default in an action against the drawer of a foreign bill, it was objected in arrest of judgment, that it was not stated in the declaration that the defendant promised to pay the money after the protest was made; but it was answered, that the law did raise the promise upon the custom of merchants, and therefore it was not necessary to lay an actual promise; and the plaintiff had judgment.

[A declaration which stated that the defendant by his note promised to pay A. B. or bearer, and alleging the plaintiff to be the bearer, was on demurrer held good, though it did not allege notice to the defendant, and a consequent liability and promise by him to pay the plaintiff. Dole v. Weeks, 4 Mass. R. 451.]

[(*a*) The endorser of a note died before it became due. In an action on the note against his executors, the declaration alleged notice of the non-payment to him, and a consequent liability, and promise to pay by him. The court held that as the endorser was dead at the time of the notice to him, and alleged promise by him, the evidence did not support the declaration, and nonsuited the plaintiffs. Stewart v. Eden, 2 Cain. R. 121.]

(146) Simmonds v. Parminter, 1 Wils. 185. 4 Bro. Parl. Cas. 604. The declaration upon two foreign bills for the payment of 4000 and 5000 dollars did not state what their value was, and after a demurrer this was urged as a ground to arrest the judgment; but the court gave judgment for the plaintiff, and upon a writ of error that judgment was affirmed.

[In a declaration in Virginia on a bill payable in pounds sterling, it seems that not averring the value of the pounds sterling in the declaration, is not a material defect, the value of pounds sterling being fixed there by statute; but if it is a defect it is cured by verdict. Brown v. Barry, 3 Dall. R. 365.]

(147) Cox v. Earle, 3 Barnew. and Ald. 430. Declaration against acceptor on bill paid by plaintiff under protest for the honor of the second endorser stated, that plaintiff, according to the usage and custom of merchants, paid the bill under protest: special demurrer, on the

ground that it was not alleged to whom plaintiff paid it, or that he paid it to the holder, or that plaintiff thereby became the legal holder thereof: sed per cur. on argument, payment to a wrong person would be no payment; this payment is alleged to have been according to the usage and custom of merchants, and plaintiff would be bound to prove payment to the person entitled to receive. Judgment for plaintiff.

[(*a*) Action on a note dated 15th July, acknowledging a certain sum to be due the plaintiff with interest from the 1st day of June. Demurrer for uncertainty in not stating what June. Per Curiam. "The count is good. When a day or month is mentioned as antecedent or subsequent to a contract, and the precise day or month is not specified, it means the time nearest to the date of the contract. Here the 1st of June must mean the preceding 1st of June." Whitney v. Crosby, 3 Cain. R. 89.

In Massachusetts it has been held that notes not negotiable, may be declared on like negotiable notes, in an action by the payee against the maker, or the endorsee against his endorser. See Jones v. Fales, ante, p. 7.

In Virginia, a declaration by the assignee of a note against the maker is not sufficient to maintain the action, if it do not state that the defendant failed to pay the money to the payee of the note as well as to the plaintiff. Norvell v. Hudgins, 4 Munf. 496.

In an action of debt by the assignee against the maker of a note, which is authorized by statute in Virginia, the averment that the assignment of it to the plaintiff was *for value received*, is immaterial. For the assignee without value, can as well maintain the action, as the assignee for a valuable consideration. In such case, where the defendant pleaded the bankruptcy of the assignor, a replication stating that the note was giving to the assignor *in trust for the plaintiff*, was held to be no departure from the declaration. Marshall C. J. said that the majority of the court were of opinion that "the duty created by the trust, and which was discharged by the assignment, might be considered as constituting a valuable consideration to support the averment, and prevent the replication from being a departure." Wilson v. Codman, 3 Cranch, 193.

But where the payee of a note endorsed it without recourse, and his assignee brought an action against him on the note on the ground that he had received the money from the maker, the court appeared to think the count defective for "not stating the endorsement was for a valuable consideration." Welch v. Lindo, 7 Cranch, 159.

Where the declaration stated the assignment to be for *value received*, and the assignment produced in evidence contained no expression of a valuable consideration, but was expressed to be "*without recourse*," the variance was held immaterial. Wilson v. Codman, 3 Cranch, 193.

In an action of debt, under the Virginia statute, against the endorser of a bill, the declaration which was for the principal, interest, damages, and *charges of protest*, without averring the amount of the charges, was on that account held bad. The court said that it was "material in the action of debt, that the declaration should state the demand with certainty." Wilson v. Lenox, 1 Cranch, 194.]

CHAP. X.

Remedy upon a Bill or Note by proving it under a Commission of Bankruptcy, or suing out a Commission thereon.

WHEREVER the holder of a bill or note is entitled to compel a person to pay it, he (1) may, in the event of such person's bankruptcy, prove the amount under his commission; and whatever would be a defence to a suit, (2) will be an answer to such proof.

And a bill or note (3) may be proved before it has become

---

(1) In ex parte Dewdney, 15 Ves. 495. Lord Eldon C. held that where recovery in an action on a bill would be barred by a plea of the statute of limitations, and all relief in equity would be equally defeated by lapse of time, to which courts of equity, in analogy to the statute of limitations, give similar effect, the bill could not be proved under a commission of bankruptcy; and after reasoning on the inconsistency which would result from a contrary doctrine, his lordship observed, "that consideration, among others, furnishes a ground for concluding that the real meaning of the legislature in those acts (the bankruptcy statutes) requiring the Lord Chancellor to give execution to all the creditors, was, that this species of execution should be given to those creditors, who, if a commission of bankruptcy had not issued, could, by legal or equitable remedies, have compelled payment." See 1 Sch. and Lefr. 48. Where the holder has bought bills or notes for less than the money payable upon them, (as in ex parte Lee, 1 P. Wms. 782., where he bought notes for 10*s.* in the pound,) or where he has discounted them, (as in ex parte Marlar, 1 Atk. 150.) as he might have recovered in an action, so he may prove under a commission of bankruptcy, to the full amount.

(2) As to such objections as arise from the form of the bill or note, vide ante, c. 1., also ex parte Adney, Cowp. 460., and ex parte Tootell, 4 Ves. 372. As to the sufficiency of the stamp, vide ante, c. 3. As to the transfer, vide ante, chap. 5. Acceptance, chap. 6. As to the effect of laches, vide ante, chap. 7. As to the legality of the consideration, vide post, chap. 12.

(3) By 7 Geo. 1. c. 31. § 1, after reciting that traders had been obliged to sell their goods upon trust or credit, "and to take bills, bonds, promissory notes, or other persons' securities for their moneys, payable at the end of three, four, or six months, or other future day of payment," and that it had become a question whether "such persons giving such credit on such securities," could be let in to prove their debts before the securities became payable, it is enacted, "That all and every person and persons who have given credit, or at any time or times hereafter shall give credit on such securities as aforesaid to any person or persons, who is, are, or shall become bankrupts, upon a good and valuable consideration *bonâ fide* for any sum or sums of money or other matter or thing whatsoever which is or shall not be due or paya-

due, deducting, on payment of the dividend, a rebate of legal interest for such time as it may then have to run; and it may (under certain (4) restrictions) be proved, though the bankrupt's liability commenced after his act of bankruptcy, and within two calendar months before the date of his commission.

So the money payable upon a bill or note, if of the requisite amount, though not yet due, (5) will be a good petitioning creditor's debt to support a commission of bankruptcy.

And a commission may issue against the drawer of a bill before it becomes due. (6)

And the commission will stand, though the bill when due is paid by the drawee. (6)

---

ble at or before the time of such person's becoming bankrupt, shall be admitted to prove his, her, and their several and respective bills, bonds, notes, or other securities, promise, or agreements for the same, in like manner as if they were made payable presently, and not at a future day; and shall be entitled unto and shall have and receive a proportionable part, share, and dividend of such bankrupt's estate in proportion to the other creditors of such bankrupt, deducting only thereout a rebate of interest and discounting such securities payable at future times after the rate of five pounds per centum per annum for what he shall so receive to be computed from the actual payment thereof to the time such debt, duty, or sum of money should or would have become due and payable in and by such securities as aforesaid."—And by § 2. the bankrupt shall be discharged by his certificate, of and "from all and every such bond, note, or other security as aforesaid."

(4) Vide post, p. 293. to 295., and 46 Geo. 3. c. 135. § 2., post, p. 294. n. (12).

(5) By 7 Geo. 1. c. 31. § 3. it was provided, "That no such creditor (i. e. upon bill, bond, promissory note, or other persons' securities not yet due), shall be deemed or taken to be a sufficient creditor, for or in respect of such debt, to petition or join in any petition for the obtaining or suing forth of any commission of bankruptcy, until such time as such debt shall become actually due and payable." But by 5 Geo. 2. c. 30. § 22., after reciting such provision, it is enacted, "That so much of the said act as disables any such person from petitioning for, or joining in any petition for a commission against any person or persons who have before committed any act of bankruptcy, is hereby repealed: and it shall and may be lawful hereafter, for such person to petition for, or join in petitioning for any such commission of bankruptcy; any thing in the said act contained to the contrary thereof, in any wise notwithstanding."

Note, that in 7 G. 1. c. 31. § 1. the language is, "other persons' securities," (and it is so in the parliament roll) but in 5 G. 2. c. 30. § 22. (which professes to recite the substance of the former) it is, "other personal securities."

(6) Ex parte Douthat, 4 Barnew. and Ald. 67. Douthat owed Wade £148, and in order to pay him drew on Eyre and Miller, in favor of

And it is sufficient, if the money payable to the holder, be, at the time of (7) petitioning, of the requisite amount, though, by reason of the rebate of interest, it was not of that amount at the time of the act of bankruptcy; but it must be of the requisite amount at the time of the petition.

If, therefore, the bill or note be not *then* due, it would (8) seem that he must be a creditor for such sum as, after deducting the rebate of interest for the time which the bill or note has to run, will leave a debt of the requisite amount.

And upon bills or notes which are due at the time of the

Wade or order, at four months' date: Eyre and Miller acccepted the bill, and paid it when due; but in the interim Douthat committed an act of bankruptcy, and Wade sued out a commission against him, and proved the bill. Case from chancery on the question, whether under these circumstances there was at the date of the commission a good petitioning creditor's debt? the court certified that there was, and their opinion seemed to be founded not on there being a pre-existing debt to Wade, but on the ground that the statutes 7 G. 1. c. 31. and 5 Geo. 2. c. 30. § 22. extended to drawers and endorsers of bills as well as acceptors; and that if such drawer or endorser committed an act of bankruptcy before the bill was due, a commission might at once be sued out thereon.

(7) Brett v. Levett, 13 East. Rep. 213. In an action by the assignee of a bankrupt against the sheriff, and verdict for the plaintiff, a rule nisi to set aside the verdict was granted, on a question as to the sufficiency of the petitioning creditor's debt. The debt arose on two bills of exchange, each for £50, drawn by the bankrupt, and transferred to the petitioning creditor before the act of bankruptcy; both were dishonored by the drawee. The act of bankruptcy was on the 28th Dec. 1809, and the commission was dated 8th Feb. 1810. Each bill became due before the petition for the commission, but *after the act of bankruptcy.* At the time of the *act of bankruptcy*, therefore, there was not a debt of £100 due to the petitioning creditor, but only that sum minus the rebate of interest for the time which the bills had to run; and it was contended that at *that* time there ought to have been such debt due. But the court, after referring to 7 Geo. 1. c. 31. § 3., which disabled a creditor, by a bill or note, payable at a future day, from petitioning for a commission in respect of such debt, "until such time as such debt shall become actually due and payable," and to 5 Geo. 2. c. 30. § 22., which removes such disability, held clearly, that it was sufficient if a debt of the requisite amount were due at the time of petitioning. Rule discharged. See also the judgment of Lord Kenyon in Glaister v. Hewer, infra.

(8) See 7 G. 1. c. 31. § 1. & 3., and 5 G. 2. c. 30. § 22. & 23. The petitioning creditor must, at the time of petitioning, make an affidavit that £100 is due to him from the bankrupt. But if this debt arise from a bill or note for £100 not then due, the sum *then* due to him is £100 minus the amount of discount; and if the bill or note be drawn payable at a very distant day, the discount may greatly diminish the sum then payable, and may possibly nearly exhaust it.

petition, interest cannot be taken into the account, unless it is expressly made payable on the face of the bill or note. (9)

Where it is so payable it may. (9)

The holder (10) may petition for a commission of bankruptcy, in respect of the money payable upon a bill or note, or may prove the amount under a commission when issued, notwithstanding the bill or note may not have been transferred to him until after the act of bankruptcy committed, provided the bankrupt's liability had commenced before the act of bankauptcy.

For the case of a bill or note being one in which the law admits of the assignment of a chose in action, the assignee becomes a creditor as from the time of the original creation of the debt, and not from that of the assignment.

---

(9) Cameron v. Smith, 2 Barnew. and Ald. 305. A commission was founded on an acceptance for £96, 17*s.* 8*d.* The bill was so long over due that near £5 was due for interest, but no interest was expressly made payable by the bill. The point was reserved whether this debt would support the commission, and, after argument, the court was clear it would not; for, though interest, if expressly reserved constituted part of the debt, if it was not expressly reserved, it constituted damages only, and damages cannot be considered part of the debt.

(10) Glaister v. Hewer, 7 Term Rep. 498. The plaintiff being indebted to Hewer in a sum below £100, and to Wilson on a note for £11, 12*s.*, committed an act of bankruptcy; on which, Wilson, for a valuable consideration, endorsed his note to Hewer to enable him to petition for a commission: the two sums together amounting to above £100. In an action of trover for goods taken by the assignees, brought to try the validity of the commission, the only question was, whether Hewer's were a sufficient debt to support the commission, it not being so when the act of bankruptcy was committed, inasmuch as the whole did not then exist in *him.* Rooke J. thought it was, and on a rule nisi to enter a verdict for the plaintiff, Lord Kenyon said the statute only required that there should be an existing debt of £100 in the petitioning creditor; this petitioning creditor had such a debt at the time of petitioning, and that is sufficient to support the commission. Rule discharged.

Bingley v. Maddison, Co. B. L. 20. A note was given by the bankrupt in January, which became due in June. The act of bankruptcy was in October following, and the endorsement in November. The endorsee was the petitioning creditor, and sued out the commission. It was contended, that at the time of the bankruptcy the petitioning creditor had no debt, and that therefore the commission could not be supported. But the court said that this was a case in which the law allowed the assignment of a chose in action: that the assignment related to the original debt: that the endorsee always came in under the commission, because the endorsement related to the original debt: that it stood thus upon principle; and that the cases were clear, explicit, and positive, and of the highest nature: they therefore held the commission valid.

And though the bankrupt may have committed an act of bankruptcy before he became a party to the bill or note, it will not (11) invalidate a commission of bankruptcy issued on the petition of the holder, (12) or prevent his proving the amount under a commission, provided, in the former case, there is a subsequent act of bankruptcy sufficient to support the commission, (13) and in the latter that he had become such party before the (14) date of the commission;

(11) By 46 G. 3. c. 135. § 5. it is enacted, "That no commission of bankrupt that shall be hereafter issued, shall be avoided or defeated by reason of any act of bankruptcy having been committed by the person or any of the persons against whom such commission shall have issued, prior to the contracting the debt of the creditor or any of the creditors upon whose petition such commission shall have issued, if such petitioning creditor had not any notice of such act of bankruptcy at the time when the debt to him was contracted; but that such commission of bankrupt, and all the proceedings under the same shall be valid and effectual to all intents and purposes, notwithstanding that such prior act or acts of bankruptcy shall have been committed by such bankrupt."

(12) By 46 G. 3. c. 135. § 2. it is enacted, "That in all cases of commissions of bankrupt hereafter to be issued, all and every person and persons with whom the bankrupt shall have really and bonâ fide contracted any debt or debts before the date and suing forth of such commission, which, if contracted before any act of bankruptcy committed, might have been proved under such commission, shall, notwithstanding any prior act of bankruptcy may have been committed by the bankrupt, be admitted to prove such debt or debts, and to stand, and be a creditor under such commission, to all intents and purposes whatever, in like manner, as if no such prior act of bankruptcy had been committed by such bankrupt, provided such creditor or creditors had not, at the time of such debt or debts being contracted, any notice of any prior act of bankruptcy by such bankrupt committed."

(13) E. Moss v. Smith, 1 Campb. N. P. C. 489. To an action against the sheriff for a false return of nulla bona to a writ of fi. fa. issued against David Moss's goods, the defence was the bankruptcy of D. M. before the delivery of the writ. On the 8th of December, 1807, he committed an act of bankruptcy; on which a commission issued, founded on a debt contracted for goods sold on a credit which did not expire until the 11th of December. On the 29th his goods were taken under the fi. fa.; but the execution was withdrawn on notice of the bankruptcy. Lord Ellenborough held that the commission could not be supported, as the petitioning creditor's debt was not due when the act of bankruptcy was committed; and that it was not a case within 46 G. 3. c. 135. Verdict for the plaintiff. And on motion afterwards for a new trial, the court refused a rule. And per Lord Ellenborough, the grievance which that statute meant to remedy was the practice of upsetting commissions of bankrupt, by unexpectedly proving an act of bankruptcy prior to that relied upon by the assignees.

(14) See 46 G. 3. c. 135. § 2. supra. note (12).

and in each, that the holder had not any (15) notice of a prior act of bankruptcy.

If an endorser of a bill or note be obliged, in consequence of the bankruptcy of an antecedent party to pay it, he (16) may prove the amount under his commission, though he did not make the payment until after the commission issued. And though the endorsement were lent merely to give credit to the bill or note, (17) he may prove it independently of 49 G. 3. c. 121. § 8., unless the bankrupt were the person to whom such endorsement was lent.

---

(15). See 46 G. 3. c. 135. § 2 and 5. ante, p. 294. note (12). and p. 294. note (11).

(16) Joseph v. Orme, 2 New Rep. 180. The plaintiff being holder of a bill accepted by the defendant, endorsed it for a valuable consideration to Adams. Before the maturity of the bill, a commission of bankruptcy issued against the defendant: and the plaintiff was afterwards obliged to pay the bill to Adams, and now sued the defendant as acceptor. The defendant having received his certificate, obtained a rule nisi to enter an exoneretur on the bail piece; and after cause shewn, the court held that the plaintiff might have proved the bill under the commission, and therefore made the rule absolute.

(17) Ex parte Brymer, Cooke, B. L. 165. To enable Scott and Pearson to raise money, Forsyth drew three bills on Wilkins, which the latter accepted, dated the 28th of May, 1787, for £800 each, payable three months after date; two to the order of Span, and the third to the order of the drawer, which last was endorsed in blank by the drawer. They were then sent to Scott and Pearson, and by them to Span, who endorsed them, got them discounted, and remitted the money to Scott and Pearson. Before the bills became due Scott and Wilkins became bankrupt; Span was afterwards obliged to take up the bills, and was admitted to prove under Wilkins's commission; and on a petition to have that proof expunged, the chancellor said, the debt accrued by the acceptance, and Span became a holder in a fair way. Petition dismissed. And on a second petition for a rehearing, the chancellor continued of the same opinion.

Houle v. Baxter, 3 East's Rep. 177. The defendant, a retail silversmith, ordered goods of Capper, a working silversmith, and to enable him to obtain silver for the order, accepted a bill drawn on him by Capper; and to increase the credit of the bill, Capper prevailed on the plaintiff to lend his endorsement. Capper then passed the bill to Abud, who supplied the silver of which the goods were made and delivered to the defendant. On the 7th of November, 1796, the defendant became bankrupt, and afterwards obtained his certificate. On the 24th of December, 1796, the day before the bill became due, the plaintiff took it up from Abud, and now sued the defendant as acceptor. A verdict was found for the plaintiff subject to the opinion of the court. And Grose J., who delivered the opinion of the court, said, that here the plaintiff never became surety to the *defendant;* his demand arises solely on the bill, and there was nothing to prevent his proving it under the commission. The bankrutcy and certificate is therefore a bar. Nonsuit entered.

If the bankrupt were the person to whom the endorsement was lent, in which case the endorser is a mere surety, he will be entitled under 49 G. 3. c. 121 § 8. on taking up the bill or note to stand in the place of the holder, if he had proved under the commission, and to prove himself, if the holder had not, provided in such case he had not notice, when he lent his endorsement, that the person to whom he lent it had committed any act of bankruptcy or become insolvent, or stopped payment.

And a surety has this right, though he did not become surety until after the principal had committed an act of bankruptcy.

The issuing of a commission, though such commission may afterwards be superseded (18) will be deemed such notice.

---

(18) By 49 Geo. 3. c. 121. § 8. it is enacted, That in all cases of commissions of bankrupt already issued, under which no dividend has yet been made, or under which the creditors, who have not proved, can receive a dividend equally in proportion to their respective debts without disturbing any dividend already made, and in all cases of commissions of bankrupts hereafter to be issued, where at the time of issuing the commission any person shall be surety for or be liable for any debt of the bankrupt, it shall be lawful for such surety or person liable, if he shall have paid the debt, or any part thereof in discharge of the whole debt, although he may have paid the same after the commission shall have issued, and the creditor shall have proved his debt under the commission, to stand in the place of the creditor as to the dividends upon such proof; and when the creditor shall not have proved under the commission, it shall be lawful for such surety, or person liable, to prove his demand in respect of such payment as a debt under the commission, not disturbing the former dividends, and to receive a dividend or dividends proportionably with the other creditors taking the benefit of such commission, notwithstanding such person may have become surety or liable for the debt of the bankrupt after an act of bankruptcy had been committed by such bankrupt, provided that such person had not at the time when he became such surety, or when he so became liable for the debt of such bankrupt, notice of any act of bankruptcy by such bankrupt committed, or that he was insolvent, or had stopped payment; provided always, that the issuing a commission of bankrupt, although such commission shall afterwards be superseded, shall be deemed such notice; and every person against whom any such commission of bankrupt has been or shall be awarded, and who has obtained or shall obtain his certificate, shall be discharged of all demands at the suit of every such person having so paid, or being hereby enabled to prove as aforesaid, or to stand in the place of such creditor as aforesaid, with regard to his debt in respect of such suretyship or liability, in like manner to all intents and purposes as if such person had been a creditor before the bankruptcy of the bankrupt for the whole of the debt in respect of

If an acceptance for the accommodation of the drawer of a bill be given before, and renewed after, he has committed an act of bankruptcy, such renewal is a continuation of the same suretyship; and therefore if a commission of bankruptcy be issued against the drawer, and the acceptor afterwards pay the bill, he (19) will be entitled to prove the amount under such commission; though, before the renewal of the acceptance, he had notice of such act of bankruptcy having been committed.

Nor will the case be varied in principle, by the circumstance of the holder of the first bill, having, before the renewal (20) given time to the drawer; or by that of (21) an additional name, as that of an endorser, having been lent upon the second bill.

---

which he was surety or was so liable as aforesaid. Vide Stedman v. Martinnant, next note. For the law before this act, vide Snaith v. Gale, 7 Term Rep. 364.

(19) Stedman v. Martinnant, 13 East's Rep. 127., and vide S. C. 12 East's Rep. 664. On 5th of January, 1807, the plaintiff accepted a bill for the accommodation of the defendant, the drawer, which became due on the 19th of March, when it was dishonored. On the 18th of March, 1807, a docket was struck against the defendant, and on the 21st a commission of bankrupt was issued, which was superseded on the 15th of April. A meeting of the defendant's creditors was then held, when time was given to pay his debts by instalments. On the 9th of June, 1807, the plaintiff accepted a second bill for the defendant, in order to take up the former one, for the same sum with the addition of interest and stamp: and the endorsement of a third person was lent as an additional security, which was required by the holders of the former bill, On the 6th of August, 1807, a valid commission was issued against the defendant, founded on an act of bankruptcy committed in the preceding March. The second bill became due on the 12th of September, 1807, when the plaintiff paid it. The first dividend under the commission was declared and made on the 6th of August, 1808. On the 4th of September, 1809, the defendant obtained his certificate. In an action for money paid, and the bankruptcy and certificate pleaded, a verdict was found for the plaintiff subject to the opinion of the court, as to whether the certificate were a discharge. The court (Le Blanc J. absente) held that the second acceptance was a continuation of the same suretyship, which was created by the first; and that as such suretyship commenced before any act of bankruptcy committed, and consequently before the plaintiff could have any notice of such act, the plaintiff might, by 49 G. 3. c. 121. § 8., have proved his demand under the commission, and therefore the certificate was a bar. Postea to the defendant.

(20) Vide Stedman v. Martinnant, supra, n. (19). It must be presumed that the holder was ignorant of the bills having been accepted for the *accommodation* of the drawer. Vide Laxton v. Peat, ante, p. 224. note (20).

(21) Vide Stedman v. Martinnant, supra, n. (19).

Counter acceptances are good mutual considerations for such acceptances.

Therefore if two traders exchange acceptances and afterwards become bankrupt, each (22) may prove the other's acceptances under his commission.

Though the acceptances of neither be due at the time of such bankruptcy.

Especially where each has (23) engaged to pay his own acceptances.

And if one be obliged to pay the acceptances of both,

---

(22) Rolfe v. Caslon, 2 H. Blackst. 570. Rolfe and Caslon drew two bills of the same tenor and date on each other, and each accepted the other's bill, neither having effects of the other in his hands. Twenty days before the bills were due Caslon became bankrupt. He had endorsed the bill which Rolfe had accepted in part satisfaction of a larger debt, and the creditor proved his whole debt; Rolfe paid the difference of the bill he accepted, allowing for the dividend, and now sued Caslon on his acceptance and for money paid; Caslon pleaded his bankruptcy. Verdict for the plaintiff, with liberty to the defendant to move to set it aside. On motion accordingly and rule nisi, it was urged for the plaintiff that this acceptance could not have been proved under the commission, because it created no debt to Rolfe, unless he paid the bill which Caslon drew; and at the time of the bankruptcy it was uncertain and contingent whether he would pay such bill; but the court was clear that the mutual acceptances constituted a debt on each side; and that the defendant's acceptance might have been proved under the commission, and that therefore the certificate was a bar. Rule absolute. Vide also Buckler v. Buttevant, post, p. 299. note (25).

(23) Cowley v. Dunlop, 7 Term Rep. 565. The Peters and Dunlops exchanged acceptances to the amount of £3000 and upwards, under an agreement that each should provide for their own acceptances. Both houses became bankrupt, and obtained their certificates. The Peters paid part of their acceptances, and their assignees paid dividends upon the rest, and also upon Dunlop's acceptances. Dunlop's acceptances were also proved under Dunlop's commission, and a dividend paid thereon. The Peters' assignees having paid considerably more than the Peters' proportion upon the bills, brought an action for money paid against the Dunlops; the question was, whether their bankruptcy was a bar. After two arguments, the court was divided: Lawrence and Grose, Js. thought it was, because the assignees had no claim in respect of the Peters' acceptances, inasmuch as by the agreement they were to provide for them; and the claim on the acceptances of the Dunlops was barred by the certificate, because at the time of the bankruptcy, they were debita solvenda in futuro; Rolfe v. Caslon: and the assignees had no better claim than if the Peters had been holders at the time of the bankruptcy. Ashhurst J. thought it no bar, because the Peters were to be considered as sureties. Lord Kenyon thought the Peters could not be remitted to their original right as drawers, because the bills had been already proved and a dividend paid under the Dunlops' commission.

and the other afterwards obtain his certificate, the party paying (24) cannot recover any of the money so paid from the other; for as to his own acceptances the party paying was bound by his engagement to provide for them; and as to the other's, they were provable under his commission, and therefore his certificate is a discharge.

And it is immaterial whether the acceptances exchanged be the acceptances of the parties themselves, or of (25) other persons.

Nor is it (26) essential that the bills exchanged should agree precisely in amount, or in the times at which they respectively become due; any difference, however, in these respects is evidence of the bills not having been given in exchange for each other.

But the money payable upon such counter acceptances, will (27) not be a good petitioning creditor's debt to support

---

(24) Vide Cowley v. Dunlop in the last note.

(25) Buckler v. Buttivant, 3 East's Rep. 72. The defendants gave the plaintiff their bills, accepted by third persons, in exchange for the plaintiff's acceptances of bills drawn by the defendants on him. Each bill tallied in amount with that for which it was exchanged, excepting that in one instance two bills were given in exchange for one of the aggregate amount of both; and in another instance there was a difference (between the bills last exchanged) of a few shillings which were paid at the time, in order (as it was expressed) "to finish the transaction." They also agreed in dates, excepting that in two instances bills were made payable two days earlier than those for which they were respectively exchanged. And the defendants' letters, in which they enclosed their remittances, always spoke of "valuing" on the plaintiff "for the same amount:" and the whole correspondence pointed at nothing else than an exchange of paper. The defendants became bankrupt; when the commission was issued the plaintiff had paid the whole amount of his acceptances to the holders, excepting £49, and he proved the money so paid, under the commission. He afterwards paid the balance of £49, and brought this action for money paid, to recover that sum. All the bills received by the plaintiff from the defendants were dishonored. A verdict was found for the plaintiff, subject to the opinion of the court. The court held that this was an absolute exchange of acceptances; that each party's remedy against the other was upon the other's bills only; and that therefore this action, which was founded on an implied promise, and not on the bills, could not be supported. Postea to the defendant. Vide Toussaint v. Martinnant, 2 Term Rep. 100.

(26) Vide Buckler v. Buttivant, in the last note.

(27) Sarratt and another v. Austin, 4 Taunt. 200. In trover by the assignees of a bankrupt against the sheriff for goods taken in execution the only question was as to the sufficiency of the petitioning creditor's

a commission; unless it appear that the petitioning creditor has taken up his own acceptances.

And though such counter acceptances may be proved, yet the party who has given the bankrupt his own acceptances in exchange, will not be allowed to (28) receive a dividend upon such proof, until he take up his own acceptances.

---

debt. He and the bankrupt had drawn two bills on each other of precisely the same tenor and dates, and each had accepted the other's bills. Before any of the bills became due, the bankrupt committed an act of bankruptcy, upon which a cammission was issued founded upon the acceptances so given by the bankrupt. None of the bills was due or paid when this action was brought. A verdict was found for the plaintiffs, with liberty to the defendant to move to set it aside and enter a nonsuit. On rule nisi accordingly and cause shewn, three manuscript cases were cited to shew that where there are cross acceptances neither party can prove under a commission of bankruptcy, until he has taken up his own acceptance. Mansfield C. J. said, "If those cases had not been mentioned, I should have had no doubt that either party might prove; that the debt is barred by the certificate has been decided; why is it barred? because it might have been proved under the commission: it is strange to say then that it cannot be proved; either the one or the other must be wrong." And after time taken to consider, his Lordship, in delivering the opinion of the court, said, this question depends on the construction of 7 Geo. 1. c. 31. and 5 Geo. 2. c. 30. taken together: the preamble of the former act only contemplates the case of bills and other securities being taken for *goods sold*, and has not the least mention of their being taken where a debt is not clearly due. The act does not apply to debts in their nature contingent. This debt, though not contingent on the face of the instrument, is thus far in its nature contingent, that, until the party taking the bankrupt's acceptance have paid his counter bill, the court of chancery will restrain him from receiving any dividend: and it would be a singular construction of the statutes that a man, who will not be entitled to receive a shilling out of the bankrupt's estate, unless he take up his own acceptance, should be able to petition for a commission. And no case being cited to shew that he can, the court upon principle think the debt not sufficient to support the commission. Rule absolute.

The enacting part of 7 Geo. 1. c. 31. § 1. only requires that the security be taken upon good and valuable consideration. And according to Rolfe v. Caslon, (ante, p. 298.) a counter acceptance is a good consideration to enable the holder of the bankrupt's acceptance to *prove;* though from this case it appears that it is not so, to enable him to petition.

(28) Whether the not having taken up the counter acceptance will prevent the proof the bankrupt's acceptance, or whether it will only occasion a suspension of the dividend, is a point upon which there have been contradictory decisions; and the text writers have adopted different opinions. In Cooke, B. L. p. 162. it is considered as settled that the proof cannot be permitted until the counter bill be taken up. Mr. Cooke cites ex parte Brown, 23d of December, 1797. That was a

So where a banker from time to time advances money and accepts and discounts bills for a customer, and in return, the latter remits bills drawn by him and accepted by others, and afterwards becomes bankrupt, the banker, though his own acceptances may not then be due, (29) may prove the bills so remitted, under a commission issued against the customer.

But it seems that mere reciprocal accommodations without any specific exchange of bills or notes, will (30) not

---

petition to prove upon an indemnity bond forfeited before the bankruptcy, but the surety the petitioner had not paid his own bond at the time of the petition being heard. The chancellor said, "The debt cannot be twice proved, there is no equity, but by taking up the original bond;" and he dismissed the petition. It must however be observed that here the payment of the money upon the original bond must have been the very condition upon which the bond of indemnity was to be paid. This was the case of principal and surety, which that of cross acceptances has been decided not to be. In Cullen, p. 134. and in Montagu, vol. i. p. 139. it is said that the proof is allowed, but the dividend withholden. And see the judgment of Mansfield C. J. in Sarratt v. Austin, ante, p. 300. n. (27) to the same effect. See also ex parte Bloxham in the next note.

(29) Ex parte Bloxham, 8 Ves. 531. The bankrupt kept an account with the Bloxhams as his bankers; in the course of which they advanced money, and accepted and discounted bills for him; and he, from time to time, remitted bills to them drawn by him and accepted by others; these remittances were made previously to the bankruptcy, some before and some after the acceptances of the bankers. At the date of the commission the bankers were under acceptances, and they held bills so remitted: neither the acceptances or bills being then due. On petition, the chancellor, after referring to ex parte Maydwell, Cooke, B. L. 159. in which Lord Thurlow held that the liability by the acceptance was a good consideration for a promissory note, ordered that the bankers should be permitted to prove the bills upon which the bankrupt's name appeared, to cover their acceptances. See also Bosanquet v. Dudman, post.

(30) Ex parte Walker, 4 Ves. 373. Various accommodation transactions had for many years taken place between Caldwell and Co. and the Brownes. The former were the bankers of the latter. A commission of bankruptcy issued against Caldwell and Co. in March, 1793, and in the same month the Brownes became bankrupt. An account was then taken of the mutual debts and credits. That account consisted, first, of a cash account, which included good bills as well as payments in cash; and secondly, of a bill account which related exclusively to bills which had been passed by one house to the other, and which were all ultimately dishonored. The result was, that on the cash account the Brownes were indebted to Caldwell and Co. in the sum of 40,716*l.* and that on the bill account Caldwell and Co. had received from the Brownes bad bills to the amount of 305,149*l.* 19*s.* 10*d.* and the Brownes had received from Caldwell and Co. bad bills to the amount of 204,910*l.*

create a debt on either side; each party, in such case, becomes surety for the other, and until obliged to pay bills or notes negotiated by the other, acquires no right to sue the other, or in the event of his bankruptcy, to prove under his commission.

And even after he has been so obliged to pay bills or notes negotiated by the other, his right of action, or of proof, does not arise on the other's bills or notes, but in respect of the money paid to the use of the other.

And if both become bankrupt, and the holders of the bills or notes negotiated by each, prove, and receive the dividends upon them, under both commissions, though the one party may have negotiated bills or notes to a greater amount than the other, the assignees of neither will be permitted to (31) prove or claim, under the commission of the other, any

---

5*s*. Of the bad bills received from Caldwell and Co. the Brownes had negotiated bills to the amount of 196,589*l*. 6*s*. 4*d*. and of those received from the Brownes Caldwell and Co. had negotiated bills to the amount of 126,855*l*. 11*s*. 10*d*. having retained the residue (viz. 178,294*l*. 8*s*.) at the request of the Brownes. All the bills received by the Brownes were discountable, and upon most of them they had received the full value; and Caldwell and Co. had no consideration for them but the bad bills received from the Brownes. All the bills (or nearly so) which the Brownes had negotiated were proved against the estate of Caldwell and Co. and by far the greater part against the estate of the Brownes also; but to a large amount, viz. 80,000*l*. the Brownes had deposited bills as a security for the payment of a much smaller sum, so that the proof against them in respect of those bills was only for the sum really due, whereas against Caldwell and Co. the proof was for the whole sum payable on the bills: and the consequence of this and of the unequal negotiation of each other's bills, was, that a much larger sum was proved against Caldwell and Co. in respect of bills negotiated by the Brownes, than against the latter in respect of bills negotiated by the former. And Caldwell and Co. on petition claimed the right to prove the bills which still remained in their hands in order to be reimbursed the difference. But the chancellor said, "Till Caldwell and Co. pay all the creditors of Browne, who are likewise creditors of theirs, 20*s*. in the pound, they would be, by proving, sharing with the creditors of Browne, who are likewise creditors of theirs. If I allow this petition I must do two things that are quite impossible. I must hold that the bankruptcy creates a debt which did not exist antecedently; and I must hold that the same debt may be proved twice." The proof was confined to the balance on the cash account only. This abstract is taken not only from Mr. Vesey's but also Mr. Cooke's report of this case. Cooke, B. L. 162. See also ex parte Earle, 5 Ves. 833.

(31) See ex parte Walker, ante, p. 301. n. (30), The assignees of Caldwell and Co. were not permitted to prove, either on the bills which

dividends which they may have paid on the bills or notes negotiated by the other; because it would be permitting the same debt (to the extent of such dividends) to be twice charged on the same estate.

If a creditor receive bills from his debtor, and negotiate them, and both become bankrupt, the creditor (33) will not be allowed to receive dividends upon his debt until he take up the bills which he has so negotiated; for otherwise the debtor's estate would be charged with both the debt and bills.

Though the drawee of a bill may have no effects of the drawer's in hand, yet if it be drawn *on account* of a person who has, and the drawee accept it on his account, he renders himself responsible to the same extent as that person

---

remained in their hands, because no consideration had been given for them; or for money paid, because it had been paid after the Brownes' bankruptcy, and because after full proof by the holders of the negotiated bills, there would have been a double proof as to part. The decision would have been the same, had the case arisen subsequently to the 49 Geo. 3. c. 121. That statute only applies where the surety pays the whole debt, or a part in discharge of the whole; it does not embrace the case of a surety, or (if a bankrupt) his assignees, paying part of the debt, after the creditor has proved and received dividends under the principal's commission; such surety, or his assignees, can derive no advantage from the creditor's proof; nor can he or they make any distinct proof in respect of the part so paid, because the creditor has already proved, and to the extent of such part there would be a double proof against the principal's estate. In ex parte Walker the Caldwells had clearly sustained an injury; but the decision only related to the right of proof, and nothing was said as to the right of action, which, it would seem, the assignees of each party had against the other for the dividends paid by them on the bills which the other ought to have taken up: nor does the right of action, in such case, appear to have been affected by the 49 G. 3. c. 121. § 8.

(33) Ex parte Metcalfe, 11 Ves. 404. Palmer had received from Williamson in cash and bills 6424*l.* 9*s.* 3*d.*, and Williamson had received from Palmer in cash 5824*l.* 19*s.* 7*d.* Both became bankrupt. Palmer had negotiated the bills; some of which to the amount of 1098*l.* were dishonored by the drawee, and Palmer's assignees contended that the amount of these bills should be deducted from the 6424*l.* 9*s.* 3*d.* which would reduce the sum received by him to 5326*l.* 9*s.* 3*d.*, making a balance of 498*l.* 10*s.* 4*d.* in his favor, which balance they contended they were entitled to prove against Williamson's estate. On petition to prevent such proof, Lord Eldon C. ordered that the proof of the 498*l.* 10*s.* 4*d.* should be allowed; but that Williamson's assignees should retain the dividends upon such proof in order to exonerate that estate from any demand which might be made in respect of the bills, which should have been taken up by Palmer.

would have been had he been the drawee and acceptor; and therefore if he refuse payment, and the drawer be obliged to take up the bill, the latter (34) may prove it under a commission of bankruptcy issued against such acceptor.

If more than one of the persons liable on account of the non-acceptance or non-payment of a bill or note become bankrupts, the holder may prove, under the separate commission of each, the full (35) amount of the money due to

---

(34) Ex parte Marshall and others, 1 Atk. 131. Watkin having dealings with Garway, and Garway with Hatton, it was agreed between the two latter that Hatton should answer such bills as Watkin should draw on him on Garway's account. Watkin drew accordingly on Hatton for 4000*l.* having effects in Garway's hands beyond that amount. Hatton accepted the bill, though he had no effects either of Garway or Watkin in hand; he afterwards refused payment, and Watkin was obliged to pay the bill, and proved it under a commission of bankruptcy issued against Hatton. Hatton's assignees petitioned to have the debt expunged, but the Chancellor held that Watkin was entitled to prove, because of his having had effects in Garway's hands beyond the amount of the bill. Petition dismissed.

Ex parte Matthews, 6 Ves. 235. Matthews being indebted to Garland and Co. directed Caldwell and Co., his bankers, to give an order to Burton, Forbes, and Gregory (on whom they drew) to accept a bill to be drawn by Garland and Co. for the amount of their debt. The bill was drawn and accepted accordingly. Before it became due Caldwell and Co., and Burton, Forbes, and Gregory became bankrupt. Garland and Co. proved the bill under the acceptor's commission, but afterwards received the whole amount of the bill from Matthews; on which the proof was expunged; and on petition that it might be restored for Matthews' benefit, it appearing that Matthews had effects in the hands of Caldwell and Co. beyond the amount of the bill, and that he had given them credit for that amount, the proof was ordered to be reinstated.

(35) Ex parte Wildman, 1 Atk. 109. 2 Vez. 113. Wildman held bills drawn by Buckle and accepted by Vanhylik: Vanhylik failed, and made a composition with his creditors, and Buckle became bankrupt, Wildman having received nothing under Vanhylik's composition, proved his whole debt under Buckle's commission, but before any dividend was made he received 2*s.* 6*d.* in the pound out of Vanhylik's estate: Buckle's assignees then contended that he ought to deduct the 2*s.* 6*d.* in the pound out of his proof, and take a dividend upon the balance only: but Lord Hardwicke held, that as the whole sum was due when he proved his debt, and the dividend and composition would not amount to 20*s.* in the pound upon his debt, he was entitled to a dividend upon his whole debt; and per Lord Hardwicke, "In cases of bills or notes, where there is a drawer, and perhaps several endorsers, suppose two of these persons become bankrupts, the holder may prove his *whole debt* under each commission, and is entitled to receive satisfaction out of both estates, according to the dividends to be made, until he has receiv-

him upon the bill or note at the time he makes his proof, and receive dividends under each upon the sums proved, until he shall in the whole have received such amount.

But after the (36) receipt, (or even the (37) declaration,) of a dividend under one commission, he cannot prove under any of the rest more than the sum remaining due after deducting such dividend.

If a bill or note be pledged with a person as a collateral security for the payment of a smaller sum than that for which it is drawn, the pawnee (38) may prove the full amount of

---

ed satisfaction for his whole debt; for he has a double security, and it is neither law nor equity to take it from him: but if before the bankruptcy of one he had received payment of part from the other, he could only have proved the residue under the latter bankruptcy, as the form of proving his debt shews, because no more would remain due to him." To the same effect are the cases of ex parte Royd and ex parte Bennett, cited 2 Ves. 114.

And see Cooke's Bankrupt Laws, 170.

(36) See ex parte Wildman, ante, p. 304, note (35).

Cooper v. Pepys, 1 Atk. 106. The holders of notes drawn by Reeves, and payable to Andree, accepted 6*s*. in the pound from Andree; and Reeves having become bankrupt, the question was, whether they might prove the whole debt under his commission? and Lord Hardwicke held they could not, but that the 6*s*. in the pound must go in discharge of so much of the debt, and they could only prove the remaining 14*s*. The same point was ruled in ex parte Ryswick, 2 P. Williams, 89, ex parte Lefebvre, 2 P. Williams, 407.

See Cooke's Bankrupt Laws, 170.

(37) Ex parte Leers, 6 Ves. 644. Leers was holder of a bill which had been drawn upon, and accepted by persons at Hambro', endorsed by the payees to Pierre de Ruesnas at Hambro', and by him to Leers. It was protested for non-payment. A commission under the great seal issued against the payees, and the acceptors and last endorser were also made bankrupts. Leers had the amount of the bill claimed against the estates of each of the last mentioned parties, according to the due course at Hambro', and a dividend was declared of each estate. He had not received any part of either of these dividends; and the question now was, whether he might prove the whole bill against the estate of the payees? Lord Eldon, after hearing that the practice (the principle of which he doubted) was against such proof, ordered that these dividends should be deducted.

(38) Ex parte King, Cooke's B. L. 156. Davies gave his note for 500*l*. to Turner and Toye, expressed to be for value received but in fact for their accommodation, and they being indebted to King in 300*l*. endorsed this note to him, to enable him to raise that sum. Turner and Toye, and Davies afterwards became bankrupt; and on petition, King was allowed to prove the whole amount against Davies's estate, and to receive dividends not exceeding 300*l*.

Ex parte Crossley, Cooke's B. L. 157. 3 Bro. Ch. Cas. 237. Hartley being indebted to Crossley in 147*l*. 10*s*. gave him a bill for 200*l*.

the bill or note against all parties who are liable to the full amount, excepting against him from whom he received it; so as he do not by that means receive more than the sum which it was pledged to secure.

Nor will such proof be prevented by the circumstance of the bill or note having been drawn (39) by way of accommodation.

But against the party from whom he received it, he can only prove the (40) actual debt.

Under a commission of bankruptcy, the holder of a bill or note is not (41) entitled, (unless the bankrupt's estate should produce a (42) surplus,) to any interest or charges accrued or incurred after the commission issued, nor where the act

---

which had been drawn on Livesay and Co. by a partner in that house, payable to Hartley's order. The bill was accepted, but afterwards dishonored. Livesay and Co. became bankrupts; but before a commission issued, Hartley paid Crossley £101, 10*s*. in part of his debt. It appearing that Livesay and Co. had lent this bill to Hartley, the commissioners refused to allow Crossley to prove under Livesay's commission more than the balance of £46 remaining due to him from Hartley. But on petition, the Chancellor ordered the proof to be admitted for the whole £200 and dividends to be received until the petitioner should be satisfied the £46. Ex parte King was relied on.

See also ex parte Bloxham, 6 Ves. 449, in which Lord Eldon C. said, "I looked upon it as settled that you cannot hold the paper of the bankrupt, and prove beyond your actual debt upon it; but that you may have the paper of third persons, those persons being indebted to your debtor in more, and you may prove to the whole amount; not exceeding 20*s*. in the pound upon the original debt."

(39) Vide ex parte King, and ex parte Crossley, ante, p. 305. n. (38). See also Cooke's B. L. 5th ed. p. 156.

(40) Vide ex parte Bloxham, supra, note (38)., and Cooke's B. L. p. 156.

(41) Anon. 1 Atk. 140. The question was, whether the costs and charges incurred by protesting bills after a commission of bankruptcy issued could be proved; and Lord Hardwicke ordered that the costs of the protests arisen before the commission should be proved, but no part of the costs arisen afterwards.

As to re-exchange see ex parte Hoffman, Cooke, B. L. 173. and Francis v. Rucker, Ambl. 672. and as to the latter see 2 Bro. Cha. Cas. 599. It is observable that, in that case, the drawer was (in effect) allowed to prove re-exchange under the acceptor's commission. It has been held indeed that the acceptor is not liable for re-exchange; vide ante, p. 236. Pothier (pl. 117.) expressly says that he is in like manner as the drawer: and it seems reasonable that he should be liable to all parties where he has effects; and to all, excepting the drawer, where he has not.

(42) Vide ex parte Mills, 2 Ves. 295. and Butcher v. Churchill, 14 Ves. 573.

of bankruptcy to which the commission relates is ascertained, (43) to any accrued or incurred after that act of bankruptcy.

Mutual debts and (44) credits between a bankrupt and any other person, (45) may be set off against each other

(43) Ex parte Moore, 2 Bro. Cha. Cas. 597. Previous to the 5th of May, 1785, Mrs. Tyler accepted several bills drawn upon her by Moore, and on that day committed an act of bankruptcy, but no commission issued until the 9th of March, 1786; the bills became due between May, 1785, and March, 1786, and Mrs. Tyler not paying them, Moore did; he also paid £298 for damages and charges, and the interest amounted to £46, 10*s.*; the commissioners allowed Moore to prove the sum for which the bills were drawn, but would not let him prove the interest, or the sum paid for damages and charges, upon which he petitioned the Chancellor, but the Chancellor held, that as the time when the act of bankruptcy was committed was ascertained, he could not carry the damages beyond that time; and the petition was disallowed.

(44) Ex parte Prescott, 1 Atk. 230. The petitioner was a creditor for £110 and at the same time debtor to the bankrupt on a bond for £340 with interest. The interest was payable annually, but the principal was not payable until March, 1756, this petition being in August, 1753. The petitioner prayed that he might be allowed to set off the £110 against the principal and interest on the bond: it was objected that the bond not being yet due, these were not mutual debts. But Lord Hardwicke C. held that the case came within the expression of "mutual credit," in 5 Geo. 2. c. 30. § 28., and that that act was to be construed with reference to 7 Geo. 1. c. 31., permitting certain debts to be proved before they became due. He therefore allowed the set off.

Atkinson v. Elliot, 7 Term. Rep. 378. In May, 1796, Hodges bought a parcel of goods from the defendants for £430, and in September following another parcel for £230; each at six months' credit: on each occasion he gave his acceptance for the price. The first bill became due on the 6th of November, 1796, and the other on the 9th of March, 1797. On the 9th of November, 1796, in order to take up the first bill, he gave them a bill for £100, and the next day endorsed to them another for £500, taking from them a written engagement to pay over to him the surplus, viz. £170 when those bills should be paid. Those bills, viz. for £100 and £500, became due and were paid on the 11th of Dec. 1796. On the 13th of December, 1796, Hodges became bankrupt, and the plaintiffs, his assignees, immediately claimed the £170. The defendants however contended that they were entitled to retain the £170 in part satisfaction of Hodges' acceptance for £230, though not then due; and therefore refused to pay the £170. On which the plaintiffs in Feb. 1797, brought this action for money had and received. But on a case reserved the court held that this case was clearly within the authority of ex parte Prescott, which Lord Kenyon said was properly decided, and therefore postea to the defendants.

(45) By 5 G. 2. c. 30. § 28. it is enacted, "That where it shall appear to the commissioners, or the major part of them, that there hath been mutual credit given by the bankrupt and any other person, or mutual debts between the bankrupt and any other person, at any time before such person became bankrupt, the said commissioners, or the major part of them, or the assignees of such bankrupt's estate, shall state the accounts between them, and one debt may be set against an-

under a commission of bankruptcy, provided they accrued or were given before any act of bankruptcy has been committed by such bankrupt.

So also they may be set off, (46) notwithstanding any prior act of bankruptcy committed by such bankrupt before the credit was given to, or debt contracted by such bankrupt, provided the credit was given to the bankrupt two calendar months before the date and suing forth of his commission, and the party claiming the benefit of such set-off had not, at the time of giving the credit, notice of such prior act of bankruptcy, or that the bankrupt was insolvent, or had stopped payment: but not otherwise.

Therefore the amount of a bill or note cannot be the subject of set-off under a commission of bankruptcy, if either the bankrupt or the person claiming the benefit of such set-off, became party to, or holder of the bill or note after such act, and either within such two months, or after such notice.

Unless perhaps where the credit upon the bill or note forms part of a credit previously created, as where goods are sold upon a credit with liberty, before the credit expires, to draw a bill or demand a note for the price.

If an endorser of a bill take it up after the bankruptcy of

---

other; and what shall appear to be due on either side on the balance of such account, and on setting such debts against one another, and no more, shall be claimed or paid on either side respectively." See Tamplin v. Diggins, 2 Campb. N. P. C. 312.

(46) By 46 Geo. 3. c. 135. § 3. it is enacted, "That in all cases in which, under commissions of bankrupt hereafter to be issued, it shall appear that there has been mutual credit given by the bankrupt and any other person, or mutual debts between the bankrupt and any other person, one debt or demand may be set off against another notwithstanding any prior act of bankruptcy committed by such bankrupt before the credit was given to or the debt was contracted by such bankrupt, in like manner as if no such prior act of bankruptcy had been committed, provided such credit was given to the bankrupt two calendar months before the date and suing forth of such commission, and provided the person claiming the benefit of such set-off, had not at the time of giving such credit any notice of any prior act of bankruptcy by such bankrupt committed, or that he was insolvent or had stopped payment: provided always, that the issuing of a commission of bankrupt against such bankrupt, although such commission shall afterwards be superseded, shall be deemed notice of a prior act of bankruptcy for the purposes of this act, if it shall appear that an act of bankruptcy had been actually committed at the time of issuing such commission." Vide 49 G. 3. c. 121. § 1.

the acceptor, he (47) cannot set off any debt due from him to the bankrupt against the amount of such bill, because the right of set-off did not exist at the time of the bankruptcy.

A bill or note may however be the subject of set-off, though it do not (48) become due until after an act of bankruptcy committed. (*a*) (*b*)

---

(47) Ex parte Hale, 3 Ves. 304. The acceptor of a bill for £200 became bankrupt, and Hale, who had endorsed it before the bankruptcy, was obliged after the bankruptcy to take it up, and being indebted to the bankrupt in £90, he petitioned that he might be allowed to set it off. But the Chancellor said the petitioner must pay the £90 and then prove the £200. There was a debt created upon the estate and due at the time of the bankruptcy, but that was not due to the petitioner; in that respect therefore the set-off fails. The petition was dismissed so far as it sought to set off the £90.

(48) Ex parte Wagstaff, 13 Ves. 65. A commission of bankruptcy issued against the Kershaws on the 29th of June, 1804. At that time Wagstaff was a creditor for £2277, and he had accepted a bill drawn on him by the bankrupts for £399 which became due, and was paid by Wagstaff, on the 5th of July, 1804. He was at the same time debtor to the bankrupt in £363, the greatest part of which was for goods sold on a credit which did not expire until the 1st of May, 1805 : the residue was for money had and received. He claimed to be allowed to prove his debt of £2277, contending that he had a right to set off the £363 against the £399 on the acceptance, though not due until after the bankruptcy. The commissioners however refused to allow the set-off. But Lord Erskine C. on petition ordered the set-off to be allowed, and said that this was mutual credit to all intents and purposes. See ex parte Prescott, and Atkinson v. Elliot, ante, p. 307. n. (44).

[(*a*) Johnson being insolvent made an assignment of all debts due to him to trustees for the benefit of his creditors, Jan. 16th, 1793. In an action in Johnson's name for the benefit of his assignees, against one of his debtors, the defendant claimed to set off a note made by the plaintiff and endorsed to the defendant, and which the defendant purchased in 1793 and after it was due, for twelve shillings in the pound, for the purpose of setting it off against this demand. The defendant denied any knowledge of the assignment at the time of purchasing the note. A majority of the Court, Radcliff, Kent, and Benson, Js. were against allowing the set-off, on the ground, that the defendant purchasing the note after it was due, " at a depreciated rate, for the purpose of a set-off, though he may not in fact know of the assignment, yet he is properly chargeable with having acted under an implied notice of it." Lewis J. and Lansing C. J. contra. Johnson v. Bloodgood, 1 Johns. Cas. 51. S. C. 2 Cain. Err. 302.

A. failing, assigned his property and debts, including a demand against B. B. afterwards purchased a note of A. which was overdue. In an action by A. for the benefit of his assignees against B., it was held that B. could not set off A's note, if he had notice of the assignment, and that actual notice need not be proved, but it was sufficient to prevent the allowance of the offset, that the note was purchased under circumstances sufficient to put him on inquiry. Anderson v. Van Allen, 12 Johns. R. 343.

See also Goodwin v. Cunningham, 12 Mass. R. 193.

Where a note was purchased after a commission of bankruptcy against the maker, and proved under the commission, it was held that the assignees might set off any demand of the maker of the note against the person from whom the holder purchased it. Humphries v. Blight, 4 Dall. 370.]

[(*b*) The following note, as to the effect of the bankruptcy of a factor or banker, as it regards bills in his possession at the time of his bankruptcy, is chiefly extracted from Chitty on Bills, (5th ed. p. 620 to 623., 6th ed. p. 482 to 486.)

In the case of the bankruptcy of a factor or banker, bills remitted to him, and entered short while unpaid, and bills paid in generally, to be received, and not discounted or treated as cash, and bills sent for a particular purpose, are not affected by the bankruptcy of the factor or banker, and the property in them is not altered, and they, or the proceeds received by the assignees, must be returned by them to the principal, subject to such lien as the factor or banker may have thereon. Zinck v. Walker, 2 Bla. R. 1154: Brown v. Kewley, 2 Bos. & Pull. 523; Bolton v. Richard, 6 T. R. 139; 5 T. R. 215, 494; Parke v. Eliason, 1 East, 547; Paley, P. & A. 71; Ex parte Waring and others, 19 Ves. 345.

Ex parte Sargeant, 1 Rose, 153. Ex parte Sollers, 18 Ves. 229, S. P. Where short bills were in the possession of a bankrupt at the time of his bankruptcy, their proceeds were ordered to be returned, unless upon inquiry, it should appear that with the knowledge of the party depositing them, or from habits of dealing between the parties, they were to be considered as cash; the onus of proving which lies on the assignees of the bankrupt banker.

Ex parte Pease, 1 Rose, 232. 19 Ves. Jr. 25. Bills remitted by a country bank to their banker in London, remaining at his bankruptcy in his hands undue or unapplied according to the authority given, or afterwards coming into the hands of the assignees, and the proceeds received, restored and paid to the remitter, taking up the acceptances on their account, and subject to the banker's lien for any balance, by the contract remaining the property of the remitters in the hands of the banker, as agent for a particular purpose, namely, to hold until due, and receive the proceeds, then first forming an item in the cash account. The circumstance of the bills being written short, is only evidence of a trust, which may also be proved by express declaration, or other evidence equivalent. The statute 21 Jac. 1. c. 19. § 11. is not applicable to bills in the hands of a banker written short, or sent for a particular purpose, the trust accounting for the possession, being considered as goods in the hands of a factor, but if the bills are dealt with before bankruptcy, the money cannot be followed, as if dealt with afterwards it may.

Ex parte Rowton, 17 Ves. Jr. 426; 1 Rose, 15, S. C. Short bills remitted by a country bank, to their banker in London, standing at the bankruptcy of the latter entered short in the usual way, not being due; ordered, on petition in the bankruptcy, to be delivered up by the assignees to the country bank, who not being creditors when the petition was presented, the cash balance being against them, had since become so, turning it in their favor by taking up the bankrupt's acceptances on their account.

Ex parte Buchanan, 1 Rose, 280. An order was made upon the provisional assignee to deliver up short bills in the hands of bankers at the time of their bankruptcy, the estate being indemnified against their outstanding acceptances on account of the petitioner.

See also ex parte the Burton Bank, 2 Rose, 162, and Thompson v. Giles, ante, p. 79.

A customer paying bills, not due, into his bankers in the country, whose practice it was to credit their customers for the amount of such bills, if approved, as cash, (charging interest,) is entitled recover back such bills in specie from the bankers becoming bankrupt; the balance of his cash account, independent of such bills being in his favor at the time of the bankruptcy; and if payment be afterwards received upon such bills by the assignees, they are liable to refund it to the customer in an action for money had and received. Giles v. Perkins, 9 East, 12. See also Thompson v. Giles, ante, p. 79.

Where A. abroad commissions B. in London, to send him foreign coin, with particular directions, as to the manner and time of sending it, and remits bills, which B. discounts, and the coin required not being to be had in England, sends two remittances, not equal to the amount of A.'s bills, to Lisbon for the purpose of procuring it; with directions, if it cannot be had, to return the bills. The coin not being to be had, bills nearly to the amount of the remittances to Lisbon, are returned, and B. in the interval becoming bankrupt, are received by his assignees; A. was held to have a right to those bills upon the particular circumstances, the Lord Chancellor expressing much doubt, whether such right could exist in the case of a remittance to buy goods in the way of trade. Ex parte Sayers, 5 Ves. 169.

So it has been held that a remittance in bills and notes for a specific purpose, viz. to answer acceptances, received by the administrator, in consequence of the death of the party to whom it was remitted, was not general assets, the specific purpose operating as a lien, which would also be the effect upon a bankruptcy. Hassall v. Smithers, 12 Ves. 119.

But if the holder of bills deliver them to a banker, expressly on the terms of discount, or if, by the course of dealing between the customer and banker, bills received by the latter are understood by both parties as cash minus the discount, and the customer is at liberty to draw on account thereof, beyond the amount of cash in the hands of the banker, then in the event of the bankruptcy of the banker, the assignees are entitled to the bills. See Chitty, 5th ed. p. 158; 6th ed. p. 122; and Carstairs v. Bates, 3 Camp. 301; Giles v. Perkins, 9 East, 12.

So where a person having three bills of exchange applied to a country bank, with whom he had had no previous dealings, to give for them a bill on London of the same amount, and the bill given by the banker was afterwards dishonored, held, that this was a complete exchange of securities, and that trover would not lie for the three bills of exchange; and it was also held, that if the exchange had not been complete, still that the banker having become a bankrupt, and the three bills having come to the possession of his assignees, must be considered as goods and chattels in the order and disposition of the bankrupt at the time of his bankruptcy, within the statute 21 Jac. 1. c. 19. Hornblower v. Prowd, 2 B. & A. 327.

Lord Hardwicke, in the case of ex parte Oursell, Amb. 297, said, "If bills are sent by a correspondent to a merchant here to be received, and the money to be applied to a particular use, and the merchant becomes bankrupt before the money is received on the bills, the correspondent has a special lien in respect of those bills, and the money shall not be divided amongst the creditors at large. But where bills are sent on a general account between the correspondent and the merchant, and as an item in the account, it is otherwise." See also Bent v. Puller, 5 T. R. 294, in which the same doctrine is recognised.]

CHAP. XI.

Of the Evidence necessary to entitle the plaintiff to recover upon a Bill or Note.

To recover in respect of a bill or note upon a count for money lent, money paid, or money had and received, the plaintiff must prove such of those facts which are not admitted, as he ought to state upon a special count; and upon a special count, he must prove such of the facts which are not admitted as appear upon the face of that count necessary.

[In an action against any party to a bill or note the instrument itself must in general be produced. (*a*)

But the plaintiff in an action on a bill or note which is dated, is not bound to prove the day on which it was issued, or to show at what time he received it. (*b*)]

An acceptance admits the (1) ability of the drawer to make the bill, and, if made after sight of the bill, his (2)

[(*a*) As to cases in which an action may be maintained on a bill lost or destroyed, see Long v. Bailie, ante, p. 262, and other cases p. 262, 263.

The statutes of Kentucky provide that no person shall be permitted to deny his signature as maker or assignor of a note in a suit against him, unless he will make an affidavit denying the execution or assignment. It was held that this statute did not render the production of the original instrument unnecessary in a suit against the assignor, and that the record of a judgment against the maker of the note, and which contained a copy of it, was not admissible in evidence. Story J. who delivered the opinion of the court, said, "It would be dangerous to allow that, because proof of the execution of an instrument was dispensed with, therefore no proof of its existence, or of the right of the party to hold it by assignment, was to be required." Sebree v. Dorr, 9 Wheat. R. 558.]

[(*b*) Bayley v. Taber, 6 Mass. R. 451.]

(1) Porthouse v. Parker and others, 1 Camp. N. P. C. 82. This was an action by the payee against the drawers of a bill. The bill purported to have been drawn by Wood as agent of the defendants, upon John Parker one of the defendants. There was no proof of Wood's authority; but it was proved that the bill had been accepted by the agent of John Parker, the drawee: and Lord Ellenborough held that the bill having been accepted by order of one of the defendants, this was sufficient evidence of its having been regularly drawn.

(2) Wilkinson v. Lutwidge, Str. 648. In an action against the acceptor of a bill, Raymond, C. J. allowed the plaintiff to read the bill without proving the drawer's hand, because he thought the acceptance a sufficient acknowledgment on the part of the defendant, but he said it would not be conclusive; and if the defendant could shew the contrary,

signature; an endorsement admits the ability, and (3) signature of every antecedent party.

---

the reading the bill should not preclude him. See Cooper v. Le Blanc, post, note (26).

Jenys v. Fawler, Str. 946. In an action against the acceptor of a bill, Raymond, C. J. held it was not necessary for the plaintiff to prove the drawer's hand, and on the defendant's offering to call witnesses to swear they believed it was not the drawer's hand, the chief justice would not admit the evidence, and he inclined strongly that actual proof of forgery would not excuse the defendant.

Price v. Neale, Burr. 1354. Blackst. 390. Two forged bills were drawn upon the plaintiff, which he accepted and paid; on discovering the forgery he brought this action for money had and received to recover back the money, but on a case reserved, the court held it would not lie; and Lord Mansfield said, "It was incumbent on him to have been satisfied before he accepted or paid them, that the bills were the drawer's hand:" and in Smith v. Chester, 1 Term. Rep. 655, Buller J. says, "When a bill is presented for acceptance, the acceptor looks to the handwriting of the drawer, which he is afterwards precluded from disputing, and it is on that account that he is liable, even though the bill is forged."

Smith v. Mercer, 6 Taunt. 76. A bill was drawn on Evans payable to Temple, endorsed by him to Le Souef, and by Le Souef to defendants: defendants endorsed it, that their correspondents in town might get it paid: it had upon it, when defendants took it, this acceptance, "Smith, Payne, and Smith's, Maurice Evans." This was a forgery; but defendants did not know it: when the bill became due, Smith, Payne, and Smith paid it, but at the end of a week they discovered the forgery, and gave notice thereof to defendants, and on their refusal to refund the money, brought money had and received against them. On a special case, Chambre J. thought plaintiffs entitled to recover, because defendants, by endorsing the bill with the forged acceptance thereon, had impliedly vouched for its authenticity, and because there was no blame or negligence imputable to plaintiffs, and it was against conscience in defendants to keep their money, for which they got nothing; but the other judges thought plaintiffs not entitled; Dallas and Heath Js. because it was plaintiffs' duty to know their customer's hand before they paid the bill; and Gibbs C. J., because plaintiff's conduct had prevented notice to those parties defendants might have sued, and had therefore destroyed the remedy against them. Postea to defendants.

[See also Levy v. Bank of the United States, ante, p. 259.]

(3) Lambert v. Pack, Salk. 127. Lord Raym. 443. 12 Mod. 244. Holt. 117. In an action against the endorser of a bill, Holt, C. J. ruled that it was not necessary to prove the drawer's hand, for though the bill was forged, the endorser would be liable.

Williams v. Seagrove, 2 Barnard. B. R. 82. A rule was made absolute for delivering up a note to an endorsee, though it was proved to have been forged, upon the ground that he might notwithstanding bring actions upon it against the endorsers. See also Str. 442.

Critchlow v. Parry, 2 Campb. N. P. C. 182. Endorsee against the endorser of a bill. The plaintiff was the immediate endorsee of the defendant. The declaration stated several prior endorsements, and the question was, whether it were necessary to prove them. Lord Ellenborough held the proof unnecessary, and the plaintiff had a verdict.

But an acceptance, though made after sight of an endorsement, does not admit the ability or (4) signature of the endorser.

Nor does it admit the endorsement of the drawer where the bill is payable to the drawer's order. (5)

And if such bill imports to be drawn and endorsed by procuration, though the acceptance admits the procuration as to the drawing, it does not as to the endorsement. (5)

But upon a bill payable to the drawer's order, an acceptance admits the drawer's ability to endorse; for if he cannot endorse, he was not of ability to draw. (6)

---

(4) Smith v. Chester, 1 Term Rep. 654. In an action by the endorsee of a bill against the acceptor, the plaintiff was nonsuited because he could not prove the handwriting of the first endorser, though the endorsement was on the bill at the time of the acceptance. A motion was made to set aside the nonsuit on the ground that as the endorsement was on the bill when it was accepted the acceptance admitted it, but the court thought it did not, because the acceptor only looks to the handwriting of the drawer, and *that* he is afterwards precluded from disputing. Rule discharged.

Carvick v. Vickery, Dougl. 630—653. n. 134. ante, p. 40. note (16). A bill payable to the order of father and son, who were not partners, was endorsed by the son only, after which it was presented, and the drawee wrote upon it a direction to his banker to pay it. In an action against the drawee the question was, Whether the endorsement by the son alone was sufficient? and Willes J. inclined to think the order to the banker was a recognition of the endorsement. But Ashhurst and Buller, Js. thought not. However in Hankey v. Wilson, Say. 223. in an action by the endorsee of a bill against the acceptor, there was no actual proof of the handwriting of one of the endorsers, but it appearing that the endorsement was upon the bill when the defendant accepted it, and that he promised to pay it; Ryder, C. J. left the case to the jury, who found for the plaintiff, and upon a rule to shew cause why there should not be a new trial, the court thought it a question for the jury, Whether the acceptance and promise did not amount to an admission that the name of every endorser was authentic? and refused the rule.

(5) Robinson v. Yarrow, 7 Taunt. 455. Action by endorsee against acceptor on bill importing to be drawn by Henry, per procuration for Stachen and Co. payable to the order of Stachen and Co., and to be endorsed by Henry per procuration for Stachen and Co. Plaintiff proved the acceptance, but he did not prove Henry's signature to the endorsement, nor his authority to endorse, upon which Burrough J. directed a verdict for defendant; and on rule nisi for new trial, and cause shewn, the court held the acceptance admitted Henry's authority to draw, and his signature as drawer, but that it was no admission of his authority to endorse, or of his endorsement, for the drawing and endorsing would have contrary effects, the one would bring the amount to Stachen and Co., the latter would carry it from them; and rule discharged.

It precludes the acceptor therefore from relying upon infancy in such drawer and endorser. (6)

So if a bill is drawn in the name of a firm purporting to consist of several persons, the acceptance admits that there is such a firm. (7)

And that it consists of several. (7)

And the acceptor will be precluded from proving the contrary, if it is only to let in a technical objection. (7)

In an action, therefore, against the acceptor of a bill or maker of a note, the plaintiff must prove the defendant's signature, and the necessary endorsements; and in the former case, if the acceptance was made without sight of the bill, the signature of the drawer: in an action against the drawer of a bill, or the endorser of a bill or note, he must prove the defendant's signature, the necessary endorsements (8) between him and the plaintiff, the presentment, the non-acceptance or non-payment, the notice of dishonor (or the facts to shew such notice unnecessary), and, in the case of a foreign bill, the protest.

In an action indeed against the drawer (9) or acceptor of a bill, or the maker of a note, all the endorsements stated, though some may have been stated unnecessarily, must be proved; but against an (10) endorser, the defendant's en-

---

(6) See Taylor v. Croker, ante, p. 34.

(7) Bass v. Clive, 4 Maule, 13. Endorsee against acceptor on bill purporting to be drawn by Ellis, Needham Jun., and Co., and payable "to our order." Plaintiff declared upon it as drawn by certain persons trading under the firm of Ellis, Needham jun., and Co., and payable to their own order; defendant proved at the trial that only one person constituted that firm, upon which Lord Ellenborough nonsuited, with liberty to plaintiff to move to enter a verdict. On a rule nisi inde and cause shewn, he and the rest of the court were clear that by the acceptance defendant had admitted conclusively that there was such a firm as that stated on the face of the bill, and was not at liberty to prove the contrary; and rule absolute. [See Williamson v. Johnson, ante, p. 278.]

(8) Vide Critchlow v. Parry, ante, p. 313. n. (3).
[See also Blakely v. Grant, 6 Mass. R. 386.]

(9) Waynam v. Bend, 1 Campb. N. P. C. 175. In an action against the maker of a promissory note payable to T. L. or bearer, the declaration averred an endorsement by T. L., and Lord Ellenborough held that the plaintiff, having stated such endorsement, though unnecessarily, was bound to prove it. See also Smith v. Chester, ante, p. 314. n. (4), and Bosanquet v. Anderson, 6 Esp N. P. C. 43.

(10) See Critchlow v. Parry, ante, p. 313. n. (3).

dorsement, and such endorsements only as are stated to have been made subsequently to his, need be proved.

If a bill, in consequence of having an acceptance upon it pointing out a particular house for payment, is presented there for payment, and not at the drawee's residence or personally to the drawee, such acceptance must in general be proved in an action against the drawer or an endorser; because otherwise the presentment at that particular house will not be a valid presentment. (11)

But if it can be shewn that such acceptance was upon the bill when the defendant passed it, proof of the acceptance will be unnecessary. (11)

Proof that it was upon the bill when the plaintiff took it, if he did not take it immediately from the defendant, will not be sufficient. (11)

Where plaintiffs have no title upon a bill or note, unless they constitute a particular firm, they must prove that they constitute that firm.

As if they sue upon a bill or note payable to that firm by its name of business, without specifying its members;

Or specially endorsed to it.

But though several persons join in suing as endorsees, yet if they claim under an endorsement in blank, they need not shew that they are partners, or that they have a joint interest. (12)

---

(11) Smith v. Bellamy, 2 Stark. 223. Second endorsee of bill against payee, on bill drawn on Stevenson, payable in London, with an acceptance thereon payable at Spooner and Atwood's. It had been presented there and there only; the acceptance was upon the bill when the plaintiff took it, but there was no evidence that it was so when defendant endorsed it and passed it away: it was urged that the jury might presume it was on the bill when plaintiff took it; Lord Ellenborough thought not, and as proof of the acceptance was necessary to make the presentment valid, he nonsuited the plaintiff.

(12) Ord v. Portal, 3 Campb. 239. Three persons sued as endorsees on a bill; the endorsement to them was in blank: it was urged that it ought to be shewn that they were partners, or had a joint interest. Sed per Lord Ellenborough, It is not necessary; the endorsement in blank gives a joint right of action to as many as agree in suing. Verdict for plaintiffs.

Rordasnz v. Leach, 1 Stark. 446. Two persons sued as endorsees; the endorsement to them was in blank: and on question whether they

It is indeed stated to have been held, that if a bill endorsed in blank is sent to a particular house, and an action is afterwards brought thereon by some of the members of that house and additional parties, there must be some evidence that that house transferred the bill to the plaintiffs, or consented to their suing upon it. (13)

And this, though the bill was sent to the house for the benefit of the persons who sue. (13)

[The holder of a bill or note is *primâ facie* the rightful owner, and need not prove a consideration, except where circumstances of suspicion appear. (*a*)

A bill or note importing on its face to be for "*value received*," is *primâ facie* evidence of that fact, not only between the parties to the note, but against third persons, whenever the bill or note is admissible as evidence. (*b*)

But the presumption of *value received* arising from those words on the face of a bill, may be rebutted by circumstances; as if the payee should neglect entirely to present it for acceptance. (*b*)]

---

were bound to shew a joint title, Lord Ellenborough held they were not.

[In an action by surviving partners as endorsees of a bill endorsed in blank, they declared in their own right, without describing themselves as surviving partners, though it appeared that when they received the bill there was another person in their firm, who died before the action was brought. It was held that the action was properly brought. Park J. said that in case of a special endorsement strict evidence must be given that the plaintiffs composed the firm to whom it is endorsed, but that "an endorsement in blank conveys a joint right of action to as many as agree to sue on the bill." Attwood v. Rattenbury, 6 Moore, 579.]

(13 Machell, Boucher, and Birkbeck v. Kinnear, 1 Stark. 499. Plaintiffs were trustees of the estate of Holder, an insolvent; two of them were partners in the house of Langton and Co.: defendant being indebted to Holder, sent a bill endorsed in blank to Langton and Co. on account of Holder's estate: the trustees sued thereon; but on an objection that Langton and Co. did not appear to have transferred the bill to the plaintiffs or to have sanctioned their suing thereon, Lord Ellenborough held that proof essential, and nonsuited the plaintiffs.

[(*a*) Cruger v. Armstrong, 3 Johns. Cas. 5; Conroy v. Warren, 3 Johns. Cas. 259. See also Dugan v. The United States, ante, p. 212.

In a case in Pennsylvania in 1792 in an action by the drawers who were also payees and endorsers of a bill, against the acceptor, it was held that the production of the bill and protest was not sufficient evidence to prove that the plaintiffs had paid the amount to the endorsee, and judgment was given for the defendant. Gorgerat v. M'Carty, 1 Yeates, 94. S. C. 2 Dall. 144.]

[(*b*) Mandeville v. Welch, 5 Wheat. R. 277.]

And in many cases the plaintiff is compellable to prove that either he or some preceding party took the bill or note bonâ fide, and for value.

As in case of a bill or note originally given without consideration, and whilst the person giving it was under duress. (14)

Or in case of a bill or note obtained by fraud. (15)

Or in case of a transfer by delivery by a person not entitled to make it. (16)

As in the instance of bills or notes which have been stolen or lost. (16)

---

(14) Duncan v. Scott, 1 Campb. N. P. C. 100. Endorsee against the drawer of a bill. It appeared that the defendant gave the bill while under duress abroad, and under a threat of personal violence and confiscation of his property, and that it was given without consideration. Lord Ellenborough held that the defendant not having been a free agent when he drew the bill, it was incumbent on the plaintiff to give some evidence of consideration; and no such evidence being given, the plaintiff was nonsuited.

(15) Rees v. Marquis of Headfort, 2 Campb. N. P. C. 574. In an action by an endorsee of a bill against the acceptor, it appeared that the drawer had received no consideration for the bill, and had been tricked out of it by a gross fraud; and Lord Ellenborough held that this made it incumbent on the plaintiff to shew what consideration he gave for the bill; and the plaintiff not being prepared to do so, was nonsuited.

[In an action against the endorser of a note, he gave notice to the plaintiff before the trial that evidence would be required of him of the consideration paid by him, and of the circumstances under which the note came into his hands. At the trial the defendant offered to prove that the note was fraudulently put into circulation by the maker. The court refused to admit the evidence; or to make the plaintiff prove the manner in which he became possessed of the note. On Error, Tilghman C. J. "The defendant was not permitted to make out a case which would have entitled him to a verdict, unless the plaintiff had come forward and cleared himself of suspicion. I am of opinion that the District Court erred in rejecting the evidence." Judgment reversed. Holme v. Karsper, 5 Bin. 469. See also Garriges v. Vogdes, 2 Browne's R. 262; and Coster v. Merest, 7 Moore, 87.]

(16) Vide Anon. ante, p. 72. and Miller v. Race, Grant v. Vaughan, ante, p. 73. n. (21). Peacock v. Rhodes, ante, p. 67. n. (9.)

Solomons v. the Bank of England, 13 East's Rep. 135. n. Trover for a bank note for 500*l*. It appeared that the note had been fraudulently obtained by means of a forged draught, and therefore when presented for payment it was stopped by the bank, who informed the plaintiff of the circumstances. The plaintiff had received it from his correspondents at Middleburgh, and by desire of the bank, wrote to learn how they came by it. In answer, they wrote that they had received it in payment for goods, from a stranger. The note was three years old, and

To compel a plaintiff, however, to give such proof, it has been held necessary he should be apprized before the trial that such proof would be required from him. (17)

It is laid down in (18) some cases, that in an action against the endorser of a bill, the plaintiff must prove an application to the drawer for payment; but it (19) is now fully settled he need not.

And an offer, after the bill or note has become due, to give the holder another bill in lieu of it, is an (20) admission of the holder's title, so as to supersede the necessity of proving the endorsements or other special facts.

So (21) part payment of a bill or note after it has be-

---

was stated by the plaintiff to have been taken by him in reduction of a balance due to him from his correspondents; but how this was did not appear. Bank notes of this value were not usually current at Middleburgh. Lord Kenyon said that as it did not appear that the plaintiff had given a valuable consideration for the note before notice, he should consider him as agent to his correspondents, and he thought that they had not satisfactorily accounted for their possession of the note. The plaintiff consented to a nonsuit; and on a rule nisi to set it aside and cause shewn the court refused to interfere. See Lowndes v. Anderson, 13 East's Rep. 130.

(17) Paterson v. Hardacre, 4 Taunt. 114. In an action by endorsee against acceptor, the defence was, that an agent employed by defendant to get the bill discounted had appropriated it to his own use, and absconded: it was urged upon this that plaintiff was bound to prove how he got the bill, and what consideration he gave for it; he was not prepared with such proof, and was allowed to take a verdict subject to the question, whether he was bound to give it? and on rule nisi for a nonsuit on this ground and time to consider, the court held that where such a defence was contemplated, it was incumbent on the defendant to give distinct notice to the plaintiff that such proof would be called for at the trial: and because no such notice had been given, the rule was discharged.

(18) Vide Burr. 671.

(19) This was decided after two arguments in the case of a foreign bill in Bromley v. Frazier, Str. 441; and in the case either of a foreign or inland bill, but which does not appear, in Lawrence v. Jacob, Str. 515; and in the case of an inland bill, Heylin v. Adamson, Burr. 669.

(20) Bosanquet v. Anderson, 6 Esp. N. P. C. 43. Endorsee of a bill against the acceptor. The bill was drawn in favor of the drawer, who had endorsed it; and his endorsement and several others were stated in the declaration. The plaintiff proved the first endorsement, and that when the bill became due the defendant, being unable to take it up, came to the plaintiff and offered another in lieu of it. Lord Ellenborough held that this was an admission of the plaintiff's title, and dispensed with the proof of the several endorsements.

(21) Sidford v. Chambers, 1 Stark. 326. Plaintiffs sued as endorsees of Niblock and Co., who were endorsees of Sheckles, to whom defend-

come due, without any objection being made for want of notice, or a (22) promise to pay, furnish grounds from which

---

ant had endorsed: they could not prove the endorsement of Sheckles, but they proved a letter from defendant to plaintiffs offering to substitute another bill, saying they had not money to take up the bill in question, and expressing a hope that it was not in the hands of Niblock and Co. Lord Ellenborough thought this evidence of the channel through which the bill had passed to plaintiffs, and made proof of the endorsement by Sheckles unnecessary; and plaintiffs had a verdict.

Horford v. Wilson, 1 Taunt. 12. In an action by the endorsee against the drawer of a bill, which had been dishonored by the acceptor, it appeared that the defendant had paid part of the money due upon the bill, without making any objection for want of notice of the dishonor; and the court held, upon a motion for a new trial, that from this the jury were warranted in presuming that due notice had been given.

(22) Lundie v. Robertson, 7 East's Rep. 231. Endorsee against an endorser of a bill. No evidence was given of presentment or notice; but it was proved that on being called upon by the plaintiff's clerk some months after the bill was due, the defendant said, "he had not the cash by him, but if the clerk would call in a day or two, and bring the account (meaning of the expenses) he would pay it;" the bill was shewn him at the time. On a second application, he offered a bill on London for the debt and expenses, which was refused: he then said that "he had not had regular notice, but as the debt was justly due, he would pay it." Chambre J. thought this sufficient; and verdict for the plaintiff. On a rule nisi for a new trial, and cause shewn, Lord Ellenborough said the case admits of no doubt: it was to be presumed primâ facie from the promise to pay that the bill had been presented in time, that due notice had been given, that no objection could be made to payment, and that every thing had been rightly done; this superseded the necessity of the ordinary proof: the other conversation does not vary the case; for though the defendant said he had not had notice, he waived that objection. Rule discharged.

See Gibbon v. Coggon, 2 Campb. N. P. C. 188., where, from the drawer's promising to pay a bill, Lord Ellenborough directed the jury to presume that it had been duly protested. See also Taylor v. Jones, 2 Campb. N. P. C. 105.

Greenway v. Hindley, 4 Campb. 52. In an action by the endorsees of a foreign bill against the drawer, it was proved that long after the bill became due defendant called on the holder, and said he came to arrange the payment; and on being shewn it, added, "it was regular, it was due from him and his partner, and that he was come to arrange for paying principal and interest." The declaration having alleged presentment and protest, it was urged that evidence ought to be given upon those points; but Lord Ellenborough said the defendant's acknowledgment was a sufficient foundation from which the jury might infer those facts; and verdict for plaintiffs.

Hodge v. Fillis, 3 Campb. 463. A bill was made payable in London, and accepted payable at Sir John Perring and Co.'s; and in an action against the acceptor, plaintiff had alleged presentment at Sir John Perring's, but could not prove it; Lord Ellenborough held the proof essential, unless there were something to dispense with it: plaintiff then proved that after the bill was due defendant promised payment, and Lord Ellenborough thought that made the other proof unnecessary; and verdict for plaintiff.

a jury may presume that it has been properly presented, that notice has been duly given, and that a protest (where necessary) has been made.

And such presumption may be made (23), though the promise were not made to the plaintiff or in his presence, but to a subsequent endorsee who then held the bill or note.

Though there has been no due presentation, yet if there has been a subsequent application from an endorser for indulgence, it is for the jury to consider whether at the time of the application the endorser knew there had not been a due presentation. (24)

A nonsuit, without leaving that point to the jury, is improper. (24)

If there have been laches in not giving notice, an endorser who may be prejudiced thereby in his remedies over against other endorsers, will not be precluded from insisting on such laches by having desired that the bill may be sent to him

---

Wood v. Brown, 1 Stark. 217. In an action against the drawer of a bill, plaintiff proved a letter from defendant after the bill was due, in which he said he was an accommodation drawer only, and that the bill would be paid before the following term; Lord Ellenborough held that this made proof of notice of the dishonor unnecessary, and the plaintiff had a verdict without such proof.

(23) Potter v. Rayworth, 13 East's Rep. 417. Endorsee of a note against the payee and endorser. It appeared that the note (which had been negotiated in the country) had been endorsed by the defendant to Fulford, by him to the plaintiff, by the plaintiff to Kirton, and by him to others, before it became due. A fortnight after it had become due, Kirton, who had taken it up, called on the defendant, who until then had received no notice of its dishonor: the defendant then promised Kirton to pay him the next day; having failed in this, Kirton resorted to the plaintiff, who paid the amount; and the defence now being the want of notice, the question was whether the plaintiff could avail himself of this promise so made to Kirton. Graham B. directed a verdict for the plaintiff: and on motion to set it aside, the court (Grose and Le Blanc, Js. absent.) held that this promise was an acknowledgment by the defendant, either of notice, or that without notice he was the proper person to pay the note, and refused the rule.

(24) Hopley v. Dufresne, 15 East. 275. Endorsee against endorser; the bill was accepted payable at Hammersley's, and there was no presentment there proved till after the banking-hours; but after the declaration delivered, defendant had applied to plaintiff for further time to pay the bill: nonsuit, on the ground that no sufficient presentment was proved; but on rule nisi for new trial, and cause shewn, the court thought it should have been left to the jury to say, whether at the time of his promise defendant did not know there had been no due presentation; and on that account, rule absolute.

or some other person he names as soon as he receives notice, unless the bill when so sent is kept an improper time. (25)

[Where there is a subscribing witness to a note, in an action upon it, he ought to be produced at the trial to prove the signature of the party, or his absence accounted for. (*a*)

But it has been held that proof of the confession of the party signing the instrument, that he executed it, rendered it unnecessary in an action against him to produce the subscribing witness. (*b*)

And in a case where the subscribing witness was out of the government, it was held that other evidence might be produced of the signature of the maker of the note, without first proving the signature of the witness. (*c*)]

A confession of his signature is sufficient evidence (26)

---

(25) Borradaile v. Lowe, 4 Taunt. 93. Bill due 19th January; defendant was fifth endorser, Trevor and Co. the fourth; 25th January, letter to defendant that it was dishonored, with reasons assigned for not writing sooner; defendant wrote for answer, "I cannot think of remitting till I receive the draught, therefore if you think proper you may return it to Trevor and Co., if you think me unsafe." It was accordingly sent to Trevor and Co., but they returned it in a few days, saying, they had applied to the third endorser, and received it back from him as out of time; and as the delay was with plaintiff, they thought themselves and defendant discharged. Action inde: laches in plaintiff were admitted, but defendant's letter was relied upon as an answer; the distinction between the situation of an endorser, whose remedy over may be lost by the holder's laches, and of a drawer, was strongly relied on for defendant; and on rule nisi for nonsuit, and cause shewn, Mansfield C. J. said this letter contained no express promise to pay at all events, and he thought it would be too much to fix defendant here: in most cases where a defendant had been held liable there had been an express, promise to pay, or a promise under full knowledge of being discharged, or where there was a debt binding in conscience due from defendant. Rule absolute.

[(*a*) January v. Goodman, 1 Dall. 208.]

[(*b*) Hall v. Phelps, 2 Johns. R. 451.]

[(*c*) The subscribing witness to a note in suit being out of the Commonwealth in a neighboring State, other evidence was admitted of the signature of the maker, without proving the handwriting of the witness. Parker C. J. giving the opinion of the Court, said, "As the instrument in question is good without a subscribing witness, we do not think this strictness necessary; however it might be in relation to deeds or instruments under seal, where something more is necessary to be proved than the signature of the party." Homer v. Wallis, 11 Mass. R. 309.]

(26) Cooper v. Le Blanc, Str. 1051. The plaintiff, on discounting a note, sent to the defendant to know whether an endorsement upon it was his, and the defendant said it was, and the note would be paid when due: he would notwithstanding have given evidence by similitude of

against the party making it, but (27) not against any other party; and it is (28) sufficient, though made pending a treaty for a compromise.

[But it has been held that the confession of his signature by a party to an instrument, was not conclusive evidence, even in an action against him. (*a*)

In an action against A. as maker of a note payable to B. or bearer, to which there is a subscribing witness, the admission of A. that he gave a note to B, and a promise to pay it, made without seeing the note in suit, or having its date or amount stated, are not sufficient evidence to dispense with the production of the subscribing witness. (*b*)

---

hands that the endorsement was a forgery; but Lord Hardwicke would not allow it: he seemed inclined, however, to admit proof of actual forgery; but the defendant could not adduce it, and the plaintiff had a verdict. See Wilkinson v. Lutwidge, ante, p. 113. 312.

Leach v. Buchanan, 4 Esp. N. P. C. 226. The plaintiff, before he took a bill, sent a person with it to the defendant to inquire whether the acceptance upon it were his handwriting; the defendant said that it was, and that it would be duly paid. He now offered evidence of the actual forgery of the acceptance; but Lord Ellenborough held that that proof would not discharge the defendant; that after having so accredited the bill and induced a person to take it, he was bound to pay it. Verdict for the plaintiff.

(27) Hemmings v. Robinson, Barnes, 3d ed. 436. In an action by the endorsee of a note against the maker, it was reserved as a point whether the acknowledgment of an endorser was sufficient evidence to prove his endorsement; and the court held not. See Gray v. Palmer, p. 325. n. (33).

(28) Waldridge v. Kennison, Espinasse, 143. In an action against two as acceptors of a bill, the only evidence of the signature by one was an admission he made pending a treaty for settling the cause: it was objected that this admission ought not to be received in evidence, because it was made under the faith of a compromise; but Lord Kenyon held that the admission of a handwriting might be received in evidence, though it was made under faith of a compromise; and he admitted it accordingly.

[(*a*) In an action against Huse as the maker of a note, an acknowledgment by him of the signature was proved at the trial. The defendant was allowed to produce witnesses acquainted with his writing to prove that in their opinion the signature was not genuine; and also to prove the same by a signature known to be his. After a verdict for the defendant, the Court refused a new trial, saying that "it was merely a question of evidence, of which the jury were the judges." Hall v. Huse, 10 Mass. R. 39. The defendant in this case was 70 years old, and the evidence did not show that he had any reason to suspect, or did in fact suspect the signature, when he said it was his.

[(*b*) Shaver v. Ehle, 16 Johns. R. 201. Per Curiam. "The identity of the note to which the defendant's confession related is not proved

In an action on a bill, it has been made a question, whether an affidavit of the defendant, which implied that the plaintiff was rightful holder of the bill, should be permitted to go to the jury to prove the signature of an endorser. (*a*)]

Proof of the signature by a person who has no knowledge of the handwriting, except from having seen the party once write his name, may be sufficient, if the party then wrote his name at length. (29)

Or as much thereof as the signature to be proved contains. (29)

Otherwise it is not sufficient. (29)

[In Massachusetts a comparison by the jury of a disputed signature with genuine signatures of the party, is competent evidence. (*b*)]

In an action against the drawer of a lost bill, Holt C. J. (30) held proof that the defendant owned he had made the bill sufficient.

---

with reasonable certainty. Although there was a genuine note from him to A. or bearer, in existence somewhere, *non constat*, but that the note produced on the trial was a forgery."]

[(*a*) In an action on a bill against Coolidge and Co. in order to prove an endorsement by the payee, the plaintiffs offered the affidavit of Coolidge filed in the case, in which he referred to the bill in such a manner as implied that the plaintiffs were rightful holders of the bill. Story J. permitted the affidavit to be read to the jury. Payson v. Coolidge, 2 Gallis. 233. On Error to the Supreme Court of the United States, the court were divided on the question whether the affidavit ought to have been admitted. Coolidge v. Payson, 2 Wheat. 66.]

(29) Powell v. Ford, 2 Stark. 164. To prove an acceptance in which the defendant wrote his Christian name at length, plaintiff called a witness who had no other knowledge of defendant's handwriting but from having once seen him sign his name, where he put the initial only for his Christian name, "M. Ford." Lord Ellenborough thought his evidence might have been sufficient, had he ever seen defendant write his name at length; but that as he had never seen him write his Christian name, the Christian name could not be inferred to be gennine from evidence as to the sirname, any more than proof by a person who had seen him write some only of the letters which occurred in the sirname could be competent to prove the whole sirname. Nonsuit.

[(*b*) Parker C. J. in delivering the opinion of the Court, says, "Whatever doubt there may now be in England as to this species of evidence; (for in former times it was holden admissible, and has never yet to our knowledge been absolutely settled otherwise;) we have no doubt, that a comparison by the jury of the contested signature with other writings proved to be genuine, has become by long and invariable usage in this State, competent evidence." Homer v. Wallis, 11 Mass. R. 309. See also Hall v. Huse, ante, p. 323.]

(30) This was the case of Hart v. King, 12 Mod. 309.

So in an action against an endorser, proof that the defendant admittted to have received a bill corresponding with that upon which the action was brought, that after issue joined he had declared that he came to town to hasten the trial of a cause brought against him on an endorsement he had made upon a bill, and that he carried the cause down by proviso, was (31) held sufficient.

But in an action by the endorsee of a bill against the drawer, proof that one of the endorsers had confessed his signature (32) is insufficient; and in an action against several drawers, endorsers, or acceptors, an admission upon the pleadings by one of his signature will (33) not exempt the plaintiff from proving it against the others, if they contest it.

Though a person sued as acceptor of a bill prove that the acceptance was forged, yet if it appear that he and the party who committed the forgery had been connected in business, and that the defendant had paid other bills drawn by such party and accepted similarly to that on which the action is brought, it will be sufficient, because it shews that he (34)

---

(31) Dale v. Lubbock, 1 Barnard. B. R. 199. In an action against an endorser the evidence was, that he had written a letter stating that he had received a bill from A. upon B. bearing date such a day, and payable to him or order six months after date (in all which circumstances the bill stated in the letter corresponded with the bill declared upon), but not mentioning the sum; that he had said he came up to town to hasten on the trial of an action brought against him on an endorsement he had made upon a bill, and that in fact he carried down the cause by proviso; and Raymond C. J. held this sufficient evidence to prove that the defendant endorsed the bill stated; and the jury found for the plaintiff.

(32) Hemmings v. Robinson, p. 323. n. (27).

(33) Gray v. Palmer, Espinasse, 125. Action against James Palmer, John Palmer, and Hodgson, as makers of a note; Hodgson pleaded a judgment recovered, and each of the Palmers non-assumpsit: upon the trial on the non-assumpsits, the plaintiff proved the subscription by each of the Palmers, and there rested his case. The Palmers contended that he ought to prove Hodgson's subscription also, but the plaintiff insisted that *that* was admitted by the plea of nul tiel record; Lord Kenyon, however, held that it was only admitted as against Hodgson, not against the Palmers, and that the plaintiff could not recover against them without proving it.

(34) Barber v. Gingell, 3 Esp. N. P. C. 60. In an action against the defendant as acceptor of a bill, he proved that the acceptance was forged by Taylor the drawer; in answer to which it was proved that the defendant had been connected in business with Taylor, and that he had paid several bills drawn as the present by Taylor, and to which

had sanctioned such acceptances, and rendered himself liable to pay them.

[So in an action against a person as endorser of a note, where it appeared that the endorsement had been forged by the maker, it was held that the defendant having previously had notice of several similar forged endorsements of his name previously made by the maker, without objecting to them, had virtually authorized this, and made it his own. (*a*)

Where an old and a new bank had been incorporated by the same name, and the new bank had received and issued notes of the old bank, it was held that the new bank was not liable on notes of the old bank not actually issued by the new bank. (*b*)

A bank receiving notes appearing to be its own, but in fact forged, and paying cash for them, cannot afterwards recover back the amount paid, from the party who presented them, if a *bonâ fide* holder. (*c*)

Taylor (as it was supposed) had written the acceptances in the defendant's name. And Lord Kenyon held that this was an answer to the case of forgery set up by the defendant; for though he might not have accepted the bill, he had adopted the acceptance, and thereby made himself liable to pay the bill. Verdict for the plaintiff.

See Gibson v. Hunter, 2 H. Bl. 288.

[(*a*) Hartford Bank v. Hart, 3 Day, 491.]

[(*b*) The President, Directors, and Co. of the Hallowell and Augusta Bank were incorporated in 1804. Another corporation was incorporated by the same name in 1812, which had the same president and cashier as the old one. In an action against the new bank, in order to charge it with notes made by the old bank, it was proved that the new bank had received and passed or issued bills of the old bank; that the cashier and some of the directors of the new bank had frequently declared that there was no distinction between the notes which were issued before, and those issued after the incorporation of the new bank, and that this conduct of the new bank and these declartions had occasioned many of the notes of the old bank, and probably those in suit, to become current and be received as good. Parker C. J. who tried the case, being of opinion, that nothing short of proof that the notes sued or some of them, were issued by the new bank, as their own notes, with an intent to have them considered as evidence of promises on their part, would entitle the plaintiff to recover, nonsuited the plaintiff. And the whole court overruled a motion to set aside the nonsuit. Parker C. J. giving the opinion of the court, said, "We are not clear that with such proof the defendants would be answerable, unless it were likewise proved that the company, by some vote or legal act, had authorized the directors or officers of the corporation to bind them in this unusual way." Wyman v. Hallowell and Augusta Bank, 14 Mass. R. 58.]

So a bank receiving notes as its own, and crediting them as cash to the party who presented them, cannot afterwards in an action by the party who paid them in, a *bonâ fide* holder, be permitted to prove that they were forged. (*c*)

But where a sealed package was given to an officer of a bank, represented to contain notes of the bank to a certain amount, and he, without examining the notes, paid that amount to the party presenting them, a *bonâ fide* holder, and the bank on examination found some of the notes were forged, the court was of opinion that the bank might have reclaimed the amount of the forged notes from the party passing them, if notice had been immediately given. But the bank having neglected for fifteen days to give notice to the party who passed the notes to it, it was held that the bank had by this delay made the notes its own, and could not afterwards be allowed to reclaim the money paid, on account of the notes being forged. (*a*)

[(*c*) In an action by the United States Bank against the Bank of Georgia, the latter set up as a defence a payment from the former of certain notes of the Bank of Georgia, which had been fraudulently altered by some persons unknown from a small to a larger amount, which payment had been credited as cash to the United States Bank, and was the amount claimed in the suit. The Bank of Georgia did not give notice of this alteration of the notes until eighteen days after receiving them, and did not offer to return them until the nineteenth day. Story J. delivered the opinion of the court. "We think the defendants were bound to know their own notes, and having once accepted the notes in question as their own, they are concluded by their act of adoption, and cannot be permitted to set up the defence of forgery against the plaintiffs." United States Bank v. Bank of Georgia, 10 Wheat. R. 333.]

[(*a*) One of the directors of the Gloucester Bank, received from the Salem Bank, at the banking house of the latter bank, a sealed package represented by the Salem Bank to contain notes of the Gloucester Bank to the amount of $8500; and paid for them without opening the package, and the next day delivered the package unopened to the cashier of the Gloucester Bank. Fifteen days afterwards the Gloucester Bank, for the first time, intimated to the Salem Bank that some of the notes were forged, and a month afterwards offered to return the notes to the Salem Bank. The Gloucester Bank then sued the Salem Bank to recover the amount of part of the notes as being forged. At the trial Parker C. J. nonsuited the plaintiffs. On motion for new trial, Parker C. J. delivered the opinion of the court. "As the delivery of the notes was not at the bank, nor in banking hours, and was accompanied with a declaration that they were good bills, a reasonable time should have been allowed to count and examine them. Had this been done the next morning at the Gloucester Bank, and the notes been immediately returned, or a tender of these made, there can be no doubt an action

Where the notes of a bank after being signed by the cashier, were stolen from the banking-house, and the signature of the president forged upon them; it was held that the bank was not liable to a *bonâ fide* holder of the notes for the negligence of its officers in so keeping the paper that it was stolen, and put into circulation with a forged signature; it was also held that the bank was not liable in assumpsit to the holder of such notes, though the officers of the bank did not pronounce them counterfeit when first presented for payment, but expressed an opinion that they were genuine, though they refused to pay them. (*a*)]

The signature of a partner or servant, importing to have been made on the partnership or master's account, is to be considered as the signature of the (35) partnership or master.

On a signature by a servant, the servant's authority must be proved.

An authority by parol is (36) sufficient.

Subsequent assent is (37) evidence of precedent authority.

Usual employ is evidence (38) of a general authority; and a general authority is supposed to continue until its determination is notorious.

Therefore, after the discharge of a servant usually employed, a (39) man will be bound by his signature until his discharge is generally known.

The clerk who signs bank notes need not have authority for the purpose under the common seal of the bank. (40)

---

might have been maintained."—"The party receiving such notes must examine them as soon as he has opportunity, and return them immediately. But if he pays them, and continues silent, after he has had sufficient opportunity to examine them, he should be considered as having adopted them as his own." Motion overruled. Gloucester Bank v. Salem Bank, 17 Mass. R. 33.]

[(*a*) Salem Bank v. Gloucester Bank, 17 Mass. R. 1.]

(35) Vide Pinkney v. Hall, Lord Raym. 175., Smith v. Jarvis, Lord Raym, 1484., Carvick v. Vickery, Dougl. 630. n. 134.

(36) 12 Mod. 564.

(37) Comb. 450.

(38) 12 Mod. 346., Malynes, B. 3. c. 5. § 6. p. 264., 10 Mod. 110.

(39) Vide Beawes, § 231. p. 445. Molloy. B. 2. c. 10. § 27.

(40) Brown v. Messiter, ante, p. 263.

And now, by 1 G. 4. c. 92. s. 3., his signature may be impressed by machinery.

[In an action against the endorser of a note, evidence that the defendant has said that the maker of the note informed him that payment had been duly demanded of him, will not prove a demand. (*a*)]

Where notice is to be sent by the post, proof of putting it into the post is (41) sufficient.

Proof of sending one of two duplicate notices by the post may be established by the duplicate notice, without giving notice to produce that which was sent. (42)

Proof of sending notice by letter may be established, without giving notice to produce that letter. (42)

Proof that duplicate notices were written in order that one might be sent, and that a letter was sent to defendant at that time, will be sufficient evidence that such letter contained the notice, if defendant, on notice, does not produce such letter. (42)

[(*a*) Tower v. Durell, 9 Mass. R. 337.]

(41) Saunderson v. Judge, ante, p. 128. 178.; [and other cases cited p. 178. note, (3).]

[The court were unanimously of opinion that " evidence of the letter containing notice having been put into the postoffice, directed to the defendant, (an endorser,) at his place of residence, was sufficient proof of notice to be left to the jury; and that it was unnecessary to give notice to the defendant to produce the letter before such evidence could be admitted." Lindenberger v. Beall, 6 Wheat. R. 104.]

(42) Roberts v. Bradshaw, 1 Stark. 28. In an action by endorsee of a bill against drawer, plaintiff's clerk proved that on the day the bill was dishonored his master gave him two papers to compare, purporting to be notices of the dishonor of the bill, one of which he produced; it was objected that the one produced could not be read unless notice had been given to produce the other; Lord Ellenborough thought otherwise, and said a letter acquainting a party with the dishonor of a bill was in nature of a notice, and it was unnecessary to prove notice to produce such a letter; plaintiff could not then prove specifically that any notice was sent, but he proved that the same day he sent a letter to defendant, the contents of which his witness did not know, and that he had given due notice to produce that letter; Lord Ellenborough thought this sufficient evidence that the letter amounted to notice, for if it did not, defendant might produce it; and plaintiff had a verdict. Defendant moved for a new trial, but the Court of King's Bench refused a rule.

[So notice by letter may be proved by a copy of the letter, without giving notice to produce the original. Kine v. Beaumont, 3 Brod. and Bing. 288; S. C. 7 Moore, 112. See also Lindenberger v. Beall, supra, and Johnson v. Haight, 13 Joh . R. 470.]

But it has been held that proof that a notice was put into the post either the day it ought to have been sent *or the day following* is not (though notice to produce is given) sufficient evidence that the notice was sent in time. (43)

And that it cannot be submitted to the jury for their consideration. (43)

[After the death of a person, usually employed to make presentment to the makers, and give notice to the endorsers of notes, as a sworn bank messenger or notary public, the book of such person in which he recorded his proceedings upon notes, is admissible evidence to prove a presentment or notice. (*a*)

The protest of a note by a notary, is after his decease evidence of the demand and notice stated in the protest. (*a*)

---

(43) Lawson v. Sherwood, 1 Stark. 314. In an action against an endorser, it was necessary for plaintiff to prove that notice was sent to the defendant the second day after the bill became due; a witness proved that he sent him a notice two or three days after the bill became due, but whether it was the second or third day he could not state; notice to produce was proved, and it was urged for plaintiff, that as defendant did not produce what had been sent, this was evidence to go to the jury that the notice was sent on the second day: but Lord Ellenborough thought otherwise: he said the non-production only entitled plaintiff to give parol evidence of its contents; plaintiff was bound to give notice on the second day, and evidence that he gave it either on that or the following day could not be left to the jury as evidence that he gave it on the second. Plaintiff was theorfore nonsuited.

[(*a*) The messenger of the State Bank kept a book in which he entered his doings with respect to notices to makers and endorsers of notes belonging to the bank and of those left for collection. The by-laws of the bank made it his duty to keep such a book, and to take an oath faithfully to perform his duty. In an action against the endorser of a note which had been left in the bank for collection, it was held that the book of a deceased messenger, after proving his handwriting, was admissible evidence to go to the jury to show a demand on the maker and notice to the endorser. Welsh v. Barrett, 15 Mass. R. 380.

In an action against the endorser of a note payable at the Nashville Bank, the notary who made the demand and gave the notice having died before the trial, the plaintiff offered in evidence his protest, which stated that he had made a regular demand and given notice to the endorser, and the deposition of a witness which stated that the notary kept a book in which be recorded copies of the notes protested by him and of the protests, and memorandums of the manner of giving notice. A copy of the protest was annexed to the deposition. This evidence, though objected, to was admitted; and a verdict given for the plaintiff. On Error,—Story J. delivered the opinion of the court. "Memorandums made by a person in the ordinary course of his business, of acts or matters which his duty in such business requires him to do for others,

But where a memorandum in the register of a notary deceased before the trial, merely stated that notice to the endorser of a note was put into the post-office, but did not state where the endorser resided, or to what place the notice was directed, or that any inquiry was made to ascertain his place of residence, it was held that the memorandum was not sufficient evidence of notice. (*a*)

It has however been ruled at *nisi prius*, that the entry of

---

in case of his death, are admissible evidence of the acts and matters so done. *A fortiori* we think the acts of a public officer, like a notary public, admissible, although they may not be strictly official, if they are according to the customary business of his office, since he acts as a sworn officer, and is clothed with public authority and confidence." Judgment affirmed. Nicholls v. Webb, 8 Wheat. R. 326. See also Halliday v. Martinet, infra; and Sharpe v. Bingley, 1 S. Car. R. 373.]

[(*a*) In an action against the endorser of two notes, the plaintiff offered in evidence the protests of Bleecker, a notary public who had died before the trial, which stated that he had made diligent inquiry for the maker, in the city of New York where the notes were dated, but could not find him: he also offered the register of the notary in which were inserted copies of the notes and protests, and which stated that he had put notices for the endorser in the post-office. A clerk of the notary testified that it was the usual course of business in the notary's office to make inquiry to ascertain the place of the endorser's residence, and if it could not be found to put a notice in the post-office, and that he had no doubt such inquiry was made in this case, and that the endorser's residence could not be ascertained, though he did not *know* the fact. Nonsuit. Woodworth J. delivered the opinion of the court. "I am satisfied on principle and authority that the evidence was competent, and that there was due diligence to demand payment of the maker."—"It remains wholly uncertain whether diligent inquiry was made for the endorser, and that he could not be found; and whether he resided in the city of New York or at what other place. If the notary had stated, that the endorser could not be found, he would have made out sufficient to entitle the plaintiff to recover; but to charge an endorser by merely proving the general practice of the office in other cases, accompanied by the opinion of a witness not resting on any recollection or knowledge, but manifestly derived from such usual practice only, would in my judgment be dangerous." Judgment affirmed. Halliday v. Martinet, 20 Johns. R. 168.

But in a previous case where the evidence of notice to the endorser of a bill consisted of the deposition of the notary who protested the bill, who stated that it was his usual practice on the evening of the day of protest in all cases to give notice in writing to endorsers residing at a distance by putting a notice directed to the party at his place of residence into the post-office, and that he had no doubt notice in this case was duly given, though he could not recollect positively; and that it was possible he might have given the notice to the holder to be forwarded; the evidence of notice was held to be sufficient in the first instance. Miller v. Hackley, 5 Johns. R. 375.]

a clerk of a notary in his books, stating search for the maker, and notice to the endorser, could not be received in evidence in an action against the endorser, though the clerk at the time of the trial was absent on a voyage. (*a*)

In an action against the drawer of a bill by endorsees, an agreement between the defendant and the plaintiff's endorser, which recited that the bill in suit among others was *overdue*, and *was or ought* to be in the hands of the endorser, was held to be evidence of notice to the drawer, though the plaintiff was no party to the agreement. (*b*) (*c*)]

Production of the instrument is (44) sufficient evidence of a protest.

[A protest of an inland bill or note is not evidence of a demand or notice. (*d*)

In an action upon a lost note the plaintiff must prove its loss and contents by the best evidence in his power.

It seems that a notarial copy may be received in connexion with other evidence, to prove the contents of the

---

[(*a*) By Van Ness J. in Cummings v. Fisher, Anth. N. P. 1.]

[(*b*) Gunson v. Metz, 2 Dow. and Ryl. 334; S. C. 1 Barn. and Cres. 193.]

[(*c*) As to what is evidence of notice or a waiver of it, see Jones v. Fales, and other cases, ante, p. 204. note, (*c*.)]

(44) Anon. 12 Mod. 345. To prove a protest, the plaintiff produced an instrument attested by a notary public; and though it was insisted that he should prove this instrument or at least give some account how he came by it, Holt C. J. ruled that it was not necessary.

[See also Fenwick v. Sears, 1 Cranch, 259. In this case the questions,—whether the acts of a notary public, who certifies himself to be duly commissioned and sworn, are valid if he be duly appointed, but not sworn: and whether between the parties to a bill, the certificate of the notary who protested it, that he is "duly commissioned and sworn," be not conclusive evidence of the fact,—were argued, but no opinion given.

The certificate of a notary under his notarial seal, is *primâ facie* evidence that he is duly commissioned by the governor. The court said that it had been the daily practice to receive such certificates without objection. Browne v. Philadelphia Bank, 6 Serg. and Raw. 484.]

[(*d*) Nicholls v. Webb, 8 Wheat. R. 326; Union Bank v. Hyde, 6 Wheat. R. 572; Cummings v. Fisher, Anth. N. P. 1.

In Pennsylvania a protest of a note by a notary has been held to be evidence of the demand and notice stated in the protest, by virtue of the statute of that State of January 2, 1815, which enacts that the *official* acts, protests, and attestations of all notaries public, may be received as evidence of the facts therein certified. Browne v. Philadelphia Bank, 6 Serg. and Raw. 484.]

note, but it is not necessary for the plaintiff to produce a notarial copy. (*a*)

In an action on a lost bill after its existence was proved, the plaintiff was in one case allowed to prove its loss by his own oath. (*b*)]

On a judgment by default in an action upon a bill or note, no (45) evidence need be given. (*c*)

[(*a*) In an action upon a lost note a notarial copy was permitted to go to the jury connected with other evidence which showed that the makers had admitted their liability upon the note, although the notarial copy was the only evidence of the date and amount of the note. Peabody v. Denton, 2 Gallis. 351. See also Anderson v. Robson, 2 Bay, 495.

In an action on a lost note, Thompson J. who delivered the opinion of the court, said, "Proof of the contents of a lost paper ought to be the best the party has in power to produce, and at all events such as to leave no reasonable doubt as to the substantial parts of the paper. But to have required a notarial copy, would have been demanding that of the existence of which there was no evidence, and which the law will not presume was in the power of the party; it not being necessary that a promissory note should be protested." Renner v. Bank of Columbia, 9 Wheat. R. 581.]

[(*b*) Meeker v. Jackson, 3 Yeates, 442. The court said that the plaintiff was a witness from the necessity of the case.]

(45) Bevis v. Lindsell, Str. 1149. On executing a writ of inquiry in an action on a note, the plaintiff did not produce the subscribing witness, but offered other evidence that it was the defendant's hand, and the court held *that* sufficient; "for the note being set out in the declaration is admitted, and the only use of producing it is to see whether any payment is endorsed upon it."

Mills v. Lyne, B. R. H. 26 G. 3. On a writ of inquiry in an action upon a note, the sheriff directed the jury to give nominal damages only, because the plaintiff could not prove the note. Lawrence insisted that the plaintiff was bound to produce the note (because a receipt of part might have been endorsed thereon) and to prove the defendant's signature; but per Buller J. "If you had paid part you might have pleaded it, but you have let judgment go for the whole;" and the court set aside the inquisition.

Green v. Herne, 3 Term. Rep. 301. Upon a rule nisi to set aside an inquisition against the acceptor of a bill of exchange, it was urged that the bill, though *produced* before the jury, was not *proved;* but the court held that by suffering the judgment the defendant admitted the acceptance of the bill, and that he was liable to its amount: and Buller J. said, "the only reason of producing the bill is to see whether any part of it is paid."

[(*c*) But the note itself must be produced, or its absence accounted for, though it is not necessary to prove the note. And if a note be produced varying from the declaration, the plaintiff will not be allowed to prove that the variance was occasioned by mistake, and that the note produced was the one intended to be described in the declaration. Sheehy v. Mandeville, 7 Cranch, 208.]

The court (46) will therefore upon such judgment, even in assumpsit, if the bill or note is for the payment of British money, refer it to an officer to ascertain the sum due for principal, interest, and costs, and give the plaintiff final judgment without a writ of inquiry.

And if the bill or note be lost pending the action, they will refer it on a verified copy. (47)

But the (48) court will not refer it, if the bill or note is for the payment of foreign money.

Nor will they refer it, to ascertain the amount of (49) charges and expenses; or to compute (50) re-exchange upon a foreign bill.

And though the action be in fact brought to recover the money due upon a bill or note, yet the court will not refer

---

(46) Shepherd v. Charter, 4 Term Rep. 275. The defendant having suffered judgment by default in an action on a bill, the plaintiff obtained a rule to shew cause why it should not be referred to the master, to compute what was due for principal and interest. The rule was opposed upon the general ground that a reference in such cases was improper; but the court thought otherwise; and Grose J. observed, that the judges in the common pleas gave the case before them great consideration before they referred the question to one of the prothonotaries; and the rule was made absolute. The same had previously been done in Rashleigh v. Salmon, 1 H. Bl. 252., Andrews v. Blake, 1 H. Bl. 529., Longman v. Fenn, 1 H. Bl. 541.; and it is now every day's practice in the king's bench and common pleas, but not in the exchequer, vide Chilton v. Harborn, 1 Anstr. 249.

(47) Brown v. Messiter, ante, p. 263.

(48) Maunsell v. Lord Massareene, 5 Term Rep. 87. The court discharged a rule nisi for referring it to the master to compute principal, interest, and costs, upon a bill of exchange, because the bill was for the payment of 200*l.* Irish money. See also Napier v. Schneider, infra, n. 50.

(49) Goldsmid v. Taite, 2 Bos. and Pull. 55. On a rule to shew cause why a bill of exchange should not be referred to the prothonotary to compute principal, interest, exchange, re-exchange, charges, expenses, and costs, it was objected that charges and expenses were not matter of mere computation; and the counsel for the rule consenting to strike out those words, the court made the rule absolute. But as to re-exchange, see the next note.

(50) Napier v. Schneider, 12 East's Rep. 420. A bill was drawn in Scotland upon and accepted by the defendant in England, and on motion to refer it to the master to compute principal, interest, and costs on this bill, the court was prayed to direct the master to allow re-exchange; but this they refused, saying that they would not refer it to the master to try foreign customs and facts, but only to compute what was due upon the bill itself. They therefore granted the rule in the common form.

it to the officer (51), unless the bill or note be stated in the declaration.

Nor will the court make such reference, in an action of debt brought on a (52) judgment recovered on a bill or note.

Where one count in the declaration is on a bill or note, and the defendant demurs to that count, and judgment is given for the plaintiff, the court (53) will refer it to the officer to ascertain what is due for principal, interest, and costs, on that count, though there are other counts on which the parties are at issue.

---

(51) Osborne v. Noad, 8 Term Rep. 648. The declaration contained only counts for goods sold, and work and labor, and the common money counts. On judgment by default, the plaintiff obtained a rule nisi to refer it to the master to compute principal and interest on two notes; and in support of the rule an affidavit was produced, stating that the action was brought to recover the amount of these notes, and that such amount was recoverable under the money counts. The court, however, said that the rule was confined to cases in which it appeared by the declaration that the action was brought on the notes or bills. Rule discharged.

(52) Nelson v. Sheridan, 8 Term Rep. 395.

(53) Duperoy v. Johnson, 7 Term Rep. 473. The declaration contained many counts, one of which was on a bill; to that there was a demurrer, on which the plaintiff had judgment; to the others there was a plea, on which issue was joined: a rule nisi was obtained to refer it to the master to compute principal, interest, and costs on the bill; and on shewing cause against this rule, it was urged that the plaintiff ought either to have waited for the result of the trial of the issue on the other counts, or to have entered a nolle prosequi as to those counts. In support of the rule, Fleming v. Langton, 1 Str. 532., was cited; and the court thought that case decisive of the present, and made the rule absolute.

See Tidd's Practice, 5th ed. 569., stating that a nolle prosequi must be entered on the other counts; but that such entry need not be made *before* the reference to the master; that it is sufficient if done at any time before final judgment.

CHAP. XII.

Defence to an Action on a Bill or Note.

One species of defence sometimes attempted upon a bill or note is, that there was some bargain when they were given or transferred, for a renewal or indulgence.

But it is a settled rule that no such defence can be supported by oral evidence, where it is inconsistent with the tenor of the bill or note. (1)

Thus upon a bill or note payable at a specified time, parol evidence of a bargain when it was issued, that it was not to be paid till I. S. should die, or certain estates should be sold, is inadmissible. (1) (*a*)

---

(1) Woodbridge v. Spooner, 3 Barnew. and Ald. 233. Action against executors, on note payable on demand for value received: evidence was given that the bargain was at the time the note was given, that it should not be payable till after the maker's death, and should then be in nature of a legacy, and on that ground nonsuit: but on rule nisi to enter verdict for plaintiff, and cause shewn, the whole court held the evidence should not have been received, because it imported a different bargain and intention from what the note expressed; and rule absolute.

Free v. Hawkins, 8 Taunt. 92. In an action upon a note by endorsee against endorser, defendant insisted upon want of notice of the dishonor: plaintiff offered parol evidence that at the time the note was given and defendant (who only lent his name) endorsed it, it was understood that payment was not to be required until certain estates of the maker were sold, nor then unless they produced sufficient, and that therefore the defendant knew the note had not been honored. Gibbs C. J. rejected the evidence, and nonsuited the plaintiff; and on a rule nisi for a new trial, the court held the evidence rightly rejected, because it contradicted the note, and the rule was discharged.

Rawson v. Walker, 1 Stark. 361. In an action by the payee against the maker, on a note payable on demand, defendant offered parol evidence, that it was given for goods sold to a bankrupt by his assignees, and that defendant was not to be called upon, unless his allowance under the commission should not be sufficient to pay the amount: per Lord Ellenborough, I am ready to admit evidence to shew the consideration illegal, but I cannot receive parol evidence inconsistent with the terms of the note; upon a note payable on demand, parol evidence to shew it was not to be payable upon demand, but on a contingency only, is not admissible. Verdict for plaintiff.

Same point, Campbell v. Hodgson, Gow. 74.

[See also Renner v. Bank of Columbia, 9 Wheat. R. 587, and Britten v. Webb, ante, p. 214.

It is held in many American cases that in an action against an endorser, parol evidence is not admissible to contradict or vary the legal

[In an action on a note payable immediately, parol evidence cannot be received that it was to be paid at a future day. (*b*)]

So upon a general endorsement of a bill or note, the like evidence of a bargain at the time of the endorsement, that the bill should be renewed, cannot be received. (2)

But parol evidence of a bargain after a bill or note was given or transferred, will be admissible; and the bargain, if there is a sufficient consideration to support it, will be binding. (2)

---

effect of the endorsement. Field v. Nickerson, 13 Mass. R. 138; Sice v. Cunningham, 1 Cowen, 397; the opinion of Hosmer J., in Bishop v. Dexter, 2 Conn. R. 422; Price v. Perry, 2 S. Car. R. 31; Rugely v. Davidson, 2 S. Car. R. 33.

But in a case in Pennsylvania, in an action against the endorser of a note endorsed by him in blank, it was held that he might prove by parol evidence, that at the time of the endorsement, the plaintiff received the note under an agreement not to have recourse upon it to the endorser. Duncan J. delivering the opinion of the Court, said, "The parol evidence is not to contradict any written instrument, but to prevent the party from making use of a blank endorsement, with which he was entrusted, contrary to his agreement when he received it; and as parol evidence in an action between drawer and payee of fraud or want of consideration to impeach a note, is constantly received, the same evidence may be given to impeach an endorsement between the endorser and the endorsee." Hill v. Ely, 5 Serg. and Raw. 363.]

[(*a*) It has been held in Massachusetts, in an action on a note payable at a day certain, that a written agreement given by the payee to the maker at the time the note was made, "to wait for the money due him, till the maker turned his property to the best advantage," and a parol agreement to wait five years, could not be received in evidence. Parsons C. J. said, "This agreement, although made at the same time, must be considered as a collateral promise of the promisee's, for the breach of which, if there be a legal consideration, an action would lie." Dow v. Tuttle, 4 Mass. R. 414.]

[(*b*) In an action brought in New York on the following note, "I promise to pay Samuel Thompson eighty dollars, Montego Bay, Ap. 21, 1807," it was held, that the note was payable immediately, and being made in Jamaica, parol evidence was not admissible that it was to be paid in New York. Kent C. J. delivered the opinion of the Court. "The time of payment is part of the contract, and if no time be expressed, the law adjudges that the money is payable immediately, and the parol proof went to alter in a very material degree its operation and effect, by making it not payable, until some distant and undefined period when the parties should arrive in New-York." Thompson v. Ketcham, 8 Johns. R. 146.]

(2) Hoare v. Graham, 3 Campb. 57. Endorsee against payee of a note payable two months after date. Defence, that defendant refused to endorse unless plaintiffs would agree the note should be renewed when due, and that plaintiff acceded to that condition: sed per Lord

Where the ground of defence is an engagement to renew, it will be incumbent on the defendant to shew that he has taken the proper steps towards such renewal. (3)

It is a defence to an action on a bill, that it was passed to plaintiff by the first endorser for the special purpose of his getting it discounted for the first endorser, and that instead of so doing he claimed to hold it for a debt owing to him by the second endorser. (4)

[So where a note made by two persons was received by the payee for him to get it discounted at a particular bank, on specified terms, part of the money received on it to go to one of the makers, and the remainder to be retained by the payee on account of a debt due to him from the other maker, and the bank refused to discount the note; it was held that an endorsee of the payee who sued for the benefit

---

Ellenborough, I cannot admit this evidence; it is inconsistent with the written instrument: I will receive evidence that the note was endorsed to plaintiffs as a trust; there may, after a bill is drawn, be a binding promise for a valuable consideration to renew it, but if the promise be contemporaneous with the drawing, the law will not enforce it; it would be incorporating with a written contract an incongruous parol agreement. Verdict for plaintiff.

[After a note made by A. Winship to J. Winship became due, in consideration of A. W.'s becoming a surety for J. W. in a bond J. W. agreed that a balance should remain unpaid upon the note for A. W.'s security, which should not be claimed by J. W. if A. W. was obliged to pay the bond. J. W. became bankrupt and A. W. afterwards paid the bond. In an action by J. W.'s assignee against A. W. on the note, it was held that the above facts were a good defence for the amount paid on the bond. Parker C. J. delivering the opinion of the Court, said, "The agreement is not inconsistent with the written contract, it being made subsequently, and after the contract was broken by non-payment." Ward v. Winship, 12 Mass. R. 481.]

(3) Gibbon v. Scott, 2 Stark. 286. In an action by drawer against acceptor on a bill for the freight of a chartered ship, the defence was, that plaintiff had engaged to renew the bill if the charterer did not return before the bill was due; but no application appearing to have been made to plaintiff to renew, Lord Ellenborough thought the defence failed, and the plaintiff had a verdict.

(4) Delaunay v. Mitchell, 1 Stark. 439. E. Clewer held a bill payable to herself or order, and endorsed first by herself, and secondly by her son: to prevent a commission against her son she delivered the bill to plaintiff, that he might get it discounted for her; he did not get it discounted, but insisted on holding it for a debt the son owed him, and sued the acceptor; but Lord Ellenborough thought it clear he could not maintain the action, and directed a nonsuit.

of the payee, could not maintain an action upon the note against the makers. (*a*)

In an action by an endorser of a bill against the drawer, the defendant may prove that the plaintiff holds the bill as agent or trustee of the payee, and that the payee has requested the defendant not to pay the bill to the plaintiff. (*b*)

In an action against A. and B. two joint makers of a note, a plea by A. of an agreement by the payee when the note was made, that A. should only be held to pay a certain sum upon the note less than the full amount of it, and that he had paid that amount, has been held bad on demurrer. (*c*) And it is immaterial whether the agreement is verbal or written. (*c*)

It is a good defence to an action against the endorser of a note, that the holder, who had received it from the maker, knew at the time of receiving it that the maker had no right to transfer it. (*d*)

[(*a*) Denniston v. Rogers, 10 Johns. R. 207.]

[(*b*) In an action by Barker as endorsee against Prentiss as drawer of a bill payable to Robinson and Co. and endorsed by them and also by Taber and Son, it was held to be a good defence that Taber and Son acted as agents of Robinson and Co. and endorsed the bill to Barker merely as agent of Robinson and Co. and for their use; and that Robinson and Co. before this action was brought had requested Prentiss not to pay the bill to Barker; and that the agency of Taber and Son and Barker, which did not appear by the endorsements, might be proved by parol evidence. Barker v. Prentiss, 6 Mass. R. 430.]

[(*c*) Shed v. Pierce, 17 Mass. R. 623. Parker C. J. giving the opinion of the Court, said, "The agreement is in direct contradiction to the promise contained in the note; and whether in writing or merely verbal, we think, cannot be set up against the note. Being inconsistent with the express terms of the contract, and relating to one only of the promisers, it ought not to defeat the action against the other; as it will if it should be held a good bar."]

[(*d*) Warren endorsed a note for the accommodation of the makers, for them to raise money on it, but they becoming insolvent with the note in their hands, he directed them not to part with it. They however passed it to Skilding and Haight for a valuable consideration, but informed them at the time of the above facts. It was held that Skilding and Haight could not maintain an action against Warren as endorser. Spencer C. J. giving the opinion of the Court, said, "The plaintiffs are *mala fide* holders of the note, and they took it with a view to charge a person who had endorsed it to aid men who were in good circumstances, but who became insolvent. The plaintiffs were warned that the note was *functus officio*, and yet they took it." Skilding v. Warren, 15 Johns. R. 270.]

In an action on a note against an endorser, it is no defence that he endorsed the note for the accommodation of the maker, and that it was intended to be discounted at a particular bank, but that the maker, the bank refusing to discount it, had it discounted by A. B. who knew these circumstances. (*a*)]

Another species of defence to an action in respect of a bill or note, is (5) want or inadequacy of consideration for giving or transferring it.

A total failure of consideration is, where it can be insisted upon, a total bar: inadequacy, or a partial failure, a bar pro tanto only. (6) (*b*)

[(*a*) In an action by J. and T. Powell against Waters, as endorser of a note made by Wood, it appeared that the note was a renewal of one which was made by Wood and endorsed by Waters for Wood's accommodation for the purpose of having it discounted at the Bank of Newburgh for Wood's use. The bank refusing to discount it, it was offered to Parish, one of the firm of J. and T. Powell and Co., who immediately discounted it, being at the time informed of the purpose for which it was made. Waters did not know when he endorsed the note in suit, that the first note had been discounted by Powell and Co. The note in suit was endorsed to the plaintiffs by Powell and Co. Spencer C. J. giving the opinion of the Court, said, "It was entirely immaterial whether the first note was discounted at the Bank of Newburgh or elsewhere. It did not alter or increase the responsibility of the endorser. If the plaintiffs knew when they received the note, that it was intended to be discounted at the Bank of Newburgh, and had been refused, it would not affect them, or establish any fraud." Powell v. Waters, 17 Johns. R. 176.]

(5) Jefferies v. Austen, Str. 647. In an action by the payee of a note against the maker, Eyre C. J. of the common pleas, allowed the defendant to prove, that it was given as a reward in case the plaintiff procured the defendant to be restored to an office, and that the defendant was not restored; and on this proof the defendant had a verdict.

Jackson v. Warwick, 7 Term Rep. 121. The defendant's son was apprenticed by indenture to the plaintiff; and the defendant gave the plaintiff a note for £10 as an apprentice fee; but this premium was not mentioned in the indentures, nor were they stamped pursuant to 8 Ann. c. 9. The son remained part of his time, and then absconded. In an action on the note, and failure of consideration (the apprenticeship) relied on as a defence, it was contended that the avoiding the indentures could not collaterally affect the note, and that at all events the consideration had not wholly failed, inasmuch as the plaintiff had maintained the apprentice during his stay. Lawrence J., however, thought that the consideration was entire, and had wholly failed; but he allowed a verdict to be taken for the plaintiff, with liberty to the defendant to move to enter a nonsuit. The court concurred in opinion with Lawrence, and directed a nonsuit to be entered.

(6) Barber v. Backhouse, Peake, 61. In an action on a bill of ex-

Thus in an action against an acceptor, it is a good defence either wholly or in part, that the acceptance was either wholly or in part for the accommodation of the plaintiff; (7)

---

change by the payee, the defendant paid part of the money into court, and it appeared upon the trial that there was no consideration for the other part. Law, however, urged that the payment of the money into court admitted the bill was good for part, and if it was good for part, it was good in toto; but Lord Kenyon declared himself clearly of a contrary opinion, upon which the jury found for the defendant; and this case being afterwards mentioned by Lord Kenyon in the course of argument, Law said he was perfectly satisfied with the decision.

Ledger v. Ewer, Peake, 216. In an action by the payee of a bill against the acceptor, the consideration appeared to be that the plaintiff had taken the defendant into partnership; but on the defendant's friend's advice he broke off the connexion: there was evidence of fraud on the plaintiff's part in drawing the defendant into the engagement, which Lord Kenyon left to the jury; but he told them if they were against the defendant on the evidence of fraud, they should take into consideration the damages the plaintiff had really sustained by the non-performance of the contract, and were not obliged to find the whole amount of the bill; the jury, however, found for the defendant.

[(*b*) Livingston owing Maule a large sum, and Maule holding land for Livingston's use, Maule conveyed the land to Winter, on his becoming security for Livingston's debt to Maule. By an agreement between Winter and Livingston, Livingston made his notes to Winter, and Winter agreed to convey the land to him on payment of the notes, but this agreement to be void if Livingston did not pay his notes as they fell due. He did not pay them as they fell due, and Winter exercised acts of ownership over the land by selling parcels of it, &c. It was held that Winter could not maintain an action against Livingston on the notes, on account of the failure of the consideration. Per Curiam. "Livingston has received nothing for his notes, and Winter has a complete and perfect title to the lands." Winter v. Livingston, 13 Johns. R. 54.

In an action by Shepard against Hawley and Loomis, as endorsers of a note, it was held to be a complete defence to the action, that Shepard holding Loomis' drafts on Ward, agreed to return them, on receiving certain notes, and among others that in suit, which were accordingly given him, but that he refused to deliver up the drafts—that Shepard received part of the money of Ward, and gave him a receipt in full, erased the acceptances,—and three months after the notes were received, offered to return the drafts in that state to Loomis, who refused to receive them. Shepard v. Hawley, 1 Conn. R. 367.

It was held in a subsequent case that Shepard could not maintain an action against the maker of one of the notes mentioned in the preceding case. Shepard v. Hall, 1 Conn. R. 494.

Where after non est inventus returned on the *ca. sa.* against the principal in a suit, the bail gave his note for the amount of the judgment, and the judgment against the principal was afterwards reversed on a writ of error, it was held that the consideration for the note of the bail had failed, and that no action could be maintained upon it. Tappen v. Van Wagenen, 3 Johns. R. 465.

A note given to aid a fund for support of the parish minister was held to be void for want of consideration. Boutell v. Cowdin, 9 Mass. R. 254.]

Or for some person for whom the plaintiff is trustee. (8)

So if a bill or note is given either wholly or as to a specific part, as the consideration of a special contract, and that contract either fails in toto or is in toto rescinded, it will be an answer to an action on the bill or note either wholly or pro tanto, if the plaintiff stands in a situation which makes him liable to such a defence. (9) (*a*)

---

(7) Darnell v. Williams, 2 Stark. 166. Payee against acceptor on bill for £19, 12*s*. Defendant proved that he had value for £10 only, and that he accepted for the rest to accommodate the plaintiff: and per Lord Ellenborough, "Though this, as to third persons, is a bill for £19, 12*s*., yet as between these parties, their acceptance is for £10 only;" and that sum having been paid before the action, he nonsuited the plaintiff.

(8) Jones v. Hibbert, 2 Stark. 304. Defendant accepted a bill for £415 to accommodate Philips and Co.: Philips and Co. endorsed it to their bankers for value, and became bankrupts: the bankers knew it to be an accommodation acceptance, and their demand against Philips and Co. was £265 only: in an action by them upon this acceptance, it was held that they could only recover the £265; and they had a verdict accordingly.

(9) Lewis v. Cosgrave, 2 Taunt. 2. This was an action on a banker's check drawn by the defendant, and given to the plaintiff for the price of a horse sold by the plaintiff to the defendant, and warranted sound. The horse was in fact unsound, and that was relied on as a defence. The defendant proved that he had sent back the horse, but the plaintiff refused to take it; he, however, sent it again, and left it in the plaintiff's stable without his knowledge. Heath J. told the jury that as the plaintiff had refused to receive back the horse, the contract for the sale was not rescinded, and that the defendant was therefore bound to pay the check, and had his remedy by action for the deceit. They found a verdict for the plaintiff; but on a rule nisi for a new trial, and cause shewn, the court, on the ground of there being clear evidence of fraud, made the rule absolute. See Weston v. Downes, Dougl. 23., Power v. Wells, Cowp. 818., and Towers v. Barrett, 1 Term Rep. 133.

[See also Reed v. Prentiss, 1 N Hamp. R. 174.]

[(*a*) It is a good defence to an action on a note, that it was given in consideration of the assignment of a void patent right from the plaintiff to the defendant. And it seems that the defence is good, although the assignment should contain covenants, on which the defendant might maintain an action against the plaintiff. A note in such a case was held to be void notwithstanding the plaintiff had furnished the defendant with materials, and given him instructions in the art described in the patent, the materials and instructions being of no value to the defendant, except as subservient to the art pretended to be conveyed. Bliss v. Negus, 8 Mass. R. 46.

In an action on notes given for the price of a shearing machine, it was held that the defendant under the general issue might prove that the plaintiff made certain representations with respect to the usefulness of the machine, which were utterly false, and that known to him at the time, and that the machine was in fact worth nothing and totally use-

But the partial failure of consideration will constitute no defence if the quantum to be deducted on that account is

---

less; and that this evidence proved the note to be without consideration and void, and was a complete defence to the action. Sill v. Rood, 15 Johns. R. 230.

Getman agreed with his slave Tom that if Tom would procure him good notes to the amount of $200, and give his own note for $75, that he would immediately manumit him and his family. Tom procured the notes and delivered them to his master, and among them one made by Christy payable to Petry and not to his order, and by him assigned to Getman to be collected at his own risk. Getman made out an instrument of manumission, and procured a certificate from the overseers of the poor. Getman however kept the papers two years and 5 months, and then gave them to the town clerk to be recorded, and during all that time kept and treated the negroes as his slaves. In an action against Christy upon his note in the name of Petry, the court considered Getman as the real plaintiff, as there was no evidence that the note was ever delivered to Petry; and that there was a failure of consideration, as the agreement of Getman was to manumit the slaves *immediately* on receiving the notes, and he had refused to do so for two years and five months; and that it made no difference whether the manumission was legally consummated or not, without any delivery of the certificate, since Getman's actually holding the negroes as his slaves was a violation of his agreement. Judgment for the defendant. Petry v. Christy, 19 Johns. R. 53.

In an action by an insurance company against the endorser of a note given to secure a premium of insurance, the insurance company having before the suit commenced become liable to pay the insured, who was the maker of the note, a return of part of the premium, it was held that the defendant was entitled to have the amount of the return of premium deducted from the amount of the note, although the maker was insolvent, and indebted to the insurers upon other premium notes. Per Curiam. "The consideration for the note was the premium of insurance, and the only question is, what was the amount of that premium. If the plaintiffs are bound to return part, then the premium really and ultimately due, is not as much as it was at first understood to be."—"The surety is no further bound than his principal, and is entitled to the same defence." Phœnix Ins. Co. v. Fiquet, 7 Johns. R. 383.

Stow claiming a certain sum of Wadley on account of an alleged mistake in settling their accounts, which mistake Wadley denied, Wadley made his note for the amount payable to Stow, and lodged it with Ten Eyck, the parties agreeing that if Wadley within 60 days should exhibit Ten Eyck proof from which Ten Eyck should think that Wadley ought not to pay the note, then it should be delivered to Wadley, otherwise it should belong to Stow. Wadley within the 60 days insisted on giving parol evidence to Ten Eyck, which he thinking himself not authorized to admit, returned the papers to Stow. It was held that Stow could not maintain an action against Wadley on the note. Per Curiam. "There was no consideration for the note. Ten Eyck declined to act, and would not receive the parol evidence that the defendant offered. The defendant was not in default, and his default, or a decision of Ten Eyck against him, was a condition precedent to the validity and binding operation of the note." Stow v. Wadley, 8 Johns. R. 96.

Olmsted made a note payable to E. Stewart or bearer, but at the time

matter, not of definite computation, but of unliquidated damages.

Thus if a bill or note is given for the stipulated price of goods previously delivered, it is no ground of partial defence that the price was exorbitant. (10)

---

of making it informed C. Stewart, to whom the note was delivered as the agent of E. Stewart, that he did not owe E. Stewart so much as the note was given for, that he had mislaid his papers, but that he would give the note, and let it lie until he could find them. In an action on the note by C. Stewart against Olmsted, it was held that the defendant might prove the amount really due from him to E. Stewart, and that that amount was all which could be recovered by the plaintiff. Olmsted v. Stewart, 13 Johns. R. 238.

March 8th, 1810, Dennis of Philadelphia drew a bill upon Liverpool payable to Smith or order, at 60 days' sight. Smith endorsed it in blank, and Dennis handed it to Eddy and Co. to secure a balance supposed to be due by him to them. The bill was not passed to the credit of Dennis by Eddy and Co. but they delivered it to Chancellor to be sent on for collection, and took from him a receipt promising to account for the bill. On the 6th Aug. Eddy and Co. assigned this receipt, *inter alia*, to Evans, on account of a pre-existing debt, Evans knowing nothing of the transaction between the original parties. The bill being returned dishonored, was delivered to Evans, who brought a suit upon it against Smith. A majority of the referees to whom the case was referred, as is usual in Pennsylvania, considered that the bill was not taken by Evans in the usual course of business, and was liable to the same equity in his hands as in those of Eddy and Co., and that of course his right to recover depended upon there being a balance due to that house by Dennis. They awarded in favor of Evans, without particularly examining the accounts, thinking any balance was sufficient to carry the whole bill. Yeates J. "The bill did not go into the hands of the plaintiff in the usual course of business, and seems to me analogous to the case of a promissory note negotiated after it becomes due. The plaintiff then stands precisely on the same footing with Eddy and is only entitled to the real balance as it stood between the latter and the drawer of the bill." Report set aside. Evans v. Smith, 4 Bin. R. 367.

Where A., a debtor of B., knowing that B. has made an assignment of his effects and demands for the benefit of his creditors, buys of C. a note made by B. at a discount, to enable him to offset it against B.'s demand against him, and pays for it by his own note with an endorser, it has been held that these facts afford a sufficient defence to the endorser on A.'s note in an action by C., the sale of B.'s note being an attempt to defraud the creditors of B. Richter v. Selin, 8 Serg. and Raw. 425.]

(10) Solomon v. Turner, 1 Stark. 51. In an action by payee of a note against the maker, the defence was that that and another note, which had been paid, had been given as the price of certain pictures, and that the pictures were not worth the amount of the other note: and per Lord Ellenborough, I will not admit evidence for the purpose of reducing the damages, that the pictures were of inferior value; if by inadequacy of value, and other circumstances, you can prove fraud, so as to shew there was no contract at all, the evidence will be admissible; if it fall short of that, it will be unavailable: it did fall short, and plaintiff had a verdict.

Or that the goods were damaged when they ought to have been sound ; (11)

Unless the contract was rescinded on that ground. (12)

[It is a defence to an action on a note given for the price of an article sold, that the property in the article never passed. (*a*)

So where a note was given for the price of land, and the title of the vendor wholly failed, it was held that this was a good defence to an action on the note, even though the deed contained covenants on which the vendor was liable. (*b*)

But a failure of title to part of the land, or an incumbrance

---

(11) Morgan v. Richardson, 1 Campb. N. P. C. 40. n. To an action by the drawer against the acceptor of a bill, drawn payable to the drawer's order, the defence was, that the bill had been accepted for the price of some hams, and that they had proved to be so bad as to be almost unmarketable. The sum for which they were actually sold was paid into court. Lord Ellenborough held, that this partial failure of consideration was no defence to this action, but that the defendant must take his remedy by action. S. P. Fleming v. Simpson, 1 Campb. N. P. C. 40. n. From 2 Campb. N. P. C. 346. it appears, that the case of Morgan v. Richardson was afterwards brought before the court of king's bench, and that the court approved of the direction of the chief justice.

In Tye v. Gwynne, 2 Campb. N. P. C. 346., the same point again arose in an action by the drawer of a bill against the acceptor, and Lord Ellenborough said that he should certainly adhere to the judgment of the court given in Morgan v. Richardson.

[See also Reed v. Prentiss, 1 N. Hamp. R. 174.]

Vide Broom v. Davis, cit. 7 East's Rep. 480. See also Basten v. Butter, 7 East's Rep. 479., and the cases therein cited.

(12) Lewis v. Cosgrave, ante, p. 342. n. (9).

[(*a*) See Reed v. Prentiss, 1 N. Hamp. R. 174. See also Fowler v. Shearer, infra.]

[(*b*) Where notes were given for the purchase money of land conveyed by the payee to the maker by deed with warranty ; and at the time of the conveyance, there was a judgment against the payee, under which the land was afterwards sold and conveyed by the sheriff; it was held that the payee could maintain no action against the maker of the notes. Per Curiam. "The consideration for the note has entirely failed; for the defendant has no title, it having been extinguished by the sale under the judgment. Although the defendant has not yet been evicted by the purchaser under the sheriff's sale, he is liable to be so, and will be responsible for the mesne profits. To allow a recovery in this case would lead to a circuity of action, for the defendant on this failure of title would be entitled immediately to recover back the money." Frisbee v. Hoffnagle, 11 Johns. R. 50.

But see Lloyd v. Jewell, infra.

A note given in consideration of a void deed is *nudum pactum* between the parties, and the payee cannot maintain an action on it. Fowler v. Shearer, 7 Mass. R. 14.]

upon it, is no defence to an action upon a note given for the purchase money. (*a*)]

It is no answer to an action on a bill or note, that it was given as the condition of a lease to be executed by the plaintiff and of letting the defendant into possession of the premises, and that plaintiff had refused to execute the lease, for he is not bound to execute till the price is paid; and as the defendant was let into possession, the consideration fails in part only; and the sum to be allowed for such failure is matter, not of mere calculation, but of unliquidated damages. (13)

[(*a*) In an action on a note by the payee against the maker, it was held to be no defence that the note was given in consideration of a bond from the payee to the maker, conditioned for the conveyance of land, and that the land was then under mortgage, and continued so at the time the action was brought. Smith v. Sinclair, 15 Mass. R. 171.

In an action by the payee against the makers of one of six notes given for land, it was held to be no defence that the deed contained a condition that upon the breach of any of the covenants, the grantor should only be liable to the amount of the consideration expressed in the deed, payable in cash to the amount received on the notes, and the residue by delivering up the unpaid notes; and that the grantor had no title to a part of the land, which part was in the possession of a stranger, and was of greater value than the note in suit, estimating the whole at the price in the deed. Mellen C. J. giving the opinion of the Court, said, "In an action on a note, given for the price of real estate conveyed by the promisee to the promiser, by deed containing the usual covenants of seizin and warranty, the action being between the original parties, a total or partial failure of title, or want of title in the grantor, at the time of the conveyance," is no defence. The Court thought that the special covenants in this case did not render the defence tenable, for the clause relied on was introduced for the benefit of the plaintiff, and reserved no rights to the defendants. Lloyd v. Jewell, 1 Greenleaf, 352. The Court said that they were inclined to believe, had the defence been admissible against *either* of the notes, the plaintiff might elect to have the damages paid by giving up one of the other notes, three of which were unpaid.

Although the consideration of a note fail, by reason of the want of title to lands which were agreed to be conveyed to the maker, yet if a new agreement as a substitute for the old one be entered into between the original parties to the note, the failure of the original consideration creates no equity in favor of the maker of the note against an endorsee, even in Virginia; and a court of equity will not relieve against a judgment at law obtained by the endorsee against the maker. Young v. Grundy, 7 Cranch, 543.]

(13) Moggridge v. Jones, 14 East, 486. In an action on a bill for £200 by drawer against acceptor, the defence was, that the acceptance was given as part of the consideration for a lease plaintiff was to execute to defendant, and which he had refused to execute: by the agreement plaintiff agreed to let, and defendant to take, for twenty-one

So it is no answer to an action on a bill or note that it was for an apprentice fee, and that the apprenticeship had been dissolved for misconduct in the master; (14)

Unless it appears that the fee was not to be paid unless the apprenticeship continued till a given period, and the dissolution occurred before that period had arrived. (14)

[It has been held that a note given by a person as executor or administrator was not binding on him unless he had assets. (*a*)

---

years, from 29th December next; and plaintiff, in consideration of 500*l.* to be paid by defendant by three bills, agreed to execute the lease: defendant was let into possession and gave the bills, of which that sued on was one. Lord Ellenborough held the refusal to execute the lease no answer to the action; and verdict for plaintiff. Motion for new trial; but the court thought the verdict right, and that defendant must resort to his remedy upon the agreement, if plaintiff persisted in refusing to execute the lease. Lord Ellenborough's reason at the trial was, that the consideration had not wholly failed, because plaintiff had been let into possession.

(14) Grant v. Welchman, 16 East, 207. Payee against maker, on note for 6*l.* of three years' standing: defence, first, that it was in part for an apprentice fee, and that the apprenticeship was for less than seven years; secondly, that a year before the action the apprentice was discharged, because plaintiff had enticed him to commit felony: Graham B. overruled both objections; and on motion for nonsuit, the court answered to the first objection, that the apprenticeship was voidable only, not void; and on the second, they inquired how the consideration for the apprentice was reserved, and it appearing that it was all to be paid at the time of the binding, but that the note was taken as an indulgence, they thought that decisive against defendant; and rule refused. Sed vide Ledger v. Ewer, Peake, 216. contra.

[(*a*) The delaration on a note stated that the defendant as administrator of Peter Bregan promised to pay the plaintiffs $61.72, "for value received by Peter Bregan and heirs." On demurrer to the declaration —per Curiam. "The declaration does not state a consideration for the promise. The note states that the value was received by third persons, and there is no consideration for the promise." Judgment for the defendant. Ten Eyck v. Vauderpoel, 8 Johns. R. 93.

Action on a note by the payee against the makers. The defendants as executors of De Witt referred all demands between their testator and the plaintiff to an arbitrator; and the plaintiff and defendants executed notes payable to each other and gave them to the arbitrator. The arbitrator endorsed on the note signed by the defendants, an award that a certain amount was due from the estate of their testator, and endorsed a payment to reduce the note to that amount, and endorsed on the other note that it was fully satisfied. It was agreed verbally at the time of the submission that the defendants were only to be liable on the award as executors. It was held that the action could not be maintained. Per Curiam. "The defendants were executors, and the note they gave was a mode adopted, to submit their difference with the plaintiff as to

It has been held that a note made by a person in his last sickness, and delivered to the payee without consideration, but in expectation of dissolution, and intended as a gift, was a good *donatio causâ mortis*; and that an action lay upon it by the payee against the executors of the maker. (*a*)

An endorsee of a note in an action against the maker is subject to the same defence as his endorser, if the endorsee took it with a knowledge of such defence, or if he received it otherwise than in the usual course of business, and under circumstances which ought to have excited his suspicions; or if he is a mere agent or trustee of his endorser. (*b*)

The mere circumstance of a note's being sold to an endorser at a considerable discount, unless much less than the customary rate, is not of itself sufficient to justify a jury in

---

the matter of account between him and their testator to arbitration. The award endorsed by the arbitrator shows, that it was intended merely that he should ascertain what was due from the estate of the intestate, and that the defendants should be liable only in their representative capacity, or so far only as they had assets. It was incumbent then on the plaintiff to show affirmatively that the defendants had assets; for a promise by an executor to pay is not binding unless he has assets." Schoonmaker v. Roosa, 17 Johns. R. 301.

But see Childs v. Monins, Thacher v. Dinsmore, and Foster v. Fuller, ante, p. 50.]

[(*a*) Wright v. Wright, 1 Cowen, 598. See also 1 P. Will. 441.]

[(*b*) See Nowell v. Hutchins, 4 Munf. 496; and Evans v. Smith, ante, p. 344.

In an action by endorsee of a bill against the drawer, it appeared that the bill was endorsed to the plaintiff in the words following—"Pay Thos. Wilson Esq. or order for our use, value received in account. Benson, Abbott, and Briggs;" and the defendant was permitted to give in evidence an obligation of the payees to the drawer to pay the amount of the bill, when that should appear to have been paid, and in case of its being dishonored to exchange the bill for the obligation, the drawer being liable to no damages but to pay expenses of protest, &c. Verdict directed for defendant subject to opinion of court. Parsons C. J. gave the opinion of the Court. "Wilson appearing to have no property" in the bill, "unless as a mere factor, the evidence was properly admitted, the direction of the judge and the verdict are right, and a new trial cannot be granted." Wilson v. Holmes, 5 Mass. R. 543.

Where a note is assigned for a valuable consideration and in the usual course of business, the assignee cannot be affected by any transactions between the assignor and the parties to such note, to which the assignee is not privy, and evidence to that effect is not relevant in a suit by the assignee against the parties to the note. But such evidence is relevant if it also shows that the assignee was a trustee, or had notice of the transactions, or did not receive the note in the usual course of negotiation. Harrisburg Bank v. Meyer, 6 Serg. and Raw. 537.]

inferring that the endorsee was acquainted with the fact of there being no valid consideration for the note. (*a*)

Nor does a note's being sold to an endorsee at his own risk render him liable in an action against the maker to the defence that the note was given without consideration or obtained from him by fraud. (*b*)

The assignee of a note not negotiable, takes it subject to all the equity between the original parties, existing at the time of the assignment, and notice to the maker. (*c*)]

The want of consideration, in toto or in part, cannot be insisted upon, if the plaintiff, or any intermediate party between him and the defendant, took the bill or note bonâ fide, and upon a valid consideration. (15)

Where it is so taken, it is no defence that the bill or note was originally accommodation paper, and known so to be. (16)

[(*a*) Perkins v. Challis, 1 N. Hamp. R. 254.]

[(*b*) Russel brought an action against the makers of a note. An endorsement by the payee ordered the contents to be paid to the plaintiff at his own risk, and continued, "I am not to be made liable to pay the same, as the note was taken without my knowledge, Z. Booth." It appeared that Booth objected to endorsing the note to Russel, as it had been taken by his partner, and he did not know for what it was taken. It was held that the defendants could not be permitted to show a want of consideration for the note or fraud in obtaining it, without showing that the endorsee was not a bonâ fide holder for a valuable consideration. Livingston J. giving the opinion of the court, said, "There is nothing disclosed in this case which would have rendered it proper to receive evidence, either of a want of a consideration, or of a fraud in obtaining it, to which the plaintiff was not himself a party." Russel v. Ball, 2 Johns. R. 50.]

[(*c*) Chamberlain v. Gorham, 20 Johns. R. 144.]

(15) Morris v. Lee, B. R. H. 26 G. 3. In an action by the endorsee against the maker of a note thirteen years old, the defendant obtained a rule nisi to set aside a judgment by default on an affidavit by a third person that he believed the defendant was swindled out of the note. An affidavit was made on the other side, that the plaintiff took the note bonâ fide, and gave a valuable consideration for it; and the court held, that however improperly it might have been obtained, a third person, who took it fairly and gave a consideration for it, was entitled to recover, and discharged the rule. And see Com. 43. 1 Term. Rep. 40. 2 Term Rep. 71. 2 Atk. 182. Bull. Nisi Prius, 274. See also De Bras v. Forbes, 1 Esp. N. P. C. 117.

[See also Warren v. Lynch, 5 Johns. R. 239; and Perkins v. Challis, 1 N. Hamp. R. 254.]

(16) Smith v. Knox, 3 Esp. N. P. C. 46. In an action by the endorsee of the drawer of a bill against the acceptor, it was urged in defence

And to support the defence against a person who may be a bonâ fide holder for value, the plaintiff should be apprized before the trial that he will be required to shew from whom he took the bill or note, and on what consideration; otherwise that defence may be excluded. (17)

If a banker is under acceptance for a customer to an amount beyond the cash balance in his hands, every bill he holds of that customer's he is to be considered as holding for value. (18)

And it makes no difference, though he holds other collateral securities more than sufficient to cover the excess of his acceptances. (18)

[Where A. gives his note to B. for a consideration passing from B. to C.; a want or failure of consideration between B. and C. is no defence to an action on the note by B. against A. (*a*)

---

that this was an accommodation acceptance. But Lord Eldon said, if a person give a bill for a particular purpose, and that is known to the party taking the bill, as for example, to answer a particular demand, then the party taking the bill cannot apply it to a different purpose; but where a bill is given under no such restriction, but given merely for the accommodation of the drawer or payee, and that is sent into the world, it is no answer to an action brought on that bill, that the defendant accepted it for the accommodation of the drawer, and that that fact was known to the holder.

Charles v. Marsden, 1 Taunt. 224. Endorsees of the drawer of a bill against the acceptor. The defendant pleaded that he had accepted the bill for the accommodation of the drawer, without any consideration, and that after the bill became due it was endorsed to the plaintiffs, they knowing that it was an accommodation one. On special demurrer to the replication, the argument turned on the validity of the plea; and the whole court held, that there being no fraud or collusion alleged, the plea was bad, and gave judgment for the plaintiffs.

(17) See Paterson v. Hardacre, ante, p. 319.

(18) Bosanquet v. Dudman, 1 Stark. 1. Plaintiffs sued as endorsees of a bill, and it was made a question whether they were holders for value: they had it from Clarkson and Co., for whom they were bankers, and they took this and many other securities to cover their advances and acceptances: they were under acceptances for Clarkson and Co. beyond the amount of the cash balance in their hands; and a question being put as to the amount of the acceptances and cash balance, and the value of the other securities, Lord Ellenborough said he should hold, that if the acceptances exceeded the cash balance, plaintiffs held all the collateral securities for value. The inquiry was dropped, and plaintiffs had a verdict.

[(*a*) Nickerson assigned an apprentice who was bound to him to E. Howard, and in part payment of the consideration W. B. Howard gave

And where A. gives his note to B. for a consideration passing from C. to A., a want or failure of consideration between C. and A. is no defence to an action on the note. (*b*) (*c*)]

---

his note to Nickerson. In an action on this note against the maker, it was held that the defendant could not set up as a defence that the assignment was invalid. Platt J. giving the opinion of the Court, said, "Whether the assignment was valid or not, it must be presumed that the note was made at the request of E. Howard; and as between him and the defendant it can never be material whether the assignment of the indenture passed any interest or not." Nickerson v. Howard, 19 Johns. R. 113.]

[(*b*) Ebenezer Clark, one of the heirs, and also the administrator of Seth Clark, gave a bond to Mrs. Sanger, another heir, conditioned that he should pay all the debts of the deceased, and should procure a decree of the judge of probate assigning her all the real estate of the deceased. Afterwards she and her husband released all her right in the said real estate to Ebenezer, and he by her request conveyed it to Cleveland by deed with warranty. And Cleveland gave two notes to Mrs. Sanger for the price, one of which he afterwards paid. And a memorandum was made on the bond by her agent, acknowledging the deed to Cleveland to be equivalent to procuring a decree of the judge of probate. In an action by Sanger and wife against Cleveland on the other note, it appeared that the land was afterwards sold by leave of court to pay the debts of Seth Clark, and purchased by Cleveland; and he claimed to have the amount paid by him deducted from the note. But it was held to be no defence, and judgment was given for the whole amount of the note. Sanger v. Cleveland, 10 Mass. R. 415.

Carmer gave his bond to Bartlett, for a certain sum, on payment of which Bartlett was to convey a certain parcel of land to him. Bartlett being indebted to Freligh, gave him the bond and authorized him to receive payment. Freligh received of Carmer as principal and Gaylord as surety, their joint and several note for the amount due Bartlett, and gave up the bond to Carmer. There was some evidence that Freligh, when he received the note, promised to give it up if Bartlett should refuse to consider the note as payment. Bartlett afterwards did refuse to consider the note as payment, and becoming bankrupt could give no title to the land. In an action on this note it was held that these facts were no defence. Spencer J. giving the opinion of the Court, said, "The giving the note by Carmer, and his taking possession of the bond under the authority given by Bartlett to Freligh, amounted in law to a payment. The agreement that Bartlett should allow the note as a payment, was in effect performed, since he could not legally disallow it; and his subsequent dissent, after he was thus concluded by the acts of his agent, was vain and idle. The subsequent bankruptcy of Bartlett cannot vary the case. If Carmer chose to part with his money before he acquired a title for the land, it was a want of caution on his part, for which he must blame himself." Parsons v. Gaylord, 3 Johns. R. 463.]

[(*c*) If the endorser of a note agree with the maker to pay it when it becomes due, this undertaking is a good consideration for a note from the maker to the endorser.

Cushing being an endorser on notes of Gore and Grafton for their accommodation, Grafton before the note became due gave the company's note to Cushing, to enable him to indemnify himself by an attach-

Illegality in the consideration, either wholly or in part, is another ground of defence.

---

ment of property or otherwise; it being understood that Cushing was to take up and discharge the notes endorsed by him as they became due; and to hold the note then given as good only for the amount of the others which he should take up. There was no evidence however of any express promise by Cushing. Cushing brought an action immediately upon the note given him, and attached property, which was also subsequently attached by creditors whose demands were due before either of the notes endorsed by Cushing became due. It was held that Cushing might recover the amount of the notes endorsed by him with interest. Parker C. J. said, "When an endorser has either expressly or impliedly undertaken to pay the note by him endorsed, there can be no question that such an undertaking is a good and valuable consideration for a promissory note." Cushing v. Gore, 15 Mass. R. 69.

A submission to arbitration, is a good consideration for a note deposited with the arbitrators, on which they make an endorsement so as to leave the amount due on the note as their award.

Watrous being under arrest in an action of slander at the suit of Shepard, made a note to Shepard for $200, and delivered it to certain arbitrators who were to decide upon the subject in dispute between him and Shepard; and in consequence of this arrangement was discharged from custody. The arbitrators endorsed $100, and returned the note to Shepard. It was held that the note was given for a good consideration; and that in an action on it no evidence could be received to show that the plaintiff had no cause of action in the original suit. Shepard v. Watrous, 3 Cain. R. 166.

Where referees, having agreed on an award, wrote a note, which one of the parties to the submission signed with a surety, not knowing the amount for which the note was given, the body of the note being concealed from sight, and the parties also signed mutual receipts; it was held that there was a sufficient consideration for the note in any view of the case, either in the adjustment of the controversy by the receipts, or in the award itself. Page v. Pendergast, 2 N. Hamp. R. 233. Quære whether any such defence would be permitted in an action on the note between the original parties, as would be admissible in an action on the award. *Ib.*

A note accepted in satisfaction of a breach of covenants, is a bar to any future action on the covenants, although no release of such covenants be executed at the time of giving the note; and consequently the note is good, being given for a sufficient consideration. Moody v. Leavitt, 2 N. Hamp. R. 171.

In an action by a turnpike company declaring upon a note made by the defendant for $125, for five shares of the capital stock of the corporation, to be paid in such manner and proportion, and at such time and place, as the company should require, it was held that there was a sufficient consideration on the face of the note, and that the action was maintainable notwithstanding the statute remedy in case of non-payment, of a forfeiture of the shares and all previous payments. Goshen Turnpike Co. v. Hurtin, 9 Johns. R. 217. S. P. Dutchess Cotton Manufactory v. Davis, 14 Johns. R. 238.

Where A. agreed to serve B. for a year at a certain rate per day, and at the end of three months B. gave A. a note for his services for that

The (19) debt of a third person, or a debt barred by (20) the statute of limitations, by a discharge under an insolvent or fugitive act, by a (21) bankruptcy and certificate, or by a composition, is a good consideration; and so is an apprentice fee, though the apprenticeship is for less than seven years. (22)

[Where the act incorporating an insurance company required their capital stock to be invested in a certain manner, it was held that an action might be maintained against a stockholder on a note given to the company for a part of the stock held by him, although this was a different investment from that directed in the act of incorporation. (*a*) (*b*)]

---

time, and A. left B.'s service without his consent before the year was ended; it was held that A. might maintain an action against B. on the note, notwithstanding the original contract was entire, the note being pro tanto a change or modification of the original contract. Thorpe v. White, 13 Johns. R. 53.]

(19) Popplewell v. Wilson, Str. 264. A. gave a note to pay so much to B. for a debt due from C. to B.; and on error it was objected that the debt of a third person was no consideration; but the court thought otherwise, and the judgment was affirmed.

(20) Vide Lord Raym. 389. 6 Mod. 309. Burr. 2630. Blackst. 703. Cowp. 290.

(21) Trueman v. Fenton. Cowp. 544. Birch v. Sharland, 1 Term Rep. 715. Cowp. 290.

(22) See Grant v. Welchman, ante, p. 347.

[(*a*) The act incorporating the Un. Mar. & Fire Ins. Co. required that their capital stock should, within six months after payment, be invested in the funded debt of the United States or of this commonwealth, or in the stock of some incorporated banking company. Instead of such an investment, the company received notes of the several stockholders with collateral security for the payment of them. They from time to time renewed such notes either partially or in the whole. It was held that these facts did not constitute a defence to an action brought for the use of the company on a note given for a balance of instalments due from the defendant, as one of the stockholders.

The court said, "Whether for this misbehavior of the corporation the government might not seize their franchises, upon due process, is a question not now betore us. It does not lay in the mouth of a stockholder for this cause to avoid his contract, which, as between him and the company, was made on a sufficient consideration." Little v. Obrien, 9 Mass. R. 423.]

[(*b*) It has been held in Massachusetts that the sale of a license from the enemy to protect a ship from capture and condemnation, on a voyage to a neutral port, was a legal consideration for a note. Coolidge v. Inglee, 13 Mass. R. 410. But it has been since decided in the Supreme Court of the United States, that a contract for the purchase or sale of such a license was void on account of the illegality of the consideration. Patton v. Nicholson, 3 Wheat. R. 204.]

45

But the consideration of (23) signing a bankrupt's certificate, or withdrawing a petition (24) against it, or (25) joining in the acceptance of a composition, is illegal.

And if the creditor of a banker is also an acting commissioner under his commission, and takes a bill or note for his debt whilst the commission is in progress, he cannot enforce payment of such bill or note. (26)

Especially if he afterwards signed the bankrupt's certificate as such commissioner. (26)

Though he did not prove his debt under the commission. (26)

---

(23) Sumner v. Brady, 1 H. Bl. 647.

(24) By 5 G. 2. c. 30. § 11. it is enacted, that every bill, note, contract, agreement, or other security whatsoever, to be made or given by any bankrupt, or by any other person, unto or to the use of or in trust for any creditor or creditors, or for the security of the payment of any debt or sum of money due from such bankrupt at the time of his becoming bankrupt, or any part thereof, between the time of his becoming bankrupt and such bankrupt's discharge, as a consideration, or to the intent to persuade him, her or them, to consent to or sign any such allowance or certificate, shall be wholly void and of no effect; and the monies thereby secured or agreed to be paid shall not be recovered or recoverable. And see Smith v. Bromley, 2 Dougl. 670.

[Rice and Bush had made several notes to Forsaith, which he had endorsed to the Wiggins, residents at Boston. Bush being about to obtain a discharge under the insolvent laws, Forsaith, being at New York, opposed it. In consideration of Forsaith's withdrawing his opposition, Bush, April 22, 1812, made a note payable to Forsaith or order for $1000, dating it May 24th, 1812, and a memorandum of the day when it was executed was endorsed. On the 1st of May Bush obtained his discharge. Forsaith on his return endorsed the note to the Wiggins, without informing them how he obtained it. It was held that an action by the Wiggins against Bush on this note could not be maintained. Yates J. giving the opinion of the court, said, "The note was void in law, as a fraud upon other creditors.—But it is contended that this is a defence set up against third persons, who are subsequent holders, for a valuable consideration, and without notice. This could not give validity to the note if void *ab initio*. By the endorsement on the note of the real date, the plaintiffs had such information as ought to have led to an inquiry into the manner the payee obtained it. The neglect of the plaintiffs to make any inquiry, ought to subject them to the consequences of the transaction between the defendant and Forsaith, the immediate parties. It is, however, manifest, from the face of the transaction, that Forsaith acted as the agent of the plaintiffs; they of course are bound by his acts, and are subject to the same consequences, as if the whole had been conducted by themselves." Wiggin v. Bush, 12 Johns. R. 306.]

(25) Spurett v. Spiller, 1 Atk. 105. Cockshott v. Bennett, 2 Term Rep. 763. Jackson v. Lomas, 4 Term Rep. 166. Cooling v. Noyes, 6 Term Rep. 263.

(26) Haywood v. Chambers, 5 Barnew. and Ald. 753. 1 Dowl. and

[A note given to the creditor of an insolvent, to induce him to become a petitioning creditor under an insolvent act, is void, on account of illegality of the consideration. (*a*)

And where such a note was given to the creditor by a third person, it was held that the note being void *ab initio*, the maker was not liable upon it, although he had been indemnified by the original debtor. (*b*)]

Where however a creditor *has* joined in a deed of composi-

Ryl. 411. In an action by payee of a note against the maker, it appeared that defendant had been a bankrupt and obtained his certificate; that the note was given to plaintiff between the second and third meetings for a debt due before the bankruptcy; that plaintiff was one of the acting commissioners under the defendant's commission; that he did not prove his debt under the commission, but that after he had received the note he signed the defendant's certificate as one of the commissioners. Abbott C. J. thought defendant not a free agent when he gave the note, and nonsuited the plaintiff; and on motion to enter a verdict for plaintiff, the court said a security to induce a commissioner to sign a bankrupt's certificate would be clearly void, and it was against public policy to allow any thing which led to that result: a commissioner has an important public duty to perform, and this would have a tendency to warp his conduct in the discharge of it; and in giving a security under such circumstances, the bankrupt could not be deemed a free agent. Rule refused.

[(*a*) Eden being about to take the benefit of the "act for giving relief in cases of insolvency," applied to Hurtin, one of his creditors, to sign the petition, and gave Hurtin a note for the amount of his debt, leaving the date blank, and Hurtin, without annexing any affidavit of his debt, put his name, which was the very last, to the petition; though exclusive of him there was a sufficiency in number and value to exonerate the defendant. After Eden obtained his discharge, Hurtin filled up the blank as if the note had been then given, and endorsed it to a third person in trust for one of his relations. Eden afterwards promised to pay the note. It was held that the endorsee could not maintain an action against Eden on the note. Thompson J. giving the opinion of the Court, said, "The transaction was founded in fraud, and against the policy of the insolvent act. The note was void in its creation, and being so, the subsequent promise will avail nothing. As the note was held by the plaintiff as trustee, and for the benefit of some relation of Hurtin, we consider the cause in the same point of view as if the original parties were now before us." Payne v. Eden, 3 Cain. R. 213.]

[(*b*) At a meeting of the creditors of Ketcham, an insolvent, Chatterton, one of them, refused to become a petitioning creditor, unless some person would give him a good note for $50, to be deducted from his demand. Yeomans gave him such a note, and Chatterton then signed the petition, deducting $50 from his demand. It was held, in an action by Chatterton against Yeomans upon this note, that the "note was void, as being given against the policy, and in fraud of the insolvent act; and that the note being void *ab initio*, testimony that Ketcham had indemnified Yeomans was improper." Yeomans v. Chatterton, 9 Johns. R. 295.]

tion, it is (27) not illegal to obtain the security of a third person for such composition.

And therefore a bill given by a third person, as such security, is (27) good;

Though such creditor's composition be thereby secured to be paid at an (27) earlier period than that of the other creditors.

But to stipulate privately for such additional security before joining in the acceptance of the composition, is a (28) fraud on the other creditors.

And if there is a private stipulation for more than the composition money from a third person, and the third person pays the money, he cannot recover upon any bill or note the debtor may give him for reimbursement. (29)

Though the creditor was induced originally to trust the debtor upon upon a representation by such third person of his responsibility. (29)

And refused to consent to the composition without such additional security on the ground of that representation. (29) (*a*)

---

(27) Feise v. Randall, 6 Term Rep. 146.

(28) Leicester v. Rose, 4 East's Rep. 372.

(29) Bryant v. Christie, 1 Stark. 329. Back trusted Christie to the amount of £332, on a representation by Bryant of Christie's responsibility. Christie became embarrassed, and offered to compound with his creditors at 10*s.* in the pound. Back considered himself guarantied by Bryant, and therefore refused to sign the composition deed unless Bryant would promise him the remainder of his debt. Bryant promised accordingly, and Back signed the deed which released Christie: the composition was paid, and Bryant paid the difference: Christie accepted bills to reimburse Bryant, and Bryant sued thereon. But Lord Ellenborough considered this as a circuitous mode of securing Back the full amount of his debt, and a fraud upon the creditors at large, and he nonsuited the plaintiff.

[(*a*) Where a creditor of an insolvent debtor, who had petitioned to be discharged under the Insolvent Act, obtained from his debtor while in prison, a bill of exchange for his debt; and the debtor was afterwards discharged from the debts in his schedule, which included the debt for which the bill was given, and the creditor endorsed the bill to an innocent holder for a valuable consideration; it was held, that however improper the circumstances might be, under which the bill was obtained from the insolvent, still his discharge was no bar to an action by a *bonâ fide* endorsee for a valuable consideration. Simpson v. Pogson, 3 Dow. & Ryl. 567.]

Past (30) seduction is a good consideration; future (31) prostitution an illegal one.

A note given to parish officers for a sum certain, to defray the future expenses of a bastard child, is (32) illegal; the officers being authorized by law to take an indemnity only.

[A note given to a person to induce him not to bid at a sale of land on execution, is void on account of the illegality of the consideration. (*b*)]

Dropping (33) a criminal prosecution, or suppressing evidence thereon, is an illegal consideration: but where a person has been convicted of a misdemeanor, and the court offer that if he will pay a certain sum for the expenses of the prosecution, the sentence shall be for a shorter period of imprisonment than it otherwise would, a note given by him for such sum is (34), as far as respects the consideration, unobjectionable.

And where there are both civil and criminal proceedings, an agreement to compound the civil proceedings and to take a given sum for costs, and to give a bill for the amount, will not make the bill illegal, if the criminal costs do not appear to have been included, and it is no part of the bargain that the criminal proceedings shall be abandoned. (35)

---

(30) Annandall v. Harris, 2 P. Wms. 432. Cray v. Rooke, Forrest, 153. Turner v. Vaughan, 2 Wils. 339.

(31) Walker v. Parkins, Burr. 1568.

(32) Cole v. Gower, 6 East's Rep. 110.

[(*b*) Caswell and Noble, after a judgment against Eggleston, (which was a lien on his land,) but without any knowledge of it, purchased land of him for a good consideration. The land being for sale on an execution on the judgment, Caswell and Noble agreed with the judgment creditor, that if he would not bid against them, they would pay his execution and $150. Notes were accordingly given by them for this sum. It was held that no action could be maintained upon the notes against the makers, by a person receiving them after they were due, and who was also acquainted with the nature of the consideration. Kent J. said, "It was a consideration against public policy, which encourages bidding at sales on execution." Jones v. Caswell, 3 Johns. Cas. 29.]

(33) 3 P. Wms. 279. Collins v. Blantern, 2 Wils. 349.

(34) Beely v. Wingfield, 11 East's Rep. 46.

(35) Harding v. Cooper, 1 Stark 467. In an action against the acceptor of a bill, it appeared that plaintiffs had sued the drawer, and taken out a commission of bankruptcy against him, and, on his having obtained his discharge as an insolvent, had indicted him for fraud in obtaining it. They then came to an agreement that plaintiffs should have

So the release by an excise officer of a person apprehended for penalties under the excise laws, is a (36) sufficient consideration for a note given, with the approbation of the commissioners, for the amount of such penalties.

Or if an officer who has a warrant to levy excise penalties take a note for the amount, though such a transaction is to be looked upon with extreme jealousy, yet if there has been no extortion in the officer, nor other improper conduct, the consideration will be unobjectionable, and the note valid. (37)

Especially if the commissioners afterwards approve what has been done. (37)

A (38) recommendation to an office in the king's household, though of a private nature, and not within the statute of the 5th and 6th Edw. 3. a (39) smuggling, an (40) usurious, a (41) stock-jobbing contract, a wager upon the future

---

2*s.* 6*d.* in the pound for their debt, £220 for costs, without taxation, and that the commission should be superseded, and defendant gave his acceptance for the amount. Plaintiffs afterwards consented that the indictment should be quashed. It was urged that this was an illegal consideration; and Lord Ellenborough said, a stipulation to drop the prosecution would, without doubt, have been illegal, but if the civil rights only were compounded, and plaintiffs chose afterwards to forego the prosecution, the transaction was not illegal: and there being no evidence that the costs of the prosecution were mentioned during the negotiation, or included in the £220, or that there was any stipulation for dropping the prosecution, the plaintiffs had a verdict.

(36) Pilkington v. Green, 2 Bos. and Pull. 151.

(37) Sugars v. Brinkworth, 4 Campb. 46. Defendant was convicted in excise penalties to the amount of £340, and plaintiff, a supervisor, had a warrant to levy the amount. Plaintiff took defendant's note at two months for that sum, and though he had no previous authority from the commissioners to take it, they approved of it when they knew it. In an action upon the note it was urged, that there might be great abuses if the taking a note for penalties were allowed: and Lord Ellenborough said if there were any reason to think the law had been abused by plaintiff, he would not be allowed to enforce payment; that such a transaction was to be looked to with extreme jealousy; but that here plaintiff appeared to have acted with perfect good faith; and defendant, to whom indulgence had been extended, was not to criminate his benefactor when nothing wrong had been done. Verdict for plaintiff.

(38) Harrington v. Du Chatel, Bro. C. C. 114.

(39) Guichard v. Roberts, Blackst. 445.

(40) 12 Ann. St. 2. c. 16. post, note (63).

(41) 7 G 2. c. 8. See Faikney v. Reynous, Burr. 2069. Petrie v. Hannay, 3 Term Rep. 418. and Steers v. Lashley, 6 Term Rep. 61.

amount of any branch of the (42) public revenue, or selling spiritous liquors in small quantities, contrary to 24 G. 2. c. 40. § 12., is an illegal consideration. (43)

So money lost by gaming, (except (44) in some part of a royal palace in which the King is then actually resident, the freehold and inheritance of which part is in the crown, and which is not in lease) or betting on the sides of persons so gaming, money knowingly lent for such gaming or betting, or money lent at the time and place of such play to any person either then gaming or betting, or who shall, during the play, play or bet, is (46) an illegal consideration.

Betting on a game at cricket, (47) a horse race, or (48) a foot race against time, is gaming within 9 Anne : insuring (49) in the lottery not.

So also the (50) ransom, or money knowingly (51) lent to enable the owner to obtain the ransom, of the ship or vessel of any British subject, or any merchandize or goods on board the same, (unless in the case of extreme necessity, to be allowed by the court of admiralty,) is an illegal consideration. (*a*)

[A note given by the loser to the winner of a bet on the result of an election, even after the polls are closed, is void, as being against public policy. (*b*) (*c*)]

---

(42) Shirley v. Sankey and others, 2 Bos. and Pull. 130. and Atherfold v. Beard, 2 Term Rep. 610.

(43) See Scott v. Gilmore, post. p. 360.

(44) 9 Ann. c. 14. § 9.

(46) 9 Ann. c. 14. § 1.

(47) Jeffryes v. Walter, 1 Wils. 220.

(48) Lynall v. Longbotham, 2 Wils. 36.

(49) Lewis v. Piercy, 1 H. Bl. 29.

(50) 45 Geo. 3. c. 72. § 16. 17.

(51) See Webb v. Brooke, post, p. 365. n. (65).

[(*a*) A bill of exchange, expressed to be for the ransom of a vessel, and given as security for the payment of the ransom bill, was held to be a contract on which an action might be sustained in a court of common law, the plaintiff and payee being an alien friend, and the capturing vessel belonging to a friendly nation. Maisonnaire v. Keating, 2 Gallison, 325. In an action upon such bill, the capture must be taken to be justifiable, and the ransom regular. Ib.]

[(*b*) Lansing v. Lansing, 8 Johns. R. 354.]

[(*c*) A deputy sheriff instead of taking bail of a defendant took from him as indemnity the note of a third person, which the defendant endorsed. It was held that the assignment to the officer was illegal and

If a bill or note is in part upon a consideration which the law has made illegal, and in part upon a good consideration, it has been held that the illegality will taint the whole bill or note; and that the holder, if barred at all by such illegality, will be barred in toto as to his claim on the bill or note. (52)

But if there be a privity between him and the defendant as to the good part of the consideration, he may recover that part exclusively of the bill or note. (53)

If a new bill or note be substituted for one which was given upon an illegal consideration, it will be open to the same objections as the original bill or note, unless it is reformed so as to exclude what made it illegal. (54) (*a*)

---

void, being contrary to a statute of New York; and that he could not maintain an action upon the note against the maker. Strong v. Tompkins, 8 Johns. R. 76.

By the statute of Massachusetts of 1783, c. 15, the sale of shingles either not of the statute dimensions, or not surveyed, is expressly prohibited; and in each case, under the penalty of forfeiture, and both buyer and seller are liable to a penalty, if they are sold without being surveyed. In an action on a note given in payment for shingles of a different quality from that required by the statute and not surveyed, the court said, "that the shingles, for the price of which the note in suit was given, having been sold in direct violation of the statute, the consideration of the promise was clearly illegal and insufficient to support it;"—and nonsuited the plaintiff. Wheeler v. Russell, 17 Mass. R. 258.]

(52) Scott v. Gillmore, 3 Taunt. 226. Action against acceptor: the bill was given to the keeper of a coffee-house by the drawer, partly for money lent, and partly for spirits in small quantities under 20*s.* worth at each time: nonsuit on the ground of 24 G. 2. c. 40. § 12. On motion for new trial, Mansfield C. J. said the statute makes the consideration illegal, not merely void, and the security is entire, and cannot be apportioned; and since it is partly given for an illegal consideration, the whole bill is void. See Spencer v. Smith, 3 Campb. 9.

N. The case does not state whether plaintiff was endorsee: if plaintiff were the coffee-house keeper, still as defendant was a stranger to the original transaction, he could not be liable otherwise than on the bill.

[It has however been held in Pennsylvania, that where a note was given partly for a good and partly for an illegal consideration, it was good as to the amount of the good consideration. Yundt v. Roberts, 5 Serg. & Raw. 139.]

(53) See Robinson v. Bland, post, p. 363. n. 60.

[(*a*) But where *bonâ fide* endorsees of a note which had been given on a usurious consideration to the payee, obtained judgment upon it, it was held that another note given to them as collateral security for the judgment, could not be avoided on account of usury in the first note; and therefore that a promise to pay the new note by a person not a

Though the new bill or note is given to an endorsee who took the first security innocently, and gave value for it. (54)

Especially if he was apprised of the illegality in the first bill or note, before he took the second. (54)

If the new bill or note is so reformed as to exclude what made the first illegal, it will be unobjectionable. (55)

Thus if a bill or note is substituted for one which was given upon an usurious contract, it will be open to the same objections as the original bill or note, if it is not confined to what remains due for principal and legal interest. (56)

And if it were given to an endorsee of the first bill or note, who took it bonâ fide and for value, he could not before 58 G. 3. have sued any of the parties whom the usury would have protected from the first bill or note. (56)

Especially if he knew of the usury when he took the substituted security. (56)

But a bill or note substituted for one given upon an usurious contract will be valid, if it is given for principal and legal interest only; (57)

Or for what remains due for principal and legal interest, after reforming all prior payments, and excluding all usurious interest. (57)

---

party to it, made for a good consideration, was binding on him. Stewart v. Eden, 2 Cain R. 150.]

(54) See Chapman v. Black, infra. [See also Tuthill v. Davis, 20 Johns. R. 285.]

(55) See Preston v. Jackson, infra, note (57).

(56) Chapman v. Black, 2 Barnew. 588. White got money from Akers upon usurious interest, and endorsed to Akers a bill for £40 upon the transaction: this bill came into plaintiff's hands bonâ fide and for valuable consideration, but when it became due it was not paid, and plaintiff was apprised of the usury; it was then arranged that Akers should draw for the amount upon defendant, and that defendant should accept for the accommodation of White, which was done accordingly: nonsuit; and on rule nisi to set aside the nonsuit, and cause shewn, the court thought that as defendant really stood in the place of White, whatever would be a defence for White was also a defence for defendant, and as plaintiff's recovery in this action would enable Akers to keep the usurious interest he had received, and plaintiff by taking this new security, in which White's name was studiously omitted, was lending himself to screen Akers, the usury was a bar to this action, and the nonsuit right.

(57) Preston v. Jackson, 2 Stark. 237. Wyer lent defendant two sums on usurious interest, and took defendant's bonds for the amount;

If a bill or note is given in part upon a legal, and in part upon an illegal consideration, and several bills or notes are afterwards substituted in lieu thereof, the effect of the illegality may be confined to some only of the substituted bills or notes, and the other stand exempt. (58)

As where a bill or note is given as to half for a gaming debt, and as to the residue for money lent, and two bills or notes of equal amount are afterwards substituted for it, if the giver does any thing which may be considered an election to ascribe the gaming debt to the one, he will be liable upon the other. (58)

Promising to pay one whilst both remain unpaid, shall be deemed an election to ascribe the gaming debt to the other. (58)

But it is no objection to a bill or note that it was drawn in order to be discounted, and that the brokerage for getting it discounted was exorbitant, if the broker did not discount

---

the bonds were afterwards given up, the account settled, and a note given for the usurious interest: Wyer endorsed that note to the plaintiff, and Holroyd J. held, that though a new security for principal and legal interest had been held binding, such a security for the usurious interest was not so, and he would not allow the plaintiff to recover on the note.

[In an action by an endorsee against Watts, the maker of a note endorsed by Lancaster, the defence set up was usury. Watts had made a note to Lancaster and another person, on which interest at the rate of 12 per cent. was to be paid. He made several payments on this note amounting to more than the interest, and it was then cancelled, and he gave a new note to Lancaster for the balance, on which only lawful interest was paid. After several payments on this note, Watts gave the note declared on, for the balance remaining due to Lancaster. Sewall C. J. giving the opinion of the Court, said, that there was no pretence that the note in suit included unlawful interest; and the defendant was defaulted. Chadbourn v. Watts, 10 Mass. R. 121.]

(58) Hubner v. Richardson, Michas. 1819. Richardson lost to Brown at gaming £90 and owed him other money; and for upwards of £20 of the gaming debt, and upwards of £70 of the other, gave him a £100 note: he paid part, and then gave Brown two notes for £43 each, one of which was endorsed to plaintiff for a valuable consideration, and he knew nothing of the gaming debt; defendant promised him payment: and in an action on the note, case on question whether the gaming consideration vitiated the note in plaintiff's hands, and after argument, the court held it did not, for it was for defendant to make out that some of the gaming debt made part of the consideration of this note: it might be wholly included in the other note, which did not appear to have been paid, and defendant's promise to pay this, implied an election on his part that it should be so included in the other.

them himself, and the person who did knew nothing of his charge. (59)

The objection of illegality of consideration is in some cases confined to those persons who were parties or privy to such illegality, and those to whom they have passed the bill or note without value; in other cases it is extended even to holders bonâ fide, and for value. (*a*)

The latter cases are, where the consideration is either (60) wholly or in part (61) signing a bankrupt's certificate, money (62) lost by gaming as aforesaid, or by betting on the sides

---

(59) See Acland v. Pearce, 2 Campb. 599. Young v. Wright, 1 Campb. 139. Dagnell v. Willey, 11 East. 43.

[(*a*) The Court in South Carolina, (in 1792,) say that there is no difference between a note void by common law or by statute, for illegality of consideration; and that a *bonâ fide* endorsee of a note, void at common law for illegality and turpitude in the consideration, could not maintain a suit upon it against the maker. 1 Bay, 249. See also Wiggin v. Bush, ante, p. 354. But the law is well settled that a note given for an illegal consideration, is available in the hands of a bonâ fide holder, unless made void by statute. See Chitty on Bills, 5th ed. p. 105.]

(60) Robinson v. Bland, Burr. 1077. A bill of exchange was partly for money lent at the time and place of play, and partly for money lost at play: and on a case reserved the court held that the plaintiff could recover nothing upon the bill, but that he might recover the money lent on a count for money lent.

(61) Vide 5 G. 2. c. 30. § 11. ante, p. 354. note (24).

(62) By 9 Ann. c. 14. § 1. It is enacted that all notes, bills, or other securities whatsoever, given, granted, drawn, or entered into, or executed by any person or persons whatsoever, where the whole or any part of the consideration of such conveyances or securities shall be for any money, or other valuable thing whatsoever, won by gaming, or playing at cards, dice, tables, tennis, bowls, or other game or games whatsoever, or by betting on the sides or hands of such as do game at any of the games aforesaid, or for the reimbursing or repaying any money knowingly lent or advanced for such gaming or betting as aforesaid, or lent or advanced at the time and place of such play, to any person or persons so gaming as aforesaid, or that shall, during such play, so play or bet, shall be utterly void, frustrate, and of none effect, to all intents and purposes whatsoever.

Bowyer v. Bampton, Str. 1155. Several notes given by Bampton to Church for money lent to game with, were endorsed by Church to the plaintiff for a full and valuable consideration, and the plaintiff had no knowledge that any part of the consideration from Church to Bampton was money lent for gaming; and after two arguments upon a case reserved, the court held that the plaintiff could not maintain the action; for it would be making the notes of use to the lender, if he could pay his debts with them, and it would tend to evade the act, on account of the difficulty of proving notice on an endorsee; and the plaintiff would not be without remedy, for he might sue Church on his endorsement.

[Benson was sued as acceptor of a bill drawn by Duckworth payable

of persons so gaming, money knowingly lent for such gaming or betting, money lent at the time and place of such play to any person either then gaming or betting, or who shall, during the play, play or bet, (63) money lent on an usurious contract, the (64) ransom, or money knowingly (65) lent to

---

to his own order and by him endorsed. Duckworth drew and endorsed the bill without any consideration at the request of an agent of O'Reilly, and O'Reilly obtained Benson's acceptance on account of a sum won at cards by O'Reilly of Benson. Duckworth the drawer was a stranger to Benson. The plaintiffs were bonâ fide endorsees for a valuable consideration without notice. The court held that the action could not be maintained, the bill being void within the statute of 9 Anne, c. 14, § 1. Richards C. B. said that the bill was "*drawn* for the purpose and on account of this very gambling debt;" but expressed an opinion that an acceptance was within the meaning of the statute. Graham B. said, "I allow that the statute only extends to bills drawn; but a bill is only in an inchoate state before acceptance. It has no binding force as a bill of exchange until acceptance. It is not drawn for any purpose until accepted; and when once accepted, the act of acceptance has relation to the drawing." Henderson v. Benson, 8 Price, 281.]

(63) By 12 Ann. St. 2. c. 16. It is enacted, that no person or persons whatsoever, upon any contract, take directly or indirectly, for loan of any monies, wares, merchandise, or other commodities whatsoever, above the value of £5 for the forbearance of £100 for a year, and so after that rate for a greater or lesser sum, or for a longer or shorter time; and that all contracts and assurances whatsoever, made after the time aforesaid, for payment of any principal, or money to be lent or covenanted to be performed upon or for any usury, whereupon or whereby there shall be reserved or taken above the rate of £5 in the hundred, as aforesaid, shall be utterly void.

Lowe v. Waller, Dougl. 708—736. The defendant was acceptor of a bill, which he gave to Harris and Stratton upon an usurious contract; Harris and Stratton endorsed it to the plaintiff for a valuable consideration, and the plaintiff had no notice of the usury; upon a case reserved, the question was, whether the usury between Harris and Stratton and the defendant was a defence against an endorsee who took the bill bonâ fide, and paid a valuable consideration for it; and after time taken to consider, the court held it was, and though Lord Mansfield had a wish the law should turn out in favor of the plaintiff, the court found the words of the act too strong, and could not get over the case of Bowyer v. Bampton, Str. 1155.

[In an action by the endorsee of a note against the endorser, it is a bar that the note was given by the maker to the endorsee on a usurious consideration. Levy v. Gadsby, 3 Cranch, 180.]

(64) By 45 Geo. 3. c. 72. (which repeals the former act 43 Geo. 3. c. 160. relating to the same subject) sect. 16. it is enacted, "That it shall not be lawful for any of his Majesty's subjects to ransom, or to enter into any contract or agreement for ransoming any ship or vessel belonging to any of his Majesty's subjects, or any merchandise or goods on board the same which shall be captured by the subjects of any state at war with his Majesty, or by any persons committing hostilities against his Majesty's subjects, unless in the case of extreme necessity to be allowed by the court of admiralty."

enable the owner to obtain the ransom, of the ship or vessel of any British subject, or any merchandise or goods on board the same, as before mentioned.

Where usury is the defence, letters between the parties at the time the bill or note is given, to fix the usurer's terms, (66) are admissible in evidence against a subsequent holder, if the usury is as against him a valid defence. (*a*)

And by sect. 17. "All contracts and agreements which shall be entered into, and all bills, notes, and other securities which shall be given by any person or persons for ransom of any ship or vessel, or of any merchandise or goods on board the same contrary to this act, shall be absolutely null and void in law, and of no effect whatever."

(65) Webb v. Brooke, 3 Taunt. 6. The plaintiff and defendant (British subjects) were made prisoners by the French at Oporto, where the defendant's ship was at the same time taken; they jointly petitioned for the release of themselves, and for the ransom of the defendant's ship, and to enable the defendant to pay for the ransom, the plaintiff lent him 3000 dollars, and for this sum the defendant drew a bill in his own favor, which he endorsed to the plaintiff. Their liberation and the ransom were accordingly effected, and they returned (as had been agreed upon) in the ship to England. The drawee refused to accept the bill, and this action was brought against the defendant as endorser. The defence was the illegality of the purpose for which the money was lent according to 45 Geo. 3. c. 72. A verdict was found for the plaintiff, and the point of law reserved. And after a rule nisi to enter a nonsuit, and cause shewn, Mansfield C. J. said, there is a manifest distinction between the cases of Faikney v. Reynous, and Petrie v. Hannay, and the other cases, in which a man having a debt of honor borrows money to pay it, and those cases where the plaintiff previously advances the money for effectuating an illegal transaction, or causing it to be done. Here the plaintiff and the defendant are equally ransomers; equally solicitous to procure the ransom, for they were to return home by this ship. The ransom is as much the deed of the plaintiff as of the defendant. Rule absolute.

(66) Kent v. Lowen, 1 Campb. N. P. C. 177. 180. d. This was an action against the maker of a note, endorsed by the payees to Watson, and by him to the plaintiff. The defence was usury in the original consideration for the note; to prove which the defendant tendered letters from the payees to the defendant setting forth the consideration. Lord Ellenborough held that it was first necessary to shew, either by the post mark, or otherwise, that the letters were contemporaneous with the making of the note, after which they would be evidence of an act done by the payees through whom the plaintiff claimed. From the post mark it appeared that they had been written just before the date of the note, and they were read in evidence. The defendant had a verdict; and on a motion for a new trial, the court held that the letters had been properly received.

[(*a*) The oath of the maker of a note to prove that it was given on a usurious consideration, which is permitted in Massachusetts by statute, 1783, c. 55. § 2, is only admissible where the original party to the usurious consideration is plaintiff; and it is not admissible even where the plain-

But now 58 G. 3. c. 93. removes the objection of usury from an endorsee for valuable consideration, if he was ignorant of the usury at the time he took the bill or note and gave the consideration. (67) (*b*)

If the consideration upon which a bill or note was made is not illegal, an illegallity in the consideration upon which it is afterwards transferred will be no (68) defence, if the plaintiff took it bonâ fide, and upon a good consideration, and is not bound in making out his title to state or prove the signature of the person making such transfer.

Where he is bound to state or prove such signatures, the authorities are contradictory upon the question whether the illegality is a defence.

If the bill or note were originally given upon an unobjectionable consideration, but endorsed over by the payee upon an illegal consideration, Lord Kenyon thought a subsequent endorsee, if he took the bill bonâ fide, and upon a valuable consideration, was entitled to keep it in opposition to such payee; (69)

---

tiff is a mere trustee for the original creditor, the party to the usurious consideration. Binney v. Merchant, 6 Mass. R. 190.]

(67) By 58 G. 3. c. 93. no bill or note that shall be made after 10th June, 1818, shall, though it may have been given for an usurious consideration, or upon an usurious contract, be void in the hands of an endorsee for valuable consideration, unless such endorsee had, at the time of discounting or paying such consideration for the same, actual notice that such bill or note had been originally given for an usurious consideration, or upon an usurious contract.

[(*b*) In New Hampshire the maker of a note including in it usurious interest reserved upon the remaining part of the note, cannot set this up as a defence in an action by a *bonâ fide* endorsee, the statute of that State of 12 February, 1791, not declaring the contract void, but only prohibiting the taking of more than six per cent. interest. The court said that if the action had been brought by the original payee, the illegal interest would have been deducted. Young v. Bradley, 2 N. Hamp. R. 410.

In Massachusetts, by a late statute, (passed March 4, 1826,) no contract or assurance is rendered void on account of usurious interest being taken or reserved upon it, but it is valid for the recovery of the principal sum without interest.]

(68) Daniel v. Cartony, Espinasse, 274.

(69) Parr v. Eliason, 1 East's Rep. 92. A bill was drawn in favor of the plaintiff, he endorsed it to Persent and Bodeker upon an usurious consideration, and they endorsed it over; it was afterwards endorsed back to the assignees of Persent and Bodeker, who had become bank-

And to enforce payment in case of a bill, against the acceptor. (70)

In Lord Ellenborough's time, the court of king's bench thought he could not enforce such payment. (71) (*a*)

---

rupts, for a debt due to their estate; upon which the plaintiff brought trover to recover back the bill. Lord Kenyon directed a nonsuit, and after a rule nisi for a new trial, the court held, that as the bill was originally good, and as the endorsement by Persent and Bodeker was unimpeached, their endorsee had a good right to the bill, and that right was transferred to the defendants. Rule discharged.

(70) Daniel v. Cartony, Espinasse, 274. Scott drew a bill on the defendant payable to his own order, and discounted it with Greensill, who took 18*l.* per cent. discount; it was afterwards endorsed to the plaintiff, and the defendant could not impeach *that* transaction; and per Lord Kenyon, This is no defence; had the note been originally given on an usurious transaction, or for an usurious consideration, it would have been void in the hands of even a bonâ fide holder; but usury in an intermediate transaction respecting it, can never make it void in the hands of a bonâ fide endorsee, where there was no usury in the original transaction.

(71) Lowes v. Massaredo, 1 Stark. 385. In an action by endorsees against acceptor on a bill payable to Lowes or order, it appeared that Lowes endorsed it to Bloxham upon usurious terms, that Bloxham endorsed it to Ambrose, and that Ambrose endorsed it to the plaintiffs upon questionable terms: Lord Ellenborough thought plaintiffs precluded from recovery by the usury between Bloxham and Lowes, independent of the usury between them and Ambrose, but upon being strongly pressed by Parr v. Eliason, he suffered plaintiffs to take a verdict, subject to a motion for entering a nonsuit; a rule nisi was accordingly granted, and on cause shewn, the court thought the usury between Bloxham and Lowes a bar to the plaintiff's claim, because they could not bring themselves in connexion with the defendant but through the medium of Lowes's endorsement, which was tainted with usury: they also thought the terms upon which Ambrose endorsed to the plaintiffs usurious, and the rule for a nonsuit was made absolute.

[But see Munn v. Commission Company, p. 368. note (*a*)].

[(*a*) If a bill or note be made for the purpose of raising money upon it, and it is discounted at a higher premium than the legal rate of interest, and where none of the parties whose names are on it could, as between themselves, maintain a suit on the bill or note when it becomes due, provided it had not been discounted, then such discounting the bill is usurious, and the bill void. Munn v. Commission Company, 15 Johns. R. 44. See also Powell v. Waters, 17 Johns. R. 176; and Levy v. Gadsby, ante, p. 364.

Roosevelt endorsed a note made by Mark and Co. for their accommodation, this note Goodrich discounted for Mark and Co. at a usurious rate of interest. In an action by an endorsee to whom Goodrich had passed it against Roosevelt, the court held that the note was usurious and void. Radcliff J. "Notwithstanding the note was made payable to Roosevelt, and endorsed by him, it was essentially an original contract between Mark and Co. on the one part, and Goodrich on the other, and as between them, was clearly founded on usury and void." Wilkie v. Roosevelt, 3 Johns. Cas. 66.

It is no objection in an action against an endorser that the bill or note was drawn upon a gaming, or usurious, or

---

In an action against M'Cullum and Merriam, as makers of a note payable to Averill or bearer, it was proved that the note was made for the purpose of passing it to Averill for a good consideration, but it had in fact never been passed to him. The defendants at the trial before Woodworth J. offered to prove that Merriam afterwards sold it to Hudson for less than the amount due on the note. The judge rejected the evidence. Platt J. delivered the opinion of the court. "As to Averill this note had no inception. And if, as the defendants offered to prove, the agreement between Hudson and the makers was *usurious*, and the note was first given to Hudson as security for an usurious loan; then it follows that it was corrupt and illegal in its inception." New trial. Marvin v. M'Cullum, 20 Johns. R. 288.

See Henderson v. Benson, ante, p. 363.

The defendants made their notes payable to Fitch or bearer, to enable him to raise money upon them at a usurious rate of interest, and Fitch sold them to Humphreys at 21 per cent. discount; and it did not appear whether Humphreys knew the manner in which Fitch obtained the notes. In an action on these notes by a person to whom Humphreys passed them against the makers, it was held that they were void. Van Ness J. said, "The case of Munn v. Commission Company is decisively against the plaintiff. We decided that a note made for the purpose of being discounted at an usurious interest, and endorsed for the accommodation of the maker, was void in its original formation." Bennet v. Smith, 15 Johns. R. 355.

Eaton held a note made by Blanchard and Ford, and endorsed by Hubbard, and given by Blanchard and Ford to Eaton for a usurious consideration. When the note fell due Eaton agreed to give Blanchard and Ford further credit, provided he had other security. They offered to give him Hubbard's note endorsed by Sumner. They procured and delivered him such a note, and the other note was cancelled. An action was brought against Hubbard by persons to whom Eaton had transferred this note, without endorsing it himself. A majority of the court, Parker C. J. Thacher and Wilde Js. held that the note was usurious, and therefore that the plaintiffs could not recover. Parker C. J. said, "The proposition made by one party and acceded to by the other, was that this note should be taken as security for a pre-existing usurious debt. For this purpose it was made and delivered to the usurious lender." Jackson and Putnam, Js. dissented. Jackson J. said, "I say the note was made for a lawful and sufficient consideration; because that is the legal presumption in the absense of all evidence to the contrary: we must presume that it was either given for a preceding debt due to Blanchard and Ford; or that they paid the value for it at the time; or that they gave satisfactory security to Hubbard to pay the amount at a future day." Bridge v. Hubbard, 15 Mass. R. 96.

See also Towsend v. Bush, 1 Conn. R. 260.

But where the original consideration for which a bill or note is given is good, and it is afterwards sold at a greater discount than the legal rate, this is no defence in an action against the maker by a purchaser.

H. Ruggles drew a bill, in favor of O. Ruggles on Darling, agent of the Commission Company, which was accepted by the drawee. O. Ruggles sold the bill by a broker, deducting more than the legal rate of interest, and endorsed the bill, but there was no evidence of any usu-

other illegal consideration; for though the statute against gaming, &c. makes such bill void to all intents and purposes, the proper construction upon those words is, that it makes it void as far as can be necessary to further the objects of the act, but it does not avoid it in favor of a party whom the statute meant to punish, not to protect. (72) (*a*)

---

rious agreement between O. Ruggles and H. Ruggles or Darling. Spencer J. giving the opinion of the court, said, "The bill, while in the hands of O. Ruggles and before it was discounted by the plaintiffs, was a perfect and available bill, and when it became due, he could have maintained an action upon it, against either the defendants or H. Ruggles, the drawer. The principle is too well settled to be questioned that a bill free from usury in its concoction, may be sold at a discount, by allowing the purchaser to pay less for it, than it could amount to at the legal rate of interest for the time the bill has to run." Judgment for the plaintiffs. Munn v. Commission Company, 15 Johns. R. 44.

See also the opinion of Jackson J. in Bridge v. Hubbard, supra.]

(72) Edwards v. Dick, Hil. 1 and 2 Geo. 4. 4 Barnew. 212. Action on bill drawn by defendant on Lord Rossmere, payable to defendant's order, and endorsed by him; defence, that defendant drew the bill for money won by him of Lord Rossmere at play. Bayley J. thought this no defence, because by endorsing the bill defendant affirmed it to be free from exception, with which this defence was inconsistent, and rejected the evidence. On motion for new trial, the court thought he did right, for defendant was not within the spirit of the act against gaming; it was not for a person standing as he did that the act intended protection; compelling payment from him was not advancing any practice the statute meant to suppress, and giving him protection would assist a winner, whom the act meant to discountenance, and would enable him to set up his own misconduct to bar the honest claim of an innocent endorsee. Rule refused.

[(*a*) The statute of Massachusetts, 1804, c. 58, § 1. enacts that all bills, notes, &c. under five dollars, payable to bearer or order, shall be wholly in writing; and that all bills notes, &c. under that amount and so payable, issued after April 1, 1805, and having the impression of types, plates, or printing, shall be utterly void, and no action shall be thereon sustained in any court of law. In an action on printed or engraved notes payable to bearer, each for less than $5. but dated previously to April 1, 1805, it was held that evidence that the notes were issued after that date was admissible, and constituted a good defence to the action. Bayley v. Taber, 5 Mass. R. 286.

The statute of Pennsylvania of March 19th, 1810, declared it unlawful for any incorporated association of persons to perform the operations of banking, or to loan money on any note, and unlawful for any person to offer any note for discount at any such bank. It seems that the endorser of a note discounted by such an association, and who has taken it up, cannot maintain an action on account of it against the maker of the note. Myers v. Irwin, 2 Serg. and Raw. 368.

The act of Pennsylvania of 21 March, 1814, made all notes in the nature of bank notes issued after January 1, 1815, issued by any unincorporated bank null and void, and "irrecoverable in any court." By the statute of 22 March, 1817, so much of any act as prevents the holder of such a note from recovering upon it against the bank, association, or partnership is repealed. The Supreme Court of Pennsylvania held that notes in the nature of bank notes issued by an unincorporated association between 1 January, 1815 and 22 March, 1817, might be recovered upon in a suit against the members of the association as partners. Hess v. Werts, 4 Serg. and Raw. 356. Though such notes contain a promise to pay "out of their joint funds, according to their articles of association," yet the members are personally liable. *Ib.*

Where a bill, drawn in New York on a person in Great Britain, during a time of war between that country and the United States, for supplies furnished by the payee to a British packet, authorized by an act of Congress, (passed 6th of July, 1812, 1 Sess. 12th. Cong. c. 129,) to sail from New York to Great Britain, was sold by the payee, and remitted by the purchaser to Great Britain for collection; in an action by the holder against the drawer, it was held that the remittance of the bill was within the protection afforded to the original transaction, and was not illegal, and that the plaintiff was equally protected with the payee who furnished the supplies. Suckley v. Furse, 15 Johns. R. 338.

It is no bar to an action on a bill or note, that it was made on Sunday. Geer v. Putnam, 10 Mass. R. 312. See also Smith v. De Fontaine, 1 Taunt. 131. The contrary has been held in Connecticut. 1 Root, 474. See also 1 Root, 98. and 145.

In case of an endorsement of a note after it is due, the maker may set up any defence to the action of the endorsee, which he might have done against the payee; but where the maker had confessed judgment on the note, the court refused to set aside the judgment to let in a defence of the illegality of the consideration of the note, where both parties to the original contract were in *pari delicto*. Sebring v. Rathbun, 1 Johns. Cas. 331.]

CHAP. XIII.

Competence of Witnesses.

In an an action against one of several makers of a note, another maker is a competent witness for the plaintiff, for he stands indifferent; if the plaintiff recovers, he will be liable to pay contribution to the defendant; if plaintiff fails and forces him to pay, he will be entitled to contribution from the defendant. (1)

It was at one time held, that no person who had signed a negotiable bill or note was admissible as a witness to impeach its validity, because his conduct had sanctioned what his testimony would defeat.

But the contrary is now fully settled.

Thus the drawer of a bill dated abroad and not stamped is a competent witness to prove that it was made in England, and therefore not admissible in evidence. (2)

And the only objection which can now be made against the testimony of a party to the bill or note is, that he has a direct interest in the event of the suit: if he has such an interest he is not admissible, otherwise he is.

Therefore in an action against one of several makers of a note, any of the others is a competent witness for the plaintiff; for if the plaintiff succeeds in the suit, the witness

---

(1) York v. Blott, 5 Maule, 71. Assumpsit against one of two makers of a note; plaintiff called the other maker, and Graham B. admitted him: on motion for a new trial, the court thought the witness stood indifferent, and was properly admitted, and refused the rule.

(2) Jordaine v. Lashbrooke, 7 Term Rep. 601. In an action against the acceptor of a bill purporting to have been drawn at Hamburg, the defence was that it was drawn in London, and therefore inadmissible in evidence without a stamp: the payee and endorser was called to prove where it was drawn; but it was objected that he was incompetent. Lord Kenyon, however, admitted him; and on his testimony the defendant had a verdict upon the counts on the bill. On a rule nisi for a new trial, and cause shewn, Ashhurst J. thought the witness inadmissible; but Lord Kenyon, Grose, and Lawrence, Js. held that as he was neither interested in the event, nor rendered infamous by a conviction for any crime, he was properly admitted. Rule discharged. See also Adams v. Lingard, Peake, N. P. C. 117.

will be liable to pay contribution; if the plaintiff fails in the suit and makes the witness pay, the witness will be entitled to receive contribution. (3)

So in an action against the acceptor of a bill, the drawer is a competent witness either for the plaintiff (4) or for the defendant (5) (6); for if the plaintiff recovers against the acceptor, the drawer pays the bill by the hands of the acceptor; if the plaintiff fails against the acceptor, the drawer is liable to pay the bill himself. (4)

And the drawer has accordingly been admitted for the plaintiff, to prove the defendant's hand-writing; and for the defendant, to prove that (5) the plaintiff discounted the bill upon an usurious consideration, or that (6) the bill had been paid.

And it is no objection to the competence of the drawer, when called to prove the acceptor's handwriting, that he is in custody upon a charge of having forged it. (7)

But in an action against the acceptor upon an acceptance

---

(3) See York v. Blott, supra, n. (1).

(4) Dickinson v. Prentice, 4 Esp. N. P. C. 32. This was an action against the defendant as acceptor of a bill; the defence intended to be set up was that the acceptance was a forgery: to prove the defendant's handwriting the plaintiff called the drawer. It was objected, that having drawn the bill, the forgery of the acceptance could only be imputable to him; and that as he might be committed for a capital offence, if the forgery were established, he had such an interest as ought to disqualify him. But Lord Kenyon said that this was matter of observation as to his credit, but was no objection to his admissibility. He was admitted, and the plaintiff had a verdict. See also Barber v. Gingell, 3 Esp. N. P. C. 62.

(5) Rich v. Topping, Peake, N. P. C. 224. The drawer himself had endorsed the bill to the plaintiff for an usurious consideration; he had a release from the acceptor, which Lord Kenyon thought was necessary. The reporter, however, in a note upon the case, considers that the witness stood indifferent, and ought to have been received even without a release; and in Brard v. Ackerman, 5 Esp. N. P. C. 119., the drawer (under precisely similar circumstances) was admitted without a release; at least it is not stated that he had any.

(6) Humphrey v. Moxon, Peake, N. P. C. 52. This was an action by an endorsee; and a distinction was attempted to be taken between this case and one wherein the payee was the plaintiff: but Lord Kenyon held that there was no difference in principle, and admitted the drawer.

(7) See Dickinson v. Prentice, supra, n. (4.), and in Barber v. Gingell, 3 Esp. N. P. C. 62., the drawer was called to prove that he had paid the bill. Being at that time a prisoner on a charge of having forged the bill, and brought up by habeas corpus, he was objected to as incompetent; but Lord Kenyon overruled the objection.

for the accommodation of the drawer, the drawer or his wife is not a competent witness for the defendant; for he has a direct interest to defeat the suit, because if plaintiff recovers against the acceptor, the drawer will be liable to the acceptor not only for the amount of the bill, but for all the costs the acceptor may sustain: whereas, if plaintiff fails against the acceptor, the drawer will be liable for the amount of the bill only, not for the costs. (8) (*a*)

[In an action by the endorsee of a bill against the acceptor, it has been held that the endorser is not a competent witness for the defendant, to prove that the plaintiff had no right to recover upon the bill, having merely received it from the endorser in trust to obtain payment of it from the acceptor on account of the endorser himself. (*b*)]

In an action by endorsee of a note against an endorser, the maker is a competent witness for the plaintiff: for if the endorser is made to pay, the maker will be liable to pay him; if the endorser is not made to pay, the maker will be liable

---

(8) Jones v. Brooke, 4 Taunt. 464. Action against acceptor of a bill: the acceptance was without value, to accommodate the drawer; the drawer's wife was called as a witness for the defendant, to prove that the drawer endorsed away the bill upon an usurious consideration; the witness was objected to, but admitted: but on rule nisi, cause shewn, and time to consider, the court held the drawer had a direct interest to defeat the action, because otherwise he must indemnify defendant against the costs as well as pay him the amount of the bill; that the wife therefore was incompetent. Rule absolute.

[(*a*) It has been held that the drawer of a bill was not a competent witness for the plaintiff, in an action against the acceptor; "because if the plaintiff prevailed the witness would be liable to account to the defendant for the amount of the bill only; but if the defendant succeeded, the witness, as drawer, would be answerable to the plaintiff as holder, not only for the amount of the bill, but also for charges, damages, and interest." Scott v. M'Lellan, 2 Greenleaf, 199.]

[(*b*) Buckland v. Tankard, 5 Term Rep. 578. This was an action by an endorsee against the acceptor of a bill. The bill was drawn by Gregson payable to his own order, and endorsed by him in blank. And the defendant called Gregson to prove that he had endorsed and delivered it to the plaintiff that he might get it paid, and not to give him any interest in it; and that he had no consideration for it, and was still entitled to it. The witness had a release from the acceptor. Lord Kenyon thought him interested and rejected him. And on a rule nisi for a new trial, the court held that his sitnation would be better or worse according to the event of the verdict, and therefore that he was properly rejected. Rule discharged.]

to pay the endorsee; and his liability to the one cannot exceed in extent his liability to the other. (9)

So in an action by endorsee against drawer or acceptor, an endorser is in general a competent witness either for plaintiff or defendant: for plaintiff, because, though the plaintiff's succeeding in the action *may* prevent him from calling for payment from the endorser, it is not certain that it will (*a*); and whatever part of the bill or note the endorser is compelled to pay, he may recover again from the drawer or acceptor; and he is competent for defendant, because, if plaintiff fails against drawer or acceptor, he is driven either to sue the endorser or to abandon his claim.

---

(9) Venning v. Shuttleworth, 24th February, 1796, at Guildhall. In an action by Venning, as endorsee of a note, against Shuttleworth as payee and endorser, the plaintiff called the drawer to prove notice to the defendant; he was objected to, but per Lord Kenyon, stat indifferenter, and he was accordingly admitted.

[In an action against the endorser of a note, it was held that the maker was a competent witness to prove that time had been given him by a previous holder after the note became due. Spencer C. J. giving the opinion of the Court, said, "The witness was answerable on the note, whether the plaintiff succeeded in the suit or failed; and in either event no additional burthen was thrown on him. If this were an accommodation note, then on the authority of Jones v. Brooke, (4 Taunt. 466,) the objection to the witness would be well founded; because if the defendant was rendered liable in this action, he would have a remedy over against the maker of the note, not only for the principal and interest, but for the costs." Hubbly v. Brown, 16 Johns. R. 70.

But it has been held in Massachusetts, that in an action against the endorser of a note, the maker was not a competent witness for the defendant without a release. Jackson J. giving the opinion of the Court, said, "The maker is directly interested in the event of the suit; because a verdict against defendant may be used as evidence in an action by the latter against him. If there has been any uncertainty in the practice of other courts, there has been none in this; and such witnesses have always been released by the defendant before they were examined by him." Pierce v. Butler, 14 Mass. R. 303.

Where the maker of a note had given a mortgage to the endorser, defeasible on the former's paying the contents of the note to the latter, it was held, in an action against the endorser by an endorsee, that the maker was not a competent witness for the defendant. By the Court. "The object of the mortgage was to indemnify the endorser. Not only payment of the note by the maker would defeat the mortgage, but should the note be avoided by other means, so that the endorser should be saved harmless from it, the result would be the same. The witness was interested in the event of the suit." Cowles v. Wilcox, 4 Day, 108.]

[(*a*) In Massachusetts, in an action against the maker of a note, a release was in one case considered necessary in order to render an en-

Thus he has been admitted upon a bill drawn for his accommodation to prove for the plaintiff that (10) the plaintiff gave him value for it, and he has been admitted for the defendant to prove that he had paid the bill (11), or to prove that an unstamped bill, dated abroad, had in fact been made here. (12)

So he has been admitted for the plaintiff to prove his own endorsement. (13)

---

dorser a competent witness for the plaintiff, to prove the handwriting of the defendant. Barnes v. Ball, 1 Mass. R. 73.

And in Virginia in an action by an endorser against the drawer of a bill, it was held, that an endorser, who purchased the bill merely as agent of the plaintiff, was not a competent witness for the plaintiff, unless the agency was first proved by other evidence than the endorser's, or the endorser released; but that after the agency was proved, or the release given, he would be competent. Murray v. Carrett, 3 Call, 373. See also Steinmitz v. Currie, 1 Dall. 269.]

(10) Shuttleworth v. Stephens, 1 Campb. 408.

[In an action against the drawer of a bill, an endorser who has endorsed it without recourse to himself, is a competent witness for the plaintiff to support his title as endorsee. Cowles v. Harts, 3 Conn. R. 516.]

(11) Charrington v. Milner, Peake, N. P. C. 6. The note had been endorsed by Monk to the plaintiff, and the defendant was allowed by Lord Kenyon to call Monk to prove that he had paid the note to the plaintiff.

Birt v. Kershaw, 2 East's Rep. 458. The defendant drew a bill in favor of Wilby, which Wilby endorsed to Glover, whose assignees now sued the defendant on the bill. The defendant called Wilby to prove that he had paid the bill to Glover, and had been reimbursed by the defendant. It was objected that Wilby (who had no release from Kershaw) came to discharge himself, and was therefore interested; his evidence, however, was received, and a verdict found for the defendant. And on rule nisi to set it aside, and cause shewn, the court was clearly of opinion that this testimony had been properly admitted; that this case fell directly within the principle of that of Ilderton v. Atkinson, 7 Term Rep. 480.: that the witness stood indifferent. Rule discharged. Lord Ellenborough said, it is true that in an action by the defendant against Wilby for the money received by him, if the plaintiffs recover, Wilby may also be liable for the costs of this action; but that argument was urged in Ilderton v. Atkinson, without effect.

(12) See Jordaine v. Lashbrooke, ante, p. 371.

(13) Richardson v. Allen, 2 Stark. 334. In an action by endorsee against acceptor, a witness called to prove the endorsement said it was not the supposed endorser's writing; plaintiff then proposed to call other witnesses to prove it was, but Lord Ellenborough held that as plaintiff was not obliged to have called the witness he did, from his being an attesting witness, it was not competent for him to call other witnesses to contradict him; plaintiff then proposed to call the endorser himself, and Lord Ellenborough thought he might, because he could speak from knowledge, other witnesses from belief only, and he came to charge

And, where the endorsement has been negatived by another witness (not being an attesting witness) whom plaintiff had called, he, or some person who saw it written, is the only witness who can be called to prove it. (14)

[It has been held, that in an action against the maker of a note, a person who passed it to the plaintiff without endorsing it, was not a competent witness to prove the signature of the maker, because he was liable on an implied warranty that the note was not forged. (*a*)

But a person who sells a note, without endorsing it himself, is a competent witness for the plaintiff in an action by the holder against an endorser, after the execution of the note is proved. (*b*)]

In an action against the drawer of a bill, it has been held that the acceptor is not a competent witness for defendant to prove a set-off, on the ground that he is answerable to the drawer only to the amount to which plaintiff recovers against defendant. (15) (*d*)

---

himself; he was examined accordingly, but negatived the handwriting; and the plaintiff was nonsuited.

(14) See Richardson v. Allen, ante, p. 375.

[(*a*) Herrick v. Whitney, 15 Johns. R. 240. Per Curiam. "The witness was responsible upon an implied warranty that the note was not forged. He therefore had a direct interest in establishing the fact which he was called to prove; for by obtaining a verdict for the plaintiff on the plea of *non assumpsit*, he protected himself against his own warranty."

A witness in a similar case was held to be incompetent, who had passed the note to the plaintiff to be collected at the plaintiff's risk For this means the risk of the maker's solvency, not the risk of the note's being a forgery. Shaver v. Ehle, 16 Johns. R. 201.

But in a case in Massachusetts, an endorser who had endorsed a note to A. B. "at his own risk," was held to be a competent witness to prove the execution of the note. The defendant's counsel objected that the witness was interested in the event of the suit, on account of his liability in case the note was forged. But the court said that he had no interest in the event of the suit. The court however says nothing as to his liability, in case the maker's name was a forgery. Rice v. Stearns, 3 Mass. R. 226.]

[(*b*) Williams v. Matthews, 3 Cowen, 252.]

(15) Mainwaring v. Mytton, 1 Stark. 83. In an action against the drawer of two bills, he called the acceptor to prove that the acceptor had endorsed to defendant a bill drawn by him on the plaintiff, and accepted by plaintiff, and that defendant was therefore entitled to set off this acceptance; objection being made to his competence, it was urged that he was indifferent, for if plaintiff failed against the drawer, he might

But if the drawer is protected against the holder by a cross-demand he has against the holder, quære, is not such cross-demand, when set off, equivalent to payment; and will not the drawer be entitled to call upon the acceptor for the full amount of the bill, as much as if he had paid the full amount in money?

[It has been held, that in an action on a bill or note, a person interested in the event of the suit, or even the plaintiff himself, was competent to prove the loss of the instrument. (*e*) (*f*)]

---

sue the witness; but Dampier J. said the witness was interested in lessening the balance, being answerable to defendant for what plaintiff should recover; and he was rejected, and plaintiff recovered his whole demand.

[(*d*) In an action against the drawer of a bill, it has been held that the acceptor, though he had funds of the drawer's in his hands sufficient to pay the bill, at the time he accepted it, was a competent witness for the defendant, because not liable for the costs of the suit. Barnwell v. Mitchell, 3 Conn. R. 101.]

[(*e*) In an action on a note not negotiable, brought in the name of the payee for the benefit of an assignee, it was held that the party in interest might be a witness to prove the preliminary point of the loss of the note, in order to let in parol evidence of its contents. Chamberlain v. Gorham, 20 Johns. R. 144.

So it has been held that the plaintiff was a competent witness to prove the loss of a bill of exchange. Meeker v. Jackson, 3 Yeates, 442.

Parties to suits have, in some American cases, been admitted to prove the loss or destruction of deeds, preparatory to the admission of evidence of their contents. See Jackson v. Frier, 16 Johns. R. 193; Seekright v. Bogan, 1 Hayer. 176.]

[(*f*) It was formerly held in England, that a party to a negotiable instrument, could not be a witness to impeach its validity. Walton v. Shelly, 1 T. R. 296.

This rule, though abandoned in England, (See Jordaine v. Lashbrooke, ante, p. 371,) has been adhered to in many of the courts of the United States.

Thus it has been held that the endorser of a note was not a competent witness to prove that it was given for a usurious consideration. Parker v. Lovejoy, 3 Mass. R. 565; Winton v. Saidler, 3 Johns. Cas. 185; Churchill v. Suter, 4 Mass. R. 156.

In the case of Churchill v. Suter, Parsons C. J., after a review of the English cases which had been decided before that time, (1808,) says, "From this review of the adjudged cases, no conclusion, on either side, can be drawn."—"More than twenty years ago, after a full argument, the court unanimously decided that the testimony of the parties to the note should not be admitted; and the decision has been uniformly adhered to. We admit, as a general rule, that infamy and interest are the tests of the competency of witnesses. But we are satisfied that the exclusion of parties to a negotiable security, from testifying that it was originally void, is another exception, established to assist commerce and discourage fraud. No man shall be admitted to allege his own turpitude, when the allegation will tend to encourage or support fraud or illegality."

So it has been held that the maker is not a competent witness in an action against an endorser, to prove that the note was given for a usurious consideration. Widgery v. Munroe, 6 Mass. R. 449.

So in an action against one of two makers of a joint and several note, the other, though released, is not a competent witness for the defendant, to prove that the note was given for a usurious consideratfon. Jones v. Coolidge, 7 Mass. R. 199; Houghton v. Page, 1 N. Hamp. R. 60.

The maker of a note who signed it for the accommodation of the endorser, is not a competent witness, in an action against the endorser, to prove that the defendant after receiving the note got it discounted at a usurious rate of interest; "because the note was made to all substantial purposes, when the endorser procured it to be discounted, which was the purpose for which it was made." Hartford Bank v. Barry, 17 Mass. R. 94.

It has been held in Massachusetts, that a person signing the note as agent for the maker, was not a competent witness to prove the note usurious in its creation. Packard v. Richardson, 17 Mass. R. 122.

The expressions reported to be used by the Supreme Court of Massachusetts in the case of Butler v. Damon, imply that an endorser of a note could not be a witness to prove that the note was not given for any value, but was merely an accommodation note. The Court said, "The principle of the decision in Churchill v. Suter is applicable here. A party to a negotiable security shall not be received to show facts antecedent to the transfer, whereby the holder is to be defeated of his recovery." 15 Mass. R. 223.

But though a party to a note is not permitted to prove that it was void at its original formation, yet he is a competent witness to prove any subsequent facts, which invalidate the title of the holder.

In Powell v. Waters, 17 Johns. R. 180, the court says, "A party whose name is on a negotiable paper, may be permitted to testify, as to any facts which arise subsequent to the signatnre of the witness."

Thus in an action against the maker of a note, the endorser is a competent witness, to prove that neither he nor the maker received any consideration for the note, that he delivered it to a third person in order to get it discounted at the bank, who, instead of offering it at the bank, put it into the hands of a broker. The Court said, "The principle sanctioned in the case of Winton v. Saidler, (supra,) which excludes the party to negotiable paper from invalidating it, does not apply to this case. Such persons have been admitted under that rule, to testify to facts *subsequent* to the due execution of the note, and which go to destroy the title of the holder." Woodhull v. Homes, 10 Johns. R. 231.

So the maker or endorser of a note is a competent witness to prove payment. Warren v. Merry, 3 Mass. R. 27; White v. Kibling, 10 Johns. R. 231; Bryant v. Ritterbush, 2 N. Hamp. R. 212.

So where the maker and payee of a note agreed that if the maker did not take certain goods of the payee, the note was to be void and returned; and the maker a few days after gave notice to the payee that he should not take the goods; and the payee afterwards endorsed it to secure a debt; it was held that the endorser was a competent witness in an action against the maker, to prove these facts, and also that the plaintiff, when he received the note, had notice of the condition on which the note was given, and of its having failed. Spencer C. J. giving the opinion of the Court, said, "The defendant was not testifying to any fact which showed that the note was void in its inception, but that it became so by the determination of the defendant not to take the goods; and this fact being communicated to the plaintiff, he took the note subject to that condition." M'Fadden v. Maxwell, 17 Johns. R. 188.

So the endorser of a note is a competent witness to prove whether he endorsed the note previously or subsequently to its becoming due. Baker v. Arnold, 1 Cain. R. 258. See also Baird v. Cochran, 4 Serg. & Raw. 397.

So the endorser of a note was held to be a competent witness to prove that the date of the note had been altered after it was made. In this case the note had been in the hands of a third person previously to the making of the endorsement, although the endorser was payee of the note; and he could not state whether the alteration had been made when he endorsed the note or not. The Court said, "The note is not objected to as originally void, but as having been fraudulently altered; and this the witness was competent to prove." Parker v. Hanson, 7 Mass. R. 470.

In an action against the drawer of a bill endorsed by Robinson and Co. to Taber and Son, and by the latter to the plaintiff, without recourse to them, it was held that Taber was a competent witness to prove that Taber and Son were merely agents of Robinson and Co. to procure payment of the bill, and that Taber and Son endorsed it to the plaintiff merely as the agent of Robinson and Co. and for their use, and that Robinson and Co. had requested the drawer before this suit was brought, not to pay the bill to the plaintiff. Barker v. Prentiss, 6 Mass. R. 430.

In an action against the payee of a note, who had endorsed it for the accommodation of the makers for them to raise money on it, but they becoming insolvent with the note in their hands, had directed them not to part with it; it was held that one of the makers of the note was a competent witness to prove that they afterwards sold the note to the plaintiffs, and at the same time informed the plaintiffs of all the above facts in relation to the note. Skilding v. Warren, 10 Johns. R. 270.

See also Hubbly v. Brown, ante, p. 374.

So the drawer of a bill is a competent witness to prove a conversation which he had with the payee, respecting the terms on which the drawee had agreed to accept the bill. Storer v. Logan, 9 Mass. R. 55.

Where the plaintiff is himself a party to the illegal consideration of a bill or note, or to a fraud in its transfer, the rule which prevents parties to negotiable instruments from being witnesses to impeach them, does not apply, and a party to the bill or note if not interested, may prove the illegal consideration or fraud.

Thus it has been held, in an action on a note, that an endorser who had negotiated the note to the plaintiff was a competent witness to prove that the plaintiff, since the note was discounted, had admitted to him that it was usuriously discounted. Spencer C. J. giving the opinion of the Court, said, "The situation in which the witness stood did not incapacitate him from testifying to that fact. He was not asked any question involving his own turpitude, as whether the note which he passed as a good and available note, was void within his knowledge when he offered it to the plaintiff. In Winton v. Saidler, Mr. Justice Thompson considered it as contrary to sound policy and morality, that a party to a negotiable note should be a witness to invalidate it; meaning, undoubtedly, that a person whose name was on a negotiable paper, and who had thereby contributed to its circulation, should not be heard to say that the paper thus sanctioned by his name, was tainted when it passed into his hands. But if it receives its taint when it is negotiated to the party plaintiff by the facts then happening, it is not contrary to public policy or morality, nor would it come within the princicle of the decision of Winton v. Saidler, to hear the witness as to such facts. The principle in Winton v. Saddler, was intended as a protection for the fair and *bonâ fide* holders of a negotiable note or bill, against any prior transaction, which had already invalidated the paper." Powell v. Waters, 17 Johns. R. 176.

So in an action against the first endorsers of a note for $4000, it was held that the maker and second endorser were competent witnesses for the defendants, to prove that for the accommodation of the makers and second endorser, the first endorsers endorsed a blank paper, on which the maker was to draw a note for $2000, and that the plaintiff, without the privity or consent of the defendants, afterwards persuaded the maker to draw the note for $4000. Per Curiam. "It is insisted that this case comes within the rule that the party to a promissory note, shall not be admitted to impeach its original validity. It would however be a misapplication and abuse of the rule to extend it to this case. The reason and policy of the rule is to protect *bonâ fide* holders of negotiable paper, which they have honestly received in the usual course of business. Here the party who asks for the benefit of the rule is the very person who committed the fraud, which is now relied on by the defendant to annul the contract." Myers v. Palmer, 18 Johns. R. 167.

So an endorser of a note, in a suit against the maker, is a competent witness to prove that it was given to the plaintiff to take up two other notes endorsed by the witness to the plaintiff, and on which two notes the plaintiff had received more than legal interest. Platt J. giving the opinion of the Court, says, "If the decision in the case of Winton v. Saidler be still considered as sound law, it has no application in this case. Skilding v. Warren, and Powell v. Waters, give the rule for this case." Tuthill v. Davis, 20 Johns. R. 287.

So in an action by the administrators of the payee of a note against the administrator of the maker, a person who was a several promiser on the note as surety, was held to be a competent witness to prove that the note was given to the intestate for a usurious consideration. Fox v. Whitney, 16 Mass. R. 118.

But in some cases, parties to negotiable instruments, though not interested, have been held not to be competent witnesses to prove an illegal consideration in the origin or transfer of a bill or note, where the plaintiff was himself a party to the illegal consideration. Mann v. Swann, 14 Johns. R. 270; Manning v. Wheatland, 10 Mass. R. 502. See also Houghton v. Page, 1 N. Hamp. R. 60; and Cumming v. Fisher, Auth. N. P. 1.

The rule excluding parties to negotiable instruments from being witnesses to impeach them, only applies to the case of *bonâ fide* holders of bills and notes passed to them in the usual course of business, and before they are due.

Thus in an action against partners as makers of a note, it was held that the payee, who endorsed it, was a competent witness, to prove that the note was given by one of the partners for his separate debt to the witness, and that he endorsed it to the plaintiff some time after the day of payment. Baird v. Cochran, 4 Serg. & Raw. 397.

In Connecticut it has been decided, after much argument, that a party to a negotiable instrument, if not interested in the event of the suit, is a competent witness to prove that it was usurious in its creation. Townsend v. Bush, 1 Conn. R. 260.]

CHAP. XIV.

Forgery of Bills or Notes.

Forging or causing to be forged, or assisting in forging, any bill or note, or any endorsement or assignment thereof, with intention to defraud any person whatever; or uttering the same as true, knowing it to be forged, with a like intent, was made a capital offence by 2 Geo. 2. c. 25. (1)

This act did not extend to Scotland. (2)

By 7 Geo. 2. c. 22. it is applied to acceptances, and the term *alter* is used as well as forge. (3)

By 31 Geo. 2. c. 22. s. 78. (4) the second of Geo. 2. is

---

(1) By 2 Geo. 2. c. 25. s. 1, made perpetual by 9 Geo. 2. c. 18, if any person after 29th June, 1729, shall falsely make, forge, or counterfeit; or cause or procure to be falsely made, forged, or counterfeited: or willingly act or assist in the false making, forging, or counterfeiting, amongst other things, any bill of exchange or promissory note for payment of money, or any endorsement or assignment of any bill of exchange or promissory note for payment of money, with intention to defraud any person whatsoever; or shall utter or publish as true any false, forged, or counterfeit bill of exchange or promissory note for payment of money, or any endorsement or assignment of any bill of exchange or promissory note for payment of money, with intention to defraud any person, knowing the same to be false, forged, or counterfeited; then every such person shall be deemed guilty of felony, without benefit of clergy.

(2) By 2 Geo. 2. c. 25. s. 4, provided always, that nothing in this act contained shall extend to that part of Great Britain called Scotland.

(3) By 7 Geo. 2. c. 22, which recites that by 2 Geo. 2. c. 25. no punishment is inflicted upon any person who shall falsely make, alter, forge, or counterfeit, or cause or procure to be falsely made, altered, forged or counterfeited, or willingly act or assist in the false making, altering, forging, or counterfeiting, any acceptance of any bill of exchange, or who shall knowingly utter or publish the same as true: it is therefore enacted, that if any person, after the 24th day of June, 1734, shall falsely make, alter, forge, or counterfeit, or cause or procure to be falsely made, altered, or counterfeited, or willingly act or assist in the false making, altering, forging, or counterfeiting any acceptance of any bill of exchange with intention to defraud any person whatsoever; or shall utter or publish as true any false, altered, forged, or counterfeited acceptance of any bill of exchange, with intention to defraud any person, knowing the same to be false, altered, forged, or counterfeited; then every such person shall be deemed guilty of felony, without benefit of clergy.

(4) By 31 Geo. 2. c. 22. § 78., which recites that doubts might arise whether the punishment inflicted by 2 Geo. 2. c. 25. extends to the

extended to cases where the intent is to defraud, not an individual, but a corporation; and by 18 Geo. 3. c. 18. (5) the seventh of Geo. 2. c. 22. is in like manner extended.

And by 45 Geo. 3. c. 89. (6) forging or altering or caus-

---

commission of forgeries with intention to defraud any corporation, it is enacted, that if any person from and after the 1st of July, 1758, shall falsely make, forge, or counterfeit, or cause or procure to be falsely made, forged, or counterfeited, or willingly act or assist in the false making, forging, or counterfeiting, any bill of exchange or promissory note for payment of money, or the endorsement or assignment of any bill of exchange or promissory note for payment of money, with an intention to defraud any corporation whatsoever; or shall utter or publish as true, any false, forged, or counterfeited bill of exchange or promissory note for payment of money, or the endorsement or assignment of any bill of exchange or promissory note for payment of money, with intention to defraud any corporation, knowing the same to be falsely forged or counterfeited; then every such person shall be deemed guilty of felony, without benefit of clergy.

(5) By 18 Geo. 3. c. 18, which recites that doubts had arisen whether the punishment inflicted by 7 Geo. 2. c. 22. extended to such forgeries when committed with an intention to defraud any corporation, it is enacted, that if any person after the 25th of March, 1778, shall falsely make, alter, forge, or counterfeit, or cause or procure to be falsely made, altered, forged or counterfeited, or willingly act or assist in the false making, altering, forging, or counterfeiting, any acceptance of any bill of exchange, with intention to defraud any corporation whatsoever; or shall utter or publish as true any false, altered, forged, or counterfeited acceptance of any bill of exchange with intention to defraud any corporation whatsoever, knowing the same to be false, altered, forged, or counterfeited; every such person, being thereof lawfully convicted, shall be deemed guilty of felony, and shall suffer death as a felon without benefit of clergy.

(6) By 45 Geo. 3. c. 89, § 1, which recites 2 Geo. 2. c. 25. and certain other acts, and states that certain provisions had been made and enacted for the preventing and punishing the forgery of bank notes, and other notes, bills, and instruments, in those acts respectively mentioned; and that it was expedient that such provisions should extend and be in force in every part of Great Britain, with such alterations and amendments therein as were thereby made; it is enacted, that if any person or persons shall from and after the passing of this act, falsely make, forge, counterfeit, or alter, or cause or procure to be falsely made, forged, counterfeited, or altered, or willingly act or assist in the false making, forging, counterfeiting, or altering (among other instruments) any bill of exchange, promissory note for payment of money, endorsement or assignment of any bill of exchange or promissory note for payment of money, or acceptance of any bill of exchange, with intention to defraud any person or persons, body or bodies politic or corporate whatsoever; or shall offer, dispose of, or put away any false, forged, counterfeited, or altered bill of exchange, promissory note for payment of money, endorsement or assignment of any bill of exchange or promissory note for payment of money, or acceptance of any bill of exchange, with intention to defraud any person or persons, body or bodies politic or corporate,

ing to be forged or altered, or willingly acting or assisting in the forging or altering any bill or note, or any endorsement or assignment, or acceptance thereof, with intent to defraud any person or body politic, or offering, disposing of, or putting away any such forged or altered bill, note, endorsement, assignment, or acceptance, with a like intent, knowing it to be forged or altered, is a capital offence; and this act extends to every part of Great Britain. (7)

By 43 Geo. 3. c. 139. s. 1. forging or uttering any bill or note purporting to be the bill or note of any foreign prince, state, or country, or of any person or company of persons residing in any foreign country, or of any body corporate, or body in the nature thereof, constituted by any foreign prince or state, with intent to deceive his Majesty, or any such foreign prince, &c. or any person or body politic here or abroad, is made a felony, and punishable by transportation for a term not exceeding fourteen years.

There are other provisions as to bank notes, bank post bills, and certain other securities, as to which the different statutes which refer to them must be consulted.

Forgery may be committed either by altering or adding to what has a genuine signature, or by introducing a false signature.

And a signature will be false, though in a man's own name, if he attaches to it or adopts the description or addition of any other person of the same name.

And a signature in a false name assumed for the purpose, or in the name of a non-existing person, will be as much a forgery as a signature in the name of an existing person.

Altering a bill or note from a lower to a higher sum is a forgery; the instrument, as altered, is a false instrument. (8)

---

knowing the same to be false, forged, counterfeited, or altered, then every person or persons so offending shall be deemed guilty of felony, without benefit of clergy.

(7) And by 45 Geo. 3. c 89. § 8. all and every the clauses and provisions in this act contained, shall extend to every part of Great Britain.

(8) Rex v. Teague, Mich. 1802. Prisoner altered a 10*l.* country bank bill to 50*l*; it was on a sixteen-penny stamp, and had been thrice paid and reissued. The indictment charged, first, that the prisoner forged the bill, and secondly, that he uttered it knowing it to be forged: two

Discharging one endorsement and inserting another, is altering the endorsement; (9)

And forging it.

If a bill or note import to be payable at any of several places, substituting a new place for one of those named, if with intent to defraud, is a forgery. (10)

Substituting the new place by introducing over the old

---

objections; first, that the charge should have been for altering; and secondly, that this being a bill, not a note, could not legally be reissued without a new stamp. Prisoner was convicted, and the judges held the conviction right.

Rex v. Elsworth, Pasch. 1781. An indictment stated that a bill was drawn for 8*l.*; that persons unknown feloniously did alter it by falsely forging and adding a cipher to the 8*l.* and a *y* to the eight; that the prisoner had in his possession the said false, forged, altered, and counterfeitod bill, and that he feloniously did utter as a true bill, the said false, forged, altered, and counterfeited bill with intent, &c., and knowing, &c. Motion in arrest of judgment, on the ground that the forgery was stated to be by persons unknown, and that the statement should have been that they feloniously *forged*, not that they feloniously *altered;* the statute 2 Geo. 2. c. 25. s. 1. making it capital to *forge*, but saying nothing as to altering; but it was answered that the *altering* was *forging*, and the judges were unanimous that the conviction was right. And see Rex v. Post, ante, p. 7.

(9) Rex v. Birkitt, July, 1813. After conviction generally upon a bank indictment, it appeared there was one count only upon which the conviction could be supported; that count stated that the prisoner had in his possession a bank bill of exchange with a falsely altered endorsement thereon, and that he disposed thereof. The genuine endorsement was by Grant, Burbey, and Co., to Ladbrooke and Co.; the prisoner discharged the whole of that endorsement, and wrote de novo, "Grant, Burbey, and Co.;" the judges thought this alteration made the bill what the indictment described it, and that on this count the conviction was right.

Rex v. Bigg, 3 P. Wm. 419. By 8 and 9 W. 3. c. 20. s. 36. altering or rasing any endorsement on any bank bill or note of any sort is made felony, without clergy. Upon a bank note for 100*l.* the bank paid 90*l.* and wrote upon the face of the note in red ink, "paid ninety pounds;" this writing the prisoner discharged by some liquid, probably lemon-juice: indictment thereon. The indictment stated that quoddam scriptum, anglice an endorsement, on the said note was duly made, specifying that 90*l.* was paid, and that the prisoner feloniously erased that endorsement: special verdict, finding inter al. that at the time of the act and till the 28th Nov. 1696, the only way used for endorsing bank notes, was by writing in black ink on the back side of the notes, but from the 28th Nov. 1696, it was by writing in front in red ink; special verdict. Many objections were taken; one that this was not an endorsement: after argument, the judges differed, but the majority held the conviction right. The prisoner was transported, not executed.

(10) See Rex v. Treble, ante, p. 61.

place a piece of paper containing the new one, is a forgery. (10)

Adding a false addition to a fictitious name to delude a party to present a second time a bill he had before presented without success, under pretence that it was for want of that addition that the bill had been before dishonored, is a forgery. (11)

If there are two persons of the same name, but of different descriptions or additions, and one signs his name with the description or addition of the other, it is a forgery. (12)

Thus, if a bill be addressed to A. B. of London, merchant, and A. B. not of London, or not a merchant, accept it, the acceptance will be a forgery, if there be any A. B. of London, merchant; (12)

If there be no person of that name, description, and addition, not. (12)

So if a man of the same name as the payee or special endorsee of a bill or note endorse the bill or note, such endorsement is a forgery, because an endorsement by any other person than the right, is a false endorsement. (13)

But if the real payee or endorser of a bill or note endorse his own name thereon, without any false description

---

(11) Rex v. Francis, Mich. 1811. John Francis took a lodging in the name of Cooke; and in less than a month passed to his landlord's wife a draft he drew on Praeds and Co. for 15*l.*, and she gave him a bank note for it to that amount. It was returned, on the ground that no person of that name kept cash there: the prisoner said it was a mistake for want of his adding "jun." to his name; which he accordingly added, and the note was again taken to Praeds, who again refused payment; but before it was brought back the prisoner absconded. Chambre J. left it to the jury whether he did not assume the name of Cooke, or at least of Cooke, *jun.*, with intent to defraud his landlord; and the jury thought he did, and he was convicted. On case, the conviction was held right.

(12) Rex v. Webb, Mich. 1819. A bill was addressed to Thomas Bowden, baize manufacturer, Rumford, and prisoner uttered it with an acceptance thereon made by a Thomas Bowden, who did not live at Rumford, and was not a baize manufacturer; and on indictment for uttering a forged acceptance, it appeared that there was no such baize manufacturer at Rumford; and on case, the majority of the judges held that the adopting a false description and addition, where a false name was not assumed, and where there was no person answering that description or addition, was not a forgery; and the prisoner was pardoned.

(13) See Mead v. Young, ante, p. 76.

or addition, his assuming at the time he utters it to be a different person of the same name, but with a different description or addition, will not make his signature a forgery, nor his uttering a capital offence.

If the signatures to a bill or note are genuine, a false pretence by the person who utters it that he bears a character he does not, will not make him liable to a prosecution for forgery. (14)

So as to any other genuine signatures upon a bill or note, though they may be intended to be passed as and for the signatures of other persons, and are passed accordingly, yet if there be nothing upon the bill or note to apply them to those persons, they are not forgeries.

A signature in an assumed name is a forgery if the name was assumed to defraud in that particular instance. (15)

---

(14) Rex v. Hevey, Hil. 1782. The prisoner uttered a bill purporting to be payable to Bernard M'Carthy or order, and having the endorsement "B. M'Carthy," thereon, he was indicted for forging that endorsement, and uttering it knowing it to be forged: the jury found that there was such a man as B. M'Carthy, and that the endorsement was his handwriting, but that the prisoner passed himself off as that B. M'Carthy when he uttered the bill: and on case, the judges were unanimous that as the endorsement was not forged, the prisoner was not liable to be convicted.

(15) Rex v. Marshall, R. Michaelmas, 1804. Prisoner was paying away a bill payable to Ward, or order, and endorsed by Ward, and was desired to put his name upon it, and he wrote, Luke Marsden, when his real name was Thomas Marshall: he paid the bill to Harland for a horse: Harland did not know him before, but supposed from his writing it that Luke Marsden was his name. Question for the judges whether this was forgery, and they held it was.

Rex v. Whiley, Trinity, 1805. Whiley assumed the name of Milward 27th of December, and ordered goods of Thurston in that name: on 5th January following he gave Thurston a draft in the name of Milward, on Stephenson and Co., for ten guineas more than the amount of the goods, and Thurston gave him the difference. Thurston would have trusted the prisoner equally if he had used his own name: the draft was not paid, and prisoner was indicted as for a forgery. Thomson B. left it to the jury whether the prisoner assumed the name of Milward, when he ordered the goods and gave the note, with intent to defraud the prosecutor: they found that he did, and on case, the judges held the conviction right.

Rex v. Dunn, Michaelmas, 1765. Indictment that prisoner forged a note for payment of money, the tenor of which is as follows: "London, 27th July, 1765. I promise to pay Mr. Edward Hooper the sum of three pounds thirteen shillings and sixpence, or order, seven days after date, value received by me Mary ⋈ Wallace, her mark," with intent to defraud

Or for a system of fraud within which that signature fell. (16)

And it makes no difference, though the bill or note would have been equally taken had the party used his own name. (17)

And though it was taken upon the credit of other names upon the bill or note, not upon the fictitious name. (18)

And though the party had passed for some time by that name. (19)

Edward Hooper: it appeared that her real name was Dunn; that she assumed the name of Wallace to represent herself as a seaman's widow; that she got three guineas and a half of Cooper, a navy agent, under that pretence, and that he wrote the note in question as security for it, and she put her mark to it; that he then asked her what name he should put to her mark, and she said "Mary Wallace;" upon which he wrote "Mary Wallace, her mark." The recorder doubted whether this addition after her signature could be deemed part of the note she forged; but Perrot B. and Aston J. held it was. Case on the ground that this was the prisoner's own note, and offered as her own; and nine judges against Aston J. held it a case within 2 G. 2. c. 25., and that the prisoner was properly convicted.

Rex v. Toft, Pasch. 1777. A bill of exchange for 150*l.* endorsed in blank, was stolen at Leicester; the same night the prisoner got cash for it at the Harboro' bank; but before it was cashed he was told it was the rule of the house that the person for whom they cashed a bill should endorse it, and he wrote the name John Williams; his real name was Toft. The jury found him guilty, and the judges were of opinion it was forgery.

Rex v. Peacock, Pasch. 1814. Prisoner went to Nuneham, in Gloucestershire, with intent to defraud by getting money upon bills he should draw: he went in the name of White, and in that name he drew a bill; he was indicted for forging this bill, and it was proved that his real name was Peacock; but it was not proved by what name he had passed for six years before he went to Nuneham: the jury found that he assumed that name, and went to Nuneham under it with a view to get money on bills he should draw in that name; and on case the judges held his conviction right; and that if he had used the name of White before he went to Nuneham, it was incumbent on him to prove it.

And see Rex v. Francis, ante, p. 385.

(16) See Rex v. Whiley, p. 386. and Rex v. Peacock, supra.

(17) See Rex v. Marshall, Rex v. Whiley, (ante, p. 386.) and Rex v. Francis, ante, p. 385.

Rex v. Shepherd, Michaelmas, 1781. The prisoner bought some things at a silversmith's, and uttered a forged check in payment: the silversmith took it as *his* draught, and he knew it. On conviction a doubt was entertained, as much as the silversmith gave credit to the prisoner, not to the draught, for he supposed it to be the prisoner's check; but on point saved the judges were unanimous the conviction was right.

(18) See Rex v. Hough, post, p. 391.

(19) See Rex v. Whiley, ante, p. 386.

But a signature in an assumed name will not be a forgery though the name were assumed for concealment or fraud, if it were not assumed with a view to that transaction, or for a system of which that is part.

Signing a mark in an assumed name, and suffering the assumed name to be ascribed to the mark, is forging the name. (20)

And it makes no difference, though the assumed name is not ascribed to the mark till after the mark is made, if it be ascribed to it in the prisoner's presence. (20)

Procuring a man to forge a bill or note is a capital offence.(21)

Procuring to utter, a common law felony only. (21)

But procuring to utter, if the person procured is ignorant of the forgery, and therefore free from crime, may make the procurer chargeable for the uttering, and subject him to an indictment capitally on that charge.

Shewing a man forged notes to raise a false idea in him of the party's substance, would probably not be an uttering within 2 G. 2.; it has been held not to be an uttering of the sham notes to which 13 G. c. 3. 79. applies. (22)

Nor would the leaving them sealed up, under color that he may take charge of them as being too valuable to be carried about. (22)

---

(20) See Rex v. Dunn, ante, p. 386.

(21) Rex v. Morris, Pasch. 1814. The prisoner was convicted of procuring his wife to utter a forged order for payment of money, and the judges held he could only be punished as for a common law felony; but they held that had he been found guilty of procuring her to forge it, the offence would have been capital.

(22) Rex v. Shuckard, Michaelmas, 1811. Prisoner had two sham notes for paying 550*d.*, but the numbers were in white letters on a black ground, so that they had the appearance of bank notes for 550*l.* he shewed them to J. S. with intent to make him suppose he was a man of fortune, but they were folded up so that the numbers only were visible: he then said he did not like to carry so much property about him, sealed them up in a cover, and delivered them to J. S. that he might take charge of them for the prisoner; the prisoner was afterwards suspected; J. S. opened the cover, discovered what the notes were, and the prisoner was indicted on 13 G. 3. c. 79. for uttering and publishing them; but on case, the judges held, that what he had done did not amount to an uttering or publishing within the statute, and that the conviction was wrong.

To constitute an uttering it probably would not be deemed necessary it should be uttered in payment.

Uttering under the false pretence that it had been given in change by the person to whom it is uttered, in order to obtain from him a good note in lieu thereof, would probably be deemed an uttering; it has been so held in the case of counterfeit coin. (23)

And under 45 G. 3. c. 89., offering, disposing of, or putting away, is described as the offence; uttering is not mentiened.

The offence of disposing of and putting away may be complete, though the person to whom they were disposed of was an agent to detect utterers. (24)

And though the prisoner was applied to by such agent for the bill or notes. (24)

And though he might not have them when the agent first applied. (24)

And though he disposed of them, not as genuine, but as forged. (24)

Giving a confederate a forged bank note that he may utter it, is a dispcsing and putting away thereof. (25)

---

(23) Rex v. Franks, Leach, 736. The prisoner sold Redit some apricots, and Redit paid him a good shilling, the prisoner put it into his mouth, and took from thence a counterfeit, and gave it to Redit as the shilling received from him, desiring him to change it, which he did: the prisoner practised the same trick with a second and third good shilling Redit gave him, on which Redit apprehended him. Conviction.—Objection that the indictment did not state that the shilling was uttered as and for a good one; the court thought an uttering not in payment within the statute, and the indictment right.

(24) Rex v. Holden, Michaelmas, 1809. Indictment charged that prisoner disposed of and put away a forged bank note with intent to defraud the bank, he knowing it at the time to be forged. The evidence was, that Shaw and Whitehead were employed by the magistrates, with the approbation of the agents for the bank, to detect utterers: that they applied to the prisoner, who procured the notes, and sold them, not as genuine, but as forged: it did not appear by any direct evidence that prisoner had the notes in his possession when first applied to, but he produced them at a subsequent meeting. It was urged, 1st, That the indictment was insufficient as not stating in what manner and to whom the notes were disposed of; and 2dly, That the disposal was insufficient, as the prisoner was solicited to commit the act by the bank's agent: but Chambre J. overruled the objections, and, on case for the twelve judges, they were unanimous that the objections had no weight.

(25) Rex v. Palmer, Pasch. 1804. Palmer and Hudson were jointly

Forging or uttering a bill or note for less than 20*s*., or a bill or note for (26) less than 5*l*. which does not comply with the requisites of 17 G. 3. c. 30., or any other bill or note the legislature has declared void, is not within the statutes against forgery.

But a bill or note for payment of so many pound, instead of pounds, is. (27)

And so is a bill or note for payment of ten, twenty, thirty, &c. omitting "Pounds," if the figures with an £. affixed are put upon it to denote the amount. (28)

And so is a bill on the commissioners of the navy, though it is not warranted by 35 G. 3. c. 94., if it has the requisites of a bill of exchange. (29)

---

indicted, 1st, for uttering a forged bank note; and 2dly, for disposing and putting away: Hudson tendered it in payment, but Palmer was not with her: the shop-keeper stopped it as suspicious, and Palmer came afterwards with Hudson, and claimed it as his, and said he would have either the note or change. The jury found Palmer alone guilty; and seven judges against four, held him well convicted on the second count.

(26) Rex v. Moffat, Hil. 1787. Indictment for uttering a forged acceptance on a bill for 3*l*. 3*s*. The bill did not specify the payee's place of abode, and had no subscribing witness, and was therefore void by 17 G. 3.; and on a case reserved the judges held this not a forgery within 7 G. 2.

(27) See Rex v. Post, ante, p. 7.

(28) Rex v. Elliot, Michaelmas, 1777. The prisoner was found guilty of forging this note, " No. 17.73 I promise to pay to Mr. Jos. Crook, or bearer, on demand, the sum of fifty, London, the 20th day of June. For the governor and company of the Bank of England. Thos. Thompson. £Fifty. Entered C. Blewerse." One count called it a note for payment of money only, describing it however as for payment of fifty pounds, and setting out the tenor; on the trial, the judge left it to the jury whether it was not to be considered as for 50*l*.: the prisoner was found guilty, and on case, the judges were unanimous of opinion the conviction was right.

(29) Rex v. Chisholme, Pasch. 1815. Prisoner was convicted of uttering a bill on the commissioners of the navy for 22*l*. 6*s*. 9*d*. for pay due to J. S. as acting lieutenant of the Zealous. Acting lieutenants have no power under 35 G. 3. to draw, and it was admitted therefore that the indictment could not be maintained on 35 G. 3.; it was urged, that it could not be deemed a bill of exchange, because the commissioners of the navy were removeable, and the instrument, if genuine, would not have been drawn for the purpose of being accepted by the commissioners, but in order to obtain an assignment under 35 G. 3.; but the judges on case held, that it was, in form, a bill of exchange, and 35 G. 3. would not prevent its being so.

But a bill or note is not within the statutes against forgery, unless it is for payment of money in specie; (30)

And at all events.

Therefore a bill or note to pay in cash or bank notes is not. (30)

And it is questionable whether a bill or note payable to , or order, leaving a blank for the payee's name, is within the statutes. (31)

Forging or uttering a note without a maker's name is not a capital offence. (31*)

Forging or uttering a bill or note importing to be payable to A. B., or order, is a complete offence, though there is no endorsement upon it in A. B.'s name. (32)

---

(30) See Rex v. Wilcox, ante, p. 6.

(31) See Rex v. Randall, ante, p. 23.

(31*) Rex v. Pateman, Pasch. 1821. Prisoner was convicted of uttering and publishing as true forged a promissory note. The note was as follows: "No. 16,209. Bedford Bank. I promise to pay the bearer forty pounds on demand, here, or at Sir Charles Price, Baronet, and Co.'s, bankers, London. Value received. Bed d, the 17th day of October, 1817. For Barnard Barnard and Green." It was objected that this was no note, because it had no maker's name, and imported to bind nobody: the point was saved for the consideration of the judges, and they held the objection good, and the conviction wrong.

(32) Rex v. Birkett, Pasch. 1805. Indictment for forging and uttering a note payable to the prisoner's order: it appeared that he deposited it for his bill at an inn unendorsed, with a promise that he would pay the bill in a few days, saying, he wished not to discount it. Conviction.—Doubts whether it should not have been left to the jury to consider, whether he did not really mean to pay his bill, and get back the note, and make no further use of it. The judges thought not, and the conviction stood.

Rex v. Hough, Michaelmas, 1806. Indictment for uttering a forged bill importing to be drawn by Hastings, payable to Higgins, or order, with intent to defraud Green: the indictment did not state any endorsement in Higgins's name; the prisoner passed it to Green, and Green, at the time, inquired who Hastings and Higgins were, and the prisoner said he did not know much about Hastings, but he spoke of Higgins as a considerable manufacturer, and Green took the bill on the prisoner's representation of Higgins. Sutton B. doubted whether prisoner could properly be convicted, as Green took the bill on the credit of Higgins, and there was nothing in the indictment about his endorsement; but all the other judges thought the conviction right.

Rex v. Wicks, Pasch. 1809. Prisoner uttered a forged bill importing to be payable to the order of the drawers, Rimmington and Co.; it had not their endorsement thereon, though it had one endorsement beside prisoner's. On conviction thereon a case was reserved, and on consideration, the judges (nine) held the conviction right; for the instrument

Forging on unstamped paper a bill or note which requires a stamp is as much an offence as if it were on stamped paper. (33)

And altering a bill which has once been paid, and which has been reissued without having a new stamp thereon, where such new stamp is requisite, is as much an offence as if the bill had never been paid, or as if it had had the additional stamp. (34)

An intent to defraud the person who would have to pay the bill or note if it were genuine, is to be inferred. (35)

And this inference ought to be drawn, though, from the manner of executing the forgery, or from that person's ordinary caution, it would not be likely to impose on him. (35)

And though, from its being negotiable, it would be likely to defraud others, before it reached him. (35)

And though the object was general, to defraud whoever might take the instrument, and the particular intention of defrauding the person who would have to pay it, if genuine, never entered into the prisoner's contemplation. (35)

An intent to defraud a body politic or corporate is equally criminal with an intent to defraud an individual. (36)

Where the forgery is by alteration, the indictment may charge that that the prisoner forged the altered instrument (37); or that he altered by forging; for altering is forging. (38)

---

was a bill, and though it would not be available against the drawers without their endorsement, they might be compelled to endorse it, if they passed it away for good consideration. Lawrence J. for some time doubted, but at last seemed satisfied.

(33) See Rex v. Hawkeswood, ante, p. 55.

(34) See Rex v. Teague, ante, p. 383.

(35) Rex v. Mazagora, Pasch. 1815. On indictment for disposing of forged bank notes, the intent was charged to be to defraud the bank: the jury stated that the intent was to defraud whoever might take the notes, but that the intention of defrauding the bank in particular did not enter into the prisoner's contemplation, and they found the prisoner guilty. On case, the judges thought it too clear for discussion; that the prisoner must be taken to have intended to defraud the bank, and that the conviction was right.

(36) See 45 G. 3. c. 89. ante, p. 382.

(37) See Rex v. Teague, ante, p. 383.

(38) See Rex v. Elsworth, ante, p. 384.

And discharging one endorsement, and inserting another, may be charged as altering the endorsement. (39)

If the bill or note omit the word pounds in the body, but has an £. with figures prefixed to the amount in the margin, it may be described as a bill or note for payment of that amount. (40)

The indictment must set out the bill or note in the very words: it is not sufficient to set out the substance. (41) (*a*)

And if the bill or note contain figures, the indictment must follow it in that respect. (42)

And if the bill or note be in a foreign language, a translation of it must be set out, that it may appear upon the record in a language the courts understand that it is what the law considers a bill or note. (43)

---

(39) See Rex v. Birkitt, ante, p. 384. 391.

(40) See Rex v. Eliot, ante, p. 390.

(41) Rex v. Mason, Pasch. 1793. Indictment stated that the prisoners having in their possession a bill of exchange purporting to be drawn by J. S. on J. N., thereby requiring J. N., two months after date, to pay A. B., or order, 91*l*., and purporting to have been endorsed by A. B., together with a forged acceptance, written on the same bill, and purporting to have been written by the said J. N., feloniously did utter, &c. Thomson B. saved the question whether the indictment ought not to have set out the bill and acceptance in their words and figures; and the judges held it ought, and that for want thereof it was bad.

Note. It would not otherwise appear on the record whether the bill was what the law considers a bill.

[(*a*) But see Commonwealth v. Ross, 2 Mass. R. 373. An indictment for uttering a forged promissory note did not set forth the words of the note, nor the date, nor the time when it was payable. The attorney-general said, that the reason why the note was not more particularly described, was that the defendant when arrested swallowed the note, and thus put it out of the power of the government to give a more particular description. The indictment was held sufficient.]

(42) See Rex v. Powell, post, 394.

(43) Rex v. Goldstein, Michaelmas, 1821. The prisoner was convicted under 43 G. 3. c. 139. of forging a note purporting to be a note of the king of Prussia: the note was in the German language, and was set out verbatim: the indictment did not set out any English translation of it, and on that account an application was made to arrest the judgment: the point was saved for the consideration of the twelve judges; they directed it to be argued, and after argument, the opinion of the majority was, that a translation ought to have been set out upon the indictment, for it might be a question whether the instrument was within the statute; a court of error ought to have the means of deciding upon that point, to give them those means they ought to have the instrument before them in a language they understand, and unless they had a translation sanctioned by the jury which tried the indictment, they had no

Alleging that the prisoner forged a bill or note "as follows," or that he had a bill or note "as follows," implies, that what follows is in the very words of the bill or note, and makes it necessary to prove the bill or note verbatim. (44)

On an indictment for forging a bill or note with a false name ascribed to the prisoner's mark, the words ascribing the name to the mark, if written in the prisoner's presence, may be described as part of the bill or note. (45)

If the false signature contain an initial only for the christian name, it is not necessary to aver what christian name it means. (46)

The indictment ought not describe the bill or note *as signed* by the person whose name is supposed to have been forged; such an allegation is inconsistent with the charge of forgery, and makes the indictment bad. (47)

And an indictment must not describe a bill or note as having a purport different from what appears upon the face of the instrument. (48)

---

means of getting a translation upon which they could judicially rely; and the judgment was arrested.

(44) Rex v. Powell, Michaelmas, 1771. Indictment against prisoner for forging a stock receipt with intent to defraud, 1st, Taylor Barrow, and secondly, T. Sykes. The indictment stated that the prisoner forged a certain receipt as follows, viz. &c. The receipt, as set out, contained certain sums in figures, and it was signed T. Barrow. Three objections: 1st, That this was not equivalent to setting out the tenor; but the judges held it was, and that any variance would be fatal: 2dly, That the sums should not have been set out in figures; but the judges held the receipt must be pursued literatim, or it would be a variance; and thirdly, That it should have been averred that T. Barrow, as signed, meant Taylor Barrow; but the judges thought not, and prisoner was executed.

(45) See Rex v. Dunn, ante, p. 386.

(46) See Rex v. Powell, supra, n. 44.

(47) Rex v. Carter, Hil. 1801. Indictment for forging and uttering a bill in Hutchinson's name, described it as signed by Hutchinson; and after conviction the judges held it bad upon the face of it, and that the prisoner might be indicted de novo.

(48) Rex v. Reading, Hil. 1794. East, 981. Upon a bill directed to John Ring, there was an acceptance in the name of John King. The indictment described the bill as purporting to be directed to John King by the name of John Ring; and after conviction for forging and uttering, the judges held this a repugnant and absurd description, for the bill could only purport to be what it appeared upon the face of it to be; and the judgment was arrested.

S. P. Rex v. Gilchrist, East, 982; and see Rex v. Jones, Dougl. 302, East, 883.

On an indictment for forging the endorsement of a payee, it is not necessary to shew by the drawer or maker who was intended as payee, if there is proof that the prisoner has himself admitted who it was. (49)

To support a charge of forgery by subscribing a fictitious name, there must be evidence on the part of the prosecution that that is not the party's real name. (50)

And if there is no evidence affirmatively what the real name is, there ought to be proof that it was assumed for the transaction in question; (50)

Or for a system of which that was part. (50)

But if there is proof affirmatively what the real name is, it is for the prisoner to shew a prior independent use of the assumed name. (50)

And in such case an absence of proof on the part of the prosecution by what name the prisoner has passed for several years, will not be material. (50)

On an indictment for uttering, proof that the prisoner had in his possession other bills or notes ejusdem generis is admissible, because if unexplained it tends to shew that he knew the bill or note in question was a forgery. (51)

And bills on the same house with a bill in question, importing to be drawn by persons not known at that house, will be deemed ejusdem generis with the bill in question. (51)

---

(49) Rex v. Downs, Michaelmas, 1789. Indictment for forging the payee's endorsement on a bill payable to John Sowerby, or order; when prisoner passed the bill, he said Sowerby was a cheesemonger at Liverpool, and John Sowerby of Liverpool, cheesemonger, was called; who proved that there was no other cheesemonger at Liverpool of that name but himself, and that the endorsement was not his; there were letters from the prisoner after his apprehension implying guilt generally in this transaction. It was urged, that the drawer should have been called to prove what John Sowerby he meant; but Wilson J. left the case as it was to the jury, who convicted; and on a case reserved the judges thought the evidence sufficient to go to the jury, and that the conviction was right.

(50) See Rex v. Peacock, ante, p. 387.

(51) Rex v. Hough, Michaelmas, 1806. Indictment for uttering a forged bill, purporting to be drawn by Hastings on Esdailes, and proof that no such person as Hastings kept cash at Esdailes': when the prisoner was apprehended, which was four months after the uttering, there were found upon him two other bills, importing to be drawn by

And proof that the prisoner had pointed out where bills or notes ejusdem generis were hid, is admissible, because if unexplained it raises a presumption that he had hid them. (52)

So proof that he had uttered other bills or notes ejusdem generis, is also admissible. (53)

But such bills or notes must be produced, and their being forgeries proved. (54)

Walters on Esdaile, and another, importing to be drawn by Newman on Esdaile; and evidence was given that no such person as Walters or Newman kept cash at Esdailes': Sutton B. allowed these bills to be read as evidence that prisoner knew the bill he uttered to be forged: and after conviction the judges thought it right.

(52) Rex v. Rowley, Pasch. 1806. Waring, a person employed by the solicitor to the bank, applied to the prisoner, who twice procured him forged bank notes; he applied a third time, prisoner went out, and after some time returned, and told Waring they were in an old shoe, in a particular lane; they went together, and prisoner threw a stone into a bush, and said, there they are: Waring found the shoe there, and the notes in it: the prisoner was indicted on 45 G. 3. c. 89. § 6. for having these notes in his possession, and Graham B. told the jury that if prisoner had the notes in his possession on their passage to the shoe, it was sufficient, and they convicted prisoner: the judges held the conviction right.

(53) Rex v. Wylie, 1 New Rep. 92. Upon an indictment for uttering a forged bank note, knowing, &c. the uttering was proved, and its being forged, and to prove the knowledge evidence was offered that the prisoner had passed other forged notes: this was objected to on the ground that it was evidence of other felonies, and the prisoner could not be prepared to resist it, but Lord Ellenborough, Heath J. and Thompson B. held it admissible, and the prisoner was found guilty.

Rex v. Ball, Michaelmas, 1807, P. C. 1 Campb. 324. P. C. On indictment for uttering a forged bank note, evidence was given that three months before prisoner had passed another note, forged in the same manner, namely, with a camel-hair pencil, by the same hand, and with the same materials, and that fifteen other notes of the same fabrication had been found filed at the bank with the prisoner's writing thereon: point saved whether the evidence was admissible: all the judges except Chambre J. thought it was, though its weight would depend on the number of notes issued, and the time, and the probability, from the prisoner's situation in life, of his taking them in businesss.

See Rex v. Hough, pp. 391. 395.

(54) Rex v. Millard, Pasch. 1813. The prisoner was tried for uttering a £5 bank note, and to prove the guilty knowledge it was proved that he had before uttered two £1 Leicester notes; that in about a fortnight one having been objected to as bad, he changed it, and that when under charge for the uttering in question, the other was brought to him with the word "forged" upon it, and he changed that, but neither of these bills were produced, nor had any notice been given for producing them; and on case, the judges held that this evidence should not have been admitted, without proper proof that these notes were

Proof that the prisoner took them back and changed them with the word "forged" written thereon, is not sufficient. (54)

And evidence may be given of the prisoner's conduct on such other utterings, and that he passed by different names. (55)

But quære, whether other evidence to impeach his conduct on those occasions is admissible? because he cannot be expected to be ready to meet such evidence.

Proof that the prisoner had uttered other forged bills or notes of a different kind is questionable.

On an indictment for forgery, the person whose name is forged, or upon whose genuine name a forgery is committed, is not a competent witness to prove the forgery if he has an interest in the destruction of what is supposed to be forged. (56)

And the reason perhaps is, that the indictment may be considered in some degree as a proceeding in rem, and a conviction would warrant a judicial cancellation of the forgery.

And he is not competent to prove any fact which has a tendency to make out the forgery. (56)

When the forgery is established by other evidence, whether he is competent on the part of the prosecution to any points unconnected with the forgery, is not settled. (56)

---

forged, and without deciding whether bills of a different description and denomination were admissible, (which Le Blanc J. thought they were); an application for a pardon was recommended.

(55) See Rex v. Millard, p. 396.

(56) Rex v. Crocker, 2 New Rep. 87. Indictment for forging a note. There was an endorsement on it in the prisoner's writing that a year's interest had been paid, and Le Blanc J. permitted the party whose name was forged to prove that he had never paid interest on this or any other note; but on case on this and another point, the prisoner was pardoned, and it was understood that a majority of the judges were of opinion that he ought not to have been admitted.

Note. Lord Ellenborough, Lawrence C. B. and Le Blanc J. thought him admissible, because it was sufficiently proved before that the note was not signed by him, and they thought him admissible to all points but that of the forgery: some of the other judges seemed to think that to points perfectly collateral he would have been admissible, but they considered the point to which he was called as contributing to prove the forgery. Le Blanc's MSS.

If he has no interest in the destruction of the forgery, he is a competent witness.

Thus if the holder of a forged note release the person in whose name it is made, such person will be a competent witness to prove the name forged. (57)

And he will be competent though the note was not payable to order or to bearer, so as to be negotiable, but simply to the prisoner, if the prisoner passed it to the owner for full value. (57)

So on an indictment against the payee of a bill for forging an acceptance, a release from the endorsee will make the supposed acceptor competent to prove the forgery. (58)

And so will an abandonment of his claim by the person who would be entitled to sue the supposed acceptor if the acceptance were genuine.

And it will have that effect though such endorsee advanced the payee only part of the amount of the bill, and would be liable to him, if the bill were genuine and paid, for the residue. (58)

And the endorsee in such case is a competent witness also. (59)

---

(57) Rex v. Akehurst, Leach, 136. Akehurst was indicted for forging a note payable to himself, but not payable to order; he paid it away in part discharge of a debt, but did not endorse it; the holder gave the drawer a general release, and the drawer being offered as a witness to prove the forgery, Lord Mansfield, after argument, admitted him.

(58) Rex v. Mott, Hil. 1821. Indictment against payee of a bill for uttering it with the forged acceptance of Dover thereon; prisoner had endorsed it to Hood and Co. on having value to the amount of half the bill; Hood was examined as a witness, and so, on release from Hood, was Dover: case saved on the question whether Dover was competent without release from prisoner also, for if the acceptance were genuine, prisoner would have a claim against Dover for one half the bill; but the judges thought the release from Hood and Co. sufficient, because the endorsement vested the whole legal interest in them, and if the release destroyed any claim by prisoner on Dover, it gave a claim pro tanto against Hood and Co.: it was then urged that Hood was incompetent, for he had a direct interest in the prisoner's conviction; for if he was acquitted and could prove the acceptance genuine, he might sue Hood and Co. for giving the release: but a great majority of the judges held him competent.

(59) Rex v. Usher, Leach, 44. Usher forged the acceptance of a bill, making it payable at Sir Charles Asgill's in the name of Mr. Merry. Sir C. Asgill paid the bill, and charged it to Mr. Merry's account; but on being satisfied of the forgery, they gave him credit to the amount of

Where the forgery consists in altering a genuine instrument, and consists in what gives the bill or note a better credit, but does not vary the responsibility of the drawer or maker, the drawer or maker is a competent witness to prove the forgery.

He has been held competent where the forgery introduced a new place for payment. (60)

---

the charge. Usher was indicted for the forgery, and Mr. Merry produced as a witness against him; upon which his counsel objected to Mr. Merry's admissibility; but Lord Mansfield, Smythe B., and Wilmot J. held, that as Sir C. Asgill had given up his claim, it was immaterial to Mr. Merry whether Usher was convicted or acquitted, inasmuch as no demand could be made upon Mr. Merry for the money, and they therefore over-ruled the objection.

(60) Rex v. Treble, Pasch. 1810. Indictment for forgery by substituting in a country bank note the name of a solvent town banker as one of the places where it was payable, instead of an insolvent one: the signature was genuine, the maker was admitted a witness, and on point saved, the judges held it right.

TABLE

OF

PRINCIPAL MATTERS.

TABLE

OF

CITED CASES.